SAS® System for Mixed Models

Ramon C. Littell, Ph.D.

George A. Milliken, Ph.D.

Walter W. Stroup, Ph.D.

Russell D. Wolfinger, Ph.D.

Comments or Questions?

The author assumes complete responsibility for the technical accuracy of the content of this book. If you have any questions about the material in this book, please write to the author at this address:

> SAS Institute Inc.
> Books by Users
> Attn: SAS System for Mixed Models
> SAS Campus Drive
> Cary, NC 27513

If you prefer, you can send e-mail to sasbbu@sas.com with "comments for SAS System for Mixed Models" as the subject line, or you can fax the Books by Users program at (919) 677-4444.

The correct bibliographic citation for this manual is as follows: Littell, Ramon C., Milliken, George A., Stroup, Walter W., and Wolfinger, Russell D., *SAS® System for Mixed Models*, Cary, NC: SAS Institute Inc., 1996. 633 pp.

SAS® System for Mixed Models

Contents

Preface

Introduction

The topic of mixed linear models is presented in graduate level statistics courses and is familiar to most statisticians. However, many persons who are engaged in analyzing data sets for which mixed models are appropriate are not aware of the need for mixed models. Also, mixed model methodology has advanced rapidly in recent years, and even statisticians who studied the topic five years ago may not be aware of the tremendous new capabilities available for applications of mixed models. Most of the mixed model advancements in the SAS System are in the MIXED procedure. We firmly believe that valid statistical analysis of most data sets requires mixed model methodology.

This book presents mixed model methodology in the setting of numerous applications. The scope of the book is both broad and deep. Examples are included from several applications areas and they range from basic to advanced. The book is intended to be useful to as broad an audience as possible although persons with some knowledge of analysis of variance and regression analysis will benefit most. Sections 2 and 3 of the preface give entry-level descriptions of types of data-producing projects and statistical models. Section 4 describes fixed and random effects, which are concepts that may be new even to persons with considerable data analysis experience. Section 5 follows with a definition and illustration of mixed models. Finally, section 6 gives overviews of the 12 chapters in the book.

Not everyone will want to read the book from cover to cover. Persons who have little or no exposure to mixed models will be interested in the early chapters and can progress through later chapters as their needs require. Persons with good basic skills may want to jump into the chapters on topics of specific interest and refer to earlier material to clarify basic concepts.

Good statistical applications require a certain amount of theoretical knowledge. The more advanced the application, the more theoretical skills will help. This book is certainly applied. Theoretical developments are given to describe how mixed model methodology works and when it is useful.

Types of Projects That Produce Data

Data sets presented in this book come from three types of sources: (1) designed experiments, (2) sample surveys, and (3) observational studies. Almost any data set is produced by one of these sources. In designed experiments, some form of treatment is applied to experimental units and responses are observed. An example is a food processing experiment in which portions of fruit, such as slices of apples, are treated with different preservative compounds. Then the shelf lives of the portions of fruit are determined. In sample surveys, data are collected on units according to a plan, called a survey design, but treatments are not applied to units. The units, typically people, already possess certain attributes such as age and occupation. A value, such as amount of indebtedness, is determined for each unit. In observational studies, data are collected on units that are available, rather than on units chosen according to a plan. An example is a study at a veterinary clinic in which dogs that enter the clinic are diagnosed according to their skin condition, and blood samples are drawn for measurement of trace elements.

You choose to run a designed experiment, a sample survey, or an observational study depending on the objectives of the project and the type of resources available. Even though the three types of projects are carried out quite differently, some statistical terminology is common to data sets coming from each type of project. For example, the terms **factor**, **level**, and **effect** are used alike in designed experiments, sample surveys, and observational studies. In the food processing experiment, preservative is a **factor**, and each compound is a **level** of the factor. Also, each level has its **effect**; that is, applying any one of the compounds has an effect on the shelf life of the fruit portion. In the sample survey of indebtedness, occupation is a factor, and each level of the factor (each different occupation) has its effect on indebtedness. That is, a particular occupation does not cause a certain amount of indebtedness, but persons in one occupation may tend to have greater or less indebtedness than persons in another occupation. In the veterinary observational study, diagnosis is a factor and each skin condition is a level of the factor. Differences in the blood trace elements between the diagnostic groups are effects of the factor levels. These concepts are defined more precisely in the next section.

From now on, the term **study** refers to whatever type of project is relevant: designed experiment, sample survey, or observational study.

Statistical Models

Statistical models for data are mathematical descriptions of how data conceivably can be produced. Consider the food processing experiment with five compounds (say, A, B, C, D, and E) that are applied as preservatives to portions of fruit. Then preservative is a **treatment factor**, and A, B, C, D, and E are the **level**s of the factor. Let μ_A stand for the mean shelf life of portions of fruit that have been treated with compound A, and define μ_B, μ_C, μ_D, and μ_E similarly for the other compounds. The **effect** of compound A is $\alpha_A = \mu_A - \mu$, where μ is an overall mean. If y is the shelf life of one randomly chosen portion of fruit treated with compound A, then y is a random variable with mean μ_A and variance σ^2. The value of y deviates from μ_A by a random amount e, called the **error** in y. Because y is a random variable with mean μ_A and variance σ^2, it follows that e is a random variable with mean zero and variance σ^2. This gives the equation $y = \mu_A + e$, which is an example of a simple **linear statistical model** called a **means** model. It says that the data value y obtained as a result of applying compound A is equal to the fixed mean μ_A plus the random error e. Taking an additional step, the model equation can be written $y = \mu + \alpha_A + e$. This equation says the data y is equal to the overall mean μ plus the effect α_A of compound A plus the random error e. In this form, the model is called an **effects** model.

In the previous paragraph, discussion centered on the effect of compound A. Similar equations and statements apply to all other levels of the factor, that is, compounds B through E. You can combine all five equations into a single equation by letting μ_i generically represent any one of the five means; that is, let i stand for A, B, C, D, or E. Likewise, $\alpha_i = \mu_i - \mu$, generically represents the effects of the five compounds. Letting y_i be an observation obtained from using compound i, you can write the model $y_i = \mu + \alpha_i + e_i$. The subscript i on e indicates that this is the error that goes with the observation y_i.

Now suppose that each compound is applied to several portions of fruit, say, n. Assignment of fruit portions to compounds is completely at random. The experiment then has a **completely randomized design**. Shelf lives are determined for each treated portion. Then y_{A1} stands for the shelf life of the first portion of fruit treated with compound A. In general, y_{ij} stands for the jth portion of fruit treated with compound i. Then you can write the model equation $y_{ij} = \mu + \alpha_i + e_{ij}$, where e_{ij} is a random variable with mean zero and variance σ^2. Of course, shelf lives of all portions of fruit treated with one of the compounds are not the same because of random variation among the fruit portions themselves. This variation is represented by the e_{ij} quantities in the model. Notice that the variance of e_{ij}, σ^2 is assumed to be the same for each compound. This is an assumption for mathematical convenience and may or may not be valid in a given situation.

Notation note: When data values are summed or averaged over a subscript, that subscript is replaced with a period. For example, $y_{i.}$ stands for the sum $y_{i1} + ... + y_{in}$.

Fixed and Random Effects

Factor effects are either fixed or random depending on how levels of factors that appear in the study are selected. An effect is called **fixed** if the levels in the study represent all possible levels of the factor, or at least all levels about which inference is to be made. In the fruit preservative designed experiment, the effects of the preservative compounds are fixed effects if the five specific compounds are the only candidates for use as preservatives and if conclusions of the experiment are restricted to these five compounds. You can examine differences among the five compounds to see which are essentially equivalent and which are better or worse than others. In terms of the model $y_{ij} = \mu + \alpha_i + e_{ij}$, the overall mean μ can represent the average of the compound means μ_A through μ_E. The effects α_A, α_B, etc. then stand for differences between the mean for a particular compound and the average of the means for all five compounds. The parameters α_A, α_B, etc. represent fixed, unknown quantities.

Data from the study provide estimates about the five compound means and differences among them. For example, the sample mean from compound A, $\bar{y}_{A.}$ is an estimate of the population mean μ_A. The difference between two sample means, such as $\bar{y}_{A.} - \bar{y}_{B.}$ is an estimate of the difference between the two population means $\mu_A - \mu_B$. The variance of the estimate $\bar{y}_{A.}$ is σ^2/n, and the variance of the estimate $\bar{y}_{A.} - \bar{y}_{B.}$ is $2\sigma^2/n$. In reality, σ^2 is unknown and must be estimated. Denote the sample variance for compound A by s_A^2 and similarly for compounds B, C, D and E. Each of these sample variances is an estimate of σ^2 with $n-1$ degrees of freedom. Therefore, the average of the sample variances, $s^2 = (s_A^2 + ... + s_E^2)/5$ is also an estimate of σ^2 with $5(n-1)$ degrees of freedom. This estimate can be used to estimate standard errors of the mean estimates, which in turn can be used to make inference about the mean estimates. For example, an estimate of the standard error of $\bar{y}_{A.} - \bar{y}_{B.}$ is $(2s^2/n)^{1/2}$, which can be used to obtain a confidence interval for $\mu_A - \mu_B$. The confidence interval is $(\bar{y}_{A.} - \bar{y}_{B.} - t_\alpha(2s^2/n)^{1/2}, \bar{y}_{A.} - \bar{y}_{B.} + t_\alpha(2s^2/n)^{1/2})$, where t_α is the α level, two-sided critical value of the t-distribution with $5(n-1)$ degrees of freedom.

Factor effects are **random** if the levels of the factor that are used in the study represent only a random sample of a larger set of potential levels. The factor effects corresponding to the larger set of levels constitute a population of effects with a probability distribution. In the food preservative designed experiment, preservative effects are considered random if there are actually a large number of potential compounds. Only five compounds, however, were randomly selected for use in the study. In these circumstances, the effects of the five compounds in the study may not be of any particular interest to the investigator except for the information they contain about the entire population of preservative effects. The distribution of the population of preservative effects has mean zero and variance σ_P^2. The subscript P refers to variance of the preservative effects. In terms of the model $y_{ij} = \mu + a_i + e_{ij}$, the overall mean μ represents the mean of all compounds in the population,

not just those which appear in the study. Note that the preservative effect is denoted a_i, rather than α_i as in the previous model. A frequently used convention is to denote fixed effects using Greek symbols and random effects using Latin symbols. This book follows this convention. Because the compounds in the study were randomly selected, the effects a_i of the compounds are random variables with a mean zero and variance σ_P^2. The variance of y_{ij} from a randomly chosen portion of fruit treated with a randomly chosen compound is
$\text{Var}(y_{ij}) = \text{Var}(\mu + a_i + e_{ij}) = \sigma_P^2 + \sigma^2$.

The random preservative effects in the food preservative designed experiment represent **random treatment** effects. Other types of random effects are not treatment effects because they are not the result of treating something. For example, suppose there are five portions from each of n individual fruit and that the five preservatives are randomly assigned to the five portions from each fruit. If the n fruit are randomly chosen from a larger population of fruit, then fruit is also a factor with random effects. The experiment as now described has a **randomized blocks design**. The factor fruit has **random block** effects. A model is $y_{ij} = \mu + a_i + b_j + e_{ij}$, where b_j stands for the effect of the jth fruit. The random fruit effects, the b_j's, are random variables with mean zero and variance σ_F^2. The variance of y_{ij} from a randomly chosen portion of a randomly chosen fruit treated with a randomly chosen compound is
$\text{Var}(y_{ij}) = \sigma_P^2 + \sigma_F^2 + \sigma^2$. The variance of the mean for a randomly chosen compound is
$\text{Var}(\bar{y}_{i.}) = \sigma_P^2 + (\sigma_F^2 + \sigma^2)/n$, and the variance of the difference between the means of two randomly chosen compounds is $\text{Var}(\bar{y}_{i.} - \bar{y}_{i'.}) = 2(\sigma_P^2 + \sigma^2/n)$.

Mixed Models

Fixed and random effects were described in the preceding section. A **mixed model** is one that contains both **fixed** and **random effects**. Consider the food preservative designed experiment as described in the previous paragraph in which the five compounds are assigned to five portions from each of n fruit. Return to the assumption that preservative effects are fixed; that is, the five compounds in the study are the only compounds of interest. Retain the assumption, however, that the n fruit are randomly chosen from a larger lot of fruit. Then preservative is a treatment factor with fixed effects and fruit is a blocking factor with random effects. The design is **randomized blocks** with **fixed treatment** effects and **random block** effects.

A model is $y_{ij} = \mu + \alpha_i + b_j + e_{ij}$, where α_A, α_B, etc. represent fixed, unknown parameters, and the b_j are random variables with mean zero and variance σ_F^2. The variance of y_{ij} from a randomly chosen portion of fruit from a randomly chosen fruit treated with a particular one of the five compounds is $\text{Var}(y_{ij}) = \sigma_F^2 + \sigma^2$. The difference between two preservatives (say, A and B) on the same fruit is $y_{Aj} - y_{Bj}$. It is noteworthy that this difference expressed in terms of the model equations is $y_{Aj} - y_{Bj} = \alpha_A + e_{ij} - \alpha_A - e_{ij}$, which contains no fruit effect; that is, the b_j term dropped out of the expression. Thus the variance of this difference is $2\sigma^2$. The difference between preservatives can be measured free of block effects.

The randomized blocks design is just the beginning for mixed models. Numerous other experimental designs produce data for which mixed models are appropriate. Some examples are nested (also called hierarchical) designs, split-plot designs, and repeated measures designs. Each of these experimental designs has its own model structure depending upon how the treatments were applied to experimental units and how data were recorded. In nested and split-plot designs there are typically two or more sizes of experimental units. For example, if the fruit preservatives are applied to an entire fruit and portions from the same fruit are stored under different conditions, then a fruit is an experimental unit for the preservative factor and a portion of a fruit is the experimental unit for the storage condition factor. Variances of means and differences between means must be correctly assessed in order to make valid statistical inferences.

In repeated measures designs the random effects in the model structure are affected by the fact that measurements taken close in time are more highly correlated than measurements taken far apart in time. Take care to build the appropriate covariance structure into the model. Otherwise, tests of hypothesis and confidence intervals are not valid.

Overview of Chapters

There are 12 chapters in this book. We anticipate that Chapters 1 through 4 will be of greatest interest to the most readers because they provide an introduction to mixed model applications and theory. Also, they cover the topics we have found to be the most popular.

Chapter 1, "A Setting for Mixed Models Applications: Randomized Block Designs," contains an introduction to mixed models in the context of randomized blocks designs. The chapter opens with a randomized blocks design with fixed treatments and random blocks and illustrates the importance of accounting for random effects in such a basic situation as computing a variance for a treatment mean. The use of PROC MIXED is introduced with explanations of how to set up the MODEL and RANDOM statements. The chapter continues with illustrations of CONTRAST, ESTIMATE, and LSMEANS statements, which will be familiar to users of the GLM procedure in the SAS System. Then PROC GLM is applied to the same example to illustrate similarities and differences between PROC GLM and PROC MIXED and to emphasize which basic applications are handled correctly by PROC MIXED and not by PROC GLM. A brief explanation of mixed model theory is presented in relation to the randomized blocks design, including explicit descriptions of the matrices in the general linear mixed model. Then, an incomplete block design is used to illustrate some of the issues that occur with unbalanced mixed model data.

Chapter 2, "Common Mixed Models," continues with several examples of mixed model applications in somewhat more complex experimental designs. This chapter focuses on models with more than one error term, that is, models with two or more sizes of experimental units. The two working examples are split-plot models and models arising from multilocation trials. The main emphasis is on the various estimable functions (treatment combination means, marginal means, main-effect differences, simple-effect differences, contrasts) and their associated inference. Derivation of standard errors and obtaining approximate degrees of freedom via Satterthwaite's approximation receive a lot of attention. Similarities and differences to traditional ANOVA, contrasts, etc. using PROC GLM are discussed.

Chapter 3, "Analysis of Repeated Measures Data," covers basic repeated measures analysis using a typical repeated measures data set. The REPEATED statement in PROC MIXED is used to illustrate modelling the covariance structure of repeated measures. Three structure types are shown: compound symmetric, unstructured, and autoregressive order one. Then, PROC GLM is applied to the same example showing the similarities and differences of the two procedures for repeated measures analysis. Finally, the data set is modified to have missing values. Basically, the same analyses are applied using PROC MIXED and PROC GLM to show the advantages of PROC MIXED.

Chapter 4, "Random Effects Models," covers models with random effects only. These are models in which the only fixed parameter is the mean. All other model terms are random variables, that is, random effects. The objective may be to estimate the mean parameter. The standard error of the estimate is a function of the variances of the random effects, and therefore these variances need to be estimated from the data. In some cases, the objective is to estimate the variances of the random effects. This is the case, for example, in quality improvement experiments in which the objective is to determine the amount of variation attributable to several sources of variation such as differences between machines or operators.

The next five chapters, 5 through 9, discuss topics that are somewhat more advanced or at least specialized in application level.

Chapter 5, "Analysis of Covariance," presents analysis of covariance in mixed model situations. Covariance models are useful for comparing groups when there is a continuous independent variable, called a **covariable**. The covariable can account for extraneous variation in the response variable and also can adjust group means to comparable values of the covariable. In mixed model situations, such as split-plot experiments, the covariable may be measured separately on each of the smallest-sized units, or it may be measured only on larger-sized experimental units.

Chapter 6, "Best Linear Unbiased Prediction," (BLUP), covers a topic that is relatively new in most areas of application although it has been used in dairy cattle breeding for several decades. Only in the last fifteen years has its use been recognized in many areas. BLUP is concerned with estimating random effects. In the dairy cattle breeding industry, the problem is to estimate genetic quality of bulls used for artificial insemination. This chapter lays out basic concepts, definitions, and terminology associated with BLUP. The distinctions between BLUP and BLUE (best linear unbiased estimation) and between estimable and predictable functions are defined. Examples of predictable functions that arise naturally from various models are presented. Considerable discussion of the inference space concept is presented.

Chapter 7, "Random Coefficient Models," discusses models in which the regression coefficients are assumed to be a random sample from a population of regression coefficients. In other words, regression lines representing the data are assumed to be a sample from a population of regression lines. For example, growth curves for individual animals may be assumed to be a random sample from a population of growth curves. The objective is to estimate the mean growth curve for the population. In some cases, the samples are from several populations of regression lines and the objective is to compare mean regression lines.

Chapter 8, " Heterogeneous Variance Models," covers models that handle variability and correlations that change over the range of the data. Both between-subject and within-subject heterogeneity are discussed in the context of three examples. The first example considers high flux hemodialyzer data that exhibit a marked increase in variability over transmembrane pressure. Several covariance structures are contrasted and compared, including heterogeneous versions of the standard autoregressive and compound symmetry structures as well as a power-of-the-mean model. The second example, involving grip strength data, shows how between-subject and within-subject heterogeneity can be combined in the same model. Here, the unstructured and random coefficient models serve as useful illustrations. The third example considers a log-linear variance model applied to robust design data from the semiconductor industry. Random effects are also incorporated in this final analysis.

Chapter 9, "Spatial Variability," discusses a popular topic of current statistical research and application. This chapter shows how to use PROC MIXED for data with spatially correlated errors. The first section contains a brief introtion to linear models with spatially correlated errors and describes typical situations where such models may arise. A series of examples of increasing complexity drawn from environmental and agricultural research is presented.

Chapter 10, "Case Studies," provides examples from numerous case studies illustrating a variety of applications.

The final two chapters, 11 and 12, cover topics which the general linear mixed model is not designed to represent. Therefore, PROC MIXED is not directly applicable. However, PROC MIXED can be adapted to handle the essential computations, making solutions available within the SAS System. These applications utilize two macros written by Russell Wolfinger.

Chapter 11, " Generalized Linear Mixed Models," covers models with nonnormal error structure, which comprise another topic of intense current research and application. The first section contains an introduction to generalized linear **fixed effect** models and then develops the extension to generalized linear models with **random** effects. Two examples, a multisite clinical trial with binomial errors and a plant ecology study with Poisson errors, are presented. These models use the GLIMMIX macro to allow you to use PROC MIXED with link functions and variance functions required for generalized linear models.

Chapter 12, " Nonlinear Mixed Models," discusses nonlinear random coefficient models. These are arguably the most complex models considered in this book, and the appropriate analysis methods reflect this complexity. Because of inherent nonlinearities, the standard likelihood-based methods are much more difficult to carry out than with linear mixed models. Hence, three Taylor-series-based approximation methods are discussed and compared, and theoretical details behind the three methods are presented. The methods are implemented in the NLINMIX macro and are illustrated with two examples. The first example considers a traditional data set measuring the growth of orange trees, and the second example models the pharmacokinetics of phenobarbital.

The book concludes with four appendices: Appendix 1, "Mixed Model Theory," is a detailed presentation of mixed model theory as implemented by PROC MIXED. It includes descriptions of the model components in matrix notation, the mixed model equations for estimation, and the statistical foundation for tests of hypotheses and confidence intervals. Appendices 2 and 3 describe the GLIMMIX and NLINMIX macros, which were applied in Chapters 11 and 12, respectively. Finally, Appendix 4, "SAS Data Sets," contains the data sets used in the examples for each chapter.

All PROC MIXED output is produced using Release 6.11 of the SAS System. A special thanks is due to Bill Duckworth of SAS Institute for running the examples.

Chapter 1 A Setting for Mixed Models Applications: Randomized Blocks Designs

1.1 Introduction

Blocking is a research technique that is used to diminish the effects of variation among experimental units. The units can be people, plants, animals, manufactured mechanical parts, or numerous other objects that are used in experimentation. **Blocks** are groups of units that are formed so that units within the blocks are as nearly homogeneous as possible. Then levels of the factor being investigated, called **treatments**, are **randomly assigned to units within the blocks**. An experiment conducted in this manner is called a **randomized blocks design**. The primary objectives usually are to estimate and compare treatment means. In most cases, the **treatment effects** are considered **fixed** because the treatments in the experiment are the only ones to which inference is to be made. That is, no conclusions will be drawn about treatments which were not employed in the experiment. **Block effects** are usually considered **random** because the blocks in the experiment are only a small subset of the larger set of blocks over which inference about treatment means is to be made. In other words, the investigator wants to estimate and compare treatment means with statements of precision (confidence intervals) and levels of statistical significance (from tests of hypothesis) that are valid in reference to the entire population of blocks, not just those in the experiment. To do so requires proper specification of random effects in model equations. In turn, computations for statistical methods must properly accommodate the random effects. The model for data from a randomized blocks design usually should contain fixed effects for treatment contributions and random effects for block contributions, making it a **mixed** model.

Section 1.2 presents the randomized blocks model as it is usually found in a basic statistical methods textbook. The standard analysis of variance methods are given, followed by an example to illustrate the standard methods. Section 1.3 illustrates using the MIXED procedure to obtain the results for the example, followed by results using the GLM procedure and the VARCOMP procedures for comparison. Then, basic mixed model theory for the randomized blocks design is given in section 1.4, including a presentation of the model in matrix notation. Section 1.5 presents an analysis of data from an incomplete blocks design to illustrate PROC MIXED and PROC GLM with unbalanced data.

1.2 Mixed Model for a Randomized Complete Blocks Design

A randomized blocks design that has each treatment applied in each block is called a **randomized complete blocks design** (RCBD). In the most common situation each treatment appears once in each block. Assume there are r blocks and t treatments and there will be one observation per experimental unit. Because each of the t treatments is applied in each of the r blocks, there are tr experimental units altogether. Letting y_{ij} denote the response from the experimental unit that received treatment i in block j, the equation for the model is

$$y_{ij} = \mu + \tau_i + b_j + e_{ij} \tag{1.1}$$

where

$i=1,...,t$
$j=1,...,r$
μ and τ_i are fixed parameters such that the mean for the ith treatment is $\mu_i = \mu + \tau_i$
b_j is the random effect associated with the jth block
e_{ij} is random error associated with the experimental unit in block j that received treatment i.

Assumptions for random effects are
- block effects are distributed **normally and independently** with mean 0 and variance σ_b^2; that is, the b_j are distributed iid $N(0,\sigma_b^2)$
- errors e_{ij} are distributed **normally and independently** with mean 0 and variance σ^2; that is, the e_{ij} are distributed iid $N(0,\sigma^2)$. They are also independent of the b_j.

These are the conventional assumptions for a randomized blocks model.

1.2.1 Means and Variances from Randomized Blocks Design

Recall that the usual objectives of a randomized blocks design are to estimate and compare treatment means using statistical inference. Mathematical expressions are needed for the variances of means and differences between means in order to construct confidence intervals and conduct tests of hypotheses. It follows from model equation 1.1 that a treatment mean, for example, $\bar{y}_{1\bullet}$, can be written

$$\bar{y}_{1\bullet} = \mu_1 + \bar{b}_\bullet + \bar{e}_{1\bullet} \tag{1.2}$$

Likewise, the difference between two means, such as $\bar{y}_{1\bullet} - \bar{y}_{2\bullet}$, can be written

$$\bar{y}_{1\bullet} - \bar{y}_{2\bullet} = \mu_1 - \mu_2 + \bar{e}_{1\bullet} - \bar{e}_{2\bullet} \tag{1.3}$$

From these expressions, you see that the variances of $\bar{y}_{1\bullet}$ and $\bar{y}_{1\bullet} - \bar{y}_{2\bullet}$ are

$$\text{Var}(\bar{y}_{1\bullet}) = (\sigma^2 + \sigma_b^2)/r \tag{1.4}$$

and

$$\text{Var}(\bar{y}_{1\bullet} - \bar{y}_{2\bullet}) = 2(\sigma^2)/r \tag{1.5}$$

Notice that the variance of a treatment mean $\text{Var}(\bar{y}_{1\bullet})$ contains the block variance component σ_b^2, but the variance of the difference between two means $\text{Var}(\bar{y}_{1\bullet} - \bar{y}_{2\bullet})$ does *not* contain σ_b^2. This is the manifestation of the RCBD controlling block variation; differences between treatments are estimated free of block variation.

1.2.2 The Traditional Method: Analysis of Variance

Almost all statistical methods textbooks present analysis of variance (ANOVA) as a key component in analysis of data from a randomized blocks design. Our assumption is that readers are familiar with fundamental concepts for analysis of variance, such as degrees of freedom, sums of squares (SS), mean squares (MS), and expected means squares (Exp MS). Readers needing more information concerning analysis of variance may consult Littell, Freund, and Spector (1991), Milliken and Johnson (1984), or Winer (1991). Table 1.1 is a standard ANOVA table for the RCB, showing sources of variation, degrees of freedom, mean squares, and expected mean squares.

Table 1.1 *ANOVA Table for Randomized Complete Blocks Design*

Source of Variation	df	MS	Exp MS
Blocks	$r-1$	MS(Blks)	$\sigma^2 + t\sigma_b^2$
Treatments	$t-1$	MS(Trts)	$\sigma^2 + r\phi^2$
Error	$(r-1)(t-1)$	MS(Error)	σ^2

1.2.3 Using Expected Mean Squares

Expected means squares are the quantities that are estimated by mean squares in an analysis of variance. They can be used to motivate test statistics. The basic idea is to examine the expected mean square for a factor and see how it differs under the null and alternative hypotheses. For example, the expected mean square for treatments, $E(\text{MS(Trts)}) = \sigma^2 + r\phi^2$, can be used to determine how to set up a test statistic for treatment differences. The null hypothesis is $H_o:\mu_1=...=\mu_t$. The expression ϕ^2 in Exp MS(Trts) is $\phi^2=\Sigma(\mu_i - \bar{\mu}_\bullet)^2/(t-1)$, where $\bar{\mu}_\bullet$ is the mean of $\mu_1,...,\mu_t$. Thus $\phi^2=0$ is equivalent to $\mu_1=...=\mu_t$ So, if the null hypothesis $H_o:\mu_1=...=\mu_t$ is true, MS(Trts) simply estimates σ^2. On the other hand, if $H_o:\mu_1=...=\mu_t$ is false, then Exp MS(Trts) estimates a quantity larger than σ^2. Now, MS(Error) estimates σ^2 regardless of whether H_0 is true or false. Therefore, MS(Trts) and MS(Error) tend to be approximately the same magnitude if H_o is true, and MS(Trts) tends to be larger than MS(Error) if $H_o:\mu_1=...=\mu_t$ is false. So a comparison of MS(Trts) with MS(Error) is an indicator of whether $H_o:\mu_1=...=\mu_t$ is true or false. In this way the expected mean squares show that a valid test statistic is the ratio F=MS(Trt)/MS(Error).

Expected mean squares also can be used to estimate variance components, variances of treatment means, and differences between treatment means. They reveal that estimates of the variance components are

$$\hat{\sigma}^2 = MS(Error) \tag{1.6}$$

and

$$\hat{\sigma}_b^2 = [MS(Blks) - MS(Error)]/t \tag{1.7}$$

These are called **analysis of variance** estimates of the variance components. It follows that estimates of $Var(\bar{y}_{1\bullet})$ and $Var(\bar{y}_{1\bullet} - \bar{y}_{2\bullet})$ are

$$\hat{V}ar(\bar{y}_{1\bullet}) = (\hat{\sigma}^2 + \hat{\sigma}_b^2)/r$$

$$= MS(Blks)/rt + (t-1)MS(Error)/rt \tag{1.8}$$

and

$$\hat{V}ar(\bar{y}_{1\bullet} - \bar{y}_{2\bullet}) = 2MS(Error)/r \tag{1.9}$$

The expression for $Var(\bar{y}_{1\bullet})$ points out a common misconception that the estimate of the variance of a treatment mean from a randomized blocks design is simply $MS(Error)/r$. This misconception prevails in some text books and results in incorrect calculation of standard errors by computer program packages. The good news is that it gives a starting point for illustrating the MIXED procedure in the SAS System.

1.2.4 Example: A Randomized Complete Blocks Design

An example from Mendenhall, Wackerly, and Scheaffer (1990) is used to illustrate analysis of data from a randomized blocks design.

Data for an RCB designed experiment are presented in Data Set 1.1, "BOND," in Appendix 4, "SAS Data Sets." Blocks are ingots of a composition material and treatments are metals (nickel, iron, or copper). The response is the amount of pressure required to break a bond of two pieces of material from an ingot that used one of the metals as the bonding agent.

Table 1.2 *ANOVA Table for BOND Data*

Source of Variation	df	SS	MS	F	P
Ingots	6	268.29	44.72		
Metal	2	131.90	65.95	6.36	0.0131
Error	12	124.46	10.37		

The ANOVA table and the metal means provide the essential computations for statistical inference about the population means.

The ANOVA F = 6.36 for metal gives a test of the null hypothesis H_o: $\mu_c = \mu_i = \mu_n$. The significance probability for the F-test is $p = 0.0131$, indicating strong evidence of differences between metal means. Estimates of the variance components are $\hat{\sigma}^2 = 10.37$ and $\hat{\sigma}_b^2 = (44.72 - 10.37)/3 = 11.45$. Thus, an estimate of the variance of a metal mean is $(\hat{\sigma}^2 + \hat{\sigma}_b^2)/7 = 3.11$, and the estimated standard error is $3.11^{1/2} = 1.77$. An estimate of the variance of a difference between two metal means is $2\hat{\sigma}^2/7 = 2*10.37/7 = 2.96$, and the standard error is $(2.96)^{1/2}$.

A Note for PROC GLM Users

It might seem natural at this point to illustrate the use of PROC GLM to obtain the analysis described in the previous subsection. Indeed, this was strongly considered. However, the main focus of this book is on PROC MIXED, and we decided that this procedure should be the first introduced rather than forever linking PROC MIXED through PROC GLM. It is important to show relationships between the two procedures, and this is done throughout the book. Readers who want to see PROC GLM results for the RCBD first may turn to subsection 1.3.3.

1.3 Using PROC MIXED to Analyze RCBD Data

PROC MIXED is a procedure based on likelihood. That is, many of the estimation and inferential methods are implemented on the basis of the likelihood function and associated principles and theory. Most readers are probably more familiar with the analysis of variance approach described in the previous section. In fact, section 1.2 is presented as a frame of reference rather than as an indication of how PROC MIXED works. In section 1.3.1 results from PROC MIXED are shown that duplicate many of the results of the previous section.

1.3.1 Basic PROC MIXED Statements and Output

Program

Here are the basic PROC MIXED statements for the RCBD data analysis:

```
proc mixed data=rcb;
   class ingot metal;
   model pres=metal;
   random ingot;
run;
```

The PROC MIXED statement calls the procedure.

The CLASS statement specifies that INGOT and METAL are classification variables as opposed to continuous variables.

The MODEL statement is an equation whose left-hand side contains the name of the response variable to be analyzed, in this case PRES. The right-hand side of the MODEL statement contains a list of the **fixed-effect** variables, in this case the variable METAL. In terms of the statistical model, this specifies the τ_i parameters. (The intercept parameter μ is implicitly contained in all models unless otherwise declared.)

The RANDOM statement contains a list of the **random** effects, in this case INGOT, and represent the b_j terms in the statistical model.

The MODEL and RANDOM statements are the core essential statements for many mixed model applications. Results from these statements appear in Output 1.1.

Results

Output 1.1 *Results of the RCBD Data Analysis*

```
                    The MIXED Procedure

                Class Level Information❶

          Class      Levels  Values

          INGOT        7     1 2 3 4 5 6 7
          METAL        3     c i n



             REML Estimation Iteration History❷

        Iteration Evaluations    Objective     Criterion

            0           1       79.32809232
            1           1       74.70841482    0.00000000


                Convergence criteria met.



          Covariance Parameter Estimates (REML)❸

        Cov Parm      Ratio       Estimate     Std Error      Z

        INGOT      1.10376333   11.44777778   8.72036577    1.31
        Residual   1.00000000   10.37158730   4.23418279    2.45



          Covariance Parameter Estimates (REML)

          Pr > |Z|


             0.1893
             0.0143



             Model Fitting Information for PRES❹
          Description                      Value


          Observations                   21.0000
          Variance Estimate              10.3716
          Standard Deviation Estimate     3.2205
          REML Log Likelihood           -53.8951
          Akaike's Information Criterion -55.8951
          Schwarz's Bayesian Criterion  -56.7855
          -2 REML Log Likelihood        107.7902


                Tests of Fixed Effects❺


        Source      NDF   DDF   Type III F  Pr > F

        METAL        2     12       6.36    0.0131
```

Interpretation

The first feature you notice in Output 1.1 is that the PROC MIXED output reflects its likelihood orientation, as opposed to the analysis of variance orientation of the ANOVA and GLM procedures. Here are annotations of key portions of the output.

❶ **Class Level Information** lists the variables in the CLASS statement and their levels.

❷ **REML Estimation Iteration History** shows the sequence of evaluations to obtain (restricted) maximum likelihood estimates of the variance components. This portion of the output is not critical to most applications, such as the present RCBD analysis.

❸ **Covariance Parameter Estimates (REML)** show estimates of the variance component parameters. The estimate of σ_b^2, the block variance component, is 11.45 (labeled INGOT), and the estimate of σ^2, the error variance component, is 10.37 (labeled Residual). For this example of a balanced data set, these variance component estimates are exactly the same as the estimates obtained from the analysis of variance method. That is, the estimate of σ^2 is MS(Error) from the ANOVA table, and the estimate of σ_b^2 is (MS(Blocks)−MS(Error))/7. In more complicated unbalanced data sets, the REML estimates are not necessarily equal to the ANOVA estimates.

❹ **Model Fitting Information for PRES** shows the "Number of Observations" equal to 21. Next is the "Variance Estimate," 10.3716, which is the same as the Residual variance component. This is followed by the Standard Deviation Estimate, 3.2205, which is simply the square root of the Variance Estimate, equal to $10.3716^{1/2}$. Remaining computations are more complicated to explain and are not essential to this analysis.

❺ **Tests of Fixed Effects** is like an abbreviated ANOVA table showing a line of computations for each term in the MODEL statement, in this example, METAL. Included is an F-test for testing the null hypothesis H_0: $\mu_c = \mu_i = \mu_n$. With 2 numerator and 12 denominator degrees of freedom, the F-value of 6.36 is significant at the $p=0.0131$ level. If the true METAL means are equal, then an F-value as large as 6.36 would occur less than 131 times in 10,000 by chance. This is the same F-test that was obtained from the analysis of variance in Table 1.2.

In summary, the basic PROC MIXED computations are based on likelihood principles, but many of the statistical computions are the same as those obtained from analysis of variance methods for a balanced data set.

1.3.2 Estimating and Comparing Means: LSMEANS, ESTIMATE, and CONTRAST Statements

You can obtain treatment means from the LSMEANS (Least Squares MEANS) statement

```
lsmeans metal / pdiff;
```

Results appear in Output 1.2.

Results Using the LSMEANS Statement

Output 1.2 *Results of Using the LSMEANS Statement*

```
                          Least Squares Means


    Level            LSMEAN      Std Error    DDF      T    Pr > |T|


    METAL c       70.18571429   1.76551753    12    39.75   0.0001
    METAL i       75.90000000   1.76551753    12    42.99   0.0001
    METAL n       71.10000000   1.76551753    12    40.27   0.0001



                   Differences of Least Squares Means


    Level 1   Level 2   Difference    Std Error    DDF      T     Pr > |T|


    METAL c   METAL i   -5.71428571   1.72142692    12    -3.32    0.0061
    METAL c   METAL n   -0.91428571   1.72142692    12    -0.53    0.6050
    METAL i   METAL n    4.80000000   1.72142692    12     2.79    0.0164
```

Interpretation

For the case of balanced data, the LS means are simply the averages for treatments. Also printed are standard errors for the means. The value is 1.766 for each of the means. This estimate is equal to $((\hat{\sigma}^2+\hat{\sigma}_b^2)/7)^{1/2}$, which is a valid estimate of the true standard error $((\sigma^2+\sigma_b^2)/7)^{1/2}$ because it uses the correct linear combinations of variance components.

Pairwise comparisons of means are obtained by the PDIFF option on the LSMEANS statement. In Output 1.3 you see pairwise differences and standard errors of the differences. Each standard error has the value 1.721, equal to $(2\hat{\sigma}^2/7)^{1/2}$. You also see results of *t*-tests for the statistical significance of the difference between the means in each pair. The results declare both copper and nickel different from iron but copper and nickel not different from each other.

Linear combinations of means can be estimated with the ESTIMATE statement. For illustration, consider the linear combination equal to the nickel mean, μ_n. First of all, express the nickel mean as a linear combination of the model parameters, $\mu_n=\mu+\tau_n$. More explicitly, $\mu_n=1\mu+0\tau_c+0\tau_i+1\tau_n$. Then insert these coefficients of the model parameters into the ESTIMATE statement:

```
estimate 'nickel mean' intercept 1 metal 0 0 1;
```

In a similar fashion, the difference between the means for copper and iron is $\mu_c-\mu_i=\tau_c-\tau_i$, so the ESTIMATE statement is

```
estimate 'copper vs iron' metal 1 -1 0;
```

Results of these ESTIMATE statements appear in Output 1.3.

Output 1.3 *Inference about Linear Combinations of Means*

```
                          ESTIMATE Statement Results

Parameter       Estimate        Std Error     DDF       T       Pr > |T|
nickel mean     71.10000000     1.76551753     12      40.27    0.0001
copper vs iron  -5.71428571     1.72142692     12      -3.32    0.0061


                          CONTRAST Statement Results

Source          NDF             DDF           F       Pr > F
copper vs iron  1               12            11.02    0.0061
```

You see that the estimates of the nickel mean and differences between the copper and iron means are the same as those obtained from the LSMEANS statement in Output 1.2.

The CONTRAST statement is a companion to the ESTIMATE statement. It is used to test hypotheses about linear combinations of model parameters. To test the null hypothesis $H_o:\mu_c-\mu_i = 0$, submit the statements

```
contrast 'copper vs iron' metal 1 -1 0;
```

This CONTRAST statement produces the F-test shown in Output 1.3.

The F-value of 11.02 is equal to the square of the *t*-value from the corresponding ESTIMATE statement.

The general use of the ESTIMATE and CONTRAST statements is to estimate and test linear combinations of *all* terms in the mixed model, including random effects.

1.3.3 Comparison of PROC MIXED with PROC GLM for the RCBD Data

PROC GLM was the principal SAS procedure for analyzing mixed models data prior to the advent of PROC MIXED, even though the basic computations of PROC GLM are for fixed effect models. The GLM procedure uses statements similar to those used by PROC MIXED. In this section you will see differences and similarities in the statements and output. However, you will not see complete coverage of PROC GLM capabilities. Refer to Littell, Freund, and Spector (1991) for more detailed PROC GLM coverage.

Program

Statements for PROC GLM to obtain the ANOVA table, mean estimates, and comparisons analogous to those discussed in Section 1.3.1 and 1.3.2 are

```
proc glm data=rcb;
   class ingot metal;
   model pres=ingot metal;
   lsmeans metal/stderr pdiff;
   estimate 'nickel mean' intercep 1 metal 0 0 1;
   estimate 'copper vs iron' metal 1 -1 0;
   contrast 'copper vs iron' metal 1 -1 0;
   random ingot;
run;
```

Results of these statements appear in Output 1.4.

Results

Output 1.4 *Randomized Blocks Analysis with PROC GLM*

```
                    General Linear Models Procedure
                      Class Level Information

            Class      Levels     Values

            INGOT        7      1 2 3 4 5 6 7

            METAL        3      c i n


          Number of observations in data set = 21


            General Linear Models Procedure

Dependent Variable: PRES
```

Source	DF	Sum of Squares	F Value	Pr > F
Model	8	400.19047619	4.82	0.0076
Error	12	124.45904762		
Corrected Total	20	524.64952381		

R-Square	C.V.	PRES Mean
0.762777	4.448490	72.3952381

Source	DF	Type I SS	F Value	Pr > F
INGOT	6	268.28952381	4.31	0.0151
METAL	2	131.90095238	6.36	0.0131

Source	DF	Type III SS	F Value	Pr > F

INGOT	6	268.28952381	4.31	0.0151
METAL	2	131.90095238	6.36	0.0131

General Linear Models Procedure
Least Squares Means

METAL	PRES LSMEAN	Std Err LSMEAN	Pr > |T| H0:LSMEAN=0	LSMEAN Number
c	70.1857143	1.2172327	0.0001	1
i	75.9000000	1.2172327	0.0001	2
n	71.1000000	1.2172327	0.0001	3

Pr > |T| H0: LSMEAN(i)=LSMEAN(j)

i/j	1	2	3
1	.	0.0061	0.6050
2	0.0061	.	0.0164
3	0.6050	0.0164	.

NOTE: To ensure overall protection level, only probabilities associated with pre-planned comparisons should be used.

General Linear Models Procedure

Source	Type III Expected Mean Square
INGOT	Var(Error) + 3 Var(INGOT)
METAL	Var(Error) + Q(METAL)

Contrast	Contrast Expected Mean Square
copper vs iron	Var(Error) + Q(METAL)

General Linear Models Procedure

Dependent Variable: PRES

Contrast	DF	Contrast SS	F Value	Pr > F
copper vs iron	1	114.28571429	11.02	0.0061

Parameter	Estimate	T for H0: Parameter=0	Pr > |T|	Std Error of Estimate
copper vs iron	-5.7142857	-3.32	0.0061	1.72142692
nickel mean	71.1000000	58.41	0.0001	1.21723265

Interpretation

Following is a comparison of syntax and output for PROC GLM and PROC MIXED statements:

- First, both procedures use the same CLASS statements; if a variable is a classification variable in PROC GLM, then so it is with PROC MIXED.

- You see that the MODEL statements of PROC MIXED and PROC GLM are *not* exactly the same. This is a very important distinction between the procedures: In PROC MIXED, you list only the *fixed* effects in the right-hand side of the MODEL statement. But in PROC GLM you list all effects, both fixed and random, although PROC GLM does not really treat the random effects as random. The options in PROC GLM for inference accommodating random effects are adaptations of the fixed effect computations for this procedure. PROC MIXED, on the other hand, was conceived from the outset for mixed models. The distinction between MODEL statements in PROC MIXED and PROC GLM carries over to the output from the two procedures. In Output 1.6, from PROC GLM, you see an ANOVA table listing all the terms in the MODEL statement, with no distinction between fixed and random. But in Output 1.2, from PROC MIXED, the list of Tests of Fixed Effects contains only terms in the MODEL statement.

- The LSMEANS statements for the two procedures are essentially the same, except that you need the STDERR option in the LSMEANS statement for PROC GLM. Here is another important distinction between the procedures: In comparing Output 1.3 with Output 1.4, you see that the LSMEANS estimates are the same for the two procedures, but their standard errors are *not* the same. This is due to the inherent fixed-effect nature of PROC GLM. The standard errors for the LSMEANS computed by PROC GLM are $(\hat{\sigma}^2/7)^{1/2}$, which would be appropriate if INGOT (the blocks) were fixed. Recall from section 1.3.1 that PROC MIXED performed correct computations for the LSMEAN standard errors with INGOT random.

- Syntax for ESTIMATE statements is the same in PROC GLM as in PROC MIXED for estimating linear combinations of fixed effects. The remarks comparing standard errors of LSMEANS estimates from PROC MIXED and PROC GLM also hold pertaining to ESTIMATE statements. You see in Output 1.5 from PROC GLM that the standard error of the estimate of the nickel mean is the same as for the nickel LSMEAN, which previously was stated to be incorrect.

  Estimates, their standard errors and tests of the difference between the COPPER and IRON means are the same for PROC GLM (Output 1.4) and PROC MIXED (Outputs 1.2 and 1.3). This is true for the present example, but not for all mixed model data sets, as you will see in the case of an incomplete block design in subsection 1.5.2.

- The RANDOM statements for PROC MIXED and PROC GLM represent another major distinction between the two procedures although they have the same appearance for the present example. In PROC MIXED, listing INGOT in the RANDOM statement causes all standard errors and test statistics to incorporate the information that the effect is random. This is not true in PROC GLM. The RANDOM statement in PROC GLM (as used here) merely computes expected mean squares for terms in the MODEL statement and for linear combinations in the CONTRAST statement. You must then digest the information in the expected means squares table and formulate appropriate tests. (The TEST option in the PROC GLM RANDOM statement will do this automatically for terms in the MODEL statement, but not for CONTRAST statements.) In the RCBD example, the default tests computed by PROC GLM are correct, so no modification is needed for the test of differences from the MODEL and CONTRAST statements.

These comparisons of PROC MIXED and PROC GLM are summarized in Table 1.3 in the next section.

1.3.4 Comparison of PROC VARCOMP with PROC MIXED and PROC GLM for the RCBD Data

Program

The VARCOMP procedure is used to obtain estimates of the variance components in a mixed model. For the RCBD data, submit the statements

```
proc varcomp method=reml data=rcb;
   class ingot metal;
   model pres=metal ingot / fixed=1;
run;
```

PROC VARCOMP uses the same CLASS statement as PROC GLM and PROC MIXED. The MODEL statement in PROC VARCOMP contains a list of all fixed-effect variables followed by all random-effect variables. The designation FIXED=1 tells VARCOMP how many of the variables are fixed. Only classification variables are allowed in the MODEL statement of PROC VARCOMP. Results appear in Output 1.5.

Results

Output 1.5 *Variance Component Estimation Procedure*

```
            Variance Components Estimation Procedure
                   Class Level Information

            Class      Levels     Values

            INGOT         7       1 2 3 4 5 6 7

            METAL         3       c i n


         Number of observations in data set = 21


            REML Variance Components Estimation Procedure

Dependent Variable: PRES


    Iteration        Objective      Var(INGOT)      Var(Error)

          0        50.87068437     11.44777778     10.37158730
          1        50.87068437     11.44777778     10.37158730

                Convergence criteria met.
```

```
             Asymptotic Covariance Matrix of Estimates


                           Var(INGOT)        Var(Error)


            Var(INGOT)     76.04477922       -5.97610129
            Var(Error)     -5.97610129       17.92830386
```

Interpretation

You see iterative computations toward estimation of the variance components σ_b^2 and σ^2. The estimates are 11.45 and 10.37. These are the same estimates produced by PROC MIXED. The "Asymptotic Covariance Matrix of Estimates" contains estimates of the large sample variances and covariances of the variance component estimates. The variance estimate of the INGOT variance component estimate is 76.04; its square root of 8.72 is the standard error of the variance component estimate printed by PROC MIXED in Output 1.1. Likewise, the variance estimate of the ERROR variance component estimate is 17.93, and its square root of 4.23 is the standard error of the variance component estimate labeled Residual in Output 1.1. The estimate of the covariance between the variance component estimates is -5.98.

Comparisons of PROC VARCOMP, PROC GLM, and PROC MIXED for the RCBD data are summarized in Table 1.3.

Table 1.3 *Summary Comparison of Syntax and Output for PROC GLM, PROC MIXED, and PROC VARCOMP*

Statement	PROC MIXED	PROC GLM	PROC VARCOMP
CLASS	list classification variables	same	same
MODEL	specify dependent variable and list fixed effect	specify dependent variable and list all terms in model	specify dependent variable and list all terms in model, fixed effects preceding random
RANDOM	specify random effects	obtain table of expected mean squares	not applicable
LSMEANS	estimate means for fixed effect factors	estimate means for fixed effect factors	not applicable
ESTIMATE	estimate linear combination of model terms	estimate linear combination of model terms	not applicable
CONTRAST	test set of linear combinations of model terms	test set of linear combination of model terms	not applicable

1.4 Introduction to the Theory of Linear Models

You have seen an application of PROC MIXED to the RCBD data set. Before introducing other example data sets, a brief introduction to mixed model theory is presented to help you understand the basis for applications. Also, this introduction to theory helps you understand the differences between results produced by PROC MIXED and PROC GLM. This is a very brief and incomplete presentation of mixed model theory. Complete results are presented in Appendix 1. The use of matrix notation makes the results more concise and easily comprehensible than the use of summation notation.

1.4.1 Some Basic Theory Results

You are probably already familiar with the standard linear regression model in matrix notation,

$$\mathbf{Y} = \mathbf{X}\boldsymbol{\beta} + \mathbf{e} \tag{1.10}$$

where

$\mathbf{Y}$ is the vector of observations
$\mathbf{X}$ is the matrix of values of independent variables
$\boldsymbol{\beta}$ is the vector of regression parameters
$\mathbf{e}$ is a vector of errors.

Ordinary least squares (OLS) estimates of the parameters in $\boldsymbol{\beta}$ are given by solving the normal equations

$$\mathbf{X'X}\boldsymbol{\beta} = \mathbf{X'Y} \tag{1.11}$$

A solution is given by

$$\hat{\boldsymbol{\beta}} = (\mathbf{X'X})^{-}\mathbf{X'Y} \tag{1.12}$$

where $(\mathbf{X'X})^{-}$ is a generalized inverse of $\mathbf{X'X}$.

Notice that we have not made any assumptions about the probability distribution of the vector $\mathbf{e}$ of errors. The estimator $\hat{\boldsymbol{\beta}}$ is an OLS estimator of $\boldsymbol{\beta}$ regardless of the distribution of $\mathbf{e}$. Now assume that the errors are independently and normally distributed with common variance σ^2. Then the covariance matrix of $\hat{\boldsymbol{\beta}}$ is $\sigma^2(\mathbf{X'X})^{-}$. Also, $\hat{\boldsymbol{\beta}}$ is the best estimate of $\boldsymbol{\beta}$ in the following sense: if $\mathbf{K}$ is a vector of coefficients such that the linear combination $\mathbf{K'}\boldsymbol{\beta}$ is estimable, then the best linear unbiased estimate (BLUE) of $\mathbf{K'}\boldsymbol{\beta}$ is $\mathbf{K'}\hat{\boldsymbol{\beta}}$. These results provide the foundation for statistical inference about linear combinations of the parameter vector $\boldsymbol{\beta}$.

The regression model is a special case of the general linear mixed model (GLMM), which has the equation

$$\mathbf{Y} = \mathbf{X}\boldsymbol{\beta} + \mathbf{Zu} + \mathbf{e} \tag{1.13}$$

In this equation $\mathbf{u}$ is distributed multivariate normal with mean vector $\mathbf{0}$ and covariance matrix $\mathbf{G}$ (which we denote MVN($\mathbf{0},\mathbf{G}$)), and $\mathbf{e}$ is distributed MVN($\mathbf{0},\mathbf{R}$). The only requirement of the matrices $\mathbf{G}$ and $\mathbf{R}$ is that they be positive definite (that is, they are covariance matrices). Then the covariance matrix of $\mathbf{Y}$ is

$$V(\mathbf{Y}) = \mathbf{ZGZ'} + \mathbf{R} \tag{1.14}$$

The **RANDOM** statement in PROC MIXED **defines G**, and the **REPEATED** statement, which will be introduced in Chapter 4, **defines R**.

It follows that $\mathbf{Y}$ is distributed MVN($\mathbf{X}\boldsymbol{\beta},\mathbf{ZGZ'} + \mathbf{R}$). Thus the generalized least squares (GLS) estimate of $\boldsymbol{\beta}$ is

$$\hat{\boldsymbol{\beta}} = (\mathbf{X'V}^{-1}\mathbf{X})^{-}\mathbf{X'V}^{-1}\mathbf{Y} \tag{1.15}$$

where $\mathbf{V} = V(\mathbf{Y}) = \mathbf{ZGZ'} + \mathbf{R}$. Also,

$$V(\hat{\boldsymbol{\beta}}) = (\mathbf{X'V^{-1}X})^- \tag{1.16}$$

If $\mathbf{K'\beta}$ is estimable, then the BLUE of $\mathbf{K'\beta}$ is $\mathbf{K'}\hat{\boldsymbol{\beta}}$, and the variance of $\mathbf{K'}\hat{\boldsymbol{\beta}}$ is $\mathbf{K'(X'V^{-1}X)^-K}$.

Analogous to the regression model, the preceding results provide the foundation for statistical inference about linear combinations of the parameter vector $\boldsymbol{\beta}$. That is, they can be used to test hypotheses and to construct confidence intervals about linear combinations of parameters. These are some of the basic theoretical results used by PROC MIXED.

In reality, the covariance matrices **G and R are usually functions of unknown parameters**, which must be estimated. Typically, the parameters are variance components or correlation parameters. PROC MIXED uses either ML or REML to estimate the parameters of **G** and **R** (ML and REML are described in Appendix 1). Then these estimates are substituted in place of the true parameters values in **G** and **R** to compute estimates of $\boldsymbol{\beta}$ and $V(\boldsymbol{\beta})$. Also, the matrix $\mathbf{X'V^{-1}X}$ typically is singular so that a generalized inverse is used.

1.4.2 The RCBD Model in Matrix Notation

The RCBD model in equation (1.1) can be written in matrix notation. In explicit detail, the model equation is

$$
\begin{bmatrix} Y_{11} \\ \cdot \\ \cdot \\ Y_{t1} \\ \cdot \\ \cdot \\ \cdot \\ Y_{1r} \\ \cdot \\ \cdot \\ Y_{tr} \end{bmatrix}
=
\begin{bmatrix} 1 & 1 & . & . & . & 0 \\ & . & . & . & & . \\ & & & & & \\ 1 & 0 & & & & 1 \\ & . & . & & & \\ . & & . & & . \\ . & & & & . \\ 1 & 1 & . & . & . & 0 \\ & . & . & . & & . \\ & . & . & & & . \\ 1 & 0 & & & & 1 \end{bmatrix}
\begin{bmatrix} \mu \\ \tau_1 \\ \cdot \\ \cdot \\ \tau_t \end{bmatrix}
+
\begin{bmatrix} 1 & . & . & . & 0 \\ \cdot & & & & \cdot \\ \cdot & & & & \cdot \\ 1 & . & . & . & 0 \\ \cdot & & & & \cdot \\ . & . & & . \\ 0 & . & . & . & 1 \\ \cdot & & & & \cdot \\ \cdot & & & & \cdot \\ 0 & . & . & . & 1 \end{bmatrix}
\begin{bmatrix} b_1 \\ \cdot \\ \cdot \\ b_r \end{bmatrix}
+
\begin{bmatrix} e_{11} \\ \cdot \\ \cdot \\ e_{t1} \\ \cdot \\ \cdot \\ e_{1r} \\ \cdot \\ \cdot \\ e_{tr} \end{bmatrix}
\tag{1.17}
$$

with terms defined following equation (1.1). In more compact matrix notation the equation is

$$\mathbf{Y} = \mathbf{X\beta} + \mathbf{Zu} + \mathbf{e} \tag{1.18}$$

where
   Y is the vector of observations
   X is the treatment design matrix
   $\boldsymbol{\beta}$ is the vector of treatment fixed effect parameters
   Z is the block design matrix
   u is the vector of random block effects
   e is the vector of experimental errors.

The equation states that the vector **Y** of observations can be expressed as a sum of fixed treatment effects **Xβ**, random block effects **Zu**, and random experimental errors **e**. The **Xβ** portion is defined by the MODEL statement, and the **Zu** portion is defined by the RANDOM statement. It is not necessary in this example to define the experimental errors **e**.

For the RCBD model in matrix notation, the random vector **u** has a multivariate normal distribution with mean vector **0** and covariance matrix $\sigma_b^2\mathbf{I}_r$ (**V** is distributed MVN($\mathbf{0}, \sigma_b^2\mathbf{I}_r$)), and the random vector **e** is distributed MVN($\mathbf{0}, \sigma^2\mathbf{I}_{tr}$).

The variance of the observation vector **Y** is

$$\mathbf{V} = \mathbf{V(Y)} = \mathbf{ZGZ'} + \mathbf{R}$$

$$= \begin{bmatrix} \sigma_b^2\mathbf{J}_r & \Phi_r & \dots & \Phi_r \\ \Phi_r & \sigma_b^2\mathbf{J}_r & \dots & \Phi_r \\ \cdot & & \cdot & \cdot \\ \cdot & & \cdot & \cdot \\ \cdot & & \cdot & \cdot \\ \Phi_r & \Phi_r & \dots & \sigma_b^2\mathbf{J}_r \end{bmatrix} + \sigma^2\mathbf{I}_{tr}$$

$$= \begin{bmatrix} \mathbf{V}_b & \Phi_r & \dots & \Phi_r \\ \Phi_r & \mathbf{V}_b & \dots & \Phi_r \\ \cdot & & \cdot & \cdot \\ \cdot & & \cdot & \cdot \\ \cdot & & \cdot & \cdot \\ \Phi_r & \Phi_r & \dots & \mathbf{V}_b \end{bmatrix}$$

where $\mathbf{V}_b = \sigma_b^2\mathbf{J}_r + \sigma^2\mathbf{I}_r$ is the covariance matrix of all the observations in a particular block, Φ_r is an $r{\times}r$ matrix of zeros, and $\mathbf{J}_r$ is an $r{\times}r$ matrix of 1's.

The matrix $\mathbf{X'V^{-1}X}$ is singular, so a generalized inverse must be used to obtain a GLS estimate β of the fixed effect parameter vector. But the treatment means and differences between treatment means are estimable parameters. Thus, no matter what generalized inverse is used, there will be a **K** vector for which **K'β** is equal to a mean or a difference between means. For example, choosing **K'**=(1,1,0,...,0) gives **K'β**= $\mu + \tau_1 = \mu_1$. Then the general theory gives $\mathbf{V(K'\beta)} = (\sigma_b^2 + \sigma^2)/r$. Likewise, **K'**=(0,1,−1,0...,0) gives **K'β**=$\mu_1 - \mu_2$, and $\mathbf{V(K'\beta)} = 2(\sigma^2)/r$. These are the expressions presented in section 1.2.1.

In the case of a relatively simple, balanced design such as an RCBD, the variance expressions can be derived directly from the model as was done in subsection 1.2.1. But in more complicated unbalanced situations, the general theoretical results must be invoked. In this subsection, we have illustrated the general results in the RCBD setting to confirm their validity and to assist you in becoming more comfortable in using the general linear mixed model.

1.5 Example of an Unbalanced Two-way Mixed Model: Incomplete Block Design

In some applications of blocking there are not enough experimental units in each block to accommodate all treatments. **Incomplete block designs** are designs in which only a subset of the treatments are applied in each block. The treatments that go into each block should be selected in order to provide the most information relative to the objectives of the experiment.

Two types of incomplete block designs are the so-called **balanced** incomplete block design (BIBD) and the **partially balanced** incomplete block design (PBIBD). This does not mean "balanced" in the more common sense of the word, in which each treatment appears the same number of times in each block. In fact, any incomplete block design is "unbalanced" by the common definition.

The BIB and PBIB designs result in all treatments having the same variance (and hence the same standard error). Also, the variances of differences between two treatment means are the same for all pairs of treatments with BIBDs and for sets of treatments with PBIBDs. As you may suspect, it is not possible to construct BIB or PBIB designs for all possible numbers of treatments and blocks. Discovery of numbers of blocks and treatments for which BIBDs and PBIBDs can be constructed was once an active area of statistical research. With the advent of fast computers and good statistical software, the existence of BIBDs and PBIBDs for given numbers of blocks and treatments has become a less important problem. Mead (1988) has an excellent discussion of this issue.

This section presents analyses for a PBIBD using PROC GLM and PROC MIXED to further illustrate some of the similarities and differences between the two procedures. You can see some distinctions between PROC MIXED and PROC GLM that did not occur in the analyses of the RCB design. Although the example is a PBIBD, data analysis methods of this section apply to incomplete block designs in general.

Model

The equation for the model of an incomplete blocks design is the same as for an RCBD. That is, the response Y_{ij} that results from applying treatment i in block j is assumed to be equal to a treatment mean $\mu_i = \mu + \tau_i$ plus a block effect b_j, plus experimental error e_{ij}. Thus the equation

$$Y_{ij} = \mu + \tau_i + b_j + e_{ij} \tag{1.19}$$

where the block effects b_j are iid $N(0, \sigma_b^2)$, the experimental errors e_{ij} are iid $N(0, \sigma^2)$, and the b_j are independent of the e_{ij}. An analysis of variance table for an incomplete blocks design is shown in Table 1.4.

Table 1.4 *Analysis of Variance Table for Incomplete Blocks Design*

Source of Variation	df	F
Blocks	r-1	
Treatments (adjusted for blocks)	t-1	MS(Trts adj.)/MS(Error)
Error	N-r-t+1	

In the table, r is the number of blocks, t is the number of treatments, and N is the total number of observations. Notice that the Treatments source of variation is adjusted for blocks. The Treatments cannot be compared simply on the basis of the usual sum of squared differences between treatment means because this would contain effects of blocks as well as treatment differences. Instead, a sum of squared differences must be computed between treatment means that have been adjusted to remove the block effects.

Analyses of BIBD and PBIBD data that are presented in most statistics textbooks are called **intra-block** analyses because treatments are compared on the basis of differences computed within blocks. You can perform this type of analysis with PROC GLM. It is discussed first in subsection 1.5.1 because this is the analysis with which you are most likely familiar. In subsection 1.5.2, an analysis is presented using PROC MIXED that utilizes information about treatment means contained in differences between blocks. This type of analysis combines intra- and inter-block information.

1.5.1 The Usual Intra-block Analysis of PBIB Data Using PROC GLM

Data Set 1.5.1, PBIB, in Appendix 4, "SAS Data Sets," contains data from Cochran and Cox (1957, p. 456). The design is a PBIBD with fifteen blocks, fifteen treatments, and four treatments per block. Data are pounds of seed cotton per plot. The **block size** is the number of treatments per block. This PBIBD has a block size of four. Each treatment appears in four blocks. Some pairs of treatments appear together in one block (e.g., treatments 1 and 2) and others do not appear together in the same blocks (e.g., treatments 1 and 6).

Program

An intra-block analysis of the PBIBD data is obtained from submitting the statements

```
proc glm data=pbib;
   class blk treat;
   model response=blk treat;
   means treat;
   lsmeans treat / stderr pdiff;
   estimate 'treat 1 mean' intercep 1 treat 1;
   estimate 'trt 1 mean' intercep 15 treat 15
            blk 1 1 1 1 1 1 1 1 1 1 1 1 1 1 1 / divisor=15;
   estimate 'trt 1 blk 1' intercep 1 treat 1 blk 1;
   estimate 'trt 1 vs trt 2' treat 1 -1;
   contrast 'trt 1 vs trt 2' treat 1 -1;
   random block;
run;
```

Results appear in Output 1.6.

Results

Output 1.6 *Incomplete Blocks Design: PROC GLM Analysis*

```
                    General Linear Models Procedure
                       Class Level Information

        Class     Levels    Values

        BLK          15      1 2 3 4 5 6 7 8 9 10 11 12 13 14 15

        TREAT        15      1 2 3 4 5 6 7 8 9 10 11 12 13 14 15



              Number of observations in data set = 60



                    General Linear Models Procedure

Dependent Variable: RESPONSE

Source                   DF     Sum of Squares    F Value     Pr > F

Model                    28        6.32855556       2.62      0.0050

Error                    31        2.67077778

Corrected Total          59        8.99933333

                 R-Square            C.V.           RESPONSE Mean

                 0.703225          10.72546           2.73666667


Source                   DF      Type III SS     F Value     Pr > F

BLK                      14        3.33422222       2.76      0.0090
TREAT                    14        1.48922222       1.23      0.3012



                    General Linear Models Procedure

        Level of          ----------RESPONSE----------
        TREAT      N         Mean                SD

          1        4       2.77500000        0.17078251
          2        4       2.40000000        0.21602469
          3        4       2.45000000        0.23804761
          4        4       2.95000000        0.36968455
          5        4       2.80000000        0.14142136
          6        4       2.92500000        0.80156098
          7        4       2.82500000        0.17078251
          8        4       2.72500000        0.34034296
```

```
                9        4       2.82500000       0.51881275
               10        4       2.45000000       0.12909944
               11        4       2.97500000       0.32015621
               12        4       3.12500000       0.29860788
               13        4       2.52500000       0.37749172
               14        4       2.42500000       0.05000000
               15        4       2.87500000       0.55000000
```

General Linear Models Procedure

Least Squares Means

TREAT	RESPONSE LSMEAN	Std Err LSMEAN	Pr > |T| H0:LSMEAN=0	LSMEAN Number
1	2.84555556	0.16342514	0.0001	1
2	2.41277778	0.16342514	0.0001	2
3	2.45166667	0.16342514	0.0001	3
4	2.68333333	0.16342514	0.0001	4
5	2.80666667	0.16342514	0.0001	5
6	2.90388889	0.16342514	0.0001	6
7	2.77111111	0.16342514	0.0001	7
8	2.81000000	0.16342514	0.0001	8
9	2.93333333	0.16342514	0.0001	9
10	2.51500000	0.16342514	0.0001	10
11	2.85388889	0.16342514	0.0001	11
12	3.01277778	0.16342514	0.0001	12
13	2.66833333	0.16342514	0.0001	13
14	2.53333333	0.16342514	0.0001	14
15	2.84833333	0.16342514	0.0001	15

Pr > |T| H0: LSMEAN(i)=LSMEAN(j)

i/j	1	2	3	4	5	6	7	8
1	.	0.0711	0.0989	0.4887	0.8677	0.8093	0.7500	0.8789
2	0.0711	.	0.8677	0.2515	0.0989	0.0420	0.1450	0.0962
3	0.0989	0.8677	.	0.3248	0.1354	0.0599	0.1776	0.1450
4	0.4887	0.2515	0.3248	.	0.5981	0.3482	0.7072	0.5882
5	0.8677	0.0989	0.1354	0.5981	.	0.6774	0.8789	0.9886
6	0.8093	0.0420	0.0599	0.3482	0.6774	.	0.5705	0.6879
7	0.7500	0.1450	0.1776	0.7072	0.8789	0.5705	.	0.8677
8	0.8789	0.0962	0.1450	0.5882	0.9886	0.6879	0.8677	.
9	0.7072	0.0318	0.0458	0.3049	0.5882	0.8996	0.4887	0.5981
10	0.1634	0.6619	0.7863	0.4727	0.2328	0.1031	0.2772	0.2121
11	0.9725	0.0661	0.0923	0.4669	0.8397	0.8361	0.7231	0.8509
12	0.4756	0.0178	0.0214	0.1648	0.3802	0.6414	0.3211	0.3879
13	0.4498	0.2782	0.3729	0.9488	0.5545	0.3168	0.6602	0.5587
14	0.1873	0.6063	0.7267	0.5360	0.2468	0.1196	0.3124	0.2412
15	0.9905	0.0694	0.0967	0.4814	0.8631	0.8120	0.7410	0.8696

Pr > |T| H0: LSMEAN(i)=LSMEAN(j)

i/j	9	10	11	12	13	14	15
1	0.7072	0.1634	0.9725	0.4756	0.4498	0.1873	0.9905
2	0.0318	0.6619	0.0661	0.0178	0.2782	0.6063	0.0694
3	0.0458	0.7863	0.0923	0.0214	0.3729	0.7267	0.0967
4	0.3049	0.4727	0.4669	0.1648	0.9488	0.5360	0.4814

5	0.5882	0.2328	0.8397	0.3802	0.5545	0.2468	0.8631
6	0.8996	0.1031	0.8361	0.6414	0.3168	0.1196	0.8120
7	0.4887	0.2772	0.7231	0.3211	0.6602	0.3124	0.7410
8	0.5981	0.2121	0.8509	0.3879	0.5587	0.2412	0.8696
9	.	0.0805	0.7338	0.7338	0.2612	0.1052	0.7160
10	0.0805	.	0.1533	0.0395	0.5127	0.9374	0.1742
11	0.7338	0.1533	.	0.4977	0.4290	0.1761	0.9810
12	0.7338	0.0395	0.4977	.	0.1469	0.0468	0.4829
13	0.2612	0.5127	0.4290	0.1469	.	0.5641	0.4428
14	0.1052	0.9374	0.1761	0.0468	0.5641	.	0.1835
15	0.7160	0.1742	0.9810	0.4829	0.4428	0.1835	.

NOTE: To ensure overall protection level, only probabilities
associated with pre-planned comparisons should be used.

General Linear Models Procedure

Source	Type III Expected Mean Square
BLK	Var(Error) + 3.2143 Var(BLK)
TREAT	Var(Error) + Q(TREAT)

Contrast	Contrast Expected Mean Square
trt1 vs trt2	Var(Error) + Q(TREAT)

General Linear Models Procedure

Dependent Variable: RESPONSE

Contrast	DF	Contrast SS	F Value	Pr > F
trt1 vs trt2	1	0.30101240	3.49	0.0711

Parameter	Estimate	T for H0: Parameter=0	Pr > |T|	Std Error of Estimate
treat 1 mean	2.84555556	17.41	0.0001	0.16342514
trt 1 mean	2.84555556	17.41	0.0001	0.16342514
trt 1 blk 1	2.39666667	11.74	0.0001	0.20406165
trt 1 vs trt 2	0.43277778	1.87	0.0711	0.23153188

From Output 1.6, you can construct the analysis of variance table, as shown in Table 1.5.

Table 1.5 *Analysis of Variance Table for Incomplete Blocks Design from Cochran and Cox (1957)*

Source of Variation	df	SS	MS	F	p
Blocks	14	3.334	0.238		
Treatments					
(adjusted for blocks)	14	1.489	0.106	1.23	0.3012
Error	31	2.671	0.086		

Interpretation

The F-test for differences between (adjusted) treatment differences has a significance probability of $p=0.3012$, which presents no evidence of differences between treatments. In agreement with this conclusion, the table of significance probabilities for the lsmeans shows only six (out of 120) p-values less that 0.05. You would expect that many by chance.

Least squares means, obtained from the LSMEANS statement, are usually called **adjusted means** in standard textbooks. These means and their standard errors come from the OLS estimation of the treatment means. Thus, they do not take into account the fact that blocks are random. The adjustment of treatment means to remove block effects is a computation that treats blocks simply as another fixed effect. This analysis of variance, along with adjusted treatment means and differences between them and their standard errors, comprise the so-called **intra-block** analysis of PBIBD data.

In the PROC GLM statements following the LSMEANS statement, you see three ESTIMATE statements and a CONTRAST statement. The first ESTIMATE statement (with the label "treat1 mean") specifies coefficients for the INTERCEPT and the TREAT 1 parameter. By default, PROC GLM averages across the BLK parameters to form the linear combination of model terms. The second ESTIMATE statement (with the label "trt 1 mean") explicitly specifies the same linear combination of model terms; that is, it specifies coefficients 1/15 for each of the BLK terms. The results of these two ESTIMATE statements are identical, including their standard errors. Moreover, they duplicate the LSMEAN for TREAT 1 and its standard error. These standard errors do not take into account the random block effects. Subsection 1.5.2 shows analogous ESTIMATE statements in PROC MIXED that produce different results. This is the purpose for showing these first two ESTIMATE statements. The fourth ESTIMATE statement (with label "trt 1 vs trt 2") simply computes the difference between the lsmeans for TREAT 1 and TREAT 2. The CONTRAST statement with the label "trt 1 vs trt 2" computes an F-test that is equivalent to the t-test from the ESTIMATE statement with the same label.

The RANDOM statement in GLM, as already mentioned, causes only expected mean squares to be computed. The expected mean squares table in Output 1.7 shows that the correct denominator for the F-test for TREAT is MS(Error).

1.5.2 The Combined Intra- and Inter-block Analysis of PBIB Data Using PROC MIXED

Program

When blocks are treated as random, the result is then combined intra- and inter-block analysis. You can obtain this using PROC MIXED by submitting the statements:

```
proc mixed data=pbib;
   class blk treat;
   model response=treat;
   random blk;
   lsmeans treat / pdiff;
   estimate 'treat 1 mean' intercept 1 treat 1;
   estimate 'trt 1 mean' intercept 15 treat 15 |
            blk 1 1 1 1 1 1 1 1 1 1 1 1 1 1 1 / divisor=15;
   estimate 'trt 1 blk 1' intercept 1 treat 1 | blk 1;
   estimate 'trt 1 vs trt 2' treat 1 -1;
   contrast 'trt 1 vs trt 2' treat 1 -1;
run;
```

Results appear in Output 1.7 for the combined intra- and inter-block analysis.

Results

Output 1.7 *Incomplete Block Design: PROC MIXED Analysis*

```
                    The MIXED Procedure

               Class Level Information

    Class      Levels  Values

    BLK        15    1 2 3 4 5 6 7 8 9 10 11 12 13
                     14 15
    TREAT      15    1 2 3 4 5 6 7 8 9 10 11 12 13
                     14 15




           REML Estimation Iteration History

    Iteration  Evaluations     Objective      Criterion

          0            1   -24.83873612
          1            3   -30.71608590    0.00022046
          2            1   -30.71956742    0.00000043
          3            1   -30.71957397    0.00000000


           Convergence criteria met.
```

Covariance Parameter Estimates (REML)

Cov Parm	Ratio	Estimate	Std Error	Z	Pr > |Z|
BLK	0.54373914	0.04652189	0.02795193	1.66	0.0960
Residual	1.00000000	0.08555921	0.02157637	3.97	0.0001

Model Fitting Information for RESPONSE

Description	Value
Observations	60.0000
Variance Estimate	0.0856
Standard Deviation Estimate	0.2925
REML Log Likelihood	-25.9924
Akaike's Information Criterion	-27.9924
Schwarz's Bayesian Criterion	-29.7991
-2 REML Log Likelihood	51.9849

Tests of Fixed Effects

Source	NDF	DDF	Type III F	Pr > F
TREAT	14	31	1.53	0.1576

ESTIMATE Statement Results

Parameter	Estimate	Std Error	DDF	T	Pr > |T|
treat 1 mean	2.81752245	0.16641271	31	16.93	0.0001
trt 1 mean	2.81752245	0.15681751	31	17.97	0.0001
trt 1 blk 1	2.52880832	0.18454599	31	13.70	0.0001
trt 1 vs trt 2	0.41220751	0.22206087	31	1.86	0.0729

CONTRAST Statement Results

Source	NDF	DDF	F	Pr > F
trt 1 vs trt 2	1	31	3.45	0.0729

Least Squares Means

Level	LSMEAN	Std Error	DDF	T	Pr > |T|
TREAT 1	2.81752245	0.16641271	31	16.93	0.0001
TREAT 2	2.40531494	0.16641271	31	14.45	0.0001
TREAT 3	2.45494317	0.16641271	31	14.75	0.0001
TREAT 4	2.78383061	0.16641271	31	16.73	0.0001
TREAT 5	2.80489797	0.16641271	31	16.86	0.0001
TREAT 6	2.91069390	0.16641271	31	17.49	0.0001
TREAT 7	2.78898509	0.16641271	31	16.76	0.0001
TREAT 8	2.78160548	0.16641271	31	16.72	0.0001
TREAT 9	2.89131103	0.16641271	31	17.37	0.0001
TREAT 10	2.49106159	0.16641271	31	14.97	0.0001
TREAT 11	2.89869913	0.16641271	31	17.42	0.0001
TREAT 12	3.05282147	0.16641271	31	18.34	0.0001
TREAT 13	2.61776910	0.16641271	31	15.73	0.0001
TREAT 14	2.49131103	0.16641271	31	14.97	0.0001
TREAT 15	2.85923304	0.16641271	31	17.18	0.0001

Differences of Least Squares Means

Level 1	Level 2	Difference	Std Error	DDF	T
TREAT 1	TREAT 2	0.41220751	0.22206087	31	1.86
TREAT 1	TREAT 3	0.36257929	0.22206087	31	1.63
TREAT 1	TREAT 4	0.03369184	0.22206087	31	0.15
TREAT 1	TREAT 5	0.01262448	0.22206087	31	0.06
TREAT 1	TREAT 6	-0.09317145	0.22720031	31	-0.41
TREAT 1	TREAT 7	0.02853736	0.22206087	31	0.13
TREAT 1	TREAT 8	0.03591697	0.22206087	31	0.16
TREAT 1	TREAT 9	-0.07378858	0.22206087	31	-0.33
TREAT 1	TREAT 10	0.32646086	0.22206087	31	1.47
TREAT 1	TREAT 11	-0.08117667	0.22720031	31	-0.36
TREAT 1	TREAT 12	-0.23529902	0.22206087	31	-1.06
TREAT 1	TREAT 13	0.19975335	0.22206087	31	0.90
TREAT 1	TREAT 14	0.32621142	0.22206087	31	1.47
TREAT 1	TREAT 15	-0.04171059	0.22206087	31	-0.19
TREAT 2	TREAT 3	-0.04962822	0.22206087	31	-0.22
TREAT 2	TREAT 4	-0.37851567	0.22206087	31	-1.70
TREAT 2	TREAT 5	-0.39958303	0.22206087	31	-1.80
TREAT 2	TREAT 6	-0.50537896	0.22206087	31	-2.28
TREAT 2	TREAT 7	-0.38367015	0.22720031	31	-1.69
TREAT 2	TREAT 8	-0.37629054	0.22206087	31	-1.69
TREAT 2	TREAT 9	-0.48599609	0.22206087	31	-2.19
TREAT 2	TREAT 10	-0.08574665	0.22206087	31	-0.39
TREAT 2	TREAT 11	-0.49338418	0.22206087	31	-2.22

TREAT 2	TREAT 12	-0.64750653	0.22720031	31	-2.85
TREAT 2	TREAT 13	-0.21245416	0.22206087	31	-0.96
TREAT 2	TREAT 14	-0.08599609	0.22206087	31	-0.39
TREAT 2	TREAT 15	-0.45391810	0.22206087	31	-2.04
TREAT 3	TREAT 4	-0.32888744	0.22206087	31	-1.48
TREAT 3	TREAT 5	-0.34995480	0.22206087	31	-1.58
TREAT 3	TREAT 6	-0.45575074	0.22206087	31	-2.05
TREAT 3	TREAT 7	-0.33404192	0.22206087	31	-1.50
TREAT 3	TREAT 8	-0.32666232	0.22720031	31	-1.44
TREAT 3	TREAT 9	-0.43636786	0.22206087	31	-1.97
TREAT 3	TREAT 10	-0.03611842	0.22206087	31	-0.16
TREAT 3	TREAT 11	-0.44375596	0.22206087	31	-2.00
TREAT 3	TREAT 12	-0.59787830	0.22206087	31	-2.69
TREAT 3	TREAT 13	-0.16282594	0.22720031	31	-0.72
TREAT 3	TREAT 14	-0.03636786	0.22206087	31	-0.16
TREAT 3	TREAT 15	-0.40428988	0.22206087	31	-1.82
TREAT 4	TREAT 5	-0.02106736	0.22206087	31	-0.09
TREAT 4	TREAT 6	-0.12686330	0.22206087	31	-0.57
TREAT 4	TREAT 7	-0.00515448	0.22206087	31	-0.02
TREAT 4	TREAT 8	0.00222513	0.22206087	31	0.01
TREAT 4	TREAT 9	-0.10748042	0.22720031	31	-0.47
TREAT 4	TREAT 10	0.29276902	0.22206087	31	1.32
TREAT 4	TREAT 11	-0.11486852	0.22206087	31	-0.52
TREAT 4	TREAT 12	-0.26899086	0.22206087	31	-1.21
TREAT 4	TREAT 13	0.16606150	0.22206087	31	0.75
TREAT 4	TREAT 14	0.29251958	0.22720031	31	1.29
TREAT 4	TREAT 15	-0.07540244	0.22206087	31	-0.34
TREAT 5	TREAT 6	-0.10579594	0.22206087	31	-0.48
TREAT 5	TREAT 7	0.01591288	0.22206087	31	0.07
TREAT 5	TREAT 8	0.02329249	0.22206087	31	0.10
TREAT 5	TREAT 9	-0.08641306	0.22206087	31	-0.39
TREAT 5	TREAT 10	0.31383638	0.22720031	31	1.38
TREAT 5	TREAT 11	-0.09380116	0.22206087	31	-0.42
TREAT 5	TREAT 12	-0.24792350	0.22206087	31	-1.12
TREAT 5	TREAT 13	0.18712887	0.22206087	31	0.84
TREAT 5	TREAT 14	0.31358694	0.22206087	31	1.41
TREAT 5	TREAT 15	-0.05433507	0.22720031	31	-0.24
TREAT 6	TREAT 7	0.12170882	0.22206087	31	0.55
TREAT 6	TREAT 8	0.12908842	0.22206087	31	0.58
TREAT 6	TREAT 9	0.01938288	0.22206087	31	0.09
TREAT 6	TREAT 10	0.41963231	0.22206087	31	1.89
TREAT 6	TREAT 11	0.01199478	0.22720031	31	0.05
TREAT 6	TREAT 12	-0.14212756	0.22206087	31	-0.64
TREAT 6	TREAT 13	0.29292480	0.22206087	31	1.32
TREAT 6	TREAT 14	0.41938288	0.22206087	31	1.89
TREAT 6	TREAT 15	0.05146086	0.22206087	31	0.23
TREAT 7	TREAT 8	0.00737961	0.22206087	31	0.03
TREAT 7	TREAT 9	-0.10232594	0.22206087	31	-0.46
TREAT 7	TREAT 10	0.29792350	0.22206087	31	1.34
TREAT 7	TREAT 11	-0.10971404	0.22206087	31	-0.49
TREAT 7	TREAT 12	-0.26383638	0.22720031	31	-1.16
TREAT 7	TREAT 13	0.17121599	0.22206087	31	0.77
TREAT 7	TREAT 14	0.29767406	0.22206087	31	1.34
TREAT 7	TREAT 15	-0.07024795	0.22206087	31	-0.32
TREAT 8	TREAT 9	-0.10970555	0.22206087	31	-0.49

TREAT 8	TREAT 10	0.29054389	0.22206087	31	1.31
TREAT 8	TREAT 11	-0.11709364	0.22206087	31	-0.53
TREAT 8	TREAT 12	-0.27121599	0.22206087	31	-1.22
TREAT 8	TREAT 13	0.16383638	0.22720031	31	0.72
TREAT 8	TREAT 14	0.29029445	0.22206087	31	1.31
TREAT 8	TREAT 15	-0.07762756	0.22206087	31	-0.35
TREAT 9	TREAT 10	0.40024944	0.22206087	31	1.80
TREAT 9	TREAT 11	-0.00738810	0.22206087	31	-0.03
TREAT 9	TREAT 12	-0.16151044	0.22206087	31	-0.73

Differences of Least Squares Means

Level 1	Level 2	Difference	Std Error	DDF	T
TREAT 9	TREAT 13	0.27354192	0.22206087	31	1.23
TREAT 9	TREAT 14	0.40000000	0.22720031	31	1.76
TREAT 9	TREAT 15	0.03207798	0.22206087	31	0.14
TREAT 10	TREAT 11	-0.40763754	0.22206087	31	-1.84
TREAT 10	TREAT 12	-0.56175988	0.22206087	31	-2.53
TREAT 10	TREAT 13	-0.12670751	0.22206087	31	-0.57
TREAT 10	TREAT 14	-0.00024944	0.22206087	31	-0.00
TREAT 10	TREAT 15	-0.36817145	0.22720031	31	-1.62
TREAT 11	TREAT 12	-0.15412234	0.22206087	31	-0.69
TREAT 11	TREAT 13	0.28093002	0.22206087	31	1.27
TREAT 11	TREAT 14	0.40738810	0.22206087	31	1.83
TREAT 11	TREAT 15	0.03946608	0.22206087	31	0.18
TREAT 12	TREAT 13	0.43505236	0.22206087	31	1.96
TREAT 12	TREAT 14	0.56151044	0.22206087	31	2.53
TREAT 12	TREAT 15	0.19358842	0.22206087	31	0.87
TREAT 13	TREAT 14	0.12645808	0.22206087	31	0.57
TREAT 13	TREAT 15	-0.24146394	0.22206087	31	-1.09
TREAT 14	TREAT 15	-0.36792202	0.22206087	31	-1.66

Interpretation

You will note several differences from the intra-block analysis given by PROC GLM.

First of all, referring to the results of the first two ESTIMATE statements (with labels "treat 1 mean" and "trt 1 mean"), the estimates of the treatment means are different. Granted, the differences are not major, but they are certainly numerically different. In other applications the distinction can be dramatic. The PROC MIXED estimate of the treatment 1 mean is 2.817, compared with the PROC GLM estimate of 2.846. The distinction is that the PROC GLM estimate is OLS, whereas the MIXED estimate is (estimated) GLS. Theoretically, the GLS estimate is superior. PROC MIXED accounts for BLK being random and computes the BLUE estimates accordingly. Estimates of the variance components are used to compute $\mathbf{V}$ in equation (1.15) because the true variance components are unknown. The standard errors in PROC MIXED likewise are different from those in PROC GLM. The standard error of the OLS estimate is 0.163 from GLM. This is not a valid estimate of the true standard error of the OLS estimate for the same reason that PROC GLM did not compute a valid standard error estimate for a treatment mean for the RCBD data in subsection 1.1.1; the random effects of blocks were ignored. You see different standard errors for the "treat 1 mean" and "trt 1 mean" estimates from PROC MIXED. The ESTIMATE statement with label "treat 1 mean" did not specify coefficients for the block terms, whereas the ESTIMATE statement with label "trt 1 mean" did specify coefficients for blocks. This made no difference with PROC GLM, but it does with PROC MIXED. The standard error from the ESTIMATE statement labeled "treat 1 mean" correctly estimates the standard error of the GLS estimate considering blocks to be random. Thus it can be used to produce a confidence interval for the mean that would be valid for inference across the population of blocks from which those in the experiment were randomly drawn. The standard error from the ESTIMATE statement labelled "trt 1 mean," however, does not involve the block variance component. Thus a confidence interval based on this standard error is valid only for the blocks in the experiment. Standard errors of the LSMEANS are the same as for the "treat 1 mean" estimate. The "trt 1 mean" is an example of a *best linear unbiased predictor* (BLUP), and linear combination of fixed and random effects. BLUPs are unique to mixed model theory and are discussed in Chapter 6.

1.6 Summary

Chapter 1 begins with an example of a randomized blocks design with fixed treatments and random blocks. The importance of accounting for random effects in such a basic situation as computing a variance for a treatment mean is demonstrated. The use of PROC MIXED is introduced with explanations of how to set up the MODEL and RANDOM statements. The chapter continues with illustrations of CONTRAST, ESTIMATE, and LSMEANS statements. Then, PROC GLM is applied to the same example to illustrate similarities and differences of PROC GLM and PROC MIXED and to emphasize what basic applications are handled correctly by PROC MIXED and not by PROC GLM. A brief explanation of mixed model theory is presented in relation to the randomized blocks design, including explicit descriptions of the matrices in the general linear mixed model. Then, an incomplete block design is used to illustrate some of the issues confronted with unbalanced mixed model data.

1.7 References

Cochran, W.G. and Cox, G.M. (1957), *Experimental Designs, Second Edition*, New York: John Wiley & Sons.

Littell, R.C., Freund R.J., and Spector, P.C. (1991), *SAS System for Linear Models, Third Edition*, Cary, NC: SAS Institute Inc.

Mead, R. (1988), *The Design of Experiments*, New York: Cambridge University Press, 620 pp.

Mendenhall, W., Wackerly, D.D., and Scheaffer, R.L. (1990), *Mathematical Statistics with Applications*, 4th Edition, Belmont, CA: Duxbury Press.

Milliken, G.A. and Johnson, D.E. (1994), *Analysis of Messy Data, Volume 1: Designed Experiments*, London: Chapman Press.

Winer, B.J. (1971), *Statistical Principles in Experimental Design, Second Edition*, New York: McGraw-Hill, Inc.

Chapter **2 Common Mixed Models**

2.1 Introduction

Many studies use designs which require analysis of variance models with two or more error terms. Widely used examples include split-plot and split-block experiments, multi-location trials, and regression models with random coefficients. In the past, such studies have been analyzed using computational procedures appropriate for fixed-effects models modified to obtain relevant statistics, e.g., PROC GLM with optional statements to specify error terms. In many cases, such modified fixed-effects procedures yield appropriate statistics. However, these methods are often awkward to use. More importantly, in many cases fixed-effects procedures simply cannot be modified to produce statistics appropriate for the objectives of interest. In this chapter, mixed model methods are presented to analyze common mixed models with multiple error terms.

2.2 Examples: Split-Plot Experiments

A **split-plot experiment** is a factorial design conducted such that the experimental unit with respect to one or more factors is a subunit of the experimental unit with respect to other factors. Split-plot experiments are often used out of necessity when a factor, or factorial combination, must be applied to relatively large experimental units, whereas other factors are more appropriately applied to subunits. Split-plot experiments are also frequently used for convenience: it is often simply easier to apply different factors to different sized units. Split-plot experiments may also be used to increase the precision of the estimated effect of the factor applied to the subunits.

The following examples, discussed by Littell, Freund, and Spector (1991), illustrate the main features of split-plot experiments.

The first example is an experiment conducted to evaluate the effect of three bacterial inoculation treatments applied to two grass cultivars on dry weight yield. The experiment was conducted using four blocks (denoted BLOCK in the example). Each block was divided in half, and cultivar (CULT) A or B was randomly assigned to each half, or **whole-plot unit**. Each whole-plot unit consisted of three plots, or **split-plot units**; 3 inoculation treatments (INOC) were randomly assigned to sub-plot units within each whole plot. The SAS data set for this experiment is Data Set 2.2(a), "Data from Cultivar-Inoculation Trial," in Appendix 4, "SAS Data Sets."

The model for this experiment is

$$y_{ijk} = \mu_{ij} + r_k + w_{ik} + e_{ijk} \tag{2.1}$$

where

μ_{ij} is the mean of ij^{th} CULT*INOC combination
r_k is the kth BLOCK effect
w_{ik} is the whole-plot error effect
e_{ijk} is the split-plot error effect.

Assumptions for the random effects are
- the whole-plot errors (w_{ik}) and split-plot errors (e_{ijk}) are independent of one another
- the whole-plot errors are assumed iid $N(0,\sigma_w^2)$, and
- the split-plots errors are assumed iid $N(0,\sigma^2)$.

The whole-plot error in this model is equivalent to BLOCK*CULT. The model can also be written as

$$y_{ijk} = \mu + r_k + \alpha_i + w_{ik} + \beta_j + (\alpha\beta)_{ij} + e_{ijk} \tag{2.2}$$

where

$\mu_{ij} = \mu + \alpha_i + \beta_j + (\alpha\beta)_{ij}$
α_i is the effect of the ith level of CULT
β_j is the effect of the jth INOC
$(\alpha\beta)_{ij}$ is the ij^{th} CULT*INOC interaction effect.

Usually, the block effect is considered random with r_k assumed iid $N(0,\sigma_R^2)$ and independent of the w_{ik} and e_{ijk}.

The second example is an experiment conducted in a semiconductor plant to study the effect of several modes of a process condition (ET) on resistance in computer chips. Twelve silicon wafers (WAFER) were drawn from a lot, and three wafers were randomly assigned to four modes of ET. Resistance in the chips was measured on chips at four different positions (POS) on each wafer after processing. The measurement was recorded as the variable RESISTA. The data are given in Data Set 2.2(b), "Data from Semiconductor Example," in Appendix 4, "SAS Data Sets."

The semiconductor experiment consists of two factors, ET and POS. The experimental unit with respect to ET is the wafer. The experimental unit with respect to POS is the individual chip, a subdivision of the wafer. Thus, the wafer is the whole-plot unit, and chip is the split-plot unit.

For this experiment, the model is

$$y_{ijk} = \mu + \alpha_i + w_{ik} + \beta_j + (\alpha\beta)_{ij} + e_{ijk} \tag{2.3}$$

where

$\mu_{ij} = \mu + \alpha_i + \beta_j + (\alpha\beta)_{ij}$ is the mean of the ij^{th} ET*POS combination
α_i, β_j, and $(\alpha\beta)_{ij}$ are the ET, POS, and ET*POS effects, respectively
w_{ik} is the whole-plot error effect, assumed iid $N(0,\sigma_w^2)$
e_{ijk} is the split-plot error effect, assumed iid $N(0,\sigma^2)$
w_{ik} and e_{ijk} are assumed to be independent of one another.

Littell, et. al. (1991) mention that correlation among the chips may actually depend on their proximity on the wafer, thus violating the assumption of independence among split-plot errors. If so, the data may be analyzed by revising the model to assume spatially-dependent correlated errors. This is discussed in Chapter 3, "Analysis of Repeated Measures Data," and Chapter 9, "Spatial Variability."

These experiments are similar in several respects:

- Each experiment has two factors under study. In the first experiment, they are CULT and INOC; in the second experiment, they are ET and POS. In both cases, the two factors are crossed in a complete factorial arrangement.

- In each experiment, one factor is assigned to a larger experimental unit, or whole plot— CULT in the first experiment, ET in the second experiment. The relevant error for evaluating CULT or ET main effects comes from variability among whole-plot experimental units.

- In each experiment, one factor is assigned to the split-plot experimental unit, which is a subunit of the whole plot. The split-plot factors are INOC in the first experiment and POS in the second. The relevant error for evaluating INOC or POS main effects and their interactions, respectively, with CULT or POS, comes from variability among split-plot experimental units.

The factorial treatment structure in conjunction with the different experimental units for different factors are the common features of all split-plot experiments. However, there are some differences:

- In the first experiment, the whole-plot experimental units are arranged in blocks. Thus, the experiment is a **randomized complete block design** with respect to the whole plot. On the other hand, the whole-plot experimental units in the second experiment are not blocked. The experiment is a **completely randomized design** with respect to the whole plot. Figure 2.1 illustrates the difference between these two designs.

Figure 2.1 *Example Layouts of a Split-Plot Experiment*

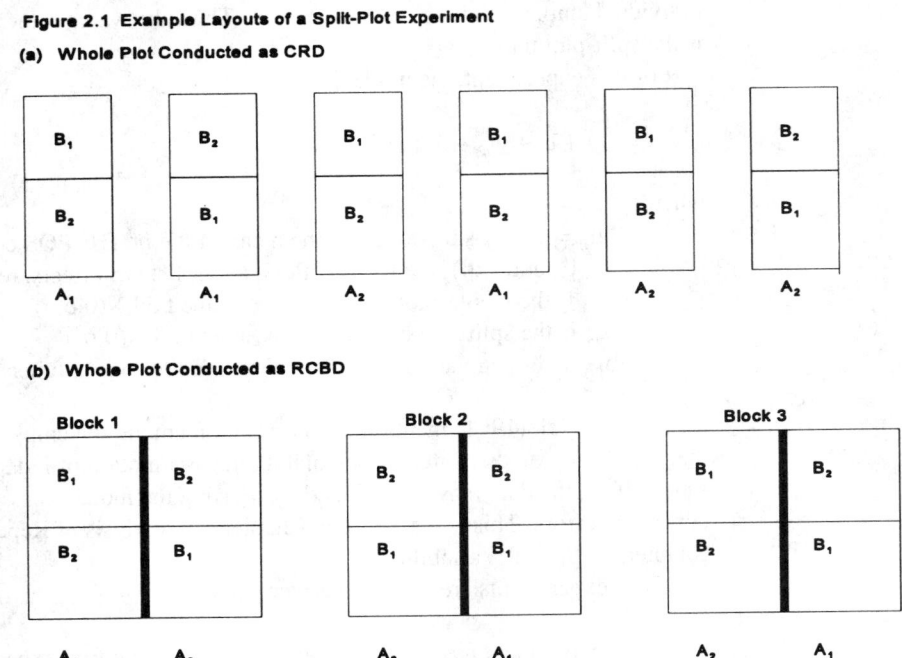

In the first experiment, the assignment of INOC levels to split-plot experimental units is random. In the second experiment, POS is determined by the location of the chip on the wafer; it cannot be randomized. As a result, the assumption of independent split-plot errors is reasonable in the first experiment, whereas it may be violated in the second experiment.

These are examples of simple split-plot experiments. In general, there are any number of variations. Whole plots may be arranged as incomplete block designs, Latin Squares, etc. Whole plots or split plots may consist of a single factor or may themselves be factorial combinations. The split-plot principle may be expanded by assigning additional factors to subunits of the split-plot experimental units, giving rise to the **split-split-plot experiment**. Or a block may consist, for example, of experimental units running in an east-to-west direction for one factor and experimental units running in a north-to-south direction for the other factor—the **strip-split-plot** or **split-block** experiment. Combinations of split-plot and split-block arrangements may also be used.

You can obtain further information on split-plot experiments in experimental design texts such as Cochran and Cox (1957) and Mead (1988). Milliken and Johnson (1984) have a comprehensive discussion of the analysis of split-plot experiments.

Chapter 10 presents examples of elaborations of the split-plot principle. This chapter gives detailed presentations of the cultivar-inoculation and semiconductor examples described above. These two examples permit illustration of the main features of mixed model analysis.

2.2.1 Estimating Treatment Means and Differences in the Split-Plot Experiment

This section presents methods for estimating treatment means, differences, or other linear combinations of means and determining their standard errors. These include the following:

$$\mu_{11} = \mu + \alpha_1 + \beta_1 + (\alpha\beta)_{11}$$

a treatment combination mean, here, the 1st level of the whole-plot factor and the 1st level of the split-plot factor

$$\mu_{1\bullet} = \mu + \alpha_1 + \beta_\bullet + (\alpha\beta)_{1\bullet}$$

a main effect mean, here, the mean of the 1st level of the whole-plot factor

$$\mu_{\bullet 1} = \mu + \alpha_\bullet + \beta_1 + (\alpha\beta)_{\bullet 1}$$

the mean of the 1st level of the split-plot factor

$$\mu_{1\bullet} - \mu_{2\bullet} = \alpha_1 - \alpha_2 + (\alpha\beta)_{1\bullet} - (\alpha\beta)_{2\bullet}$$

whole-plot main effect, here the difference between the means of the first two levels of the whole-plot factor

$$\mu_{\bullet 1} - \mu_{\bullet 2} = \beta_1 - \beta_2 + (\alpha\beta)_{\bullet 1} - (\alpha\beta)_{\bullet 2}$$

split-plot main effect, here the difference between the means of the first two levels of the split-plot factor

$$\mu_{11} - \mu_{12} = \beta_1 - \beta_2 + (\alpha\beta)_{11} - (\alpha\beta)_{12}$$

the simple effect of the split-plot factor given a whole-plot level, the difference between the means of two split-plot factors levels at a given level of the whole-plot factor

$$\mu_{11} - \mu_{21} = \alpha_1 - \alpha_2 + (\alpha\beta)_{11} - (\alpha\beta)_{21}$$

the simple effect of the whole-plot factor for a given split-plot factor level.

For balanced split-plot experiments, the best linear unbiased estimates of μ_{ij}, $\mu_{i\bullet}$, and $\mu_{\bullet j}$ are $\bar{y}_{ij\bullet}$, $\bar{y}_{i\bullet\bullet}$, and $\bar{y}_{\bullet j\bullet}$, respectively. Their standard errors can be determined from the form of the variance of the estimator.

For the semiconductor example

$$\text{Var}(\bar{y}_{ij\bullet}) = \text{Var}\left[(1/3)\sum_k y_{ijk}\right]$$

$$= (1/9)[\Sigma \text{Var}(y_{ijk})]$$

$$= (1/9)[\Sigma \text{Var}(\mu_{ij} + w_{ik} + e_{ijk})]$$

$$= (1/9)[3\sigma_w^2 + 3\sigma^2]$$

$$= (1/3)[\sigma_w^2 + \sigma^2]$$

Similar derivations yield

$$\text{Var}(\bar{y}_{i..}) = (1/12)[4\sigma_w^2 + \sigma^2], \text{ and}$$

$$\text{Var}(\bar{y}_{.j.}) = (1/12)[\sigma_w^2 + \sigma^2]$$

The variance of a difference can be determined in a similar manner. For example, for a whole-plot main effect, whose estimate in the above example is $\bar{y}_{1..} - \bar{y}_{2..}$, the variance is

$$\text{Var}(\bar{y}_{1..} - \bar{y}_{2..}) = \text{Var}[(1/12)\underset{j\,k}{\Sigma\Sigma}(y_{1jk} - y_{2jk})]$$

$$= (1/12)^2\{\text{Var}[\Sigma\Sigma(\mu_{1j} - \mu_{2j} + w_{1k} - w_{2k} + e_{1jk} - e_{2jk})]\}$$

$$= (1/12)^2\{\text{Var}[4\Sigma(w_{1k} - w_{2k})] + \text{Var}[\Sigma\Sigma(e_{1jk} - e_{2jk})]\}$$

$$= (1/12)^2[4^2(3*2\sigma_w^2) + 12*2\sigma^2]$$

$$= (1/12)[2*(4\sigma_w^2 + \sigma^2)]$$

$$= (1/6)(4\sigma_w^2 + \sigma^2)$$

Similar derivations yield

$$\text{Var}(\bar{y}_{.1.} - \bar{y}_{.2.}) = (1/6)\sigma^2$$

$$\text{Var}(\bar{y}_{11.} - \bar{y}_{12.}) = (2/3)\sigma^2$$

$$\text{Var}(\bar{y}_{11.} - \bar{y}_{21.}) = (2/3)(\sigma_w^2 + \sigma^2)$$

In general, estimates of functions of the μ_{ij} and their variances can be determined from the mixed model equations and their properties (see Appendix 1 for details). In the semiconductor example, the matrix form of the model is

$$\mathbf{y} = \mathbf{X\mu} + \mathbf{Zw} + \mathbf{e}$$

where

      $\mathbf{y}$ is the vector of observations
      $\mathbf{\mu}' = [\mu_{11}, \mu_{12}, \ldots, \mu_{14}, \ldots, \mu_{44}]$, the vector of ET*POS means
      $\mathbf{w}' = [w_{11}, w_{12}, \ldots, w_{43}]$, the vector of whole-plot errors
      $\mathbf{e}$ is the vector of split-plot errors
      $\mathbf{X}$ is the design matrix with respect to ET*POS treatment combinations
      $\mathbf{Z}$ is the design matrix with respect to whole-plot experimental units (WAFERS).

In matrix form, the model assumptions are

- $\mathbf{w}$ is distributed $\text{MVN}(\mathbf{0}, \mathbf{I}\sigma_w^2)$ and
- $\mathbf{e}$ is distributed $\text{MVN}(\mathbf{0}, \mathbf{I}\sigma^2)$.
- The resulting distribution of $\mathbf{y}$ is $\text{MVN}(\mathbf{X\mu}, \mathbf{V})$, where $\mathbf{V} = \mathbf{Z}(\mathbf{I}\sigma_w^2)\mathbf{Z}' + \mathbf{I}\sigma^2$.

In this model, $\mathbf{X}\boldsymbol{\mu}$ could be expressed in terms of the fixed effects. That is,

$$\mathbf{X}\boldsymbol{\mu} = \mathbf{1}\mu + \mathbf{X}_A\boldsymbol{\alpha} + \mathbf{X}_B\boldsymbol{\beta} + \mathbf{X}_{AB}(\boldsymbol{\alpha\beta})$$

where

> $\mathbf{1}$ is a vector of ones
> $\boldsymbol{\alpha}' = [\alpha_1, \ldots, \alpha_4]$, the vector of ET effects
> $\mathbf{b}' = [\beta_1, \ldots, \beta_4]$, the vector of POS effects
> $(\boldsymbol{\alpha\beta})' = [(\alpha\beta)_{11}, (\alpha\beta)_{12}, \ldots, (\alpha\beta)_{44}]$, the vector of ET*POS effects
> $\mathbf{X}_A$, $\mathbf{X}_B$, and $\mathbf{X}_{AB}$ are the design matrices with respect to ET, POS, and ET*POS respectively.

The solution to the mixed model equations provides best linear unbiased estimates of the fixed effects, $\boldsymbol{\mu}$, or, alternatively, **estimable functions** of μ, α, β, and $(\alpha\beta)$. For any linear combination $\mathbf{K}'\boldsymbol{\mu}$ (or estimable linear combination of μ, α, β, and $\alpha\beta$), the variance of the estimate is $\mathbf{K}'[\mathbf{X}'\mathbf{V}^{-1}\mathbf{X}]^{-1}\mathbf{K}$.

For example, for a main-effect mean for the first level of ET,

$$\mu_{1.} = (1/4)(\mu_{11} + \mu_{12} + \mu_{13} + \mu_{14})$$

$$= (1/4)[1\ 1\ 1\ 1\ 0\ 0\ 0\ 0\ 0\ 0\ 0\ 0\ 0\ 0\ 0\ 0]'\boldsymbol{\mu}.$$

Thus $\mathbf{K}' = (1/4)[1\ 1\ 1\ 1\ 0\ 0\ 0\ 0\ 0\ 0\ 0\ 0\ 0\ 0\ 0\ 0]'$. Applying the formula $\mathbf{K}'[\mathbf{X}'\mathbf{V}^{-1}\mathbf{X}]^{-1}\mathbf{K}$ yields

$$\mathrm{Var}(\hat{\mu}_{1.}) = \mathrm{Var}\{(1/4)[1\ 1\ 1\ 1\ 0\ 0\ 0\ 0\ 0\ 0\ 0\ 0\ 0\ 0\ 0\ 0]'\boldsymbol{\mu}\}$$

$$= (1/12)[4\sigma_w^2 + \sigma^2]$$

This approach can also be used for a treatment difference. For example, for the main-effect difference $\mu_{1.} - \mu_{2.}$, $\mathbf{K}'\boldsymbol{\mu}$ is

$$(1/4)[1\ 1\ 1\ 1\ -1\ -1\ -1\ -1\ 0\ 0\ 0\ 0\ 0\ 0\ 0\ 0]'\boldsymbol{\mu}$$

Applying the variance formula, the variance of $\hat{\mu}_{1.} - \hat{\mu}_{2.}$ is $(1/6)(4\sigma_w^2 + \sigma^2)$.
Applying these results gives a general formula for the confidence interval for linear combinations of the treatment combination means:

$$\mathbf{K}'\boldsymbol{\mu} \pm t_\nu \sqrt{\mathbf{K}'(\mathbf{X}'\mathbf{V}^{-1}\mathbf{X})^{-1}\mathbf{K}}$$

The degrees of freedom, ν, is determined by the degrees of freedom required to estimate the linear combination of variance components in $\mathbf{K}'[\mathbf{X}'\mathbf{V}^{-1}\mathbf{X}]^{-1}\mathbf{K}$. These can be determined from the expected means squares of the analysis of variance associated with the model and, if necessary, Satterthwaite's approximation.

For example, in the semiconductor example, the analysis of variance is given in Table 2.1.

Table 2.1 *Analysis of Variance for Semiconductor Example*

Source of Variation	d.f.	Expected Mean Square
ET	3	$\sigma^2 + 4\sigma_w^2 + \phi_{ET}$
WAFER(ET) (whole-plot error)	8	$\sigma^2 + 4\sigma_w^2$
POS	3	$\sigma^2 + \phi_{POS}$
ET*POS	9	$\sigma^2 + \phi_{ET*POS}$
split-plot error	24	σ^2

In Table 2.1, the ϕ are quadratic expressions for the fixed effects and have no bearing on variance component estimation. Littell, et. al. (1991) discuss them in detail. The variance components can be estimated as

$$\hat{\sigma}^2 = MS(\text{split-plot } error), \text{ or } MS(SPE) \text{ for convenience, and}$$

$$\hat{\sigma}_w^2 = (1/4)\{MS[WAFER(ET)] - MS(SPE)\}$$

For a whole-plot main effect mean, $\mu_{i\bullet}$, the variance is $(1/12)[4\sigma_w^2 + \sigma^2]$, which is estimated as $(1/12)\{MS[WAFER(ET)]\}$. Thus, the degrees of freedom for a confidence interval correspond to the degrees of freedom for WAFER(ET), $\nu = 8$.

For a split-plot main effect difference, $\mu_{\bullet 1} - \mu_{\bullet 2}$, the variance is $(1/6)\sigma^2$, which is estimated by $(1/6)[MS(SPE)]$. Thus, the degrees of freedom for the confidence interval correspond to the degrees of freedom for split-plot error, $\nu = 24$.

As a final example, consider the simple effect difference $\mu_{11} - \mu_{21}$, whose variance is $(2/3)(\sigma_w^2 + \sigma^2)$. The linear combination $\sigma_w^2 + \sigma^2$ cannot be estimated by a single mean square. Instead, it is estimated by

$$\hat{\sigma}_w^2 + \hat{\sigma}^2 = MS(SPE) + (1/4)\{MS[WAFER(ET)] - MS(SPE)\}$$
$$= (3/4)[MS(SPE)] + (1/4)[MS(WAFER(ET)]$$

The degrees of freedom can be approximated using Satterthwaite's formula. Let $MS = a_1 MS_1 + ... + a_k MS_k$. The approximate degrees of freedom for MS is

$$\nu \cong \frac{(MS)^2}{\dfrac{(a_1 MS_1)^2}{df_1} + \; . \; . \; . \; + \dfrac{(a_k MS_k)^2}{df_k}}$$

Thus, the approximate degrees of freedom for the simple effect of ET for a given POS is

$$\nu \cong \frac{\left(\dfrac{3}{4}MS(SPE) + \dfrac{1}{4}MS[WAFER(ET)]\right)^2}{\dfrac{[\frac{3}{4}MS(SPE)]^2}{24} + \dfrac{[\frac{1}{4}MS(WAFER(ET))]^2}{8}}$$

2.2.2 Hypothesis Testing with the Split-Plot Experiment

This section presents methods for testing hypotheses of interest in split-plot experiments. For example, in the semiconductor experiment, hypothesis tests might include

H_0: $\mu_{1\bullet} = \mu_{2\bullet} = ... = \mu_{4\bullet}$

all ET main-effect means equal

H_0: $\mu_{\bullet 1} = \mu_{\bullet 2} = ... = \mu_{\bullet 4}$

all POS main-effect means equal

H_0: $\mu_{ij} - \mu_{ij'}$ for all i, given $j \neq j'$; i.e., all $(\alpha\beta)_{ij} = 0$

no ET*POS interaction

H_0: $\mu_{1\bullet} - \mu_{2\bullet} = 0$

main-effect contrast of ET; here, ET1 versus ET2

H_0: $\mu_{\bullet 1} - \mu_{\bullet 2} = 0$

main-effect contrast of POS; here, POS1 versus POS2

H_0: $\mu_{11} - \mu_{12} = 0$

simple-effect contrast of POS; here, POS1 versus POS2 given ET1

H_0: $\mu_{11} - \mu_{21} = 0$

simple-effect contrast of ET; here, ET1 versus ET2 given POS1

H_0: $\frac{1}{2}(\mu_{12} + \mu_{22}) - \frac{1}{2}(\mu_{32} + \mu_{42}) = 0$

contrast; here average of ET1 and ET2 versus average of ET3 and ET4 given POS2.

The first three hypotheses are tested using F-ratios from the analysis of variance. From the ANOVA table for the semiconductor experiment, the required test statistics are

MS(ET) / MS[WAFER(ET)]   for the ET main effect
MS(POS) / MS(SPE)   for the POS main effect
MS(ET*POS) / MS(SPE)   for the ET*POS interaction

The remaining hypotheses are all single-degree-of-freedom contrasts. They can be tested in one of two equivalent ways.

First, for the difference of interest, the **estimate** and the **standard error** can be computed as shown in section 2.2.1. Their ratio

$$t = \frac{estimate}{stderr}$$

has a t-distribution whose degrees of freedom, ν, depends on the form of the standard error.

For example, the main-effect comparison of ET1 versus ET2 can be tested using the ratio

$$t = \frac{\hat{\mu}_{1\bullet} - \hat{\mu}_{2\bullet}}{\sqrt{\frac{1}{12}\left(\hat{\sigma}^2 + 3\hat{\sigma}_w^2\right)}} = \frac{\hat{\mu}_{1\bullet} - \hat{\mu}_{2\bullet}}{\sqrt{\frac{1}{12}MS[WAFER(ET)]}}$$

Thus, the degrees of freedom for the *t*-test correspond to the degrees of freedom for WAFER(ET), $\nu=8$.

In many cases, the degrees of freedom for the *t*-test must be determined using Satterthwaite's approximation. For example, the *t*-ratio for the test of ET1 and ET2 versus ET3 and ET4 in POS2 is

$$t = \frac{\hat{\mu}_{12} + \hat{\mu}_{22} - \hat{\mu}_{32} - \hat{\mu}_{42}}{\sqrt{\frac{4}{3}\left(\hat{\sigma}^2 + \hat{\sigma}_w^2\right)}}$$

Since $\hat{\sigma}^2 + \hat{\sigma}_w^2$ is estimated by $(1/4)MS[WAFER(ET)] + (3/4)MS(SPE)$, the approximate degrees of freedom are determined as shown in section 2.2.1.

Alternatively, the single-degree-of-freedom hypotheses can be tested using F-ratios of the form

$$F = t^2 = \frac{estimate^2}{std\ err^2} = \frac{MS(contrast)}{MSE}$$

where MSE is the appropriate mean square or linear combination of mean squares. Thus, the F-ratio for the main effect of ET1 versus ET2 is

$$F = \frac{MS(ET1\ versus\ ET2)}{MS[WAFER(ET)]}$$

The numerator has one degree of freedom and the denominator has $\nu=8$, corresponding to the degrees of freedom for WAFER(ET). For the test of ET1 and ET2 versus ET3 and ET4 in POS2, the F-ratio is

$$F = \frac{MS(ET1,\ ET2\ versus\ ET3,\ ET4\ given\ POS2)}{\left(\frac{1}{4}\right)MS[WAFER(ET)] + \left(\frac{3}{4}\right)MS(SPE)}$$

There is one degree of freedom for the numerator. For the denominator, the degrees of freedom are determined from the Satterthwaite approximation for the linear combination of MS[WAFER(MS)] and MS(SPE).

All of the above F-ratios, for the overall main effects, interactions, and single-degree-of-freedom tests, are special cases of a general result for mixed models. In general, you can test hypotheses with one or more degrees of freedom by defining a **K** matrix consisting of any number of *independent* **k** vectors.

Common examples of multiple-degree-of-freedom hypotheses are overall main-effect or interaction terms in the analysis of variance. For example, consider the main effect of ET.

The overall hypothesis of no ET main-effect is

$$H_0: \mu_{1\bullet} = \mu_{2\bullet} = ... = \mu_{4\bullet}$$

This can be expressed in terms of a **K** matrix several ways. Because there are 4 levels of ET, there are 3 degrees of freedom for the ET main effect. Therefore, **K** consists of 3 independent **k** vectors, one per degree of freedom. *Any set of 3 comparisons such that H_0 is true* can be used to form **K**. For example,

$$\mathbf{K'} = \left(\frac{1}{4}\right)\begin{bmatrix} 1 & 1 & 1 & 1 & -1 & -1 & -1 & -1 & 0 & 0 & 0 & 0 & 0 & 0 & 0 & 0 \\ 1 & 1 & 1 & 1 & 0 & 0 & 0 & 0 & -1 & -1 & -1 & -1 & 0 & 0 & 0 & 0 \\ 1 & 1 & 1 & 1 & 0 & 0 & 0 & 0 & 0 & 0 & 0 & 0 & -1 & -1 & -1 & -1 \end{bmatrix}$$

defines the comparisons $\mu_{1\bullet} = \mu_{2\bullet}$, $\mu_{1\bullet} = \mu_{3\bullet}$, and $\mu_{1\bullet} = \mu_{4\bullet}$. If all 3 equalities hold, then $\mu_{1\bullet} = \mu_{2\bullet} = ... = \mu_{4\bullet}$, i.e., H_0 is true. On the other hand,

$$\mathbf{K'} = \begin{bmatrix} 1 & 1 & 1 & 1 & -1 & -1 & -1 & -1 & 0 & 0 & 0 & 0 & 0 & 0 & 0 & 0 \\ 1 & 1 & 1 & 1 & 1 & 1 & 1 & 1 & -2 & -2 & -2 & -2 & 0 & 0 & 0 & 0 \\ 1 & 1 & 1 & 1 & 1 & 1 & 1 & 1 & 1 & 1 & 1 & 1 & -3 & -3 & -3 & -3 \end{bmatrix}$$

defines the comparisons $\mu_{1\bullet} = \mu_{2\bullet}$, $(1/2)(\mu_{1\bullet} + u_{2\bullet}) = \mu_{3\bullet}$, and $(1/3)(\mu_{1\bullet} + \mu_{2\bullet} + \mu_{3\bullet}) = \mu_{4\bullet}$. If these 3 equalities hold, they *also* guarantee that $H_0: \mu_{1\bullet} = \mu_{2\bullet} = ... = \mu_{4\bullet}$ is true. For the main effect of ET, **K** can be composed of any 3 comparisons sufficient to guarantee that $\mu_{1\bullet} = \mu_{2\bullet} = ... = \mu_{4\bullet}$. For any **K** so constructed, the resulting *F*-statistic, discussed below, will be the same.

For any linear combination **K'μ** (or estimable linear combination of the fixed effects μ, α, β, and (αβ)),

$$(\mathbf{K'\hat{\mu}})'[\mathbf{K'(X'V^{-1}X)K}]^{-1}(\mathbf{K'\hat{\mu}})$$

has an approximate χ^2 distribution with rank(**K**) degrees of freedom *when V is known*. When **V** is unknown and the components of **V** are estimated (by far the more common case)

$$\{(\mathbf{K'\hat{\mu}})'[\mathbf{K'(X'\hat{V}^{-1}X)K}]^{-1}(\mathbf{K'\hat{\mu}})\}/[\text{rank}(\mathbf{K})]$$

has an approximate *F*-distribution, whose numerator degrees of freedom are rank(**K**) and whose denominator degrees of freedom correspond to the degrees of freedom required to estimate [**K'(X'V⁻¹X)K**]. For balanced split-plot experiments, [**K'(X'V⁻¹X)K**] is estimated from either a single mean square or a linear combination of mean squares from the analysis of variance.

For example, for the main-effect comparison of ET1 versus ET2,

$$\mathbf{K'} = (1/4)[1 \ 1 \ 1 \ 1 \ -1 \ -1 \ -1 \ -1 \ 0 \ 0 \ 0 \ 0 \ 0 \ 0 \ 0 \ 0]$$

$$[\mathbf{K'(X'\hat{V}^{-1}X)K}] \propto \text{MS[WAFER(ET)]}$$

For the comparison of ET1 and ET2 versus ET3 and ET4 in POS2,

$$\mathbf{K'} = (1/2)[0\ 0\ 0\ 0\ \ 1\ 1\ -1\ -1\ \ 0\ 0\ 0\ 0\ \ 0\ 0\ 0\ 0]$$

$$[\mathbf{K'}(\mathbf{X'\hat{V}^{-1}X})\mathbf{K}] \propto (1/4)MS[WAFER(ET)] + (3/4)MS(SPE)$$

The F-ratio for other main effects and interactions, e.g., POS and ET*POS, can be constructed from appropriately defined $\mathbf{K}$ using the same logic as for ET. The numerator degrees of freedom for the resulting F-test is the rank of $\mathbf{K}$. The denominator degrees of freedom is determined by the ANOVA mean square implied by $[\mathbf{K'}(\mathbf{X'V^{-1}X})\mathbf{K}]^{-1}$. For the semiconductor example, the following results hold regarding degrees of freedom.

Table 2.2 *Degrees of Freedom for Semiconductor Example*

	Numerator d.f.	Denominator d.f
Effect tested	Rank	$[\mathbf{K'}(\mathbf{X'V^{-1}X})\mathbf{K}]^{-1}$ depends on
ET	3	MS[WAFER(ET)]
POS	3	MS(SPE)
ET*POS	9	MS(SPE)

2.3 Using PROC MIXED to Analyze a Balanced Split-Plot Experiment

This section shows how to compute the estimates described in section 2.2.1 and the hypothesis tests described in section 2.2.2 using PROC MIXED. As in the previous sections, the semiconductor experiment is used to demonstrate.

2.3.1 Fitting the Split-Plot Model

Program

To fit the split-plot model, the essential SAS statements are

```
proc mixed;
    class et wafer pos;
    model resista=et pos et*pos;
    random wafer(et);
run;
```

The results appear in Output 2.1.

Results

Output 2.1 *Basic Output from PROC MIXED*

```
                        The MIXED Procedure

                     Class Level Information

                     Class     Levels  Values

                      ET          4    1 2 3 4
                      WAFER       3    1 2 3
                      POS         4    1 2 3 4


                        The MIXED Procedure

                   REML Estimation Iteration History

            Iteration  Evaluations    Objective      Criterion

                  0          1      0.67743239
                  1          1     -8.16157109    0.00000000


                     Convergence criteria met.



                 Covariance Parameter Estimates (REML)

Cov Parm          Ratio       Estimate     Std Error       Z   Pr > |Z|

WAFER(ET)      0.95178532    0.10579028    0.06726878    1.57    0.1158
Residual       1.00000000    0.11114931    0.03208604    3.46    0.0005




                Model Fitting Information for RESISTA

                Description                      Value

                Observations                   48.0000
                Variance Estimate               0.1111
                Standard Deviation Estimate     0.3334
                REML Log Likelihood           -25.3252
                Akaike's Information Criterion -27.3252
                Schwartz's Bayesian Criterion -28.7910
                -2 REML Log Likelihood          50.6505



                     Tests of Fixed Effects

            Source      NDF   DDF   Type III F   Pr > F

             ET          3     8       1.94      0.2015
             POS         3    24       3.39      0.0345
             ET*POS      9    24       0.81      0.6125
```

Interpretation

The main items of information are

- The estimates of σ^2 and σ_w^2, printed as the "Covariance Parameter Estimates" for Residual and WAFER(ET), respectively. The default variance component estimation procedure used by PROC MIXED is the REML algorithm. For balanced experiments, REML estimates are identical to the estimates obtained from the expected mean squares discussed in section 2.2.1, provided all estimates are positive.

- The F-tests for the ET and POS main effects and the ET*POS interaction, given under "Tests of Fixed Effects."

There are other items in the output. Under "Covariance Parameter Estimates" there is a standard error, a Z-statistic, and the PR > |Z|. These are based on asymptotic properties, and are not very reliable if the degrees of freedom to estimate the variance component is small. For example, in certain instances you may want to know if there is significant variability among wafers. Formally, variability among wafers is tested by the hypothesis H_0: $\sigma_w^2 = 0$. The Z-statistic is 1.57 with a probability of 0.1158. However, because there are only 8 degrees of freedom to estimate σ_w^2, this is not a good test.

A better test of H_0: $\sigma_w^2 = 0$ is provided by the **likelihood ratio statistic**, which is based on REML log-likelihood given under "Model Fitting Information for RESISTA." Specifically, the likelihood ratio statistic is computed by taking the difference between the -2 REML log-likelihood of the model containing the random effect WAFER(ET) and the model without WAFER(ET). In Output 2.1, the -2 REML log-likelihood for the model with WAFER(ET) is 50.6505. You can obtain the -2 REML log-likelihood for the model without WAFER(ET) by rerunning the PROC MIXED statements given above, but deleting RANDOM WAFER(ET). That is, submit the program

```
proc mixed;
    class et wafer pos;
    model resista=et pos et*pos;
run;
```

The resulting -2 REML log-likelihood is 59.4895. Thus, the likelihood ratio statistic is $58.4895 - 50.6505 = 8.8390$.

Self and Liang (1987) discussed the distribution of the likelihood ratio statistic for this test. The model with WAFER(ET) has one more parameter (σ_w^2) than the model without. However, σ_w^2 must be non-negative. As a result, the p-value for likelihood ratio statistic can be obtained by taking half of the probability of a greater χ^2 from a χ^2 distribution with 1 degree of freedom. For this example, the probability of a χ^2 statistic greater than 8.8390 is 0.0029. Thus, the p-value is 0.0015 — considerably stronger evidence of variation among wafers than the Z-test provides.

Alternatively, you can test H_0: $\sigma_w^2 = 0$ using the analysis of variance table from PROC GLM. The SAS program statements and the corresponding output for this example are discussed in Section 2.4.

The other information in the tables is of limited interest for interpreting split-plot experiments. The model fitting criteria, Akaike's Information Criterion and Schwarz's Bayesian Criterion, are of interest when comparing competing models and are discussed elsewhere in this book.

The estimates of the μ_{ij} and the main effect means $\mu_{i.}$ and $\mu_{.j}$ are obtained by the following command:

```
lsmeans et pos et*pos;
```

The results are shown in Output 2.2.

Output 2.2 *LSMEANS Using PROC MIXED Default*

```
                        The MIXED Procedure

                        Least Squares Means

        Level           LSMEAN      Std Error    DDF       T   Pr > |T|

        ET 1           5.62583333   0.21101154     8   26.66   0.0001
        ET 2           5.96583333   0.21101154     8   28.27   0.0001
        ET 3           6.08750000   0.21101154     8   28.85   0.0001
        ET 4           6.33250000   0.21101154     8   30.01   0.0001
        POS 1          6.02083333   0.13445556    24   44.78   0.0001
        POS 2          6.13416667   0.13445556    24   45.62   0.0001
        POS 3          5.74750000   0.13445556    24   42.75   0.0001
        POS 4          6.10916667   0.13445556    24   45.44   0.0001
        ET*POS 1 1     5.61333333   0.26891113    24   20.87   0.0001
        ET*POS 1 2     5.45000000   0.26891113    24   20.27   0.0001
        ET*POS 1 3     5.55333333   0.26891113    24   20.65   0.0001
        ET*POS 1 4     5.88666667   0.26891113    24   21.89   0.0001
        ET*POS 2 1     5.99333333   0.26891113    24   22.29   0.0001
        ET*POS 2 2     6.18666667   0.26891113    24   23.01   0.0001
        ET*POS 2 3     5.76666667   0.26891113    24   21.44   0.0001
        ET*POS 2 4     5.91666667   0.26891113    24   22.00   0.0001
        ET*POS 3 1     6.13666667   0.26891113    24   22.82   0.0001
        ET*POS 3 2     6.34666667   0.26891113    24   23.60   0.0001
        ET*POS 3 3     5.77333333   0.26891113    24   21.47   0.0001
        ET*POS 3 4     6.09333333   0.26891113    24   22.66   0.0001
        ET*POS 4 1     6.34000000   0.26891113    24   23.58   0.0001
        ET*POS 4 2     6.55333333   0.26891113    24   24.37   0.0001
        ET*POS 4 3     5.89666667   0.26891113    24   21.93   0.0001
        ET*POS 4 4     6.54000000   0.26891113    24   24.32   0.0001
```

The standard errors are obtained from the method presented in section 2.2.1. For example, for the main-effect mean of ET1, $\mu_{1\cdot}$, the standard error is

$$\sqrt{\left(\frac{1}{12}\right)(\hat{\sigma}^2 + 4\hat{\sigma}_W{}^2)}$$

Using the variance component estimates given in Output 2.1, the standard error for μ_1 is

$$\sqrt{\left(\frac{1}{12}\right)[0.1111 + 4*(0.1058)]} = 0.2110$$

The *t*-ratios and their probabilities are obtained by the ratio of the estimate to the standard error, as given in section 2.2.2. For example, the *t*-ratio to test $H_0: \mu_{1\cdot} = 0$ is

$$t = \frac{\bar{y}_{1\cdot\cdot}}{std\ err(y_{1\cdot\cdot})} = \frac{5.6258}{0.2110} = 26.66$$

2.3.2 Degrees of Freedom

Default Degrees of Freedom in PROC MIXED

The default denominator degrees of freedom for the t-values for all LSMEANS is the degrees of freedom for the random effect containing the effect of interest. If no random model effect contains the LSMEAN effect, then the degrees of freedom for error is used. Here, ET is contained within MS[WAFER(ET)], and therefore the degrees of freedom equal 8. POS and ET*POS are not contained in any random effect, so they have default denominator degrees of freedom of 24.

Overriding the Default

Depending on the form of the standard error, the default may or may not be correct. For example, the standard error for the estimated ET mean is a function of the WAFER(ET) expected mean square *only*, so the default degrees of freedom is correct. However, from Section 2.2.1, the standard errors of the estimated POS and ET*POS means involve linear combinations the WAFER(ET) and error expected mean squares.

For example, the variance of an estimated POS mean is $(1/12)(\sigma_w^2 + \sigma^2)$. The estimate of $\sigma_w^2 + \sigma^2$ is $(3/4)[MS(SPE)]+(1/4)\{MS[WAFER(ET)]\}$. Using Satterthwaite's procedure, the approximate degrees of freedom are

$$v = \frac{\left(\frac{3}{4}MS(SPE) + \frac{1}{4}MS[WAFER(ET)]\right)^2}{\dfrac{[\frac{3}{4}MS(SPE)]^2}{24} + \dfrac{[\frac{1}{4}MS(WAFER(ET))]^2}{8}}$$

MS[WAFER(ET)] be obtained from its expected mean square formula $\sigma^2 + 4\sigma_w^2$. Thus,

$$MS[WAFER(ET)] = 0.1111 + 4(0.1058) = 0.5343$$

Also, MS(SPE) = $\hat{\sigma}^2$ = 0.1111. The approximate degrees of freedom are

$$v = \frac{\left[\left(\frac{3}{4}\right)0.1111 + \left(\frac{1}{4}\right)0.5343\right]^2}{\dfrac{\left[\left(\frac{3}{4}\right)(0.1111)\right]^2}{24} + \dfrac{\left[\left(\frac{1}{4}\right)(0.5343)\right]^2}{8}} = 18.7$$

To get the correct degrees of freedom, you must overide the default. PROC MIXED provides you with several ways to override the default and obtain the correct degrees of freedom.

One way is to directly specify the degrees of freedom. For example you can use the statement

```
lsmeans pos/df=18.7;
```

The results are given in Output 2.3.

Results

Output 2.3 *LSMEANS for POS Using Corrected Degrees of Freedom*

```
                        Least Squares Means


        POS 1           6.02083333     0.13445556  18.7   44.78   0.0001
        POS 2           6.13416667     0.13445556  18.7   45.62   0.0001
        POS 3           5.74750000     0.13445556  18.7   42.75   0.0001
        POS 4           6.10916667     0.13445556  18.7   45.44   0.0001
```

Interpretation

The estimate, standard error, and t-ratio are the same, but the denominator degrees of freedom are different and probability values may be affected. In this case, the probabilities are the same because the t-ratios are large.

The other way is to specify that the Satterthwaite approximation be applied for all estimates and test-statistics computed by PROC MIXED. The Satterthwaite option is discussed in the next section. The point to emphasize here is that for any model with multiple error terms, you often need to override the default to obtain the correct degrees of freedom.

2.3.3 Estimates and Contrasts

Program for Estimates

Estimates of contrasts, such as the main-effect differences and simple effects presented in section 2.2.1, are obtained as follows:

```
estimate 'et1 vs et2' et 1 -1 0 0;
estimate 'pos1 vs pos2' pos 1 -1 0 0;
estimate 'pos1 v pos2 in et1' pos 1 -1 0 0 et*pos 1 -1 ;
estimate 'et1 v et2 in pos1' et 1 -1 0 0 et*pos 1 0 0 0 -1;
estimate 'et1,et2 v et3,et4 - pos 2'
         et 0.5 0.5  -0.5 -0.5
         et*pos 0 0.5 0 0 0 0.5 0 0 0  -0.5 0 0 0  -0.5 0 0;
```

The coefficients for the main-effect comparisons are self-evident, but the coefficients for the simple effects may seem strange. The simple effects presented in section 2.2.1 were given in terms of the cell means model, (μ_{ij}), but PROC MIXED is generally specified in terms of individual treatment effects, as in the above SAS program. Thus, the coefficients in the ESTIMATE statement must be written in terms of the effects model, $\mu + a_i + b_j + (ab)_{ij}$. For example, for the simple effect of POS1 versus POS2 in ET1, labelled 'POS1 v POS2 in ET1', the comparison is

$$\mu_{11} - \mu_{12} \qquad = [\mu + a_1 + b_1 + (ab)_{11}] - [\mu + a_1 + b_2 + (ab)_{12}]$$

$$= b_1 - b_2 + (ab)_{11} - ab_{12}$$

The coefficients for POS, 1 -1 0 0, correspond to $b_1 - b_2$, and the coefficients for ET*POS, 1 -1 0 0 0 0 0 0 0 0 0 0 0 0 0 0, correspond to $(ab)_{11} - (ab)_{12}$. Notice that the list of coefficients in the SAS statement may be shortened, as they were in this example, since

SAS understands the remaining coefficients not given to be 0. The coefficients for the average of ET1 and ET2 versus the average of ET3 and ET4 at POS2 result from

$$\tfrac{1}{2}[\mu_{12} + \mu_{22} - \mu_{32} - \mu_{42}] = \tfrac{1}{2}[a_1 + a_2 - a_3 - a_4] +$$

$$\tfrac{1}{2}[(ab)_{12} + (ab)_{22} - (ab)_{32} - (ab)_{42}]$$

Alternative Program for Estimates

The resulting ESTIMATE statement can be alternatively written as

```
estimate 'et1,et2 v et3,et4 - pos 2'
         et 1 1 -1 -1
         et*pos 0 1 0 0 0 1 0 0 0 -1 0 0 0 -1 0 0/divisor=2;
```

or as it was originally written above. The DIVISOR=2 option divides every coefficient in the ESTIMATE statement by 2. Any number may be used in the DIVISOR= option; it is generally more convenient to work with fractional coefficients using the DIVISOR= option. For further details on the construction of ESTIMATE statements, see *SAS System for Linear Models* (Freund, Littell, and Spector, 1991).

The results of these statements appear in Output 2.4.

Results

Output 2.4 *Estimates of Main-Effect and Simple-Effect Differences Using PROC MIXED Default*

```
                         The MIXED Procedure

                     ESTIMATE Statement Results


                     ESTIMATE Statement Results

Parameter                Estimate      Std Error    DDF       T    Pr > |T|

et1 vs et2             -0.34000000    0.29841538      8    -1.14    0.2875
pos1 vs pos2           -0.11333333    0.13610615     24    -0.83    0.4132
pos1 v pos2 in et1      0.16333333    0.27221230     24     0.60    0.5541
et1 v et2 in pos1      -0.38000000    0.38029776     24    -1.00    0.3277
et1,et2 v et3,et4 -    -0.63166667    0.26891113     24    -2.35    0.0274
```

Interpretation

The standard errors are obtained by the method presented in section 2.2.1. For example, the standard error for the simple effect of ET1 versus ET2 in POS1 is

$$\sqrt{\left(\frac{2}{3}\right)(\hat{\sigma}_w^2 + \hat{\sigma}^2)} = \sqrt{\left(\frac{2}{3}\right)(0.1111 + 0.1058)} = 0.3803$$

The standard error may be used to compute a confidence interval or to test the hypothesis that the difference is zero. The default degrees of freedom are determined in the same manner as for LSMEANS. The same caution given above applies.

Default Degrees of Freedom for ESTIMATE

PROC MIXED uses a **containment method** to determine default degrees of freedom.

The default degrees of freedom are correct for the main effects (ET1 versus ET2 and POS1 versus POS2) and the simple effect of POS1 versus POS2 given ET1, but not for the simple effects of ET given POS1. The containment method works as follows.

The standard error for the ET1 versus ET2 main effect is a function of $\sigma^2 + 4\sigma_w^2$, the expected value of MS[WAFER(ET)]; hence, the degrees of freedom for ET1 versus ET2 are 8. The default uses the degrees of freedom for WAFER(ET) because the ET effect on which the estimate is defined is **contained** within WAFER(ET).

For the main effect of POS and the simple effect of POS given ET, the standard error is a function of σ^2 alone. The denominator degrees of freedom are thus 24, the degrees of freedom for split-plot error. This corresponds to the default because the main effect of POS and all simple effects are defined on POS and ET*POS respectively. These effects are not contained in any random effect, so they use the SPE degrees of freedom.

The default is appropriate when the standard error is a function of a single MS, but not when it involves a linear combination of MS. For the simple effects of ET given POS1, the standard errors are a function of $\sigma^2 + \sigma_w^2$, the expected (1/4)MS[WAFER(ET)] + (3/4)MS(SPE). Because the standard error is a linear combination of mean squares, you must determine the degrees of freedom using Satterthwaite's approximation. This is the same linear combination of variance components used in the standard error of the estimated POS mean discussed above. The approximate degrees of freedom are thus 18.7.

Overriding the Default Degrees of Freedom for ESTIMATE

The appropriate *t*-tests can be obtained in PROC MIXED either by specifiying the correct degrees of freedom directly using the DF= option in the ESTIMATE statements, or by using the Satterthwaite option. Using the DF= option, the modified ESTIMATE statements are

```
estimate 'et1 v et2 in pos1' et 1 -1 0 0
         et*pos 1 0 0 0 -1/df=18.7;
 estimate 'et1,et2 v et3,et4 - pos 2' et 1 1 -1 -1
          et*pos 0 1 0 0 0 1 0 0 0 -1 0 0 0 -1 0 0/divisor=2 df=18.7;
```

These produce the results given in Output 2.5.

Output 2.5 *Estimates of Main Effects and Simple Effects Using PROC MIXED with Corrected Degrees of Freedom*

The MIXED Procedure					
ESTIMATE Statement Results					
Parameter	Estimate	Std Error	DDF	T	Pr > |T|
et1 v et2 in pos1	-0.38000000	0.38029776	18.7	-1.00	0.3304
et1,et2 v et3,et4 -	-0.63166667	0.26891113	18.7	-2.35	0.0300

The DDFM=SATTERTH Option

Determining the correct degrees of freedom for every estimate and test of interest is needlessly time consuming. Another way to obtain the correct degrees of freedom is to use the Satterthwaite option, DDFM=SATTERTH. You include this command in the MODEL statement, e.g., with the wafer data:

```
model resista=et pos et*pos/ddfm=satterth;
```

Once included, this option controls the computation of degrees of freedom for the "Test of Fixed Effects" table and the LSMEANS, ESTIMATE, and CONTRAST statements. Once it is used, no additional DF= options are needed. The complete SAS program using all of the estimates and tests discussed above is

```
proc mixed;
    class et wafer pos;
    model resista=et pos et*pos/ddfm=satterth;
    random wafer(et);
    lsmeans et pos et*pos;
    estimate 'et1 vs et2' et 1 -1 0 0;
    estimate 'pos1 vs pos2' pos 1 -1 0 0;
    estimate 'pos1 v pos2 in et1' pos 1 -1 0 0 et*pos 1 -1;
    estimate 'et1 v et2 in pos1' et 1 -1 0 0 et*pos 1 0 0 0 -1;
    estimate 'et1,et2 v et3,et4 - pos 2'
            et 1 1 -1 -1
            et*pos 0 1 0 0 0 1 0 0 0 -1 0 0 0 -1 0 0/divisor=2;
run;
```

The results are given in Output 2.6.

Output 2.6 *PROC MIXED Analysis Using the Satterthwaite Option (DDFM=SATTERTH) to Correct Degrees of Freedom*

```
                          Tests of Fixed Effects

                Source      NDF    DDF   Type III F   Pr > F

                ET           3      8       1.94      0.2015
                POS          3     24       3.39      0.0345
                ET*POS       9     24       0.81      0.6125




                      ESTIMATE Statement Results

Parameter              Estimate      Std Error    DDF       T    Pr > |T|

et1 vs et2           -0.34000000    0.29841538      8   -1.14     0.2875
pos1 vs pos2         -0.11333333    0.13610615     24   -0.83     0.4132
pos1 v pos2 in et1    0.16333333    0.27221230     24    0.60     0.5541
et1 v et2 in pos1    -0.38000000    0.38029776   18.7   -1.00     0.3305
et1,et2 v et3,et4 -  -0.63166667    0.26891113   18.7   -2.35     0.0300
```

The output is identical to previous output in every respect except the degrees of freedom. The main drawback of the Satterthwaite option is that it is computationally very intensive. Depending on the memory available on your computer, you may need to run large models without the Satterthwaite option and determine the needed degrees of freedom as shown above.

Confidence Intervals

Confidence intervals can be determined for any of the means or contrasts estimated using the formula

```
estimate ± tᵥ*(standard error)
```

For the main-effect mean of ET1, the degrees of freedom $v=8$. The t-value for $v=8$ and 95% confidence is 2.306. The resulting 95% confidence interval is

$$5.626 \pm 2.306*0.2110$$

or (5.139, 6.113).

For the simple effect of ET1 versus ET2 given POS1, the approximate degrees of freedom, $v=18.7$. To construct a confidence interval, you need to look up a t-value from a published t-table or use a computer software function, such as TINV in SAS. A typical textbook table only has integer values of v; rounding v down to be conservative is appropriate. Using a published table, for 95% confidence the t-value for $v=18$ is 2.101. The resulting 95% confidence interval is

$$-0.38 \pm 2.101*0.3803$$

or (−1.18, 0.42).

Contrasts

If you are only interested in tests of hypotheses, the F-ratios for all of the contrasts discussed may be obtained using the following statements:

```
contrast 'et1 vs et2' et 1 -1 0 0;
contrast 'pos1 vs pos2' pos 1 -1 0 0;
contrast 'pos1 v pos2 in et1' pos 1 -1 0 0 et*pos 1 -1;
contrast 'et1 v et2 in pos1' et 1 -1 0 0
         et*pos 1 0 0 0 -1 / df=18.7;
contrast 'et1,et2 v et3,et4 - pos 2' et 1 1 -1 -1
         et*pos 0 1 0 0 0 1 0 0 0 -1 0 0 0 -1 0 0 / df=18.7;
```

Note the coefficients for 'ET1, ET2 v ET3, ET4 −POS 2'. Unlike ESTIMATE, where the fractional values of the coefficients are essential to get the right estimate, for CONTRAST the fractions are optional because the resulting F-value is the same whether they are used or not.

Degrees of Freedom Using CONTRAST

The CONTRAST statement uses the same degree of freedom default as LSMEANS and ESTIMATE. For many contrasts, e.g., the simple effects of ET for a given POS in this example, you must modify the degrees of freedom by either direct specification using the DF= option, as shown above, or by using the DDFM=SATTERTH option in the MODEL statement. If you use the Satterthwaite option, you do not need the DF= options. The degrees of freedom are determined exactly as described above in this section. The CONTRAST results are shown in Output 2.7.

Output 2.7 *Contrasts to Test Main Effects and Simple Effects Using PROC MIXED with Corrected Degrees of Freedom*

```
                        CONTRAST Statement Results

           Source                    NDF    DDF       F    Pr > F


           et1 vs et2                  1      8     1.30   0.2875
           pos1 vs pos2                1     24     0.69   0.4132
           pos1 v pos2 in et1          1     24     0.36   0.5541
           et1 v et2 in pos1           1   18.7     1.00   0.3305
           et1,et2 v et3,et4 -         1   18.7     5.52   0.0300
```

2.3.4 Simple Effect Estimation and Testing

This example shows simple-effect ESTIMATE and CONTRAST statements in some detail to illustrate many of the essential principles associated with common mixed models with complex random effects such as the split plot. In practice, writing a separate ESTIMATE or CONTRAST statement for every simple effect of interest can be tedious. To simplify matters, PROC MIXED offers an option called SLICE with the LSMEANS statement to compute desired simple effects. For example, to obtain simple effects of ET for given values of POS, you use the following statement.

Program for the SLICE Option

```
lsmeans et*pos / slice=pos diff;
```

The results are given in Output 2.8.

Output 2.8 *Results of Using the SLICE Option to Obtain Simple Effects in WAFER Example*

```
                      Tests of Effect Slices

          Effect   Slice   NDF    DDF       F    Pr > F


          ET*POS   POS 1     3   18.7     1.30   0.3038
          ET*POS   POS 2     3   18.7     3.19   0.0477
          ET*POS   POS 3     3   18.7     0.28   0.8383
          ET*POS   POS 4     3   18.7     1.26   0.3181



                 Differences of Least Squares Means


Level 1         Level 2        Difference     Std Error    DDF       T   Pr > |T|


ET*POS 1 2      ET*POS 2 2     -0.73666667    0.38029776   18.7   -1.94    0.0680
ET*POS 1 2      ET*POS 3 2     -0.89666667    0.38029776   18.7   -2.36    0.0295
ET*POS 1 2      ET*POS 4 2     -1.10333333    0.38029776   18.7   -2.90    0.0093
ET*POS 2 2      ET*POS 3 2     -0.16000000    0.38029776   18.7   -0.42    0.6788
ET*POS 2 2      ET*POS 4 2     -0.36666667    0.38029776   18.7   -0.96    0.3473
ET*POS 3 2      ET*POS 4 2     -0.20666667    0.38029776   18.7   -0.54    0.5933
```

Interpretation

From this output, you can see that there are signficant differences among levels of ET for POS2 *only*. The DIFF option prints a table of simple-effect differences. This table is quite long as it includes all possible simple effects. For the sake of space, the table given in Output 2.8 is abridged to include only ET simple-effect differences for POS2. From the output, you can see that the significant ET effect at POS2 results from differences between ET1 and ET3 and between ET1 and ET4.

2.4 Comparison with the Analysis of a Split-Plot Experiment Using PROC GLM

Until PROC MIXED became available, the standard method of analyzing a split-plot experiment used PROC GLM. This section compares the results using PROC GLM and PROC MIXED. There are a number of similarities but some important differences.

2.4.1 Split-Plot Analysis Using PROC GLM

For the semiconductor example, the PROC GLM statements required to reproduce (as closely as possible) the statistics computed in section 2.2.3 using PROC MIXED are as follows.

Program

```
proc glm;
    class et wafer pos;
    model resista = et wafer(et) pos et*pos;
    random wafer(et) / test;

    lsmeans et/stderr e=wafer(et);
    lsmeans pos et*pos/stderr;

    contrast 'et1 vs et2' et 1 -1 0 0/e=wafer(et);
    contrast 'pos1 vs pos2' pos 1 -1 0 0;
    contrast 'pos1 v pos2 in et1' pos 1 -1 0 0 et*pos 1 -1;
    contrast 'et1 v et2 in pos1' et 1 -1 0 0 et*pos 1 0 0 0 -1;
    contrast 'et1,et2 v et3,et4 - pos 2'
            et 1 1 -1 -1 et*pos 0 1 0 0 0 1 0 0 0 -1 0 0 0 -1 0 0;

    estimate 'et1 vs et2' et 1 -1 0 0;
    estimate 'pos1 vs pos2' pos 1 -1 0 0;
    estimate 'pos1 v pos2 in et1' pos 1 -1 0 0 et*pos 1 -1;
    estimate 'et1 v et2 in pos1' et 1 -1 0 0 et*pos 1 0 0 0 -1;
    estimate 'et1,et2 v et3,et4 - pos 2' et 1 1 -1 -1
            et*pos 0 1 0 0 0 1 0 0 0 -1 0 0 0 -1 0 0/divisor=2;
run;
```

The results are given in Output 2.9 .

Results

Output 2.9 *Analysis of Semiconductor Experiment Using PROC GLM*

```
                    General Linear Models Procedure

Dependent Variable: RESISTA
                                Sum of         Mean
Source                  DF      Squares       Square    F Value    Pr > F

Model                   23    9.32500833    0.40543514     3.65    0.0013
Error                   24    2.66758333    0.11114931
Corrected Total         47   11.99259167


              R-Square         C.V.        Root MSE      RESISTA Mean

              0.777564       5.553811       0.33339         6.00292


Source                  DF    Type I SS   Mean Square   F Value    Pr > F

ET                       3    3.11215833   1.03738611      9.33    0.0003
WAFER(ET)                8    4.27448333   0.53431042      4.81    0.0013
POS                      3    1.12889167   0.37629722      3.39    0.0345
ET*POS                   9    0.80947500   0.08994167      0.81    0.6125
Source                  DF   Type III SS  Mean Square   F Value    Pr > F

ET                       3    3.11215833   1.03738611      9.33    0.0003
WAFER(ET)                8    4.27448333   0.53431042      4.81    0.0013
POS                      3    1.12889167   0.37629722      3.39    0.0345
ET*POS                   9    0.80947500   0.08994167      0.81    0.6125


Source        Type III Expected Mean Square

ET            Var(Error) + 4 Var(WAFER(ET)) + Q(ET,ET*POS)
WAFER(ET)     Var(Error) + 4 Var(WAFER(ET))
POS           Var(Error) + Q(POS,ET*POS)
ET*POS        Var(Error) + Q(ET*POS)


          Tests of Hypotheses for Mixed Model Analysis of Variance

Source: ET *
Error: MS(WAFER(ET))
                         Denominator   Denominator
     DF    Type III MS       DF            MS       F Value    Pr > F
      3    1.0373861111        8      0.5343104167   1.9415    0.2015
* - This test assumes one or more other fixed effects are zero.


Source: WAFER(ET)
Error: MS(Error)
                         Denominator   Denominator
     DF    Type III MS       DF            MS       F Value    Pr > F
      8    0.5343104167       24      0.1111493056   4.8071    0.0013
```

```
Source: POS *
Error: MS(Error)
```

DF	Type III MS	Denominator DF	Denominator MS	F Value	Pr > F
3	0.3762972222	24	0.1111493056	3.3855	0.0345

* - This test assumes one or more other fixed effects are zero.

```
Source: ET*POS
Error: MS(Error)
```

DF	Type III MS	Denominator DF	Denominator MS	F Value	Pr > F
9	0.0899416667	24	0.1111493056	0.8092	0.6125

Least Squares Means

Standard Errors and Probabilities calculated using the Type III MS for
WAFER(ET) as an Error term

ET	RESISTA LSMEAN	Std Err LSMEAN	Pr > |T| H0:LSMEAN=0
1	5.62583333	0.21101154	0.0001
2	5.96583333	0.21101154	0.0001
3	6.08750000	0.21101154	0.0001
4	6.33250000	0.21101154	0.0001

POS	RESISTA LSMEAN	Std Err LSMEAN	Pr > |T| H0:LSMEAN=0
1	6.02083333	0.09624158	0.0001
2	6.13416667	0.09624158	0.0001
3	5.74750000	0.09624158	0.0001
4	6.10916667	0.09624158	0.0001

ET	POS	RESISTA LSMEAN	Std Err LSMEAN	Pr > |T| H0:LSMEAN=0
1	1	5.61333333	0.19248316	0.0001
1	2	5.45000000	0.19248316	0.0001
1	3	5.55333333	0.19248316	0.0001
1	4	5.88666667	0.19248316	0.0001
2	1	5.99333333	0.19248316	0.0001
2	2	6.18666667	0.19248316	0.0001
2	3	5.76666667	0.19248316	0.0001
2	4	5.91666667	0.19248316	0.0001
3	1	6.13666667	0.19248316	0.0001
3	2	6.34666667	0.19248316	0.0001
3	3	5.77333333	0.19248316	0.0001
3	4	6.09333333	0.19248316	0.0001
4	1	6.34000000	0.19248316	0.0001
4	2	6.55333333	0.19248316	0.0001
4	3	5.89666667	0.19248316	0.0001
4	4	6.54000000	0.19248316	0.0001

Main-effects and simple effects using ESTIMATE

Parameter	Estimate	T for H0: Parameter=0	Pr > |T|	Std Error of Estimate
et1 vs et2	-0.34000000	-2.50	0.0197	0.13610615
pos1 vs pos2	-0.11333333	-0.83	0.4132	0.13610615
pos1 v pos2 in et1				
	0.16333333	0.60	0.5541	0.27221230
et1 v et2 in pos1				
	-0.38000000	-1.40	0.1755	0.27221230
et1,et2 v et3,et4 -				
	-0.63166667	-3.28	0.0031	0.19248316

Contrast	Contrast Expected Mean Square
et1 vs et2	Var(Error) + 4 Var(WAFER(ET)) + Q(ET,ET*POS)
pos1 vs pos2	Var(Error) + Q(POS,ET*POS)
pos1 v pos2 in et1	Var(Error) + Q(POS,ET*POS)
et1 v et2 in pos1	Var(Error) + Var(WAFER(ET)) + Q(ET,ET*POS)
et1,et2 v et3,et4 -	Var(Error) + Var(WAFER(ET)) + Q(ET,ET*POS)

Following hypotheses use default error term (ERROR)

Contrast	DF	Contrast SS	Mean Square	F Value	Pr > F
pos1 vs pos2	1	0.07706667	0.07706667	0.69	0.4132
pos1 v pos2 in et1	1	0.04001667	0.04001667	0.36	0.5541
et1 v et2 in pos1	1	0.21660000	0.21660000	1.95	0.1755
et1,et2 v et3,et4 -	1	1.19700833	1.19700833	10.77	0.0031

Tests of Hypotheses using the Type III MS for WAFER(ET) as an error term

Contrast	DF	Contrast SS	Mean Square	F Value	Pr > F
et1 vs et2	1	0.69360000	0.69360000	1.30	0.2875

2.4.2 Comparison of PROC GLM and PROC MIXED for Split-Plot Analysis

This example using PROC GLM is discussed in detail by Littell, Freund and Spector (1991); the discussion here focuses on the highlights:

- The default F-tests all use MS(error), that is MS(SPE). These tests are correct for POS and ET*POS but not for ET.

- The F-tests produced by the RANDOM statement are based on the expected mean squares. The F-ratios and degrees of freedom are all correct.

  For the fixed effects, ET, POS, and ET*POS, the F-values and associated probabilities are identical to those obtained by PROC MIXED. For balanced data, the F-values obtained by PROC MIXED and PROC GLM agree. For unbalanced data, they do not, in general, agree.

  For the random effect of WAFER(ET), an F-test for H_0: $\sigma_w^2 = 0$ is computed. The F-value is 4.41 with a probability of 0.0013. PROC MIXED does not compute an F-test for the variance components of random effects. It does compute a Z-test and can be used to construct a likelihood ratio χ^2 test. For small degrees of freedom, as is the case for MS[WAFER(ET)], the small-sample properties of the Z-test are poor. But the likelihood ratio test is more reliable, and its probability of 0.0015 is comparable to the F-test produced by PROC GLM.

- The default standard error for the LSMEAN in PROC GLM is

$$\sqrt{\frac{\hat{\sigma}^2}{(no.\ observations\ per\ mean)}}$$

  For example, each ET mean is based on 12 observations, so the default standard error for the main-effect means ET1, ET2, etc. is

$$std\ err(\hat{\mu}_{1.}) = \sqrt{\frac{\hat{\sigma}^2}{12}}$$

  which is incorrect. In this example, you can use WAFER(ET) mean square to obtain the standard error of the ET main-effect means. This is because in a balanced split plot without blocking, the expected WAFER(ET) mean square corresponds to the form of the standard error of the estimated ET mean. This is one of the few cases in which life is so convenient.

  The POS main-effect means and ET*POS means are more troublesome. As shown in section 2.2.1, their standard errors are functions of $\sigma^2 + \sigma_w^2$, which must be estimated by $(3/4)MS(SPE) + (1/4)MS[WAFER(ET)]$. There is no provision for obtaining standard errors using a linear combination of mean squares in PROC GLM. PROC MIXED computes the correct standard errors, but PROC GLM cannot.

- The standard errors used to obtain estimates of the main-effect and simple-effect differences all use the formula

$$std\ err = \sqrt{\frac{2\sigma^2}{no.\ obs\ per\ mean}}$$

  This is correct only for the POS1 versus POS2 main effect and POS1 versus POS2 given ET1 simple effect. PROC GLM has no option to specify the alternative standard errors when the default is inappropriate. Thus, the standard errors and resulting t-statistics computed by PROC GLM for the ET main effect and ET given POS simple effects are wrong. They can be obtained using PROC MIXED.

- The contrasts in PROC GLM use the split-plot error mean square as the default denominator for all F-statistics. This is correct for the POS main effect and the POS given ET simple effect. PROC GLM provides limited ability to override the default; an alternative mean square can be specified, as it is in this example for the ET1 versus ET2 main effect. The TEST option of the RANDOM statement in PROC GLM does *not* apply to CONTRAST, ESTIMATE, or LSMEANS statements.

  However, PROC GLM does not allow linear combinations of mean squares to be used with contrasts. Thus, there is no way to compute the correct F-statistic for the ET given POS simple effects. They can only be computed using PROC MIXED.

2.5 Split-Plot Experiments with Whole Plots in Randomized Blocks

This section presents the analysis of split-plot experiments with the whole-plot experiments arranged in blocks. The variety-inoculation trial described previously in this chapter and whose data are given in Appendix 4, Data Set 2.2(a) serves as an example.

In most respects, the methods are similar to those used for a completely random arrangement of whole-plot units. This section focuses primarily on differences between the blocked and completely random cases. These differences are minor unless there are missing data. Section 2.7.1 presents an example with missing data.

Program

For the cultivar-inoculation trial, the following statements specify the basic mixed model using PROC MIXED:

```
proc mixed;
   class block cult inoc;
   model drywt = cult inoc cult*inoc/ddfm=satterth;
   random block block*cult;
   lsmeans cult inoc cult*inoc;
run;
```

The results are given in Output 2.10.

Results

Output 2.10 *Basic PROC MIXED Results for Variety-Inoculation Trial*

```
                        The MIXED Procedure

             Covariance Parameter Estimates (REML)

Cov Parm          Ratio       Estimate     Std Error      Z    Pr > |Z|

BLOCK          1.24748966   0.88000000   1.22640094    0.72    0.4730
BLOCK*CULT     1.15987399   0.81819444   0.86538380    0.95    0.3444
Residual       1.00000000   0.70541667   0.28798515    2.45    0.0143
```

```
                  Model Fitting Information for DRYWT

             Description                        Value

             Observations                      24.0000
             Variance Estimate                  0.7054
             Standard Deviation Estimate        0.8399
             REML Log Likelihood              -32.5313
             Akaike's Information Criterion   -35.5313
             Schwartz's Bayesian Criterion    -36.8669
             -2 REML Log Likelihood            65.0626


                         Tests of Fixed Effects


             Source     NDF   DDF   Type III F   Pr > F

             CULT         1     3        0.76    0.4471
             INOC         2    12       83.76    0.0000
             CULT*INOC    2    12        1.29    0.3098



                       Least Squares Means


   Level              LSMEAN      Std Error    DDF        T   Pr > |T|

   CULT a           30.10000000   0.69522179   4.97   43.30    0.0001
   CULT b           30.73333333   0.69522179   4.97   44.21    0.0001
   INOC con         27.96250000   0.64066480   4.06   43.65    0.0001
   INOC dea         29.95000000   0.64066480   4.06   46.75    0.0001
   INOC liv         33.33750000   0.64066480   4.06   52.04    0.0001
   CULT*INOC a con  27.90000000   0.77517919   7.5    35.99    0.0001
   CULT*INOC a dea  29.25000000   0.77517919   7.5    37.73    0.0001
   CULT*INOC a liv  33.15000000   0.77517919   7.5    42.76    0.0001
   CULT*INOC b con  28.02500000   0.77517919   7.5    36.15    0.0001
   CULT*INOC b dea  30.65000000   0.77517919   7.5    39.54    0.0001
   CULT*INOC b liv  33.52500000   0.77517919   7.5    43.25    0.0001
```

Interpretation

In this example, the BLOCK effect is assumed to be random. The whole-plot error consists of variability among block-cultivar combinations—the whole-plot units. Hence, the whole-plot error effect is denoted BLOCK*CULT.

The variance component estimates for BLOCK, BLOCK*CULT, and RESIDUAL are the estimates of block (σ_R^2), whole-plot error (σ_W^2), and split-plot error (σ^2) variance, respectively. The standard errors and Z-tests are based on asymptotic normality. For the BLOCK effect in particular, which is estimated with only 3 degrees of freedom, this is not a reliable test.

Tests for σ_R^2 and σ_W^2 can be obtained by dropping BLOCK*CULT from the model, rerunning the analysis, and and then dropping BLOCK. The resulting likelihood ratio χ^2 tests H_0: $\sigma_R^2 = 0$. The method is similar to that discussed for the semiconductor example above. The difference between the "-2 REML Log-Likelihood" computed by the analysis with BLOCK*CULT in the model and the analysis without BLOCK*CULT is the χ^2 statistic for H_0: $\sigma_W^2 = 0$. These results are presented in Output 2.11.

Output 2.11 *Information for Testing Hypotheses about BLOCK and BLOCK*CULT Effects in Variety-Inoculation Trial*

```
                      The MIXED Procedure

                Model Fitting Information for DRYWT

           Description                        Value

           Observations                      24.0000
           Variance Estimate                  1.1963
           Standard Deviation Estimate        1.0938
           REML Log Likelihood              -34.2437
           Akaike's Information Criterion   -36.2437
           Schwartz's Bayesian Criterion   -37.1341
           -2 REML Log Likelihood           68.4874



Likelihood ratio χ² to test BLOCK*CULT



     χ² =    -2 REML Log-Likelihood for reduced model - (-2 REML Log-
             Likelihood for full model)


        =    68.4874 - 65.0626


     Probability (P-VALUE) obtained using PROBCHI function



              OBS      CHISQ     P_VALUE

               1      3.4248    0.064224
```

For these data the likelihood-ratio χ^2 statistic for H_0: $\sigma_R^2 = 0$ is 6.6976 with a probability of 0.0093 (and thus a p-value of 0.0047), and the likelihood-ratio χ^2 statistic for H_0: $\sigma_w^2 = 0$ is 3.4248 with a probability of 0.0642, i.e, a p-value of 0.0321. The dramatic difference in results between the Z-tests and likelihood-ratio tests is typical of random effects with few degrees of freedom. The Z-test has little sensitivity under these conditions.

The standard errors for the LSMEANS are obtained using the same method as shown in the semiconductor example. For example, the main-effect mean for CULT, $\mu_{i.}$ is estimated by $\bar{y}_{i..}$ whose variance is

$$\text{Var}(\bar{y}_{i..}) = \text{Var}[(1/12)\underset{j}{\sum}\underset{k}{\sum}y_{ijk}]$$

$$= (1/12)^2\{\text{Var}[\Sigma\Sigma(\mu_{ij} + r_k + w_{ik} + e_{ijk})]\}$$

$$= (1/12)^2\,\text{Var}(3\Sigma r_k + 3\Sigma w_{ik} + \Sigma\Sigma e_{ijk})$$

$$= (1/12)(3\sigma_R^2 + 3\sigma_w^2 + \sigma^2)$$

Thus, the standard error for a CULT mean is the square root of the estimate of $(1/12)(3\sigma_R^2 + 3\sigma_W^2 + \sigma^2)$, which is

$$std\ err(\hat{\mu}_{i.}) = \frac{\sqrt{3*0.8800 + 3*0.8182 + 0.7054}}{12} = 0.6952$$

The variances and standard errors for INOC and CULT*INOC means can be obtained in the same way. The variances are

INOC $Var(\bar{y}_{.j.}) = (1/8)(2\sigma_R^2 + \sigma_W^2 + \sigma^2)$

CULT*INOC $Var(\bar{y}_{ij.}) = (1/4)(\sigma_R^2 + \sigma_W^2 + \sigma^2)$

None of the standard errors for main-effect or treatment combination means are functions of single mean squares. For each effect, degrees of freedom for the LSMEANS must be determined using Satterthwaite's approximation. For example, the standard error for a CULT mean can be expressed in terms of ANOVA means squares as

$$\sqrt{\left(\frac{1}{12}\right)\left[\left(\frac{1}{2}\right)MS(BLOCK) + \left(\frac{1}{2}\right)MS(BLOCK*CULT)\right]}$$

In other words, $4\sigma_R^2 + 4\sigma_W^2 + \sigma^2$ can be estimated by $(1/2)MS(BLOCK) + (1/2)MS(BLOCK*CULT)$. Using this expression, the approximate degrees of freedom are

$$DF = \frac{\left(\frac{1}{2}MS(BLOCK) + \frac{1}{2}MS[BLOCK*CULT]\right)^2}{\dfrac{[\frac{1}{2}MS(BLOCK)]^2}{3} + \dfrac{[\frac{1}{2}MS(BLOCK*CULT)]^2}{3}}$$

For these data, MS(BLOCK)=8.4400 and MS(BLOCK*CULT)=3.1600. Thus,

$$DF = \frac{\left[\frac{1}{2}(8.4400) + \frac{1}{2}(3.1600)\right]^2}{\dfrac{[\frac{1}{2}(8.4400)]^2}{3} + \dfrac{[\frac{1}{2}(3.1600)]^2}{3}} = 4.97$$

The DDFM=SATTERTH option computes the appropriate test statistics for $H_0: \mu_{i.} = 0$. Alternatively, you can specify the degrees of freedom directly, e.g.:

```
lsmeans cult / df=4.97;
```

Comparison with PROC GLM

The results for the analysis using PROC GLM are given in Output 2.12.

Output 2.12 *Basic PROC GLM Analysis for Variety-Inoculation Trial*

```
                    General Linear Models Procedure

Dependent Variable: DRYWT
                             Sum of          Mean
Source              DF       Squares        Square   F Value   Pr > F

Model               11    157.208333     14.291667    20.26    0.0001
Error               12      8.465000      0.705417
Corrected Total     23    165.673333


Source              DF    Type III SS   Mean Square   F Value   Pr > F

BLOCK                3     25.320000      8.440000     11.96    0.0006
CULT                 1      2.406667      2.406667      3.41    0.0895
BLOCK*CULT           3      9.480000      3.160000      4.48    0.0249
INOC                 2    118.175833     59.087917     83.76    0.0001
CULT*INOC            2      1.825833      0.912917      1.29    0.3098


Source          Type III Expected Mean Square

BLOCK           Var(Error) + 3 Var(BLOCK*CULT) + 6 Var(BLOCK)
CULT            Var(Error) + 3 Var(BLOCK*CULT) + Q(CULT,CULT*INOC)
BLOCK*CULT      Var(Error) + 3 Var(BLOCK*CULT)
INOC            Var(Error) + Q(INOC,CULT*INOC)
CULT*INOC       Var(Error) + Q(CULT*INOC)


                      Least Squares Means

   Standard Errors and Probabilities calculated using the Type III MS for
                   BLOCK*CULT as an Error term


          CULT          DRYWT        Std Err      Pr > |T|
                        LSMEAN       LSMEAN      H0:LSMEAN=0


           a         30.1000000     0.5131601      0.0001
           b         30.7333333     0.5131601      0.0001


          INOC          DRYWT        Std Err      Pr > |T|
                        LSMEAN       LSMEAN      H0:LSMEAN=0


          con        27.9625000     0.2969463      0.0001
          dea        29.9500000     0.2969463      0.0001
          liv        33.3375000     0.2969463      0.0001


       CULT   INOC       DRYWT        Std Err      Pr > |T|
                         LSMEAN       LSMEAN      H0:LSMEAN=0


        a     con      27.9000000    0.4199454      0.0001
        a     dea      29.2500000    0.4199454      0.0001
        a     liv      33.1500000    0.4199454      0.0001
        b     con      28.0250000    0.4199454      0.0001
        b     dea      30.6500000    0.4199454      0.0001
        b     liv      33.5250000    0.4199454      0.0001
```

Interpretation: PROC GLM versus PROC MIXED Results

Comparing the two analyses, the main points are

- The random statement produces the same F-statistics and probability values for the fixed effects of CULT, INOC, and CULT*INOC. F-tests for BLOCK and BLOCK*CULT are also calculated. These produce similar results to the likelihood-ratio tests computed by PROC MIXED.

- The default standard errors for the LSMEANS computed by PROC GLM are functions of σ^2 only and are therefore incorrect. PROC GLM does allow the default to be overridden, but only by a *single* alternative mean square. However, *all* of the *correct* standard errors are functions of all three variance components and are estimated by linear combinations of mean squares. PROC MIXED computes the correct standard errors by default, but none can be computed using PROC GLM.

- Although not shown here, the methods for estimating and testing main-effect and simple-effect contrasts and the resulting standard errors and denominator degrees of freedom are identical to those presented in the semiconductor example. In some cases, PROC GLM uses the right defaults; in other cases, where the standard error involves a single mean square, PROC GLM allows you to override the default by using the correct mean square to obtain the correct result; in some cases, the standard error involves a linear combination of mean squares and PROC GLM has no option to allow these to be computed. In all cases, PROC MIXED computes the correct standard errors and test statistics by default. If the denominator degrees of freedom are something other than split-plot error, an override option in PROC MIXED is available and must be used.

2.6 Standard Errors and Implied Inference Space

In the examples in the previous sections, the default standard errors computed by PROC MIXED are always correct, whereas those computed by PROC GLM are correct only in certain special cases. Correct standard errors can be obtained by overriding the PROC GLM default in a few cases. In many other cases, the correct standard errors cannot be obtained at all using PROC GLM. Examining the functions of model effects used by each program to obtain estimates and their standard errors provides an insight into the scope of inference—or **inference space**—implied by each estimate. Chapter 6 contains a more general and systematic discussion of the conceptual ideas in mixed models underlying the notion of inference space.

2.6.1 Estimable Functions

A little background on estimable functions can help clarify things. In linear model theory, a linear combination of model effects is **estimable** if it can be written as a linear combination of expected values of the observations. In the split-plot experiments presented in the previous section, the expected value of an observation is

$$E(\bar{y}_{ijk}) = \mu_{ij} = \mu + \alpha_i + \beta_j + (\alpha\beta)_{ij}$$

and thus any linear combination of the μ_{ij}'s is estimable. For example, in the cultivar-inoculation experiment, the cultivar main-effect means

$$\mu + \alpha_i + (1/3)\sum_j \beta_j + (1/3)\sum_j (\alpha\beta)_{ij}$$

are estimable because they are equal to

$$(1/3)\sum_j \mu_{ij} = \mu_{i\bullet}$$

The important point is that the random effects, e.g., BLOCK and BLOCK*CULT in the cultivar-inoculation example, are not included in the estimates of fixed-effect treatment means, differences, and contrasts—normally, the items of primary interest to researchers.

2.6.2 How PROC MIXED and PROC GLM Handle Estimable Functions in Split-Plot Models

Estimable Functions in PROC MIXED

The coefficients of LSMEANS and ESTIMATE used by PROC MIXED can be obtained using the E option, that is:

```
lsmeans cult/e;
```

Output 2.13 shows the coefficients as presented by PROC MIXED for the cultivar main-effect means using the above option.

Output 2.13 *Coefficients for Cultivar LSMEAN Using PROC MIXED*

Parameter	Row 1	Row 2
INTERCEPT	1	1
CULT a	1	0
CULT b	0	1
INOC con	0.3333333333	0.3333333333
INOC dea	0.3333333333	0.3333333333
INOC liv	0.3333333333	0.3333333333
CULT*INOC a con	0.3333333333	0
CULT*INOC a dea	0.3333333333	0
CULT*INOC a liv	0.3333333333	0
CULT*INOC b con	0	0.3333333333
CULT*INOC b dea	0	0.3333333333
CULT*INOC b liv	0	0.3333333333

```
NOTE that coefficients for random effects (BLOCK and BLOCK*CULT)
default to zero.
```

Estimable Functions in PROC GLM

The same option can be used in PROC GLM to show the coefficients the procedure is using. These are given in Output 2.14. These coefficients are computed as if BLOCK (and hence BLOCK*CULT) were a fixed effect. PROC GLM thus assumes that

$$E(\bar{y}_{ijk}) = \mu_{ijk} = \mu + \alpha_i + r_k + ra_{ik} + \beta_j + (\alpha\beta)_{ij}$$

and thus a cultivar mean must be

$$\mu_{i\bullet\bullet} = (1/12)\sum_j\sum_k \mu_{ijk} = \mu + \alpha_i + \tfrac{1}{4}[\Sigma r_k + \Sigma ra_{ik}] + 1/3[\Sigma\beta_j + \Sigma(\alpha\beta)_{ij}]$$

Output 2.14 *Coefficients for Cultivar LSMEAN Using PROC GLM*

CULT			a	b
Effect			Coefficients	
INTERCEPT			1	1
BLOCK	1		0.25	0.25
	2		0.25	0.25
	3		0.25	0.25
	4		0.25	0.25
CULT	a		1	0
	b		0	1
BLOCK*CULT	1 a		0.25	0
	1 b		0	0.25
	2 a		0.25	0
	2 b		0	0.25
	3 a		0.25	0
	3 b		0	0.25
	4 a		0.25	0
	4 b		0	0.25
INOC	con		0.3333333333	0.3333333333
	dea		0.3333333333	0.3333333333
	liv		0.3333333333	0.3333333333
CULT*INOC	a con		0.3333333333	0
	a dea		0.3333333333	0
	a liv		0.3333333333	0
	b con		0	0.3333333333
	b dea		0	0.3333333333
	b liv		0	0.3333333333

Interpretation: PROC GLM versus PROC MIXED Results

There are two problems with the PROC GLM approach:

1. Because PROC GLM's LSMEANS and ESTIMATE algorithms assume *all* model effects are fixed—even those that are actually random—computation of standard errors is based on the assumption that the only source of random variation is error, and therefore all standard errors must be some function of only σ^2.

2. By assuming all model effects to be fixed, PROC GLM falsely declares correct estimable functions in mixed models—namely those with zero coefficients for *all* random effects—to be nonestimable.

These two problems help explain why PROC GLM computes the wrong standard errors so frequently. An example in the next section also illustrates how these misconceptions lead to frustrating, and unnecessary, difficulties in working with unbalanced data.

2.6.3 Inference Space

In mixed model theory, PROC GLM is actually computing Best Linear Unbiased Predictors (BLUPs) of the LSMEANS *conditional on the specific BLOCK and BLOCK*CULT combinations actually observed.* BLUP is discussed in detail in Chapter 6. In balanced experiments, these BLUPs yield the same point estimators as the usual LSMEANS, but the standard errors are limited to variation *within* the BLOCK*CULT whole-plots. This restricts the inference that can legitimately occur: the resulting confidence intervals and test statistics apply *only* to predictions regarding the BLOCK*CULT combinations actually used in the experiment and cannot be extended to a larger population. Extending inference to a larger population requires including the uncertainty associated with variation among whole-plots and BLOCKs. For this reason, the BLUP

$$\mu + \alpha_i + \tfrac{1}{4}[\textstyle\sum_k r_k + \sum_k (ra)_{ij}] + 1/3[\textstyle\sum_j \beta_j + \sum_j (\alpha\beta)_{ij}]$$

is said to apply to the "narrow" inference space. The term "narrow" is used in contrast to "broad" inference used to characterize the estimable function

$$\mu + \alpha_i + 1/3[\Sigma\beta_j + \Sigma(\alpha\beta)_{ij}]$$

consistent with the model.

As mentioned in the previous section, researchers often attempt to fix the main-effect LSMEANS standard error by using the whole-plot mean square (e.g., MS(BLOCK*CULT)) in place of the split-plot mean square, that is, using the statement

```
lsmeans cult/e=block*cult;
```

This fix is incorrect. In terms of mixed model theory, it is equivalent to computing the BLUP

$$\mu + \alpha_i + \tfrac{1}{4}\textstyle\sum_k r_k + 1/3[\textstyle\sum_j \beta_j + \sum_j (\alpha\beta)_{ij}]$$

In balanced experiments, this is equivalent to regarding BLOCK as fixed but BLOCK*CULT as random. Inference is restricted to the BLOCKs actually observed, but BLOCK*CULT effects are regarded as representative of variation among whole-plots in the population at large. This BLUP is said to apply to the intermediate inference space. In certain instances, this may be a reasonable way to model the data, but it is not consistent with the model most researchers assume when they conduct a split-plot experiment.

Program

The three inference spaces may be computed by PROC MIXED. For example, for the main-effect mean of cultivar A in the cultivar-inoculation experiment, the commands are

```
estimate 'cult=1 broad' intercept 12 cult 12 0 inoc 4 4 4
         cult*inoc 4 4 4 0 0 0 | block 0 0 0 0
         block*cult 0 0  0 0  0 0  0 0/e divisor=12;

estimate 'cult=1 intermediate' intercept 12 cult 12 0 inoc 4 4 4
         cult*inoc 4 4 4 0 0 0 | block 3 3 3 3
         block*cult 0 0  0 0  0 0  0 0/e divisor=12;

estimate 'cult=1 narrow' intercept 12 cult 12 0 inoc 4 4 4
         cult*inoc 4 4 4 0 0 0 | block 3 3 3 3
         block*cult 3 0  3 0  3 0  3 0/e divisor=12;
```

Output 2.15 gives the results of these commands. Note that all produce identical point estimates. The standard error for the **narrow** term corresponds to the PROC GLM default. The standard error for the **intermediate** term corresponds to the PROC GLM computation using MS(BLOCK*CULT) in place of MS(error). The **broad** term corresponds to the LSMEANS computed by PROC MIXED. With few exceptions, researchers' objectives are addressed by broad inference.

Output 2.15 *Estimates, Standard Errors, and Coefficients for Broad, Intermediate, and Narrow Inference Space LSMEANS for CULT 1*

```
                    Coefficients for cult=1 broad


              Parameter                      Row 1
              INTERCEPT                         1
              CULT a                            1
              CULT b                            0
              INOC con          0.3333333333
              INOC dea          0.3333333333
              INOC liv          0.3333333333
              CULT*INOC a con   0.3333333333
              CULT*INOC a dea   0.3333333333
              CULT*INOC a liv   0.3333333333
              CULT*INOC b con                   0
              CULT*INOC b dea                   0
              CULT*INOC b liv                   0
              BLOCK 1                           0
              BLOCK 2                           0
              BLOCK 3                           0
              BLOCK 4                           0
              BLOCK*CULT 1 a                    0
              BLOCK*CULT 1 b                    0
              BLOCK*CULT 2 a                    0
              BLOCK*CULT 2 b                    0
              BLOCK*CULT 3 a                    0
              BLOCK*CULT 3 b                    0
              BLOCK*CULT 4 a                    0
              BLOCK*CULT 4 b                    0


              Coefficients for cult=1 intermediate
              Parameter                      Row 1

              INTERCEPT                         1
              CULT a                            1
              CULT b                            0
              INOC con          0.3333333333
              INOC dea          0.3333333333
              INOC liv          0.3333333333
              CULT*INOC a con   0.3333333333
              CULT*INOC a dea   0.3333333333
              CULT*INOC a liv   0.3333333333
              CULT*INOC b con                   0
              CULT*INOC b dea                   0
              CULT*INOC b liv                   0
              BLOCK 1                        0.25
              BLOCK 2                        0.25
              BLOCK 3                        0.25
```

```
                              BLOCK 4                        0.25
                              BLOCK*CULT 1 a                    0
                              BLOCK*CULT 1 b                    0
                              BLOCK*CULT 2 a                    0
                              BLOCK*CULT 2 b                    0
                              BLOCK*CULT 3 a                    0
                              BLOCK*CULT 3 b                    0
                              BLOCK*CULT 4 a                    0
                              BLOCK*CULT 4 b                    0


                        Coefficients for cult=1 narrow


                        Parameter                    Row 1


                        INTERCEPT                        1
                        CULT a                           1
                        CULT b                           0
                        INOC con             0.3333333333
                        INOC dea             0.3333333333
                        INOC liv             0.3333333333
                        CULT*INOC a con      0.3333333333
                        CULT*INOC a dea      0.3333333333
                        CULT*INOC a liv      0.3333333333
                        CULT*INOC b con                  0
                        CULT*INOC b dea                  0
                        CULT*INOC b liv                  0
                        BLOCK 1                       0.25
                        BLOCK 2                       0.25
                        BLOCK 3                       0.25
                        BLOCK 4                       0.25
                        BLOCK*CULT 1 a                0.25
                        BLOCK*CULT 1 b                   0
                        BLOCK*CULT 2 a                0.25
                        BLOCK*CULT 2 b                   0
                        BLOCK*CULT 3 a                0.25
                        BLOCK*CULT 3 b                   0
                        BLOCK*CULT 4 a                0.25
                        BLOCK*CULT 4 b                   0



                        ESTIMATE Statement Results
```

Parameter	Estimate	Std Error	DDF	T	Pr > |T|
cult=1 broad	30.10000000	0.69522179	12	43.30	0.0001
cult=1 intermediate	30.10000000	0.51316014	12	58.66	0.0001
cult=1 narrow	30.10000000	0.24245561	12	124.15	0.0001

2.7 Unbalanced Split-Plot Experiments

Both split-plot examples presented in the previous sections are balanced. That is, there are an equal number of whole-plot experimental units per whole-plot treatment and each split-plot treatment is observed an equal number of times within each whole plot. Additionally, when blocking is used, as in the cultivar-inoculation example, the whole plot is a randomized complete block design with no missing cells.

In many practical situations, split-plot experiments are not balanced. This may occur because observations are lost from experiments originally set up as balanced split-plots or because the experiment was intentionally designed to be unbalanced. For example, the whole plot may be set up as an incomplete block design. Chapter 10 presents examples of complex, unbalanced split plots. This section presents a simpler example.

In principle, there is no difference between the analysis of balanced and unbalanced split-plot experiments. For example, if blocking is used, the model is the same for a whole plot arranged as a randomized complete block as it is for an incomplete block. Given the implied **X** and **Z** matrices, you can use the same methods to solve the mixed model equations, determine relevant estimable functions, and compute their estimates, standard errors, and test statistics.

2.7.1 Example: Cultivar-Inoculation Data with Missing Whole Plot

Consider the cultivar-inoculation experiment, but suppose that all of the observations for BLOCK 1, CULTIVAR 'A' were lost. You use the same model and PROC MIXED statements to obtain the analysis used in section 2.5.

Program

```
proc mixed;
   class block cult inoc;
   model drywt = cult inoc cult*inoc/ddfm=satterth;
   random block block*cult;
   lsmeans cult/e;
   lsmeans inoc cult*inoc;
   estimate 'cult diff' cult 1 -1 /e;
   contrast 'cult diff' cult 1 -1 /e;
run;
```

Output 2.16 gives the results of the analysis.

Output 2.16 *Analysis of Unbalanced Split Plot Using PROC MIXED*

```
                        The MIXED Procedure


             Covariance Parameter Estimates (REML)

Cov Parm          Ratio        Estimate      Std Error      Z   Pr > |Z|

BLOCK          1.56969539     0.97050863    1.67039941    0.58    0.5612
BLOCK*CULT     1.78082688     1.10104666    1.30382775    0.84    0.3984
Residual       1.00000000     0.61827832    0.27650247    2.24    0.0253



                    Tests of Fixed Effects

            Source      NDF   DDF   Type III F   Pr > F

            CULT         1    2.28       0.42    0.5756
            INOC         2    10        73.01    0.0001
            CULT*INOC    2    10         1.76    0.2213
```

Coefficients for cult diff

Parameter	Row 1
INTERCEPT	0
CULT a	1
CULT b	-1
INOC con	0
INOC dea	0
INOC liv	0
CULT*INOC a con	0.3333333333
CULT*INOC a dea	0.3333333333
CULT*INOC a liv	0.3333333333
CULT*INOC b con	-0.333333333
CULT*INOC b dea	-0.333333333
CULT*INOC b liv	-0.333333333

ESTIMATE Statement Results

Parameter	Estimate	Std Error	DDF	T	Pr > |T|
cult diff	-0.58366500	0.89939562	2.28	-0.65	0.5756

CONTRAST Statement Results

Source	NDF	DDF	F	Pr > F
cult diff	1	2.28	0.42	0.5756

Coefficients for CULT Least Squares Means

Parameter	Row 1	Row 2
INTERCEPT	1	1
CULT a	1	0
CULT b	0	1
INOC con	0.3333333333	0.3333333333
INOC dea	0.3333333333	0.3333333333
INOC liv	0.3333333333	0.3333333333
CULT*INOC a con	0.3333333333	0
CULT*INOC a dea	0.3333333333	0
CULT*INOC a liv	0.3333333333	0
CULT*INOC b con	0	0.3333333333
CULT*INOC b dea	0	0.3333333333
CULT*INOC b liv	0	0.3333333333

Least Squares Means

Level	LSMEAN	Std Error	DDF	T	Pr > |T|
CULT a	30.14966834	0.85132531	4.85	35.41	0.0001
CULT b	30.73333333	0.75459394	4.36	40.73	0.0001
INOC con	28.14288972	0.71060937	3.6	39.60	0.0001
INOC dea	29.97205639	0.71060937	3.6	42.18	0.0001

INOC liv	33.20955639	0.71060937	3.6	46.73	0.0001
CULT*INOC a con	28.26077945	0.92852031	6.74	30.44	0.0001
CULT*INOC a dea	29.29411278	0.92852031	6.74	31.55	0.0001
CULT*INOC a liv	32.89411278	0.92852031	6.74	35.43	0.0001
CULT*INOC b con	28.02500000	0.82003561	6	34.18	0.0001
CULT*INOC b dea	30.65000000	0.82003561	6	37.38	0.0001
CULT*INOC b liv	33.52500000	0.82003561	6	40.88	0.0001

Interpretation

You interpret resulting output just as the output for the balanced split plots in the previous sections are interpreted. The main issues in unbalanced split plots are best seen by comparing the PROC MIXED output to that obtained by a conventional analysis of variance program, e.g. PROC GLM. The equivalent PROC GLM program is

```
proc glm;
    class block cult inoc;
    model drywt = rep cult rep*cult inoc cult*inoc;
    random rep cult*rep/test;
    lsmeans cult/e stderr e=rep*cult;
    lsmeans inoc cult*inoc/stderr;
    estimate 'cult diff' cult 1 -1 /e;
    contrast 'cult diff' cult 1 -1 /e e=rep*cult;
run;
```

The results are given in Output 2.17.

Output 2.17 *Analysis of Unbalanced Split Plot Using PROC GLM*

General Linear Models Procedure

Dependent Variable: DRYWT

Source	DF	Sum of Squares	Mean Square	F Value	Pr > F
Model	10	133.197222	13.319722	21.54	0.0001
Error	10	6.182778	0.618278		
Corrected Total	20	139.380000			

Source	DF	Type I SS	Mean Square	F Value	Pr > F
BLOCK	3	28.95500000	9.65166667	15.61	0.0004
CULT	1	0.46722222	0.46722222	0.76	0.4051
BLOCK*CULT	2	7.73777778	3.86888889	6.26	0.0173
INOC	2	93.86000000	46.93000000	75.90	0.0001
CULT*INOC	2	2.17722222	1.08861111	1.76	0.2213

Source	DF	Type III SS	Mean Square	F Value	Pr > F
BLOCK	3	26.31111111	8.77037037	14.19	0.0006
CULT	1	0.46722222	0.46722222	0.76	0.4051
BLOCK*CULT	2	7.73777778	3.86888889	6.26	0.0173
INOC	2	90.28198413	45.14099206	73.01	0.0001
CULT*INOC	2	2.17722222	1.08861111	1.76	0.2213

```
Source          Type III Expected Mean Square

BLOCK           Var(Error) + 3 Var(BLOCK*CULT) + 5 Var(BLOCK)

CULT            Var(Error) + 3 Var(BLOCK*CULT) + Q(CULT,CULT*INOC)

BLOCK*CULT      Var(Error) + 3 Var(BLOCK*CULT)

INOC            Var(Error) + Q(INOC,CULT*INOC)

CULT*INOC       Var(Error) + Q(CULT*INOC)
```

Tests of Hypotheses for Mixed Model Analysis of Variance

Dependent Variable: DRYWT

Source: BLOCK
Error: MS(BLOCK*CULT)

DF	Type III MS	Denominator DF	Denominator MS	F Value	Pr > F
3	8.7703703704	2	3.8688888889	2.2669	0.3207

Source: CULT *
Error: MS(BLOCK*CULT)

DF	Type III MS	Denominator DF	Denominator MS	F Value	Pr > F
1	0.4672222222	2	3.8688888889	0.1208	0.7614

* - This test assumes one or more other fixed effects are zero.

Source: BLOCK*CULT
Error: MS(Error)

DF	Type III MS	Denominator DF	Denominator MS	F Value	Pr > F
2	3.8688888889	10	0.6182777778	6.2575	0.0173

Source: INOC *
Error: MS(Error)

DF	Type III MS	Denominator DF	Denominator MS	F Value	Pr > F
2	45.140992063	10	0.6182777778	73.0109	0.0001

* - This test assumes one or more other fixed effects are zero.

Source: CULT*INOC
Error: MS(Error)

DF	Type III MS	Denominator DF	Denominator MS	F Value	Pr > F
2	1.0886111111	10	0.6182777778	1.7607	0.2213

Least Squares Means
Coefficients for CULT Least Square Means

CULT	a	b

```
Effect                              Coefficients

INTERCEPT                                   1          1

BLOCK        1                           0.25       0.25
             2                           0.25       0.25
             3                           0.25       0.25
             4                           0.25       0.25

CULT         a                              1          0
             b                              0          1

BLOCK*CULT 1 b                              0       0.25
           2 a                    0.3333333333         0
           2 b                              0       0.25
           3 a                    0.3333333333         0
           3 b                              0       0.25
           4 a                    0.3333333333         0
           4 b                              0       0.25

INOC         con                  0.3333333333 0.3333333333
             dea                  0.3333333333 0.3333333333
             liv                  0.3333333333 0.3333333333

CULT*INOC    a con                0.3333333333         0
             a dea                0.3333333333         0
             a liv                0.3333333333         0
             b con                          0 0.3333333333
             b dea                          0 0.3333333333
             b liv                          0 0.3333333333
```

Least Squares Means

Standard Errors and Probabilities calculated using the Type III MS for
BLOCK*CULT as an Error term

CULT	DRYWT LSMEAN	Std Err LSMEAN	Pr > |T| H0:LSMEAN=0
a	Non-est	.	.
b	30.7333333	0.5678093	0.0003

Least Squares Means

(NOTE the following used MS(error) as Error term)

INOC	DRYWT LSMEAN
con	Non-est
dea	Non-est
liv	Non-est

CULT	INOC	DRYWT LSMEAN	Std Err LSMEAN	Pr > |T| H0:LSMEAN=0
a	con	Non-est	.	.
a	dea	Non-est	.	.
a	liv	Non-est	.	.
b	con	28.0250000	0.3931532	0.0001
b	dea	30.6500000	0.3931532	0.0001
b	liv	33.5250000	0.3931532	0.0001

Coefficients for estimate cult diff

(NOTE: same coefficients would be used for contrast for cult diff)

Coefficients for estimate cult diff

		Row 1
INTERCEPT		0
BLOCK	1	0
	2	0
	3	0
	4	0
CULT	a	1
	b	-1
BLOCK*CULT	1 b	-0.25
	2 a	0.3333333333
	2 b	-0.25
	3 a	0.3333333333
	3 b	-0.25
	4 a	0.3333333333
	4 b	-0.25
INOC	con	0
	dea	0
	liv	0
CULT*INOC	a con	0.3333333333
	a dea	0.3333333333
	a liv	0.3333333333
	b con	-0.333333333
	b dea	-0.333333333
	b liv	-0.333333333

Estimate and contrast for cult diff both NON-ESTIMABLE under GLM

In comparing the PROC MIXED and PROC GLM results, the following main points emerge:

- To compute the F-statistics for the CULT, INOC, and CULT*INOC effects, PROC GLM uses the ratio of mean squares implied by the expected mean squares. PROC MIXED uses the generalized F-ratio

$$F = \frac{(\mathbf{K}'\hat{\mu})'[\mathbf{K}'(\mathbf{X}'\hat{\mathbf{V}}^{-1}\mathbf{X})^{-1}\mathbf{K}]^{-1}(\mathbf{K}'\hat{\mu})}{rank(\mathbf{K})}$$

   The F-values are similar but not identical. In this case, the F-values for INOC and CULT*INOC are the same, but F for CULT is 0.42 in PROC GLM, and 0.12 in PROC MIXED. Discrepancies between F-values arise in two ways. First, PROC MIXED uses REML estimates of the variance components to compute the F-ratio, whereas the conventional mean square ratio implicitly depends on method of moments estimates. Second, the F-ratio in PROC MIXED uses generalized least squares estimates of treatment differences, whereas PROC GLM uses ordinary least squares estimates.

- PROC GLM declares least squares means for cultivar A, all levels of INOC, and all CULT*INOC combinations involving cultivar A to be non-estimable. They are, in fact, all estimable, and their estimates and standard errors appear in the PROC MIXED Output 2.18.

Why GLM has Estimability Problems with Unbalanced Split Plots

Coefficients used by PROC GLM and PROC MIXED to compute CULT least squares means are given in the output. Both sets of coefficients are identical with respect to the fixed effects. However, whereas PROC MIXED correctly sets the other coefficients—those for the random effects—equal to zero, PROC GLM tries to find an estimable linear combination over all the effects, as if they were all fixed. Because there is a missing BLOCK*CULT cell, no estimable combination can be found.

As discussed in the previous section, PROC GLM is implicitly working with the narrow inference space, which is rarely appropriate in practical applications.

Estimability problems like these illustrate a major frustration in trying to use non-mixed model software to analyze complex, unbalanced data sets. As long as there are no missing fixed effect cells—e.g., no missing cultivar-by-inoculation cells in this example—unbalanced split-plots do not have estimability problems. This example underlines the importance of working with the correct inference space.

Although not shown here, all of the estimates and contrasts presented in section 2.5 for the balanced cultivar-inoculation experiment can be computed for the unbalanced example as well, using PROC MIXED. The correct estimates, standard errors, and test statistics are computed by default. You should be aware of the degrees of freedom PROC MIXED uses for t-tests and in the denominator of F-tests because the default in PROC MIXED is not always correct. As in the balanced examples presented in previous sections, the corrected degrees of freedom using Satterthwaite's approximation can be obtained using the DDFM=SATTERTH option in the MODEL statement.

2.8 Multilocation Trial

Many studies are conducted at several locations. Agricultural experiments, for example, may be conducted at a number of different farms. Clinical trials may be conducted at a number of different centers. The common feature of all multilocation trials is the attempt to represent a relatively large target population by a number of representative elements. For example, the farms in an on-farm trial are intended to represent all farms with similar characteristics in a given geographical area.

Multilocation trials generally consist of two or more treatments. Each treatment may be observed at all locations so that the design resembles a randomized complete block design with locations as blocks. Or, there may be subsets of treatments observed at given locations so that the design resembles an incomplete block design, again with locations as blocks. Often, a replicated design—typically a completely random or randomized block design—is used at each location.

The objectives of a given multilocation trial affect how the locations are selected and modelled in the analysis. Section 2.8.1 discusses possible models and their uses. In general, multilocation trials are intended to address one of three objectives:

1. Compare treatments averaged over the entire population represented by locations (treatment main effect).

2. Estimate or test treatment-by-location interaction.

3. Determine if subpopulations exist among the locations and, if they do, to what extent they interact with treatments. These subpopulations may be either unanticipated or anticipated but poorly understood prior to conducting the trial.

Both objectives (2) and (3) imply the possible need for location-specific treatment recommendations. Objective (3) in particular calls for location-specific best linear unbiased predictors, introduced in Chapter 6. This section focuses on objectives (1) and (2) and defers objective (3) until Chapter 6.

2.8.1 Models for Multilocation Trials

Like the split-plot experiment, there is no one design for multilocation trials, but there are design features that all multilocation trials have in common. These basic features and the statistical issues associated with them are illustrated by an example of a multilocation design presented in this section. In practice, most trials use variations on the design presented here.

Data Set 2.8, "Multilocation Trial Example," given in Appendix 4, is from a multicenter trial to compare 4 treatments. The treatments were observed at each of 9 centers in the study. At each center, a randomized complete block design with 3 blocks was used. The model for this trial is thus

$$y_{ijk} = \mu + \tau_i + L_j + R(L)_{jk} + (\tau L)_{ij} + e_{ijk}$$

where

y_{ijk} is the observation
μ is the overall mean
τ_i is the treatment effect
L_j is the location effect
$R(L)_{jk}$ is the effect of block within location
$(\tau L)_{ij}$ is the treatment-by-location interaction
e_{ijk} is error.

Block within location effects and error effects are assumed random in all models. The assumptions for the random effects are

- $R(L)_{jk}$ are iid $N(0, \sigma_R^2)$
- e_{ijk} are iid $N(0, \sigma^2)$
- block and error effects are independent of one another.

Depending on the trial's design and objectives, locations may be fixed or random. The decision to consider locations fixed or random has a considerable effect on the resulting interpretation of the model.

Locations are classified as fixed if the locations have known characteristics and are intentionally selected for the trial. In this type of trial, inference is restricted to the locations observed, or, at most, to locations sharing the same characteristics. The primary initial focus of the analysis is on location effects and, especially, their interaction with treatments.

Locations are considered random if they are selected by randomly sampling the target population. The focus of the analysis is on treatment effects. Locations act as block effects and, thus, location-by-treatment interaction acts as experimental error. Typically, the location effects L_j are assumed iid $N(0,\sigma_L^2)$ and the location-by-treatment effects, $(\tau L)_{ij}$, are assumed iid $N(0,\sigma_T^2)$.

In many trials with random locations, subpopulations may be suspected but not known at the time the trial is conducted. The researcher may want to identify these subpopulations retrospectively and to determine if they interact with treatments. For example, in a multi-farm trial, a given treatment may perform very well at one set of farms but poorly at another set. The difference may not have been anticipated, but, with further study, some factor distinguishing the farms may be revealed. In the past, means for treatment-location combinations have been calculated, but these means are appropriate only if locations are fixed. For random locations, the mixed model procedure of best linear unbiased prediction (BLUP) is more appropriate for looking at location-specific effects.

2.8.2 Estimation and Hypothesis Testing for Multilocation Trials—Fixed Locations

The next two sections present methods to estimate means, differences, and other contrasts and to test hypotheses about them. The methods are presented in two parts: this section considers models with fixed locations and section 2.8.3 considers models with random locations. Section 2.8.4 discusses features common to fixed and random locations. Sections 2.8.5 and 2.8.6 present the SAS programs for working with these models.

For fixed locations, the multilocation model can be rewritten as

$$y_{ijk} = \mu_{ij} + R(L)_{jk} + e_{ijk}$$

where μ_{ij} is the mean of the ij^{th} treatment-location combination, and y_{ijk}, $R(L)_{jk}$, and e_{ijk} are defined as before.

The following are examples of parameters of interest to researchers:

$\mu_{i\bullet}$ the main-effect mean of the ith treatment

$\mu_{\bullet j}$ the main-effect mean of the jth location

$\mu_{1\bullet} - \mu_{2\bullet}$ the main-effect difference between two treatments

$\mu_{\bullet 1} - \mu_{\bullet 2}$ the main-effect difference between two locations

$\mu_{11} - \mu_{21}$ the simple effect of treatment 1 versus treatment 2 at a given location—in this case, location 1.

For balanced experiments, the estimates of the μ_{ij} are equal to the corresponding sample means, $y_{ij\bullet}$ and their estimates can be determined using the same methods as shown for split-plot experiments. For example, the multicenter data have 9 locations and 3 blocks per location, and therefore

$$\text{Var}(\hat{\mu}_{i\cdot}) = \text{Var}(\bar{y}_{i\cdot\cdot}) = \text{Var}[(1/27)\Sigma\Sigma y_{ijk}]$$

$$= (1/27)^2 \text{Var}[\Sigma\Sigma(\mu_{ij} + R(L)_{jk} + e_{ijk}]$$

$$= (1/27)^2(\sigma_R^2 + \sigma^2)$$

where the denominator 27 is the product of the number of locations and the number of blocks per location, i.e., the number of observations per treatment.

For the other estimators listed above, the variances are

$$\text{Var}(\hat{\mu}_{\cdot j}) = (1/12)(4\sigma_R^2 + \sigma^2),$$

where the denominator 12 is the product of the number of treatments and the number of blocks, i.e., the number of observations per location, and the coefficient 4 multiplied by σ_R^2 is the number of treatments.

$$\text{Var}(\hat{\mu}_{ij}) = (1/3)(\sigma_R^2 + \sigma^2)$$

$$\text{Var}(\hat{\mu}_{1\cdot} - \hat{\mu}_{2\cdot}) = (2/27)\sigma^2$$

$$\text{Var}(\hat{\mu}_{\cdot 1} - \hat{\mu}_{\cdot 2}) = (2/12)(4\sigma_R^2 + \sigma^2)$$

$$\text{Var}(\hat{\mu}_{11} - \hat{\mu}_{21}) = (2/3)\sigma^2$$

Once the variance component estimates are obtained, you can use these terms to compute standard errors. These, in turn, can be used to compute confidence intervals and t-test statistics. The degrees of freedom depend on the mean square used to estimate σ^2 alone, or the linear combination of mean squares needed to estimate functions of σ_R^2 and σ^2 using Satterthwaite's approximation.

The overall main effects of treatment and location, and the treatment-by-location interaction can be tested using standard F-tests with the mean square for error as the denominator.

2.8.3 Estimation and Hypothesis Testing for Multilocation Trials—Random Locations

For random locations, you can re-express the model as

$$y_{ijk} = \mu_i + L_j + R(L)_{jk} + (\tau L)_{ij} + e_{ijk}$$

where μ_i is the ith treatment mean, and L_j, $R(L)_{jk}$, $(\tau L)_{ij}$, and e_{ijk} are defined as before.

Normally, the test of no overall treatment effect is of interest as well as estimate of treatment means, μ_i and differences such as $\mu_1 - \mu_2$. Treatment effects can be tested using the F-test,

$$F = \frac{MS(treatment)}{MS(location * treatment)}$$

You can determine standard errors from the variance of the estimates. For example, with balanced data,

$$\text{Var}(\hat{\mu}_i) = (1/27)[3(\sigma_L^2 + \sigma_{TL}^2) + \sigma_R^2 + \sigma^2]$$

$$\text{Var}(\hat{\mu}_1 - \hat{\mu}_2) = (2/27)(3\sigma_{TL}^2 + \sigma^2)$$

In some applications, location main-effect estimates or treatment simple effects for given locations may be of interest. Traditionally, data analysts have obtained location-specific estimates by reanalyzing the data as if locations were fixed. However, computing BLUPs for locations or location-by-treatment combinations is the more appropriate procedure. Section 2.8.4 discusses this in more detail.

2.8.4 Common Features of Fixed and Random Locations

All of the expressions given in this section for variances of estimates and the resulting standard errors and test statistics are special cases of general mixed model results.

In matrix form, the multilocation model is

$$\mathbf{y} = \mathbf{X}\boldsymbol{\beta} + \mathbf{Z}\mathbf{u} + \mathbf{e}$$

where $\text{Var}(\mathbf{e}) = \mathbf{R} = \mathbf{I}\sigma^2$, and the fixed effects $\mathbf{X}\boldsymbol{\beta}$ and random effects $\mathbf{Z}\mathbf{u}$ depend on whether locations are fixed or random.

In the fixed locations model, the fixed effects vector $\boldsymbol{\beta}$ consists of the location effects, $\mathbf{L}_j$ and the treatment-location means μ_{ij} and the random effects vector, $\mathbf{u}$, consists of the block in location effects, $\mathbf{R}(\mathbf{L})_{jk}$. The fixed effects can be partitioned as

$$\mathbf{X}\boldsymbol{\beta} = \mathbf{1}'\boldsymbol{\mu} + \mathbf{X}_T\boldsymbol{\tau} + \mathbf{X}_L\mathbf{L} + \mathbf{X}_{TL}(\boldsymbol{\tau}\mathbf{L})$$

where $\boldsymbol{\tau}$, $\mathbf{L}$, and $(\boldsymbol{\tau}\mathbf{L})$ are vectors of treatment, location, and treatment-by-location effects, respectively, and $\mathbf{X}_T$, $\mathbf{X}_L$, and $\mathbf{X}_{TL}$ are the corresponding design matrices. In the fixed locations model, $\mathbf{G} = \text{Var}(\mathbf{u}) = \mathbf{I}\sigma_R^2$.

In the random effects model, the fixed effect vector $\boldsymbol{\beta}$ consists of the μ_i and the random effects vector, $\mathbf{u}$, consists of the location effects, $\mathbf{L}_j$, the block in location effects, $\mathbf{R}(\mathbf{L})_{jk}$, and the treatment-by-location effects, $(\boldsymbol{\tau}\mathbf{L})_{ij}$. The random effects can be partitioned as

$$\mathbf{Z}\mathbf{u} = \mathbf{Z}_L\mathbf{L} + \mathbf{Z}_R\mathbf{R} + \mathbf{Z}_{TL}(\boldsymbol{\tau}\mathbf{L})$$

where $\mathbf{L}$, $\mathbf{R}$, and $\boldsymbol{\tau}\mathbf{L}$ are vectors of location, block in location, and treatment-by-location effects respectively, and $\mathbf{Z}_L$, $\mathbf{Z}_R$, and $\mathbf{Z}_{TL}$ are the corresponding design matrices. In the random effects model,

$$\mathbf{G} = \begin{bmatrix} \mathbf{I}\sigma_L^2 & 0 & 0 \\ 0 & \mathbf{I}\sigma_R^2 & 0 \\ 0 & 0 & \mathbf{I}\sigma_{TL}^2 \end{bmatrix}$$

Whether the model is defined with locations fixed or random, the vectors β and $\mathbf{u}$ may be estimated solving the mixed model equations. All of the main-effect means, differences, and simple effects discussed in this section are specific estimable functions of the fixed effects, $\mathbf{K'}\beta$. For example, for the random locations model, the difference

$$\mu_1 - \mu_2 = [1\,{-}1\ \ 0\ \ 0]\begin{bmatrix}\mu_1\\\mu_2\\\mu_3\\\mu_4\end{bmatrix}$$

That is, $\mathbf{K'} = [1\ \ {-}1\ \ 0\ \ 0]$.

The standard errors may be computed using the general formula

$$s.e.(\mathbf{K'}\hat{\beta}) = \sqrt{\mathbf{K'}(\mathbf{X'}\hat{\mathbf{V}}^{-1}\mathbf{X})^{-1}\mathbf{K}}$$

here $\mathbf{V} = \mathbf{ZGZ'} + \mathbf{R}$. F-ratios are computed using the general formula

$$\mathbf{F} = (\mathbf{K'}\hat{\beta})'[\mathbf{K}'(\mathbf{X'}\hat{\mathbf{V}}^{-1}\mathbf{X})^{-1}\mathbf{K}]^{-1}(\mathbf{K'}\beta)/rank(\mathbf{K})$$

In balanced experiments, these formulas result in the standard errors and F-ratios given above. In unbalanced experiments, the standard error and F-ratio formulas do not reduce to the same simple forms, but they can be calculated using the mixed model equations as easily as for balanced data.

In the next two sections, the example data given in Appendix 4, Data Set 2.8, "Multilocation Trial Example" are analyzed using PROC MIXED. In section 2.8.5, the example is analyzed using a fixed locations model. In section 2.8.6, the same data are analyzed using the random locations model.

2.8.5 Example: Analysis of Fixed Locations Model Using PROC MIXED

For the Data Set 2.8, with locations assumed to be fixed, you can use the following PROC MIXED statements to obtain the basic analysis discussed in section 2.8.2.

Program

```
proc mixed;
   class loc block trt;
   model adg=loc trt loc*trt;
   random block(loc);
   lsmeans loc trt loc*trt;
   contrast 'trt1 vs trt2' trt 1 -1 0;
   contrast 'loc1 vs loc2' loc 1 -1 0;
   contrast 'trt 1 v 2 at loc 1' trt 1 -1 0 loc*trt 1 -1 0/e;
   estimate 'trt1 vs trt2' trt 1 -1 0;
   estimate 'loc1 vs loc2' loc 1 -1 0;
   estimate 'trt 1 v 2 at loc 1' trt 1 -1 0 loc*trt 1 -1 0/e;
   title 'Analysis with Locations Fixed';
run;
```

Output 2.18 gives the results of this analysis.

Results

Output 2.18 *Analysis of Multilocation Example with Fixed Locations Using PROC MIXED*

```
                    Covariance Parameter Estimates (REML)

Cov Parm              Ratio       Estimate     Std Error       Z    Pr > |Z|

BLOCK(LOC)         0.16253660    0.00562043   0.00503774    1.12    0.2646
Residual           1.00000000    0.03457946   0.00665482    5.20    0.0000


                          Tests of Fixed Effects

            Source       NDF    DDF   Type III F   Pr > F

            LOC            8     18      25.11      0.0000
            TRT            3     54      11.78      0.0000
            LOC*TRT       24     54       1.20      0.2829


                       ESTIMATE Statement Results

Parameter                  Estimate     Std Error    DDF        T    Pr > |T|

trt1 vs trt2             0.24636593   0.05061069     54      4.87    0.0000
loc1 vs loc2             0.70261833   0.09752024     54      7.20    0.0000
trt 1 v 2 at loc 1       0.13350667   0.15183207     54      0.88    0.3831


                       CONTRAST Statement Results

          Source            NDF    DDF       F    Pr > F

          trt1 vs trt2       1      54    23.70   0.0000
          loc1 vs loc2       1      54    51.91   0.0000
          trt 1 v 2 at loc 1 1      54     0.77   0.3831


                           Least Squares Means

   Level               LSMEAN       Std Error    DDF        T    Pr > |T|

   LOC A             2.99968083    0.06895722    18      43.50   0.0000
   LOC B             2.29706250    0.06895722    18      33.31   0.0000
   LOC C             3.04861083    0.06895722    18      44.21   0.0000
   LOC D             2.55051917    0.06895722    18      36.99   0.0000
   LOC E             2.84687750    0.06895722    18      41.28   0.0000
   LOC F             3.25858333    0.06895722    18      47.26   0.0000
```

LOC G	2.84249167	0.06895722	18	41.22	0.0000
LOC H	3.32249000	0.06895722	18	48.18	0.0000
LOC I	2.52147333	0.06895722	18	36.57	0.0000
TRT 1	2.92401667	0.03858607	18	75.78	0.0000
TRT 2	2.67765074	0.03858607	18	69.39	0.0000
TRT 3	2.94945852	0.03858607	18	76.44	0.0000
TRT 4	2.86566926	0.03858607	18	74.27	0.0000
LOC*TRT A 1	3.04719667	0.11575822	18	26.32	0.0000
LOC*TRT A 2	2.91369000	0.11575822	18	25.17	0.0000
LOC*TRT A 3	3.02933333	0.11575822	18	26.17	0.0000
LOC*TRT A 4	3.00850333	0.11575822	18	25.99	0.0000
LOC*TRT B 1	2.37762667	0.11575822	18	20.54	0.0000
LOC*TRT B 2	2.10154000	0.11575822	18	18.15	0.0000
LOC*TRT B 3	2.28341000	0.11575822	18	19.73	0.0000
LOC*TRT B 4	2.42567333	0.11575822	18	20.95	0.0000
LOC*TRT C 1	3.09178667	0.11575822	18	26.71	0.0000
LOC*TRT C 2	2.99275667	0.11575822	18	25.85	0.0000
LOC*TRT C 3	3.20531333	0.11575822	18	27.69	0.0000
LOC*TRT C 4	2.90458667	0.11575822	18	25.09	0.0000
LOC*TRT D 1	2.42544333	0.11575822	18	20.95	0.0000
LOC*TRT D 2	2.43504333	0.11575822	18	21.04	0.0000
LOC*TRT D 3	2.60821333	0.11575822	18	22.53	0.0000
LOC*TRT D 4	2.73337667	0.11575822	18	23.61	0.0000
LOC*TRT E 1	2.87348667	0.11575822	18	24.82	0.0000
LOC*TRT E 2	2.60093333	0.11575822	18	22.47	0.0000
LOC*TRT E 3	3.00384667	0.11575822	18	25.95	0.0000
LOC*TRT E 4	2.90924333	0.11575822	18	25.13	0.0000
LOC*TRT F 1	3.31300000	0.11575822	18	28.62	0.0000
LOC*TRT F 2	3.04600000	0.11575822	18	26.31	0.0000
LOC*TRT F 3	3.31800000	0.11575822	18	28.66	0.0000
LOC*TRT F 4	3.35733333	0.11575822	18	29.00	0.0000
LOC*TRT G 1	3.15025333	0.11575822	18	27.21	0.0000
LOC*TRT G 2	2.60980333	0.11575822	18	22.55	0.0000
LOC*TRT G 3	2.89007667	0.11575822	18	24.97	0.0000
LOC*TRT G 4	2.71983333	0.11575822	18	23.50	0.0000
LOC*TRT H 1	3.45095333	0.11575822	18	29.81	0.0000
LOC*TRT H 2	3.04126667	0.11575822	18	26.27	0.0000
LOC*TRT H 3	3.42447667	0.11575822	18	29.58	0.0000
LOC*TRT H 4	3.37326333	0.11575822	18	29.14	0.0000
LOC*TRT I 1	2.58640333	0.11575822	18	22.34	0.0000
LOC*TRT I 2	2.35782333	0.11575822	18	20.37	0.0000
LOC*TRT I 3	2.78245667	0.11575822	18	24.04	0.0000
LOC*TRT I 4	2.35921000	0.11575822	18	20.38	0.0000

Interpretation

The variance components estimates are 0.00562 for BLOCK(LOC), corresponding to σ_R^2, and 0.0346 for Residual, corresponding to σ^2. The F-statistics for LOC, TRT, and LOC*TRT correspond to the F-ratios that would be computed using the effect mean square and the error mean square in a conventional analysis of variance program.

The standard errors for the three estimates computed correspond to the variance formulas given in section 2.8.2 using the estimated variance components. For example, the standard error for the main-effect difference TRT1 vs TRT2 is

$$s.e.(trt1 \ \ vs \ \ trt2) \ = \ \sqrt{\left(\frac{2}{27}\right)\hat{\sigma}^2} \ = \ \sqrt{\left(\frac{2}{27}\right)0.0346} \ = \ 0.0506$$

The *t*-ratios are computed by dividing the estimate by the standard error.

The F-ratios for the contrasts correspond to the ratio between the contrast mean square and the error mean square that a conventional analysis of variance program computes. They are actually obtained from the general formula

$$F \ = \ \frac{(\mathbf{K'\hat{\beta}})'[\mathbf{K'}(\mathbf{X'\hat{V}^{-1}X})^{-1}\mathbf{K}](\mathbf{K'\hat{\beta}})}{rank(\mathbf{K})}$$

discussed in section 2.8.2. The specific coefficients of **K** depend on the contrast. The coefficients for the treatment 1 versus treatment 2 main effect can be produced by adding the E option to the first ESTIMATE statement in the preceding PROC MIXED code.

The standard errors of the least squares means given in the LSMEANS section correspond to the formulas given in section 2.8.2. For example, for the main-effect mean of TRT, the standard error is

$$s.e.(trt1 \ \ lsmean) = \sqrt{\left(\frac{1}{27}\right)(\hat{\sigma}_R^2 + \hat{\sigma}^2)} \ = \ \sqrt{\left(\frac{1}{27}\right)(0.00562 + 0.0346)} = 0.0386$$

To reiterate, the fixed locations analysis is appropriate only if the locations are selected intentionally and inference is restricted to those locations observed only.

2.8.6 Example: Analysis of Random Locations Model Using PROC MIXED

You can obtain the analysis of Data Set 2.8 assuming random locations using the following PROC MIXED statements.

Program

```
proc mixed;
    class loc block trt;
    model adg=trt/ddfm=satterth;
    random loc block(loc) loc*trt;
    lsmeans trt;
    contrast 'trt1 vs trt2' trt 1 -1 0;
    estimate 'trt1 vs trt2' trt 1 -1 0;
    title 'PROC MIXED Analysis with Locations Random';
run;
```

Output 2.19 gives the results.

Results

Output 2.19 *Analysis of Multilocation Example with Random Locations Using PROC MIXED*

```
              Covariance Parameter Estimates (REML)

Cov Parm              Ratio      Estimate    Std Error       Z   Pr > |Z|

LOC              3.29904879    0.11407934   0.05973844    1.91    0.0562
BLOCK(LOC)       0.16253660    0.00562043   0.00503774    1.12    0.2646
LOC*TRT          0.06692009    0.00231406   0.00456992    0.51    0.6126
Residual         1.00000000    0.03457946   0.00665482    5.20    0.0001


                      Tests of Fixed Effects

Source        NDF     DDF   Type III F   Pr > F

TRT             3      24         9.81    0.0002


                    ESTIMATE Statement Results

Parameter            Estimate     Std Error    DDF       T   Pr > |T|

trt1 vs trt2       0.24636593    0.05545879     24    4.44     0.0001


                       The MIXED Procedure

                    CONTRAST Statement Results

Source                     NDF     DDF      F    Pr > F

    trt1 vs trt2             1      24   19.73   0.0001


                       The MIXED Procedure

                      Least Squares Means
Level               LSMEAN     Std Error    DDF       T   Pr > |T|

TRT 1            2.92401667    0.12008949   9.43   24.35     0.0001
TRT 2            2.67765074    0.12008949   9.43   22.30     0.0001
TRT 3            2.94945852    0.12008949   9.43   24.56     0.0001
TRT 4            2.86566926    0.12008949   9.43   23.86     0.0001
```

Interpretation

This analysis is probably more consistent with the manner in which most multilocation trials are conducted and with their primary objectives.

The variance component estimates are 0.114 for LOC (σ_L^2), 0.00562 for BLOCK(LOC) (σ_R^2), 0.00231 for LOC*TRT (σ_{TL}^2), and 0.0346 for residual (σ^2). Because the data are balanced, the estimates of σ_R^2 and σ^2 are identical to those obtained with the fixed locations model. These are REML estimators, which correspond to ANOVA EMS-based method of moments estimators for balanced data provided the estimates are positive. For unbalanced data, or when at least one variance component estimate is negative, this is not necessarily the case.

Note that the standard errors and the Z-statistics for the variance components are based on asymptotic normality. They are not reliable for variance components estimated with relatively few degrees of freedom, as is the case here, particularly for LOC. Either the likelihood ratio test, as demonstrated in section 2.2.3, or the F-test computed in analysis of variance programs such as PROC GLM are preferable methods for testing the variance components.

The F-statistic for the overall TRT effect is obtained from the general F-ratio for the mixed model, discussed in sections 2.3.2 and 2.3.3. In this case, it corresponds to

$$F = \frac{MS(TRT)}{MS(LOC*TRT)}$$

The standard errors for the estimates are obtained using the formulas given in section 2.3.3. For example, for treatment 1 versus treatment 2, the standard error is

$$s.e.(trt1 \ vs \ trt2) = \sqrt{\left(\frac{2}{27}\right)\left(3\hat{\sigma}_{TL}^2 + \hat{\sigma}^2\right)}$$

$$= \sqrt{\left(\frac{2}{27}\right)\left(3(0.00231) + 0.0346\right)}$$

$$= 0.0555$$

The standard errors of the treatment least squares means correspond to the formula given in section 2.8.3. Because

$$\mathrm{Var}(\hat{\mu}_i) = (1/27)[3(\sigma_L^2 + \sigma_{TL}^2) + \sigma_R^2 + \sigma^2]$$

the standard error is

$$\sqrt{\left(\frac{1}{27}\right)\left[3(0.114 + 0.00231) + 0.00562 + 0.0346\right]}$$

or 0.120.

Because this example contains balanced data, the standard errors can be written conveniently in terms of the variance components. However, they are all special cases of the general formula

$$s.e.(\mathbf{K'\hat{\beta}}) = \sqrt{\mathbf{K'(X'V^{-1}X)^{-1}K}}$$

for the variance of estimable functions of the fixed effects.

In a practical analysis of these data with random locations, if there is evidence of a location-by-treatment interaction, it is often of interest to look at simple effects of treatments at specific locations or sets of locations. Because locations are random, simple-effect means like those computed in the semiconductor example in section 2.3 are inappropriate. The appropriate method of inference for location specific effects when locations are random is BLUP. BLUP for this multilocation example is discussed in Section 6.5.

2.9 Summary

This chapter shows how to use PROC MIXED to analyze common mixed models with multiple error terms. **Split-plot** and **multilocation** experiments are used as examples for explaining the basic principles. Section 2.2 gives some fundamental results. Section 2.3 presents a detailed PROC MIXED example of a simple split-plot. Section 2.4 compares PROC MIXED results with PROC GLM analyses traditionally used for multiple error term models. Section 2.5 presents the analysis of a split-plot with blocking. Section 2.6 provides additional theoretical background to explain differences between PROC MIXED and PROC GLM. Section 2.7 shows a split-plot example with missing data. Section 2.8 presents a multilocation example.

2.10 References

Cochran, W.G. and Cox, G.M. (1957), *Experimental Designs, 2nd Edition,* New York: John Wiley & Sons, Inc.

Littell, R.C., Freund, R.J., and Spector, P.C. (1991), *SAS System for Linear Models, Third Edition.* Cary, NC: SAS Institute Inc.

Mead, R. (1988), *The Design of Experiments,* Cambridge, UK: Cambridge University Press.

Milliken, G.A. and Johnson, D.E. (1994), *Analysis of Messy Data, Volume 1: Designed Experiments,* London: Chapman Hall.

Self, S.G. and Liang, K-Y. (1987), Asymptotic properties of maximum likelihood estimators and likelihood ratio tests under nonstandard conditions, *Journal of the American Statistical Association,* **82**, 605–610.

Chapter **3 Analysis of Repeated Measures Data**

3.1 Introduction

The term **repeated measures** refers to data sets with multiple measurements of a response variable on the same experimental unit. In most applications, the multiple measurements are made over a period of time. An example is growth curve data such as monthly weight measurements of babies for the first year of their lives. Another example is drug effects data such as measurements of pulse or respiration on patients following administration of a drug. But repeated measures can also refer to multiple measurements over space such as thicknesses of the vertebrae of animals. In a general sense, any data measured repeatedly over time or space are repeated measures data. Most of this chapter, however, uses the term in the more traditional sense, referring to sequences of measurements on experimental units in a designed experiment, sample survey, or retrospective study.

3.1.1 Basic Concepts of Repeated Measures

The basic repeated measures study consists of a completely randomized experimental design with data collected in a sequence of equally spaced points in time. In other words, treatments have been assigned to experimental units, and data are collected at a sequence of times from each experimental unit. Because of the human psychological heritage of repeated measures, experimental units are often called **subjects**. In this basic setup, there are two factors, **treatments** and **time**. In this sense, all repeated measures experiments are factorial experiments. **Treatment** is called the **between-subjects** factor because levels of treatment can change only between subjects; all measurements on the same subject will represent the same treatment. **Time** is called a **within-subjects** factor because different measurements on the same subject are at different times. In repeated measures experiments, interest centers on 1) how treatment means change over time and 2) how treatment differences change over time. In other words, is there a **time main-effect**, and is there a **treatment-by-time interaction**? These are the types of questions we may want to ask in any factorial experiment. There is nothing peculiar about the objectives of a repeated measures study. What makes repeated measures data analysis distinct is the **covariance structure** of the observed data. In Chapters 1 and 2, all of the models assume **independent errors**. Assuming independent errors means that all observations within a given block, i.e., within a subject in a repeated measures design, are equally correlated. However, in a typical repeated measures experiment, two measurements taken at adjacent times are typically more highly correlated than two measurements taken several time points apart. The objectives of repeated measures data analysis usually are to compare treatment means or treatment regression curves over time. A lot of effort, however, is usually needed at the beginning of the statistical analysis to assess the covariance structure of the data. Several pages in subsections 3.2.1 and 3.2.2 are devoted to modelling the covariance structure of the example data although the covariance structure itself is not of primary interest. Modelling an appropriate covariance structure is essential so that inferences about means are valid.

There are similarities between repeated measures experiments and split-plot experiments. The treatment factor in a repeated measures experiment corresponds to the main-plot factor in a split-plot experiment. The time factor in repeated measures corresponds to the sub-plot factor. In short, the between-subjects factor corresponds to the main-plot factor, and the within-subjects factor corresponds to the sub-plot factor. The experimental units to which the treatments are assigned in the repeated measures experiment are analogous to main-plot units in the split-plot experiment, and the experimental units **at particular times** correspond to sub-plot units. However, in a true split-plot experiment, levels of the sub-plot factor are randomly assigned to sub-plot units within main-plot units. Consequently, responses from different sub-plot units in the same main-plot unit are equally correlated with each other. But in repeated measures experiments, responses from points close in time are usually more highly correlated with each other than are responses from points far apart in time. Therefore, special methods of analysis are usually needed to accommodate the correlation structure of the repeated measures.

3.1.2 Types of Repeated Measures Analyses

Three general types of statistical analyses are most commonly used for repeated measures. One method treats repeated measures data as having come from a split-plot experiment. This method, often called a **univariate analysis of variance**, can be implemented in the SAS System using PROC GLM with the RANDOM statement, as was discussed in Chapter 2. Another method applies **multivariate and univariate analysis methods to linear transformations** of the repeated measures. The linear transformations can be means, differences between responses at different time points, slopes of regression curves, etc. These techniques are invoked by the REPEATED statement in PROC GLM. The third method applies **methods based on the mixed model with special parametric structure on the covariance matrices**. This type of methodology has been computationally feasible only in recent years. It is applied in PROC MIXED, typically using the REPEATED statement. The third method is illustrated first, and then it is related to the other two methods.

3.2 Example: Mixed Model Analysis of Data from Basic Repeated Measures Design

This repeated measures example is from Littell, Freund, and Spector (1991). Subjects in an exercise therapy study were assigned to one of three weightlifting programs. In the first program (RI) the number of repetitions of weightlifting was increased as subjects became stronger. In the second program (WI) the amount of weight was increased as subjects became stronger. In the third program (CONT) subjects did not participate in weightlifting. Strengths of the subjects were measured every other day for two weeks following the beginning of the study.

Data were entered in a multivariate mode into a SAS data set named "WEIGHTS" which is partially printed in Data Set 3.2(a) in Appendix 4, "SAS Data Sets." In order to use PROC MIXED for the mixed model analysis, you must transform the data set from a multivariate mode to a univariate mode. A univariate form of the data is in a SAS data set named "WEIGHT2" that contains variables PROGRAM, SUBJ, TIME, and STRENGTH, and is shown in Data Set 3.2(b) in Appendix 4. PROC MIXED requires the univariate version of the data set. A third data set named "AVG," which was created by PROC MEANS, is printed in Data Set 3.2(c) in Appendix 4. Figure 3.1 contains a plot of the STRENGTH means for each PROGRAM over the seven levels of TIME. The objectives are to compare the program strength increase trends over time.

Figure 3.1 *Plot of the STRENGTH MEANS over Time for Each PROGRAM*

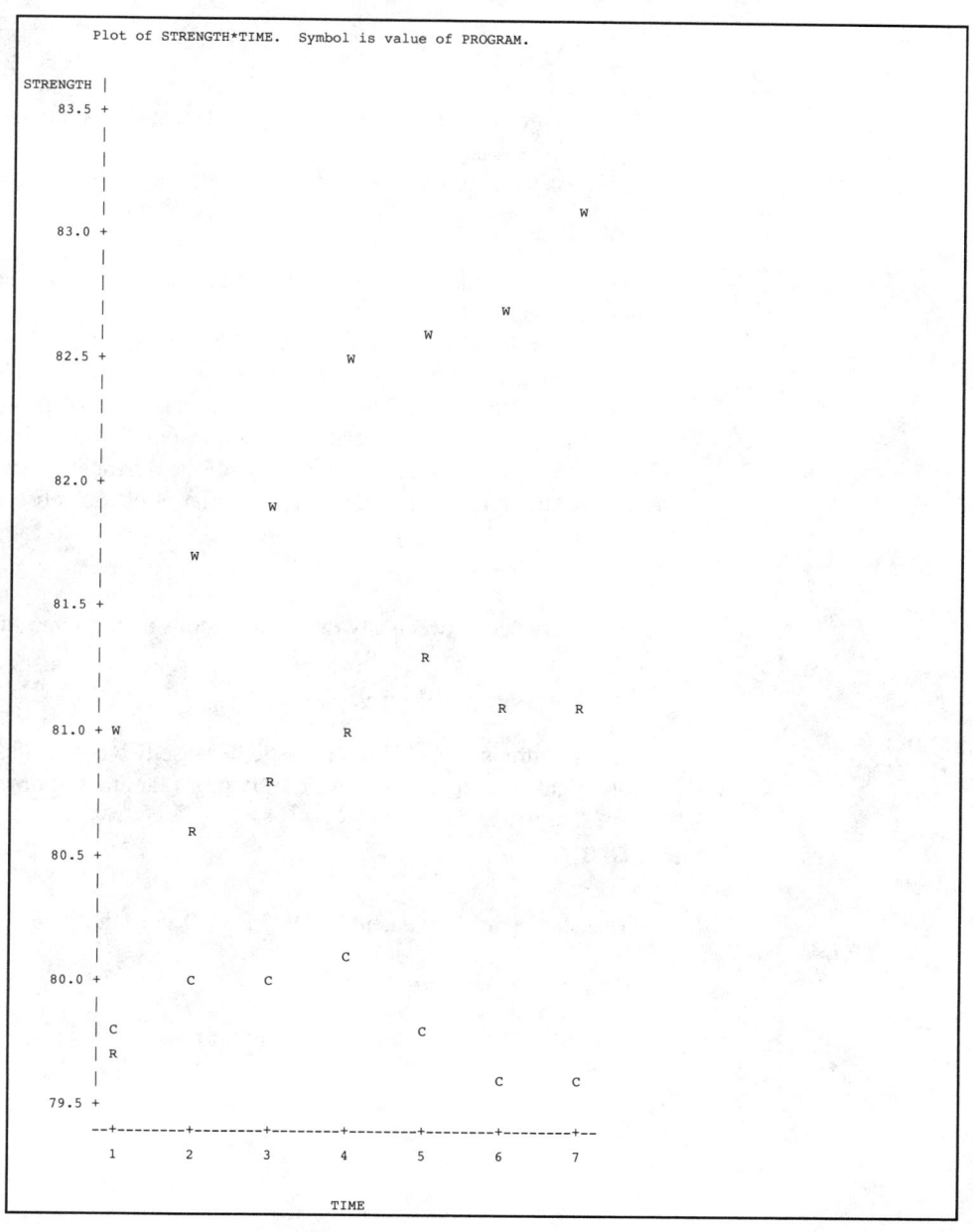

3.2.1 Mixed Model Analysis Using the RANDOM Statement in PROC MIXED

A RANDOM statement in PROC MIXED is first used to produce an analysis similar to the semiconductor experiment in Chapter 2. The factors PROGRAM and TIME are considered fixed. But SUBJ is considered random because inference is to be made to entire populations of subjects who conceivably could have received one of the three exercise therapies.

Model

A statistical model is

$$y_{ijk} = \mu + \alpha_i + d_{ij} + \tau_k + (\alpha\tau)_{ik} + e_{ijk} \tag{3.1}$$

where:

$i = 1,\ldots,t$

$j = 1,\ldots,r$

μ, α_i, τ_k, and $(\alpha\tau)_{ik}$ are fixed parameters such that the mean for the ith program at time k is $\mu_{ik} = \mu + \alpha_i + \tau_k + (\alpha\tau)_{ik}$

d_{ij} is the random effect associated with the jth subject in program i

e_{ijk} is random error associated with the jth subject in program i at time k.

Note that this model equation is the same as the model equation for the semiconductor example in Chapter 2.

In the general linear mixed model $\mathbf{Y} = \mathbf{X\beta} + \mathbf{Zu} + \mathbf{e}$, Equation 1.13, the d_{ij} make up the $\mathbf{u}$ term and the e_{ijk} make up the $\mathbf{e}$ term. The d_{ij} are taken to be MVN$(\mathbf{0},\sigma_S^2\mathbf{I})$ and the e_{ijk} are taken to be MVN$(\mathbf{0}, \sigma_T^2\mathbf{I})$. This results in a covariance matrix $\mathbf{V(Y)} = \sigma_S^2\mathbf{ZZ'} + \sigma_T^2\mathbf{I}$. This matrix is block diagonal, with each block corresponding to a single subject. Each block is 7x7 with $\sigma_S^2 + \sigma_T^2$ on the diagonal and σ_S^2 off the diagonal. This describes **compound symmetric** structure. It specifies that the variance of each observation is

$$\text{Var}(y_{ijk}) = \text{Var}(d_{ij} + e_{ijk}) = \sigma_S^2 + \sigma_T^2 \tag{3.2}$$

and the covariance between any two observations on the same subject is

$$\text{Cov}(y_{ijk},y_{ijk'}) = \text{Var}(d_{ij}) = \sigma_S^2$$

This structure is probably not realistic because two observations close in time are likely to be more highly correlated than two observations far apart in time.

Program

These statements implement PROC MIXED to fit the statistical model 3.1:

```
proc mixed data=weight2;
   class program subj time;
   model strength = program time program*time;
   random subj(program);
run;
```

Fixed effects for **program**, **time,** and **program*time** interaction are placed in the MODEL statement, and random effects for **subjects** nested **within program** are placed in the RANDOM statement.

Results appear in Output 3.1.

Results

Output 3.1 *Mixed Model Analysis of Repeated Measures Using the RANDOM Statement in PROC MIXED*

```
                      The MIXED Procedure

                 Class Level Information

       Class      Levels  Values

       PROGRAM       3   CONT RI WI
       SUBJ         21   1 2 3 4 5 6 7 8 9 10 11 12 13
                         14 15 16 17 18 19 20 21
       TIME          7   1 2 3 4 5 6 7


                REML Estimation Iteration History

       Iteration  Evaluations    Objective     Criterion

           0           1      1339.1654525
           1           1       726.10266507   0.00000000

                   Convergence criteria met.



         ❶ Covariance Parameter Estimates (REML)

 Cov Parm            Ratio      Estimate    Std Error      Z    Pr > |Z|

 SUBJ(PROGRAM)    8.02368623   9.60333050   1.88111525   5.11    0.0001
 Residual         1.00000000   1.19687264   0.09403520  12.73    0.0001

           Model Fitting Information for STRENGTH

           Description                        Value

           Observations                     399.0000
           Variance Estimate                  1.1969
           Standard Deviation Estimate        1.0940
           REML Log Likelihood             -710.410
           Akaike's Information Criterion  -712.410
           Schwarz's Bayesian Criterion    -716.345
           -2 REML Log Likelihood          1420.820
```

```
          ❷ Tests of Fixed Effects

     Source        NDF   DDF  Type III F  Pr > F
     PROGRAM        2     54       3.07   0.0548
     TIME           6    324       7.43   0.0001
     PROGRAM*TIME  12    324       2.99   0.0005
```

Interpretation

Two basic portions of the output are

❶ Under "Covariance Parameter Estimates," the estimate of σ_S^2 is equal to 9.603 and the estimate of σ_T^2 is equal to 1.197.

❷ At the bottom of Output 3 under "Tests of Fixed Effects," you see F-statistics for the fixed effects of PROGRAM, TIME, and PROGRAM*TIME.

Note in particular the significance level $p=0.0005$ for PROGRAM*TIME interaction. As shown in subsection 3.3.1, this is the F-test that is obtained in a univariate analysis of variance. It probably is not valid because the covariance structure imposed with the RANDOM statement (compound symmetry) probably does not provide a good fit to the data. The point of illustrating this application of PROC MIXED is to provide a springboard to the REPEATED statement, which allows a much more satisfactory analysis of the data. The first task is to obtain a better model for the covariance structure of the repeated measures of STRENGTH on the same subject.

3.2.2 Modelling Covariance Structure: Using the REPEATED Statement in PROC MIXED

As you saw in Chapters 1 and 2 and the preceding subsection, the RANDOM statement defines the **Zu** portion of the general linear mixed model. The RANDOM statement allows you to model variation *between* experimental units, such as the main-plot units in a split-plot experiment. The REPEATED statement is used to model variation *within* experimental units. When analyzing repeated measures data, you normally use the REPEATED statement to model the covariance structure within subjects. PROC MIXED provides a rich assortment of covariance types from which to select.

Three of the most commonly used structures are **compound symmetric, autoregressive order one**, and "**unstructured**." You can specify these as options in the REPEATED statement as CS, AR(1), and UN, respectively. First, define these structures in terms of the general linear mixed model,

$$\mathbf{y} = \mathbf{X}\boldsymbol{\beta} + \mathbf{Zu} + \mathbf{e}$$

The REPEATED statement is used to define covariance structure on **e**; that is, to define the **R** matrix. In repeated measures analyses you normally define **R** to be block diagonal with each block corresponding to a subject.

The variance-covariance matrix of the observations, Var(y), is $\mathbf{ZGZ'} + \mathbf{R}$. For model 3.1, the resulting $\mathbf{ZGZ'} + \mathbf{R}$ is

$$
\text{Var}\begin{pmatrix} \mathbf{Y}_{11} \\ . \\ . \\ . \\ \mathbf{Y}_{a1} \\ \mathbf{Y}_{12} \\ . \\ . \\ \mathbf{Y}_{a2} \\ . \\ . \end{pmatrix} = \begin{bmatrix} \sigma_s^2\mathbf{J} + \Sigma & ... & 0 & 0 & ... & 0 & ... \\ . & . & . & . & . & . & . \\ 0 & ... & \sigma_s^2\mathbf{J} + \Sigma & 0 & ... & 0 & ... \\ 0 & ... & 0 & \sigma_s^2\mathbf{J} + \Sigma & ... & 0 & ... \\ . & . & . & . & . & . & . \\ 0 & ... & 0 & 0 & ... & \sigma_s^2\mathbf{J} + \Sigma & ... \\ . & . & . & . & . & . & . \end{bmatrix}
$$

where $\mathbf{Y}_{ij}$ is the vector of observations over the time periods for the ij^{th} subject, and Σ is the ij^{th} block diagonal element of $\mathbf{R}$, i.e., $\mathbf{R} = \text{diag}\,(\Sigma)$.

Case 1: **compound symmetry**

Here, $\Sigma = (\mathbf{J}\rho + \mathbf{I}(1-\rho))\sigma_T^2$

where ρ is the correlation between observations on the ij^{th} subject. You can see that in this case, σ_s^2 and $\rho\sigma_T^2$ are confounded. Thus, this compound symmetry model is equivalent to the model described in section 3.2.1.

Case 2: **AR(1)**

Here the correlation between observations w time periods apart is assumed to be ρ^w. Thus,

$$
\Sigma = \sigma^2 \begin{bmatrix} 1 & \rho & \rho^2 & . & . & \rho^{k-1} \\ \rho & 1 & \rho & \rho^2 & . & \rho^{k-2} \\ . & . & . & . & . & . \\ \rho^{k-1} & . & . & . & \rho & 1 \end{bmatrix}
$$

Notice that in this case, σ_s^2 and $\rho\sigma^2$ are not confounded.

In some repeated measures experiments, the contribution of the subject effects is negligible, i.e., $\sigma_s^2 = 0$. In such cases, $\mathbf{Zu}$ may be dropped from the model. The model equation is now

$$\mathbf{y} = \mathbf{X}\beta + \mathbf{e}$$

where $\mathbf{X}\beta$ models the fixed effects of PROGRAM, TIME and PROGRAM*TIME, and $\mathbf{e}$ models the random variation, $\mathbf{Var(y)} = \mathbf{Var(\,e)} = \mathbf{R}$. As already stated, the REPEATED statement defines the covariance matrix $\mathbf{R}$ of $\mathbf{e}$. Recall that $\mathbf{R}$ is to be block diagonal. This can be specified with the SUB= option in the REPEATED statement.

Compound Symmetric Covariance

Here are statements that use the REPEATED statement in PROC MIXED to model compound symmetric covariance structure:

```
proc mixed data=weight2;
   class program subj time;
   model strength = program time program*time;
   repeated / type=cs sub=subj(program) r rcorr;
run;
```

In the REPEATED statement, TYPE=CS specifies the covariance structure type to be compound symmetric. The option SUB=SUBJ(PROGRAM) specifies that the compound symmetric structure pertains to submatrices corresponding to each SUBJect in each PROGRAM. The matrix **R** is block diagonal with a block for each subject. This is explained more thoroughly in the description of the output in the next paragraph. The options R and RCORR in the REPEATED statement request printing of the covariance matrix **R** and the correlation matrix derived from **R**. Notice that the RANDOM SUBJ(PROGRAM) statement must be dropped because the SUBJ (PROGRAM) variance component (σ_s^2) and the compound symmetry covariance component ($\rho\sigma^2$) are confounded.

Results appear in Output 3.2.

Results

Output 3.2 *REPEATED Statement in PROC MIXED with Compound Symmetric Covariance*

```
                 R Matrix for SUBJ(PROGRAM) 1 CONT


   Row          COL1          COL2          COL3          COL4


    1      10.80020314    9.60333050    9.60333050    9.60333050
    2       9.60333050   10.80020314    9.60333050    9.60333050
    3       9.60333050    9.60333050   10.80020314    9.60333050
    4       9.60333050    9.60333050    9.60333050   10.80020314
    5       9.60333050    9.60333050    9.60333050    9.60333050
    6       9.60333050    9.60333050    9.60333050    9.60333050
    7       9.60333050    9.60333050    9.60333050    9.60333050



                 R Matrix for SUBJ(PROGRAM) 1 CONT
                      COL5          COL6          COL7


                9.60333050    9.60333050    9.60333050
                9.60333050    9.60333050    9.60333050
                9.60333050    9.60333050    9.60333050
                9.60333050    9.60333050    9.60333050
               10.80020314    9.60333050    9.60333050
                9.60333050   10.80020314    9.60333050
                9.60333050    9.60333050   10.80020314
```

```
                R Correlation Matrix for SUBJ(PROGRAM) 1 CONT

   Row          COL1           COL2           COL3           COL4

    1       1.00000000     0.88918054     0.88918054     0.88918054
    2       0.88918054     1.00000000     0.88918054     0.88918054
    3       0.88918054     0.88918054     1.00000000     0.88918054
    4       0.88918054     0.88918054     0.88918054     1.00000000
    5       0.88918054     0.88918054     0.88918054     0.88918054
    6       0.88918054     0.88918054     0.88918054     0.88918054
    7       0.88918054     0.88918054     0.88918054     0.88918054


                R Correlation Matrix for SUBJ(PROGRAM) 1 CONT

                COL5           COL6           COL7

            0.88918054     0.88918054     0.88918054
            0.88918054     0.88918054     0.88918054
            0.88918054     0.88918054     0.88918054
            0.88918054     0.88918054     0.88918054
            1.00000000     0.88918054     0.88918054
            0.88918054     1.00000000     0.88918054
            0.88918054     0.88918054     1.00000000


                Covariance Parameter Estimates (REML)

   Cov Parm         Ratio       Estimate    Std Error      Z    Pr > |Z|

   DIAG CS       8.02368623   9.60333050   1.88111525   5.11     0.0001
   Residual      1.00000000   1.19687264   0.09403520  12.73     0.0001


                Model Fitting Information for STRENGTH

       Description                            Value

       Observations                         399.0000
       Variance Estimate                      1.1969
       Standard Deviation Estimate            1.0940
       REML Log Likelihood                 -710.410
       Akaike's Information Criterion      -712.410
       Schwarz's Bayesian Criterion        -716.345
       -2 REML Log Likelihood              1420.820
       Null Model LRT Chi-Square            613.0628
       Null Model LRT DF                      1.0000
       Null Model LRT P-Value                 0.0000
```

```
                        Tests of Fixed Effects


          Source              NDF   DDF  Type III F  Pr > F


          PROGRAM              2     54        3.07  0.0548
          TIME                 6    324        7.43  0.0001
          PROGRAM*TIME        12    324        2.99  0.0005
```

Interpretation

First, under the heading "Covariance Parameter Estimates (REML)," are parameter estimates that are identical to those in Output 3.1 from the RANDOM statement although they are labelled differently. In other words, models have been fitted with equivalent random effects in Outputs 3.2 and 3.3. Because the MODEL statements are identical, the two models have the same fixed effects; that is, $X\beta$ is the same for both models. Therefore, the two models are equivalent.

Specifying TYPE=CS with SUB=SUBJ(PROGRAM) in the REPEATED statement defines a compound symmetric covariance structure for each subject. The covariance matrix for a particular subject is printed as a result of the r specification. That covariance matrix is printed under the heading "R Matrix for SUBJ(PROGRAM) 1 CONT." This means the covariance for subject number 1 in the CONT program. But all subjects have the same covariance matrix, namely,

$$\text{Cov}(Y_{ij}) = \begin{bmatrix} 10.800 & 9.603 & \dots & 9.603 \\ 9.603 & 10.800 & \dots & 9.603 \\ . & . & \dots & . \\ . & . & \dots & . \\ . & . & \dots & . \\ 9.603 & 9.603 & \dots & 10.800 \end{bmatrix}$$

where Y_{ij} is the vector of data for subject j in program i.

Elements of the diagonal are $10.800 = 9.603 + 1.197$. The overall covariance matrix is

$$R = \begin{bmatrix} R_{1(1)} & & & \\ & R_{1(2)} & & \\ & & \dots & \\ & & & R_{21(3)} \end{bmatrix}$$

where each $R_{j(i)} = \text{Cov}(Y_{ij})$ and blank spaces indicate zeros. The compound symmetric covariance structure specifies that the covariance between two measurements on the same subject is 9.603 and the variance of a measurement is 10.800.

Recall that the general definition of correlation between two random variables, say W and Z, is $r_{WZ} = Cov(W,Z)/(V(W)V(Z))^{1/2}$. Applying this formula with the covariance parameter estimates shows the correlation between two measurements on the same subject is $r = 9.603/((10.800)(10.800))^{1/2} = 0.889$. Thus, the correlation estimate is the same regardless of the length of time interval between the measurements. This does not agree with the concept discussed above that correlations between repeated measurements are larger between measurements close in time than between measurements far apart in time. This is a clue that compound symmetric covariance structure may not be satisfactory. This being the case, other covariance structures will be investigated.

Autoregressive Order 1 Covariance

A covariance structure with the desired property of correlations being larger for nearby times than far-apart times is **autoregressive of order 1**, which is usually denoted **AR(1)**. The mathematical expression for the covariance is $\sigma^2\rho^w$, where w is the number of time intervals between the measures. Autoregressive (order 1) covariance structure specifies that the covariance between two measurements w time intervals apart is $\sigma^2\rho^w$. The parameter σ^2 stands for the variance of an observation, $Var(y_{ijk}) = \sigma^2$. The parameter ρ stands for the correlation between adjacent observations on the same subject, for example, $Corr(y_{ij1}, y_{ij2}) = Corr(y_{ij3}, y_{ij4}) = \rho$. Thus, the correlation between measurements at times one and two is ρ, between measurements at times one and three is ρ^2, between measurements at times one and four is ρ^3, and so on.

You fit the model with AR(1) covariance with the statements

```
proc mixed data=weight2;
   class program subj time;
   model strength = program time program*time;
   repeated / type=ar(1) sub=subj(program) r rcorr;
run;
```

Results appear in Output 3.3.

Results

Output 3.3 *REPEATED Statement in PROC MIXED with Autoregressive Covariance*

R Matrix for SUBJ(PROGRAM) 1 CONT			
Row	COL1	COL2	COL3	COL4
1	10.75999023	10.24111032	9.74725240	9.27720983
2	10.24111032	10.75999023	10.24111032	9.74725240
3	9.74725240	10.24111032	10.75999023	10.24111032
4	9.27720983	9.74725240	10.24111032	10.75999023
5	8.82983416	9.27720983	9.74725240	10.24111032
6	8.40403232	8.82983416	9.27720983	9.74725240
7	7.99876397	8.40403232	8.82983416	9.27720983

R Matrix for SUBJ(PROGRAM) 1 CONT		
COL5	COL6	COL7
8.82983416	8.40403232	7.99876397
9.27720983	8.82983416	8.40403232
9.74725240	9.27720983	8.82983416

```
        10.24111032      9.74725240      9.27720983
        10.75999023     10.24111032      9.74725240
        10.24111032     10.75999023     10.24111032
         9.74725240     10.24111032     10.75999023
```

R Correlation Matrix for SUBJ(PROGRAM) 1 CONT

Row	COL1	COL2	COL3	COL4
1	1.00000000	0.95177692	0.90587930	0.86219500
2	0.95177692	1.00000000	0.95177692	0.90587930
3	0.90587930	0.95177692	1.00000000	0.95177692
4	0.86219500	0.90587930	0.95177692	1.00000000
5	0.82061730	0.86219500	0.90587930	0.95177692
6	0.78104461	0.82061730	0.86219500	0.90587930
7	0.74338023	0.78104461	0.82061730	0.86219500

R Correlation Matrix for SUBJ(PROGRAM) 1 CONT

COL5	COL6	COL7
0.82061730	0.78104461	0.74338023
0.86219500	0.82061730	0.78104461
0.90587930	0.86219500	0.82061730
0.95177692	0.90587930	0.86219500
1.00000000	0.95177692	0.90587930
0.95177692	1.00000000	0.95177692
0.90587930	0.95177692	1.00000000

Covariance Parameter Estimates (REML)

Cov Parm	Ratio	Estimate	Std Error	Z	Pr > |Z|
DIAG AR(1)	0.08845518	0.95177692	0.00879593	108.21	0.0001
Residual	1.00000000	10.75999023	1.81781312	5.92	0.0001

Model Fitting Information for STRENGTH

Description	Value
Observations	399.0000
Variance Estimate	10.7600
Standard Deviation Estimate	3.2802
REML Log Likelihood	-633.402
Akaike's Information Criterion	-635.402

```
Schwarz's Bayesian Criterion        -639.337
-2 REML Log Likelihood             1266.804
Null Model LRT Chi-Square          767.0795
Null Model LRT DF                    1.0000
Null Model LRT P-Value               0.0000


                Tests of Fixed Effects
        Source        NDF   DDF   Type III F  Pr > F


        PROGRAM        2     54      3.11     0.0528
        TIME           6    324      4.30     0.0003
        PROGRAM*TIME  12    324      1.17     0.3007
```

You see the estimates of the AR(1) parameters are $\sigma^2 = 10.760$ and $\rho = 0.952$. Correlations printed under the heading "R Correlation Matrix for SUBJ(PROGRAM) 1 CONT" show correlations equal to 0.952 for adjacent measurements, $0.906 = 0.952^2$ for observations two time units apart, and so on down to $0.743 = 0.952^6$ for measurements six units apart.

You can add a RANDOM INTERCEPT / SUB=SUBJ (PROGRAM) statement to this program to fit a random intercept in addition to the AR(1) covariance structure. This addition is consistent with the delta_ij term in model (3.1). It does not significantly improve the model fit and results are not shown here.

Unstructured Covariance

The third covariance structure to be tried is "unstructured." That is, no mathematical pattern is imposed on the covariance matrix. Thus "unstructured" means "no structure."

These statements specify unstructured covariance:

```
proc mixed data=weight2;
    class program subj time;
    model strength = program time program*time;
    repeated / type=un sub=subj(program) r rcorr;
run;
```

Add a RANDOM INTERCEPT / SUB=SUBJ (PROGRAM) statement to this program would be redundant because the unstructured covariance structure is the most general one possible.

Results appear in Output 3.4.

Output 3.4 *REPEATED Statement in PROC MIXED with Unstructured Covariance*

```
              R Matrix for SUBJ(PROGRAM) 1 CONT

  Row       COL1          COL2          COL3          COL4

    1    8.78036817    8.75733025    8.96588404    8.19863316
    2    8.75733025    9.47322531    9.46334877    8.56882716
    3    8.96588404    9.46334877   10.70827822    9.92680776
    4    8.19863316    8.56882716    9.92680776   10.07755732
    5    8.67835097    9.20154321   10.66644621   10.59982363
    6    8.22056878    8.73101852   10.07043651    9.89894180
    7    8.41721781    8.68780864   10.21417549   10.04356261
```

```
                    R Matrix for SUBJ(PROGRAM) 1 CONT


                   COL5            COL6            COL7


             8.67835097      8.22056878      8.41721781
             9.20154321      8.73101852      8.68780864
            10.66644621     10.07043651     10.21417549
            10.59982363      9.89894180     10.04356261
            12.09541446     11.34470899     11.36410935
            11.34470899     11.75621693     11.65039683
            11.36410935     11.65039683     12.71036155
```

```
                R Correlation Matrix for SUBJ(PROGRAM) 1 CONT


      Row          COL1            COL2            COL3            COL4


       1      1.00000000      0.96021046      0.92464906      0.87158040
       2      0.96021046      1.00000000      0.93958503      0.87699034
       3      0.92464906      0.93958503      1.00000000      0.95559122
       4      0.87158040      0.87699034      0.95559122      1.00000000
       5      0.84211319      0.85960980      0.93723726      0.96008708
       6      0.80911771      0.82733649      0.89754179      0.90944688
       7      0.79677051      0.79173959      0.87551691      0.88742406
```

```
                R Correlation Matrix for SUBJ(PROGRAM) 1 CONT


                   COL5            COL6            COL7


             0.84211319      0.80911771      0.79677051
             0.85960980      0.82733649      0.79173959
             0.93723726      0.89754179      0.87551691
             0.96008708      0.90944688      0.88742406
             1.00000000      0.95136942      0.91652871
             0.95136942      1.00000000      0.95307696
             0.91652871      0.95307696      1.00000000
```

```
                 Covariance Parameter Estimates (REML)
```

Cov Parm	Estimate	Std Error	Z	Pr > |Z|
DIAG UN(1,1)	8.78036817	1.68978264	5.20	0.0001
UN(2,1)	8.75733025	1.72062241	5.09	0.0001
UN(2,2)	9.47322531	1.82312306	5.20	0.0001
UN(3,1)	8.96588404	1.79716702	4.99	0.0001
UN(3,2)	9.46334877	1.88068596	5.03	0.0001
UN(3,3)	10.70827822	2.06080910	5.20	0.0001
UN(4,1)	8.19863316	1.69805035	4.83	0.0001
UN(4,2)	8.56882716	1.76850936	4.85	0.0001
UN(4,3)	9.92680776	1.95530996	5.08	0.0001
UN(4,4)	10.07755732	1.93942681	5.20	0.0001
UN(5,1)	8.67835097	1.83341398	4.73	0.0001
UN(5,2)	9.20154321	1.92089381	4.79	0.0001
UN(5,3)	10.66644621	2.12260383	5.03	0.0001
UN(5,4)	10.59982363	2.08277101	5.09	0.0001

```
          UN(5,5)    12.09541446    2.32776360    5.20    0.0001
          UN(6,1)     8.22056878    1.77848075    4.62    0.0001
          UN(6,2)     8.73101852    1.86388670    4.68    0.0001
          UN(6,3)    10.07043651    2.05165937    4.91    0.0001
          UN(6,4)     9.89894180    2.00214237    4.94    0.0001
          UN(6,5)    11.34470899    2.23978644    5.07    0.0001
          UN(6,6)    11.75621693    2.26248500    5.20    0.0001
          UN(7,1)     8.41721781    1.83813114    4.58    0.0001
          UN(7,2)     8.68780864    1.90460523    4.56    0.0001
          UN(7,3)    10.21417549    2.11009684    4.84    0.0001
          UN(7,4)    10.04356261    2.05913748    4.88    0.0001
          UN(7,5)    11.36410935    2.28878130    4.97    0.0001
          UN(7,6)    11.65039683    2.29797622    5.07    0.0001
          UN(7,7)    12.71036155    2.44611022    5.20    0.0001
 Residual             1.00000000         .           .        .


              Model Fitting Information for STRENGTH


          Description                          Value


          Observations                        399.0000
          Variance Estimate                     1.0000
          Standard Deviation Estimate           1.0000
          REML Log Likelihood                -617.448
          Akaike's Information Criterion     -645.448
          Schwarz's Bayesian Criterion       -700.536
          -2 REML Log Likelihood             1234.896
          Null Model LRT Chi-Square           798.9873
          Null Model LRT DF                    27.0000
          Null Model LRT P-Value                0.0000



                  Tests of Fixed Effects


          Source         NDF    DDF   Type III F   Pr > F


          PROGRAM          2     54        3.07    0.0548
          TIME             6     54        7.12    0.0001
          PROGRAM*TIME    12     54        1.57    0.1297
```

In the correlation matrix you see the general pattern of correlations decreasing with increasing length of time interval between measurements. But you see in the covariance matrix that variances also increase with time, from the variance of 8.780 at TIME = 1 to 12.710 at TIME = 7. This increasing pattern of the variances is not accommodated by the compound symmetric or AR(1) covariance models. However, the variance increase from 8.780 at time 1 to 12.710 at time 7 is not a great increase and likely will not cause much of a problem if not built into the model.

Choosing the Covariance Structure

Now you must decide which of the three covariance structures to assume in the model for final inference. This decision process can be assisted by using two model-fit criteria computed by PROC MIXED, Akaike's Information Criterion (AIC) and Schwarz' Bayesian Criterion (SBC). These are essentially log likelihood values penalized for the number of parameters estimated. SBC imposes a heavier penalty than AIC. They appear under the heading "Model Fitting Information for STRENGTH" in Outputs 3.2–3.4. Values of the criteria for each covariance structure are

Structure	CS	AR(1)	UN
AIC	-712.12	-635.40	-645.45
SBC	-716.35	-639.34	-700.54

The covariance structure with the largest values of the criteria is considered most desirable. In this example, both AIC and SBC point to the AR(1) structure. Autoregressive covariance shows considerable improvement in the criteria over compound symmetric and at least marginal improvement over unstructured. SBC has a poor value for unstructured covariance because of the large number of parameters. On this basis and visual comparison of the estimated AR(1) correlation matrix with the unstructured matrix, we choose AR(1). It is not a perfect fit, but it is suitable for practical purposes.

3.2.3 Effects of Covariance Structure on Tests and Estimates

In most applications, such as the present one, you are not interested in the covariance structure in its own right. Instead, you are interested in obtaining a good model for the covariance structure so that computations and inferences about fixed effects are valid. In the present example, you want to obtain valid inference regarding PROGRAM, TIME, and PROGRAM *TIME effects. Now examine the tests for fixed effects that result from each of the covariance structures. F-tests are printed by PROC MIXED for each of the fixed effects in an analysis of variance format in Outputs 3.2–3.4. These are summarized as follows:

Structure	CS	AR(1)	UN
PROGRAM	0.0548	0.0528	0.0548
TIME	0.0001	0.0003	0.0001
PROGRAM*TIME	0.0005	0.3007	0.1297

You see that tests for PROGRAM and TIME result in essentially the same conclusions regardless of the covariance structure. In fact, the compound symmetric and unstructured covariances produce identical F-tests for PROGRAM. That is also the standard analysis of variance F-ratio of PROGRAM mean square divided by SUBJ(PROGRAM) mean square. But the PROGRAM*TIME interaction results differ dramatically, with p-values ranging from "highly significant" $p=0.0005$ for compound symmetric structure, to "nonsignificant" $p=0.3007$ for the autoregressive structure. Keep in mind that the compound symmetric structure does not seem appropriate for this application because of the apparent decreasing trends of the correlations. This makes the p-value unduly small. The unstructured covariance does not recognize any patterns. The nonsignificant p-value for PROGRAM*TIME interaction resulting from the autoregressive structure is somewhat disturbing at first because the plot in Output 3.4 indicates the trends over TIME for the three PROGRAMs are not parallel. However, you shall see that when regression trends are introduced into the time effects, there is, indeed, statistical evidence of interaction.

3.2.4 Modelling Time As a Regression Variable

Because the variable TIME is quantitative, you can model STRENGTH as a polynomial function of TIME. This gives smoothed trends over TIME and yields equations that can be used for comparing programs at specific times or predicting STRENGTH for a PROGRAM at a specific TIME. The plot in Figure 3.1 indicates that quadratic equations should be adequate for regressions of STRENGTH on TIME.

Program

To fit quadratic regression models, submit the PROC MIXED statements

```
proc mixed;
   class program subj;
   model strength = program time time*program
   time*time time*time*program / htype=1;
   repeated / type=ar(1) sub=subj(program);
run;
```

Notice that TIME is excluded from the CLASS statement in order to treat TIME as a continuous rather than a classification variable. Also, note that the HTYPE=1 option is used in the MODEL statement. This will provide sequentially formulated hypotheses that are appropriate for polynomial models.

Results appear in Output 3.5.

Results

Output 3.5 *REPEATED Statement in PROC MIXED with Autoregressive Covariance and Quadratic Model for TIME*

```
              Covariance Parameter Estimates (REML)

  Cov Parm           Ratio        Estimate      Std Error        Z     Pr > |Z|

  DIAG AR(1)      0.08851334     0.95226971    0.00868773    109.61     0.0001
  Residual        1.00000000    10.75848821    1.81983753      5.91     0.0001
                      Tests of Fixed Effects


       Source             NDF   DDF   Type I F  Pr > F


       PROGRAM             2     54      3.10    0.0530
       TIME                1    336     12.69    0.0004
       TIME*PROGRAM        2    336      4.75    0.0093
       TIME*TIME           1    336      7.18    0.0077
       TIME*TIME*PROGRAM   2    336      0.88    0.4167
```

Interpretation

Tests of the fixed effects, starting at the bottom of the list and working upward, indicate that quadratic effects are needed in the model. The TIME*TIME*PROGRAM effect is not significant, but this is perhaps somewhat misleading, as you shall see when examining individual regression equations in Output 3.6. In any event, the TIME*TIME effect is significant with $p=0.0077$, and indicates the need for quadratic terms. Also, TIME*PROGRAM interaction is significant with $p=0.0093$. This result establishes the presence of interaction between TIME and PROGRAM.

Results of the tests for fixed effects are useful in deciding what model should be used to represent the trends over time. Now individual quadratic curves will be obtained for each PROGRAM. These curves were actually fitted to obtain Output 3.5, but the model is parameterized in such a way that the parameter estimates that would be printed do not directly produce the equations for the three curves.

Program

In order to obtain equations for the three PROGRAMs, submit the statements

```
proc mixed;
   class program subj;
   model strength = program time*program time*time*program / noint
   s htype=1;
   repeated / type=ar(1) sub=subj(program);
run;
```

Deleting TIME and TIME*TIME from the previous MODEL statement and adding the NOINT option in the MODEL statement formulates the model so that parameter estimates directly provide quadratic equations for the three PROGRAMs. Include the S (for SOLUTION) as a MODEL statement option to print the parameter estimates when a CLASS statement is used.

See Output 3.6 for results.

Results

Output 3.6 REPEATED Statement in PROC MIXED with Autoregressive Covariance and Quadratic Model for TIME Showing Parameter Estimates

```
            Covariance Parameter Estimates (REML)

  Cov Parm          Ratio       Estimate      Std Error         Z     Pr > |Z|

  DIAG AR(1)     0.08851334    0.95226971    0.00868773    109.61     0.0001
  Residual       1.00000000   10.75848821    1.81983753      5.91     0.0001


                     Solution for Fixed Effects

  Parameter                     Estimate      Std Error    DDF        T    Pr > |T|

  PROGRAM CONT                79.57079564    0.79716499     54    99.82     0.0001
  PROGRAM RI                  78.90542310    0.89125755     54    88.53     0.0001
  PROGRAM WI                  80.49279681    0.77795337     54   103.47     0.0001
  TIME*PROGRAM CONT            0.20916699    0.23525632    336     0.89     0.3746
  TIME*PROGRAM RI              0.86061556    0.26302456    336     3.27     0.0012
  TIME*PROGRAM WI              0.58606279    0.22958666    336     2.55     0.0111
  TIME*TIME*PROGRAM CONT      -0.02929894    0.02731349    336    -1.07     0.2842
  TIME*TIME*PROGRAM RI        -0.07766501    0.03053740    336    -2.54     0.0114
  TIME*TIME*PROGRAM WI        -0.03062516    0.02665523    336    -1.15     0.2514


                     Tests of Fixed Effects

       Source            NDF    DDF   Type I F   Pr > F

       PROGRAM             3     54   12910.80   0.0001
       TIME*PROGRAM        3    336       7.39   0.0001
       TIME*TIME*PROGRAM   3    336       2.98   0.0316
```

Interpretation

Under the heading "Solution for Fixed Effects" you locate parameter estimates, and you determine the equations for the programs:

CONT: STRENGTH = 79.57 + 0.209*TIME – 0.0293*TIME*TIME
RI: STRENGTH = 78.91 + 0.861*TIME – 0.0777*TIME*TIME
WI: STRENGTH = 80.49 + 0.586*TIME – 0.0306*TIME*TIME

Notice the significance probabilities for the *t*-tests for the parameters. The quadratic coefficient for CONT is not significant because the STRENGTH profile for CONT is basically flat (see Output 3.1) except for some "waving" that is typical with autoregressive correlation. The quadratic coefficient for RI is significant and negative because the RI profile is not increasing as rapidly at later times as it was at earlier times. The quadratic coefficient for WI is not significant because the profile is still increasing at about the same rate at later times as it was at earlier times; that is, the trend is essentially linear. Differences in results from the *t*-tests for quadratic coefficients indicate interaction between TIME*TIME and PROGRAM, although the statistical test for TIME*TIME* PROGRAM was not significant in Output 3.5. This seeming contradiction is resolved by observing that 1) the quadratic coefficients for CONT and WI are nearly equal, and 2) the coefficient for RI differs from the CONT and WI coefficients by less that two of its standard errors.

3.3 Comparison of PROC MIXED and PROC GLM for Analysis of Repeated Measures Data

PROC GLM was originally written as a fixed-effects procedure that would handle models with both classification and regression variables. Statements and options were added to adapt PROC GLM to handle some mixed model and repeated measures applications. These include the TEST, RANDOM, and REPEATED statements, and the E= option to MODEL, CONTRAST, and LSMEANS statements. Two approaches using PROC GLM to analyze repeated measures data are presented in this section and are related to results obtained using PROC MIXED in section 3.2. **Univariate analysis of variance**, which essentially treats repeated measures data as if they were obtained from a split-plot experiment, is illustrated in subsection 3.3.1. The RANDOM statement in PROC GLM is a key statement for this methodology. Then, in subsection 3.3.2, **multivariate and univariate analyses of contrasts** are illustrated. These analyses are obtained from the REPEATED statement in PROC GLM.

You have already seen the RANDOM and REPEATED statements in PROC MIXED in section 3.2. Although both PROC GLM and PROC MIXED contain statements by the same name, and the statements are used in similar situations, the functions of the RANDOM and REPEATED statements differ greatly between PROC GLM and PROC MIXED. Thus, if you are accustomed to using these statements in PROC GLM, do not expect to see similar output from PROC MIXED.

Two types of repeated measures analyses can be obtained by PROC GLM: (1) univariate analysis of variance, and (2) multivariate and univariate analyses of contrasts. These two approaches are discussed in subsections 3.3.1 and 3.3.2, respectively.

This book focuses primarily on PROC MIXED. References to PROC GLM are mainly for comparison, rather than to provide a complete documentation of PROC GLM capabilities in mixed models. You can refer to Littell, Freund, and Spector (1991) and to Milliken and Johnson (1984) for more detailed information on using PROC GLM for mixed model and repeated measures analyses.

3.3.1 Univariate Analysis of Variance Using the RANDOM Statement in PROC GLM

Doing a univariate analysis of variance of repeated measures data means to analyze the data using the methods illustrated with PROC GLM in Chapter 2. In the case of the weight lifting repeated measures data, a univariate analysis of variance parallels the analysis of the semiconductor data in Chapter 2. In terms of analysis of variance, the two can be related as shown in Table 3.1.

Table 3.1 *Analysis of Variance of Semiconductor and Weightlifting Examples*

Semiconductor example		Weightlifting example	
Source of Variation	DF	Source of Variation	DF
ET	3	PROGRAM	2
WAFER(ET)	8	SUBJ(PROGRAM)	54
POS	3	TIME	6
ET*TIME	9	PROGRAM*TIME	12
RESIDUAL	24	RESIDUAL	324

All the methods illustrated in Chapter 2 can be applied, but not all would produce correct results. The difficulty lies with the covariance structure. In the semiconductor data, it is reasonable to assume that measurements at two positions on the same WAFER are equally correlated, regardless of the location of the positions. However, the analogous assumption is not reasonable with the weightlifting data. Measurements at adjacent TIMEs are more highly correlated than measurements far apart in time. This phenomenon led to the AR(1) covariance providing a better fit than compound symmetric covariance in section 3.2.

Program

To do a univariate analysis of variance with PROC GLM, submit these statements:

```
proc glm data=weight2;
   class program subj time;
   model strength = program subj(program) time program*time;
   test h=program e=subj(program);
   random subj(program);
run;
```

These statements are similar in many ways to the PROC MIXED statements shown in section 3.2. One of the most important distinctions is that the random effect SUBJ(PROGRAM) is not included in the MODEL statement of PROC MIXED, but it is included in the PROC GLM MODEL statement. These issues were discussed in more detail in Chapters 1 and 2. Another distinction is that the TEST statement is used in PROC GLM to obtain F-statistics with the appropriate denominator mean square. Also, the RANDOM statement in PROC GLM prints the expected mean squares, whereas in PROC MIXED the RANDOM statement actually defines the random effects contained in the **Zu** portion of the statistical model.

Results from the PROC GLM statements appear in Output 3.7.

Results

Output 3.7 *Univariate Analysis of Variance Using the RANDOM Statement in PROC GLM*

```
                     General Linear Models Procedure
Dependent Variable: STRENGTH
                          Sum of          Mean
Source            DF     Squares        Square   F Value    Pr > F
Model             74    4210.0529      56.8926     47.53    0.0001

Error            324     387.7867       1.1969

Corrected Total  398    4597.8396


        R-Square           C.V.       Root MSE      STRENGTH Mean


        0.915659        1.350972        1.0940           80.980




Source            DF    Type I SS   Mean Square   F Value    Pr > F


PROGRAM            2     419.4353     209.7176    175.22     0.0001
SUBJ(PROGRAM)     54    3694.6901      68.4202     57.17     0.0001
TIME               6      52.9273       8.8212      7.37     0.0001
PROGRAM*TIME      12      43.0002       3.5834      2.99     0.0005


Source            DF    Type III SS  Mean Square   F Value   Pr > F


PROGRAM            2     419.4353     209.7176    175.22     0.0001
SUBJ(PROGRAM)     54    3694.6901      68.4202     57.17     0.0001
TIME               6      53.3543       8.8924      7.43     0.0001
PROGRAM*TIME      12      43.0002       3.5834      2.99     0.0005
```

```
                         General Linear Models Procedure

Source                Type III Expected Mean Square

PROGRAM               Var(Error) + 7 Var(SUBJ(PROGRAM))
                      + Q(PROGRAM,PROGRAM*TIME)

SUBJ(PROGRAM)         Var(Error) + 7 Var(SUBJ(PROGRAM))

TIME                  Var(Error) + Q(TIME,PROGRAM*TIME)

PROGRAM*TIME          Var(Error) + Q(PROGRAM*TIME)
                         General Linear Models Procedure


Dependent Variable: STRENGTH


Tests of Hypotheses using the Type III MS for
SUBJ(PROGRAM) as an error term

Source              DF    Type III SS   Mean Square   F Value    Pr > F

PROGRAM              2     419.43526     209.71763      3.07     0.0548
```

Interpretation

You see that the test for PROGRAM differences produced by the TEST statement has $F = 3.07$, significant at the $p = 0.0548$ level. This is identical to the PROGRAM test computed by PROC MIXED in Outputs 3.2 and 3.4 when compound symmetric or unstructured covariance was specified. The test for TIME is significant at $p = 0.0001$, and the test for PROGRAM*TIME interaction is significant at $p = 0.0005$. These results are the same as those obtained from PROC MIXED with the compound symmetric covariance structure in Output 3.1. This is because a generalized least squares fit of a model with compound symmetric error structure is equivalent to ordinary least squares for balanced data.

3.3.2 Multivariate and Univariate Analyses of Contrast Variables Using the REPEATED Statement in PROC GLM

In the early 1980s, the REPEATED statement was added to PROC GLM. Its syntax and output are quite different from other PROC GLM statements. *The REPEATED statement in PROC GLM works only when repeated measures are written as multivariate responses in the MODEL statement. The repeated measures also must appear in a multivariate mode in the data set. Observations with missing data for any of the repeated measures variables are not used in the analysis.*

The methods of analysis presented in this section are obtained by computing a new set of variables that are contrasts of the original variables. Some of the possible contrast variables are orthogonal polynomials, differences between each variable and a particular variable, etc. Then standard statistical multivariate and univariate analyses of variance are applied to the contrast variables. In the weightlifting example, orthogonal polynomials of time will be used as the contrast variables.

Program

Submit the statements

```
proc glm data=weights;
   class program;
   model s1-s7 = program / nouni;
   repeated time polynomial / printe summary;
run;
```

These statements are altogether different from the PROC MIXED statements used in section 3.2.4 to fit polynomial models. First, PROC GLM is run on the multivariate version of the data set, WEIGHTS, and the MODEL statement has multivariate response variables S1 through S7. The only variable, or source of variation, on the right hand side of the MODEL statement is PROGRAM. This basically describes the *treatment* structure of this example. It is a completely randomized design with PROGRAM as the treatment factor and SUBJECTS as the experimental units. The NOUNI option is used in the MODEL statement to suppress univariate ANOVA tables that would otherwise be printed for each of the response variables, that is, analyses for each time.

The REPEATED statement in PROC GLM bears little resemblance to the REPEATED statement in PROC MIXED. Recall that the REPEATED statement in PROC MIXED defines the covariance structure in the **R** matrix of the general linear mixed model. The REPEATED statement in PROC GLM was added to the procedure to accommodate repeated measures, rather than being an original part of the procedure. Nonetheless, it provides useful information, and it is interesting to compare results with those of PROC MIXED.

The essential function of the REPEATED statement in PROC GLM is to define the contrast variables and assign a name to them. The first designation following the keyword REPEATED, TIME, is the name assigned to the contrast variables. This name has no particular function other than to label the output.

The next specification, POLYNOMIAL, specifies the set of contrast variables to be constructed. Because there are seven response variables, S1-S7, orthogonal polynomials of order 1 through 6 will be computed. The output from the REPEATED statement in PROC GLM comes from various analyses of these contrast variables.

Results from PROC GLM appear in Output 3.8.

Results

An abundance of output is produced by PROC GLM with the REPEATED statement, but not all of it will be discussed in detail.

Output 3.8 *Results Using the REPEATED Statement in PROC GLM*

```
                    General Linear Models Procedure
                      Class Level Information

              Class     Levels    Values

              PROGRAM      3       CONT RI WI



          Number of observations in data set = 57




                    General Linear Models Procedure
                  Repeated Measures Analysis of Variance
                  Repeated Measures Level Information

Dependent Variable         S1        S2        S3        S4        S5

   Level of TIME            1         2         3         4         5


Dependent Variable         S6        S7
   Level of TIME           6         7




                    General Linear Models Procedure
                  Repeated Measures Analysis of Variance
        Partial Correlation Coefficients from the Error SS&CP Matrix /
                             Prob > |r|


   DF = 54          S1        S2        S3        S4        S5        S6        S7

   S1            1.000000  0.960210  0.924649  0.871580  0.842113 0.809118   .796771
                 0.0001    0.0001    0.0001    0.0001    0.0001   0.0001     0.0001


   S2            0.960210  1.000000  0.939585  0.876990  0.859610 0.827336   .791740
                 0.0001    0.0001    0.0001    0.0001    0.0001   0.0001     0.0001


   S3            0.924649  0.939585  1.000000  0.955591  0.937237 0.897542   .875517
                 0.0001    0.0001    0.0001    0.0001    0.0001   0.0001     0.0001
```

S4	0.871580	0.876990	0.955591	1.000000	0.960087	0.909447	0.887424
	0.0001	0.0001	0.0001	0.0001	0.0001	0.0001	0.0001
S5	0.842113	0.859610	0.937237	0.960087	1.000000	0.951369	0.916529
	0.0001	0.0001	0.0001	0.0001	0.0001	0.0001	0.0001
S6	0.809118	0.827336	0.897542	0.909447	0.951369	1.000000	0.953077
	0.0001	0.0001	0.0001	0.0001	0.0001	0.0001	0.0001
S7	0.796771	0.791740	0.875517	0.887424	0.916529	0.953077	1.000000
	0.0001	0.0001	0.0001	0.0001	0.0001	0.0001	0.0001

Test for Sphericity: Mauchly's Criterion = 0.0403737
Chisquare Approximation = 166.18471 with 20 df
Prob > Chisquare = 0.0000

Applied to Orthogonal Components:
Test for Sphericity: Mauchly's Criterion = 0.0403737
Chisquare Approximation = 166.18471 with 20 df
Prob > Chisquare = 0.0000

Manova Test Criteria and Exact F Statistics for
the Hypothesis of no TIME Effect
H = Type III SS&CP Matrix for TIME   E = Error SS&CP Matrix

S=1   M=2   N=23.5

Statistic	Value	F	Num DF	Den DF	Pr > F
Wilks' Lambda	0.5588901	6.4456	6	49	0.0001
Pillai's Trace	0.4411099	6.4456	6	49	0.0001
Hotelling-Lawley Trace	0.7892604	6.4456	6	49	0.0001
Roy's Greatest Root	0.7892604	6.4456	6	49	0.0001

Manova Test Criteria and F Approximations for
the Hypothesis of no TIME*PROGRAM Effect
H = Type III SS&CP Matrix for TIME*PROGRAM   E = Error SS&CP Matrix

S=2   M=1.5   N=23.5

Statistic	Value	F	Num DF	Den DF	Pr > F
Wilks' Lambda	0.7316744	1.3808	12	98	0.1880
Pillai's Trace	0.2818894	1.3672	12	100	0.1943
Hotelling-Lawley Trace	0.3481903	1.3928	12	96	0.1827
Roy's Greatest Root	0.2825903	2.3549	6	50	0.0442

NOTE: F Statistic for Roy's Greatest Root is an upper bound.
NOTE: F Statistic for Wilks' Lambda is exact.

```
                      General Linear Models Procedure
                   Repeated Measures Analysis of Variance
               Tests of Hypotheses for Between Subjects Effects


Source              DF      Type III SS   Mean Square   F Value    Pr > F

PROGRAM             2         419.44        209.72        3.07     0.0548


Error               54       3694.69         68.42
```

```
                      General Linear Models Procedure
                   Repeated Measures Analysis of Variance
             Univariate Tests of Hypotheses for Within Subject Effects


Source: TIME

                                                          Adj   Pr > F
     DF Type III SS Mean Square   F Value   Pr > F   G - G     H - F
      6   53.354264   8.892377      7.43    0.0001   0.0003    0.0002


Source: TIME*PROGRAM

                                                          Adj   Pr > F
     DF Type III SS Mean Square   F Value   Pr > F   G - G     H - F
     12   43.000233   3.583353      2.99    0.0005   0.0130    0.0104
Source: Error(TIME)

     DF Type III SS Mean Square
    324  387.786735   1.196873


            Greenhouse-Geisser Epsilon = 0.4233
               Huynh-Feldt Epsilon = 0.4624


                      General Linear Models Procedure
                   Repeated Measures Analysis of Variance
                  Analysis of Variance of Contrast Variables


   TIME.N represents the nth degree polynomial contrast for TIME

Contrast Variable: TIME.1

Source              DF      Type III SS   Mean Square   F Value    Pr > F

MEAN                1       40.5144529    40.5144529     9.85     0.0028
PROGRAM             2       40.3913623    20.1956812     4.91     0.0110

Error               54      222.1875850    4.1145849

Contrast Variable: TIME.2

Source              DF      Type III SS   Mean Square   F Value    Pr > F

MEAN                1       10.5771313    10.5771313     8.64     0.0048
PROGRAM             2        1.4241049     0.7120525     0.58     0.5626

Error               54      66.1339569     1.2247029

Contrast Variable: TIME.3
```

```
Source              DF    Type III SS   Mean Square   F Value    Pr > F

MEAN                1      1.31320035    1.31320035     2.55      0.1163
PROGRAM             2      0.03999060    0.01999530     0.04      0.9620

Error               54    27.83720238   0.51550375
```

Contrast Variable: TIME.4

```
Source              DF    Type III SS   Mean Square   F Value    Pr > F

MEAN                1      0.08132173    0.08132173     0.12      0.7329
PROGRAM             2      0.53719750    0.26859875     0.39      0.6798

Error               54    37.31675557   0.69105103
```

Contrast Variable: TIME.5

```
Source              DF    Type III SS   Mean Square   F Value    Pr > F

MEAN                1      0.69325639    0.69325639     2.19      0.1451
PROGRAM             2      0.20663265    0.10331633     0.33      0.7234

Error               54    17.12670068   0.31716112
```

Contrast Variable: TIME.6

```
Source              DF    Type III SS   Mean Square   F Value    Pr > F

MEAN                1      0.17490098    0.17490098     0.55      0.4617
PROGRAM             2      0.40094473    0.20047237     0.63      0.5365

Error               54    17.18453412   0.31823211
```

Interpretation

Correlations of repeated measures. First, look at the matrix under the heading "Partial Correlation Coefficients from the Error SSCP Matrix / Prob > |r|." This comes from the PRINTE option, which also can be used with the MANOVA statement in PROC GLM. As the title implies, these are partial correlations computed from residuals after fitting the between-subjects model; that is, they are computed from sums of squares and cross products of deviations of strength measurements from subject means. These correlations are identical to the correlations computed from the RCORR option in the REPEATED statement in PROC MIXED when TYPE=UN is specified as the covariance structure. This is a clue that there is a relationship between the analyses obtained from the two procedures. Notice the decreasing trends in the correlations as the number of time intervals increases between the measurements.

Huynh-Feldt condition. Next in the PROC GLM output is a matrix of partial correlations based on the SSCP matrix of contrast variables defined by the POLYNOMIAL option in the REPEATED statement. Following this matrix is a "Test for Sphericity." This is a test of whether the condition holds that is necessary for univariate analysis of variance, the so-called Huynh-Feldt (H-F) condition. Specifically, it is a test of whether a set of orthonormal contrasts of the repeated measures variables (such as the polynomial contrasts) have a spherical covariance matrix; that is, they are independent and have equal variances.

Decreasing trends in correlations as a function of increasing time interval between measurements was discussed in section 3.2 and was noted in the preceding paragraph. This is an indication that the H-F condition is not met. Statistical significance of the test for sphericity ($p=0.0000$) tells you the H-F condition is not met. Consequently, portions of the univariate analysis of variance which involve TIME are possibly invalid. In the present case, the test for TIME*PROGRAM interaction has a p-value (0.0005) that is too small. In other words, significance of the PROGRAM*TIME interaction is over-assessed by the univariate ANOVA.

Multivariate tests for within-subject effects. Now look at the table of multivariate tests for TIME and TIME*PROGRAM tests. These tests do not assume any particular covariance structure. They are results of multivariate analysis of variance being applied to the contrast variables. Note the $F = 6.4456$ with $P = 0.0001$ for the four multivariate tests for TIME. There is no question of a TIME effect. It is highly significant for all test statistics. But note also the multivariate tests for TIME*PROGRAM interaction. The four tests have p-values ranging from 0.0442 to 0.1943. These p-values are in the same ballpark as the p-value equal to 0.0989 from PROC MIXED when covariance TYPE=UN is specified in the REPEATED statement. The multivariate tests from PROC GLM and the test from PROC MIXED with unstructured covariance are closely related because they are based on the same estimate of covariance structure.

Univariate tests for between-subjects effects. Under "Tests of Hypotheses for Between Subjects Effects," PROC GLM presents an F-test for the between-subjects effect, PROGRAM. This test is identical to the test from the univariate analysis of variance obtained by PROC GLM when the appropriate denominator mean square, SUBJ(PROGRAM), was specified with the TEST statement in subsection 3.3.1. It is computed by performing the usual univariate ANOVA F-test based on subject means; that is, means of S1 through S7 for each subject. It also is the same test computed by PROC MIXED in "Tests of Fixed Effects" when either compound symmetric or unstructured covariance is specified.

Univariate tests for within-subject effects and adjustments to p-values. Under "Tests of Hypotheses for Within Subject Effects," PROC GLM presents F-tests for the within-subject effects TIME and PROGRAM*TIME. These test statistics are the same as those from the univariate analysis in section 3.3.1, and the same p-values are presented. In addition, the tests from the REPEATED statement have adjustments to the p-values according to the assessed degree of failure for the Huynh-Feldt conditions to be met. Two types of adjustments to p-values are presented, the G-G, for Greenhouse-Geisser, and the H-F, for Huynh-Feldt. Each of these adjustments is obtained by discounting the degrees of freedom by a factor of "epsilon." **Epsilon** is a quantity whose value equals 1 if the H-F condition is met, and has a value which decreases with increasing failure of the H-F condition to be met. The two adjustments differ in the manner by which they estimate epsilon. Neither of these adjusted p-values corresponds directly to output from PROC MIXED.

Analysis of variance of the contrast variables. The remaining output from the REPEATED statement in PROC GLM appears under "Analysis of Variance for Contrast Variables." As the heading indicates, these are analysis of variance tables for the variables computed sequentially as the regression coefficients for polynomial models. TIME.1 is the linear coefficient in a linear model, TIME.2 is the quadratic coefficient in a quadratic model, and so on. The main thing to notice in this portion of the output is that there are "significant" p-values for TIME.1 and TIME.2, but none for higher degree polynomials. These tests are not exactly duplicated in any of the PROC MIXED results. But they correspond for practical purposes with results in Output 3.6 from running PROC MIXED with TIME treated as a regression variable. PROC MIXED can produce more complete results because you can obtain the actual equations as shown in Output 3.6, along with valid tests with properly specified covariance.

3.4 Missing Data in Repeated Measures

Missing data in repeated measures historically have caused serious statistical analysis problems. The two most common approaches using PROC GLM were 1) univariate analysis of variance utilizing the RANDOM statement, and 2) multivariate and univariate analyses of contrast variables, utilizing the REPEATED statement. Both of these approaches are heavily affected by missing data. Missing data do not cause nearly so serious a problem with PROC MIXED. The basic theory on which PROC MIXED is based holds even with unbalanced and missing data, so long as the missing data are random. In this section the weightlifting data set is modified by randomly deleting strength measurements, each with probability 0.15. This mimics data that would be obtained if each subject failed to show up for the strength measurement at any time with probability 0.15. The resulting data sets are described in section 3.4.1. Then they are analyzed using the three basic methods already discussed in sections 3.2 and 3.3. Subsection 3.4.2 presents the mixed model analysis of repeated measures using PROC MIXED, fitting polynomial models over time as was done in subsection 3.2. Then univariate analysis of variance using PROC GLM is demonstrated is subsection 3.4.3. This is followed by multivariate and univariate analysis of contrasts using PROC GLM, also presented in subsection 3.4.3.

3.4.1 Data Sets with Missing Values

The SAS data set named WTSMISS is shown in Data Set 3.4(a) in Appendix 4. This data set is in the multivariate form and has missing values for the variables S1–S7. Another SAS data set, named WT2MISS, is created with the following statements:

```
data wt2miss; set wtsmiss;
   time=1; t=time; strength=s1; output;
   time=2; t=time; strength=s2; output;
   time=3; t=time; strength=s3; output;
   time=4; t=time; strength=s4; output;
   time=5; t=time; strength=s5; output;
   time=6; t=time; strength=s6; output;
   time=7; t=time; strength=s7; output;
   keep subj program time t strength;
run;


proc sort data=wt2miss; by program time;
run;


data wt2miss; set wt2miss;
   if strength=. then delete;
run;
```

The data set WT2MISS is partially shown in Data Set 3.4(b). It has 347 observations. Notice that WT2MISS is in the univariate form and that observations with missing values have been deleted. Also notice that a variable T is contained in WT2MISS whose values are equal to those of time. A third SAS data set containing means by program and time is shown in Data Set 3.4(c) in Appendix 4, and is plotted in Figure 3.2. It shows trends for the three exercise programs similar to those in the complete data set means plotted in Figure 3.1.

Figure 3.2 *Plot of Strength Means Over Time for Each Program with Missing Values*

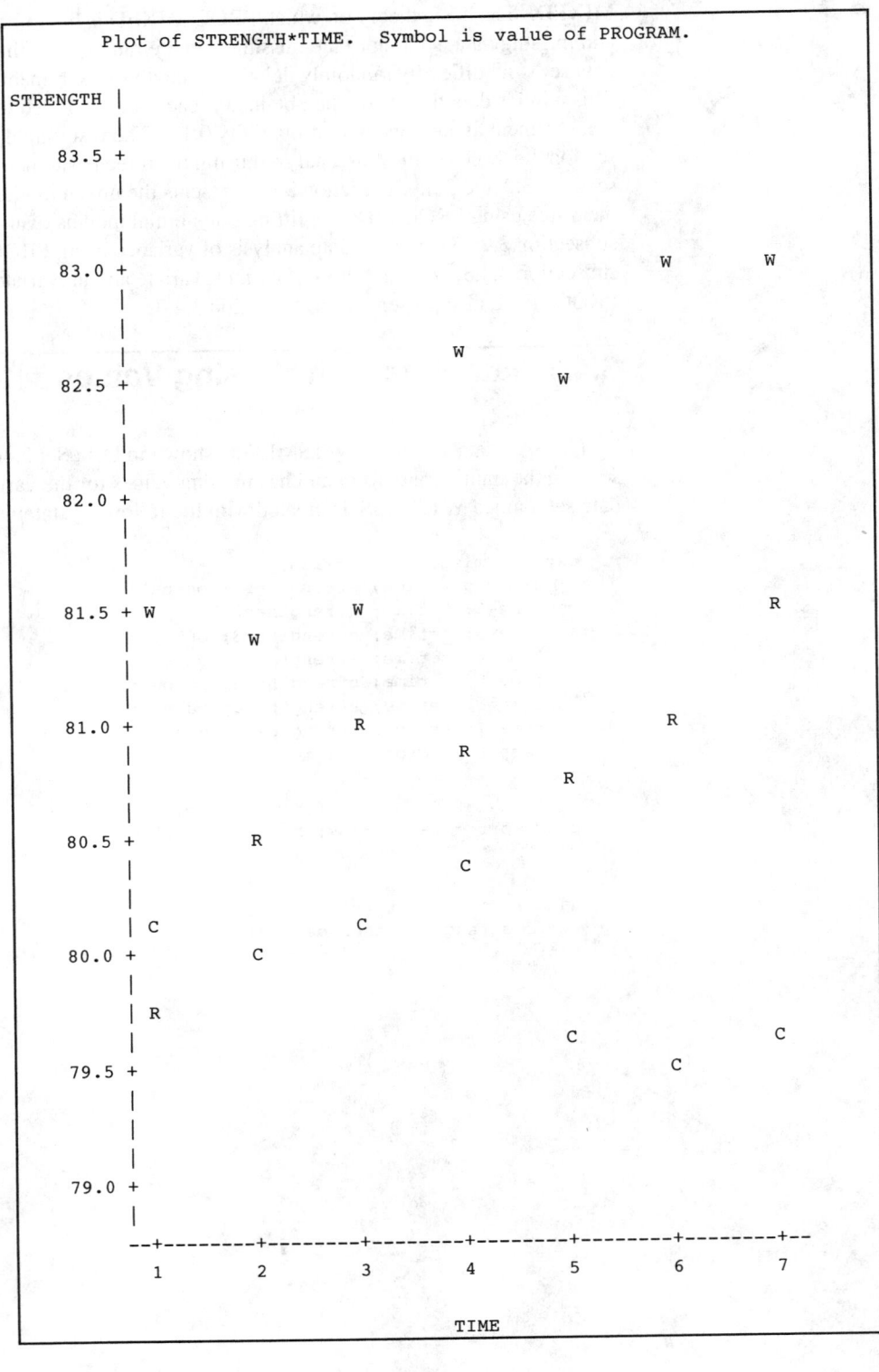

3.4.2 Effects of Missing Data on PROC MIXED

All of the PROC MIXED programs shown in subsections 3.2.1and 3.2.2 can be run directly on the data set WT2MISS, with the modification that the REPEATED statements in subsection 3.2.2 need the additional specification shown in boldface:

```
repeated time / type=covariance type sub=sub(program);
```

The variable named TIME is needed so that PROC MIXED can properly align the observations according to time. This is necessary because of the missing data. A variable in this position in the REPEATED statement must be a CLASS variable. Output from PROC MIXED has the same basic appearance as with complete data.

The final analysis using PROC MIXED in subsection 3.2, shown in Output 3.6, treated TIME as a regression variable. Therefore, TIME cannot be used in the REPEATED statement as shown above. This is the purpose of the variable T in the data set with values identical to TIME. The variable T can be a CLASS variable used in the REPEATED statement, while TIME is used as a regression variable in the MODEL statement.

Program

Following are the statements from subsection 3.2.4 that produced Output 3.6, with the modification using the variable T as discussed in the preceding paragraph:

```
proc mixed data=wt2miss;
   class program subj t;
   model strength=program program*time time*time*program / htype=1 s
         noint;
   repeated t / type=ar(1) sub=subj(program);
run;
```

Results appear in Output 3.9.

Results

Output 3.9 *Repeated Measures with Missing Values Using REPEATED Statement in PROC MIXED with Autoregressive Covariance and Quadratic Model for Time*

```
                    The MIXED Procedure

                 Class Level Information

      Class      Levels  Values

      PROGRAM        3   CONT RI WI
      SUBJ          21   1 2 3 4 5 6 7 8 9 10 11 12 13
                         14 15 16 17 18 19 20 21
      T              7   1 2 3 4 5 6 7
```

```
                    REML Estimation Iteration History

       Iteration  Evaluations     Objective      Criterion

           0           1       1196.6550837
           1           2        542.71993278    0.00000179
           2           1        542.71944619    0.00000000


                     Convergence criteria met.


              Covariance Parameter Estimates (REML)

  Cov Parm        Ratio       Estimate     Std Error      Z  Pr > |Z|


  T AR(1)       0.08824920   0.95079752   0.00907632  104.76  0.0001
  Residual      1.00000000  10.77400773   1.82041089    5.92  0.0001
```

Model Fitting Information for STRENGTH

Description	Value
Observations	347.0000
Variance Estimate	10.7740
Standard Deviation Estimate	3.2824
REML Log Likelihood	-581.961
Akaike's Information Criterion	-583.961
Schwarz's Bayesian Criterion	-587.784
-2 REML Log Likelihood	1163.922
Null Model LRT Chi-Square	653.9356
Null Model LRT DF	1.0000
Null Model LRT P-Value	0.0000

Solution for Fixed Effects

Parameter	Estimate	Std Error	DDF	T	Pr > |T|
PROGRAM CONT	79.53085203	0.82586864	54	96.30	0.0001
PROGRAM RI	78.79901492	0.90175769	54	87.38	0.0001
PROGRAM WI	80.48400056	0.80934658	54	99.44	0.0001
TIME*PROGRAM CONT	0.23305684	0.25760236	284	0.90	0.3664
TIME*PROGRAM RI	0.94112030	0.27660620	284	3.40	0.0008
TIME*PROGRAM WI	0.61612133	0.25574679	284	2.41	0.0166
TIME*TIME*PROGRAM CONT	-0.03189780	0.02937742	284	-1.09	0.2785
TIME*TIME*PROGRAM RI	-0.08690497	0.03223743	284	-2.70	0.0074
TIME*TIME*PROGRAM WI	-0.03622097	0.02954356	284	-1.23	0.2212

Tests of Fixed Effects

Source	NDF	DDF	Type I F	Pr > F
PROGRAM	3	54	12915.94	0.0001
TIME*PROGRAM	3	284	6.38	0.0003
TIME*TIME*PROGRAM	3	284	3.32	0.0204

Interpretation

Parameter estimates, standard errors, and test statistics are not greatly different from those obtained in Output 3.6 using the complete data set. Note that degrees of freedom have changed, as you would expect.

3.4.3 Effect of Missing Data on PROC GLM

This section is not a complete discourse on effects of missing data on PROC GLM output. Instead, it points out the major consequences only.

Effects on Univariate Analysis of Variance

Submit the statements for the univariate analysis of variance:

```
proc glm data=wt2miss;
   class program subj time;
   model strength=program subj(program) time program*time;
   random subj(program);
   test h=program e=subj(program);
run;
```

Results appear in Output 3.10.

Output 3.10 *Univariate Analysis of Variance with Missing Values Using RANDOM Statement in PROC GLM*

```
                    General Linear Models Procedure
                        Class Level Information

Class     Levels    Values

PROGRAM      3      CONT RI WI

SUBJ        21      1 2 3 4 5 6 7 8 9 10 11 12 13 14 15 16 17 18
                    19 20 21

TIME         7      1 2 3 4 5 6 7
                    Number of observations in data set = 399

NOTE: Due to missing values, only 347 observations can be used in
      this analysis.


                    General Linear Models Procedure

Dependent Variable: STRENGTH
                              Sum of        Mean
Source              DF       Squares      Square   F Value    Pr > F

Model               74      3737.6514    50.5088    41.64     0.0001

Error              272       329.9337     1.2130

Corrected Total    346      4067.5850
```

	R-Square	C.V.	Root MSE	STRENGTH Mean
	0.918887	1.360283	1.1014	80.965

Source	DF	Type I SS	Mean Square	F Value	Pr > F
PROGRAM	2	339.2024	169.6012	139.82	0.0001
SUBJ(PROGRAM)	54	3313.7397	61.3656	50.59	0.0001
TIME	6	48.7962	8.1327	6.70	0.0001
PROGRAM*TIME	12	35.9130	2.9927	2.47	0.0045

Source	DF	Type III SS	Mean Square	F Value	Pr > F
PROGRAM	2	362.0847	181.0423	149.25	0.0001
SUBJ(PROGRAM)	54	3302.4058	61.1557	50.42	0.0001
TIME	6	49.3246	8.2208	6.78	0.0001
PROGRAM*TIME	12	35.9130	2.9927	2.47	0.0045

General Linear Models Procedure

Source	Type III Expected Mean Square
PROGRAM	Var(Error) + 5.9445 Var(SUBJ(PROGRAM)) + Q(PROGRAM,PROGRAM*TIME)
SUBJ(PROGRAM)	Var(Error) + 6.037 Var(SUBJ(PROGRAM))
TIME	Var(Error) + Q(TIME,PROGRAM*TIME)
PROGRAM*TIME	Var(Error) + Q(PROGRAM*TIME)

General Linear Models Procedure

Dependent Variable: STRENGTH

Tests of Hypotheses using the Type III MS for
SUBJ(PROGRAM) as an error term

Source	DF	Type III SS	Mean Square	F Value	Pr > F
PROGRAM	2	362.08468	181.04234	2.96	0.0603

First, you see differences between Types I and III sums of squares. Additional differences would be present for Type II sum of squares. Also, you see that coefficients for expected mean squares do not match exactly. Even if covariance structure were not a problem (i.e., the Huynh-Feldt conditions held), the F-test for PROGRAM would not be completely valid.

Effects on Univariate and Multivariate Analysis of Contrasts

Now submit the statements for the analysis of contrasts:

```
proc glm data=wtsmiss;
   class program;
   model s1-s7=program / nouni;
   repeated time polynomial / printe summary;
run;
```

Results appear in Output 3.11.

Output 3.11 *Multivariate and Univariate Analysis of Contrasts with Missing Values Using REPEATED Statement in PROC GLM*

```
                  General Linear Models Procedure
                     Class Level Information

            Class      Levels    Values

            PROGRAM       3       CONT RI WI


          Number of observations in data set = 57


NOTE: Observations with missing values will not be included in this
      analysis.  Thus, only 20 observations can be used in this
      analysis.



                  General Linear Models Procedure
                Repeated Measures Analysis of Variance
                Repeated Measures Level Information

Dependent Variable      S1      S2      S3      S4     S5  S6  S7

    Level of TIME         1       2       3       4      5   6   7



                  General Linear Models Procedure
                Repeated Measures Analysis of Variance


Partial Correlation Coefficients from the Error SS&CP Matrix /
                       Prob > |r|

     DF = 17          S1        S2        S3        S4        S5        S6        S7

     S1            1.000000  0.952049  0.952517  0.935019  0.852760  0.811846  0.834037
                     0.0001    0.0001    0.0001    0.0001    0.0001    0.0001    0.0001

     S2            0.952049  1.000000  0.956936  0.933345  0.876181  0.829448  0.815438
                     0.0001    0.0001    0.0001    0.0001    0.0001    0.0001    0.0001

     S3            0.952517  0.956936  1.000000  0.968350  0.938247  0.894537  0.875122
                     0.0001    0.0001    0.0001    0.0001    0.0001    0.0001    0.0001
```

S4	0.935019	0.933345	0.968350	1.000000	0.961311	0.916592	0.854606
	0.0001	0.0001	0.0001	0.0001	0.0001	0.0001	0.0001
S5	0.852760	0.876181	0.938247	0.961311	1.000000	0.957192	0.885413
	0.0001	0.0001	0.0001	0.0001	0.0001	0.0001	0.0001
S6	0.811846	0.829448	0.894537	0.916592	0.957192	1.000000	0.952671
	0.0001	0.0001	0.0001	0.0001	0.0001	0.0001	0.0001
S7	0.834037	0.815438	0.875122	0.854606	0.885413	0.952671	1.000000
	0.0001	0.0001	0.0001	0.0001	0.0001	0.0001	0.0001

```
                      E = Error SS&CP Matrix

     TIME.N represents the nth degree polynomial contrast for TIME


             TIME.1    TIME.2    TIME.3    TIME.4    TIME.5    TIME.6

TIME.1    72.9878    7.3394  -10.6844   -6.3643   -5.2150    8.0015
TIME.2     7.3394   27.2340    9.0907    0.8750   -4.4224   -2.2894
TIME.3   -10.6844    9.0907   12.2881   -0.8267   -0.9634    0.5031
TIME.4    -6.3643    0.8750   -0.8267    7.0242   -1.5718    0.2220
TIME.5    -5.2150   -4.4224   -0.9634   -1.5718    4.8599   -0.2271
TIME.6     8.0015   -2.2894    0.5031    0.2220   -0.2271    6.7326

                    General Linear Models Procedure
                  Repeated Measures Analysis of Variance


      Partial Correlation Coefficients from the Error SS&CP Matrix
        of the Variables Defined by the Specified Transformation /
                           Prob > |r|


    DF = 17       TIME.1    TIME.2    TIME.3    TIME.4    TIME.5    TIME.6


    TIME.1      1.000000  0.164619 -0.356766 -0.281076 -0.276897  0.360958
                0.0001    0.5139    0.1461    0.2585    0.2660    0.1411


    TIME.2      0.164619  1.000000  0.496935  0.063260 -0.384410 -0.169076
                0.5139    0.0001    0.0359    0.8031    0.1152    0.5024


    TIME.3     -0.356766  0.496935  1.000000 -0.088980 -0.124669  0.055308
                0.1461    0.0359    0.0001    0.7255    0.6221    0.8275


    TIME.4     -0.281076  0.063260 -0.088980  1.000000 -0.269022  0.032282
                0.2585    0.8031    0.7255    0.0001    0.2804    0.8988


    TIME.5     -0.276897 -0.384410 -0.124669 -0.269022  1.000000 -0.039695
                0.2660    0.1152    0.6221    0.2804    0.0001    0.8757


    TIME.6      0.360958 -0.169076  0.055308  0.032282 -0.039695  1.000000
                0.1411    0.5024    0.8275    0.8988    0.8757    0.0001


     Test for Sphericity: Mauchly's Criterion = 0.0074646
       Chisquare Approximation = 72.375323 with 20 df
                Prob > Chisquare = 0.0000
```

```
                    Applied to Orthogonal Components:
            Test for Sphericity: Mauchly's Criterion = 0.0074646
               Chisquare Approximation = 72.375323 with 20 df
                        Prob > Chisquare = 0.0000



                Manova Test Criteria and Exact F Statistics for
                      the Hypothesis of no TIME Effect
          H = Type III SS&CP Matrix for TIME     E = Error SS&CP Matrix


                         S=1     M=2     N=5


Statistic                    Value         F      Num DF   Den DF   Pr > F


Wilks' Lambda             0.2377017     6.4139       6       12     0.0032
Pillai's Trace            0.7622983     6.4139       6       12     0.0032
Hotelling-Lawley Trace    3.2069537     6.4139       6       12     0.0032
Roy's Greatest Root       3.2069537     6.4139       6       12     0.0032

               Manova Test Criteria and F Approximations for
                  the Hypothesis of no TIME*PROGRAM Effect
       H = Type III SS&CP Matrix for TIME*PROGRAM    E = Error SS&CP Matrix


                         S=2     M=1.5     N=5


Statistic                    Value         F      Num DF   Den DF   Pr > F


Wilks' Lambda             0.3858777     1.2196      12       24     0.3259
Pillai's Trace            0.7011196     1.1695      12       26     0.3531
Hotelling-Lawley Trace    1.3660419     1.2522      12       22     0.3117
Roy's Greatest Root       1.1740043     2.5437       6       13     0.0746


      NOTE: F Statistic for Roy's Greatest Root is an upper bound.
           NOTE: F Statistic for Wilks' Lambda is exact.


                      General Linear Models Procedure
                    Repeated Measures Analysis of Variance
                 Tests of Hypotheses for Between Subjects Effects


Source            DF    Type III SS   Mean Square   F Value     Pr > F


PROGRAM            2       134.080       67.040       0.87       0.4373


Error             17      1311.770       77.163
```

General Linear Models Procedure
Repeated Measures Analysis of Variance
Univariate Tests of Hypotheses for Within Subject Effects

Source: TIME

					Adj Pr > F	
DF	Type III SS	Mean Square	F Value	Pr > F	G - G	H - F
6	22.947624	3.824604	2.98	0.0102	0.0533	0.0374

Source: TIME*PROGRAM

					Adj Pr > F	
DF	Type III SS	Mean Square	F Value	Pr > F	G - G	H - F
12	19.373469	1.614456	1.26	0.2566	0.3018	0.2923

Source: Error(TIME)

DF	Type III SS	Mean Square
102	131.126531	1.285554

Greenhouse-Geisser Epsilon = 0.4001
Huynh-Feldt Epsilon = 0.5252
General Linear Models Procedure
Repeated Measures Analysis of Variance
Analysis of Variance of Contrast Variables

TIME.N represents the nth degree polynomial contrast for TIME

Contrast Variable: TIME.1

Source	DF	Type III SS	Mean Square	F Value	Pr > F
MEAN	1	15.7036298	15.7036298	3.66	0.0728
PROGRAM	2	14.0051020	7.0025510	1.63	0.2249
Error	17	72.9877551	4.2933974		

Contrast Variable: TIME.2

Source	DF	Type III SS	Mean Square	F Value	Pr > F
MEAN	1	4.94664797	4.94664797	3.09	0.0969
PROGRAM	2	0.06122449	0.03061224	0.02	0.9811
Error	17	27.23401361	1.60200080		

```
Contrast Variable: TIME.3

Source              DF    Type III SS   Mean Square   F Value    Pr > F

MEAN                1     0.54396583    0.54396583     0.75      0.3978
PROGRAM             2     0.20357143    0.10178571     0.14      0.8697

Error              17    12.28809524    0.72282913

Contrast Variable: TIME.4

Source              DF    Type III SS   Mean Square   F Value    Pr > F

MEAN                1     1.20965387    1.20965387     2.93      0.1053
PROGRAM             2     3.46767161    1.73383581     4.20      0.0330

Error              17     7.02421150    0.41318891

Contrast Variable: TIME.5

Source              DF    Type III SS   Mean Square   F Value    Pr > F

MEAN                1     0.02127019    0.02127019     0.07      0.7883
PROGRAM             2     1.53061224    0.76530612     2.68      0.0976

Error              17     4.85986395    0.28587435

Contrast Variable: TIME.6

Source              DF    Type III SS   Mean Square   F Value    Pr > F

MEAN                1     0.52245653    0.52245653     1.32      0.2666
PROGRAM             2     0.10528757    0.05264378     0.13      0.8764

Error              17     6.73259122    0.39603478
```

The consequences of missing data on this approach using PROC GLM are easy to describe. All subjects that have any missing data are simply deleted, and the analysis is performed on the remaining subjects. In the present case, each measurement had a 0.15 chance of being deleted, so the chance of an entire observation having no missing data is $.85^7$ = 0.32. Consequently, only 20 of the original 57 multivariate observations are used in this analysis. Other than that, results would be interpreted as described in section 3.3.2. This type of analysis is basically wiped out because so much data are not usable. Note that very few effects are significant. This is due to low power in the tests as a consequence of deleting so much data.

3.5 Example: Unequally Spaced Repeated Measures

In the longitudinal data setting, in which repeated measures on subjects occur over time, it is often the case that the measurements are made on time intervals which are not equal. For example, consider the heart rate profiles in Figure 3.3, which are generated by the following SAS program. See Data Set 3.5, "HR," in Appendix 4, "SAS Data Sets," for the complete data set.

```
data hr;
    input patient drug$ basehr hr1 hr5 hr15 hr30 hr1h;
    array hra{5} hr1 hr5 hr15 hr30 hr1h;
    do i = 1 to 5;
    if (i = 1) then hours = 1/60;
    else if (i = 2) then hours = 5/60;
    else if (i = 3) then hours = 15/60;
        else if (i = 4) then hours = 30/60;
        else hours = 1;
        hours1 = hours;
        hr = hra{i};
        output;
    end;
    drop i hr1 hr5 hr15 hr30 hr1h;
    datalines;
...datalines...
run;

symbol i=join r=24 c=black;
proc gplot data=hr;
    plot hr*hours=patient / nolegend vminor=1 hminor=0;
run;
```

Figure 3.3: *Unequally Spaced Repeated Heart Rate Measurements for 24 Patients*

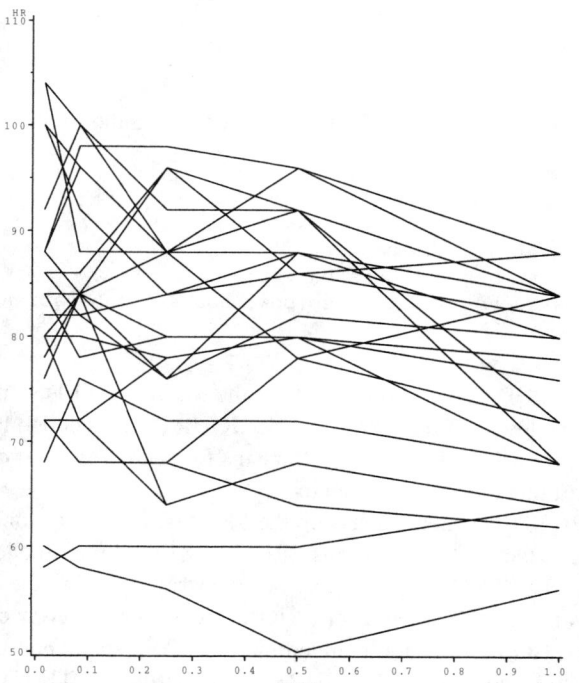

These data, from the pharmaceutical industry, consist of repeated measurements on the heart rates of 24 patients at 5 unequally spaced time intervals: 1 minute, 5 minutes, 15 minutes, 30 minutes, and 1 hour. Each patient is subjected to one of three possible drug treatment levels: a, b, and p, the last being a placebo.

Model

For data of this sort, it is sensible to consider some kind of time-series covariance structure, where the correlations of the repeated measurements are assumed to be smaller for observations that are further apart in time. However, many of the time series covariance structures available in PROC MIXED are inappropriate because they assume equal spacing. The structures that are inappropriate include AR(1), TOEP, and ARMA(1,1). The CS and UN structures are still appropriate; however, CS assumes that the correlations remain constant, and UN is often too general. Another model that may be appropriate is the random coefficient model discussed in Chapter 7. This section focuses on appropriate time-series structures.

To fit a time-series type covariance structure in which the correlations decline as a function of time, you can use any one of the spatial structures available in PROC MIXED. The most common of these are SP(POW) (spatial power law), SP(GAU) (Gaussian), and SP(SPH) (spherical). Chapter 9 discusses the use of these structures for spatial data; however, they are also useful for unequally spaced longitudinal measurements. The connection is that the unequally spaced data can be viewed as a spatial process in one dimension.

The SP(POW) structure for unequally spaced data provides a direct generalization of the AR(1) structure for equally spaced data. SP(POW) models the covariance between two measurements at times T1 and T2 as

$$cov(y_{t1}, y_{t2}) = \sigma^2 \rho^{|t1 - t2|}$$

where ρ is an autoregressive parameter assumed to satisfy $|\rho| < 1$ and σ^2 is an overall variance.

Program

You can fit this structure to the heart rate data with the following PROC MIXED program:

```
proc mixed data=hr order=data;
   class drug hours patient;
   model hr = drug|hours basehr;
   repeated hours / type=sp(pow)(hours1) sub=patient r rcorr;
run;
```

The ORDER=DATA option is used on the PROC MIXED statement to preserve the ordering of the levels of the class variable HOUR (time is coded here in hours). The fixed effects model consists of different cell means for each drug-hour combination, and the baseline heart rate is included as a covariate.

The REPEATED statement sets up the SP(POW) structure for each patient. The REPEATED effect HOURS informs PROC MIXED of the time level of the current observation. The TYPE= option specifies the structure using the continuous variable HOURS1 to indicate the time levels. HOURS1 is an exact copy of HOURS in the HR data set; however, HOURS1 is not included in the CLASS statement, and so PROC MIXED considers it to be continous. The SUB= option defines PATIENTS to be a blocking factor where data from different blocks are assumed to be independent. The R option requests the printout of the covariance matrix corresponding to the first level of PATIENT, and RCORR prints this matrix in correlation form.

The output from this code is shown in Output 3.12.

Results

Output 3.12 *Results for Unequally Spaced Model*

```
                    The MIXED Procedure

                 Class Level Information

      Class      Levels   Values

      DRUG            3    p b a
      HOURS           5    0.0166666667 0.0833333333
                           0.25 0.5 1
      PATIENT        24    201 202 203 204 205 206 207
                           208 209 210 211 212 214 215
                           216 217 218 219 220 221 222
                           223 224 232



            REML Estimation Iteration History

     Iteration  Evaluations     Objective       Criterion

             0            1   591.78708631
             1            2   543.71656066    0.00000000

            Convergence criteria met.
```

```
                        R Matrix for PATIENT 201

Row        COL1            COL2            COL3            COL4            COL5

1     75.91872308     64.99917860     44.08646758     24.62642973      7.68411323
2     64.99917860     75.91872308     51.49277878     28.76354962      8.97500671
3     44.08646758     51.49277878     75.91872308     42.40773193     13.23236122
4     24.62642973     28.76354962     42.40773193     75.91872308     23.68869831
5      7.68411323      8.97500671     13.23236122     23.68869831     75.91872308


                    R Correlation Matrix for PATIENT 201

Row        COL1            COL2            COL3            COL4            COL5

1      1.00000000      0.85616796      0.58070613      0.32437887      0.10121500
2      0.85616796      1.00000000      0.67826192      0.37887294      0.11821862
3      0.58070613      0.67826192      1.00000000      0.55859385      0.17429641
4      0.32437887      0.37887294      0.55859385      1.00000000      0.31202709
5      0.10121500      0.11821862      0.17429641      0.31202709      1.00000000


                   Covariance Parameter Estimates (REML)

Cov Parm              Ratio      Estimate      Std Error      Z    Pr > |Z|

HOURS SP(POW)      0.00128244    0.09736091    0.05788161    1.68    0.0926
Residual           1.00000000   75.91872308   13.88855692    5.47    0.0001
```

Model Fitting Information for HR

Description	Value
Observations	120.0000
Variance Estimate	75.9187
Standard Deviation Estimate	8.7131
REML Log Likelihood	−367.428
Akaike's Information Criterion	−369.428
Schwarz's Bayesian Criterion	−372.072
−2 REML Log Likelihood	734.8558
Null Model LRT Chi-Square	48.0705
Null Model LRT DF	1.0000
Null Model LRT P-Value	0.0000

Tests of Fixed Effects

Source	NDF	DDF	Type III F	Pr > F
DRUG	2	20	1.84	0.1848
HOURS	4	84	3.15	0.0182
DRUG*HOURS	8	84	1.07	0.3914
BASEHR	1	20	30.24	0.0001

Interpretation

The "Class Level Information" table shows the 3 levels of DRUG, the 5 levels of HOURS (in the order that they appeared in the data), and the 24 levels of PATIENT.

The REML fit of the model requires only 1 iteration and 3 likelihood evaluations.

The R Matrix table reveals the estimate of σ^2 to be 75.9. Note how the covariances are much smaller for time points that are further apart. The correlations in the "R Correlation Matrix" table reveal the same decline.

The estimate of ρ for this example is 0.097, as shown in the "Covariance Parameter Estimates" table. The scale of this estimate depends upon the scale selected for the HOURS1 variable; however, the fixed-effects estimates and their standard errors are scale invariant.

The "Model Fitting Information" table displays several restricted likelihood-based statistics that can be useful in comparing this covariance structures with other ones, e.g., CS and UN.

Finally, the "Tests of Fixed Effects" table reveals that the drug had little effect, that there is evidence of change over time, and that the baseline heart rate is highly associated with subsequent heart rate measurements. All of the tests in this table are based on the SP(POW) covariance model and can be regarded as adequately accounting for the unequally spaced measurements.

3.6 Example: Doubly Repeated Measures

All of the previous sections consider repeated measures that occur in one dimension, typically time. A more complicated data structure is one where repeated measures occur in two dimensions, a case referred to as **doubly repeated measures**. For example, consider the econometric data set from Example 18.1 of the PROC TSCSREG documentation in the *SAS/ETS User's Guide* (SAS Institute Inc., 1993). See Data Set 3.6, "DEMAND," in Appendix 4, "SAS Data Sets," for the complete data set.

```
data demand;
    input state$ year d y rd rt rs;
    logd = log(d);
    logy = log(y);
    logrd = log(rd);
    logrt = log(rt);
    logrs = log(rs);
    datalines;
...datalines...
run;
```

The dependent variable is *D*, measuring per capita demand deposits. *D* is measured for each of seven states over eleven years, as are four explanatory variables: *Y* (permanent per capita personal income), *RD* (service charge on demand deposits), *RT* (interest on time deposits), and *RS* (interest on savings and loan association share). The logarithm of *D* is plotted in Figure 3.4.

Figure 3.4: *Doubly Repeated Measures on 7 States and 11 Years*

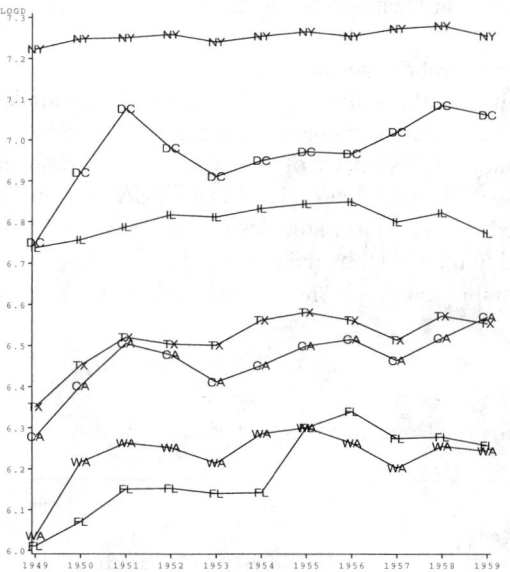

Model

The two dimensions for the doubly repeated measures in this case are represented by the STATE and YEAR variables. Data with this structure are also known as **time-series cross-sectional** or **panel** data. It is likely that observations from the same state are correlated, and it is also likely that observations from the same year are correlated. A reasonable econometric model that accounts for these correlations, as well as the possible dependence of D on the explanatory variables, is the following:

$$D_{it} = \mu Y_{it}^{\beta_Y}(RD)_{it}^{\beta_{RD}}(RT)_{it}^{\beta_{RT}}(RS)_{it}^{\beta_{RS}}\exp(v_i + e_t + \epsilon_{it})$$

Here i indexes states ($i = 1,\dots,7$) and t indexes years ($t = 1,\dots,11$). The unknown mean parameters are μ, $\beta_1, \beta_{RD}, \beta_{RT}$, and β_{RS}. The variance-covariance model involves v_i, e_t, and ϵ_{it}, which are assumed to be independent zero-mean normal random variables with unknown variances σ_v^2, σ_e^2, and σ_ϵ^2, respectively.

Even though the previous model is multiplicative, it can be transformed into a standard linear mixed model by taking the natural logarithm of both sides:

$$\log D_{it} = \beta_\mu + \beta_Y \log Y_{it} + \beta_{RD}\log(RD)_{it} + \beta_{RT}\log(RT)_{it} + \beta_{RS}\log(RS)_{it} + v_i + e_t + \epsilon_{it}$$

where $\beta_\mu = \log\mu$. This is a random effects model in which the random effects for state (v_i) and year (e_t) are crossed (Fuller and Battese, 1974).

Program

By using the log-transformed variables created in the previous DATA step, this model can be fit with PROC MIXED using the following program:

```
proc mixed data=demand;
   class state year;
   model logd = logy logrd logrt logrs / s;
   random state year;
run;
```

The CLASS statement creates dummy variables corresponding to the levels of STATE and YEAR.

The MODEL statement defines the dependent variable LOGD as a linear function of an implicitly defined intercept and the four independent regression variables LOGY, LOGRD, LOGRT, LOGRS, just as in the model equation above. The S (or SOLUTION) option requests the printout of the estimates of the mean model parameters, that is, the βs.

The RANDOM statement defines STATE and YEAR as random effects, and the dummy variables associated with them form the design matrix columns for v_i and e_t. The residual error e_{it} is included in the model by default.

The output from this analysis is shown in Output 3.13.

Results

Output 3.13 *Results for Doubly Repeated Demand Data*

```
                      The MIXED Procedure

                 Class Level Information

      Class     Levels  Values

      STATE          7  CA DC FL IL NY TX WA
      YEAR          11  1949 1950 1951 1952 1953 1954
                        1955 1956 1957 1958 1959


              REML Estimation Iteration History

     Iteration Evaluations      Objective       Criterion

             0          1   -215.1746736
             1          4   -233.0107464     0.22006779
             2          1   -267.9717598     0.15904661
             3          1   -296.8510993     0.11208075
             4          1   -319.2807546          .
             5          1   -337.0174505     0.05627078
             6          1   -349.7215967     0.03812885
             7          1   -358.6412782     0.02551634
             8          1   -364.7357435     0.01625970
             9          1   -368.6518510     0.00941044
            10          1   -370.9118508     0.00464215
            11          1   -372.0093235     0.00173742
            12          1   -372.4057479     0.00038102
            13          1   -372.4870650     0.00002714
            14          1   -372.4923740     0.00000018
            15          1   -372.4924069     0.00000000


                 Convergence criteria met.


           Covariance Parameter Estimates (REML)

   Cov Parm         Ratio      Estimate      Std Error      Z    Pr > |Z|

   STATE      26.41447173    0.02950458    0.01838350    1.60     0.1085
   YEAR        0.23693947    0.00026466    0.00021349    1.24     0.2151
   Residual    1.00000000    0.00111699    0.00021089    5.30     0.0001
```

```
              Model Fitting Information for LOGD


         Description                        Value


         Observations                       77.0000
         Variance Estimate                   0.0011
         Standard Deviation Estimate         0.0334
         REML Log Likelihood               120.0826
         Akaike's Information Criterion    117.0826
         Schwarz's Bayesian Criterion      113.6676
         -2 REML Log Likelihood           -240.165



                   Solution for Fixed Effects


    Parameter       Estimate      Std Error    DDF        T   Pr > |T|


    INTERCEPT     -1.28382915     0.72343405     6    -1.77    0.1263
    LOGY           1.06977958     0.10392545    56    10.29    0.0001
    LOGRD         -0.29532614     0.05246348    56    -5.63    0.0001
    LOGRT          0.03988053     0.02788861    56     1.43    0.1583
    LOGRS         -0.32673445     0.11438325    56    -2.86    0.0060



                    Tests of Fixed Effects


         Source       NDF    DDF   Type III F   Pr > F


         LOGY          1      56      105.96    0.0001
         LOGRD         1      56       31.69    0.0001
         LOGRT         1      56        2.04    0.1583
         LOGRS         1      56        8.16    0.0060
```

Interpretation

The "Class Levels Information" table reveals the correct levels for STATE and YEAR.

The REML algorithm requires 15 iterations to achieve convergence for this problem. The missing Criterion value in the fourth iteration is due to a constraint being dropped; evidently, one of the variance components is set to zero prior to this iteration, and then its value becomes positive.

The "Covariance Parameter Estimates" table prints the REML estimates $\hat{\sigma}_v^2 = 0.02950, \hat{\sigma}_e^2 = 0.00026,$ and $\hat{\sigma}_\epsilon^2 = 0.00112.$ For the mean parameters, $\hat{\beta}_\mu = -1.28, \hat{\beta}_Y = 1.07, \hat{\beta}_{RD} = -0.30, \hat{\beta}_{RS} = -0.33,$ with $\hat{\beta}_Y, \hat{\beta}_{RD},$ and $\hat{\beta}_{RS}$ significantly different from zero. All of these estimates are similar to the method-of-moments estimates computed by PROC TSCSREG in Example 18.1 of the *SAS/ETS User's Guide* (SAS Institute Inc. 1993).

In this example the dependent variable D remained quantitatively the same in both dimensions of the doubly repeated measures setup. This permitted the use of a single parameter to model the overall mean of the data and standard variance components to account for the covariance of measurements common in one dimension or the other.

A different type of doubly repeated measures is **multivariate repeated measures**, in which measurements are made on two or more different characteristics of a subject at different time intervals. For example, children's height and weight can be measured successively over several years. Here the characteristics, height and weight, are quantitatively different, and because the characteristics are multivariate in nature, a reasonable model should include distinct means and variances for each of the characteristics.

One reasonable choice for the covariance structure of multivariate repeated measures data involves a Kronecker product of an unstructured covariance matrix (to account for the covariance among characteristics) with some time-series covariance matrix (to account for the covariance across time). Refer to Galecki (1994) for a recent discussion. Similar structures can be fit to balanced data using PROC TSCSREG (Parks method) and PROC GLM (refer to Example 9 in the PROC GLM documentation). These structures are currently under development for PROC MIXED, and when available will provide models appropriate for data sets with missing values.

3.7 Summary

Repeated measures data need mixed models because of correlations between measurements on the same subject. Modelling the covariance structure is a preliminary step in the analysis of repeated measures data using mixed model methodology. The MIXED procedure has several covariance structures available for valid estimation of covariance in the data. An example from exercise therapy uses autoregressive (order 1) structure. Results from PROC MIXED and PROC GLM are compared.

Missing data can have a devastating effect on multivariate methods of repeated measures analysis because subjects with incomplete data are discarded. Mixed model methodology using PROC MIXED does not require complete data. The exercise therapy example data with some values randomly deleted are used for illustration.

Autoregressive covariance estimation with the AR(1) option requires equally spaced observations. But unequally spaced data with autoregressive correlation can be analyzed using spatial covariance options.

The final two sections of this chapter consider two special types of repeated measures: those which are unequally spaced and those which are repeated in more than one dimension. The models discussed for handling the former type involves generalizations of common time series structures such as AR(1) to handle the unequal spacing. The model for the latter type involves separate variance components for each dimension.

3.8 References

Fuller, W.A. and Battese, G.E. (1974), Estimation of linear models with crossed-error structure, *Journal of Econometrics*, **2**, 67-78.

Galecki, A.T. (1994), General class of covariance structures for two or more repeated factors in longitudinal data analysis, *Communications in Statistics–Theory and Methods*, **23(11)**, 3105–3119.

Littell, R.C., Freund, R.J., and Spector, P.C. (1991), *SAS System for Linear Models*, *Third Edition*, Cary, NC: SAS Institute Inc.

SAS Institute Inc. (1990), *SAS/STAT User's Guide, Version 6, Fourth Edition*, Volume 2, Cary, NC: SAS Institute Inc.

SAS Institute Inc. (1993), *SAS/ETS User's Guide, Version 6, Second Edition*, Cary, NC: SAS Institute Inc.

Chapter 4 **Random Effects Models**

4.1 Introduction: Descriptions of Random-Effects Models

Random effects models are linear models where all of the effects in the models are random variables. Random effects models are used in studies and experiments where the levels of the effects have been selected at random from a population of possible levels and you want to obtain information about the parameters of the distribution of those levels. The main goals of the analysis of random effects models are to

- estimate the parameters of the covariance structure of the random effects model
- test hypotheses about the parameters or functions of the parameters
- construct confidence intervals about the parameters or functions of the parameters.

This chapter presents methods available in PROC MIXED for estimating parameters of random effects models. This chapter also compares the information available from PROC GLM and PROC VARCOMP to that which can be obtained from PROC MIXED. Procedures for **testing hypotheses** and for constructing **confidence intervals** are presented for some simple models. Extensions of the procedures are used for some of the complex examples described in the final sections of the chapter.

The random effects model where the levels of the random effects and/or the experimental units form a **nested hierarchical** structure is also called the **unconditional hierarchical linear model** as defined by Bryk and Raudenbush (1992). **Conditional hierarchical linear models** are linear models that attempt to describe part of the variance between the levels of a random effect by either classifying the levels of a random effect into categories or by using continuous variables in the analysis of covariance context. These categorical variables are considered to be fixed effects, and the covariance part of the model is considered to be a fixed effect. Thus conditional hierarchical linear models are a form of mixed model. We describe several conditional hierarchical linear models in this chapter while additional models are discussed in other chapters.

Random effects models are applied to experiments where all of the factors in the treatment structure of the experimental design or study are random effects. All of the factors in the design structure are always considered as random effects (see Chapter 4 of Milliken and Johnson (1994) for discussions of design and treatment structures). A factor is called a **random effect** if the levels of that factor selected to be included in the study or experiment are randomly selected from a population of possible levels of that factor.

Suppose you are studying the source of nitrogen contamination in the Mississippi River at New Orleans, LA. You could go out and obtain water samples from every source of influent that eventually reaches the Mississippi River. There are hundreds of influents into the river, and it would be very expensive and time consuming to sample every one of them (also, you most likely would want to sample them over time). Another strategy would be to identify all of the influents into the river (specify the population of influents) and then randomly select, say, 100 of the influents to be actually measured. In this case, we are going to assume the concentration of nitrogen in the water from each influent in the population forms a distribution of nitrogen levels with mean μ_N and variance σ^2_N. By randomly selecting influents to be sampled, we use the sample mean and variance to provide estimates of the population parameters. A model to describe the observed nitrogen concentration from the ith sample is

$$y_i = \mu_N + a_i, \ i=1,2,...,s, \ \text{where} \ a_i \sim \text{iid N}(0, \sigma^2_N) \tag{4.1}$$

Model 4.1 is that of a single sample of size s obtained from a population with parameters μ_N and σ^2_N. This is the type of data set you may have encountered in your first course in statistical methods, but it most likely was not represented as a model. In reality, model 4.1 is a mixed model where μ_N is the fixed effects part of the model and a_i is the random effects part of the model. In this case, μ_N is the intercept or overall mean of the model. The estimates of the parameters can be obtained from PROC MIXED using the statements

```
proc mixed;
    model y=/solution;
run;
```

The above MODEL statement includes an intercept (unless you specify the NOINT option on the MODEL statement, which you would not want to do for this case) that provides the estimate of μ_N. The estimate of σ^2_N is computed from the residuals of the model, which are the deviations of the observations from the estimate of μ_N. (Using PROC MIXED in this context is like using a sledge hammer to drive a carpet tack, but the chapter uses this example to begin the introduction to using PROC MIXED for random effects models.) The normality assumption is made to provide a distributional basis for testing hypotheses and for constructing confidence intervals about the parameters of the model. The **Best Linear Unbiased Estimate** (BLUE) of μ_N is $\bar{y}.$, which has sampling distribution $\bar{y}. \sim N\left(\mu_N, \ \sigma^2_N / s\right)$. The **Best Quadratic Unbiased Estimate** of σ^2_N is

$$\hat{\sigma}^2_N = \sum_{i=1}^{s} \left(y_i - \bar{y}.\right)^2 / (s - 1)$$

The sampling distribution associated with $\hat{\sigma}^2_N$ is $(s - 1)\hat{\sigma}^2_N / \sigma^2_N \sim \chi^2_{(s-1)}$. Tests of hypotheses and confidence intervals are computed as described in any elementary or basic text on statistics. We include the **confidence intervals** for completeness. A $(1-\alpha)100\%$ confidence interval about μ_N is $\bar{y}. \pm (t_{\alpha/2,(s-1)})\hat{\sigma}_N / \sqrt{s}$. A $(1-\alpha)100\%$ confidence interval about σ^2_N is

$$\frac{(s - 1)\hat{\sigma}^2_N}{\chi^2_{\alpha/2,\,(s-1)}} < \sigma^2_N < \frac{(s - 1)\hat{\sigma}^2_N}{\chi^2_{1-\alpha/2,\,(s-1)}}$$

In our scenario, most likely the environmentalist typically wants to obtain information from multiple sites from each selected influent. In this case suppose that n_i sites were randomly selected from the population of possible sites within each randomly selected influent. The number of sites could vary from influent to influent, possibly depending on the size of the influent as there may be a desire to select the same proportion of the possible sites from each selected influent. Let y_{ij} denote the nitrogen concentration observed from the water sample taken from the jth site at the ith influent. A model to describe the collection of measurements is

$$y_{ij} = \mu_N + a_i + e_{ij} \, , \quad i=1,2,...,s, \ j=1,2,...,n_i \qquad (4.2)$$

where
$$a_i \sim \text{iid } N(0, \ \sigma^2_N)$$
$$e_{ij} \sim \text{iid } N(0, \ \sigma^2_e)$$

Model 4.2 has two variance component parameters to be estimated. The variance component σ^2_N measures the influent-to-influent variability as in Model 4.1. The variance component σ^2_e measures the site-to-site variability. Model 4.2 is a mixed effects model where μ_N is the **fixed effects part** of the model and $a_i + e_{ij}$ is the **random effects part** of the model. Model 4.2 is also called a **two level hierarchical linear model** (Bryk and Raudenbush (1992)) because the sampled sites are nested within each influent. The PROC MIXED program needed to fit model 4.2 is

```
proc mixed;
    class influent;
    model y=;
    random influent;
run;
```

Model 4.2 is the usual one-way treatment structure random-effects model where the levels of the treatment are the randomly selected influents. If you used the usual analysis of variance to compute sums of squares and evaluated their expected means squares, you would obtain the results displayed in Table 4.1. The information in Table 4.1 can be obtained by using PROC GLM to analyze the data. The PROC GLM program required to produce the results in Table 4.1 are

```
proc glm;
    class influent;
    model y=influent;
    random influent/test;
run;
```

By including the TEST option for the RANDOM statement, PROC GLM uses the expected mean squares to determine the appropriate divisor to compute F-statistics for each term in the model.

Table 4.1 *Analysis of Variance Table for a One-Way Random Effects Treatment Structure*

SOURCE	DF	Sum of Squares	Expected Mean Squares
Influents	$s - 1$	$\sum\limits_{i=1}^{s} n_i(\bar{y}_{i\bullet} - \bar{y}_{\bullet\bullet})^2$	$\sigma_e^2 + C\,\sigma_a^2$
Sites (Influents)	$\sum\limits_{i=1}^{s}(n_i - 1) = n_{\bullet} - s$	$\sum\limits_{i=1}^{s}\sum\limits_{j=1}^{n_i}(y_{ij} - \bar{y}_{i\bullet})^2$	σ_e^2

The coefficient C is computed as

$$C = \frac{n_{\bullet} - \dfrac{\sum\limits_{i=1}^{s} n_i^2}{n_{\bullet}}}{s - 1}$$

(See Chapter 18 of Milliken and Johnson (1994)). **Method of moments** estimators of the variance components are obtained by equating the observed mean squares to the expected mean squares where the variances are replaced with estimators. The **method of moments equations** are

$$MSI = \frac{\sum\limits_{i=1}^{t} n_i(\bar{y}_{i\bullet} - \bar{y}_{\bullet\bullet})^2}{s - 1} = \hat{\sigma}_e^2 + C\,\hat{\sigma}_a^2$$

$$MSsite(I) = \frac{\sum\limits_{i=1}^{s}\sum\limits_{j=1}^{n_i}(y_{ij} - \bar{y}_{i\bullet})^2}{n_{\bullet} - s} = \hat{\sigma}_e^2$$

(4.3)

The **method of moment estimators** are

$$\hat{\sigma}_a^2 = \frac{MSI - MSsite(I)}{C}$$

$$\hat{\sigma}_e^2 = MSsite(I)$$

(4.4)

4.1.1 Using PROC MIXED to Estimate the Variance Components

PROC MIXED obtains three types of estimators of the variance components. **Restricted maximum likelihood (REML)** estimators and **maximum likelihood (ML)** estimators are based on the normality assumptions stated in model 4.2. The third procedure is **MIVQUE(0)**, which provides estimates that are a form of method of moments estimator. For REML and ML estimates, PROC MIXED provides estimates of the standard errors of the estimates of the variance components that are computed from the inverse of the estimated information matrix. The z-score computed as the ratio of the estimator to the corresponding estimate of the standard error is available to be used as a test of the hypothesis H_0: $\sigma^2_a = 0$ vs H_a: $\sigma^2_a > 0$. The z-score is valid only when the sampling distribution of $\hat{\sigma}^2_a$ can be approximated by a normal distribution. As discussed above, this approximation is not appropriate when the number of levels of the random treatment, in this case number of influents, is small. When the number of levels is large, the z-score can be used to test H_0: $\sigma^2_a = 0$ vs H_a $\sigma^2_a > 0$, where the significance level needs to be divided by 2 (the alternative hypothesis is one sided).

If you are trying to decide which of the sets of estimators is better, you can use the value of –2 REML Log Likelihood as a guide. Generally, the smaller the value the better the set of estimates. For a given covariance structure, the value of –2 REML Log Likelihood is smallest for the REML estimates (the REML estimates are selected to minimize –2 REML Log Likelihood), but you can use its value to determine if estimators obtained using one of the other methods are as good as the REML estimators. The –2 REML Log Likelihood value is obtained by evaluating the likelihood at the selected estimators. If you want to compare two models for which the random effects of one model are a subset of the random effects of the other, you can formally test the additional parameters are equal to zero with a likelihood ratio test defined on the respective –2 REML Log Likelihoods of the two models. This is discussed in Appendix 1 and an example is presented in Chapter 2.

4.1.2 The Mixed Model Equations

The fixed effects part of model 4.2 is μ_N and is estimated by obtaining a solution to the mixed models equations. To review, the general mixed model can be expressed as

$$\mathbf{y} = \mathbf{X}\boldsymbol{\beta} + \mathbf{Zu} + \mathbf{e}$$

where

> $\mathbf{y}$ is the data vector
> $\boldsymbol{\beta}$ is the vector of corresponding to the fixed effects
> $\mathbf{X}$ is the design matrix for the fixed effects
> $\mathbf{u}$ is the vector coefficients corresponding to the random effects
> $\mathbf{Z}$ is the design matrix for the random effects part of the model
> $\mathbf{e}$ is the error vector.

In this chapter it is assumed that $\mathbf{u}$ and $\mathbf{e}$ are uncorrelated random variables with zero means and covariance matrices $\mathbf{G}$ and $\mathbf{R}$ respectively; thus, the covariance matrix of the data vector is $\mathbf{V} = \mathbf{ZGZ'} + \mathbf{R}$. (See Chapter 6 for more details). The solution of the mixed model equations for $\boldsymbol{\beta}$ and $\mathbf{u}$ are

$$\hat{\boldsymbol{\beta}} = \left(\mathbf{X}'\hat{\mathbf{V}}^{-1}\mathbf{X}\right)^{-1}\mathbf{X}'\hat{\mathbf{V}}^{-1}\mathbf{y}$$
$$\hat{\mathbf{u}} = \hat{\mathbf{G}}\mathbf{Z}'\hat{\mathbf{V}}^{-1}(\mathbf{y} - \mathbf{X}\hat{\boldsymbol{\beta}})$$

In PROC MIXED, requesting the SOLUTION option on the MODEL statement provides the value of $\hat{\boldsymbol{\beta}}$ and requesting the SOLUTION option on the RANDOM statement provides the value of $\hat{\mathbf{u}}$. Estimates of estimable linear combinations of $\boldsymbol{\beta}$ added to linear combinations of $\mathbf{u}$ provide predicted values of predictable functions. For model 4.2, the above matrices are $\boldsymbol{\beta} = \mu_N$, $\mathbf{X} = \mathbf{j}_s \otimes \mathbf{j}_{ni}$, $\mathbf{u} = \mathbf{a}$, $\mathbf{Z} = \mathbf{I}_s \otimes \mathbf{j}_{ni}$, $\mathbf{G} = \sigma^2_a \mathbf{I}_s$, $\mathbf{R} = \sigma^2_e \mathbf{I}_n$, and $\mathbf{e}$ is the random error. The notation $\mathbf{A} \otimes \mathbf{B}$ denotes the *right* direct product of matrices $\mathbf{A}$ and $\mathbf{B}$, $\mathbf{I}_t$ denotes a $t \times t$ identity matrix, and $\mathbf{j}_n$ denotes a $n \times 1$ vector of ones.

4.1.3 Method of Moments Estimators Using the VARCOMP Procedure

The solution to the method of moments of equations can be obtained by analyzing the data with PROC VARCOMP using the following program:

```
proc varcomp;
   class influent;
   model y=influent;
run;
```

A $(1-\alpha)100\%$ confidence interval about σ^2_e is

$$\frac{(n_\bullet - s)\hat{\sigma}^2_e}{\chi^2_{\alpha/2,\,(n_\bullet - t)}} < \sigma^2_e < \frac{(n_\bullet - s)\hat{\sigma}^2_e}{\chi^2_{1 - \alpha/2,\,(n_\bullet - t)}}$$

An approximate $(1-\alpha)100\%$ confidence interval about σ^2_a is

$$\frac{v\hat{\sigma}^2_a}{\chi^2_{\alpha/2,\,v}} < \sigma^2_a < \frac{v\hat{\sigma}^2_a}{\chi^2_{1 - \alpha/2,\,v}}$$

where v are degrees of freedom determined by using the Satterthwaite approximation. In this case, the approximate degrees of freedom are calculated by

$$v = \frac{(\hat{\sigma}^2_a)^2}{\dfrac{\left[\dfrac{MSI}{C}\right]^2}{s - 1} + \dfrac{\left[\dfrac{MSsite(I)}{C}\right]^2}{n_\bullet - s}}$$

The Satterthwaite approximation provides an approximation to the sampling distribution of linear combinations of mean squares. In this case, $\hat{\sigma}^2_a = MSI / C - MSsite(I) / C$, and the approximating sampling distribution of $v\hat{\sigma}^2_a / \sigma^2_a$ is χ^2_v. As the number of influents increases, the sampling distribution of $\hat{\sigma}^2_a$ can be approximated by a normal distribution. When the number of influents is not large, the normal approximation will not be appropriate as it is a symmetric distribution and the estimates of variances generally have a right skewed sampling distribution.

Another statistic to test the hypothesis H_0: $\sigma^2_a = 0$ vs H_a: $\sigma^2_a > 0$ is

$$F_c = \frac{MSI}{MSsite(I)}$$

and the decision rule is to reject H_0: if and only if $F_c > F_{\alpha,\,(t - 1),\,(n_\bullet - t)}$. The reality is that we know that σ^2_a cannot be equal to 0, but σ^2_a may be small enough when compared to the magnitude of σ^2_e to be considered as being negligible.

4.2 Example: One-way Random Effects Treatment Structure

The data in Data Set 4.2, "Mississippi River," in Appendix 4, "SAS Data Sets," are the nitrogen concentrations in parts per million from several sites at six of the randomly selected influents to the Mississippi River (you would want to select many more than six sites to monitor the Mississippi River, but we use only six for demonstration purposes). The model in equation 4.2 is used to describe the data where you want to estimate μ_N, σ^2_a, and σ^2_e. The model is also called a two-level hierarchical linear model. The method of moments estimates of the variance components are obtained by using PROC GLM and PROC VARCOMP.

DATA SET 4.2 *Mississippi River, the Values Are the Nitrogen Measurements in Parts Per Million (ppm)*

Influent 1	Influent 2	Influent 3	Influent 4	Influent 5	Influent 6
21	21	20	14	7	41
27	11	19	24	15	42
29	18	20	30	18	35
17	9	11	21	4	34
19	13	14	31	28	30
12	23	.	27	.	.
29	2	.	.	.	.
20	.	.	.	.	.
20	.	.	.	.	.

4.2.1 Using the MIXED Procedure

Next, PROC MIXED is used to provide the estimates of the variance components, the population mean, predicted values for each level of influent, and predicted values for the deviations of the influent effects from the population mean. The PROC MIXED program to provide REML estimates of the variance components, etc., is

```
proc mixed; class influent;
    model y=/solution;
    random influent/solution;
    estimate 'influent 1' intercept 1 |influent 1 0 0 0 0 0;
    estimate 'influent 2' intercept 1 |influent 0 1 0 0 0 0;
    estimate 'influent 3' intercept 1 |influent 0 0 1 0 0 0;
    estimate 'influent 4' intercept 1 |influent 0 0 0 1 0 0;
    estimate 'influent 5' intercept 1 |influent 0 0 0 0 1 0;
    estimate 'influent 6' intercept 1 |influent 0 0 0 0 0 1;

    estimate 'influent 1U'  |influent 1 0 0 0 0 0;
    estimate 'influent 2U'  |influent 0 1 0 0 0 0;
    estimate 'influent 3U'  |influent 0 0 1 0 0 0;
    estimate 'influent 4U'  |influent 0 0 0 1 0 0;
    estimate 'influent 5U'  |influent 0 0 0 0 1 0;
    estimate 'influent 6U'  |influent 0 0 0 0 0 1;
run;
```

The SOLUTION option on the MODEL statement provides the estimates of the fixed effects, which in this case is just the population mean and corresponds to the INTERCEPT.

The SOLUTION option on the RANDOM statement provides predicted values of the random effects with expectation zero, which are listed as a solution for the random effect. The results are in Output 4.1.

Results

Output 4.1 *The Results of Using PROC MIXED to Obtain REML Estimates of the Variance Components and to Obtain Estimated BLUP for Each INFLUENT*

```
              Covariance Parameter Estimates (REML)
Cov Parm         Ratio       Estimate     Std Error        z   Pr > |Z|
INFLUENT       1.48438019   63.32114984  45.23148440     1.40    0.1615
Residual       1.00000000   42.65830963  10.85707766     3.93    0.0001
```

```
              Model Fitting Information for Y
Description                          Value
Observations                        37.0000
Variance Estimate                   42.6583
Standard Deviation Estimate          6.5313
REML Log Likelihood               -126.176
Akaike's Information Criterion     -128.176
Schwarz's Bayesian Criterion      -129.759
-2 REML Log Likelihood             252.3511
```

```
                   Solution for Fixed Effects
Parameter      Estimate      Std Error    DDF      T    Pr > |T|
INTERCEPT     21.22311830   3.42898112     5     6.19    0.0016
```

```
                   Solution for Random Effects
Parameter      Estimate      SE Pred      DDF      T    Pr > |T|
INFLUENT 1     0.30928609   3.81929387     31    0.08    0.9360
INFLUENT 2    -6.71930751   3.91702582     31   -1.72    0.0963
INFLUENT 3    -3.89792591   4.08045211     31   -0.96    0.3468
INFLUENT 4     2.94609342   3.98696834     31    0.74    0.4655
INFLUENT 5    -6.01295462   4.08045211     31   -1.47    0.1507
INFLUENT 6    13.37480853   4.08045211     31    3.28    0.0026
```

```
                   ESTIMATE Statement Results
Parameter       Estimate      Std Error    DDF      T    Pr > |T|
INFLUENT 1     21.53240440   2.11346924     5    10.19    0.0002
INFLUENT 2     14.50381079   2.37690185     5     6.10    0.0017
INFLUENT 3     17.32519239   2.77207515     5     6.25    0.0015
INFLUENT 4     24.16921172   2.55182966     5     9.47    0.0002
INFLUENT 5     15.21016368   2.77207515     5     5.49    0.0027
INFLUENT 6     34.59792684   2.77207515     5    12.48    0.0001
INFLUENT 1U     0.30928609   3.81929387    31     0.08    0.9360
INFLUENT 2U    -6.71930751   3.91702582    31    -1.72    0.0963
INFLUENT 3U    -3.89792591   4.08045211    31    -0.96    0.3468
INFLUENT 4U     2.94609342   3.98696834    31     0.74    0.4655
INFLUENT 5U    -6.01295462   4.08045211    31    -1.47    0.1507
INFLUENT 6U    13.37480853   4.08045211    31     3.28    0.0026
```

ESTIMATE statements are used to provide predictions of predictable functions. The first set of ESTIMATE statements provides predicted values for the concentrations of nitrogen levels at each influent. These predictions are the Best Linear Unbiased Predictors (BLUP) of the nitrogen level at each influent. (See Chapter 6 for a detailed discussion of BLUP).

The second set of ESTIMATE statements is used to obtain predictions for each influent as to how it deviates from the overall mean. The second set of ESTIMATE statements is included to demonstrate that the solution for the random effects is in fact obtainable via ESTIMATE statements. To obtain predictions involving the random effects, the random effects can be included in the ESTIMATE statement after the I or bar. For comparison purposes, the results using ML, MIVQUE(0), and method of moments estimates of the variance components are included. The results are similar to those in Output 4.1 for REML estimates of the variance components. The ESTIMATE statements included with the above PROC MIXED code for computing the REML estimates of the variance components were used for the other methods but are not included in the lists of programs. The respective sets of programs are

For ML:
```
proc mixed method=ml; class influent;
   model y=/solution;
   random influent/solution;
run;
```

For MIVQUE(0):
```
proc mixed method=mivque0; class influent;
   model Y=/solution;
   random influent/solution;
run;
```

PROC MIXED does not compute standard method of moments estimates, but you can force PROC MIXED to use them. The values in the PARMS statement are the methods of moments estimates computed by PROC VARCOMP (illustrated in Output 4.6). The NOPROFILE option in the PROC statement together with the NOITER option in the PARMS statement forces PROC MIXED to use these values without modification.

```
proc mixed noprofile; class influent;
   model Y=/solution;
   random influent/solution;
   parms (56.16672059) (42.57352791)/noiter;
run;
```

The results of the above sets of code are in Outputs 4.2 through 4.4. You should notice how the values of the predictable functions change as the magnitudes of the variance components change. The variance components are somewhat variable, but the predictions of each influent's effect do not change very much. The choice between these four analyses depends on your choice of technique to estimate the variance components. Because none of the variance component estimation techniques can be shown to be superior to the others, there is no clear choice. The REML estimates seem to be used more frequently than the estimates from the other techniques.

Output 4.2 *The Results of Using PROC MIXED to Obtain ML Estimates of the Variance Components and to Obtain Estimated BLUP for Each INFLUENT*

```
                 Covariance Parameter Estimates (MLE)

Cov Parm         Ratio       Estimate      Std Error      Z     Pr > |Z|
INFLUENT       1.20031524   51.25089465   34.34981868   1.49     0.1357
Residual       1.00000000   42.69786208   10.87755464   3.93     0.0001


                    Model Fitting Information for Y
                 Description                      Value
                 Observations                    37.0000
                 Variance Estimate               42.6979
                 Standard Deviation Estimate      6.5344
```

```
                    Log Likelihood                  -128.279
                    Akaike's Information Criterion   -130.279
                    Schwarz's Bayesian Criterion     -131.889
                    -2 Log Likelihood                256.5570
```

Solution for Fixed Effects

Parameter	Estimate	Std Error	DDF	T	Pr > |T|
INTERCEPT	21.21709595	3.12190023	5	6.80	0.0010

Solution for Random Effects

Parameter		Estimate	SE Pred	DDF	T	Pr > |T|
INFLUENT	1	0.30978348	3.53651864	31	0.09	0.9308
INFLUENT	2	-6.57716312	3.63789339	31	-1.81	0.0803
INFLUENT	3	-3.78622430	3.80538616	31	-0.99	0.3275
INFLUENT	4	2.88264223	3.70988149	31	0.78	0.4430
INFLUENT	5	-5.84344434	3.80538616	31	-1.54	0.1348
INFLUENT	6	13.01440605	3.80538616	31	3.42	0.0018

ESTIMATE Statement Results

Parameter		Estimate	Std Error	DDF	T	Pr > |T|
INFLUENT	1	21.52687943	2.10052722	5	10.25	0.0002
INFLUENT	2	14.63993283	2.35821822	5	6.21	0.0016
INFLUENT	3	17.43087165	2.74202879	5	6.36	0.0014
INFLUENT	4	24.09973817	2.52854667	5	9.53	0.0002
INFLUENT	5	15.37365161	2.74202879	5	5.61	0.0025
INFLUENT	6	34.23150199	2.74202879	5	12.48	0.0001

Output 4.3 *The Results of Using PROC MIXED to Obtain MIVQUE(0) Estimates of the Variance Components and to Obtain Estimated BLUP for Each INFLUENT*

Covariance Parameter Estimates (MIVQUE0)

Cov Parm	Ratio	Estimate
INFLUENT	0.89030620	45.75410126
Residual	1.00000000	51.39142175

Model Fitting Information for Y

Description	Value
Observations	37.0000
Variance Estimate	51.3914
Standard Deviation Estimate	7.1688
REML Log Likelihood	-126.512
Akaike's Information Criterion	-128.512
Schwarz's Bayesian Criterion	-130.096
-2 REML Log Likelihood	253.0241

Solution for Fixed Effects

Parameter	Estimate	Std Error	DDF	T	Pr > |T|
INTERCEPT	21.20683430	3.01217143	5	7.04	0.0009

Solution for Random Effects

Parameter		Estimate	SE Pred	DDF	T	Pr > |T|
INFLUENT	1	0.31002928	3.49972291	31	0.09	0.9300
INFLUENT	2	-6.33343789	3.61441758	31	-1.75	0.0896
INFLUENT	3	-3.59846794	3.80035430	31	-0.95	0.3510

INFLUENT 4	2.77388940	3.69486731	31	0.75	0.4585
INFLUENT 5	-5.55822463	3.80035430	31	-1.46	0.1537
INFLUENT 6	12.40621177	3.80035430	31	3.26	0.0027

ESTIMATE Statement Results

Parameter	Estimate	Std Error	DDF	T	Pr > |T|
INFLUENT 1	21.51686359	2.27778217	5	9.45	0.0002
INFLUENT 2	14.87339642	2.54950249	5	5.83	0.0021
INFLUENT 3	17.60836637	2.94926892	5	5.97	0.0019
INFLUENT 4	23.98072371	2.72768023	5	8.79	0.0003
INFLUENT 5	15.64860967	2.94926892	5	5.31	0.0032
INFLUENT 6	33.61304607	2.94926892	5	11.40	0.0001

Output 4.4 *The Results of Using PROC MIXED to Obtain Methods of Moments Estimates of the Variance Components and to Obtain Estimated BLUP for Each INFLUENT*

Parameter Search

COL1	COL2	Variance	REML_LL	-2REML_LL	Objective
56.1667	42.5735	42.5735	-126.190	252.3802	186.2167

Covariance Parameter Estimates (Parms)

Cov Parm	Ratio	Estimate
INFLUENT	1.31928744	56.16672059
Residual	1.00000000	42.57352791

Model Fitting Information for Y

Description	Value
Observations	37.0000
Variance Estimate	42.5735
Standard Deviation Estimate	6.5248
REML Log Likelihood	-126.190
Akaike's Information Criterion	-128.190
Schwarz's Bayesian Criterion	-129.774
-2 REML Log Likelihood	252.3802

Solution for Fixed Effects

Parameter	Estimate	Std Error	DDF	T	Pr > |T|
INTERCEPT	21.21989824	3.25000763	5	6.53	0.0013

Solution for Random Effects

Parameter	Estimate	SE Pred	DDF	T	Pr > |T|
INFLUENT 1	0.30958398	3.65352726	31	0.08	0.9330
INFLUENT 2	-6.64338589	3.75327606	31	-1.77	0.0866
INFLUENT 3	-3.83805992	3.91899132	31	-0.98	0.3350
INFLUENT 4	2.91220101	3.82436204	31	0.76	0.4521
INFLUENT 5	-5.92212234	3.91899132	31	-1.51	0.1409
INFLUENT 6	13.18178316	3.91899132	31	3.36	0.0021

```
                      ESTIMATE Statement Results

Parameter                Estimate     Std Error   DDF        T   Pr > |T|
INFLUENT 1             21.52948222   2.10396681     5    10.23     0.0002
INFLUENT 2             14.57651234   2.36400823     5     6.17     0.0016
INFLUENT 3             17.38183832   2.75261064     5     6.31     0.0015
INFLUENT 4             24.13209925   2.53626019     5     9.51     0.0002
INFLUENT 5             15.29777590   2.75261064     5     5.56     0.0026
INFLUENT 6             34.40168140   2.75261064     5    12.50     0.0001
```

4.2.2 Using the GLM Procedure

PROC GLM can be used to compute the usual analysis of the random effects model that involves the computation of mean squares, expected mean squares, and statistics to test hypotheses about the importance of the individual variance components in the model. PROC GLM does not provide estimates of the variance components. You can use, however, the mean squares and expected mean squares to set up a set of equations and then solve the equations for the method of moments estimates. The PROC GLM program needed to compute the mean squares and expected mean squares and test the hypothesis $H_0: \sigma^2_a = 0$ vs $H_a: \sigma^2_a > 0$ is as follows:

```
proc glm;
   class influent;
   model Y=influent;
   random influent/test;
run;
```

The results of the above statements are in Output 4.5.

Results

Output 4.5 *The Results of Using PROC GLM to Obtain Expected Mean Squares and to Test to See if the Variance Component for INFLUENT Is Significantly Different from 0*

```
                        Dependent Variable: Y
                         Sum of          Mean
Source            DF     Squares         Square    F Value    Pr > F
Model              5  1925.1936079   385.0387216      9.04    0.0001
Error             31  1319.7793651    42.5735279
Corrected Total   36  3244.9729730


Source            DF    Type III SS   Mean Square    F Value    Pr > F
INFLUENT           5  1925.1936079   385.0387216       9.04     0.0001


Source       Type III Expected Mean Square
INFLUENT     Var(Error) + 6.0973 Var(INFLUENT)


Tests of Hypotheses for Random Model Analysis of Variance


Dependent Variable: Y
Source: INFLUENT
Error: MS(Error)

                  Denominator     Denominator
   DF    Type III MS     DF            MS       F Value    Pr > F
    5    385.03872158     31    42.573527906     9.0441    0.0001
```

Interpretation

The F-value of 9.04 has a significance level > 0.0001, which indicates there is strong evidence to believe the null hypothesis is not true.

4.2.3 Using the VARCOMP Procedure

PROC VARCOMP is a procedure that computes the estimates of the variance components. It is used here to provide the computations for obtaining the methods of moments estimates of the variance components. PROC VARCOMP can also provide REML, ML and MIVQUE(0) estimates of variance components. The PROC VARCOMP program needed to compute method of moments estimates of the variance components is

```
proc varcomp method=type1;
   class influent;
   model y=influent;
run;
```

The results of estimating the variance components are in Output 4.6.

Output 4.6 *The Results of Using PROC VARCOMP to Obtain Expected Mean Squares and to Obtain Estimates of the Variance Component for INFLUENT*

```
Dependent Variable: Y
Source                    DF        Type I SS           Type I MS
INFLUENT                   5      1925.19360789       385.03872158
Error                     31      1319.77936508        42.57352791
Corrected Total           36      3244.97297297


Source                          Expected Mean Square
INFLUENT                        Var(Error) + 6.0973 Var(INFLUENT)
Error                           Var(Error)


Variance Component                     Estimate
Var(INFLUENT)                         56.16672059
Var(Error)                            42.57352791
```

4.2.4 Confidence Intervals about the Variance Components

The final step in the analysis is to construct a 95% confidence interval about σ^2_a. There are two methods easily applied for the construction of confidence intervals about variance components. PROC MIXED provides estimates of the standard errors associated with each estimate of a variance component. Large sample normal approximation confidence intervals can be constructed using that information. The second method is to use the Satterthwaite approximation, described in the discussion following equation 4.4. The Satterthwaite confidence intervals are asymmetrical about the estimate of the variance component whereas the normal approximation confidence intervals are symmetric about the estimate of the variance component.

An asymptotic 95% confidence interval about σ_a^2 can be computed using the estimated standard error of $\hat{\sigma}_a^2$. An asymptotic 95% confidence interval about σ_a^2, computed using the estimated standard error of $\hat{\sigma}_a^2$ from Output 4.1, is

$$\hat{\sigma}_a^2 \pm z_{0.025} \ \hat{se}_{\hat{\sigma}_a^2} \ \text{or}$$
$$63.321 \pm 1.96 \times 45.231 \ \text{or}$$
$$63.321 \pm 88.652 \ \text{or}$$
$$0 < \sigma_a^2 < 151.973$$

The lower limit is truncated to zero because σ_a^2 is a nonnegative parameter.

Program

The DATA step and code used to compute the confidence interval based on the Satterthwaite approximation are

```
data satt;
   c=6.0973; * coefficient of var(influent) in e(ms influent);
   mssite=1319.77936508/31; * ms error;
   msi=1925.19360789/5; * ms influent;
   sa2=56.16672059 ; *estimate of var(influent);
   v=(sa2**2)/((((msi/c)**2)/5)+(((mssite/c)**2)/31)); * approx df;
   c025=cinv(.025,v); * lower 2.5 chi square percentage point;
   c975=cinv(.975,v); * upper 97.5 chi square percentage point;
   low=v*sa2/C975; * lower limit;
   high=v*sa2/C025; * upper limit;
run;
```

Results

Output 4.7 *Intermediate Computations for the Satterthwaite Approximation to the Confidence Interval About* σ_a^2

OBS	C	MSSITE	MSI	SA2	V	C025	C975	LOW	HIGH
1	6.0973	42.5735	385.039	56.1667	3.94765	0.46822	11.0523	20.0615	473.550

Interpretation

The intermediate computations and confidence interval about σ_a^2 are in Output 4.7 where the variable names are those as annotated in the above DATA step code. The confidence interval is based on the method of moments information in Outputs 4.5 and 4.6. The estimate of σ_a^2 is 56.17 with approximate degrees of freedom equal to 3.95. The 95% approximate confidence interval about σ_a^2 is $20.06 < \sigma_a^2 < 473.55$ (a very nonsymmetric interval). The chi-square distribution can be approximated by a normal distribution for large numbers of degrees of freedom (asymptotic distribution theory). Similarly, confidence intervals about variance components with large numbers of associated degrees of freedom can be constructed using the normal distribution and the estimated standard error of the variance components.

The sampling distribution of a sample variance is that of a chi-square distribution with the associated degrees of freedom, which is an asymmetrical distribution. When the degrees of freedom associated with an estimate of a variance are small, the resulting equal tailed confidence intervals are also asymmetric about the estimate of the variance. When the degrees of freedom are large, the confidence interval is nearly symmetric about the estimate of the variance component. Because the confidence intervals based on the normal distribution are symmetric about the estimates, the intervals can be very misleading when the number of degrees of freedom are small. For example, when there are only six levels of influent, the symmetric confidence interval based on the normal distribution most likely would be misleading as an appropriate confidence interval based on the chi-square distribution with equal tail probabilities would be asymmetric.

4.3 Example: A Simple Conditional Hierarchical Linear Model

One purpose of conditional hierarchical linear models is to attempt to explain part of the variability in the levels of a random treatment by using characteristics of the levels. For example a characteristic may be used to classify the levels into various groups. When the levels of the random factor are classified into groups, the groups are generally considered to be levels of a fixed effect. Thus, the resulting model is a mixed model where the fixed effects correspond to the means of the newly formed groups and the random effects are the levels of the random effect nested within the levels of the fixed effect. This example uses the classification technique for Data Set 4.2 in Appendix 4, "SAS Data Sets." The influents were classified as to the type of watershed above the influent. The influents were classified as to type by,

> type=1 for no farm land in watershed,
> type=2 for less than 50% farm land in watershed, and
> type=3 for more than 50% farm land in watershed.

In Data Set 4.2, influents 3 and 5 are of type 1, influents 1, 2, and 4 are of type 2, and influent 6 is of type 3. In this case the model is to determine some of the variation in the influents in Section 4.2 can be attributed to the different levels of TYPE. Thus, TYPE is considered as a fixed effect and the influents within a TYPE are considered as random effects. This section considers only the REML estimates of the variance components, but the other methods could be applied as well.

Let y_{ijk} denote the amount of nitrogen measured from the kth site at the jth influent of the ith type and a model to describe the collection of measurements is

$$y_{ijk} = \mu_i + a_{j(i)} + e_{ijk} \, , \; i=1,2,3, \; j=1,...,n_i, \; k=1,...,m_{ij} \tag{4.5}$$

where

$$a_{j(i)} \sim \text{iid } N(0, \, \sigma_a^2)$$
$$e_{ijk} \sim \text{iid } N(0, \, \sigma_e^2)$$

Model 4.5 has two variance component parameters to be estimated, the same as model 4.2. Model 4.5 is a mixed effects model where μ_i, i=1,2,3 is the fixed-effects part of the model and $a_{j(i)} + e_{ijk}$ is the random-effects part of the model. The notation $j(i)$ denotes the jth level of the ith group is nested within the ith group. By classifying the influents as to types, the $\mu_N + a_i$ of Model 4.2 has been expressed as $\mu_N + a_i = \mu_i + a_{j(i)}$ where μ_i denotes that the mean level of nitrogen for influents of type i and $a_{j(i)}$ denotes the effect of the jth randomly selected influent of type i. Model 4.5 is also called a two-level conditional hierarchical linear model (Bryk and Raudenbush (1992)) since the sampling points are nested within each influent and the influents are classified according to levels of the type, a fixed effect.

The analysis can be accomplished by using PROC MIXED, but without PROC MIXED the analysis requires the use of both PROC GLM and PROC VARCOMP. PROC MIXED is presented first followed by the analysis using PROC GLM and PROC VARCOMP.

4.3.1 Using PROC MIXED to Analyze the Data

Program

The following PROC MIXED program obtains REML estimates of the variance components, estimates of the fixed effects, and predictions of the respective influent means:

```
proc mixed;
   class type influent;
   model y=type/solution;
   random influent(type)/solution;
   estimate 'influent 1' intercept 1 type 0 1 0|influent(type) 1 0 0 0 0 0;
   estimate 'influent 2' intercept 1 type 0 1 0|influent(type) 0 1 0 0 0 0;
   estimate 'influent 3' intercept 1 type 1 0 0|influent(type) 0 0 1 0 0 0;
   estimate 'influent 4' intercept 1 type 0 1 0|influent(type) 0 0 0 1 0 0;
   estimate 'influent 5' intercept 1 type 1 0 0|influent(type) 0 0 0 0 1 0;
   estimate 'influent 6' intercept 1 type 0 0 1|influent(type) 0 0 0 0 0 1;
   lsmeans type/pdiff;
run;
```

The results in Output 4.8 correspond to the random effects part of the analysis.

Results

Output 4.8 *Results of the Random Effects Part of the Model Using PROC MIXED*

```
                      The MIXED Procedure

              Covariance Parameter Estimates (REML)

Cov Parm              Ratio      Estimate     Std Error     Z     Pr > |Z|
INFLUENT(TYPE)     0.35212727   14.97020022  17.54218970  0.85    0.3934
Residual           1.00000000   42.51360674  10.78420298  3.94    0.0001


              Model Fitting Information for Y

       Description                      Value

       Observations                    37.0000
       Variance Estimate               42.5136
       Standard Deviation Estimate      6.5202
       REML Log Likelihood           -117.262
       Akaike's Information Criterion -119.262
       Schwarz's Bayesian Criterion  -120.789
       -2 REML Log Likelihood         234.5246
```

```
                 Solution for Random Effects

Parameter                Estimate      SE Pred    DDF     T     Pr > |T|


INFLUENT(TYPE) 3 1       0.76531761    3.19319085   31    0.24    0.8122
INFLUENT(TYPE) 5 1      -0.76531761    3.19319085   31   -0.24    0.8122
INFLUENT(TYPE) 1 2       1.22952722    2.75925148   31    0.45    0.6590
INFLUENT(TYPE) 2 2      -4.32590762    2.80068591   31   -1.54    0.1326
INFLUENT(TYPE) 4 2       3.09638041    2.83136385   31    1.09    0.2826
INFLUENT(TYPE) 6 3      -0.00000000    3.86913430   31   -0.00    1.0000


                 ESTIMATE Statement Results

Parameter                Estimate      Std Error   DDF      T     Pr > |T|


INFLUENT 1              20.70337788    4.14227714    3    5.00     0.0154
INFLUENT 2              19.17274266    4.14227714    3    4.63     0.0190
INFLUENT 3              16.82952722    4.39885548    3    3.83     0.0314
INFLUENT 4              15.61215265    2.21369417    3    7.05     0.0059
INFLUENT 5              18.69638041    4.44444395    3    4.21     0.0245
INFLUENT 6              36.40000000    2.91594262    3   12.48     0.0011
```

Interpretation

The REML estimates of the variance components are $\hat{\sigma}_a^2 = 14.970$ and $\hat{\sigma}_e^2 = 42.514$. The solution of the random effects are the predicted values of the effect of the individual influents with mean zero. The ESTIMATE statements provide predictions of the predictable functions for the influents with means equal to the mean of the respective types. Output 4.9 contains the analysis of the fixed effects part of the model using the REML estimates of the variance components.

Output 4.9 *Results of the Fixed Effects Part of the Model Using PROC MIXED*

```
                    The MIXED Procedure

                 Solution for Fixed Effects

Parameter      Estimate     Std Error   DDF      T    Pr > |T|


INTERCEPT    36.40000000   4.84488613    3     7.51    0.0049
TYPE 1      -20.80000000   5.93374943    3    -3.51    0.0393
TYPE 2      -16.46193973   5.51678472    3    -2.98    0.0584
TYPE 3        0.00000000      .          .      .        .


                 Tests of Fixed Effects

      Source      NDF   DDF   Type III F   Pr > F


       TYPE        2     3       6.37      0.0832
```

```
                    Least Squares Means

      Level              LSMEAN     Std Error    DDF       T   Pr > |T|


      TYPE 1         15.60000000   3.42585183      3    4.55     0.0198
      TYPE 2         19.93806027   2.63855872      3    7.56     0.0048
      TYPE 3         36.40000000   4.84488613      3    7.51     0.0049



              Differences of Least Squares Means


  Level 1  Level 2    Difference     Std Error   DDF      T   Pr > |T|


  TYPE 1   TYPE 2    -4.33806027    4.32417077     3   -1.00    0.3897
  TYPE 1   TYPE 3   -20.80000000    5.93374943     3   -3.51    0.0393
  TYPE 2   TYPE 3   -16.46193973    5.51678472     3   -2.98    0.0584
```

The statistic to test the equal means hypothesis has a value of 6.37 with significance level 0.0832. The LSMEANS or adjusted means for the levels of type and differences between the LSMEANS are included in Output 4.9 where there is evidence that the TYPE 3 mean is different from both TYPE 1 ($p=0.0393$) and 2 ($p=0.0584$) and there is no difference between the means of TYPE 1 and 2 ($p=0.3897$).

4.3.2 PROC GLM Part of the Analysis

To start the analysis of the data in DATA 4.2 using model 4.5, use the following PROC GLM program to provide a Type III analysis for testing H_0: $\mu_1=\mu_2=\mu_3$ vs H_a (not H_0) and H_0: $\sigma_a^2 = 0$ vs H_a: $\sigma_a^2 > 0$:

```
proc glm;
   class type influent;
   model y=type influent(type);
   random influent(type)/test;
run;
```

The mixed models test of the above hypotheses is in Output 4.10.

Output 4.10 *PROC GLM Results to Provide Type III Sums of Squares and Expected Mean Squares and Tests of the Equal Type Means and the Variance Component Equal to Zero*

```
                  General Linear Models Procedure

Dependent Variable: Y
                             Sum of         Mean
Source            DF         Squares       Square    F Value    Pr > F

Model              5       1925.1936      385.0387     9.04      0.0001

Error             31       1319.7794       42.5735

Corrected Total   36       3244.9730


        R-Square        C.V.       Root MSE            Y Mean


        0.593285      31.11070      6.5248             20.973
```

Source	DF	Type I SS	Mean Square	F Value	Pr > F
TYPE	2	1503.5548	751.7774	17.66	0.0001
INFLUENT(TYPE)	3	421.6388	140.5463	3.30	0.0331

Source	DF	Type III SS	Mean Square	F Value	Pr > F
TYPE	2	1500.0332	750.0166	17.62	0.0001
INFLUENT(TYPE)	3	421.6388	140.5463	3.30	0.0331

General Linear Models Procedure

Source	Type III Expected Mean Square
TYPE	Var(Error) + 5.4393 Var(INFLUENT(TYPE)) + Q(TYPE)
INFLUENT(TYPE)	Var(Error) + 6.4848 Var(INFLUENT(TYPE))

General Linear Models Procedure
Tests of Hypotheses for Mixed Model Analysis of Variance

Dependent Variable: Y

Source: TYPE
Error: 0.8388*MS(INFLUENT(TYPE)) + 0.1612*MS(Error)

DF	Type III MS	Denominator DF	Denominator MS	F Value	Pr > F
2	750.01659014	3.36	124.75088884	6.0121	0.0777

Source: INFLUENT(TYPE)
Error: MS(Error)

DF	Type III MS	Denominator DF	Denominator MS	F Value	Pr > F
3	140.54627225	31	42.573527906	3.3013	0.0331

The F-statistic to test the equal means hypothesis has a value of 6.0121 with significance level 0.0777. The statistic to test of $\sigma_a^2 = 0$ has a value of 3.3013 with a significance level of 0.0331. Thus there is evidence that both of the hypotheses are likely to be false.

4.3.3 PROC VARCOMP Part of the Analysis

Next, use PROC VARCOMP to obtain method of moments estimates using the Type I mean squares. In the following program, the fixed effects are listed first in the MODEL statement with the option indicating the number of fixed-effects terms in the model:

```
proc varcomp method=type1;
   class type influent;
   model y=type influent(type)/fixed=1;
run;
```

The PROC VARCOMP results are in Output 4.11 where the estimates of the variance components from the Type I analysis are $\hat{\sigma}_a^2 = 15.108$ and $\hat{\sigma}_e^2 = 42.574$.

Output 4.11 *PROC VARCOMP Results to Obtain Method of Moments Estimates of the Variance Components*

```
                    Variance Components Estimation Procedure

Dependent Variable: Y

Source                      DF        Type I SS           Type I MS

TYPE                         2      1503.55479115         751.77739558

INFLUENT(TYPE)               3       421.63881674         140.54627225

Error                       31      1319.77936508          42.57352791

Corrected Total             36      3244.97297297



Source                           Expected Mean Square

TYPE                             Var(Error) + 5.516 Var(INFLUENT(TYPE))
                                 + Q(TYPE)

INFLUENT(TYPE)                   Var(Error) + 6.4848 Var(INFLUENT(TYPE))

Error                            Var(Error)



Variance Component                       Estimate

Var(INFLUENT(TYPE))                     15.10794656

Var(Error)                              42.57352791
```

4.3.4 Confidence Intervals for the Variance Components

Finally, the method of moments estimates from the Type I sums of squares of Output 4.11 are used to construct a 95% confidence interval about σ^2_a. The estimate of σ^2_a is 15.11. An approximate 95% confidence interval about σ^2_a was constructed using the Satterthwaite approximation by employing the following DATA step statements (the annotations are as in the DATA step in Section 4.2):

```
data satt;
  c=5.4393;mssite=1319.77936508/31; msit=421.6388167/3;
  sa2=15.10794656;
  v=(sa2**2)/(((((msit/c)**2)/3)+(((mssite/c)**2)/31));
  c025=cinv(.025,v);
  c975=cinv(.975,v);
  low=v*sa2/C975;
  high=v*sa2/C025;
  proc print;
run;
```

The preliminary calculations are in Output 4.12. The 95% confidence interval is $3.029 < \sigma_a^2 < 13,801.97$ (a very nonsymmetric interval). The Satterthwaite approximation to the degrees of freedom is $v=1.017$. Thus, the confidence interval is very asymmetric as there are only three degrees of freedom associated with the INFLUENT(TYPE) sum of squares. As in the previous section, an asymptotic confidence interval about σ_a^2 is $0 < \sigma_a^2 < 49.35$. There is conflicting information about the significance level associated with testing the hypothesis $H_o: \sigma_a^2 = 0$ vs $H_a: \sigma_a^2 > 0$. The F-value in Output 4.10 has a significance level of 0.0331 while the z-score in Output 4.8 has a significance level of 0.1967. Because the number of influents within a level of type is very small, the Satterthwaite approximation to the confidence interval is most likely preferable.

Output 4.12 *Intermediate Computations for the Satterthwaite Approximation to the Confidence Interval about σ_a^2*

C	MSSITE	MSIT	SA2	V	C025	C975	LOW	HIGH
5.4393	42.5735	140.546	15.1079	1.01658	.0011128	5.06906	3.02983	13801.99

4.4 Example: Three Level Nested Design Structure

The data in Data Set 4.4, "Semiconductor," in Appendix 4, "SAS Data Sets," are from a passive data collection study in the semiconductor industry where the objective is to estimate the variance components to determine assignable causes for the observed variability. The measurements are thicknesses of the oxide layer on silicon wafers determined at three randomly selected sites on each wafer. The wafers used are from eight different lots (each lot consists of 25 wafers, but only 3 wafers per lot were used in the passive data collection study). The process consisted of randomly selecting eight lots of 25 wafers from the population of lots of 25 wafers. Then three wafers were selected from each lot of 25 for use in the oxide deposition process. After the layer of oxide was deposited, the thickness of the layer was determined at three randomly selected sites on each wafer. The structure of the study involves three sizes of experimental units in the design structure with a uniform application of a single treatment in the treatment structure.

4.4.1 Three Level Nested Linear Model, an Unconditional Hierarchical Nested Linear Model

A model to describe the data in Data Set 4.4 is

$$y_{ijk} = \mu + a_i + w_{j(i)} + s_{k(ij)} \, , \quad i=1,2,\dots,8, \quad j=1,2,3, \quad k=1,2,3 \tag{4.6}$$

where

$$a_i \sim \text{iid } N(0, \sigma_L^2)$$
$$w_{j(i)} \sim \text{iid } N(0, \sigma_w^2)$$
$$s_{k(ij)} \sim \text{iid } N(0, \sigma_s^2)$$

The terms in the model are described as

a_i is the effect of the ith randomly selected lot

$w_{j(i)}$ is the effect of the jth randomly selected wafer from the ith lot

$s_{k(ij)}$ is the effect of the kth randomly selected site from the jth wafer of the ith lot.

In the linear models literature, model 4.6 has been called a **three level nested linear model** or an **unconditional hierarchical nested linear model**. The objective of the passive data collection study is to estimate the variance components, σ_L^2, σ_w^2, and σ_s^2.

4.4.2 Data Analysis Using the MIXED Procedure to Estimate the Variance Components

The PROC MIXED program to fit model 4.6 is as follows:

```
proc mixed;
    class lot wafer site;
    model y=;
    random lot wafer(lot);
run;
```

Results

Output 4.13 Results of PROC MIXED for the Three Level Nested Random Effects Model

```
                    The MIXED Procedure

              Class Level Information

        Class      Levels   Values

        LOT           8     1 2 3 4 5 6 7 8
        WAFER         3     1 2 3
        SITE          3     1 2 3


          REML Estimation Iteration History

   Iteration  Evaluations     Objective       Criterion

       0           1       436.79979609
       1           1       323.53279760     0.00000000


              Convergence criteria met.


         Covariance Parameter Estimates (REML)

Cov Parm           Ratio       Estimate     Std Error       Z    Pr > |Z|

LOT            10.33515741   129.90718695   76.72054330    1.69    0.0904
WAFER(LOT)      2.85340700    35.86574074   14.18757840    2.53    0.0115
Residual        1.00000000    12.56944445    2.56572710    4.90    0.0001
```

```
                Model Fitting Information for Y

        Description                         Value

        Observations                        72.0000
        Variance Estimate                   12.5694
        Standard Deviation Estimate          3.5453
        REML Log Likelihood               -227.011
        Akaike's Information Criterion    -230.011
        Schwarz's Bayesian Criterion      -233.405
        -2 REML Log Likelihood             454.0221
```

Interpretation

The mean is the only fixed effect, and the residual variance corresponds to the site-to-site variance. The variance components corresponding to LOT and Wafer(LOT) measure the variability in the mean thickness of the population of LOTS and the variation in the mean thickness of the wafers within the population of LOTS, respectively. The REML estimates of the variance components are in Output 4.13. For this study, the estimate of the lot-to-lot variance of 129.9 is four times larger than the wafer-to-wafer within-a-lot variance of 35.9, which is 2.85 times larger than the site-to-site within a wafer variance of 12.6. If possible, it is desired to evaluate the cause of the lot-to-lot variance in order to improve the consistency of the layer of oxide across the population of wafers.

4.4.3 Using the VARCOMP Procedure to Estimate the Variance Components

You can also use PROC VARCOMP to estimate the variance components. The following program computes Type I sums of squares, mean squares, and expected mean squares and provides method of moments estimates of the variance components:

```
proc varcomp method=type1;
   class lot wafer site;
   model y=lot wafer(lot);
run;
```

The results are in Output 4.14.

Results

Output 4.14 *Results of PROC VARCOMP for the Three Level Nested Random Effects Model*

```
Dependent Variable: Y

Source                   DF        Type I SS           Type I MS

LOT                       7       9025.31944444       1289.33134921

WAFER(LOT)               16       1922.66666667        120.16666667

Error                    48        603.33333331         12.56944444

Corrected Total          71      11551.31944442



Source                        Expected Mean Square

LOT                           Var(Error) + 3 Var(WAFER(LOT))
                              + 9 Var(LOT)

WAFER(LOT)                    Var(Error) + 3 Var(WAFER(LOT))

Error                         Var(Error)



Variance Component                   Estimate

Var(LOT)                            129.90718695

Var(WAFER(LOT))                      35.86574074

Var(Error)                           12.56944444
```

Interpretation

The method of moments estimates are

$$\hat{\sigma}^2_s = MS\,ERROR$$
$$\hat{\sigma}^2_w = \frac{MS\,WAFER(LOT) - MS\,ERROR}{3}$$
$$\hat{\sigma}^2_L = \frac{MS\,LOT - MS\,WAFER(LOT)}{9}$$

The REML and method of moments estimates of the variance components are identical as this data set is balanced. You can use the PROC VARCOMP information to construct confidence intervals about each variance component using the Satterthwaite approximation described in section 4.1.

4.4.4 Conditional Hierarchical Linear Model or Mixed Model

The next part of the analysis is to take into account the information that the lots are from two different sources, denoted by SOR in the code for model 4.7. Because the levels of source are fixed effects, we change from the unconditional hierarchical nested linear model in 4.6 to the following conditional hierarchical nested linear model:

$$y_{ijkm} = \mu_i + a_{j(i)} + w_{k(ij)} + s_{m(ijk)} \ , \ i=1,2, \ \ j=1,2,3,4, \ \ k=1,2,3, \ \ m=1,2,3 \quad (4.7)$$

where

μ_i denotes the mean of the ith level of SOR

$a_{j(i)} \sim$ iid $N(0, \ \sigma_L^2)$

$w_{k(ij)} \sim$ iid $N(0, \ \sigma_w^2)$

$s_{m(ijk)} \sim$ iid $N(0, \ \sigma_s^2)$

and where

$a_{j(i)}$ is the effect of the jth randomly selected lot from SOR i
$w_{k(ij)}$ is the effect of the kth randomly selected wafer from the jth lot from SOR i
$s_{m(ijk)}$ is the effect of the mth randomly selected site from the kth wafer of the jth lot from SOR i.

The μ_i is the fixed effects part of the model, and the $a_{j(i)} + w_{k(ij)} + s_{m(ijk)}$ is the random effects part of the model. Since the model involves both random and fixed factors, model 4.7 is also called a mixed model. The discussion here is to demonstrate the process of moving from the purely random effects linear model or unconditional hierarchical linear model to the mixed model or **conditional hierarchical linear model**.

4.4.5 Using the MIXED Procedure

The PROC MIXED program to fit the model 4.7 is

```
proc mixed;
    class sor lot wafer site;
    model y= sor/ddfm=satterth;
    random lot(sor) wafer(sor lot);
    lsmeans sor/pdiff;
run;
```

Results

Output 4.15 *Results of PROC MIXED Using Source as a Fixed Effect for the Conditional Hierarchical Linear Model for the Level Nested Random Effects Model*

Covariance Parameter Estimates (REML)					
Cov Parm	Ratio	Estimate	Std Error	Z	Pr > |Z|
LOT(SOR)	9.53840802	119.89248971	77.07335584	1.56	0.1198
WAFER(SOR*LOT)	2.85340700	35.86574074	14.18757840	2.53	0.0115
Residual	1.00000000	12.56944445	2.56572710	4.90	0.0001

```
                   Model Fitting Information for Y

          Description                            Value

          Observations                         72.0000
          Variance Estimate                    12.5694
          Standard Deviation Estimate           3.5453
          REML Log Likelihood                 -223.239
          Akaike's Information Criterion      -226.239
          Schwarz's Bayesian Criterion        -229.612
          -2 REML Log Likelihood               446.4779


                      Tests of Fixed Effects


          Source       NDF    DDF   Type III F   Pr > F

          SOR            1      6         1.53    0.2629


                       Least Squares Means


     Level          LSMEAN       Std Error    DDF       T   Pr > |T|


     SOR 1      1995.1111111    5.77157564     6   345.68     0.0001
     SOR 2      2005.1944444    5.77157564     6   347.43     0.0001


                  Differences of Least Squares Means
Level 1   Level 2    Difference      Std Error    DDF       T   Pr > |T|

SOR 1     SOR 2    -10.08333333     8.16224055     6   -1.24     0.2629
```

Interpretation

The levels of the sources, SOR, are put in the MODEL statement to denote the fixed effects part of the model. The DDFM=SATTERTH option in the MODEL statement uses a Satterthwaite approximation for the degrees of freedom associated with the estimated standard errors computed for fixed effects and predictable functions. The results of fitting the mixed model to the thickness data are in Output 4.15. The output includes estimates of the means of the fixed effects and comparisons of the means that are produced by the LMEANS statement. The estimate of the lot-to-lot variance component is a little smaller when the lot source is included in the model than when it is not included (see Output 4.13). That is because the lot-to-lot variance component now measures the variability among lots within a source (SOR). Some of the variability of the lots is attributable to the levels of SOR and thus is reflected in the smaller estimate as shown in Output 4.15. Because the data set is balanced, the wafer-to-wafer variance component and the site-to-site variance component are identical for both the unconditional and conditional hierarchical linear models.

4.4.6 Using the VARCOMP Procedure

The PROC VARCOMP program to compute Type I sums of squares and provide method of moments estimates of the variance components is

```
proc varcomp method=type1;
   class sor lot wafer site;
   model y=sor lot(sor) wafer(lot sor)/fixed=1;
run;
```

The PROC VARCOMP results are in Output 4.16.

Output 4.16 *Results of PROC VARCOMP Using Source as a Fixed Effect for the Conditional Hierarchical Linear Model for the Three Level Nested Random Effects Model*

```
Dependent Variable: Y

Source                 DF        Type I SS         Type I MS

SOR                     1     1830.12500000      1830.12500000

LOT(SOR)                6     7195.19444444      1199.19907407

WAFER(SOR*LOT)         16     1922.66666667       120.16666667

Error                  48      603.33333331        12.56944444

Corrected Total        71    11551.31944442



Source                 Expected Mean Square

SOR                    Var(Error) + 3 Var(WAFER(SOR*LOT))
                       + 9 Var(LOT(SOR)) + Q(SOR)

LOT(SOR)               Var(Error) + 3 Var(WAFER(SOR*LOT))
                       + 9 Var(LOT(SOR))

WAFER(SOR*LOT)         Var(Error) + 3 Var(WAFER(SOR*LOT))

Error                  Var(Error)



Variance Component              Estimate

Var(LOT(SOR))                  119.89248971

Var(WAFER(SOR*LOT))            35.86574074

Var(Error)                     12.56944444
```

Interpretation

The model is a mixed model, and the fixed effects must be listed first in the MODEL statement with the option (FIXED=1) specifying the number of terms in the model that are actually fixed effects. Again, because the data set is balanced, the estimates of the variance components using the method of moments estimates from the VARCOMP procedure are identical to the REML estimates from the MIXED procedure.

4.4.7 Unequal Variance Model

Oftentimes factors in an experiment have an effect on the variance of the responses as well as on the mean of the responses. Because there are two sources of lots of wafers, it is possible that the variability from lot to lot be different for each source. The last phase of the analysis is to fit a model with different lot-to-lot variance components for each source of lots. The unequal variance model is

$$y_{ijkm} = \mu_i + a_{j(i)} + w_{k(ij)} + s_{m(ijk)} \ , \ i=1,2, \ \ j=1,2,3,4, \ \ k=1,2,3, \ \ m=1,2,3 \tag{4.8}$$

where

$$a_{j(i)} \sim \text{iid } N(0, \ \sigma^2_{L_i})$$
$$w_{k(ij)} \sim \text{iid } N(0, \ \sigma^2_{w})$$
$$s_{m(ijk)} \sim \text{iid } N(0, \ \sigma^2_{s})$$

Model 4.8 has two variance components for LOTS, $\sigma^2_{L_1}$ and $\sigma^2_{L_2}$ where they are the variances of the lots within source 1 and source 2, respectively.

Program

The PROC MIXED program to fit the unequal variance model is

```
proc mixed scoring=4;
   class sor lot wafer site;
   model y= sor/ddfm=satterth;
   random lot(sor)/group=sor;
   random wafer(sor lot);
   lsmeans sor/pdiff;
run;
```

The SCORING=4 option for the MODEL statement requests that Fisher scoring be used in association with the estimation method up to iteration number 4. When the model is complex (the unequal variances make this model a little complex), the SCORING= *number* often helps the rate of convergence. The RANDOM statement asks PROC MIXED to provide a different estimate of $\sigma^2_{L_i}$ for each level of SOR, or the factor or combination of factors specified by the GROUP= option.

Results

Output 4.17 *Results of PROC MIXED Using Source as a Fixed Effect for the Conditional Hierarchical Linear Model with Unequal Variances for the Two Sources of Wafers for the Three Level Nested Random Effects Model*

```
                    Covariance Parameter Estimates (REML)

Cov Parm               Ratio      Estimate    Std Error       Z     Pr > |Z|

LOT(SOR)    SOR 1  1.35854307   17.07613169  25.28884039    0.68     0.4995
LOT(SOR)    SOR 2 17.71827297  222.70884774 192.80055304    1.16     0.2480
WAFER(SOR*LOT)     2.85340700   35.86574074  14.18757840    2.53     0.0115
Residual           1.00000000   12.56944445   2.56572710    4.90     0.0001


                    Model Fitting Information for Y

            Description                      Value

            Observations                    72.0000
            Variance Estimate               12.5694
            Standard Deviation Estimate      3.5453
            REML Log Likelihood           -221.882
            Akaike's Information Criterion -225.882
            Schwarz's Bayesian Criterion  -230.379
            -2 REML Log Likelihood         443.7631


                       Tests of Fixed Effects

            Source      NDF   DDF   Type III F   Pr > F

            SOR           1   3.76       1.53    0.2883


                       Least Squares Means

     Level         LSMEAN       Std Error   DDF        T    Pr > |T|

     SOR 1    1995.1111111    2.75807830     3   723.37    0.0001
     SOR 2    2005.1944444    7.68213349     3   261.02    0.0001


                 Differences of Least Squares Means

Level 1  Level 2    Difference     Std Error    DDF       T   Pr > |T|

SOR 1    SOR 2    -10.08333333    8.16224055   3.76   -1.24     0.2883
```

Interpretation

The results are in Output 4 .17, where the estimates of the lot-to-lot variance components are 17.08 and 222.71 for sources 1 and 2, respectively. The standard errors of the estimates of the source means reflect the unequal variances. That is, the estimated standard errors of the means are 2.76 and 7.68 for sources 1 and 2 respectively, each based on 3 degrees of freedom. The common lot-to-lot variance component model provides the same estimated standard error for the two source mean, 5.77 based on 6 degrees of freedom. (The estimated standard errors are equal for the common lot-to-lot variance model in this case because there are equal numbers of observations from each level of SOR.)

Next, compare the analysis in Output 4.17 to the analysis in Output 4.15 to see the effect unequal variances have on the analysis of the fixed effects in the model. The significance level for comparing the SOR means goes from 0.2629 for the equal variance model to 0.2883 for the unequal variance model. This change in the significance levels is due to the differences in the denominator degrees of freedom. The estimated standard errors of the differences of the two SOR means are identical for both analyses. This similarity disappears if there are unequal numbers of observations per level of SOR. The estimates of the wafer-to-wafer and site-to-site variance components are unchanged (35.87 and 12.57 respectively). The mean of the two lot-to-lot variance components is equal to the single lot-to-lot variance component for the equal variances model ((17.08 + 222.71)/2 = 119.89). This equality occurs because there are equal numbers of observations per level of SOR. Because the mean of the two lot-to-lot variance components is equal to the lot-to-lot variance component for the equal variances model, the estimate of the standard error of the difference between the two sources is the same for both models (8.162). The LSMEANS and the difference between the two means are identical for both models. A test of the equal variances hypothesis can be obtained by comparing the difference between the -2 REML Log Likelihood values to a chi-square distribution based on 1 = 4 - 3 degrees of freedom where there are four parameters in the covariance structure for the unequal variances model and there are three parameters in the covariance structure for the equal variances model. In this case, the difference is 2.7148 based on 1 degree of freedom, and the significance level is 0.3173 (from the chi-square table based on 1 degree of freedom). The results of the equal variances test indicate that the equal variance model is adequate to describe the data.

4.5 Example: A Two-way Random Effects Treatment Structure to Estimate Heritability

The data in DATA SET 4.5, "Genetics," in Appendix 4, "SAS Data Sets," represent yields of five randomly selected wheat families grown at four randomly selected locations. The wheat families were randomly selected from a population of families in a breeding program. The locations were selected from locations where the type of wheat would be grown commercially. At each location, the experimental design was a one-way treatment structure in a randomized complete block design structure. The objective of the study is to estimate the heritability of yield, a measure of possible genetic advancement under selection (Allard (1966)). Heritability is estimated by the ratio of the estimate of the genetic variance to the phenotypic variance of a family mean. A model to describe the data is

$$y_{ijk} = \mu + l_i + f_j + lf_{ij} + b_{k(i)} + e_{ijk} \tag{4.9}$$

where

$i=1,2,3,4$
$j=1,2,3,4,5$
$k=1,2,3$
$l_i \sim \text{iid } N(0, \sigma_L^2)$
$f_j \sim \text{iid } N(0, \sigma_F^2)$
$lf_{ij} \sim \text{iid } N(0, \sigma_{LF}^2)$
$b_{k(i)} \sim \text{iid } N(0, \sigma_B^2)$
$e_{ijk} \sim \text{iid } N(0, \sigma_e^2)$

The additive genetic variance component is σ_F^2, and the variance of a family mean is $\sigma_{\bar{y}_{.f}}^2 = \sigma_L^2/4 + \sigma_F^2 + \sigma_{LF}^2/4 + \sigma_B^2/12 + \sigma_e^2/12$. For this design, heritability is defined as $h^2 = \sigma_F^2 / \sigma_{\bar{y}_{.f}}^2$.

4.5.1 Using the MIXED Procedure

The following PROC MIXED program is used to fit model 4.9 to obtain REML estimates of the variance components:

```
proc mixed data=ex2_5;
   class loc fam block;
   model y=;
   random loc fam loc*fam block(loc);
run;
```

Because only the mean or intercept is the fixed effects part of the model, the MODEL statement contains no terms. All other terms in the model are random effects and thus occur in the RANDOM statement.

Results

Output 4.18 *PROC MIXED Results Providing REML Estimates of the Variance Components for the Genetics Example*

```
             Covariance Parameter Estimates (REML)


Cov Parm            Ratio       Estimate     Std Error      Z   Pr > |Z|


LOC             11.83604347  613.64953704  540.70816862   1.13   0.2564
FAM              3.62615304  188.00092593  149.52159914   1.26   0.2086
LOC*FAM          1.44392653   74.86157407   37.86473207   1.98   0.0480
BLOCK(LOC)       1.72281604   89.32083333   49.91236321   1.79   0.0735
Residual         1.00000000   51.84583333   12.96145833   4.00   0.0001


             Model Fitting Information for Y


        Description                      Value


        Observations                    60.0000
        Variance Estimate               51.8458
        Standard Deviation Estimate      7.2004
        REML Log Likelihood           -236.993
        Akaike's Information Criterion -241.993
        Schwarz's Bayesian Criterion  -247.187
        -2 REML Log Likelihood         473.9865
```

Interpretation

The results of PROC MIXED are in Output 4.18 where the estimates of the variance components are

$$\hat{\sigma}_L^2 = 613.6$$
$$\hat{\sigma}_F^2 = 188.0$$
$$\hat{\sigma}_{LF}^2 = 74.9$$
$$\hat{\sigma}_B^2 = 89.3$$
$$\hat{\sigma}_e^2 = 51.8$$
$$\hat{\sigma}_{\bar{y}_{.j}}^2 = \frac{613.6}{4} + 188.0 + \frac{74.9}{4} + \frac{89.3}{12} + \frac{51.8}{12} = 371.8$$
$$\hat{h}^2 = \frac{188.0}{371.8} = 0.506$$

The estimate of the heritability is 0.506, indicating that 50.6% of the variability in the family means is due to additive genetic variance.

The z-scores in Output 4.18 provide results for testing the hypotheses.

$$H_0: \sigma_L^2 = 0 \ vs \ H_a: \sigma_L^2 > 0$$
$$H_0: \sigma_F^2 = 0 \ vs \ H_a: \sigma_F^2 > 0$$
$$H_0: \sigma_{LF}^2 = 0 \ vs \ H_a: \sigma_{LF}^2 > 0$$

The significance levels are 0.1282, 0.1043, and 0.0240 for the respective hypotheses. (These significance levels are obtained by dividing the two- sided test significance levels printed in Output 4.18 by 2 in order to provide a one-sided test, 0.1282 = 0.2584/2, etc.)

4.5.2 Using the GLM Procedure

The analysis of variance table for model 4.9 is constructed using the following PROC GLM program:

```
proc glm data=ex2_5;
   class loc fam block;
   model y= loc fam loc*fam block(loc);
   random loc fam loc*fam block(loc)/test;
run;
```

The results of PROC GLM are in Outputs 4.19 and 4.20.

Results

Output 4.19 *PROC GLM Analysis of Variance Table for Genetics Example Model*

```
Dependent Variable: Y
                              Sum of        Mean
Source              DF        Squares      Square    F Value    Pr > F

Model               27      47217.867    1748.810     33.73     0.0001

Error               32       1659.067      51.846

Corrected Total     59      48876.933
```

	R-Square	C.V.	Root MSE	Y Mean
	0.966056	3.442973	7.2004	209.13

Source	DF	Type I SS	Mean Square	F Value	Pr > F
LOC	3	29783.333	9927.778	191.49	0.0001
FAM	4	10129.767	2532.442	48.85	0.0001
LOC*FAM	12	3317.167	276.431	5.33	0.0001
BLOCK(LOC)	8	3987.600	498.450	9.61	0.0001

Source	DF	Type III SS	Mean Square	F Value	Pr > F
LOC	3	29783.333	9927.778	191.49	0.0001
FAM	4	10129.767	2532.442	48.85	0.0001
LOC*FAM	12	3317.167	276.431	5.33	0.0001
BLOCK(LOC)	8	3987.600	498.450	9.61	0.0001

Output 4.20 *Expected Mean Squares and Tests of Hypotheses Concerning the Variance Components Using the Sums of Squares for Genetics Example*

```
                    General Linear Models Procedure

Source        Type III Expected Mean Square

LOC           Var(Error) + 5 Var(BLOCK(LOC)) + 3 Var(LOC*FAM)
              + 15 Var(LOC)

FAM           Var(Error) + 3 Var(LOC*FAM) + 12 Var(FAM)

LOC*FAM       Var(Error) + 3 Var(LOC*FAM)

BLOCK(LOC)    Var(Error) + 5 Var(BLOCK(LOC))


                    General Linear Models Procedure
          Tests of Hypotheses for Random Model Analysis of Variance

Dependent Variable: Y


Source: LOC
Error: MS(LOC*FAM) + MS(BLOCK(LOC)) - MS(Error)
```

		Denominator	Denominator		
DF	Type III MS	DF	MS	F Value	Pr > F
3	9927.7777778	13.94	723.03472222	13.7307	0.0002

```
Source: FAM
Error: MS(LOC*FAM)
```

		Denominator	Denominator		
DF	Type III MS	DF	MS	F Value	Pr > F
4	2532.4416667	12	276.43055556	9.1612	0.0012

```
Source: LOC*FAM
Error: MS(Error)
                        Denominator   Denominator
    DF    Type III MS       DF            MS       F Value   Pr > F
    12   276.43055556        32    51.845833333    5.3318    0.0001


Source: BLOCK(LOC)
Error: MS(Error)
                        Denominator   Denominator
    DF    Type III MS       DF            MS       F Value   Pr > F
     8       498.45          32    51.845833333    9.6141    0.0001
```

Interpretation

The analysis of variance table is in Output 4.19 and the expected mean squares are in Output 4.20. Also in Output 4.20 are statistics to test the following hypotheses:

$$H_0: \sigma_L^2 = 0 \ vs \ H_a: \sigma_L^2 > 0$$
$$H_0: \sigma_F^2 = 0 \ vs \ H_a: \sigma_F^2 > 0$$
$$H_0: \sigma_{LF}^2 = 0 \ vs \ H_a: \sigma_{LF}^2 > 0$$

The significance levels corresponding to the above hypotheses are 0.0002, 0.0012, and 0.0001, respectively. These tests indicate the variance components in the model are all required to adequately describe the variation in the data. The only F-statistics with appropriate denominators in Output 4.19 are those corresponding to LOC*FAM and BLOCK(LOC), as indicated by the expected mean squares in Output 4.20.

There is a large discrepancy between the significance levels from PROC MIXED and PROC GLM. One reason for the discrepancy is that PROC MIXED uses the asymptotic normal sampling distribution while PROC GLM uses the F-distribution for the F-statistics. For this example, there are very few levels of the random effects. Thus, the asymptotic normal distribution of the REML estimates is most likely not appropriate. Several more levels of the factor are necessary before the asymptotic distribution becomes appropriate.

4.6 Summary

The concept of a random effect is described where the random effect can occur in the design structure and/or the treatment structure. Procedures for estimating the parameters of a random effects model are demonstrated using PROC MIXED and PROC VARCOMP. Small sample size approximations to confidence intervals using the Satterthwaite approximation are described and are constructed for a couple of examples. Unconditional and conditional hierarchical linear models are described, which are special cases of random effects and mixed linear models respectively. When possible, PROC GLM results are provided as a comparison to the information obtained by employing PROC MIXED. Random coefficient models are a special type of mixed analysis of covariance models (see Chapter 7) and are conditional hierarchical linear models when all of the random effects are hierarchical.

4.7 References

Allard, R. W. (1966), *Principles of Plant Breeding*, New York: John Wiley & Sons, Inc.

Bryk, A. S, and Raudenbush, S. W. (1992), *Hierarchical Linear Models: Applications and Data Analysis Methods*, Newbury Park: Sage Publications.

Milliken, G. A. and Johnson, D. E. (1994), *Analysis of Messy Data: Designed Experiments, Vol I.,* London: Chapman Hall.

Chapter **5 Analysis of Covariance**

5.1 Introduction

Analysis of covariance is a strategy for analyzing data from a designed experiment where, in addition to the response variable, one or more continuous variables are measured on each experimental unit. Ideally, the additional continuous variables, called **covariates**, should be determined before the treatments have been applied to the experimental units. At a minimum, the values of the covariates should not be affected by the applied treatments. The analysis of covariance is often described as a method to remove variability in the experiment by accounting for variability in the experimental units that could not be controlled by the design structure. A more global view of analysis of covariance describes it as a **methodology to compare a series of regression models**. The analysis of covariance model is a model that consists of both **classification** or qualitative variables and **continuous**

or quantitative variables. The discussion in this chapter uses treatment or treatment combination to denote the levels of the classification variables used in the model and covariates to denote the continuous variables.

The basic series of models consists of a different **regression model** for each treatment or treatment combination in the treatment structure. **Analysis of covariance is a strategy** for making decisions about the form of the models and then comparing the models constructed for each combination of classification variables in the treatment structure. In order to establish the strategy for the analysis of covariance, Section 5.2 describes the analysis of a one-way treatment structure in a completely randomized design structure where the levels of the treatment are fixed effects. Most applications of analysis of covariance are to experimental designs with fixed treatment effects and some type of blocking. When blocking is used in the design structure, more than one size of experimental unit is generated. Models with fixed effects and more than one size experimental unit are **mixed models**. Section 5.3 presents an example of the analysis of such a design. These examples involve blocking and demonstrate the aspects of the mixed models equations concerning the combining of information from the intra-block and inter-block analyses.

Next the discussion expands to fixed-effect treatment structure models with more complex design structures including nested and split-plot types of design structures. The mixed model is very important in the analysis of complex design structures as information about the coefficients of the covariates in the model can occur at several levels of the model and the solution of the mixed models equations combines the information from all sources into a single estimate.

In the split-plot models, the covariate can be measured on any of the different sizes of experimental units. The following sections present three examples:
1. the covariate is measured on the large size of experimental unit
2. the covariate is measured on the small size of experimental unit
3. the covariate is measured on an intermediate size of experimental unit.

5.2 One-way Fixed-Effects Treatment Structure with Simple Linear Regression Models

In this type of analysis, data are collected from an experiment involving a one-way treatment structure in a completely randomized design structure where the experimental units exhibit considerable variability that cannot be controlled by using some form of blocking. Before the treatments were applied to the experimental units, the researcher measured the value of a covariate. The covariate should be considered a priori to be related to the variability observed in the experimental units. By measuring a covariate, the researcher attempts to account for variability in the experimental units that cannot conveniently be removed by blocking the experimental units into homogeneous groups. For example, in a feeding study the response to different diets may be affected by the size of the animals or the age of the animals. The animal scientist may measure the initial weight of each animal before the start of the experiment, i.e., before they are randomly assigned to the diets. The response variable can be the average daily gain of each animal computed for the amount of time the animals are in the study. At this point we have a fixed-effects treatment structure (a set of s diets), a random sample of animals from a population of animals with initial weights denoted by x, and the response, average daily gain, denoted by y. The average daily gain is calculated by dividing the total amount gained during the feeding trial by the number of days the animals were on trial. A **statistical model** that can be used to describe the relationships among the response variable y, the classification variable for diets, the covariate x, and the experimental units or animals is

$$y_{ij} = \alpha_i + \beta_i\, x_{ij} + e_{ij} \tag{5.1}$$

where

$i=1,2,...,s$

$j=1,2,...,n$

$e_{ij} \sim \text{iid } N(0,\sigma^2)$

α_i is the intercept of the model for treatment i

β_i is the slope of the model for treatment i.

Model 5.1 represents a series of **simple linear regression** lines with possibly different slopes and intercepts as exhibited in Figure 5.1.

Figure 5.1 *Three Simple Regression Lines with Unequal Slopes*

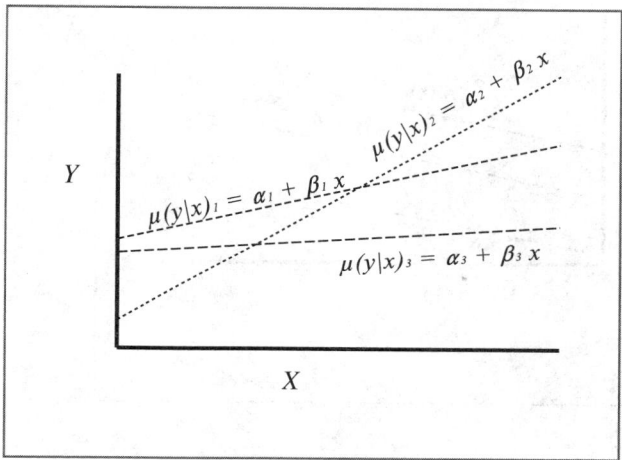

Before you use these models to describe data, you must be sure that the simple linear regression models (or the selected regression model) adequately describe the data for each treatment. This process involves the identification of outliers, testing for the equality of variances, and checking for the adequacy of the models for each treatment. This aspect of the analysis of covariance is often overlooked when put into the context of measuring variables to adjust for variability in the experimental units. When the analysis of covariance is put into the context of comparing regression models, you realize that all **regression diagnostics** used for usual regression analysis should be utilized for fitting and comparing these models.

A basic philosophy is to use the simplest possible model for the covariate part of the model; that is, don't use a more complicated model than is needed to describe the covariate part of the model. In this light, the first hypothesis to be tested is to determine if a model without the covariate can be used to adequately describe the data; i.e., test H_0: $\beta_1=\beta_2=...=\beta_s=0$ vs H_a: (not H_0), called the **slopes-equal-to-zero** hypothesis. (If you have graphed the data for each treatment, you probably already have an idea if the slopes are different from zero). If there is evidence that the slopes are not all zero, then determine if a model with a common slope can be used to describe the data; i.e., test H_0: $\beta_1=\beta_2=...=\beta_s=\beta$ vs H_a: (not H_0), where β is unspecified. If the common slope model can be used to adequately describe the data, as is described later, the process of comparing the regression models is greatly simplified. The common slope analysis of covariance model is

$$y_{ij} = \alpha_i + \beta x_{ij} + e_{ij} \qquad (5.2)$$

where

$\alpha_1, \alpha_2,..., \alpha_s$ are the intercepts for treatments 1,2,..., s
β is the common slope.

As in model 5.1, the e_{ij}'s are assumed iid $N(0, \sigma^2)$. Common slope models can be represented as shown in Figure 5.2.

Figure 5.2 *Three Simple Linear Regression Lines with Equal Slopes*

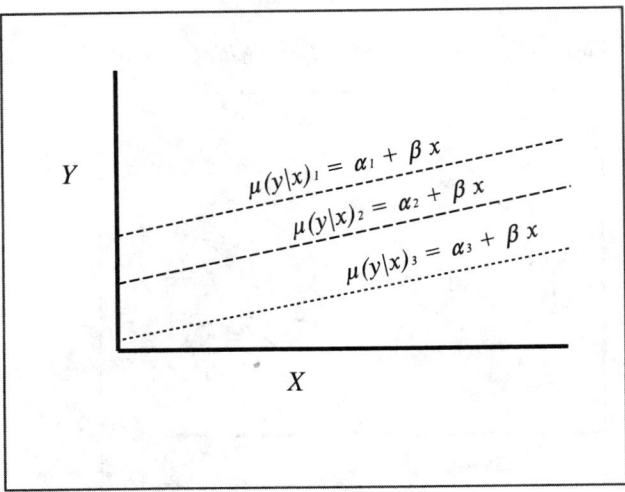

5.2.1 Comparing the Regression Models

After you decide on the form of the covariate in the model, i.e., determine the form of the slopes in the model, the next step is to make comparisons between the regression models, which may include making comparisons among the intercepts.

If the slopes are all zero, the covariate is not needed in the model, and you compare the means (intercepts for regression lines with zero slopes) using analysis of variance techniques, such as testing equality of the means, investigating contrasts of the means, or carrying out some type of multiple comparison procedure. If models with common slopes are adequate to describe the data, they form a series of parallel lines and can be compared by estimating the distance between them. The estimated regression models with common slope, i.e., the estimated mean of y for a given value of x for treatment i, are

$\hat{\mu}(y|x)_i = \hat{\alpha}_i + \hat{\beta}x$, $i=1,2,...,s$. A comparison of the regression lines for treatments one and two at $x=x^*$ is $\hat{\mu}(y|x^*)_1 - \hat{\mu}(y|x^*)_2 = \hat{\alpha}_1 - \hat{\alpha}_2$. This is a comparison of the two intercepts and is independent of the value of the covariate. The quantities $\hat{\mu}(y|x^*)_i$,$i=1,2,...s$ are predicted values obtained from the estimated regression lines evaluated at $x=x^*$, as shown in Figure 5.3, and are called **adjusted means**. Also displayed in Figure 5.3 are the estimated values of the regression lines at $x = \bar{x}$. These are the usual adjusted means that the SAS System calls LSMEANS. An important point is that adjusted means can be computed at values of x other than at $x = \bar{x}$.

For regression models with a common slope, the differences among adjusted means only involve the intercepts; i.e., they are independent of the value of the covariate used to compute the adjusted means.

Figure 5.3 *Comparison of Regression Models at x* and $\bar{x}$ Bar*

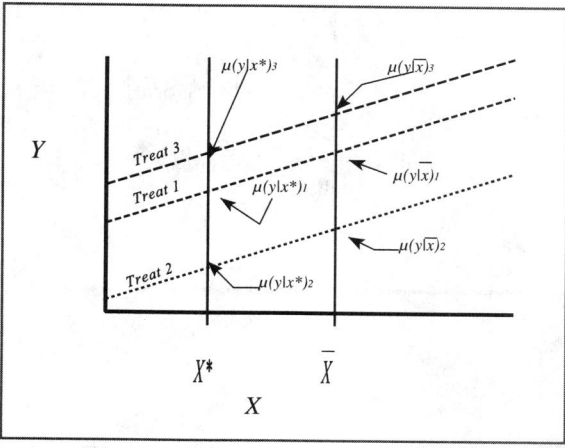

For the unequal slopes models, the estimated mean of y for a given value of x for treatment i is $\hat{\mu}(y|x)_i = \hat{\alpha}_i + \hat{\beta}_i\, x$, $i=1,2,\ldots,s$. A comparison of the regression lines for treatments one and two at $x=x^*$ is

$$\hat{\mu}(y|x^*)_1 - \hat{\mu}(y|x^*)_2 = \hat{\alpha}_1 + \hat{\beta}_1 x^* - \hat{\alpha}_2 - \hat{\beta}_2 x^* = (\hat{\alpha}_1 - \hat{\alpha}_2) + (\hat{\beta}_1 - \hat{\beta}_2)x^*$$

which is dependent on the value of the covariate, unlike for the common slope model where the differences do not depend on the value of the covariate. Because the comparison of treatments one and two depends on the value of the covariate, this model is called the **covariate by treatment interaction model**. To provide an appropriate analysis when the slopes are unequal, the models should be compared at a minimum of three values of x, such as at a low value of x, a middle value of x, and a high value of x. Potential choices are the minimum value of x, the mean value of x, and the maximum value of x, or the lower γ percentile, the median and the upper γ percentile of the distribution of the x values. Reasonable choices for γ are 5, 10, or 25. At each of the selected values of x, contrasts of interest or multiple comparisons should be used to compare the treatments. Figure 5.4 displays three models being compared at three values of x, where the points of intersection of the models with the vertical lines are the respective adjusted treatment means. Other paths of analysis consist of

- using a multiple comparison procedure to make pairwise comparisons between slopes in an attempt to form groups of treatments (*within-which* have common slopes and *between* have unequal slopes)

- constructing confidence bands about differences of models for each pair of treatments in an attempt to determine ranges of the covariate where the models are likely have similar response levels and where the models are likely to have different response levels.

These paths of analysis are used in some of the examples that follow. But first, the discussion to this point is summarized in the next section.

Figure 5.4 *Comparisons of Unequal Slope Regression Models at Three Models at Three Values of X where* μ *(y|xi)k Denotes the Mean of the* k^{th} *Treatment Evaluated at* x_i.

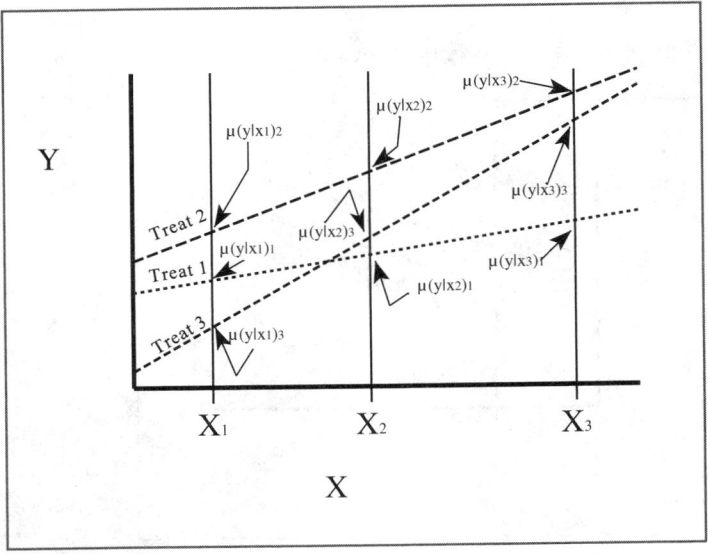

5.2.2 Summary of an Analysis of Covariance Strategy

There are several ways to approach the process of determining the form of the covariate part of the model. One strategy is summarized in Table 5.1. Following the steps in Table 5.1 provides a procedure to determine the form of the covariate part of the model. The resulting model can be used to compare the treatments by comparing the resulting regression models.

Table 5.1 *Strategy for Determining the Form of the Covariate Part of the Models for Simple Linear Regression Models*

Step	Action
1	Test the hypothesis that all the slopes are equal to zero. a) If fail to reject, go to step 2. b) If reject, go to step 3.
2	Fit a common slope model to the data and test the hypothesis that the slope is equal to zero. a) If fail to reject, compare the treatments using analysis of variance. b) If reject, use a parallel lines model and compare the treatments by comparing the intercepts or adjusted means (LSMEANS).
3	Test the hypothesis that the slopes are equal. a) If fail to reject, use a common slope model and compare the treatments by comparing the intercepts or adjusted means (LSMEANS). b) If reject, go to step 4.
4	Use the unequal slopes model. a) Compare the slopes of the treatments. b) Compare the models at a minimum of three values of the covariate. c) Construct confidence bands about the differences of selected pairs of models.

5.2.3 Extensions to More Complex Regression Models

To this point, discussion has centered around the simple linear regression model, but the same methodology can be extended to any regression model required to adequately describe the data. For example, a quadratic model in x may be required to describe the relationship between y and x for each treatment. You still need to include the simplest form of the covariate model by determining if the slopes are equal across treatments for x^2 as well for x. If there are several possible covariates, then the equality of slopes must be investigated for each possible covariate. In this case, the steps in Table 5.1 must be followed for each covariate. The strategy does not involve comparing the treatments by analysis of variance unless it is decided that the slopes for all covariates across all treatments are zero. When the slopes are unequal for a covariate, the models need to be compared at a minimum of three values for that covariate. If there are k covariates with unequal slopes and the models are to be compared at combinations of three values of each covariate, then there are 3^k combinations where the models need to be compared. Thus, it is imperative that the covariate part of the model be simplified as much as possible.

5.3 Example: One-way Treatment Structure in a Randomized Complete Block Design Structure

The data in Data Set 5.3, "Average Daily Gain," in Appendix 4, "SAS Data Sets," are average daily gains (ADG) of steers fed for 160 days. The treatments are four diets consisting of a base ration and three levels of a medicated feed additive added to the base ration. The objective of the experiment is to determine the optimal level of feed additive to maximize the average daily gain. The steers were housed in barns, the blocking factor, where each barn held four steers and the steers were individually fed.

The 32 steers were randomly assigned to the eight barns, and the four diets were randomly assigned to the four steers in each barn. Because the steers were of varying initial weights, the initial weights (IWT) were measured as a possible covariate.

5.3.1 Step 1: Fit the model to test the slopes-equal-to-zero hypothesis.

Model

A model to describe this data is

$$y_{ij} = \alpha_i + \beta_i x_{ij} + b_j + e_{ij} \tag{5.3}$$

where

$i = 1,2,3,4$
$j = 1,2,...,8$
α_i denotes the intercept of the ith diet model
β_i denotes the slope of the ith diet model
$b_j \sim$ iid N(0, σ^2_b) denotes the effect of the jth block
$e_{ij} \sim$ iid N(0, σ^2_e) denotes the experimental unit error
and b_j and e_{ij} are independent random variables.

Program

The following code fits model 5.3:

```
proc mixed;
   class trt blk;
   model adg=trt iwt*trt/noint solution;
   random blk;
run;
```

The results are in Output 5.1.

Results

Output 5.1 *The Fit of the Unequal Slope Model and the Testing of the Slopes-Equal-to-Zero Hypothesis*

```
            Covariance Parameter Estimates (REML)

Cov Parm        Ratio       Estimate     Std Error        Z    Pr > |Z|

BLK          5.24608259    0.25931025   0.14854541     1.75     0.0809
Residual     1.00000000    0.04942931   0.01703456     2.90     0.0037


            Model Fitting Information for ADG

    Description                              Value

    Observations                           32.0000
    Variance Estimate                       0.0494
    Standard Deviation Estimate             0.2223
    REML Log Likelihood                   -32.6634
    Akaike's Information Criterion        -34.6634
    Schwarz's Bayesian Criterion         -35.8415
    -2 REML Log Likelihood                 65.3268


                Solution for Fixed Effects

Parameter        Estimate     Std Error     DDF       T    Pr > |T|

TRT 0           0.43913585   0.71108869     17     0.62     0.5451
TRT 10          1.42611797   0.63754628     17     2.24     0.0390
TRT 20          0.47962757   0.54888702     17     0.87     0.3944
TRT 30          0.20010813   0.77519953     17     0.26     0.7994
IWT*TRT 0       0.00229368   0.00174730     17     1.31     0.2067
IWT*TRT 10      0.00108289   0.00148385     17     0.73     0.4755
IWT*TRT 20      0.00336566   0.00128695     17     2.62     0.0181
IWT*TRT 30      0.00444800   0.00208159     17     2.14     0.0474


                Tests of Fixed Effects

    Source     NDF    DDF    Type III F   Pr > F

    TRT         4      17       1.32      0.3011
    IWT*TRT     4      17       3.48      0.0299
```

Interpretation

The NOINT or no intercept option is used in the MODEL statement so that the model PROC MIXED is fitting to the data has a nonsingular design matrix and thus provides estimates of the intercepts and slopes. If the NOINT option is not used, the design matrix corresponding to the intercepts is singular and the estimates of the intercepts satisfy the set to includes the IWT*TRT term in the model without the IWT term. As you see a little later, excluding the IWT term enables the covariate part of the model to be nonsingular, thus excluding the IWT term enables the covariate part of the model to be nonsingular, thus providing estimates of the slopes. Including the IWT provides estimates of the slopes satisfying the set to zero restriction. The Type III F-statistic corresponding to IWT*TRT tests the hypothesis H_o: $\beta_1=\beta_2=\beta_3=\beta_4=0$ vs H_a: (not H_o:). The significance level ($p=0.0299$) indicates the slopes are most likely not all equal to zero.

5.3.2 Step 2: Determine if a common slope model will be adequate to describe the data.

Model

The following code fits the model

$$y_{ij} = \alpha_4 + (\alpha_i - \alpha_4) + \beta_4\, x_{ij} + (\beta_i - \beta_4)\, x_{ij} + b_j + e_{ij} \tag{5.4}$$

where

i=1,2,3,4
j=1,2,...,8
α_i denotes the intercept of the ith diet model
β_i denotes the slope of the ith diet model
$b_j \sim$ iid N(0, σ^2_b) denotes the effect of the jth block
$e_{ij} \sim$ iid N(0, σ^2_e) denotes the experimental unit error
b_j and e_{ij} are independent random variables.

Model 5.4 is a reparameterization of model 5.3 where the slopes have been replaced by $\beta_i = \beta_4 + (\beta_i - \beta_4)$. This reparameterization enables the Type III F corresponding to IWT*TRT to test the equal slopes hypothesis.

Program

The following code fits model 5.4 to the data:

```
proc mixed;
   class trt blk;
   model adg=trt iwt iwt*trt/solution;
   random blk;
run;
```

When the MODEL statement includes IWT (or the covariate) and IWT*TRT (the interaction), the model becomes singular and the set-to-zero restrictions are used to handle the singularity. The coefficient of IWT becomes the coefficient corresponding to the last treatment, and the coefficients of IWT*TRT become the deviations of the given treatment's coefficient from the last treatment's coefficient.

Results

The results of fitting model 5.4 are in Output 5.2, where the estimates of the fixed effects reflect the above parameterization of the model.

Output 5.2 *The Fit of the Unequal Slope Model and the Testing of the Equal Slope Hypothesis*

```
                Covariance Parameter Estimates (REML)

    Cov Parm         Ratio       Estimate     Std Error        Z

    BLK          5.24608259     0.25931025    0.14854541     1.75
    Residual     1.00000000     0.04942931    0.01703456     2.90



                Covariance Parameter Estimates (REML)


         Pr > |Z|


          0.0809
          0.0037



                    Solution for Fixed Effects


    Parameter         Estimate      Std Error    DDF       T   Pr > |T|

    INTERCEPT        0.20010813    0.77519953      7    0.26    0.8037
    TRT   0          0.23902772    1.04636989     17    0.23    0.8220
    TRT  10          1.22600984    0.95476383     17    1.28    0.2163
    TRT  20          0.27951944    0.93052742     17    0.30    0.7675
    TRT  30          0.00000000        .           .      .        .
    IWT              0.00444800    0.00208159     17    2.14    0.0474
    IWT*TRT  0      -0.00215432    0.00278626     17   -0.77    0.4500
    IWT*TRT 10      -0.00336511    0.00251483     17   -1.34    0.1985
    IWT*TRT 20      -0.00108234    0.00248755     17   -0.44    0.6690
    IWT*TRT 30       0.00000000        .           .      .        .



                    Tests of Fixed Effects


    Source        NDF    DDF    Type III F   Pr > F

    TRT            3      17        0.87      0.4755
    IWT            1      17       10.69      0.0045
    IWT*TRT        3      17        0.93      0.4471
```

By comparing Outputs 5.1 and 5.2, the estimate corresponding to IWT in Output 5.2 is that corresponding to IWT*TRT 30 in Output 5.1, and IWT*TRT 0 in Output 5.2 is (IWT*TRT 0) – (IWT*TRT 30)) in Output 5.1. The Type III *F*-statistic corresponding to IWT*TRT tests the hypothesis $H_o: \beta_1 = \beta_2 = \beta_3 = \beta_4 = \beta$ vs H_a: (not H_o). The significance level ($p = 0.4471$) indicates there is insufficient evidence to conclude the slopes are unequal.

5.3.3 Step 3: Fit a common slope model.

The preceding results indicate that the common slope model appears to be adequate to describe the data. (Plot the residuals by treatment to verify there are no patterns.)

Model

A common slope model is

$$y_{ij} = \alpha_i + \beta \, x_{ij} + b_j + e_{ij} \qquad (5.5)$$

where

$i = 1,2,3,4$
$j = 1,2,\dots,8$
α_i denotes the intercept of the ith diet model
β denotes the common slope
$b_j \sim$ iid N(0, σ^2_b) denotes the effect of the jth block
$e_{ij} \sim$ iid N(0, σ^2_e) denotes the experimental unit error
b_j and e_{ij} are independent random variables.

Program

The following program fits model 5.5 to the data with ESTIMATE statements to provide the final analysis:

```
proc mixed;
   class trt blk;
   model adg=trt iwt/ solution;
   estimate 'linear' trt -3 -1 1 3;
   estimate 'quad' trt -1 1 1 -1;
   estimate 'cubic' trt -1 3 -3 1;
   random blk;
   lsmeans trt/ pdiff ;
run;
```

Results

The results of fitting model 5.5 to the data are in Outputs 5.3 and 5.4.

Output 5.3 *The Fit of the Equal Slope Model*

Covariance Parameter Estimates (REML)					
Cov Parm	Ratio	Estimate	Std Error	Z	Pr > |Z|
BLK	4.80915375	0.24084294	0.13668343	1.76	0.0781
Residual	1.00000000	0.05008011	0.01586219	3.16	0.0016

Solution for Fixed Effects					
Parameter	Estimate	Std Error	DDF	T	Pr > |T|
INTERCEPT	0.80110822	0.35566103	7	2.25	0.0590
TRT 0	-0.55207365	0.11481310	20	-4.81	0.0001

TRT 10	-0.06856610	0.11896896	20	-0.58	0.5708
TRT 20	-0.08812911	0.11628780	20	-0.76	0.4574
TRT 30	0.00000000	.	.	.	.
IWT	0.00277971	0.00083335	20	3.34	0.0033

Tests of Fixed Effects

Source	NDF	DDF	Type III F	Pr > F
TRT	3	20	10.16	0.0003
IWT	1	20	11.13	0.0033

ESTIMATE Statement Results

Parameter	Estimate	Std Error	DDF	T	Pr > |T|
linear	1.63665795	0.36412344	20	4.49	0.0002
quad	0.39537844	0.16489047	20	2.40	0.0264
cubic	0.61076268	0.35383688	20	1.73	0.0997

Output 5.4 *The Comparison of the Treatment Means Using LSMEANS*

Least Squares Means

Level	LSMEAN	Std Error	DDF	T	Pr > |T|
TRT 0	1.33199356	0.19070136	20	6.98	0.0001
TRT 10	1.81550111	0.19136412	20	9.49	0.0001
TRT 20	1.79593811	0.19083348	20	9.41	0.0001
TRT 30	1.88406722	0.19225859	20	9.80	0.0001

Differences of Least Squares Means

Level 1	Level 2	Difference	Std Error	DDF	T	Pr > |T|
TRT 0	TRT 10	-0.48350755	0.11285282	20	-4.28	0.0004
TRT 0	TRT 20	-0.46394454	0.11205036	20	-4.14	0.0005
TRT 0	TRT 30	-0.55207365	0.11481310	20	-4.81	0.0001
TRT 10	TRT 20	0.01956301	0.11223454	20	0.17	0.8634
TRT 10	TRT 30	-0.06856610	0.11896896	20	-0.58	0.5708
TRT 20	TRT 30	-0.08812911	0.11628780	20	-0.76	0.4574

Interpretation

The estimates of the variance components are $\hat{\sigma}_e^2 = 0.05008$ and $\hat{\sigma}_b^2 = 0.24084$. Figure 5.5 is a graph of the four parallel regression models where ADG is the response variable and IWT is the regressor variable.

Figure 5.5 *Plot of Estimated Regression Lines with LSMEANS*

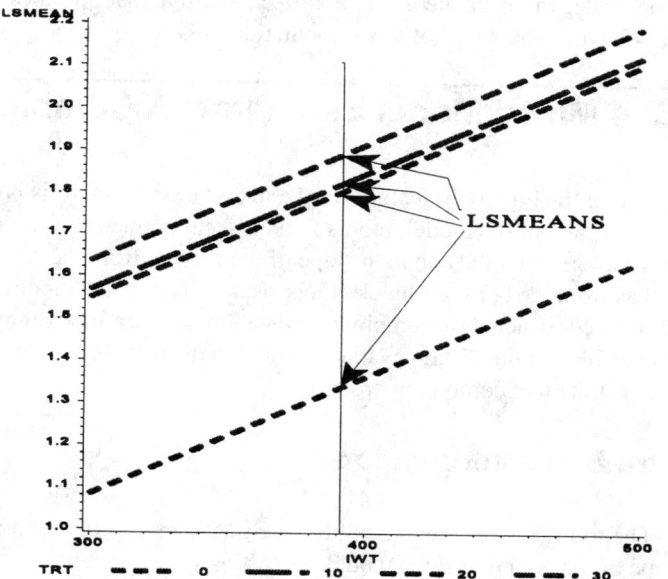

Because the treatments levels are quantitative, i.e., the levels of the feed additive are 0 pmm, 10 pmm, 20 pmm, and 30 pmm, the ESTIMATE statements are used to evaluate the shape of the response curve. The coefficients in the ESTIMATE statements correspond to the linear, quadratic, and cubic orthogonal polynomials for equally spaced levels. The response curve is the relationship between ADG and the levels of feed additive as shown in Figure 5.6.

Figure 5.6 *Plot of LSMEANS as a Function of Treatment Level*

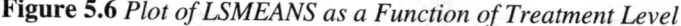

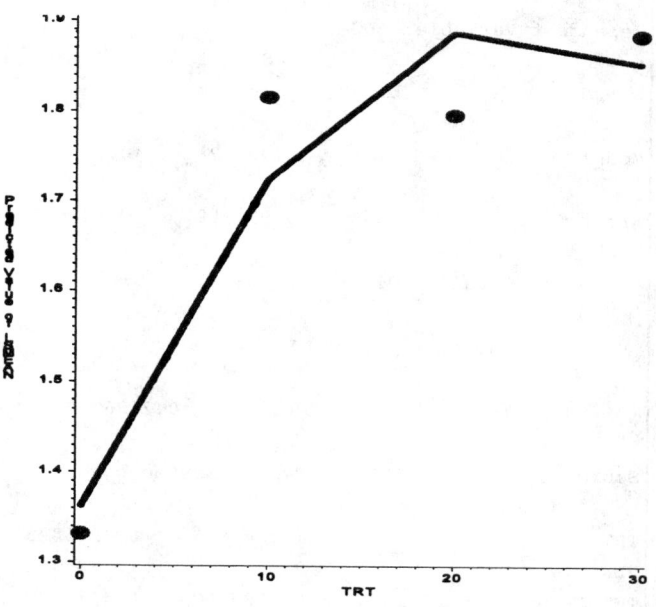

Results of the ESTIMATE statements indicate there is a strong quadratic relationship with a weak cubic trend between the LSMEANS of the ADG and the levels of feed additive. The LSMEANS in Output 5.4 are the predictions from the parallel line regression models evaluated at IWT = 389.59 (the mean of the covariate) as shown in Figure 5.5. The pairwise comparisons results indicate that treatments 10, 20, and 30 are significantly different from the control but are not different among themselves. The complete analysis involves using some strategy to estimate the level of feed additive that provides the optimal ADG response, a task beyond the scope of this presentation.

5.3.4 Mixed Model Estimator: A Combined Estimator

One of the important features of the mixed models analysis is that it combines information from all parts of the model into its fixed-effects estimates. For this example, there is information about the common slope of the models from the within-block comparisons as well as from the between-block comparisons. The mixed model estimate of the slope is an estimate constructed by combining the within- or intra-block information with the between- or inter-block information available from the data. This example provides an opportunity to demonstrate that combining process.

Intra-Block Information

The following program uses PROC GLM to extract the intra-block information about the slope of the common slope model:

```
proc glm;class blk trt;
    model adg= trt blk iwt/solution;
run;
```

The results from this code are listed in Output 5.5.

Output 5.5 *The Fit of the Equal Slope Model to Obtain the Intra-Block Information about the Common Slope Using PROC GLM*

```
                    General Linear Models Procedure

Dependent Variable: ADG
                          Sum of         Mean
Source            DF      Squares        Square    F Value    Pr > F

Model             11      10.969528      0.997230   19.95     0.0001

Error             20      0.999959       0.049998

Corrected Total   31      11.969487


        R-Square          C.V.       Root MSE          ADG Mean

        0.916458       13.10009       0.2236            1.7069


Source            DF     Type I SS   Mean Square   F Value    Pr > F

TRT               3      1.4840625    0.4946875     9.89      0.0003
BLK               7      9.0218875    1.2888411    25.78      0.0001
IWT               1      0.4635782    0.4635782     9.27      0.0064


Source            DF    Type III SS  Mean Square   F Value    Pr > F

TRT               3      1.5184618    0.5061539    10.12      0.0003
BLK               7      6.3575674    0.9082239    18.17      0.0001
IWT               1      0.4635782    0.4635782     9.27      0.0064
```

Parameter		Estimate	T for H0: Parameter=0	Pr > |T|	Std Error of Estimate
INTERCEPT		-0.183388456 B	-0.60	0.5584	0.30810597
TRT	0	-0.545646620 B	-4.75	0.0001	0.11480145
	10	-0.058470197 B	-0.49	0.6287	0.11906782
	20	-0.080218917 B	-0.69	0.4983	0.11631582
	30	0.000000000 B	.	.	.
BLK	1	0.869708466 B	5.33	0.0001	0.16317216
	2	1.220992108 B	7.30	0.0001	0.16729965
	3	1.329206546 B	7.96	0.0001	0.16695759
	4	1.593492108 B	9.52	0.0001	0.16729965
	5	1.518209105 B	9.36	0.0001	0.16213335
	6	1.093502773 B	6.87	0.0001	0.15927371
	7	0.850788122 B	5.35	0.0001	0.15898799
	8	0.000000000 B	.	.	.
IWT		0.002571550	3.04	0.0064	0.00084452

NOTE: The X'X matrix has been found to be singular and a
generalized inverse was used to solve the normal equations.
Estimates followed by the letter 'B' are biased, and are not
unique estimators of the parameters.

The estimate of the common slope and its associated estimated standard error based on the intra-block analysis are

$$\hat{\beta}_a = 0.002571550 \text{ and } \hat{\sigma}_{\hat{\beta}_a} = 0.00084452$$

Inter-Block Information

The inter-block model is constructed from the model for the block means as

$$\bar{y}_{\bullet j} = \bar{\mu}_{\bullet} + \beta \, \bar{x}_{\bullet j} + b_j + \bar{e}_{\bullet j}$$

where

$$j=1,2,...,8$$

$$\text{Var}(\bar{y}_{\bullet j}) = \text{Var}(b_j + \bar{e}_{\bullet j}) = \sigma_b^2 + \frac{\sigma_e^2}{4}$$

$$= \frac{\sigma_e^2 + 4\,\sigma_b^2}{4}$$

The inter-block model is fit to the data using PROC GLM with the following code. PROC MEANS is used to compute the block means, and the WEIGHT NADP provides weighted sums of squares which are comparable to those in Output 5.5. (We are weighting by the block size because the variance of the block means is a scalar multiple of the reciprocal of the block size.)

```
proc sort data=rcb;
   by blk;
proc means mean n;
   var adg iwt;
   by blk;
   output out=means mean=madg miwt n=NADP niwt;

proc glm;
   weight NADP;
   model madg=miwt;
run;
```

The inter-block information about the common slope is in Output 5.6 where $\hat{\beta}_r = 0.010041674$ and $\hat{\sigma}_{\beta_r} = 0.00449117$.

Output 5.6 *The Fit of the Equal Slope Model to Obtain the Inter-Block Information about the Common Slope Using PROC GLM*

```
                    General Linear Models Procedure

                Number of observations in data set = 8


Dependent Variable: MADG
Weight:             NADG
                                Sum of          Mean
Source                DF        Squares         Square    F Value    Pr > F

Model                 1        4.1004613      4.1004613    5.00       0.0667

Error                 6        4.9214262      0.8202377

Corrected Total       7        9.0218875

          R-Square         C.V.       Root MSE          MADG Mean

          0.454501       53.06011      0.9057             1.7069

Source                DF      Type I SS   Mean Square   F Value    Pr > F

MIWT                  1       4.1004613    4.1004613     5.00       0.0667

Source                DF      Type III SS  Mean Square  F Value    Pr > F

MIWT                  1       4.1004613    4.1004613     5.00       0.0667


                                    T for H0:    Pr > |T|    Std Error of
Parameter         Estimate        Parameter=0                 Estimate

INTERCEPT       -2.205298579        -1.26       0.2561       1.75704177
MIWT             0.010041674         2.24       0.0667       0.00449117
```

The estimates of the variance components using the method of moments (see Chapter 4) are

$$\hat{\sigma}_e^2 = 0.0499980$$

$$\hat{\sigma}_b^2 = \frac{MSERROR(inter) - MSERROR(intra)}{4} = 0.19255993$$

which were computed by using the expected error mean squares of the intra-block model and the inter-block model as follows:

$$E(MSERROR(intra\text{-}block)) = \sigma^2_e$$
$$E(MSERROR(inter\text{-}block)) = \sigma^2_e + 4\,\sigma^2_b$$

The combined estimate of the slope is computed by the weighted average of the intra-block estimate of the slope and the inter-block estimate of the slope where the weights are the inverses of the respective variances as

$$\hat{\beta}_c = \frac{1}{\dfrac{1}{\hat{\sigma}^2_{\beta_a}} + \dfrac{1}{\hat{\sigma}^2_{\beta_r}}} \left[\frac{\hat{\beta}_a}{\hat{\sigma}^2_{\beta_a}} + \frac{\hat{\beta}_r}{\hat{\sigma}^2_{\beta_r}} \right]$$

The combined estimate of the common slope using the method of moments estimates of the variance components is $\hat{\beta}_c = 0.0028267$ and $\hat{\sigma}_{\beta_c} = 0.00082997$. The combined estimate of the common slope using the REML estimates of the variance components from PROC MIXED is $\hat{\beta}_c = 0.0027797$ and $\hat{\sigma}_{\beta_c} = 0.000833352997$, the same as the estimate and estimated standard error of the slope computed using PROC MIXED as shown in Output 5.3. Thus, the mixed models approach to the analysis of this model extracts more information about the common slope than the intra-block analysis from PROC GLM.

5.4 Example: One-way Treatment Structure in a Balanced Incomplete Block Design Structure

The data in Data Set 5.4, "Balanced Incomplete Block," in Appendix 4, "SAS Data Sets," are from four treatments in a one-way treatment structure in a balanced incomplete block design structure with blocks of size three. The objectives of this example are to provide methodology to work with the unequal slopes model as well as demonstrate the use of PROC MIXED in the balanced incomplete block design structure. The response is Y and the covariate is X.

5.4.1 Step 1: Fit the unequal slopes model.

Model

A model that describes the data is

$$y_{ij} = \alpha_i + \beta_i\, x_{ij} + b_j + e_{ij} \, , \; (i, j)\in\mathbf{B} \tag{5.6}$$

where

α_i denotes the intercept of the ith diet model

β_i denotes the slope of the ith diet model

$b_j \sim$ iid N$(0, \sigma^2_b)$ denotes the effect of the jth block

$e_{ij} \sim$ iid N$(0, \sigma^2_e)$ denotes the experimental unit error

b_j and e_{ij} are independent random variables

$\mathbf{B}$ is the index set of observed treatment-block combinations (i,j) as denoted by
$\mathbf{B}$=[(1,1), (2,1), (3,1), (1,2), (2,2), (4,2), (1,3), (3,3), (4,3), (2,4), (3,4), (4,4), (1,5), (2,5), (3,5), (1,6), (2,6), (4,6), (1,7), (3,7), (4,7), (2,8), (3,8), (4,8)].

Program

The following program fits the unequal slopes model 5.6 to the data:

```
proc mixed data=bib;
   class blk trt;
   model y=trt x*trt/solution ddfm=satterth;
   random blk;
run;
```

The NOINT option is not used in this MODEL statement. Thus, the estimates of the intercepts satisfy the set to zero restrictions. The DDFM=SATTERTH option is included to provide approximate degrees of freedom for the denominators of each test statistic and for each estimated standard error. The approximate degrees of freedom are needed because the estimates of the slopes and intercepts are combined inter- and intra-block estimates.

The PROC MIXED results are in Output 5.7.

Results

Output 5.7 *The Fit of the Unequal Slope Model and the Testing of the Slopes-Equal-to-Zero Hypothesis*

Covariance Parameter Estimates (REML)					
Cov Parm	Ratio	Estimate	Std Error	Z	Pr > |Z|
BLK	15.20255412	18.24950714	10.02423500	1.82	0.0687
Residual	1.00000000	1.20042376	0.56359936	2.13	0.0332

```
                    Model Fitting Information for Y

            Description                     Value

            Observations                   24.0000
            Variance Estimate               1.2004
            Standard Deviation Estimate     1.0956
            REML Log Likelihood           -52.4472
            Akaike's Information Criterion -54.4472
            Schwarz's Bayesian Criterion  -55.2198
            -2 REML Log Likelihood        104.8945



                    Solution for Fixed Effects


   Parameter        Estimate     Std Error   DDF       T   Pr > |T|


   INTERCEPT      22.36785102    3.10183097  14.2    7.21    0.0001
   TRT 1           4.42948636    3.36506262   9.51   1.32    0.2189
   TRT 2          -0.43737059    2.93321906   9.39  -0.15    0.8846
   TRT 3           6.27862925    3.28205289   9.56   1.91    0.0861
   TRT 4           0.00000000         .        .      .        .
   X*TRT 1         0.21878193    0.06383358   9.47   3.43    0.0070
   X*TRT 2         0.49593121    0.05467374   9.35   9.07    0.0001
   X*TRT 3         0.26337053    0.05701116   9.51   4.62    0.0011
   X*TRT 4         0.44254746    0.08706277   9.45   5.08    0.0006



                    Tests of Fixed Effects


      Source      NDF    DDF   Type III F  Pr > F


      TRT          3    9.32        4.50   0.0329
      X*TRT        4    9.37       32.33   0.0001
```

Interpretation

The set to zero restrictions are demonstrated by reviewing the solution part of Output 5.7 where the estimate corresponding to TRT 4 is 0.00000000. The Type III F corresponding to X*TRT is the statistic testing H_o: $\beta_1=\beta_2=\beta_3=\beta_4=0$ vs H_a:(not H_o), which indicates there is evidence to reject the null hypothesis ($p<0.0001$). (If the covariate X is not in the model, the Type III F corresponding to X*TRT tests the slopes-equal-to-zero hypothesis. If X is in the model (along with X*TRT), the Type III F corresponding to X*TRT tests the slopes equal hypothesis.)

5.4.2 Step 2: Test the equality of slopes.

Program

The following program fits the unequal slope model to the data, but includes the X as well as the X*TRT so that the Type III F corresponding to X*TRT is the statistic to test: H_o $\beta_1=\beta_2=\beta_3=\beta_4=\beta$ vs H_a:(not H_o), where β is not specified.

```
proc mixed data=bib;
   class blk trt;
   model y=trt x x*trt/solution ddfm=satterth;
   estimate 'b1-b2' x*trt 1 -1 0 0;
   estimate 'b1-b3' x*trt 1 0 -1 0;
   estimate 'b1-b4' x*trt 1 0 0 -1;
   estimate 'b2-b3' x*trt 0 1 -1 0;
   estimate 'b2-b4' x*trt 0 1 0 -1;
   estimate 'b3-b4' x*trt 0 0 1 -1;
   random blk;
run;
```

The results are in Output 5.8.

Results

Output 5.8 *The Fit of the Unequal Slope Model and the Testing of the Equal Slope Hypothesis: ESTIMATE Statements Provide Pairwise Comparison between the Slopes*

Covariance Parameter Estimates (REML)					
Cov Parm	Ratio	Estimate	Std Error	Z	Pr > |Z|
BLK	15.20255412	18.24950714	10.02423500	1.82	0.0687
Residual	1.00000000	1.20042376	0.56359936	2.13	0.0332

Model Fitting Information for Y	
Description	Value
Observations	24.0000
Variance Estimate	1.2004
Standard Deviation Estimate	1.0956
REML Log Likelihood	-52.4472
Akaike's Information Criterion	-54.4472
Schwarz's Bayesian Criterion	-55.2198
-2 REML Log Likelihood	104.8945

Solution for Fixed Effects					
Parameter	Estimate	Std Error	DDF	T	Pr > |T|
INTERCEPT	22.36785102	3.10183097	14.2	7.21	0.0001
TRT 1	4.42948636	3.36506262	9.51	1.32	0.2189
TRT 2	-0.43737059	2.93321906	9.39	-0.15	0.8846
TRT 3	6.27862925	3.28205289	9.56	1.91	0.0861
TRT 4	0.00000000	.	.	.	.

```
X               0.44254746    0.08706277  9.45   5.08   0.0006
X*TRT 1        -0.22376553    0.10608323  9.46  -2.11   0.0627
X*TRT 2         0.05338375    0.09714274  9.35   0.55   0.5955
X*TRT 3        -0.17917693    0.11571014  9.6   -1.55   0.1538
X*TRT 4         0.00000000        .         .      .      .
```

```
               Tests of Fixed Effects


        Source       NDF   DDF  Type III F  Pr > F


        TRT           3    9.32      4.50   0.0329
        X             1    9.52     99.64   0.0001
        X*TRT         3    9.34      5.12   0.0233
```

```
             ESTIMATE Statement Results


Parameter            Estimate    Std Error   DDF        T     Pr > |T|


b1-b2              -0.27714928   0.07524708  9.25    -3.68    0.0048
b1-b3              -0.04458860   0.07467523  9.27    -0.60    0.5647
b1-b4              -0.22376553   0.10608323  9.46    -2.11    0.0627
b2-b3               0.23256069   0.07748868  9.39     3.00    0.0143
b2-b4               0.05338375   0.09714274  9.35     0.55    0.5955
b3-b4              -0.17917693   0.11571014  9.6     -1.55    0.1538
```

Interpretation

The Type III F-statistic corresponding to X*TRT indicates there is evidence to reject the equal slopes hypothesis (p=0.0233). The above ESTIMATE statements are used to carry out a multiple comparison procedure on the slopes, and the results are in Output 5.8. Based on these results (as well as on observing the estimates of the slopes in Output 5.7), treatments 1 and 3 are grouped together and treatments 2 and 4 are grouped together. A new variable is constructed, GRP, to denote the two groups of treatments within which the slopes are equal. The value of GRP is determined as GRP=13 for treatments 1 and 3 and GRP=24 for treatments 2 and 4. The slopes are different between groups, and they are homogeneous within groups. A grouping variable was created to take advantage of the simpler model with just two different slopes instead of using a model with four different slopes. A model with fewer slopes requires fewer comparisons between the treatments. That is, you compare treatments with a common slope at only one value of X whereas you compare treatments with unequal slopes at a minimum of three values of X.

5.4.3 Step 3: Fit Model with Unequal Slopes for Each Level of GRP

Program

The following program fits a model with unequal slopes for the two groups. Both TRT and GRP are included in the CLASS statement, but in the MODEL statement TRT is used to denote the four possible intercepts and X*GRP is used to denote the two different slopes.

```
proc mixed data=bib;
   class blk trt grp;
   model y=trt x*grp/solution ddfm=satterth;

random blk;
estimate 't1 at 25%=17' intercept 1 trt 1 0 0 0 x*grp 17 0;
estimate 't1 at 50%=28.5'intercept 1 trt 1 0 0 0 x*grp 28.5 0;
estimate 't1 at 75%=37' intercept 1 trt 1 0 0 0 x*grp 37 0;
estimate 't1 at mean' intercept 1 trt 1 0 0 0 x*grp 26 0;

estimate 't3 at 25%=17' intercept 1 trt 0 0 1 0 x*grp 17 0;
estimate 't3 at 50%=28.5' intercept 1 trt 0 0 1 0 x*grp 28.5 0;
estimate 't3 at 75%=37' intercept 1 trt 0 0 1 0 x*grp 37 0;
estimate 't3 at mean' intercept 1 trt 0 0 1 0 x*grp 26 0;

estimate 't2 at 25%=17' intercept 1 trt 0 1 0 0 x*grp 0 17;
estimate 't2 at 50%=28.5' intercept 1 trt 0 1 0 0 x*grp 0 28.5;
estimate 't2 at 75%=37'  intercept 1 trt 0 1 0 0 x*grp 0 37;
estimate 't2 at mean' intercept 1 trt 0 1 0 0 x*grp 0 26;

estimate 't4 at 25%=17' intercept 1 trt 0 0 0 1 x*grp 0 17;
estimate 't4 at 50%=28.5' intercept 1 trt 0 0 0 1 x*grp 0 28.5;
estimate 't4 at 75%=37' intercept 1 trt 0 0 0 1 x*grp 0 37;
estimate 't4 at mean' intercept 1 trt 0 0 0 1 x*grp 0 26;
****comparisons of means at 25%, 75%, and 50%;
estimate 't1-t2 75%=37'   trt 1 -1 0 0 x*grp 37 -37;
estimate 't1-t2 50%=28.5' trt 1 -1 0 0 x*grp 28.5 -28.5;
estimate 't1-t2 25%=17'   trt 1 -1 0 0 x*grp 17 -17;
estimate 't1-t4 75%=37'   trt 1 0 0 -1  x*grp 37 -37;
estimate 't1-t4 50%=28.5' trt 1 0 0 -1  x*grp 28.5 -28.5;
estimate 't1-t4 25%=17'   trt 1 0 0 -1  x*grp 17 -17;
estimate 't3-t2 75%=37'   trt 0 -1 1 0 x*grp 37 -37;
estimate 't3-t2 50%=28.5' trt 0 -1 1 0 x*grp 28.5 -28.5;
estimate 't3-t2 25%=17'   trt 0 -1 1 0 x*grp 17 -17;
estimate 't3-t4 75%=37'   trt 0 0 1 -1  x*grp 37 -37;
estimate 't3-t4 50%=28.5' trt 0 0 1 -1  x*grp 28.5 -28.5;
estimate 't3-t4 25%=17'   trt 0 0 1 -1  x*grp 17 -17;
***comparison of LSMEANS at X=26***;
estimate 't1-t2 at mean' trt 1 -1 0 0 x*grp 26 -26;
estimate 't1-t3 at mean' trt 1 0 -1 0;
estimate 't1-t4 at mean' trt 1 0 0 -1 x*grp 26 -26;
estimate 't2-t3 at mean' trt 0 1 -1 0 x*grp 26 -26;
estimate 't2-t4 at mean' trt 0 1 0 -1;
estimate 't3-t4 at mean' trt 0 0 1 -1 x*grp 26 -26;
lsmeans trt/pdiff e;
run;
```

The results are in Output 5.9, Output 5.10, Output 5.11, and Output 5.12.

Results

Ouput 5.9 *The Fit of the Unequal Slope Model for the Two Groups*

```
                    The MIXED Procedure

                  Class Level Information

           Class    Levels  Values

           BLK        8     1 2 3 4 5 6 7 8
           TRT        4     1 2 3 4
           GRP        2     13 24


             REML Estimation Iteration History

    Iteration  Evaluations     Objective    Criterion

        0           1         92.82119973
        1           3         66.09923507   0.00011577
        2           1         66.09524937   0.00000050
        3           1         66.09523267   0.00000000


                  Convergence criteria met.


          Covariance Parameter Estimates (REML)

   Cov Parm       Ratio        Estimate     Std Error       Z    Pr > |Z|

   BLK         17.85031686   18.52551842  10.12934016     1.83    0.0674
   Residual     1.00000000    1.03782575   0.44196532     2.35    0.0189


                Model Fitting Information for Y

           Description                        Value

           Observations                      24.0000
           Variance Estimate                  1.0378
           Standard Deviation Estimate        1.0187
           REML Log Likelihood              -49.5885
           Akaike's Information Criterion   -51.5885
           Schwarz's Bayesian Criterion     -52.4789
           -2 REML Log Likelihood            99.1770


                Solution for Fixed Effects

   Parameter     Estimate      Std Error   DDF       T    Pr > |T|

   INTERCEPT   20.94516525   2.06229624    16    10.16    0.0001
   TRT 1        5.34144419   1.97570610  11.4     2.70    0.0199
   TRT 2        1.13556861   0.71398863  11.2     1.59    0.1396
   TRT 3        8.18103321   1.77010040  11.4     4.62    0.0007
   TRT 4        0.00000000        .         .        .        .
```

```
X*GRP 13    0.23951987   0.04296354  11.5    5.57   0.0001
X*GRP 24    0.48923036   0.04412190  11.3   11.09   0.0001


                Tests of Fixed Effects


       Source      NDF   DDF   Type III F   Pr > F


       TRT          3   11.2      15.54    0.0003
       X*GRP        2   11.4      74.55    0.0001
```

Output 5.10 *The Adjusted Means for Each Treatment Computed at X=17, 26(mean), 28.5, and 37*

Parameter	Estimate	Std Error	DDF	T	Pr > |T|
t1 at 25%=17	30.35844731	1.66697873	9.4	18.21	0.0001
t1 at 50%=28.5	33.11292587	1.58297983	7.81	20.92	0.0001
t1 at 75%=37	35.14884480	1.61797556	8.48	21.72	0.0001
t1 at mean	32.51412618	1.58859669	7.92	20.47	0.0001
t3 at 25%=17	33.19803632	1.60914745	8.3	20.63	0.0001
t3 at 50%=28.5	35.95251488	1.59730141	8.08	22.51	0.0001
t3 at 75%=37	37.98843382	1.68436755	9.75	22.55	0.0001
t3 at mean	35.35371520	1.58685133	7.89	22.28	0.0001
t2 at 25%=17	30.39765003	1.60151095	8.16	18.98	0.0001
t2 at 50%=28.5	36.02379920	1.60435352	8.22	22.45	0.0001
t2 at 75%=37	40.18225728	1.70635049	10.2	23.55	0.0001
t2 at mean	34.80072329	1.59002121	7.95	21.89	0.0001
t4 at 25%=17	29.26208142	1.68494468	9.77	17.37	0.0001
t4 at 50%=28.5	34.88823059	1.58761945	7.9	21.98	0.0001
t4 at 75%=37	39.04668867	1.61742586	8.46	24.14	0.0001
t4 at mean	33.66515468	1.59561074	8.05	21.10	0.0001

Output 5.11 *Results from ESTIMATE Statements to Make the Necessary Comparisons among the Treatments*

Parameter	Estimate	Std Error	DDF	T	Pr > |T|
t1-t2 75%=37	-5.03341248	0.93690871	11.2	-5.37	0.0002
t1-t2 50%=28.5	-2.91087333	0.66899826	11.1	-4.35	0.0011
t1-t2 25%=17	-0.03920272	0.83732502	11.3	-0.05	0.9635
t1-t4 75%=37	-3.89784387	0.71883516	11.1	-5.42	0.0002
t1-t4 50%=28.5	-1.77530472	0.64389246	11.2	-2.76	0.0184
t1-t4 25%=17	1.09636589	1.05454697	11.4	1.04	0.3201
t3-t2 75%=37	-2.19382347	1.09257689	11.3	-2.01	0.0692
t3-t2 50%=28.5	-0.07128432	0.73391796	11.2	-0.10	0.9243
t3-t2 25%=17	2.80038630	0.69855712	11.1	4.01	0.0020
t3-t4 75%=37	-1.05825486	0.85165789	11.2	-1.24	0.2394
t3-t4 50%=28.5	1.06428429	0.63114598	11.1	1.69	0.1197
t3-t4 25%=17	3.93595491	0.88972412	11.2	4.42	0.0010
t1-t2 at mean	-2.28659711	0.64879237	11.1	-3.52	0.0047
t1-t3 at mean	-2.83958902	0.67155011	11.2	-4.23	0.0014
t1-t4 at mean	-1.15102850	0.69604176	11.2	-1.65	0.1259
t2-t3 at mean	-13.53793729	2.96867930	11.4	-4.56	0.0008
t2-t4 at mean	1.13556861	0.71398863	11.2	1.59	0.1396
t3-t4 at mean	1.68856051	0.63410543	11.1	2.66	0.0220

Output 5.12 *Information from the LSMEANS Statement. The LSMEANS are not interpretable (see text).*

```
                  Coefficients for TRT Least Squares Means

    Parameter          Row 1          Row 2          Row 3          Row 4


    INTERCEPT            1              1              1              1
    TRT 1                1              0              0              0
    TRT 2                0              1              0              0
    TRT 3                0              0              1              0
    TRT 4                0              0              0              1
    X*GRP 13            13             13             13             13
    X*GRP 24            13             13             13             13




                         Least Squares Means


        Level           LSMEAN      Std Error   DDF         T   Pr > |T|


        TRT 1        35.76036252   1.81862683  12.3      19.66   0.0001
        TRT 2        31.55448695   1.71815426  10.4      18.37   0.0001
        TRT 3        38.59995154   1.71987612  10.5      22.44   0.0001
        TRT 4        30.41891834   1.86324442  13.1      16.33   0.0001




                  Differences of Least Squares Means


    Level 1  Level 2    Difference     Std Error   DDF        T   Pr > |T|


    TRT 1    TRT 2      4.20587558    1.68411191  11.4     2.50    0.0290
    TRT 1    TRT 3     -2.83958902    0.67155011  11.2    -4.23    0.0014
    TRT 1    TRT 4      5.34144419    1.97570610  11.4     2.70    0.0199
    TRT 2    TRT 3     -7.04546459    1.47424656  11.3    -4.78    0.0005
    TRT 2    TRT 4      1.13556861    0.71398863  11.2     1.59    0.1396
    TRT 3    TRT 4      8.18103321    1.77010040  11.4     4.62    0.0007
```

Interpretation

Output 5.9 contains estimates of the slopes and intercepts for the model as well as *F*-statistics to test that the slopes are equal to zero and to test that the intercepts (models at *x*=0) are equal. Most likely these tests are not of interest. Of more interest is to compare the models at three or more values of *x*. The results in Output 5.10 are adjusted means computed from the estimated regression models at *X*=17 (25th percentile), *X*=26 (the mean of the *X* values), *X*=28.5 (the median of the *X* values) and *X*=37 (the 75th percentile), as provided by ESTIMATE statements.

The results of the ESTIMATE statements for comparing the adjusted means are in Output 5.11.

The LSMEANS comparisons are in Output 5.12. The E option on the LSMEANS statement provides the coefficients used to compute the LSMEANS. They are also displayed in Output 5.12. One very important observation is that the LSMEANS are computed by using a coefficient of 13 for both levels of X*GRP, whereas only one is required as displayed in the above ESTIMATE statements. Thus, the LSMEANS statement is not providing the appropriate information about the regression models evaluated at the average value of X. Treatments 1 and 3 and treatments 2 and 4 need to be compared only at one value of X, and they are compared at $X=26$ (mean) only. By forming groups of treatments within which there are common slopes, the required number of comparisons is greatly reduced. The graph in Figure 5.7 displays the four regression lines indicating where the models are being evaluated and compared.

Figure 5.7 *Graph of the Four Estimated Regression Lines with Vertical Lines Drawn at Values of x Where Comparisons Were Made*

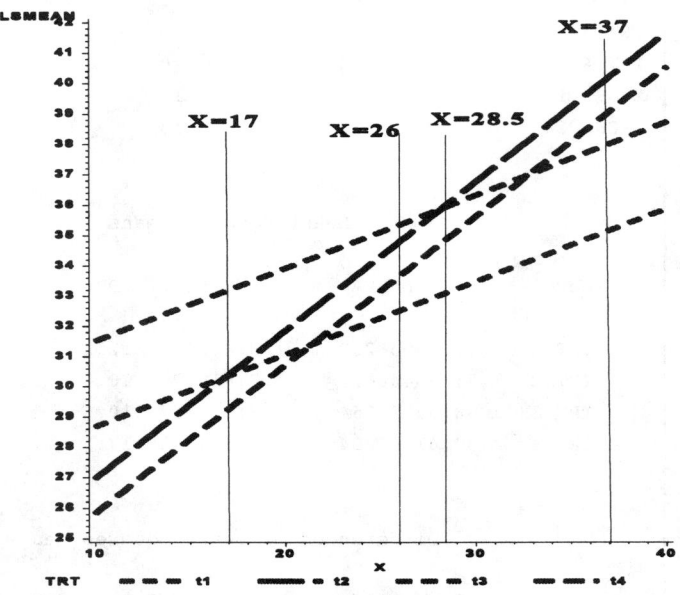

5.5 Example: One-way Treatment Structure in an Unbalanced Incomplete Block Design Structure

The data in Data Set 5.5, "Unbalanced Incomplete Block," in Appendix 4, "SAS Data Sets," are from four treatments in a one-way treatment structure in an unbalanced incomplete block design structure with blocks of size two. This design illustrates one of the advantages of the mixed model analysis. The design is **not a connected block-treatment design**. But the mixed models analysis combines the intra-block and the inter-block information about the fixed effects, thus extracting information about all of the treatments. The treatments can be compared using adjusted means such as those provided by the LSMEANS statement. The usual intra-block analysis, as you would obtain using PROC GLM, declares the comparisons 1 vs 3, 1 vs 4, 2 vs 3, and 2 vs 4 as nonestimable because the blocks and treatments are not connected. The response is Y, and the covariate is X. A model which can be used to describe the data is

$$y_{ij} = \alpha_i + \beta_i x_{ij} + b_j + e_{ij} , \ (i, j) \in \mathbf{B}$$

(5.7)

where

α_i denotes the intercept of the ith diet model

β_i denotes the slope of the ith diet model

$b_j \sim$ iid N(0, σ^2_b) denotes the effect of the jth block

$e_{ij} \sim$ iid N(0, σ^2_e) denotes the experimental unit error

b_j and e_{ij} are independent random variables

B is the index set of observed

treatment-block combinations as described in Example 5.4.

5.5.1 Step 1: Fit the unequal slope model and test the slopes-equal-to-zero hypothesis.

Program

The following program fits the unequal slopes model to the data:

```
proc mixed;
   class blk trt;
   model y=trt x*trt/noint solution ddfm=satterth;
   random blk;
run;
```

The results are in Output 5.13.

Results

Output 5.13 *Results for Fitting the Unequal Slopes Model and the Testing of the Slopes-Equal-to-Zero Hypothesis*

```
               Covariance Parameter Estimates (REML)

   Cov Parm          Ratio       Estimate     Std Error       Z    Pr > |Z|

   BLK           29.16849617    0.02495507   0.01140157    2.19     0.0286
   Residual       1.00000000    0.00085555   0.00048852    1.75     0.0799


                    Solution for Fixed Effects

   Parameter       Estimate     Std Error   DDF         T   Pr > |T|

   TRT 1          0.53522096    0.06801735  11.7      7.87    0.0001
   TRT 2          0.61263063    0.07046489    13      8.69    0.0001
   TRT 3          0.32372241    0.07905477  15.6      4.09    0.0009
   TRT 4          0.32568343    0.10768875  13.4      3.02    0.0095
   X*TRT 1       -2.72958766    0.60054628  6.34     -4.55    0.0034
   X*TRT 2       -1.91794484    0.69619194  6.34     -2.75    0.0313
   X*TRT 3       -1.40621670    0.94913699  6.92     -1.48    0.1825
   X*TRT 4       -0.99020248    1.28760823  6.92     -0.77    0.4673
```

```
                      Tests of Fixed Effects

           Source    NDF   DDF   Type III F   Pr > F

           TRT         4   9.13      23.21     0.0001
           X*TRT       4   6.47       7.66     0.0129
```

Interpretation

The Type III F-test corresponding to X*TRT in Output 5.13 tests the slopes-equal-to-zero hypothesis. There is evidence that the slopes are not all equal to zero ($p=0.0129$).

5.5.2 Step 2: Test the equal slope hypothesis.

Program

The following program is used to test the equal slopes hypothesis (X and X*TRT are both in the model).

```
proc mixed;
   class blk trt;
   model y=trt x x*trt/noint solution ddfm=satterth;
   random blk;
run;
```

The results are in Output 5.14.

Results

Output 5.14 *Results from Fitting the Unequal Slopes Model and the Testing of the Equal Slopes Hypothesis*

```
                      The MIXED Procedure

                   Class Level Information

      Class    Levels  Values

      BLK         12    1 2 3 4 5 6 7 8 9 10 11 12
      TRT          4    1 2 3 4


              REML Estimation Iteration History

      Iteration  Evaluations     Objective      Criterion

           0          1       -57.16194941
           1          2       -61.64962566    0.09072775
           2          1       -65.49410304    0.07719349
           3          1       -68.94391759    0.06085960
           4          1       -71.77307136    0.04223864
           5          1       -73.77928570    0.02382264
           6          1       -74.90919736    0.00953301
           7          1       -75.34737393    0.00204954
```

```
            8          1  -75.43525622    0.00012621
            9          1  -75.44021936    0.00000057
           10          1  -75.44024101    0.00000000


                  Convergence criteria met.


          Covariance Parameter Estimates (REML)


Cov Parm          Ratio       Estimate    Std Error       Z    Pr > |z|


BLK           29.16849617    0.02495507   0.01140157    2.19    0.0286
Residual       1.00000000    0.00085555   0.00048852    1.75    0.0799


                 Solution for Fixed Effects


Parameter        Estimate    Std Error    DDF        T    Pr > |T|


TRT 1           0.53522096   0.06801735   11.7    7.87    0.0001
TRT 2           0.61263063   0.07046489     13    8.69    0.0001
TRT 3           0.32372241   0.07905477   15.6    4.09    0.0009
TRT 4           0.32568343   0.10768875   13.4    3.02    0.0095
X              -0.99020248   1.28760823   6.92   -0.77    0.4673
X*TRT 1        -1.73938518   1.42077119   6.81   -1.22    0.2615
X*TRT 2        -0.92774236   1.46376848   6.78   -0.63    0.5470
X*TRT 3        -0.41601423   1.01695446   6.26   -0.41    0.6961
X*TRT 4         0.00000000       .          .       .        .


                  Tests of Fixed Effects


Source     NDF    DDF    Type III F    Pr > F


TRT          4    9.13      23.21      0.0001
X            1    6.96      10.08      0.0157
X*TRT        3    6.48       0.64      0.6145
```

Interpretation

The results from the Type III F-statistic corresponding to X*TRT in Output 5.14 indicates there is no evidence to believe the slopes are unequal (p=0.6145); therefore, we assume that a common slope model is adequate to describe the data.

5.5.3 Step 3: Fit a common slope model.

Program

The following program fits the common slope model to the data. The NOINT option is included in the MODEL statement so that the SOLUTION option provides estimates of the intercepts of the model. Without the NOINT option, the SOLUTION provides estimates of the intercepts that satisfy the set-to-zero restrictions. The LSMEANS statement is used to compare the treatments.

```
proc mixed; class blk trt;
   model y=trt x/noint solution ddfm=satterth;
   lsmeans trt/pdiff;
   random blk;
run;
```

The results of fitting the common slope model to the data are in Output 5.15.

Results

Output 5.15 *Results from Fitting the Common Slope Model and Results of the LSMEANS to Compare the Treatments at* x=0.044983

Covariance Parameter Estimates (REML)

Cov Parm	Ratio	Estimate	Std Error	Z	Pr > |Z|
BLK	30.19523320	0.02393202	0.01090330	2.19	0.0282
Residual	1.00000000	0.00079258	0.00037342	2.12	0.0338

Solution for Fixed Effects

Parameter	Estimate	Std Error	DDF	T	Pr > |T|
TRT 1	0.51902948	0.06526698	10.9	7.95	0.0001
TRT 2	0.62269192	0.06581960	11.3	9.46	0.0001
TRT 3	0.36016237	0.06674386	11.9	5.40	0.0002
TRT 4	0.40526149	0.06928491	13.4	5.85	0.0001
X	-2.18987167	0.39301128	9.47	-5.57	0.0003

Tests of Fixed Effects

Source	NDF	DDF	Type III F	Pr > F
TRT	4	10.2	34.12	0.0001
X	1	9.47	31.05	0.0003

Least Squares Means

Level	LSMEAN	Std Error	DDF	T	Pr > |T|
TRT 1	0.42057650	0.06446182	10.5	6.52	0.0001
TRT 2	0.52423894	0.06426935	10.3	8.16	0.0001
TRT 3	0.26170939	0.06419606	10.3	4.08	0.0021
TRT 4	0.30680851	0.06474054	10.6	4.74	0.0007

Differences of Least Squares Means

Level 1	Level 2	Difference	Std Error	DDF	T	Pr > |T|
TRT 1	TRT 2	-0.10366244	0.01648516	9.02	-6.29	0.0001
TRT 1	TRT 3	0.15886712	0.09101420	10.4	1.75	0.1104
TRT 1	TRT 4	0.11376800	0.09189905	10.8	1.24	0.2420
TRT 2	TRT 3	0.26252955	0.09085963	10.3	2.89	0.0156
TRT 2	TRT 4	0.21743043	0.09151194	10.6	2.38	0.0376
TRT 3	TRT 4	-0.04509912	0.01802636	9.09	-2.50	0.0335

Interpretation

The LSMEANS statement provides adjusted means or estimates from the common slope regression models at $X = 0.0449583$ (the mean of the covariate). Interesting observations are that the estimated standard errors of differences between treatments 1 and 2 and treatments 3 and 4 are much smaller that the estimated standard errors of the other differences. This difference in the estimated standard errors occurs because treatments 1 and 2 occur together in six blocks and treatments 3 and 4 occur together in six blocks, but all other pairs of treatments never occur together within a block (a characteristic of a nonconnected design). Thus, the within-block comparisons of treatments have estimated standard errors that do not depend on the block variance component and the between-block comparisons of treatments have estimated standard errors that do depend on the block variance component. Because the estimate of the block variance component is roughly 30 times larger than the estimate of the experimental unit variance component, those estimated standard errors involving the block effects are larger than those not involving the block effects.

5.6 Example: Split-Plot Design with the Covariate Measured on the Large Size Experimental Unit or Whole Plot

The data in Data Set 5.6, "Teaching Methods I," in Appendix 4, "SAS Data Sets," are from a study designed to evaluate the effectiveness of three teaching methods (MET). Four teachers were trained in each method. The teachers were randomly assigned to the twelve classes of eight students consisting of four females and four males. The experimental unit for the teaching method is a class of eight students. It was thought that the years of experience in teaching might influence the effectiveness of the delivery of the teaching method. Thus, the number of years of teaching experience of the twelve teachers was determined and used as a possible covariate. Part of the study was to determine if the genders respond differently to the teaching methods. Thus, gender (GEN) with two levels is considered the treatment for the small size of experimental unit, the student. This experiment involves two sizes of experimental units: (1) the class of eight students to which the teaching method is applied and (2) the students who differ by gender. The covariate, years of teaching experience, is measured on the class (really the teacher, but the teacher is completely confounded with his/her class). The treatment structure is a two-way factorial with three methods and two genders. The design structure consists of two sizes of experimental units. (The large size experimental unit is the class, and the small size experimental unit is the student which is nested within gender and class). Therefore, there are two variance components in the random part of the model. The responses are scores on a standardized test.

5.6.1 Step 1: Fit unequal slopes model and test slopes-equal-to-zero hypothesis.

Model

A model involving the covariate to describe the test scores as a function of teaching method, class taught, gender of the students, and years of teaching experience is

$$y_{ijkm} = \alpha_{ik} + \beta_{ik} x_{ij} + t_{j(i)} + e_{ijkm} \qquad (5.8)$$

where

$i=1,2,3$
$j=1,2,3,4$
$k=1,2$
$m=1,2,3,4$
α_{ik} and β_{ik} are the intercept and slope of the model for the ith teaching method and k^{th} gender
$t_{j(i)} \sim$ iid N(0, σ^2_t) is the random effect of the jth class taught by the ith method
$e_{ijkm} \sim$ iid N(0, σ^2_e) is the random effect of the mth student of the kth gender in the jth class taught by the ith method.

The **fixed effects part** of the model is $\alpha_{ik} + \beta_{ik} x_{ij}$, and the **random effects part** of the model is $t_{j(i)} + e_{ijkm}$.

Program

The following program fits model 5.8 where there are different intercepts for each gender-by-method combination obtained by GEN*MET and different slopes for each gender-by-method combination obtained by Y_EX*GEN*MET:

```
proc mixed data=splitpt;
   class teacher met gen;
   model score = gen*met y_ex*gen*met/solution noint ddfm=satterth;
   random teacher(met);
run;
```

The results are listed in Output 5.16.

Results

Output 5.16 *The Fit of the Unequal Slopes Model and the Testing of the Slopes Equal-to-Zero Hypothesis*

	Covariance Parameter Estimates (REML)				
Cov Parm	Ratio	Estimate	Std Error	Z	Pr > |Z|
TEACHER(MET)	2.78147969	1.78140660	1.07479274	1.66	0.0974
Residual	1.00000000	0.64045285	0.10255453	6.24	0.0001

```
                   Solution for Fixed Effects

   Parameter                Estimate    Std Error   DDF        T    Pr > |T|

   MET*GEN 1 f              16.42307692  2.35071565  6.53     6.99   0.0003
   MET*GEN 1 m              16.65384615  2.35071565  6.53     7.08   0.0003
   MET*GEN 2 f              20.69932432  2.06481780  6.53    10.02   0.0001
   MET*GEN 2 m              21.13513514  2.06481780  6.53    10.24   0.0001
   MET*GEN 3 f              30.98214286  1.81165477  6.53    17.10   0.0001
   MET*GEN 3 m              26.93452381  1.81165477  6.53    14.87   0.0001
   Y_EX*MET*GEN 1 f         -0.03205128  0.19956464  6.53    -0.16   0.8773
   Y_EX*MET*GEN 1 m         -0.03589744  0.19956464  6.53    -0.18   0.8627
   Y_EX*MET*GEN 2 f          0.09797297  0.16197763  6.53     0.60   0.5657
   Y_EX*MET*GEN 2 m         -0.09459459  0.16197763  6.53    -0.58   0.5788
   Y_EX*MET*GEN 3 f         -0.15178571  0.15203069  6.53    -1.00   0.3537
   Y_EX*MET*GEN 3 m         -0.18154762  0.15203069  6.53    -1.19   0.2740


                   Tests of Fixed Effects

         Source           NDF   DDF   Type III F   Pr > F

         MET*GEN           6    9.6        75.96   0.0001
         Y_EX*MET*GEN      6    9.6         1.68   0.2264
```

The solution for the fixed effects provides a list of the estimates of the intercepts (e.g., MET*GEN 1 male) and the slopes (e.g., Y_EX*MET*GEN 1 male). The Type III F for Y_EX*MET*GEN tests the slopes-equal-to-zero hypothesis. The significance level (p=0.2264) fails to provide enough evidence to believe that the slopes are not zero. For illustration purposes, the structure of the slopes is investigated further to see if a simpler model may be appropriate.

5.6.2 Step 2: Fit factorial effects model for slopes.

The model can be expressed as

$$y_{ijkm} = (\mu + \tau_i + \gamma_k + \delta_{ik}) + (\beta + \varphi_i + \theta_k + \rho_{ik})\, x_{ij} + t_{j(i)} + e_{ijkm} \qquad (5.9)$$
$$i=1,2,3,\ \ j=1,2,3,4,\ \ k=1,2,\ \ m=1,2,3,4$$

where

$$\alpha_{ik} = (\mu + \tau_i + \gamma_k + \delta_{ik})$$
$$\beta_{ik} = (\beta + \varphi_i + \theta_k + \rho_{ik})$$
$$t_{j(i)} \sim \text{iid } N(0, \sigma^2_t)$$
$$e_{ijkm} \sim \text{iid } N(0, \sigma^2_e).$$

The additional parameters in model 5.9 (over model 5.8) provide factorial effect representations for both the slopes and the intercepts. Thus, each slope and intercept is expressed with an overall mean, an effect due to teaching method, an effect due to gender, and an effect due to the interaction between method and gender. Those parameters are as follows:

> μ and β denote the overall means
> τ_i and ϕ_i denote the effect of the ith teaching method
> γ_k and θ_k denote the effect of the kth gender
> δ_{ik} and ρ_{ik} denote the interaction effect between the ith teaching method and the kth gender.

Program

The following program fits an unequal slopes model with the slopes and the intercepts expressed as factorial effects:

```
proc mixed;
   class teacher met gen;
   model score = met gen gen*met
   y_ex y_ex*met y_ex*gen y_ex*gen*met/ddfm=satterth;
   random teacher(met);
run;
```

The results of the factorial tests for the slopes and intercepts are in Output 5.17.

Results

Output 5.17 *The Fit of the Unequal Slopes Model Using Factorial Effects*

```
              Covariance Parameter Estimates (REML)

Cov Parm           Ratio        Estimate     Std Error      Z     Pr > |Z|


TEACHER(MET)    2.78147969    1.78140660    1.07479274    1.66    0.0974
Residual        1.00000000    0.64045285    0.10255453    6.24    0.0001



                    Tests of Fixed Effects


        Source         NDF    DDF    Type III F   Pr > F


        MET             2      6       10.09      0.0120
        GEN             1     78        5.30      0.0240
        MET*GEN         2     78       10.30      0.0001
        Y_EX            1      6        0.46      0.5216
        Y_EX*MET        2      6        0.33      0.7322
        Y_EX*GEN        1     78        3.48      0.0660
        Y_EX*MET*GEN    2     78        2.24      0.1138
```

Interpretation

The Type III F corresponding to Y_EX*MET*GEN is not significant ($p=0.1138$). Thus, we removed the Y_EX*MET*GEN term from the model and fit the model with just a main effects partition of the slopes.

5.6.3 Step 3: Fit model with slopes expressed as just main effects.

Model

The model where the slopes are a function of the main effects only is

$$y_{ijkm} = (\mu + \tau_i + \gamma_k + \delta_{ik}) + (\beta + \varphi_i + \theta_k) \, x_{ij} + t_{j(i)} + e_{ijkm}$$

where

$i=1,2,3$
$j=1,2,3,4$
$k=1,2$
$m=1,2,3,4$
$\alpha_{ik} = (\mu + \tau_i + \gamma_k + \delta_{ik})$
$\beta_{ik} = (\beta + \varphi_i + \theta_k).$

Program

The following program fits the model without the Y_EX*MET*GEN term:

```
proc mixed;
   class teacher met gen;
   model score = met gen gen*met y_ex y_ex*met y_ex*gen/ddfm=satterth;
   random teacher(met);
run;
```

The results are listed in Output 5.18.

Results

Output 5.18 *The Fit of the Unequal Slopes Model for the Main Effects*

Covariance Parameter Estimates (REML)

Cov Parm	Ratio	Estimate	Std Error	z	Pr > |z|
TEACHER(MET)	2.69440445	1.77893411	1.07479550	1.66	0.0979
Residual	1.00000000	0.66023277	0.10439197	6.32	0.0001

Tests of Fixed Effects

Source	NDF	DDF	Type III F	Pr > F
MET	2	6	10.09	0.0120
GEN	1	80	5.00	0.0281
MET*GEN	2	80	63.90	0.0001
Y_EX	1	6	0.46	0.5216
Y_EX*MET	2	6	0.33	0.7322
Y_EX*GEN	1	80	4.20	0.0436

Interpretation

The Type III F corresponding to Y_EX*MET is not significant. Thus, we removed the term from the model and fit a model with unequal slopes for each gender.

5.6.4 Step 4: Fit model with unequal slopes for each gender.

Model

The model where the slopes are a function of the gender effects only is

$$y_{ijkm} = (\mu + \tau_i + \gamma_k + \delta_{ik}) + (\beta + \theta_k) \, x_{ij} + t_{j(i)} + e_{ijkm}$$

where

$$i=1,2,3$$
$$j=1,2,3,4$$
$$k=1,2$$
$$m=1,2,3,4$$
$$\alpha_{ik} = (\mu + \tau_i + \gamma_k + \delta_{ik})$$
$$\beta_{ik} = (\beta + \theta_k).$$

Program

The following program fits the model with unequal slopes for each gender:

```
proc mixed;
   class teacher met gen;
   model score = met gen gen*met y_ex y_ex*gen/ddfm=satterth;
   random teacher(met);
run;
```

The results are in Output 5.19.

Results

Output 5.19 *The Fit of the Unequal Slopes Model for the Levels of Gender*

```
              Covariance Parameter Estimates (REML)

Cov Parm            Ratio        Estimate      Std Error      Z     Pr > |Z|

TEACHER(MET)     2.22111802     1.46645490    0.77460192    1.89    0.0583
Residual         1.00000000     0.66023277    0.10439197    6.32    0.0001
                      Tests of Fixed Effects
              Source      NDF    DDF   Type III F   Pr > F

              MET          2      8       77.68     0.0001
              GEN          1     80        5.00     0.0281
              MET*GEN      2     80       63.90     0.0001
              Y_EX         1      8        0.75     0.4107
              Y_EX*GEN     1     80        4.20     0.0436
```

Interpretation

The Type III F corresponding to Y_EX*GEN tests the equality of the gender slopes and presents evidence that the two slopes are unequal ($p=0.0436$). The simplified model used to investigate the relationship between the teaching methods and gender involving the covariate with unequal slopes for each gender is

$$y_{ijkm} = \alpha_{ik} + \beta_k \, x_{ij} + t_{j(i)} + e_{ijkm} \qquad\qquad (5.10)$$

where

$i=1,2,3$
$j=1,2,3,4$
$k=1,2$
$m=1,2,3,4$
$t_{j(i)} \sim$ iid N(0, σ^2_t)
$e_{ijkm} \sim$ iid N(0, σ^2_e).

Program

The following program fits model 5.10 to the data:

```
proc mixed; class teacher met gen;
    model score =gen*met y_ex*gen/noint solution;
    random teacher(met);
    lsmeans  met*gen / pdiff at means;
    lsmeans gen*met / pdiff at y_ex=5;
    lsmeans gen*met / pdiff at y_ex=10;
    lsmeans gen*met / pdiff at y_ex=20;
    estimate 'f-m m=1 y_ex=5' gen*met 1 -1 0 0 0 0 y_ex*gen 5 -5;
    estimate 'f-m m=1 y_ex=10' gen*met 1 -1 0 0 0 0 y_ex*gen 10 -10;
    estimate 'f-m m=1 y_ex=20' gen*met 1 -1 0 0 0 0 y_ex*gen 20 -20;
    estimate 'f-m m=2 y_ex=5' gen*met 0 0 1 -1    y_ex*gen 5 -5;
    estimate 'f-m m=2 y_ex=10' gen*met 0 0 1 -1    y_ex*gen 10 -10;
    estimate 'f-m m=2 y_ex=20' gen*met 0 0 1 -1    y_ex*gen 20 -20;
    estimate 'f-m m=3 y_ex=5' gen*met 0 0 0 0 1 -1    y_ex*gen 5 -5;
    estimate 'f-m m=3 y_ex=10' gen*met 0 0 0 0 1 -1  y_ex*gen 10 -10;
    estimate 'f-m m=3 y_ex=20' gen*met 0 0 0 0 1 -1  y_ex*gen 20 -20;
    estimate 'male m=1 y_ex=5' gen*met 1 0 0 0 0 0    y_ex*gen 5 0;
    estimate 'male m=1 y_ex=10' gen*met 1 0 0 0 0 0   y_ex*gen 10 0;
    estimate 'male m=1 y_ex=20' gen*met 1 0 0 0 0 0   y_ex*gen 20 0;
    estimate 'male m=2 y_ex=5' gen*met 0 0 1 0 0 0    y_ex*gen 5 0;
    estimate 'male m=2 y_ex=10' gen*met 0 0 1 0 0 0   y_ex*gen 10 0;
    estimate 'male m=2 y_ex=20' gen*met 0 0 1 0 0 0   y_ex*gen 20 0;
    estimate 'male m=3 y_ex=5' gen*met 0 0 0 0 1 0    y_ex*gen 5 0;
    estimate 'male m=3 y_ex=10' gen*met 0 0 0 0 1 0   y_ex*gen 10 0;
    estimate 'male m=3 y_ex=20' gen*met 0 0 0 0 1 0   y_ex*gen 20 0;
    estimate 'female m=1 y_ex=5' gen*met 0 1 0 0 0 0    y_ex*gen 0 5;
    estimate 'female m=1 y_ex=10' gen*met 0 1 0 0 0 0   y_ex*gen 0 10;
    estimate 'female m=1 y_ex=20' gen*met 0 1 0 0 0 0   y_ex*gen 0 20;
    estimate 'female m=2 y_ex=5' gen*met 0 0 0 1 0 0    y_ex*gen 0 5;
    estimate 'female m=2 y_ex=10' gen*met 0 0 0 1 0 0   y_ex*gen 0 10;
    estimate 'female m=2 y_ex=20' gen*met 0 0 0 1 0 0   y_ex*gen 0 20;
    estimate 'female m=3 y_ex=5' gen*met 0 0 0 0 0 1    y_ex*gen 0 5;
    estimate 'female m=3 y_ex=10' gen*met 0 0 0 0 0 1   y_ex*gen 0 10;
    estimate 'female m=3 y_ex=20' gen*met 0 0 0 0 0 1   y_ex*gen 0 20;
run;
```

ESTIMATE statements compare genders within each teaching method at 5, 10, and 20 years of teaching experience and obtain adjusted means for combinations of gender and teaching method at 5, 10, and 20 years of teaching experience. The LSMEANS compare teaching methods within each gender and compare all models at the mean years of teaching experience, 11.41667. The LSMEANS are also computed at 5, 10, and 20 years of teaching experience for comparison purposes using the "AT *value*" option, which provided predicted values from the regression lines evaluated at the "*value*," called **adjusted means**.

The estimates of the variance components and of the fixed effects are in Output 5.20.

Results

Output 5.20 *The Fit of a Model with Intercepts for the Method-by-Gender Combinations and Unequal Slopes for Each Gender*

```
                       Solution for Fixed Effects


   Parameter              Estimate      Std Error   DDF       T   Pr > |T|


   MET*GEN 1 f         16.44679565    1.18600711   8.87   13.87   0.0001
   MET*GEN 1 m         17.55592503    1.18600711   8.87   14.80   0.0001
   MET*GEN 2 f         22.28491536    1.24266500   8.87   17.93   0.0001
   MET*GEN 2 m         21.39298670    1.24266500   8.87   17.22   0.0001
   MET*GEN 3 f         29.68825574    1.16735507   8.87   25.43   0.0001
   MET*GEN 3 m         26.21440447    1.16735507   8.87   22.46   0.0001
   Y_EX*GEN f          -0.03415961    0.08883263   8.87   -0.38   0.7096
   Y_EX*GEN m          -0.11608222    0.08883263   8.87   -1.31   0.2241



                       Tests of Fixed Effects



   Source         NDF   DDF   Type III F   Pr > F


   MET*GEN          6  13.1       126.32   0.0001
   Y_EX*GEN         2  13.1         2.48   0.1221
```

Output 5.21 *The LSMEANS to Compare the Method-by-Gender Adjusted Means at the Average Value of the Covariate, Years Experience, Yr Exp=11.41667, 5, 10, and 20*

```
                         Least Squares Means


   Level          Y_EX        LSMEAN      Std Error   DDF       T   Pr>|T|


   MET*GEN 1 f    11.42    16.05680673   0.63882507  8.87   25.13   0.0001
   MET*GEN 1 m    11.42    16.23065296   0.63882507  8.87   25.41   0.0001
   MET*GEN 2 f    11.42    21.89492644   0.64075228  8.87   34.17   0.0001
   MET*GEN 2 m    11.42    20.06771463   0.64075228  8.87   31.32   0.0001
   MET*GEN 3 f    11.42    29.29826683   0.63972516  8.87   45.80   0.0001
   MET*GEN 3 m    11.42    24.88913241   0.63972516  8.87   38.91   0.0001
   MET*GEN 1 f     5.00    16.27599758   0.84624446  8.87   19.23   0.0001
   MET*GEN 1 m     5.00    16.97551391   0.84624446  8.87   20.06   0.0001
   MET*GEN 2 f     5.00    22.11411729   0.89137470  8.87   24.81   0.0001
   MET*GEN 2 m     5.00    20.81257557   0.89137470  8.87   23.35   0.0001
   MET*GEN 3 f     5.00    29.51745768   0.83184300  8.87   35.48   0.0001
   MET*GEN 3 m     5.00    25.63399335   0.83184300  8.87   30.82   0.0001
```

```
MET*GEN 1 f   10.00   16.10519952   0.64823478   8.87   24.84   0.0001
MET*GEN 1 m   10.00   16.39510278   0.64823478   8.87   25.29   0.0001
MET*GEN 2 f   10.00   21.94331923   0.66290514   8.87   33.10   0.0001
MET*GEN 2 m   10.00   20.23216445   0.66290514   8.87   30.52   0.0001
MET*GEN 3 f   10.00   29.34665961   0.64480191   8.87   45.51   0.0001
MET*GEN 3 m   10.00   25.05358222   0.64480191   8.87   38.85   0.0001
MET*GEN 1 f   20.00   15.76360339   1.00600748   8.87   15.67   0.0001
MET*GEN 1 m   20.00   15.23428053   1.00600748   8.87   15.14   0.0001
MET*GEN 2 f   20.00   21.60172310   0.95546711   8.87   22.61   0.0001
MET*GEN 2 m   20.00   19.07134220   0.95546711   8.87   19.96   0.0001
MET*GEN 3 f   20.00   29.00506348   1.02326361   8.87   28.35   0.0001
MET*GEN 3 m   20.00   23.89275998   1.02326361   8.87   23.35   0.0001
```

Output 5.22 *Needed Comparison of the LSMEANS for the Method-by-Gender Adjusted Means at the Average Value of the Covariate, Years Experience, Yr Exp = 11.41667, 5, 10, and 20*

```
                    Differences of Least Squares Means

Level 1          Level 2        Y_EX    Difference    Std Error   DDF      T   Pr > |T|

MET*GEN 1 f   MET*GEN 1 m   11.42    -0.17384623   0.28735596    80    -0.60    0.5469
MET*GEN 1 f   MET*GEN 2 f   11.42    -5.83811971   0.90564638   8.87    -6.45    0.0001
MET*GEN 1 f   MET*GEN 2 m   11.42    -4.01090790   0.90556067   8.87    -4.43    0.0017
MET*GEN 1 f   MET*GEN 3 f   11.42   -13.24146010   0.90346541   8.87   -14.66    0.0001
MET*GEN 1 f   MET*GEN 3 m   11.42    -8.83232568   0.90352677   8.88    -9.78    0.0001
MET*GEN 1 m   MET*GEN 2 f   11.42    -5.66427348   0.90556067   8.87    -6.25    0.0002
MET*GEN 1 m   MET*GEN 2 m   11.42    -3.83706167   0.90564638   8.87    -4.24    0.0023
MET*GEN 1 m   MET*GEN 3 f   11.42   -13.06761387   0.90352677   8.88   -14.46    0.0001
MET*GEN 1 m   MET*GEN 3 m   11.42    -8.65847944   0.90346541   8.87    -9.58    0.0001
MET*GEN 2 f   MET*GEN 2 m   11.42     1.82721181   0.28822286    80     6.34    0.0001
MET*GEN 2 f   MET*GEN 3 f   11.42    -7.40334039   0.90755043   8.87    -8.16    0.0001
MET*GEN 2 f   MET*GEN 3 m   11.42    -2.99420597   0.90733660   8.86    -3.30    0.0094
MET*GEN 2 m   MET*GEN 3 f   11.42    -9.23055220   0.90733660   8.86   -10.17    0.0001
MET*GEN 2 m   MET*GEN 3 m   11.42    -4.82141778   0.90755043   8.87    -5.31    0.0005
MET*GEN 3 f   MET*GEN 3 m   11.42     4.40913442   0.28776084    80    15.32    0.0001
MET*GEN 1 f   MET*GEN 1 m    5.00    -0.69951632   0.38065724    80    -1.84    0.0698
MET*GEN 1 f   MET*GEN 2 f    5.00    -5.83811971   0.90564638   8.87    -6.45    0.0001
MET*GEN 1 f   MET*GEN 2 m    5.00    -4.53657799   0.94342499   10.4    -4.81    0.0006
MET*GEN 1 f   MET*GEN 3 f    5.00   -13.24146010   0.90346541   8.87   -14.66    0.0001
MET*GEN 1 f   MET*GEN 3 m    5.00    -9.35799577   0.93601590   10.2   -10.00    0.0001
MET*GEN 1 m   MET*GEN 2 f    5.00    -5.13860339   0.94342499   10.4    -5.45    0.0002
MET*GEN 1 m   MET*GEN 2 m    5.00    -3.83706167   0.90564638   8.87    -4.24    0.0023
MET*GEN 1 m   MET*GEN 3 f    5.00   -12.54194377   0.93601590   10.2   -13.40    0.0001
MET*GEN 1 m   MET*GEN 3 m    5.00    -8.65847944   0.90346541   8.87    -9.58    0.0001
MET*GEN 2 f   MET*GEN 2 m    5.00     1.30154172   0.40095770    80     3.25    0.0017
MET*GEN 2 f   MET*GEN 3 f    5.00    -7.40334039   0.90755043   8.87    -8.16    0.0001
MET*GEN 2 f   MET*GEN 3 m    5.00    -3.51987606   0.94377376   10.4    -3.73    0.0037
MET*GEN 2 m   MET*GEN 3 f    5.00    -8.70488210   0.94377376   10.4    -9.22    0.0001
MET*GEN 2 m   MET*GEN 3 m    5.00    -4.82141778   0.90755043   8.87    -5.31    0.0005
MET*GEN 3 f   MET*GEN 3 m    5.00     3.88346433   0.37417919    80    10.38    0.0001
MET*GEN 1 f   MET*GEN 1 m   10.00    -0.28990326   0.29158863    80    -0.99    0.3231
MET*GEN 1 f   MET*GEN 2 f   10.00    -5.83811971   0.90564638   8.87    -6.45    0.0001
MET*GEN 1 f   MET*GEN 2 m   10.00    -4.12696493   0.90784751   8.96    -4.55    0.0014
MET*GEN 1 f   MET*GEN 3 f   10.00   -13.24146010   0.90346541   8.87   -14.66    0.0001
MET*GEN 1 f   MET*GEN 3 m   10.00    -8.94838271   0.90456930   8.92    -9.89    0.0001
```

MET*GEN 1 m	MET*GEN 2 f	10.00	-5.54821644	0.90784751	8.96	-6.11	0.0002
MET*GEN 1 m	MET*GEN 2 m	10.00	-3.83706167	0.90564638	8.87	-4.24	0.0023
MET*GEN 1 m	MET*GEN 3 f	10.00	-12.95155683	0.90456930	8.92	-14.32	0.0001
MET*GEN 1 m	MET*GEN 3 m	10.00	-8.65847944	0.90346541	8.87	-9.58	0.0001
MET*GEN 2 f	MET*GEN 2 m	10.00	1.71115478	0.29818764	80	5.74	0.0001
MET*GEN 2 f	MET*GEN 3 f	10.00	-7.40334039	0.90755043	8.87	-8.16	0.0001
MET*GEN 2 f	MET*GEN 3 m	10.00	-3.11026300	0.90930807	8.94	-3.42	0.0077
MET*GEN 2 m	MET*GEN 3 f	10.00	-9.11449516	0.90930807	8.94	-10.02	0.0001
MET*GEN 2 m	MET*GEN 3 m	10.00	-4.82141778	0.90755043	8.87	-5.31	0.0005
MET*GEN 3 f	MET*GEN 3 m	10.00	4.29307739	0.29004446	80	14.80	0.0001
MET*GEN 1 f	MET*GEN 1 m	20.00	0.52932285	0.45252176	80	1.17	0.2456
MET*GEN 1 f	MET*GEN 2 f	20.00	-5.83811971	0.90564638	8.87	-6.45	0.0001
MET*GEN 1 f	MET*GEN 2 m	20.00	-3.30773881	0.96538278	11.4	-3.43	0.0054
MET*GEN 1 f	MET*GEN 3 f	20.00	-13.24146010	0.90346541	8.87	-14.66	0.0001
MET*GEN 1 f	MET*GEN 3 m	20.00	-8.12915659	0.97056137	11.8	-8.38	0.0001
MET*GEN 1 m	MET*GEN 2 f	20.00	-6.36744256	0.96538278	11.4	-6.60	0.0001
MET*GEN 1 m	MET*GEN 2 m	20.00	-3.83706167	0.90564638	8.87	-4.24	0.0023
MET*GEN 1 m	MET*GEN 3 f	20.00	-13.77078295	0.97056137	11.8	-14.19	0.0001
MET*GEN 1 m	MET*GEN 3 m	20.00	-8.65847944	0.90346541	8.87	-9.58	0.0001
MET*GEN 2 f	MET*GEN 2 m	20.00	2.53038089	0.42978772	80	5.89	0.0001
MET*GEN 2 f	MET*GEN 3 f	20.00	-7.40334039	0.90755043	8.87	-8.16	0.0001
MET*GEN 2 f	MET*GEN 3 m	20.00	-2.29103688	0.96881872	11.5	-2.36	0.0366
MET*GEN 2 m	MET*GEN 3 f	20.00	-9.93372128	0.96881872	11.5	-10.25	0.0001
MET*GEN 2 m	MET*GEN 3 m	20.00	-4.82141778	0.90755043	8.87	-5.31	0.0005
MET*GEN 3 f	MET*GEN 3 m	20.00	5.11230351	0.46028390	80	11.11	0.0001

Output 5.23 *The Results of the ESTIMATE Statements to Compute and Compare Adjusted Means across Genders at Yrs Exp = 5, 10, and 20*

ESTIMATE Statement Results					
Parameter	Estimate	Std Error	DDF	T	Pr>|T|
f-m m=1 y_ex=5	-0.69951632	0.38065724	80	-1.84	0.0698
f-m m=1 y_ex=10	-0.28990326	0.29158863	80	-0.99	0.3231
f-m m=1 y_ex=20	0.52932285	0.45252176	80	1.17	0.2456
f-m m=2 y_ex=5	1.30154172	0.40095770	80	3.25	0.0017
f-m m=2 y_ex=10	1.71115478	0.29818764	80	5.74	0.0001
f-m m=2 y_ex=20	2.53038089	0.42978772	80	5.89	0.0001
f-m m=3 y_ex=5	3.88346433	0.37417919	80	10.38	0.0001
f-m m=3 y_ex=10	4.29307739	0.29004446	80	14.80	0.0001
f-m m=3 y_ex=20	5.11230351	0.46028390	80	11.11	0.0001
male m=1 y_ex=5	16.27599758	0.84624446	8.87	19.23	0.0001
male m=1 y_ex=10	16.10519952	0.64823478	8.87	24.84	0.0001
male m=1 y_ex=20	15.76360339	1.00600748	8.87	15.67	0.0001
male m=2 y_ex=5	22.11411729	0.89137470	8.87	24.81	0.0001
male m=2 y_ex=10	21.94331923	0.66290514	8.87	33.10	0.0001
male m=2 y_ex=20	21.60172310	0.95546711	8.87	22.61	0.0001
male m=3 y_ex=5	29.51745768	0.83184300	8.87	35.48	0.0001
male m=3 y_ex=10	29.34665961	0.64480191	8.87	45.51	0.0001
male m=3 y_ex=20	29.00506348	1.02326361	8.87	28.35	0.0001
female m=1 y_ex=5	16.97551391	0.84624446	8.87	20.06	0.0001
female m=1 y_ex=10	16.39510278	0.64823478	8.87	25.29	0.0001
female m=1 y_ex=20	15.23428053	1.00600748	8.87	15.14	0.0001
female m=2 y_ex=5	20.81257557	0.89137470	8.87	23.35	0.0001
female m=2 y_ex=10	20.23216445	0.66290514	8.87	30.52	0.0001

female m=2 y_ex=20	19.07134220	0.95546711	8.87	19.96	0.0001
female m=3 y_ex=5	25.63399335	0.83184300	8.87	30.82	0.0001
female m=3 y_ex=10	25.05358222	0.64480191	8.87	38.85	0.0001
female m=3 y_ex=20	23.89275998	1.02326361	8.87	23.35	0.0001

Interpretation

The Type III F-values in Output 5.20 test that the intercepts are all equal to zero and that the slopes are all equal to zero. Most likely these tests are not of much interest, but this form of the model is most convenient for constructing ESTIMATE statements because the resulting model is nonsingular and has parameters as described in model 5.10.

The LSMEANS are in Output 5.21, the comparisons of the LSMEANS are in Output 5.22, and the results of the ESTIMATE statements are in Output 5.23. For years of teaching experience of 5, 10, and 20, only comparisons of the two genders within a teaching method have been presented.

The importance of using the mixed models approach for this example is that the classes of eight students are blocks for gender and (like the RCB in section 5.2) there is information about the slopes from within blocks and between blocks. The mixed model equations combines the information from the various parts of the model into combined estimators of the slopes. Using the combined estimators should generally provide estimators with smaller variances than those based on intra-block information alone.

5.7 Example: Split-Plot Design with the Covariate Measured on the Small Size Experimental Unit or Subplot

This example is similar to the example in section 5.6 except the covariate is measured on the student instead of on the teacher. The data in Data Set 5.7, "Teaching Methods II," in Appendix 4, "SAS Data Sets," are from a study designed by a researcher to evaluate the effectiveness of three teaching methods. Four teachers were trained in each method. The twelve teachers were randomly assigned to twelve classes of eight students consisting of four males and four females.

The **experimental unit** for the teaching method is a class of eight students, the entity to which the teaching methods were randomly assigned. The researcher was interested in the possible difference in gender response to the three teaching methods. Thus, gender is treatment for the small size of experimental unit, the student.

The researcher hypothesized that the IQ of the individual might influence the student's ability to respond to the teaching method. The IQ of each of the 96 students was determined and investigated as a possible covariate.

This experiment involves two sizes of experimental units: (1) the class of eight students to which the teaching method is applied and (2) the student nested within class and gender. The covariate, IQ, is measured on the student, which is the small size of experimental unit.

The treatment structure consists of the two-way set of treatment combinations, three methods by two genders. Because the design structure consists of two sizes of experimental units (the class and the student within class), there are two variance components in the random part of the model. The responses are scores on a standardized test (SCORE).

Model

A model to describe the test scores involving the covariate is

$$y_{ijkm} = \alpha_{ik} + \beta_{ik}\, w_{ijkm} + t_{j(i)} + e_{ijkm} \tag{5.11}$$

where

$i=1,2,3$
$j=1,2,3,4$
$k=1,2$
$m=1,2,3,4$
$t_{j(i)} \sim$ iid $N(0, \sigma^2_t)$
$e_{ijkm} \sim$ iid $N(0, \sigma^2_e)$.

The intercept and slope of the model for the ith teaching method and the kth gender are α_{ik} and β_{ik}, respectively. The fixed effects part of the model is $\alpha_{ik} + \beta_{ik} w_{ijkm}$ where w_{ijkm} denotes the IQ of the mth student of the kth gender in the jth class taught by the ith method and the random effects part of the model is $t_{j(i)} + e_{ijkm}$.

5.7.1 Step 1: Fit the unequal slopes model and test the slopes-equal-to-zero hypothesis.

Program

The following program fits model 5.11, where the intercept is expressed as the factorial effect $\alpha_{ik} = \mu + \tau_i + \gamma_k + \delta_{ik}$ and there are different slopes for each gender by method combination:

```
proc mixed data=splitpt;
   class teacher met gen;
   model score = met gen gen*met iq*gen*met/solution ddfm=satterth;
   random teacher(met);
run;
```

The results are in Output 5.24 and Output 5.25.

Results

Output 5.24 *The Fit of the Unequal Slopes Model and the Testing of the Slopes-Equal-to-Zero Hypothesis*

	Covariance Parameter Estimates (REML)				
Cov Parm	Ratio	Estimate	Std Error	Z	Pr > |Z|
TEACHER(MET)	1.33788307	24.26210971	12.57483245	1.93	0.0537
Residual	1.00000000	18.13470115	2.96147981	6.12	0.0001

```
                          Solution for Fixed Effects

Parameter                 Estimate    Std Error    DDF       T  Pr > |T|

INTERCEPT               26.89117435  10.32901406   82.9   2.60   0.0109
MET 1                   -6.18497978  14.25052250   82.9  -0.43   0.6654
MET 2                   -8.72027122  14.26891081     83  -0.61   0.5428
MET 3                    0.00000000       .          .      .       .
GEN f                    1.85398396  13.41908664   76.3   0.14   0.8905
GEN m                    0.00000000       .          .      .       .
MET*GEN 1 f             -5.77823888  18.84532996   75.8  -0.31   0.7600
MET*GEN 1 m              0.00000000       .          .      .       .
MET*GEN 2 f              7.09219036  19.20647132   76.1   0.37   0.7130
MET*GEN 2 m              0.00000000       .          .      .       .
MET*GEN 3 f              0.00000000       .          .      .       .
MET*GEN 3 m              0.00000000       .          .      .       .
IQ*MET*GEN 1 f           0.43131194   0.08898591   75.1   4.85   0.0001
IQ*MET*GEN 1 m           0.41221777   0.09767593   75.4   4.22   0.0001
IQ*MET*GEN 2 f           0.45958143   0.09705282   77.1   4.74   0.0001
IQ*MET*GEN 2 m           0.53417226   0.09543340   76.2   5.60   0.0001
IQ*MET*GEN 3 f           0.50515783   0.08562135   76.3   5.90   0.0001
IQ*MET*GEN 3 m           0.47455365   0.09387714   76.5   5.06   0.0001


                          Tests of Fixed Effects


           Source        NDF   DDF  Type III F  Pr > F


           MET            2    83.4       0.41   0.6655
           GEN            1    75.8       0.09   0.7689
           MET*GEN        2    75.8       0.23   0.7967
           IQ*MET*GEN     6    76.1      25.45   0.0001
```

Output 5.25 *Tests for the Fixed Effects Including Test of the Slopes-Equal-to-Zero Hypothesis and of the Equality of Intercepts for Main Effects and Interaction at IQ=102.5, 90, and 120*

```
                      Tests of Fixed Effects


           Source        NDF    DDF  Type III F  Pr > F


           MET            2    9.07      10.26   0.0047
           GEN            1    75.1       2.49   0.1190
           MET*GEN        2    75.1       4.86   0.0103
           IQDEV*MET*GEN  6    76.1      25.45   0.0001


                      Tests of Fixed Effects


           Source        NDF    DDF  Type III F  Pr > F


           MET            2     11       8.41   0.0061
           GEN            1    75.6       1.40   0.2409
           MET*GEN        2    75.6       2.54   0.0858
           IQAT90*MET*GEN 6    76.1      25.45   0.0001
```

```
                        Tests of Fixed Effects

         Source              NDF    DDF   Type III F   Pr > F

         MET                  2     13       9.84      0.0025
         GEN                  1     75.5      0.65     0.4238
         MET*GEN              2     75.5      2.00     0.1428
         IQAT120*MET*GEN      6     76.1     25.45     0.0001
```

Interpretation

The solution for the fixed effects lists the estimates of the slopes (e.g., IQ*MET*GEN 1 male). The Type III F for IQ*MET*GEN tests the slopes-equal-to-zero hypothesis. The significance level ($p < 0.0001$) indicates there is evidence to believe that the slopes are not zero. Thus, we further investigate the structure of the slopes to see if a simpler model might be appropriate. The tests corresponding to the intercepts (MET GEN and GEN*MET) are comparing the regression lines at IQ=0, a place not of interest in this study. Output 5.25 displays the analysis of variance tables for comparing the regression models at IQ = 102.5, 90, and 120. The three analysis of variance tables in Output 5.25 were computed by replacing IQ in the above program by iqdev=iq − 102.5, iqat90=iq − 90, and iqat120 = iq − 120, respectively. By subtracting a constant from the values of the covariate, the intercept of the models are translated to that constant. Thus, the Type III F-statistics are comparing the respective regression models at the new intercept. The degrees of freedom provided by the Satterthwaite approximation depends on the value of the covariate where the models are being compared.

5.7.2 Step 2: Fit a model to test the slopes equal hypothesis.

Model

The model can be expressed as

$$y_{ijkm} = (\mu + \tau_i + \gamma_k + \delta_{ik}) + \beta_{32} w_{ijkm} + (\beta_{ik} - \beta_{32}) w_{ijkm} + t_{j(i)} + e_{ijkm} \qquad (5.12)$$

where

$i=1,2,3$
$j=1,2,3,4$
$k=1,2$
$m=1,2,3,4$
$t_{j(i)} \sim \text{iid } N(0, \sigma^2_t)$
$e_{ijkm} \sim \text{iid } N(0, \sigma^2_e)$
$\alpha_{ik} = (\mu + \tau_i + \gamma_k + \delta_{ik})$.

Program

The following code fits an unequal slopes model with the intercepts expressed as factorial effects:

```
proc mixed;
   class teacher met gen;
   model score = met gen gen*met iq iq*gen*met/solution ddfm=satterth;
   random teacher(met);
run;
```

The results of fitting model 5.12 are in Output 5.26.

Results

Output 5.26 *The Fit of the Unequal Slopes Model Using Factorial Effects, Which Tests for Parallelism of Regression Lines*

```
                    Tests of Fixed Effects (with DDFM=SATTERTH)


           Source        NDF    DDF   Type III F   Pr > F


           MET            2    83.4        0.41     0.6655
           GEN            1    75.8        0.09     0.7689
           MET*GEN        2    75.8        0.23     0.7967
           IQ             1    76.4      149.47     0.0001
           IQ*MET*GEN     5    76          0.24     0.9451




                    Tests of Fixed Effects (without DDFM=SATTERTH)


           Source        NDF    DDF   Type III F   Pr > F


           MET            2    9           0.41     0.6759
           GEN            1    75          0.09     0.7690
           MET*GEN        2    75          0.23     0.7967
           IQ             1    75        149.47     0.0001
           IQ*MET*GEN     5    75          0.24     0.9451
```

Output 5.27 *Tests for the Fixed Effects Including Test of the Equality of Slopes and of the Equality of Intercepts for Main Effects and Interaction at IQ=102.5, 90, and 120*

```
                    Tests of Fixed Effects


           Source          NDF    DDF   Type III F   Pr > F


           MET              2    9.07       10.26     0.0047
           GEN              1    75.1        2.49     0.1190
           MET*GEN          2    75.1        4.86     0.0103
           IQDEV            1    76.4      149.47     0.0001
           IQDEV*MET*GEN    5    76          0.24     0.9451
```

```
                     Tests of Fixed Effects


        Source          NDF   DDF   Type III F   Pr > F


        MET              2     11       8.41     0.0061
        GEN              1    75.6       1.40     0.2409
        MET*GEN          2    75.6       2.54     0.0858
        IQAT90           1    76.4     149.47     0.0001
        IQAT90*MET*GEN   5     76        0.24     0.9451


                     Tests of Fixed Effects


        Source          NDF   DDF   Type III F   Pr > F


        MET              2     13       9.84     0.0025
        GEN              1    75.5       0.65     0.4238
        MET*GEN          2    75.5       2.00     0.1428
        IQAT120          1    76.4     149.47     0.0001
        IQAT120*MET*GEN  5     76        0.24     0.9451
```

Interpretation

The Type III F corresponding to IQ*MET*GEN tests the equal slopes hypothesis. Its significance level ($p=0.9451$) indicates there is not sufficient evidence to believe that the slopes are unequal. (Again, the intercepts comparisons are comparisons of the models at IQ=0.) The analysis of variance table resulting from using the approximate degrees of freedom and the *usual* degrees of freedom are both included in Output 5.26. The approximate denominator degrees of freedom for MET is 83.4, the appropriate approximate degrees of freedom for comparing the intercepts at IQ=0 (a point not of interest). Output 5.27 displays the analysis of variance tables for comparing the intercepts at IQ = 102.5, 90 and 120. Again, the degrees of freedom provided by the Satterthwaite approximation depends on the value of the covariate where the models are being compared. The three analysis of variance tables were computed by replacing IQ in the above program by IQDEV=IQ − 102.5, IQAT90=IQ − 90, and IQAT120 = IQ − 120, respectively.

5.7.3 Step 3: Fit a common slope model.

Model

The following model with a common slope describes the test scores as a function of IQ and investigates the relationship between the teaching methods and gender:

$$y_{ijkm} = \alpha_{ik} + \beta\, w_{ijkm} + t_{j(i)} + e_{ijkm} \tag{5.13}$$

where

$i=1,2,3$
$j=1,2,3,4$
$k=1,2$
$m=1,2,3,4$
$t_{j(i)} \sim \text{iid } N(0, \sigma^2_t)$
$e_{ijkm} \sim \text{iid } N(0, \sigma^2_e)$

Program

The following program fits Model 5.13 to the data:

```
proc mixed;
   class teacher met gen;
   model score = met gen gen*met iq/solution ddfm=satterth;
   random teacher(met);
   lsmeans met gen met*gen/pdiff;
run;
```

The estimates of the variance components, fixed effects and analysis of variance table are displayed in Output 5.28.

Results

Output 5.28 *The Fit of the Common Slope Model*

```
                      The MIXED Procedure

             Covariance Parameter Estimates (REML)

Cov Parm             Ratio        Estimate     Std Error       Z    Pr > |Z|

TEACHER(MET)    1.41645786    24.45288179    12.54707089    1.95    0.0513
Residual        1.00000000    17.26340225     2.72942312    6.32    0.0001



                   Solution for Fixed Effects

Parameter            Estimate     Std Error    DDF       T   Pr > |T|

INTERCEPT         27.36768213    4.78158518   62.6    5.72    0.0001
MET 1            -12.25496639    3.80937059   10.7   -3.22    0.0085
MET 2             -2.83451788    3.80162959   10.6   -0.75    0.4721
MET 3              0.00000000        .          .       .        .
GEN f              5.02453427    1.47151244     80    3.41    0.0010
GEN m              0.00000000        .          .       .        .
MET*GEN 1 f       -7.32305099    2.09873647     80   -3.49    0.0008
MET*GEN 1 m        0.00000000        .          .       .        .
MET*GEN 2 f       -3.55753361    2.10779237     80   -1.69    0.0953
MET*GEN 2 m        0.00000000        .          .       .        .
MET*GEN 3 f        0.00000000        .          .       .        .
MET*GEN 3 m        0.00000000        .          .       .        .
IQ                 0.47006887    0.03725843   81.3   12.62    0.0001



                    Tests of Fixed Effects

        Source        NDF    DDF   Type III F   Pr > F

        MET             2   9.03        10.05   0.0051
        GEN             1     80         2.65   0.1074
        MET*GEN         2     80         6.09   0.0034
        IQ              1   81.3       159.17   0.0001
```

Output 5.29 *The LSMEANS from the Common Slopes Model and Comparisons of the Means*

```
                        Least Squares Means

 Level            IQ        LSMEAN      Std Error   DDF      T    Pr > |T|

 MET*GEN 1 f    102.50   60.99625861   2.68182863  10.5   22.74   0.0001
 MET*GEN 1 m    102.50   63.29477533   2.69055447  10.6   23.52   0.0001
 MET*GEN 2 f    102.50   74.18222450   2.68596242  10.6   27.62   0.0001
 MET*GEN 2 m    102.50   72.71522384   2.68455692  10.6   27.09   0.0001
 MET*GEN 3 f    102.50   80.57427599   2.68235934  10.5   30.04   0.0001
 MET*GEN 3 m    102.50   75.54974172   2.68546170  10.6   28.13   0.0001


                    Differences of Least Squares Means

 Level 1          Level 2          IQ    Difference    Std Error    DDF      T    Pr > |T|

 MET*GEN 1 f    MET*GEN 1 m    102.50   -2.29851672   1.48419338    80   -1.55   0.1254
 MET*GEN 1 f    MET*GEN 2 f    102.50  -13.18596589   3.79578544  10.5   -3.47   0.0055
 MET*GEN 1 f    MET*GEN 2 m    102.50  -11.71896523   3.79445948  10.5   -3.09   0.0108
 MET*GEN 1 f    MET*GEN 3 f    102.50  -19.57801738   3.79311947  10.5   -5.16   0.0004
 MET*GEN 1 f    MET*GEN 3 m    102.50  -14.55348311   3.79541970  10.5   -3.83   0.0030
 MET*GEN 1 m    MET*GEN 2 f    102.50  -10.88744917   3.81025306  10.7   -2.86   0.0160
 MET*GEN 1 m    MET*GEN 2 m    102.50   -9.42044851   3.79387422  10.5   -2.48   0.0313
 MET*GEN 1 m    MET*GEN 3 f    102.50  -17.27950066   3.80227997  10.6   -4.54   0.0009
 MET*GEN 1 m    MET*GEN 3 m    102.50  -12.25496639   3.80937059  10.7   -3.22   0.0085
 MET*GEN 2 f    MET*GEN 2 m    102.50    1.46700066   1.49361711  80.1    0.98   0.3290
 MET*GEN 2 f    MET*GEN 3 f    102.50   -6.39205149   3.79387422  10.5   -1.68   0.1214
 MET*GEN 2 f    MET*GEN 3 m    102.50   -1.36751722   3.79268413  10.5   -0.36   0.7256
 MET*GEN 2 m    MET*GEN 3 f    102.50   -7.85905215   3.79669177  10.6   -2.07   0.0638
 MET*GEN 2 m    MET*GEN 3 m    102.50   -2.83451788   3.80162959  10.6   -0.75   0.4721
 MET*GEN 3 f    MET*GEN 3 m    102.50    5.02453427   1.47151244    80    3.41   0.0010
```

Interpretation

The Type III F corresponding to MET*GEN indicates an interaction between gender and teaching method ($p<0.0034$). The LSMEANS in Output 5.29 are adjusted means or the estimated parallel regression lines evaluated at the average IQ value of 102.5. Because there is a significant MET*GEN interaction, to complete the analysis you need to compare the interaction adjusted means rather than the main-effect adjusted means.

5.7.4 Comparison with PROC GLM

As described in Section 5.2, **PROC MIXED extracts information from all structures of the design whereas the usual analysis obtained using PROC GLM does not**. PROC GLM extracts the information about the slopes from the within-block information (from the smallest size of experimental unit), which in this case is the classroom. PROC GLM does not use information about the slopes contained in the block or classroom totals whereas PROC MIXED does. If you use PROC GLM to carry out the analysis when there are more than one size of experimental unit in the design, you will not obtain all information about the slopes. It is particularly critical when the model involves unequal slopes, as the slopes are involved in all comparisons between the regression models. **For common slopes models,** comparisons between models do not involve the slope. **Thus, the analysis provided by PROC GLM is adequate**. As a comparison with the results from PROC MIXED, the following program uses PROC GLM to extract the within-block information about the slopes for the unequal slopes model and the common slope model.

Program

```
proc glm;
    class teacher met gen;
    * unequal slopes model;
    model score=met teacher(met) gen gen*met iq*gen*met/solution;
    random teacher(met)/test;

proc glm;
    class teacher met gen;
    * equal slopes model;
    model score=met teacher(met) gen gen*met iq/solution;
    random teacher(met)/test;
run;
```

The results are displayed in Outputs 5.30 and 5.31, respectively.

Results

Output 5.30 *The Intra-block Analysis for the Unequal Slopes Model*

```
                    General Linear Models Procedure

Dependent Variable: SCORE
                           Sum of         Mean
Source             DF      Squares       Square   F Value    Pr > F

Model              20    10734.384      536.719    29.60     0.0001

Error              75     1360.022       18.134

Corrected Total    95    12094.406

         R-Square          C.V.      Root MSE        SCORE Mean
         0.887549       5.979268      4.2584            71.219

Source             DF     Type I SS  Mean Square  F Value    Pr > F

MET                 2     5772.4375    2886.2188   159.16     0.0001
TEACHER(MET)        9     1874.3438     208.2604    11.48     0.0001
GEN                 1      225.0938     225.0938    12.41     0.0007
MET*GEN             2       90.1875      45.0938     2.49     0.0900
IQ*MET*GEN          6     2772.3215     462.0536    25.48     0.0001

Source             DF    Type III SS  Mean Square  F Value    Pr > F

MET                 2       13.6416       6.8208     0.38     0.6878
TEACHER(MET)        9     1815.1022     201.6780    11.12     0.0001
GEN                 1        1.6817       1.6817     0.09     0.7616
MET*GEN             2        8.8986       4.4493     0.25     0.7830
IQ*MET*GEN          6     2772.3215     462.0536    25.48     0.0001
```

Parameter			Estimate		T for H0: Parameter=0	Pr > |T|	Std Error of Estimate
INTERCEPT			32.73738499	B	3.35	0.0013	9.77162224
MET	1		-9.34854296	B	-0.68	0.4983	13.73854785
	2		-11.61111388	B	-0.84	0.4040	13.83392330
	3		0.00000000	B	.	.	.
TEACHER(MET)	1	1	-8.76691819	B	-4.09	0.0001	2.14611372
	2	1	-6.78407959	B	-3.18	0.0021	2.13387665
	3	1	5.09803432	B	2.39	0.0194	2.13326743
	4	1	0.00000000	B	.	.	.
	1	2	-6.05899121	B	-2.77	0.0072	2.19103378
	2	2	-2.65992135	B	-1.24	0.2170	2.13652335
	3	2	0.10909494	B	0.05	0.9611	2.22681822
	4	2	0.00000000	B	.	.	.
	1	3	-10.03953679	B	-4.46	0.0001	2.24858394
	2	3	-13.00660328	B	-5.82	0.0001	2.23322852
	3	3	-6.95767767	B	-3.15	0.0023	2.20724065
	4	3	0.00000000	B	.	.	.
GEN	f		2.83474713	B	0.21	0.8340	13.47889550
	m		0.00000000	B	.	.	.
MET*GEN	1	f	-7.36305746	B	-0.39	0.6979	18.89789290
	1	m	0.00000000	B	.	.	.
	2	f	5.98148351	B	0.31	0.7572	19.27705396
	2	m	0.00000000	B	.	.	.
	3	f	0.00000000	B	.	.	.
	3	m	0.00000000	B	.	.	.
IQ*MET*GEN	1	f	0.43653440		4.90	0.0001	0.08901890
	1	m	0.41149992		4.21	0.0001	0.09781418
	2	f	0.45326247		4.64	0.0001	0.09776591
	2	m	0.52608245		5.49	0.0001	0.09581002
	3	f	0.51164231		5.95	0.0001	0.08599203
	3	m	0.49012771		5.19	0.0001	0.09435828

NOTE: The X'X matrix has been found to be singular and a
generalized inverse was used to solve the normal equations.
Estimates followed by the letter 'B' are biased, and are not
unique estimators of the parameters.

General Linear Models Procedure

Source	Type III Expected Mean Square
MET	Var(Error) + 0.0958 Var(TEACHER(MET)) + Q(MET,MET*GEN)
TEACHER(MET)	Var(Error) + 7.5869 Var(TEACHER(MET))
GEN	Var(Error) + Q(GEN,MET*GEN)
MET*GEN	Var(Error) + Q(MET*GEN)

```
IQ*MET*GEN        Var(Error) + Q(IQ*MET*GEN)



                      General Linear Models Procedure
            Tests of Hypotheses for Mixed Model Analysis of Variance
     Dependent Variable: SCORE



     Source: MET *
     Error: 0.0126*MS(TEACHER(MET)) + 0.9874*MS(Error)


                          Denominator  Denominator
          DF   Type III MS      DF         MS      F Value  Pr > F
           2   6.8207878652    83.74  20.451014418   0.3335  0.7173
     * - This test assumes one or more other fixed effects are zero.
```

Output 5.31 *The Intra-block Analysis for the Common Slopes Model*

Source	DF	Sum of Squares	Mean Square	F Value	Pr > F
Model	15	10713.342	714.223	41.37	0.0001
Error	80	1381.065	17.263		
Corrected Total	95	12094.406			

R-Square	C.V.	Root MSE	SCORE Mean
0.885810	5.834016	4.1549	71.219

Source	DF	Type III SS	Mean Square	F Value	Pr > F
MET	2	4120.2748	2060.1374	119.34	0.0001
TEACHER(MET)	9	1907.8144	211.9794	12.28	0.0001
GEN	1	45.2364	45.2364	2.62	0.1094
MET*GEN	2	211.3993	105.6996	6.12	0.0034
IQ	1	2751.2792	2751.2792	159.37	0.0001

Parameter	Estimate	T for H0: Parameter=0	Pr > |T|	Std Error of Estimate

Source	Type III Expected Mean Square
MET	Var(Error) + 7.8436 Var(TEACHER(MET)) + Q(MET,MET*GEN)
TEACHER(MET)	Var(Error) + 7.9154 Var(TEACHER(MET))
GEN	Var(Error) + Q(GEN,MET*GEN)

```
MET*GEN          Var(Error) + Q(MET*GEN)


IQ               Var(Error) + Q(IQ)



Source: MET *
Error: 0.9909*MS(TEACHER(MET)) + 0.0091*MS(Error)

                         Denominator    Denominator
     DF    Type III MS        DF             MS      F Value   Pr > F
      2   2060.1374065       9.01   210.21325194      9.8002   0.0055
* - This test assumes one or more other fixed effects are zero.
```

Interpretation

There are slight differences between the results of the mixed model analyses and the within block model analyses because PROC GLM does not utilize the between block information about the slopes. For example, the estimate of the slope for method 1 and female student is 0.4313 for PROC MIXED (Output 5.29) and 0.4115 for PROC GLM (Output 5.30).

Again, as in Example 5.6, the classes of eight students are blocks for gender, and the mixed model equations combine the information from the various parts of the model into combined estimators of the slopes, which in turn have an effect on the LSMEANS.

5.8 Example: Complex Strip-Plot Design with the Covariate Measured on an Intermediate Size Experimental Unit

The data in Data Set 5.8, "Wafer Types," in Appendix 4, "SAS Data Sets," are from an experiment designed to study the effect of temperature (TEMP at three levels, 900°F, 1000°F, 1100°F) on the deposition rate (DELTA) of a layer of polysilicon in the fabrication of wafers in the semiconductor industry. The experiment includes two wafer types (A and B) in order to study the possibility of interaction between temperature and wafer type. The experiment consists of putting two wafers of each type into a cassette and then inserting the cassette into a furnace for treatment at a given level of temperature. The furnace is the experimental unit for the levels of temperature. Wafers of a given type are produced in groups of six wafers called **lots**. Four lots of each type of wafer were available for use in the experiment. The six wafers from one randomly selected lot of type A wafers are randomly divided into three groups of two wafers. These three groups of two type A wafers are randomly assigned to the three furnaces in the group 1 part of the experiment. Similarly, the six wafers from one randomly selected lot of type B wafers are randomly divided into three groups of two wafers. These three groups of two type B wafers are randomly assigned to the three furnaces in the group 1 part of the experiment. The diagram in Figure 5.8 exhibits the randomization process of assigning temperatures to furnaces and assigning wafer types from the wafer lots to the furnaces.

Figure 5.8 *Layout of the Wafer Experiment*

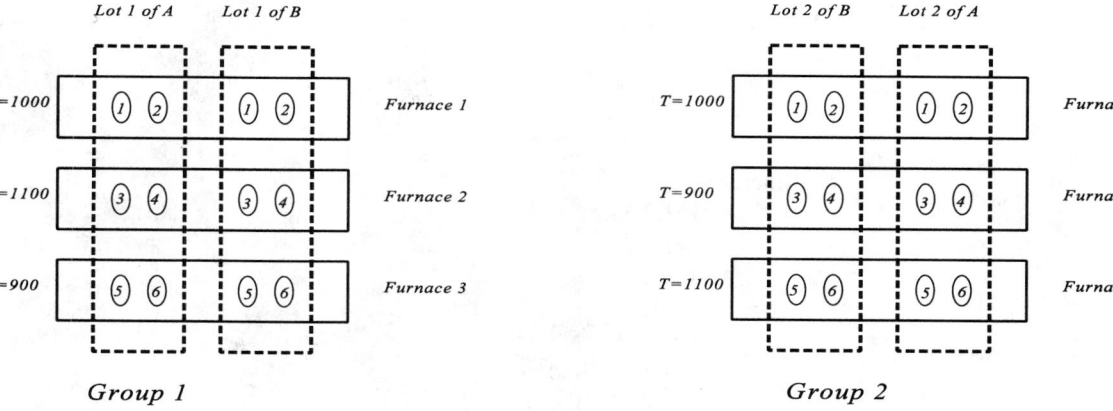

Group 1

Group 2

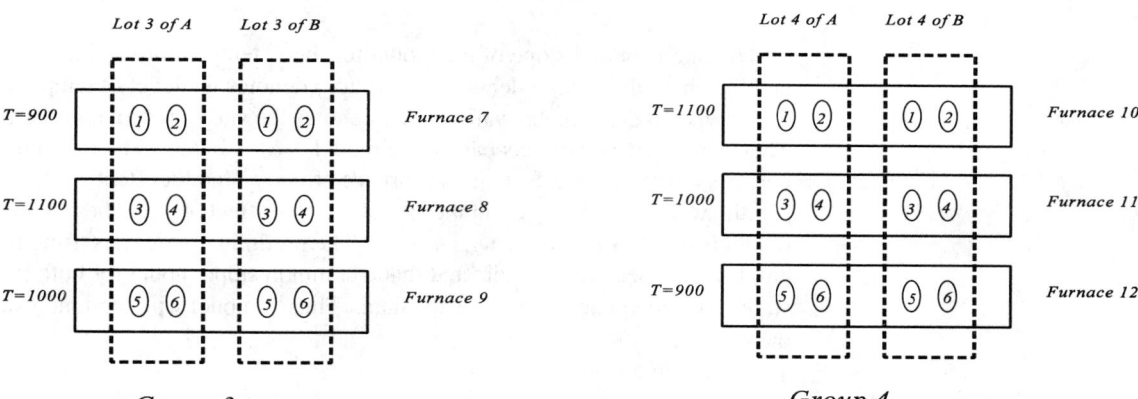

Group 3

Group 4

The lot is the experimental unit for wafer type. (Note that the type A wafer lots are different from the type B wafer lots.) Therefore each furnace has two wafers from each of two lots, and the wafers from a given lot occur in three different furnaces, one at each temperature. This process is repeated four times using a total of four lots of type A wafers, four lots of type B wafers, and twelve furnaces. (Actually, the same furnace was used each time).

The experiment was conducted by randomly assigning the three temperatures to the three furnaces in each group, thus creating a blocking factor, GROUP. The measurements are the amount of deposited material at three randomly chosen sites on each wafer. It was thought that the wafer thickness before the deposition process was applied may have an effect on the deposition rate. Therefore, the average thickness of each wafer was determined and used as a possible covariate. The covariate is measured on the wafer, the next-to-smallest size of experimental unit. The engineer also wanted to estimate the variance components associated with lots, wafers(lots), and sites(wafers lots). The design structure consists of six sizes of experimental units, the group, the furnace, the lot, the lot-furnace combination, the wafer, and the site. So there are six variance components in the random part of the model. The furnaces and the lots within a group form strip plots. The wafers are nested within lots, and the sites are nested within wafers.

Model

A model to describe the amount of material deposited as it relates to the fixed effects and the random effects is

$$y_{ijkmn} = \alpha_{jk} + \beta_{jk} t_{ijkm} + g_i + f_{ij} + l_{ik} + fl_{ijk} + w_{ijkm} + e_{ijkmn} \qquad (5.14)$$

where

$i = 1, 2, 3, 4$
$j = 1, 2, 3$
$k = 1, 2$
$m = 1, 2$
$n = 1, 2, 3$
$g_i \sim$ iid $N(0, \sigma^2_g)$
$f_{ij} \sim$ iid $N(0, \sigma^2_f)$
$l_{ik} \sim$ iid $N(0, \sigma^2_l)$
$fl_{ijk} \sim$ iid $N(0, \sigma^2_{fl})$
$w_{ijk} \sim$ iid $N(0, \sigma^2_w)$
$e_{ijkmn} \sim$ iid $N(0, \sigma^2_e)$.

The intercept and slope of the model for the jth temperature and the kth wafer type are α_{jk} and β_{jk} where the index i denotes the group, j denotes the level of temperature, k denotes the wafer type, m denotes the wafer, and n denotes the site. The covariate is denoted by t_{ijkm}. Therefore, the fixed effects part of the model is $\alpha_{jk} + \beta_{jk} t_{ijkm}$. The random part of the model consists of the group effect, g_i, the furnace effect, f_{ij}, the lot effect l_{ik}, the lot-furnace effect fl_{ijk}, the wafer effect, w_{ijkm}, and the site of a wafer effect, e_{ijkmn}. The random effects part of the model is $g_i + f_{ij} + l_{ik} + fl_{ijk} + w_{ijkm} + e_{ijkmn}$. The preliminary analysis using the strategy as employed in Section 5.6 indicated that a common slope model for both temperature and wafer type adequately describes the data. Thus, a model with common slope was fit to the data.

The common slope model is

$$y_{ijkmn} = \alpha_{jk} + \beta t_{ijkm} + g_i + f_{ij} + l_{ik} + fl_{ijk} + w_{ijkm} + e_{ijkmn} \qquad (5.15)$$

where

$i = 1, 2, 3, 4$
$j = 1, 2, 3$
$k = 1, 2$
$m = 1, 2$
$n = 1, 2, 3$
$g_i \sim$ iid $N(0, \sigma^2_g)$
$f_{ij} \sim$ iid $N(0, \sigma^2_f)$
$l_{ik} \sim$ iid $N(0, \sigma^2_l)$
$fl_{ijk} \sim$ iid $N(0, \sigma^2_{fl})$
$w_{ijkm} \sim$ iid $N(0, \sigma^2_w)$
$e_{ijkmn} \sim$ iid $N(0, \sigma^2_e)$.

Program

The following program fits the common slope model 5.15 to the data:

```
proc mixed;
    class grp temp type;
    model delta=temp|type thick/ ddfm=satterth;
    random grp grp*temp grp*type grp*type*temp wafer(grp temp type);
    lsmeans temp type;
    lsmeans temp*type/pdiff;
run;
```

The main difficulty with constructing an appropriate MODEL statement for PROC MIXED is deciding how to code terms for the five variance components (in addition to the residual). The group-to-group variance component is extracted using GRP. Because the levels of temperature and levels of wafer type form a strip plot (see Chapter 25 of Milliken and Johnson (1984)), the furnace variance component is extracted by using GRP*TEMP, the lot variance component is extracted by using GRP*TYPE and the furnace-by-lot variance component is extracted by using GRP*TEMP*TYPE. The wafer-to-wafer variance component corresponds to the term WAFER(GRP TEMP TYPE), and the site-to-site variance component is provided by the residual. When the design involves many structures, break the design down into components to determine the appropriate code to compute the desired variance components.

The results are in Output 5.32.

Results

Output 5.32 *The Estimates of the Variance Components and Analysis of the Fixed Effects for the Common Slope*

```
                     Covariance Parameter Estimates (REML)


Cov Parm                        Ratio        Estimate      Std Error
GRP                          13.60877133    51.41168488    75.97550656
GRP*TEMP                     20.27515068    76.59616229    47.65004309
GRP*TYPE                      5.92868593    22.39759381    21.49015081
GRP*TEMP*TYPE                 1.87358237     7.07808399     6.68505916
WAFER(GRP*TEMP*TYPE)          1.93161442     7.29731945     2.52572349
Residual                      1.00000000     3.77783443     0.54528343



                     Covariance Parameter Estimates (REML)


              Z    Pr > |Z|

            0.68    0.4986
            1.61    0.1080
            1.04    0.2973
            1.06    0.2897
            2.89    0.0039
            6.93    0.0001
```

```
                        Tests of Fixed Effects


              Source      NDF   DDF  Type III F  Pr > F


              TEMP         2   5.99       4.74   0.0583

              TYPE         1   3.03     134.54   0.0013

              TEMP*TYPE    2   6.09      28.97   0.0008

              THICK        1   24.8     524.74   0.0001
```

Output 5.33 *The LSMEANS Evaluated at the Averate Wafer Thickness of 1993.21 and Comparisons of the Interaction Parallel Regression Lines*

```
                         Least Squares Means


   Level                    LSMEAN     Std Error   DDF      T    Pr > |T|


   TEMP 900             328.88169496  6.01842732  6.54   54.65   0.0001

   TEMP 1000            314.15714124  6.01843484  6.54   52.20   0.0001

   TEMP 1100            310.12783047  6.01840640  6.54   51.53   0.0001

   TYPE A               296.68975586  5.07905473  3.86   58.41   0.0001

   TYPE B               338.75468858  5.07905473  3.86   66.70   0.0001

   TEMP*TYPE 900 A      313.13323028  6.35928110  8.01   49.24   0.0001

   TEMP*TYPE 900 B      344.63015963  6.35936421  8.01   54.19   0.0001

   TEMP*TYPE 1000 A     294.97723757  6.36493451  8.04   46.34   0.0001

   TEMP*TYPE 1000 B     333.33704491  6.36346948  8.03   52.38   0.0001

   TEMP*TYPE 1100 A     281.95879973  6.36006826  8.01   44.33   0.0001

   TEMP*TYPE 1100 B     338.29686121  6.36015235  8.01   53.19   0.0001



                   Differences of Least Squares Means


   Level 1              Level 2          Difference    Std Error


   TEMP*TYPE 900 A      TEMP*TYPE 900 B   -31.49692935  4.10829272

   TEMP*TYPE 900 A      TEMP*TYPE 1000 A   18.15599271  6.63686788

   TEMP*TYPE 900 A      TEMP*TYPE 1000 B  -20.20381463  7.43158956

   TEMP*TYPE 900 A      TEMP*TYPE 1100 A   31.17443055  6.63221027

   TEMP*TYPE 900 A      TEMP*TYPE 1100 B  -25.16363093  7.42874331

   TEMP*TYPE 900 B      TEMP*TYPE 1000 A   49.65292206  7.43407720

   TEMP*TYPE 900 B      TEMP*TYPE 1000 B   11.29311472  6.63442581

   TEMP*TYPE 900 B      TEMP*TYPE 1100 A   62.67135991  7.42917533

   TEMP*TYPE 900 B      TEMP*TYPE 1100 B    6.33329843  6.63185991

   TEMP*TYPE 1000 A     TEMP*TYPE 1000 B  -38.35980734  4.13836183

   TEMP*TYPE 1000 A     TEMP*TYPE 1100 A   13.01843784  6.63359222

   TEMP*TYPE 1000 A     TEMP*TYPE 1100 B  -43.31962364  7.43737560

   TEMP*TYPE 1000 B     TEMP*TYPE 1100 A   51.37824518  7.43535919

   TEMP*TYPE 1000 B     TEMP*TYPE 1100 B   -4.95981630  6.63264959

   TEMP*TYPE 1100 A     TEMP*TYPE 1100 B  -56.33806148  4.11328940
```

```
              Differences of Least Squares Means

         DDF          T   Pr > |T|

         4.78      -7.67    0.0007
         6.84       2.74    0.0298
         8.98      -2.72    0.0237
         6.82       4.70    0.0024
         8.97      -3.39    0.0081
         8.99       6.68    0.0001
         6.83       1.70    0.1336
         8.97       8.44    0.0001
         6.82       0.95    0.3722
         4.92      -9.27    0.0003
         6.83       1.96    0.0915
         9.01      -5.82    0.0003
            9       6.91    0.0001
         6.82      -0.75    0.4796
         4.81     -13.70    0.0001
```

Interpretation

The Type III F corresponding to TEMP*TYPE indicates there is a significant interaction ($p=0.0008$), and thus the temperature-wafer type models need to be used to compare the treatment combinations. The least squares means listed in Output 5.33 are the adjusted means or predicted values from the regression models at the average thickness of 1993.21.

This model involves six different sizes of experimental units, and each has information about the slope in the model. The mixed models analysis extracts the information from each part and then combines the information into a combined slope estimate.

5.9 Summary

An analysis of covariance strategy was described and demonstrated via several mixed model examples. When the model involves more than one factor in the design structure, information about the fixed effects part of the model can be extracted from several parts of the design structure. The mixed models analysis combines the information from the various parts of the design structure and provides combined estimators of the fixed effects. In particular, the estimates of the slopes corresponding to the covariates are computed from the combined information. If the design structure involves only one block, i.e., a completely randomized design structure, the usual within block analysis extracts all of the information about the slopes from the data. When the design structure is more complex, the mixed models analysis extracts more information from the data than the usual analysis provided by PROC GLM.

5.10 References

Milliken, G. A. and Johnson, D. E. (1994), *Analysis of Messy Data: Designed Experiments, Vol I*, London: Chapman Hall.

Chapter **6 Best Linear Unbiased Prediction**

6.1 Introduction

The first five chapters have focused on models whose purpose is to estimate or test fixed effects. The main role of random effects in these models is in determining the standard error of an estimated fixed effect or the proper form of a test statistic. In some cases, notably in Chapter 4, the estimates of the variance components are of intrinsic interest. One of the main features distinguishing mixed model methodology from conventional linear model methods is the ability to estimate specific random effects or linear functions of random effects. For example, Henderson (1963) developed a procedure for predicting breeding values of randomly selected sires in animal genetics experiments. To do this, he used estimates of the random sire effects in a mixed model. He called his procedure **best linear unbiased prediction**, or **BLUP**. Harville (1976) showed that Henderson's procedure had a valid theoretical basis: it can be justified as an extension of the Gauss-Markov theorem. More recently, the method of computing predictors based on estimated random effects has gained increasing acceptance and has been applied to a wide variety of statistical problems.

The purpose of this chapter is to provide an introduction to the fundamental concepts of best linear unbiased prediction, hereafter referred to as BLUP. Section 6.2 presents some introductory motivating examples. Section 6.3 discusses the basic ideas and terminology of BLUP. Sections 6.4 through 6.6 use three examples of increasing complexity to show how you can use PROC MIXED for BLUP.

6.2 Examples of BLUP

McLean, et. al. (1991) discuss various possible **inference spaces** available in working with mixed models. Robinson (1991) wrote an excellent general discussion of BLUP. This section presents a number of examples to illustrate in nontechnical terms the distinction between **estimation**—as defined in classical linear model theory—and **BLUP**. Section 6.3 presents a more technical discussion of BLUP theory and methods.

6.2.1 Random-Effects Model

The random-effects model was discussed in Chapter 4. A common example occurs in animal breeding. A group of bulls are randomly selected. Each bull is mated to a number of cows. A trait of interest (e.g., weight gain) is measured in the offspring. The model for such an experiment is

$$y_{ijk} = \mu + s_i + d(s)_{ij} + e_{ijk} \tag{6.1}$$

where

y_{ijk} is the measurement on the kth offspring of the jth dam (cow) mated to the ith sire (bull)

μ is the intercept

s_i is the effect of the ith sire

$d(s)_{ij}$ is the effect of the jth dam mated to the ith sire

e_{ijk} is the residual.

The effects s_i, $d(s)_{ij}$, and e_{ijk} are each iid normal with mean 0 and variances σ_S^2, σ_D^2, and σ^2, respectively. Additionally, all random effects are assumed to be independent of one another.

Typically, the initial purpose of such experiments is to estimate the variance associated with the random effects (e.g., sire and dam). In the animal breeding example, for instance, researchers typically want to know whether a trait can be inherited and if so, how much of the inheritance is paternal or maternal. Variance component estimates are used to estimate "heritability."

A secondary objective of many such trials is to identify superior animals for breeding purposes. For example, if the trait of interest does turn out to be strongly inherited, say, through the sire, then the animal breeder would want to identify the best sires for future breeding. In order to do this, the sire breeding value, $\mu + s_i$, must be estimated. You can see that this is a linear combination of a fixed effect, μ, and a random effect, s_i.

The difference between fixed and random effects can be further illustrated using the nested model. Suppose each of the sires represents a particular breed, e.g., sire 1 is an Angus, sire 2 is a Hereford, etc. If there is one sire per breed, then it is reasonable to regard sire (now a.k.a. "breed") as a fixed effect. The inclusion of specific breeds in the experiment is a reproducible decision, whereas the random sampling of sires from a population of bulls from the same breed is not.

6.2.2 Two-way Mixed Model

The two-way mixed model was discussed in Chapter 1. McLean, et. al. used the following example, typical of two-way models in a manufacturing application. Different machines used in a production process are to be compared. Machine operators are randomly selected from a population of possible operators. Each operator runs each machine; two observations are taken for each operator-machine combination.

The resulting model is

$$y_{ijk} = \mu + \tau_i + O_j + (\tau O)_{ij} + e_{ijk} \tag{6.2}$$

where

y_{ijk} is the kth observation on the ith machine being run by the jth operator
μ is the intercept
τ_i is the effect of the ith machine (fixed)
O_j is the effect of the jth operator (random)
$(\tau O)_{ij}$ is the ij^{th} machine-by-operator interaction
e_{ijk} is random error.

The operator, machine-by-operator, and error effects are assumed iid normal with mean 0 and variance components σ_O^2, σ_{MO}^2, and σ^2, respectively.

The analyses discussed in Chapter 1 focus on inference about fixed effects, in this case, the machine effects. For example, you can estimate the mean performance of the ith machine as $\mu + \tau_i$, or estimate or test the difference between machines, e.g., the first and second machines, $\tau_1 - \tau_2$. These estimates and tests address the objective of assessing machine performance, say for the purpose of choosing the best machine.

In this study, a manager may also be interested in assessing the performance of various operators under his or her supervision. He or she might want to know the performance of the jth operator averaged over all machines, $\mu + (1/m)\Sigma\tau_i + O_j$, where m is the number of machines in the study. The manager might also want to assess the performance of a given operator on a specific machine, $\mu + \tau_i + O_j + (\tau O)_{ij}$. These objectives must be addressed by estimating the required linear combinations of fixed and random effects, i.e., the required BLUPs.

6.2.3 A Random Coefficient Regression Model

Random coefficient regression models are discussed in detail in Chapter 7. To further illustrate the kinds of applications for which BLUP is useful, this section presents an example of random coefficient regression in nontechnical terms. A common objective of clinical trials is to assess the relationship between drug dosage and a physiological response. Suppose that a number of subjects are randomly assigned to receive a given dosage of a drug. The subjects' response is then measured. A model for the data is

$$y_{ijk} = \beta_0 + s_i + (\beta_1 + d_i)X_{ij} + e_{ij} \tag{6.3}$$

where

y_{ij} is the response of the ith subject at the jth dose level
β_0 is the fixed intercept
β_1 is the fixed slope
s_i is the random deviation of the ith subject's intercept from β_0
d_i is the random deviation of the ith subjects slope from β_1
e_{ij} is random error.

The random effects, s_i, d_i, and e_{ij} are assumed iid normal with mean 0 and variance components σ_S^2, σ_D^2, and σ^2 respectively.

In conventional regression theory, the subject-specific terms, s_i and d_i, do not appear in the model. Inference focuses on estimating the intercept and slope and using them to obtain predicted response to a given dose level, i.e., $\beta_0 + \beta_1 X_{ij}$. The estimates of intercept, slope, and predicted response are implicitly averages over the entire population of subjects.

In the above mixed model including the random regression coefficients, s_i and d_i, the same "population average" estimates used in conventional regression can also be obtained. However, in a clinical trial where the subjects happen to be patients under treatment for an illness, the specific response of a given patient to drug dosage may also be of interest. The attending physician, for example, may want to know how an individual patient responds to a given dose.

In the random coefficient mixed model, you assume that the population average relationship between dose and response is given by the conventional regression equation, $\beta_0 + \beta_1 X_{ij}$, but each subject's specific response to dosage can be estimated by

$$\beta_0 + s_i + (\beta_1 + d_i)X_{ij}$$

The terminology **population average** versus **subject-specific** is due to Zeger, et. al. (1988). The subject-specific estimate is a form of BLUP.

6.2.4 A Mixed Model with Multiple Error Terms

Mixed models with multiple error terms were introduced in Chapter 2. A common type of multierror model in which BLUP may be of interest occurs in a multilocation trial. Examples of multilocation trials include medical and pharmaceutical research, where similar experiments are often conducted at several clinics or hospitals, or technology-transfer research in agriculture, where similar experiments are often conducted at several farms. The purpose of such trials is to broaden the scope of inference, for example, to a wide variety of situations that might be encountered when an experimental treatment is adopted for practical use.

A typical multilocation trial is conducted as follows. Each of t treatments is replicated r times at each of s sites or locations. Ideally, the sites are a random sample from a target population. How well this ideal is met in practice can be a controversial matter, but assume sites are random for this discussion. The model implied by such a trial is

$$y_{ijk} = \mu + s_i + r(s)_{ij} + \tau_k + (s\tau)_{ik} + e_{ijk} \tag{6.4}$$

where

> y_{ijk} is the observation on the jth replication on the kth treatment at the ith site or location
> s_i is the site effect
> $r(s)_{ij}$ is the replication within-site effect
> τ_k is the treatment effect
> $(s\tau)_{ik}$ is the site-by-treatment interaction.

The effects s_i, $r(s)_{ij}$, $(s\tau)_{ik}$, and e_{ijk} are each assumed iid normal with mean 0 and variances σ_S^2, σ_{RS}^2, σ_{ST}^2, and σ^2, respectively. The random effects are assumed independent of one another.

In conventional fixed-effects analysis of multilocation trials, inference focuses on average treatment performance throughout the target population. Thus, estimates of treatment means, expressed as $\mu + \tau_k$, or differences between two treatments, $\tau_k - \tau_{k'}$, are the main objectives.

In many practical situations, you may be interested in the specific performance of treatments at a given site. For example, you may want to know the site-specific treatment mean, expressed as $\mu + s_i + \tau_k + (s\tau)_{ik}$, or a site-specific treatment difference, $\tau_k - \tau_{k'} + (s\tau)_{ik} - (s\tau)_{ik'}$. These estimates are of particular interest if you suspect different treatments perform better under different environmental conditions, represented by the various locations in the trial.

Traditionally, site-specific inference has been approached by first determining if a significant site-by-treatment interaction exists and then by analyzing each site separately if the interaction is present. However, this approach limits the power and precision of inference at each site. The mixed model approach using BLUP permits site-specific inference using information from the entire trial for all sites simultaneously.

6.3 Basic Concepts for BLUP

This section presents the basic concepts and terminology of best linear unbiased prediction required to follow the examples discussed the remainder of this chapter. This section focuses on application and interpretation. Appendix 1 contains additional theoretical detail.

The basic form of a linear mixed model is

$$y_j = \Sigma \beta_i X_{ji} + \Sigma u_k Z_{jk} + e_j$$

where

y_j is the jth observation
β_i's are fixed-effect parameters
X_{ji} are constants associated with the fixed effects
u_k's are random effects
Z_{jk} are constants associated with the random effects
e_j is the jth residual error

Specific forms of the linear models were discussed in section 6.2 and in the previous five chapters. Alternatively, you can write the mixed model in matrix form as $\mathbf{y} = \mathbf{X\beta} + \mathbf{Zu}$.

The expected value of an observation is

$$\mathbf{E(y)} = \mathbf{E(X\beta + Zu)} = \mathbf{X\beta}$$

since the expected value of the random effect vector, $\mathbf{u}$, is 0. This is called the **unconditional expectation**, or the mean of $\mathbf{y}$ averaged over all possible $\mathbf{u}$. The subtlety of this quantity is important: in practical terms, the observed levels of the random effects are a random sample of a larger population. The unconditional expectation is the mean of $\mathbf{y}$ over the *entire population*.

The **conditional expectation** of $\mathbf{y}$ given $\mathbf{u}$, denoted $\mathbf{E(y|u)}$ is

$$\mathbf{E(y|u)} = \mathbf{X\beta + Zu}.$$

In practical terms, this is the mean of $\mathbf{y}$ *for the specific set* of levels of the random effect *actually observed*.

The unconditional mean is thus a population-wide average whereas the conditional mean is an average specific to an observed set of random effects. Because the set of observed levels of the random factors is not an *exact* duplicate of the entire population, the conditional and unconditional means are not equal, in general.

In the previous five chapters, statistical inference is based on linear combinations of the fixed effects. Linear combinations of **fixed effects**, denoted $\Sigma K_i \beta_i$ are called **estimable functions** if they can be constructed from a linear combination of unconditional means of the observations. That is, if $\mathbf{K'\beta} = \mathbf{T'[E(y)]} = \mathbf{T'X\beta}$ for some $\mathbf{T'}$, then it is estimable. Quantities such as regression coefficients, treatment means, treatment differences, contrasts, and simple effects in factorial experiments are all common examples of estimable functions.

Estimable functions do not depend on the random effects. The examples discussed in section 6.2 introduced linear combinations of both the β_i's and $\mathbf{u}_j$'s of interest in many practical situations. A generalization of the estimable function is required for such cases. Linear combinations of the fixed and random effects, $\mathbf{K'\beta} + \mathbf{M'u}$, can be formed from linear combinations of the conditional means. Such linear combinations are called **predictable functions**. A function $\mathbf{K'\beta} + \mathbf{M'u}$ is **predictable** if its $\mathbf{K'\beta}$ component is estimable.

The mixed model equations, discussed in Appendix 1, provide solutions for both estimable and predictable functions. Using the mixed model equation solution for β in an estimable function results in the **best linear unbiased *estimate*** (BLUE) of $\mathbf{K'\beta}$. For predictable functions, the solutions for β and $\mathbf{u}$ provide the **best linear unbiased *predictor*** (BLUP) of $\mathbf{K'\beta} + \mathbf{M'u}$.

To summarize, linear combinations of fixed effects only are called **estimable functions**. The solution of the mixed model equations results in **estimates**, or BLUEs, of $\mathbf{K'\beta}$. Linear combinations of fixed *and* random effects are called **predictable functions**. Solving the mixed model equations yield **predictors**, or BLUPs, of $\mathbf{K'\beta} + \mathbf{M'u}$.

Estimates, or BLUEs, and predictors, or BLUPs, imply different targets of statistical inference. Various terminology has been developed to describe the differences. McLean, et. al. (1991) discussed the **inference space** and defined **broad** versus **narrow** inference. Zeger, et. al. (1988) discussed **population-wide** versus **subject-specific** inference. To oversimplify, **broad** and **population-wide** generally refer to inference based exclusively on fixed effects and estimable functions, whereas **narrow** and **subject-specific** generally refer to inference based on predictable functions.

Technically, the broad/narrow and population-wide/subject-specific terminology are not interchangeable, and the distinctions are somewhat more subtle. You can better understand the distinctions with the following example. Section 6.2.2 considers a study involving machines (fixed) and operators (random). The model is

$$y_{ijk} = \mu + \tau_i + O_j + (\tau O)_{ij} + e_{ijk}$$

where τ_i, O_j and $(\tau O)_{ij}$ were the machine, operator, and machine-by-operator effects, respectively. The unconditional mean of an observation is $E(y_{ijk}) = \mu + \tau_i$. If you wanted an estimate of the average performance of the ith machine over the entire population of operators—those actually observed in the study *and* those in the population but not observed—you would estimate $\mu + \tau_i$. Similarly, if you wanted to estimate the average difference between two machines over the entire population, you would estimate $\tau_i - \tau_{i'}$. Both of these terms involve only fixed effects, and thus they are **estimates**.

Alternatively, you may want to assess the performance of a machine for the specific set of operators observed. Perhaps the machine's designer wants an estimate over the entire population, but as the manager of your company, you want to know how *your operators, specifically,* are doing. If so, you want to determine the conditional mean, $\mu + \tau_i + (1/J)\Sigma O_j + (1/J)\Sigma\Sigma(\tau O)_{ij}$, where J is the number of operators. For a difference, you want to determine $\tau_i - \tau_{i'} + (1/J)\Sigma\Sigma[(\tau O)_{ij} - (\tau O)_{i'j}]$. These terms represent what McLean, et. al. called the **narrow** inference space, as contrasted to **broad** inference, which uses the unconditional mean, $\mu + \tau_i$, and difference, $\tau_i - \tau_{i'}$. Narrow inference restricts attention to only the operators observed, whereas broad inference expands attention to the entire population. Both narrow inference terms, the conditional mean and difference, are **predictors** because they involve both fixed and random effects. You can see that the narrow inference terms share the same estimable functions as their broad inference analogues, but the narrow space terms have additional random effects.

Finally, suppose, as a manager, you want to use the study to evaluate an individual employee or to determine which machine is best to assign to that particular operator. In such cases, you do not want averages. You want a quantity that is specific to a given operator. To assess a given operator, averaged over all machines, you want to determine one of two possible predictable functions:

(1) $\mu + (1/I)\Sigma\tau_i + O_j + (1/I)\Sigma\Sigma(\tau O)_{ij}$
(2) $\mu + (1/I)\Sigma\tau_i + O_j$

where I is the number of machines. The narrow space BLUP is obtained from (1), whereas (2) yields the broad space BLUP. To assess a specific operator's performance on a given machine, you want to determine the conditional mean, $\mu + \tau_i + O_j + (\tau O)_{ij}$. To compare an individual operator's performance on two specific machines, you want to determine $\tau_i - \tau_{i'} + (\tau O)_{ij} - (\tau O)_{i'j}$. Each of these are what Zeger, et. al. called **subject-specific** terms. If you drop the random-effects components of each subject-specific predictable function, you have its population-wide analogue.

The remaining sections present three examples using PROC MIXED to show how to set up, compute, and interpret various BLUPs.

6.4 Example: Obtaining BLUPs in a Random-Effects Model

This section considers a data set based on the animal breeding example introduced in Section 6.2.1. Five sires were randomly sampled from a population. Each sire was mated to two dams. Two offspring per sire-dam combination were observed. The average daily gain (ADG) of each offspring was recorded. The data are given in Appendix 4, Data Set 6.4.

The model for this data set is Model 6.1 in Section 6.2.1.

As noted in Section 6.2.1, animal breeders are often interested in the breeding value of the ith sire, that is, the BLUP of the predictable function $\mu + s_i$. Actually, three BLUPs for the ith sire might be defined. The first is $\mu + s_i$, the **population-wide** or **broad** inference space BLUP, which predicts the performance of the ith sire across the entire population of dams to which he might potentially be mated. The second is $u + s_i + (\frac{1}{2})\Sigma d(s)_{ij}$, the **narrow** inference space BLUP assessing the performance of the sire on those dams to which he was actually mated. The third is the conditional mean, $\mu + s_i + d(s)_{ij}$, a "dam-specific" BLUP assessing the performance of a specific sire-by-dam combination.

6.4.1 Program Using the MIXED Procedure

You can obtain solutions for the model effects and the three BLUPs defined above using the following PROC MIXED statements:

```
proc mixed;
   class sire dam;
   model adg=;
   random sire dam(sire);
   estimate 'sire 1 BLUP broad' intercept 1 | sire 1 0;
   estimate 'sire 1 BLUP narrow' intercept 1 | sire 1 0 0 0 0
            dam(sire) 0.5 0.5 0 0 0 0 0 0 0 0;
   estimate 'sire1 BLUP dam 1' intercept 1 | sire 1 0
            dam(sire) 1 0;
run;
```

Some things to note about this program are

- This model has no fixed effects (other than intercept). Therefore, the MODEL statement serves only to identify the dependent variable (ADG). No independent variables appear in the MODEL.
- The model effects, SIRE and DAM(SIRE), are both random and thus appear in the RANDOM statement.
- The ESTIMATE statement is used to define predictable functions. All fixed effect coefficients must appear first and then all random effect coefficients. Fixed and random effect coefficients must be separated by a vertical bar (|).
- For the BLUPs defined in this program, the only fixed effect is the intercept, μ. All other coefficients appear to the right of the vertical bar.
- In the ESTIMATE statement, for a given model effect, all coefficients after the last 0 given default to 0. For example, consider the first ESTIMATE statement, "sire 1 BLUP broad," for the broad inference space BLUP. SIRE 1 0 causes the coefficients for the remaining sire effects (s_3, s_4, and s_5) to default to zero. DAM(SIRE) 0 sets all coefficients for dam to zero. Alternatively, you can explicitly give all the coefficients for every effect in the model for the predictable function $\mu + s_1$. The ESTIMATE statement then appears as

```
estimate 'sire 1 BLUP broad' intercept 1 | sire 1 0 0 0 0
   dam(sire) 0 0 0 0 0 0 0 0 0 0;
```

The second ESTIMATE statement gives all coefficients explicitly for the predictable function defining the narrow inference space BLUP, $u + s_1 + (\frac{1}{2})\Sigma d(s)_{1j}$. The third ESTIMATE statement uses defaults to define the function specific to the sire 1, dam 1 BLUP, $\mu + s_1 + d(s)_{11}$.

The results are given in Output 6.1.

Results

Output 6.1 *PROC MIXED Output for Sire-Dam Random Effects Model*

```
                          The MIXED Procedure

                        Class Level Information

                Class     Levels  Values

                SIRE        5     1 2 3 4 5
                DAM         2     1 2




              Covariance Parameter Estimates (REML)

Cov Parm          Ratio        Estimate      Std Error       Z    Pr > |Z|


SIRE          1.32559755     0.05130062    0.05895740     0.87    0.3842
DAM(SIRE)     0.95620155     0.03700500    0.03667750     1.01    0.3130
Residual      1.00000000     0.03870000    0.01730717     2.24    0.0253



               Model Fitting Information for ADG


          Description                           Value


          -2 REML Log Likelihood               8.8976




                 ESTIMATE Statement Results


Parameter               Estimate      Std Error    DDF      T    Pr > |T|


sire 1 BLUP broad      2.20574732    0.14207621     4    15.53    0.0001
sire 1 BLUP narrow     2.16093333    0.09344944     4    23.12    0.0001
sire 1 BLUP dam 1      2.10019405    0.12282426     4    17.10    0.0001
```

Interpretation

In Output 6.1, the estimates of the variance components are given under "Covariance Parameter Estimates (REML)." The estimate of the sire variance, σ_S^2, is 0.0513. The estimated dam variance, σ_D^2, is 0.0370, and the estimated residual variance is 0.0387.

The three BLUPs are given under "ESTIMATE Statement Results." The term labeled "Estimate" in the output is the BLUP. Technically, it is not an estimate, but a predictor. The "Std Error" is technically not a standard error, but it is the square root of the estimated prediction error variance. These are fine points of linear model jargon. For practical purposes, estimates and predictors have similar roles in inference, as do standard errors and square root prediction error variances. Unless otherwise noted, the rest of this chapter uses **standard error** to refer to the square root prediction error variance.

For the three predictable functions, the results are shown in Table 6.1.

Table 6.1 *ESTIMATE Statement Results*

Label	Predictable Function	BLUP	Std. error
sire 1 broad	$\mu + s_1$	2.206	0.142
sire 1 narrow	$\mu + s_1 + (\frac{1}{2})\Sigma d(s)_{1j}$	2.161	0.093
sire 1 dam1	$\mu + s_1 + d(s)_{11}$	2.100	0.123

The BLUPs are not the same. This is typical of changes in the inference space among BLUPs. In this case, the prediction for sire 1 for the entire population of dams is higher than for the average of the dams to which he was actually mated. This relationship is specific to these data and does not necessarily hold in general. The prediction error is largest for broad inference, smallest for narrow inference, and between the two for dam-specific inference. This relationship *does* hold in general. In narrow inference, you have data on the specific sire-dam combinations you are predicting. In broad inference, your predictions apply to sire-dam combinations which are theoretically possible but have not been observed. Broad inference, therefore, is made with less precision than narrow inference: with broad inference there is more uncertainty and hence greater variability.

PROC MIXED computes the standard error by substituting the REML variance component estimates into the formula for the prediction error variance assuming known variance components. These formula are given in Appendix 1. This is often called the **naive** method of estimating prediction error variance. Kackar and Harville (1984) showed that the naive estimate is biased downward. They suggested a correction for the bias. The correction, however, is rather complex and has not been included in PROC MIXED.

6.4.2 Comparison of PROC MIXED and PROC GLM Results

In the past, researchers interested in quantities such as sire BLUPs in random effects models used procedures such as PROC VARCOMP to obtain variance component estimates and then obtained sire means using PROC GLM (or PROC ANOVA if the data were balanced). The conceptual inconsistency of this practice was obvious to all: sires were treated as random to obtain variance component estimates, but they were treated as fixed to obtain means. However, the state of software development left little alternative for researchers who were not expert programmers or who lacked access to such experts. The BLUPs computed by PROC MIXED are conceptually consistent. How different are the BLUPs and the sire means PROC GLM computes?

Traditional Analysis Using PROC GLM

You can obtain the traditional analysis using the following program:

```
proc glm;
   class sire dam;
   model adg=sire dam(sire);
   lsmeans sire /stderr;
   lsmeans sire/ e=dam(sire) stderr;
run;
```

The first LSMEANS statement obtains the default standard errors, which are based on the residual error variance, σ^2 only. The second LSMEANS statement reflects an attempt to account for the fact that dams are random.

The results are given in Output 6.2.

Output 6.2 *PROC GLM Output for Sire-Dam Random Effects Model*

Source	DF	Sum of Squares	Mean Square	F Value	Pr > F
Model	9	1.83520000	0.20391111	5.27	0.0079
Error	10	0.38700000	0.03870000		
Corrected Total	19	2.22220000			

Source	DF	Type III SS	Mean Square	F Value	Pr > F
SIRE	4	1.27165000	0.31791250	8.21	0.0033
DAM(SIRE)	5	0.56355000	0.11271000	2.91	0.0707

Least Squares Means

SIRE	ADG LSMEAN	Std Err LSMEAN	Pr > |T| H0:LSMEAN=0
1	2.13750000	0.09836158	0.0001
2	2.24000000	0.09836158	0.0001
3	2.60250000	0.09836158	0.0001
4	2.02000000	0.09836158	0.0001
5	2.65000000	0.09836158	0.0001

Least Squares Means

Standard Errors and Probabilities calculated using the Type III MS for DAM(SIRE) as an Error term

SIRE	ADG LSMEAN	Std Err LSMEAN	Pr > |T| H0:LSMEAN=0
1	2.13750000	0.16786155	0.0001
2	2.24000000	0.16786155	0.0001
3	2.60250000	0.16786155	0.0001
4	2.02000000	0.16786155	0.0001
5	2.65000000	0.16786155	0.0001

The mean for sire 1 is 2.138. The default standard error is 0.0984; the standard error accounting for random dam effects is 0.168. None of these values agree with any of the BLUPs or their square root prediction error variances. What is PROC GLM actually doing?

You can find out by running a PROC MIXED program to produce the same results as PROC GLM, as follows.

PROC MIXED Program to Duplicate PROC GLM Results

You duplicate the PROC GLM results with PROC MIXED by defining SIRE to be a fixed effect. The default standard error results from defining the narrow inference space BLUP for sire 1; it has the same coefficients as before, but now SIRE is fixed, whereas in the previous PROC MIXED program SIRE was random. The standard error accounting for random dam effects results from defining the broad space estimable function for sire 1. The PROC MIXED program is

```
proc mixed;
   class sire dam;
   model adg= sire;
   random dam(sire);
   lsmeans sire;
   estimate 'sire 1 mean broad' intercept 1 sire 1 0;
   estimate 'sire 1 mean narrow' intercept 1 sire 1 0
            | dam(sire) 0.5 0.5 0 ;
   estimate 'sire 1 - dam 1' intercept 1 sire 1 0
            | dam(sire) 1 0;
run;
```

The results are given in Output 6.3.

Output 6.3 *PROC MIXED Output for Sire-Dam Random Effects Model*

```
                Assuming Fixed Sire to Duplicate GLM Results


                    Covariance Parameter Estimates (REML)

    Cov Parm          Ratio        Estimate      Std Error      Z    Pr > |Z|

    DAM(SIRE)       0.95620155    0.03700500    0.03667750    1.01    0.3130
    Residual        1.00000000    0.03870000    0.01730717    2.24    0.0253



                      Model Fitting Information for ADG


                  Description                        Value

                  -2 REML Log Likelihood             6.0658



                          Tests of Fixed Effects


                  Source      NDF   DDF  Type III F   Pr > F

                  SIRE          4     5      2.82     0.1428
```

ESTIMATE Statement Results

Parameter	Estimate	Std Error	DDF	T	Pr > |T|
sire 1 mean broad	2.13750000	0.16786155	5	12.73	0.0001
sire 1 mean narrow	2.13750000	0.09836158	5	21.73	0.0001
sire 1 - dam1	2.07676071	0.12660174	5	16.40	0.0001

Least Squares Means

Level	LSMEAN	Std Error	DDF	T	Pr > |T|
SIRE 1	2.13750000	0.16786155	5	12.73	0.0001
SIRE 2	2.24000000	0.16786155	5	13.34	0.0001
SIRE 3	2.60250000	0.16786155	5	15.50	0.0001
SIRE 4	2.02000000	0.16786155	5	12.03	0.0001
SIRE 5	2.65000000	0.16786155	5	15.79	0.0001

The LSMEANS computed by PROC MIXED are identical to the broad space sire means. They produces identical results to the PROC GLM LSMEANS statement using the E=DAM(SIRE) option to account for random dam effects. The narrow space sire 1 mean produces the same result as the PROC GLM LSMEANS using the default standard error.

6.4.3 Relationship between Sire Means and BLUPs

These data illustrate the relationship between the estimate of a mean and its BLUP analog. Whereas a fixed-effects mean is a simple average, reflecting the assumption that the entire population of levels has been observed in the data set, the BLUP is a regression toward the overall mean based on the variance components of the model effects. Regression toward the mean is sometimes called **shrinkage estimation**. Mood (1950) gave the formula for a shrinkage estimator as

$$\hat{\mu}^s_i = \hat{\mu} + \frac{\hat{\mu}_i - \hat{\mu}}{\hat{\sigma}_S^2 / [(\hat{\sigma}_S^2 + \hat{\sigma}_W^2)/N]}$$

where

$\hat{\mu}^s_i$ is the shrinkage estimate for the ith sire mean

$\hat{\mu}$ is the overall mean

$\hat{\mu}_i$ is the ith sire mean

$\hat{\sigma}_S^2$ is the estimate of the sire variance component

$\hat{\sigma}_W^2$ is the estimate of the within variance component, obtained pooling DAM(SIRE) and ERROR

N is the number of observations per sire.

Alternatively, this can be expressed as

$$\hat{\mu}^s_i = B_i\hat{\mu} + (1-B_i)\hat{\mu}_i$$

where

$$B_i = \hat{\sigma}_i^2/(\hat{\sigma}_i^2 + \hat{\sigma}_s^2)$$
$$\hat{\sigma}_i^2 = [(\hat{\sigma}_s^2 + \hat{\sigma}_w^2)/N]$$

For example, from the PROC GLM output, the estimated mean of sire 1 (μ_i) is 2.13, and the overall mean (μ) is 2.33. The estimate of the within variance component (σ_w^2) is computed by pooling DAM(SIRE) and error, that is

$$\hat{\sigma}_w^2 = \frac{SS[DAM(SIRE)] + SSE}{df_{DAME(SIRE)} + dfe} = \frac{0.564 + 0.387}{5 + 10} = 0.0634$$

Thus, $\hat{\sigma}_i^2 = [(0.0634 + 0.0513)/4]$
$$= 0.0287$$

and $B_i = 0.0287 / (0.0287 + 0.0513) = 0.359$
Thus, the shrinkage estimator for sire 1 is

$$\mu_1^s = B_1\mu + (1 - B_1)\mu_1$$

$$= 0.359(2.33) + (1 - 0.359)(2.13)$$

$$= 2.20$$

which is the empirical BLUP of sire 1.

The basic idea of a shrinkage estimator is that it *moves* the sire mean toward the overall mean. The degree of shrinkage depends on the magnitude of the variance. A large sire variance results in very little shrinkage, whereas a smaller variance results in more shrinkage toward μ.

The advantage of the shrinkage estimate is that estimated means which are well above or below μ are regressed toward μ consistent with the magnitude of σ_s^2 relative to σ_w^2. Thus, extreme means are attenuated by knowledge of the underlying variability, and the risk of misinterpretation of the data is reduced.

6.5 Example: Two-Factor Mixed Model

The second example is based on the machine-operator study described in Section 6.2.2 and used to illustrate various BLUP concepts in Section 6.3. This example focuses on using PROC MIXED to obtain the BLUPs discussed in Section 6.3 and on relationships between these BLUPs and estimable functions frequently computed using PROC GLM.

Two different types of MACHINE were compared. Three OPERATORs were randomly sampled from a population. Two observations were taken on each operator for each machine. The response variable (Y) was a performance criterion of interest in the study. The data are given in Appendix 4, Data Set 6.5.

6.5.1 Model

The mixed model for this study is model 6.2 given in Section 6.2.2.

Section 6.3 considered three basic types of functions of the model effects of potential interest.

- **Estimable functions.** These are estimable linear combinations of fixed effects only. These correspond to broad inference for the machines in the McLean, et. al. (1991) terminology and population average inference using the Zeger, et. al. (1988) terminology.

  Consider two examples:

  e1 Machine 1 mean, $\mu + \tau_1$

  e2 Machine difference, $\tau_1 - \tau_2$

  To make it easier to relate these functions to their estimates given below, the titles *e1* and *e2* also appear by the corresponding ESTIMATE results in the relevant SAS output.

- **Narrow inference predictable functions.** These are predictable functions that limit inference to the operators actually observed. Inference is based on conditional expectations given the observed operators. This is narrow inference as described by McLean, et. al.

  Consider two examples:

  e3 Machine 1 BLUP given observed operators,

  $$\mu + \tau_1 + (1/3)\Sigma O_j + (1/3)\Sigma(\tau O)_{1j}$$

  e4 Machine difference BLUP given observed operators,

  $$\tau_1 - \tau_2 + (1/3)[\Sigma(\tau O)_{1j} - \Sigma(\tau O)_{2j}]$$

- **Subject-specific predictable functions.** These are BLUPs applicable to individual operators.

  Consider three examples:

  e5 Operator 1 BLUP, averaged over all machines.

  $$\mu + (\tfrac{1}{2})\Sigma \tau_i + O_1 + (\tfrac{1}{2})\Sigma(\tau O)_{i1}$$

  e6 BLUP for operator 1 using machine 1

  $$\mu + \tau_1 + O_1 + (\tau O)_{11}$$

  e7 BLUP for the difference between machines specific to operator 1

  $$\tau_1 - \tau_2 + (\tau O)_{11} - (\tau O)_{21}$$

6.5.2 Program to Obtain Estimates and Predictors

Program

You can obtain estimates and predictors for these functions using the following PROC MIXED statements:

```
proc mixed;
   class machine operator;
   model y=machine;
   random operator machine*operator;

   estimate 'BLUE - mach 1'  intercept 1 machine 1 0;
   estimate 'BLUE - diff' machine 1 -1;
   estimate 'BLUP - m 1 narrow'
            intercept 3 machine 3 0 | operator 1 1 1
            machine*operator 1 1 1 0 0 0/divisor=3;
   estimate 'BLUP - diff narrow'
            machine 3 -3 | machine*operator 1 1 1 -1 -1 -1/divisor=3;
   estimate 'BLUP - oper 1'
            intercept 2 machine 1 1  | operator 2 0 0
            machine*operator 1 0 0 1 0 0/divisor=2;
   estimate 'BLUP -  m 1 op 1'
            intercept 1 machine 1 0 | operator 1 0 0
            machine*operator 1 0 0 0 0 0;
   estimate 'BLUP - diff op 1'
            machine 1 -1 | machine*operator 1 0 0 -1 0 0;
run;
```

The ESTIMATE statements labeled "BLUE" are the two broad or population-averaged estimable functions. The ESTIMATE statements labeled "BLUP...narrow" correspond to the two narrow inference space BLUPs. The final set of three ESTIMATE statements refer to the subject-specific BLUPs.

The results of this program are given in Output 6.4.

Results

Output 6.4 *PROC MIXED Output for Machine-Operator Two-Way Mixed Model*

		Covariance Parameter Estimates (REML)				
Cov Parm		Ratio	Estimate	Std Error	Z	Pr > |Z|
OPERATOR		2.21208999	0.10734167	0.14977990	0.72	0.4736
MACHINE*OPERATOR		1.05109050	0.05100417	0.07655909	0.67	0.5053
Residual		1.00000000	0.04852500	0.02801592	1.73	0.0833

		ESTIMATE Statement Results				
	Parameter	Estimate	Std Error	DDF	T	Pr > |T|
e1	BLUE - mach 1	50.94833333	0.24671734	2	206.50	0.0001
e2	BLUE - diff	-1.00833333	0.22400397	2	-4.50	0.0460
e3	BLUP - m 1 narrow	50.94833333	0.08993053	2	566.53	0.0001
e4	BLUP - diff nrw	-1.00833333	0.12718097	2	-7.93	0.0155

```
e5  BLUP - oper 1        51.73655975    0.10702571    2   483.40    0.0001
e6  BLUP -  m 1 op 1     51.29789888    0.14484031    2   354.17    0.0001
e7  BLUP - diff op1      -0.87732174    0.19518415    2    -4.49    0.0461

e8  BLUP - m 1 interm    50.94833333    0.15839472    2   321.65    0.0001
e9  BLUP -op 1 intrm     51.68202865    0.17641041    2   292.96    0.0001
```

Least Squares Means

Level	LSMEAN	Std Error	DDF	T	Pr > |T|
MACHINE 1	50.94833333	0.24671734	2	206.50	0.0001
MACHINE 2	51.95666667	0.24671734	2	210.59	0.0001

Interpretation

Major points about the output are

- For the broad and narrow inference space, the **estimates** of the machine means are the same, 50.95. However, the standard errors for the two inference spaces are different. The standard error for the broad space is 0.248. For the narrow BLUP the standard error is 0.0899.

  The standard error in the broad inference space results from determining the variance of an estimated machine mean or difference, as derived in Chapters 1 and 2. The standard error for the narrow inference space is what you would get if you defined OPERATOR (and hence MACHINE*OPERATOR) as fixed, rather than random.

- The same result holds for the machine difference as well. The two inference spaces yield identical estimates, −1.008, but the standard errors, 0.224 for broad inference and 0.127 for narrow inference, are different.

  Again, the broad standard error results from the same derivations of the variance of treatment differences presented in previous chapters. The narrow standard error corresponds to the standard error you would obtain if operator effects were defined as fixed.

- The subject-specific BLUPs are computed using methods discussed in Appendix 1. Unlike the broad and narrow space estimates and predictors, they do not correspond to any straightforward, easy-to-derive formula.

6.5.3 Intermediate Inference

McLean, et. al. (1991) discussed a third inference space, which they called **intermediate** inference. For example, an alternative to the two predictable functions for the machine 1 mean presented above is

$$\mu + \tau_1 + (1/3)\Sigma O_j$$

This predictable function is conditioned on the operator main effects but not on the operator-machine interactions. For a manager assessing a machine's performance with a particular group of operators, this makes sense if operator performance averaged over machines were predictable, but specific interactions were not.

Aside from its potential application, this function has some theoretical features that help shed light on traditional ways of doing things in PROC GLM. You can compute the intermediate BLUP in PROC MIXED using the statement

```
estimate 'BLUP - m 1 interm'
          intercept 3 machine 3 0 | operator 1 1 1
          machine*operator 0 0 0 0 0 0/divisor=3;
```

The result is included in Output 6.4, above. It is labeled *e8*.

As was the case for the broad and narrow machine 1 means, the estimate is the same, 50.95. But the standard error is different. It is 0.159—less than the broad but greater than the narrow space standard error. You can derive this standard error by defining the machine and operator main effects as fixed, but the machine-by-operator effects as random.

6.5.4 Broad-Space BLUP

You can also vary the inference space for subject-specific BLUPs. For example, a broad space predictable function for operator 1 averaged across machines is

$$\mu + (\tfrac{1}{2})\Sigma\tau_i + O_1$$

This function assumes that you can estimate the machine effects and predict the operator 1 effect but that you do not want to restrict inference to the particular way in which operator 1 interacted with the machines in this study. Thus, this is broader inference than results from including the $(\tau O)_{il}$ effects.

You can compute the broad space BLUP for operator 1 in PROC MIXED using the statement

```
estimate 'BLUP - op 1 broad'
          intercept 2 machine 1 1  | operator 2 0 0
          machine*operator 0 0 0 0 0 0/divisor=2;
```

The results appear under ESTIMATE statement *e9*, in Output 6.4. The predictor ("estimate") is 51.68 with a standard error of 0.176.

6.5.5 Comparison of MIXED Procedure with PROC GLM

You can also analyze these data using PROC GLM. The estimable or predictable functions for the various inference spaces help interpret various aspects of the PROC GLM output, particular standard errors.

Program

To compute the analysis using PROC GLM, use the following statements:

```
proc glm;
   class machine operator;
   model y=machine|operator;
   random operator machine*operator/test;
   lsmeans machine operator machine*operator/stderr;
   lsmeans machine/stderr e=machine*operator;
   estimate 'diff' machine 1 -1/e;
run;
```

The results appear in Output 6.5.

Results

Output 6.5 *PROC GLM Results for Machine-Operator Two-Way Model*

```
Source                  Type III Expected Mean Square

MACHINE                 Var(Error) + 2 Var(MACHINE*OPERATOR) + Q(MACHINE)

OPERATOR                Var(Error) + 2 Var(MACHINE*OPERATOR) + 4 Var(OPERATOR)

MACHINE*OPERATOR   Var(Error) + 2 Var(MACHINE*OPERATOR)
```

MACHINE	Y LSMEAN	Std Err LSMEAN	Pr > |T| HO:LSMEAN=0
1	50.9483333	0.0899305	0.0001
2	51.9566667	0.0899305	0.0001

OPERATOR	Y LSMEAN	Std Err LSMEAN	Pr > |T| HO:LSMEAN=0
1	51.7625000	0.1101420	0.0001
2	51.5675000	0.1101420	0.0001
3	51.0275000	0.1101420	0.0001

MACHINE	OPERATOR	Y LSMEAN	Std Err LSMEAN	Pr > |T| HO:LSMEAN=0
1	1	51.3550000	0.1557642	0.0001
1	2	50.8400000	0.1557642	0.0001
1	3	50.6500000	0.1557642	0.0001
2	1	52.1700000	0.1557642	0.0001
2	2	52.2950000	0.1557642	0.0001
2	3	51.4050000	0.1557642	0.0001

Interpretation

The following are pertinent to this discussion:

- The LSMEANS for machine are computed using estimable functions with the same coefficients as the **narrow space BLUP** for machine, $\mu + \tau_i + (1/3)\Sigma O_j + (1/3)\Sigma(\tau O)_{ij}$.

The estimate of the LSMEANS for machine is the same, e.g. 50.95 for machine 1, as that obtained for the broad, narrow, and intermediate estimates in PROC MIXED.

Output 6.6 *PROC GLM Machine-Operator Output (continued)*

```
                         Least Squares Means

       Standard Errors and Probabilities calculated using the Type III MS for
                       MACHINE*OPERATOR as an Error term


              MACHINE              Y        Std Err      Pr > |T|
                                LSMEAN       LSMEAN     H0:LSMEAN=0


                 1           50.9483333    0.1583947      0.0001
                 2           51.9566667    0.1583947      0.0001




Coefficients for estimate diff




                                                Row   1


INTERCEPT                                              0


MACHINE           1                                   1
                  2                                   -1


OPERATOR          1                                   0
                  2                                   0
                  3                                   0


MACHINE*OPERATOR 1 1                            0.3333333333
                 1 2                            0.3333333333
                 1 3                            0.3333333333
                 2 1                           -0.333333333
                 2 2                           -0.333333333
                 2 3                           -0.333333333




                                         T for H0:    Pr > |T|   Std Error of
Parameter                    Estimate   Parameter=0              Estimate

diff                        -1.00833333     -7.93      0.0002    0.12718097
```

- The default standard error for the LSMEANS for machine is the standard error for the **narrow space BLUP**—0.0899.

- Traditionally, you override the default error term using the optional error term E=MACHINE*OPERATOR to account for the fact that OPERATOR effects are random. The resulting standard error is 0.159. Using this option results in the **intermediate space BLUP** estimate and standard error.

- The ESTIMATE statement to assess the difference between machines in PROC GLM uses the same coefficients and yields the same results as the **narrow space BLUP** for machine difference. The ESTIMATE statement in PROC GLM has no option to override the default standard error.

- PROC GLM has *no option* to allow computing the broad space estimates and standard errors for machine means and differences. They can be computed in PROC MIXED. This is important because in the vast majority of practical applications, the broad inference space is of primary, if not exclusive, interest.

- The LSMEANS for OPERATOR and MACHINE*OPERATOR are computed by standard linear model methods for fixed effects. They do not, in general, yield the same results as the corresponding BLUPs computed in PROC MIXED. PROC GLM cannot compute subject-specific BLUPs. For the model as defined in this example, the OPERATOR and MACHINE*OPERATOR estimates computed by PROC GLM are inappropriate.

The ANOVA table and the F-values computed using the RANDOM statement with the TEST option in PROC GLM are correct. This is one of the few aspects of the PROC GLM analysis that *is* correct for this model.

6.6 A Multilocation Example

Chapter 2, Section 2.8, considered a multilocation study which presented various aspects of using PROC MIXED for broad space inference. This section completes the multilocation example by discussing the use of PROC MIXED for prediction of location-specific effects when locations are considered random.

The example in Section 2.8 was a multicenter trial to compare 4 treatments. Treatments were observed at each of 9 centers or locations. At each location, a randomized complete block design with 3 blocks was used.

The data appear in Appendix 4, Data Set 2.8. The model is 6.4, given in Section 6.2.4.

Section 2.8 looked at two approaches to the analysis: one with fixed locations; the other with random locations. In both cases, block effects, $R(L)_{jk}$, were assumed iid normal $(0,\sigma_R^2)$, and error effects, e_{ijk}, were assumed iid normal$(0,\sigma^2)$. When locations are random, $L_j \sim NI(0,\sigma_L^2)$ and $(\tau L)_{ij} \sim NI(0,\sigma_{TL}^2)$. All random effects were assumed to be independent of one another.

Analysis assuming fixed locations is appropriate when the locations are deliberately chosen and inference is confined to just those locations. Random locations are assumed when the locations are chosen as a random sample from a population of locations. Inference may be population-wide (broad), narrow, or location-specific. The location-specific case is equivalent to subject-specific inference discussed in previous sections of this chapter.

Broad inference for this example was discussed in Section 2.8. As you have seen in previous examples in this chapter, narrow inference produces results similar to assuming a fixed-effects model. More to the point, in multilocation trials, you ordinarily would not be interested in narrow inference unless you consider locations fixed. Therefore, this section concentrates on location-specific inference.

Location-specific inference means you assess LOC main effect BLUPs, LOC*TRT BLUPs, and simple effect differences between treatments at specific locations. As in previous examples, you use BLUPs rather than means to be consistent with mixed model theory. Conventional means are not appropriate because they imply estimable functions of LOC and TRT effects, which have no meaning since LOC is not a fixed effect.

6.6.1 Obtaining BLUPs

To illustrate, suppose you want the BLUP for the main effect of location 1. In the previous sections you saw that this could imply one of two predictable functions:

(1) $\mu + (1/4)\Sigma\tau_i + L_1$

(2) $\mu + (1/4)\Sigma\tau_i + L_1 + (1/4)\Sigma\tau L_{i1}$

Function (1) represents the broader inference space and is thus ordinarily of primary interest.

The BLUP for the location-specific treatment performance is more straightforward. For example, for location 1, you can obtain the predicted response of treatment 1 using

$$\mu + \tau_1 + L_1 + (\tau L)_{11}$$

Similarly, for treatment 2 at location 1, the BLUP is

$$\mu + \tau_2 + L_1 + (\tau L)_{21}$$

Taking the difference, the BLUP for the simple effect of treatment 1 versus treatment 2 within location 1 is

$$\tau_1 - \tau_2 + (\tau L)_{11} - (\tau L)_{21}$$

6.6.2 Program Using the MIXED Procedure

You can compute these BLUPs using the following PROC MIXED statements:

```
proc mixed;
    class loc block trt;
    model adg=trt/ddfm=satterth;
    random loc block(trt) loc*trt;

    estimate 'loc 1 blup broad'
            intercept 4 trt 1 1 1 1 | loc 4 0/divisor=4;
    estimate 'loc 1 blup narrow'
            intercept 4 trt 1 1 1 1 | loc 4 0
            loc*trt 1 1 1 1 0/divisor=4;

    estimate 'trt 1 x loc 1 blup'
            intercept 1 trt 1 0 0 0 | loc 1 0 loc*trt 1 0;
    estimate 'trt 2 x loc 1 blup'
            intercept 1 trt 0 1 0 0 | loc 1 0 loc*trt 0 1 0/e;

    estimate 'trt 1 v 2 at loc 1' trt 1 -1 0 | loc*trt 1 -1 0;
run;
```

The SATTERTH option in the MODEL statement computes the approximate degrees of freedom for the BLUPs using Satterthwaite's procedure. This allows the correct test statistics to be computed and facilitates interval estimation.

Results

The BLUPs and their prediction errors are given in Output 6.6 under the ESTIMATE results. Other aspects of the analysis appeared in Chapter 2, Outputs 2.18 and 2.19.

Output 6.7 *MIXED Procedure Results for Multilocation Example*

```
                     ESTIMATE Statement Results


Parameter               Estimate    Std Error   DDF        T   Pr > |T|

loc 1 blup broad       2.99318284   0.07156714  16.2   41.82    0.0001
loc 1 blup narrow      2.99388765   0.06772582  19.3   44.21    0.0001

trt 1 x loc 1 blup     3.05997674   0.08265653    15   37.02    0.0001
trt 2 x loc 1 blup     2.83248024   0.08265653    15   34.27    0.0001


trt 1 v 2 at loc 1     0.22749650   0.07737900  2.49    2.94    0.0761
```

Interpretation

For location 1, the two inference spaces produce BLUPs of 2.99. There are minor discrepancies in the fourth decimal place. The main difference between the two is in the standard error. The narrow space BLUP yields the smaller standard error −0.068 versus 0.072 for the broad space BLUP. This is expected because the narrow space BLUP limits the sources of variation and hence uncertainty in the prediction.

You can use the output to construct interval estimates. For BLUPs, these are called **prediction intervals**. Just as BLUPs are not estimates, prediction intervals are not confidence intervals in the traditional sense. The prediction interval is constructed analogously to the confidence interval

$$\text{BLUP} \pm t_{v,\alpha}(\text{std. error})$$

For example, for the broad space BLUP for location 1, the degrees of freedom are 16.2. For a 95% prediction interval, the needed *t*-value is $t_{(16.2, 0.05)}$, which is 2.12. Thus the prediction interval is

$$2.99 \pm (2.12)(0.072)$$

or (2.84, 3.14).

You can perform the analog of hypothesis tests as well. For example, for the difference between treatment 1 and 2 at location 1, the predicted difference is 0.227, with a standard error of 0.077, and a *t*-statistic of 2.94. Using the Satterthwaite approximation, there are 2.49 degrees of freedom and the resulting *p*-value is 0.0761. This can be used as evidence of the presence or absence of a treatment difference at a specific location. This is not a true hypothesis test as, strictly speaking, **hypothesis tests** are defined for fixed parameters only.

A word of caution is in order. Distribution theory associated with BLUP is not nearly as well-understood as it is with conventional estimable functions. Thus, the *p*-values must be understood as approximate. This caution notwithstanding, *t*-tests such as this example can be very useful in assessing location-specific treatment effects.

In many multilocation trials, there are questions regarding the **stability** of treatments. In other words, do the same treatments perform well or poorly in all locations, or are there as-yet-unknown subpopulations such that some treatments perform optimally at certain types of locations whereas other treatments are better suited for other locations? By assessing the simple effects of treatments at each location using the BLUPs demonstrated in this example, the stability issue can be addressed using mixed model methods.

6.7 Summary

The chapter presents a nontechnical introduction to best linear unbiased prediction (BLUP) and the distinction between **estimation** and **prediction** in mixed models. Section 6.2 presents several examples to illustrate estimates and predictors that are of interest in practical situations. Section 6.3 develops the main ideas, illustrating them through a two-way mixed model. Sections 6.4, 6.5, and 6.6 show how to obtain BLUPs using PROC MIXED. Three data sets are used to show how to construct the programs and interpret the output.

6.8 References

Harville, D.A. (1976) Extension of the Gauss-Markov theorem to include the estimation of random effects, *Annals of Statistics*, **2**, 384–395.

Henderson, C.R. (1963), Selection index and expected genetic advance. In *Statistical Genetics and Plant Breeding* (W.D. Hanson and H.F. Robinson, eds.), 141–163. Washington, DC: National Academy of Sciences and National Research Council Publication No. 982.

Kackar, R.N. and Harville, D.A. (1984), Approximations of standard errors of estimators of fixed and random effects in mixed linear models, *Communications in Statistics, A: Theory and Methods*, **10**, 1249–1261.

McLean, R.A., Sanders, W.L., and Stroup, W.W. (1991), A unified approach to mixed linear models, *American Statistician*, **45**, 54–64.

Mood, A.M. (1950), *Introduction to the Theory of Statistics*, New York: McGraw-Hill.

Robinson, G.K. (1991), That BLUP is a good thing, *Statistical Science*, **6**, 15–51.

Zeger, S.L., Liang, K.Y., and Albert, P.S. (1988), Models for longitudinal data: a generalized estimating equation approach, *Biometrics*, **44**, 1049–1060.

Chapter 7 Random Coefficient Models

7.1 Introduction

Data that have a nested or hierarchical structure are common in a wide variety of disciplines, and similar methods for analyzing such data are found in these disciplines under different guises. The analyses considered here fall under the headings of **random coefficient models** and **empirical Bayes models** in the statistics literature (Laird and Ware, 1982; Strenio, Weisberg, and Bryk, 1983; Rutter and Elashoff, 1994; Wolfinger, 1996). Analogous terms in the educational and social science literature are **hierarchical linear models** and **multilevel linear models** (Goldstein, 1987; Bryk and Raudenbush, 1992; see also *Journal of Educational and Behavioral Statistics* (1995), **20**(2)). A primary objective of this chapter is to describe these models and illustrate how to fit them using PROC MIXED.

The basic structure of random coefficient models builds on the analysis of covariance models discussed in Chapter 5. There linear regression models are used to include continuous variables (covariates) as independent variables. The regression coefficients for the covariates are assumed to be fixed effects, that is, unknown fixed parameters that are estimated from the data.

In this chapter the regression coefficients for one or more covariates are assumed to be a random sample from some population of possible coefficients, hence the term **random coefficients**. Random coefficient models are sensible whenever the data arise from independent subjects or clusters and the regression model for each subject or cluster can be assumed to be a random deviation from some population regression model.

The standard random coefficient model involves a random intercept and slope for each subject. Letting y_{ij} denote the measurement on the jth observation on the ith subject, this model can be written as follows:

$$y_{ij} = a_i + x_{ij}b_i + e_{ij}$$

(7.1)

where

$$i=1,2,...,t$$
$$j=1,2,...,n_i$$

$$\begin{pmatrix} a_i \\ b_i \end{pmatrix} \sim \text{ iid } N\left[\begin{pmatrix} \alpha \\ \beta \end{pmatrix} , \ \Psi \ \right]$$

$$\Psi = \begin{pmatrix} \sigma_a^2 & \sigma_{ab} \\ \sigma_{ab} & \sigma_b^2 \end{pmatrix}$$

$$e_{ij} \sim \text{ iid } N(0,\sigma^2) \ .$$

The model in (7.1) can be expressed as

$$y_{ij} = \alpha + a_i^* + \beta x_{ij} + b_i^* x_{ij} + e_{ij} \qquad (7.2)$$

where

$$i=1,2,...,t$$
$$j=1,2,...n_i$$
$$a_i^* = a_i - \alpha$$
$$b^* = b_i - \beta$$

$$\begin{pmatrix} a_i^* \\ b_i^* \end{pmatrix} \sim \text{ iid } N\left[\begin{pmatrix} 0 \\ 0 \end{pmatrix} , \ \Psi \ \right]$$

$$e_{ij} \sim \text{ iid } N(0,\sigma^2) \ .$$

Model 7.2 can be expressed in terms of a mixed model as

$$y_{ij} = \alpha + \beta x_{ij} + a_i^* + b_i^* x_{ij} + e_{ij} \qquad (7.3)$$

where

$$i=1,2,...,t,$$
$$j=1,2,...n_i$$

$\alpha + \beta x_{ij}$ is the fixed effects part of the model

$a_i^* + b_i^* x_{ij} + e_{ij}$ is the random effects part of the model.

Finally, the model in 7.3 can be expressed as

$$y_{ij} = \alpha + \beta x_{ij} + e_{ij}^* \qquad (7.4)$$

where

$$i = 1, 2, \ldots, t$$

$$j = 1, 2, \ldots, n_i$$

$$E(y_{ij}) = \alpha + \beta x_{ij}$$

$$e_{ij}^* = a_i^* + b_i^* x_{ij} + e_{ij}$$

$$\mathrm{Var}(y_{ij}) = \begin{bmatrix} 1 , & x_{ij} \end{bmatrix} \Psi \begin{bmatrix} 1 \\ x_{ij} \end{bmatrix} + \sigma_e^2 .$$

A graphical representation of this model is displayed in Figure 7.1. In it the random regression lines for each subject deviate about the overall population regression line, $\mu(y|x)$. For this graph the covariance between intercept and slope σ_{ab} is positive, so if a subject's intercept is larger than others, its slope will tend to be larger as well.

Figure 7.1 *Several Simple Linear Regression Models from a Random Sample of Treatments*

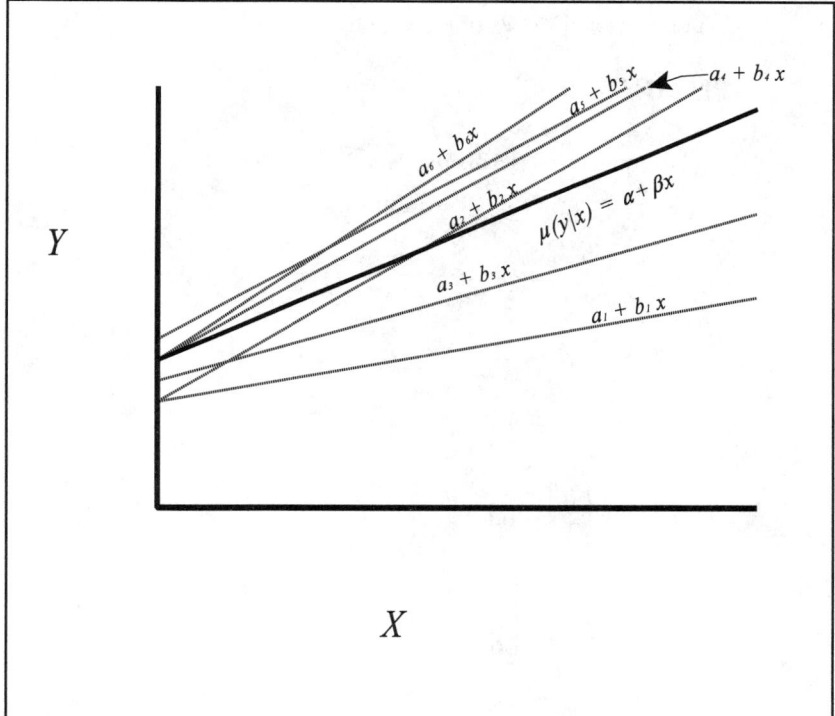

The random coefficient model is a conditional hierarchical linear model (Bryk and Raudenbush, 1992) where the experimental units are nested within the randomly selected levels of the subjects. It is possible to introduce additional levels of hierarchy as well as more than two random coefficients at each level, but the examples in the next section only consider the standard random intercept-slope model just described.

7.2 Examples

The following sections contain two examples of random coefficients models. The first example has random coefficients corresponding to a random treatment effect like that discussed in Chapter 4. The second has random coefficients arising from students in a social science experiment. Using the notation from the previous section, the analyses of the examples consist of estimating α, β, Ψ, and σ^2 and testing reasonable hypotheses about them.

7.2.1 Example: One-way Random Effects Treatment Structure in a Completely Randomized Design Structure

The data in Data Set 7.2, "Winter Wheat," in Appendix 4, "SAS Data Sets," are from ten varieties of wheat that were randomly selected from the population of varieties of hard red winter wheat adapted to dry climate conditions. The experimental units are one acre plots of land in a 60 acre field. The varieties were randomly assigned to six one acre plots of land. It was thought that the preplant moisture content of the plots could have an influence on the germination rate and hence on the eventual yield of the plots. Thus, the amount of preplanting moisture in the top 36 inches of the soil was determined for each plot. The response is yield in bushels per acre (YIELD), and the covariate is the measured amount of moisture (MOIST), which was measured before planting the varieties on the plots. Because the varieties were randomly selected, the resulting regression model for each variety is a random model selected from the population of variety models. The fixed effects of the model are the intercept and the slope, which are the expected values of the population of the intercepts and slopes of the varieties.

Model

A model to describe the data, like model 7.1, is

$$y_{ij} = a_i + x_{ij}b_i + e_{ij} \tag{7.5}$$

where

$$i = 1,2,\ldots,10$$
$$j = 1,2,\ldots,6$$

$$\begin{pmatrix} a_i \\ b_i \end{pmatrix} \sim \text{iid } N\left[\begin{pmatrix} \alpha \\ \beta \end{pmatrix}, \Psi\right]$$

$$\Psi = \begin{pmatrix} \sigma_a^2 & \sigma_{ab} \\ \sigma_{ab} & \sigma_b^2 \end{pmatrix}$$

$$e_{ij} \sim \text{iid } N(0,\sigma^2) .$$

Program

The following program fits model 7.5 to the data:

```
proc mixed scoring=8;
   class variety;
   model yield = moist/solution;
   random int moist/type=un sub=variety solution;
run;
```

The option TYPE=UN in the RANDOM statement provides estimates of the variances of the slopes and of the intercepts and the covariance between the slopes and the intercepts. The option SUBJECT=VAR in the RANDOM statement specifies that the intercept and slope of one variety is independently distributed from the intercepts and slopes of the other varieties, but the intercept and slope within each variety are correlated. Thus the covariance component $\sigma_{\alpha\beta}$ is estimated from the data. Including INT MOIST with SUB=VARIETY in the RANDOM statement generates the terms VARIETY from the INT and MOIST*VARIETY from the MOIST. The option SCORING=8 requests that PROC MIXED use Fisher's scoring for the first eight iterations. The results are in Outputs 7.1 and 7.2.

Results

Output 7.1 *Results for Covariance Parameters and Fixed Effects*

```
                        The MIXED Procedure

                    Class Level Information

            Class     Levels  Values

            VARIETY       10  1 2 3 4 5 6 7 8 9 10

            Covariance Parameter Estimates (REML)

Cov Parm                    Ratio      Estimate    Std Error        Z

INTERCEPT UN(1,1)      53.66541258   18.89424396   9.11071791     2.07
          UN(2,1)      -0.20650912   -0.07270667   0.08240034    -0.88
          UN(2,2)       0.00679834    0.00239352   0.00134857     1.77
Residual                1.00000000    0.35207488   0.07902149     4.46


            Covariance Parameter Estimates (REML)

            Pr > |Z|

              0.0381
              0.3776
              0.0759
              0.0001


            Model Fitting Information for YIELD

            Description                      Value

            Observations                   60.0000
            Variance Estimate               0.3521
            Standard Deviation Estimate     0.5934
            REML Log Likelihood           -93.0731
            Akaike's Information Criterion -97.0731
            Schwarz's Bayesian Criterion  -101.194
            -2 REML Log Likelihood        186.1463
            Null Model LRT Chi-Square      150.5228
            Null Model LRT DF               3.0000
            Null Model LRT P-Value          0.0000
```

```
                    Solution for Fixed Effects

    Parameter        Estimate     Std Error    DDF        T   Pr > |T|

    INTERCEPT      33.43385597    1.39846455      9    23.91    0.0001
    MOIST           0.66165611    0.01678188      9    39.43    0.0001




                    Tests of Fixed Effects

             Source       NDF    DDF   Type III F   Pr > F

             MOIST          1      9     1554.47     0.0001
```

The solution for the fixed effects provides $\hat{\alpha}$ = 33.43385597 and $\hat{\beta}$ = 0.66165611 . Using the RANDOM statement, REML estimates of the variance and covariance components are

$$\hat{\Psi} = \begin{pmatrix} 18.89424396 & -0.07270667 \\ -0.07270667 & 0.00239352 \end{pmatrix}$$

and $\hat{\sigma}^2_e$ = 0.35207488

Output 7.2 *Results for Random Effects*

```
                    Solution for Random Effects

    Parameter  Subject         Estimate    SE Pred  DDF       T   Pr>|T|

    INTERCEPT  VARIETY 1      0.95776229  1.51014350   40    0.63   0.5295
    MOIST      VARIETY 1     -0.04921048  0.02113403   40   -2.33   0.0250
    INTERCEPT  VARIETY 2     -2.28441488  1.52687368   40   -1.50   0.1425
    MOIST      VARIETY 2     -0.06669172  0.02741589   40   -2.43   0.0196
    INTERCEPT  VARIETY 3     -0.40800034  1.51587043   40   -0.27   0.7892
    MOIST      VARIETY 3      0.06721953  0.02230934   40    3.01   0.0045
    INTERCEPT  VARIETY 4      0.69601466  1.48188031   40    0.47   0.6411
    MOIST      VARIETY 4     -0.02330561  0.02385918   40   -0.98   0.3345
    INTERCEPT  VARIETY 5      1.11586851  1.69287673   40    0.66   0.5136
    MOIST      VARIETY 5     -0.01990302  0.02598796   40   -0.77   0.4483
    INTERCEPT  VARIETY 6      4.63919388  1.46709395   40    3.16   0.0030
    MOIST      VARIETY 6      0.02388748  0.01988611   40    1.20   0.2367
    INTERCEPT  VARIETY 7    -10.72998506  1.45532563   40   -7.37   0.0001
    MOIST      VARIETY 7      0.05642149  0.02219992   40    2.54   0.0150
    INTERCEPT  VARIETY 8      2.40122103  1.48419142   40    1.62   0.1136
    MOIST      VARIETY 8      0.02243209  0.02212984   40    1.01   0.3168
    INTERCEPT  VARIETY 9     -0.17615540  1.51676642   40   -0.12   0.9081
    MOIST      VARIETY 9      0.02335525  0.02226527   40    1.05   0.3005
    INTERCEPT  VARIETY 10     3.78849531  1.83398291   40    2.07   0.0454
    MOIST      VARIETY 10    -0.03420501  0.02872176   40   -1.19   0.2407
```

The solution for the random effects in Output 7.2 are the predicted values for the deviations of the varieties' intercepts from the population mean intercept (the first variety's intercept is denoted by INTERCEPT VARIETY 1, which is a prediction of $a_1 - \alpha$) and the deviations of the varieties' slopes from the population mean intercept (the first variety's slope is denoted by MOIST VARIETY 1, which is a prediction of $b_1 - \beta$) for each variety. These deviations of intercepts and deviations of slopes can be used with the estimates of α and β to construct a plot of the family of simple linear regression lines.

The following program fits the random coefficients model to the data assuming $\sigma_{\alpha\beta} = 0$:

```
proc mixed scoring=8;
   class variety;
   model yield = moist/solution;
   random int moist/sub=variety solution;
run;
```

The results are in Output 7.3.

Results

Output 7.3 *Results of Fitting the Random Coefficients Model to the Data*

```
                    The MIXED Procedure

                 Class Level Information

        Class      Levels   Values

        VARIETY       10    1 2 3 4 5 6 7 8 9 10


            Covariance Parameter Estimates (REML)

Cov Parm         Ratio       Estimate     Std Error      Z     Pr > |Z|

INTERCEPT    51.60785935   18.28241076   8.79723434    2.08     0.0377
MOIST         0.00646680    0.00229090   0.00129892    1.76     0.0778
Residual      1.00000000    0.35425633   0.07996434    4.43     0.0001


             Model Fitting Information for YIELD

        Description                         Value

        Observations                      60.0000
        Variance Estimate                  0.3543
        Standard Deviation Estimate        0.5952
        REML Log Likelihood              -93.5565
        Akaike's Information Criterion   -96.5565
        Schwarz's Bayesian Criterion     -99.6471
        -2 REML Log Likelihood           187.1130


                 Solution for Fixed Effects

     Parameter      Estimate     Std Error    DDF        T    Pr > |T|

     INTERCEPT    33.41079751   1.37612177     9    24.28     0.0001
     MOIST         0.66187041   0.01646834     9    40.19     0.0001
```

```
                     Tests of Fixed Effects

        Source      NDF   DDF   Type III F   Pr > F

        MOIST         1     9     1615.27     0.0001
```

The estimates of the variance components (with $\sigma_{\alpha\beta} = 0$) are

$$\hat{\Psi} = \begin{pmatrix} 18.28130046 & 0.0 \\ 0.0 & 0.00229095 \end{pmatrix}$$

and $\hat{\sigma}_e^2 = 0.35425947$

The estimates of the fixed effects intercept and slope have changed slightly. In this case, there is little evidence from Output 7.1 that $\sigma_{\alpha\beta} \neq 0$, (see Z score corresponding to UN(2,1), $p=0.3776$). The -2 REML log likelihood for the model with $\sigma_{\alpha\beta} = 0$ is 187.1130. The -2 REML log likelihood for the unstructured covariance matrix is 186.1463, a difference of 0.9667, which corresponds (asymptotically) to a chi-square distribution with 1 degree of freedom. Thus, there is little evidence to believe that $\sigma_{\alpha\beta} \neq 0$.

7.2.2 Example: Random Student Effects

Kreft et al. (1994) analyze data from the Second International Mathematics Study (SIMS). Here 3,691 eighth-grade students are measured on mathematics achievement tests, and the hierarchical structure of the data is due to the fact that these students are grouped into 190 classes.

Model

A multilevel analysis of these data begins by constructing a model at the student level involving any explanatory variables measured on the students. For this example, Kreft et al. (1994) use the standard regression model

$$(\text{GAIN})_{ij} = \beta_{0j} + \beta_{1j}(\text{PRETOT})_{ij} + e_{ij}$$

where $(\text{GAIN})_{ij}$ is the gain on the score of a particular achievement test of the ith student in the jth class and $(\text{PRETOT})_{ij}$ is the sum of some pretest core items on the same students. The residual errors e_{ij} are assumed to be independent and identically distributed Gaussian random variables with mean zero and variance σ^2.

Next, the regression coefficients β_{0j} and β_{1j} are assumed to arise from a model at the class level. Assuming initially that there are no class-level variables, the basic model to consider here is

$$\beta_{0j} = \gamma_{00} + \delta_{0j}$$

$$\beta_{1j} = \gamma_{10} + \delta_{1j}$$

where the class-level disturbance terms (d_{0j}, d_{1j}) are assumed to be independent and identically distributed bivariate Gaussian random variables with zero mean and variance-covariance matrix

$$\Omega = \begin{bmatrix} \omega_{oo} & \omega_{10} \\ \omega_{10} & \omega_{11} \end{bmatrix}$$

Substituting the expressions for β_{0j} and β_{1j} into the student-level model produces the following single equation formulation:

$$(GAIN)_{ij} = \gamma_{00} + \gamma_{01}(PRETOT)_{ij} + \delta_{0j} + (PRETOT)_{ij}\delta_{1j} + e_{ij}$$

This equation reveals that the hierarchical linear model is actually the same as the random coefficient model considered in previous sections. The mean model consists of the two parameters u_{00} and u_{10}, and the variance model has a random intercept d_{0j}, a random slope d_{1j}, and a residual error e_{ij}.

Program

The single-equation formulation is probably easiest to translate into PROC MIXED code because all mean-model effects must be placed together in the MODEL statement and the random effects are specified in the RANDOM statement. For this example, an appropriate PROC MIXED program is as follows:

```
proc mixed data=sims;
   class class;
   model gain = pretot / solution;
   random intercept pretot / subject=class type=un;
run;
```

The DATA= option on the PROC MIXED statement specifies the SAS data set to use for the analysis. The raw data are available on the ftp server ftp.stat.ucla.edu in pub/data/various/SIMS, and are assumed to be input into a SAS data set named SIMS having variables CLASS, GAIN, and PRETOT.

The CLASS statement looks a bit unusual here because the variable CLASS shares its same name. The purpose of the CLASS statement is to treat all variables included on it as classification rather than continuous variables. This is done for the variable CLASS, which indicates the class of a particular student.

The MODEL statement specifies the mean model effects. An intercept is included by default, corresponding to u_{00} and the variable PRETOT models u_{10}. Because PRETOT is not on the CLASS statement, it is treated as one-degree-of-freedom regression effect. The SOLUTION option requests that the estimates of u_{00} and u_{10} be printed along with their estimated standard errors and corresponding t-statistics.

The RANDOM statement is the mechanism for specifying the terms involving d_{0j} and d_{1j}. The INTERCEPT effect corresponds to the former; INTERCEPT is a keyword automatically interpreted by PROC MIXED as an effect with all 1's. PRETOT corresponds to the $(PRETOT)_{ij}d_{1j}$ term in the model. The SUBJECT=CLASS option is important because it instructs PROC MIXED regarding the index j and when it changes. The TYPE=UN option sets up Ω with an unstructured 2×2 form with the three parameters ω_{00}, ω_{10} and ω_{11}.

PROC MIXED includes the homogeneous residual error e_{ij} in the model by default.

The results of this analysis are shown in Output 7.4.

Results

Output 7.4 *Results of Random Student Effects Model*

```
                         The MIXED Procedure

                      Class Level Information

        Class     Levels  Values

        CLASS       190   1  2  3  4  5  6  7  8  9  10  11  12  13
                          14 15 16 17 18 19 20 21 22 23
                          24 25 26 27 28 29 30 31 32 33
                          34 35 36 37 38 39 40 41 42 43
                          44 45 46 47 48 49 50 51 52 53
                          54 55 56 57 58 59 60 61 62 63
                          64 65 66 67 68 69 70 71 72 73
                          74 75 76 77 78 79 80 81 82 83
                          84 85 86 87 88 89 90 91 92 93
                          94 95 96 97 98 99 100 101 102
                          103 104 105 106 107 108 109
                          110 111 112 113 114 115 116
                          117 118 119 120 121 122 123
                          124 125 126 127 128 129 130
                          131 132 133 134 135 136 137
                          138 139 140 141 142 143 144
                          145 146 147 148 149 150 151
                          152 153 154 155 156 157 158
                          159 160 161 162 163 164 165
                          166 167 168 169 170 171 172
                          173 174 175 176 177 178 179
                          180 181 182 183 184 185 186
                          187 188 189 190


                  REML Estimation Iteration History

        Iteration  Evaluations    Objective     Criterion

             0           1     16281.743423
             1           2     15601.343074    0.00008015
             2           1     15600.658356    0.00000211
             3           1     15600.641613    0.00000000
                    Convergence criteria met.


                 Covariance Parameter Estimates (REML)

Cov Parm                   Ratio       Estimate     Std Error        Z

INTERCEPT UN(1,1)       0.65117743   14.47972111   2.69925395     5.36
          UN(2,1)      -0.01050806   -0.23365957   0.10158234    -2.30
          UN(2,2)       0.00041336    0.00919162   0.00493989     1.86
Residual                1.00000000   22.23621475   0.55186821    40.29
```

```
           Covariance Parameter Estimates (REML)

              Pr > |Z|

                 0.0001
                 0.0214
                 0.0628
                 0.0001



                Model Fitting Information for GAIN

          Description                        Value

          Observations                    3691.000
          Variance Estimate                 22.2362
          Standard Deviation Estimate        4.7155
          REML Log Likelihood            -11190.3
          Akaike's Information Criterion  -11194.3
          Schwarz's Bayesian Criterion    -11206.7
          -2 REML Log Likelihood          22380.57
          Null Model LRT Chi-Square         681.1018
          Null Model LRT DF                  3.0000
          Null Model LRT P-Value             0.0000



                Solution for Fixed Effects

Parameter        Estimate      Std Error    DDF       T   Pr > |T|

INTERCEPT       7.05947029    0.36582540    189    19.30    0.0001
PRETOT         -0.18603178    0.01609645    189   -11.56    0.0001



                Tests of Fixed Effects

       Source        NDF    DDF   Type III F  Pr > F

       PRETOT          1    189     133.57    0.0001
```

Interpretation

The Class Level Information table prints results from the CLASS statement. The lone variable CLASS is shown to have 190 levels.

The "REML Iteration History" table shows the stages of the numerical optimization of the restricted likelihood function constructed under the Gaussian assumption on d_{0j}, d_{1j}, and e_{ij}. The Evaluations column indicates the number of likelihood evaluations and the Objective column the value of the objective function being minimized (this is -2 times the restricted log likelihood plus a constant). The Criterion column displays the value of the orthogonality criterion used to assess convergence of the algorithm. By default PROC MIXED declares convergence when this criterion drops below $1e-8$, and this is achieved in three iterations.

The "Covariance Parameter Estimates" table displays the estimates of $\omega_{00}, \omega_{10}, \omega_{11}$, and σ^2 in the Estimate column. The Ratio column are the ratios of these estimates to that of σ^2. The Std Error column displays approximate standard errors of the estimates based upon the fact that they are asymptotically normal. A corresponding Z-score and p-value are also printed, testing whether the parameter is different from zero. These tests can, however, be unreliable in small samples.

The "Model Fitting Information" table displays some basic information from the fitted model, including several statistics based upon the restricted likelihood evaluated at the parameter estimates.

The "Solution for Fixed Effects" table prints estimates of the mean model parameters u_{00} and u_{10}. These estimates are computed using the familiar estimated generalized least squares formula $(\mathbf{X}'\hat{\mathbf{V}}^{-1}\mathbf{X})^{-}\mathbf{X}'\hat{\mathbf{V}}\mathbf{y}$ and their approximate standard errors are the square roots of the diagonal elements of $(\mathbf{X}'\hat{\mathbf{V}}^{-1}\mathbf{X})^{-}$. The DDF column is the degrees of freedom to be used to assess the t-statistic, and it is computed as the number of classes minus one (for the intercept). Finally, the "Tests of Fixed Effects" table prints an F-test for $u_{10} = 0$, and this hypothesis is strongly rejected. Because this F-statistic has only 1 numerator degree of freedom, it is equal to the square of the t-statistic for PRETOT in the "Solution for Fixed Effects" table and the p-values are the same.

For comparison, Table 7.1 reproduces a portion of Table 1 from Kreft et al. (1994) as well as the results from PROC MIXED. It displays REML results for the preceding model from three other software packages. They are seen to agree closely with the PROC MIXED results.

Table 7.1 *Comparison of REML Results for SIMS Data from Other Software Packages and PROC MIXED*

Parameter	GENMOD	HLM	ML3	MIXED
u_{00}	7.060	7.060	7.060	7.060
u_{10}	−0.186	−0.186	−0.186	−0.186
ω_{00}	14.52	14.53	14.49	14.48
ω_{10}	−0.234	−0.247	−0.234	−0.234
ω_{11}	0.009	0.009	0.009	0.009
σ^2	22.23	22.23	22.24	22.24
Iterations	189	76	10	3
Sec/Iter	480	16	180	5[*]

[*] from an HP 9000/720 workstation, others from a 286 PC

The timing comparison is unfair because PROC MIXED was run on an HP 9000/720 workstation whereas the others were on a 286 PC. In spite of this, the Newton-Raphson algorithm does appear to have a performance advantage over the EM and IGLS algorithms used by the other packages. In any case, quick analyses of moderately sized data sets such as this one are certainly possible in todays computing environments.

The execution time for PROC MIXED can be decreased even further with the following program:

```
proc mixed data=sims;
   model gain = pretot / solution ddfm=bw;
   random intercept pretot / subject=class type=un;
run;
```

Two primary changes are evident. First, the CLASS statement has been removed. When a SUBJECT= effect is not on the CLASS statement, PROC MIXED assumes there is a new value for the index j whenever this variable changes. Therefore, the data set must be sorted by CLASS in order for this analysis to be valid. Second, the DDFM=BW option on the MODEL statement instructs PROC MIXED to use the Between-Within method to compute the denominator degrees of freedom as opposed to its default containment method. (See Chapter 18, "*The* MIXED Procedure," in *SAS/STAT Software: Changes and Enhancements through Release 6.11.*)

Kreft et al. (1994) also consider the inclusion of a class-level variable OTL (Opportunity to Learn). A reasonable class-level model then becomes

$$\beta_{0j} = \gamma_{00} + \gamma_{01}(OTL)_j + \delta_{0j}$$

$$\beta_{1j} = \gamma_{10} + \gamma_{11}(OTL)_j + \delta_{1j}$$

Substituting these expressions for β_{0j} and β_{10j} into the student-level model produces the following single equation formulation:

$$(GAIN)_{ij} = \gamma_{00} + \gamma_{01}(OTL)_j + \gamma_{10}(PRETOT)_{ij} + \gamma_{11}((OTL)_j(PRETOT)_{ij}) + \delta_{0j} + (PRETOT)_{ij}\delta_{1j} + e_{ij}$$

The corresponding PROC MIXED program is as follows:

```
proc mixed data=sims;
   class class;
   model gain = otl pretot otl*pretot / solution;
   random intercept pretot / subject=class type=un;
run;
```

This program is the same as in the previous analysis, except that OTL and OTL*PRETOT have been added to the MODEL statement. In general, all mean-model effects, both student-level and class-level, are included in the MODEL statement.

7.3 Summary

The data structure appropriate for this chapter consists of repeated measurements on independent subjects. The random coefficients model for such data is effectively an analysis of covariance for each subject; however, the coefficients from these regression models are assumed to have arisen from a normal probability distribution. Two examples, one where the subjects are treatments and another where the subjects are students, are used to illustrate the important features of the model.

7.4 References

Bryk, A.S. and Raudenbush, S.W. (1992), *Hierarchical Linear Models,* Newbury Park, CA: Sage Publications, Inc.

Goldstein, H. (1987), *Multilevel Models in Educational and Social Research,* New York: Oxford University Press.

Kreft, I.G.G., De Leeuw, J., and Van Der Leeden, R. (1994), Review of five multilevel analysis programs: BMDP-5V, GENMOD, HLM, ML3, VARCL, *American Statistician* **48**, 324–335.

Laird, N.M. and Ware, J.H (1982), Random-effects models for longitudinal data, *Biometrics* **38**, 963–974.

Rutter, C.M. and Elashoff, R.M. (1994), Analysis of longitudinal data: random coefficient regression modelling, *Statistics in Medicine*, **13**, 1211–1231.

Strenio, J.F., Weisberg, H.I., and Bryk, A.S. (1983), Empirical Bayes estimation of individual growth-curve parameters and their relationship to covariates, *Biometrics*, **39**, 71–86.

Wolfinger, R.D. (1996), Heterogeneous variance covariance structures for repeated measures, *Journal of Agricultural, Biological, and Environmental Statistics* (to appear).

Chapter 8 Heterogeneous Variance Models

8.1 Introduction

One of the great advantages of the likelihood-based estimation approach to mixed models is the ability to fit a variety of covariance structures. This chapter considers structures modeling variability that changes across the data, that is, variability which is **heterogeneous**.

Heterogeneous variances occur in all types of data, yet many analysts do not consider them or fail to adequately account for them in their statistical inferences. A primary motivation for modeling heterogeneous variances is the ability to appropriately downweight portions of your data that are highly variable and extract more information from portions of your data that are more precise. Failure to account for heterogeneity when it is present can lead to inefficient and possibly misleading inferences about fixed effects in your model.

Heterogeneous variance models can be placed into two categories: **within-subject** and **between-subject**. Within-subject heterogeneity occurs across data from the same subject, a typical example being variances that increase with time in a longitudinal data setting. Between-subject heterogeneity occurs when different groups of subjects display different variance patterns but are homogeneous within groups.

This chapter discusses both types of heterogeneity in the context of three examples. Refer to Wolfinger (1996) for additional examples and discussion.

8.2 Example: Within-Subject Heterogeneity

This example focuses on within-subject heterogeneity. Vonesh and Carter (1992) describe and analyze data on high flux hemodialyzers measured to assess their *in vivo* ultrafiltration characteristics. The response is the ultrafiltration rate (UFR in ml/hr) of 20 high flux membrane dialyzers measured at 7 different transmembrane pressures (TMP in dmHg). The dialyzers are evaluated *in vitro* using bovine blood and blood flow rates (QB) of either 200 dl/min or 300 dl/min.

The program to place these data into a SAS data set and plot them as in Figure 8.1 follows. Note that the data are divided by 100 here to add stability to the estimation algorithm in PROC MIXED. See Data Set 8.2, "DIAL," in Appendix 4, "SAS Data Sets," for the complete data set.

```
data dial;
    input sub qb tmp ufr index;
    tmp = tmp/100;
    ufr = ufr/100;
    datalines;
... more datalines...
symbol1 i=join r=10 l=1 c=black;
symbol2 i=join r=10 l=3 c=black;
footnote "Solid lines are QB=200 and dashed lines are QB=300";
proc gplot data=dial;
    plot ufr*tmp=sub;
run;
```

Figure 8.1 *High Flux Hemodialyzer Data*

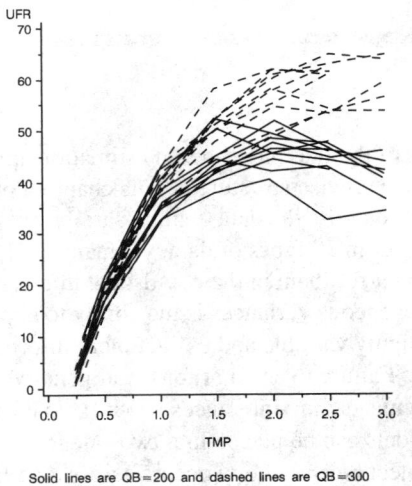

Solid lines are QB=200 and dashed lines are QB=300

The two SYMBOL statements specify the features of Figure 8.1. The I=JOIN option requests that data from the same subject be connected with straight lines. The R=10 option requests that the symbol be repeated 10 times. Thus, the SYMBOL1 statement applies to the first 10 subjects. The L= option specifies the line type, and the C= option specifies the color of the lines. Refer to *SAS/GRAPH Software: Reference, Version 6, First Edition* for further details about these options and for descriptions of the TITLE and FOOTNOTE statements.

The PROC GPLOT code generates a high resolution graph of the data. The PLOT statement is of the form Y*X=SUBJECT, and when combined with the aforementioned SYMBOL statements, produces the growth curves shown in Figure 8.1.

The curves in Figure 8.1 exhibit a definite increase in variability of UFR as TMP increases. It is this heterogeneity that we want to capture with covariance structures.

8.2.1 Basic Unstructured Covariance Model

Following the recommendations of Diggle (1988) and Wolfinger (1993), a reasonable initial model for these data should involve fairly general specifications for both the mean and the variance-covariance structure. This generality helps avoid misspecification biases that can occur with models which are too simple. Specifically what makes up a general model can be quite problem specific, especially with regard to the mean model. Preliminary plots such as Figure 8.1 are valuable in deciding upon a starting model.

Model

For the fixed-effects model in this analysis, simple linear or quadratic curves do not appear to be reasonable. Therefore, the mean model is assumed to contain additional cubic and quartic terms, and the parameters for these curves are assumed to be different for each of the two blood flow rates. This is in contrast to the nonlinear mean model of Vonesh and Carter (1992), although the quartic curves track these data fairly well. The fixed-effects component of the model is thus

$$y = \beta_0 + \tau_i + (\beta_1 + \delta_{1i})X + (\beta_2 + \delta_{2i}) X^2 + (\beta_3 + \delta_{3i})X^3 + (\beta_4 + \delta_{4i})X^4$$

where

β_0 is the intercept over both QB levels

τ_i is the ith QB level on the intercept

$\beta_1, \beta_2, \beta_3$, and β_4 are the linear, quadratic, cubic, and quartic regression coefficients averaged over QB levels

$\delta_{1i}, \delta_{2i}, \delta_{3i}$, and δ_{4i} are the effects of the ith QB level on the linear, quadratic, cubic, and quartic regression coefficients

X is the value of TMP for a given observation.

For the variance-covariance model, the basic repeated measures model from Chapter 3 is used here. In particular, it is assumed that the data from different dialyzers are independent, and that the data within a dialyzer are correlated in some fashion. More importantly, it appears sensible to allow the variances of the data to increase with higher transmembrane pressures.

The most general covariance structure possible is a 7×7 unstructured matrix, and because this is reasonable to compute, it is taken as the initial model. An advantage of considering this most general model is that its estimate can be inspected for heterogeneous patterns in both the variances and correlations.

Program

The appropriate PROC MIXED program is as follows:

```
proc mixed data=dial;
   class qb sub;
   model ufr = tmp|tmp|tmp|tmp qb|tmp|tmp|tmp|tmp;
   repeated / type=un subject=sub r rcorr;
run;
```

The MODEL statement sets up a common quartic curve using the bar (|) operator, and then different curves for the two levels of QB. Although the second set of effects contains the first set, the first set is included in order to carry out tests for whether the different curves are necessary.

The REPEATED statement requests a block-diagonal **R** matrix with blocks defined by the SUBJECT= option and the structure of each block defined by the TYPE= option. For these data, **R** is 140×140 with twenty 7×7 blocks, each one corresponding to a dialyzer. Each block has the same unstructured form with twenty-eight unknown parameters (seven variances and twenty-one covariances). The R and RCORR options print the estimate of the first block and its corresponding correlation matrix.

Results

Output 8.1 *Basic Unstructured Covariance Model*

```
                        The MIXED Procedure

                     Class Level Information

        Class     Levels  Values

        QB           2    200 300
        SUB         22    1  2  3  4  5  6  7  8  9  10 11 12 13
                          14 15 16 17 18 19 20 21 22


                 REML Estimation Iteration History

     Iteration  Evaluations      Objective       Criterion

          0            1     500.24667670
          1            2     347.17363704     0.00001437
          2            1     347.17110355     0.00000001

                 Convergence criteria met.


                      R Matrix for Subject 1

    Row          COL1            COL2            COL3            COL4

     1       2.75617181      2.90420043      3.57309738      3.04051895
     2       2.90420043      5.10239145      6.39869662      6.37525697
     3       3.57309738      6.39869662     11.15290604     12.45634204
     4       3.04051895      6.37525697     12.45634204     18.54293942
     5       0.35937423      4.13375521      8.32563064     13.37599357
     6       0.45510860      3.31876216      5.44249162     10.89993969
     7       0.64139844      1.16410956      4.01804791      7.67818314


                      R Matrix for Subject 1

                   COL5            COL6            COL7

               0.35937423      0.45510860      0.64139844
               4.13375521      3.31876216      1.16410956
               8.32563064      5.44249162      4.01804791
              13.37599357     10.89993969      7.67818314
```

```
          17.71279669    13.83472536    12.04498507
          13.83472536    20.30688607    11.32834444
          12.04498507    11.32834444    19.67404661
```

R Correlation Matrix for Subject 1

Row	COL1	COL2	COL3	COL4
1	1.00000000	0.77443782	0.64446255	0.42530969
2	0.77443782	1.00000000	0.84822411	0.65542276
3	0.64446255	0.84822411	1.00000000	0.86617813
4	0.42530969	0.65542276	0.86617813	1.00000000
5	0.05143399	0.43482479	0.59235158	0.73806259
6	0.06083314	0.32603752	0.36164468	0.56171127
7	0.08710196	0.11618769	0.27125281	0.40199655

R Correlation Matrix for Subject 1

COL5	COL6	COL7
0.05143399	0.06083314	0.08710196
0.43482479	0.32603752	0.11618769
0.59235158	0.36164468	0.27125281
0.73806259	0.56171127	0.40199655
1.00000000	0.72946642	0.64523193
0.72946642	1.00000000	0.56675836
0.64523193	0.56675836	1.00000000

Covariance Parameter Estimates (REML)

Cov Parm		Estimate	Std Error	Z	Pr > |Z|
DIAG	UN(1,1)	2.75617181	0.92208691	2.99	0.0028
	UN(2,1)	2.90420043	1.11189886	2.61	0.0090
	UN(2,2)	5.10239145	1.69425596	3.01	0.0026
	UN(3,1)	3.57309738	1.54530371	2.31	0.0208
	UN(3,2)	6.39869662	2.31837190	2.76	0.0058
	UN(3,3)	11.15290604	3.69456344	3.02	0.0025
	UN(4,1)	3.04051895	1.80897858	1.68	0.0928
	UN(4,2)	6.37525697	2.70503477	2.36	0.0184
	UN(4,3)	12.45634204	4.43179486	2.81	0.0049
	UN(4,4)	18.54293942	6.05617246	3.06	0.0022
	UN(5,1)	0.35937423	1.66520171	0.22	0.8291
	UN(5,2)	4.13375521	2.46894529	1.67	0.0941
	UN(5,3)	8.32563064	3.88079307	2.15	0.0319
	UN(5,4)	13.37599357	5.30279774	2.52	0.0117
	UN(5,5)	17.71279669	6.00231762	2.95	0.0032
	UN(6,1)	0.45510860	1.76335766	0.26	0.7963
	UN(6,2)	3.31876216	2.49928701	1.33	0.1842
	UN(6,3)	5.44249162	3.73117704	1.46	0.1447
	UN(6,4)	10.89993969	5.14730115	2.12	0.0342

```
            UN(6,5)   13.83472536    5.55586728   2.49   0.0128
            UN(6,6)   20.30688607    6.68189622   3.04   0.0024
            UN(7,1)    0.64139844    1.74216495   0.37   0.7128
            UN(7,2)    1.16410956    2.37947482   0.49   0.6247
            UN(7,3)    4.01804791    3.61587217   1.11   0.2665
            UN(7,4)    7.67818314    4.82114693   1.59   0.1112
            UN(7,5)   12.04498507    5.29877666   2.27   0.0230
            UN(7,6)   11.32834444    5.40579922   2.10   0.0361
            UN(7,7)   19.67404661    6.56607846   3.00   0.0027
  Residual             1.00007565        .          .      .
```

```
            Model Fitting Information for UFR

       Description                             Value

       Observations                         140.0000
       Variance Estimate                      1.0001
       Standard Deviation Estimate            1.0000
       REML Log Likelihood                 -293.048
       Akaike's Information Criterion      -321.048
       Schwarz's Bayesian Criterion        -361.193
       -2 REML Log Likelihood               586.0951
       Null Model LRT Chi-Square            153.0756
       Null Model LRT DF                     27.0000
       Null Model LRT P-Value                 0.0000
```

```
                 Tests of Fixed Effects

      Source              NDF   DDF   Type III F   Pr > F

      TMP                  1    110     577.35     0.0001
      TMP*TMP              1    110      72.60     0.0001
      TMP*TMP*TMP          1    110      13.94     0.0003
      TMP*TMP*TMP*TMP      1    110       4.09     0.0455
      QB                   1     20       1.19     0.2888
      TMP*QB               1    110       0.04     0.8358
      TMP*TMP*QB           1    110       0.04     0.8335
      TMP*TMP*TMP*QB       1    110       0.01     0.9355
      TMP*TMP*TMP*TMP*QB   1    110       0.05     0.8172
```

Interpretation

The REML algorithm converges in two iterations. Even those these data are perfectly balanced, these iterations are necessary because of the time-varying covariate TMP.

The "R Matrix for Subject 1" table prints the first block of **R**. Its principal diagonal with elements (2.8, 5.1, 11.2, 18.5, 17.7, 20.3, 19.7) reveals that the variances increase steadily with TMP and then level off for the last four measurements.

Even more interesting is the correlation pattern, which appears to decrease with increasing distance between TMP values. For example, the correlations with the first measurement are estimated to be (0.77, 0.64, 0.43, 0.05, 0.06, 0.09). Thus, even though TMP does not measure time, the data appear to have an autoregressive correlation structure as if it did. Some more parsimonious covariance structures exhibiting this kind of pattern may therefore fit these data well.

Note that the REML analysis has already numerically confirmed and quantified the heterogeneity of variance evident in Figure 8.1. It has also revealed a definite correlation pattern that is not so obvious in a plot of the dialyzer profiles.

The results in the "Covariance Parameter Estimates" table repeat the values from the "R Matrix for Subject 1" along with their asymptotic standard errors obtained from the inverse of the second derivative matrix from the REML algorithm. The "Residual" row in this table can be ignored because there is no separate residual variance in this model.

The "Model Fitting Information" table presents some basic likelihood-based statistics. Its final three rows indicate that this basic unstructured model fits exceedingly better than the null model with independent homogeneous errors, according to a likelihood-ratio test. Note that the degrees of freedom for this test are equal to the difference in the number of parameters between the two models, which in this case is 28−1 = 27.

The "Tests of Fixed Effects" table provides good evidence for dropping some of the higher order model terms involving QB. Type I (sequential) tests may also be useful in this regard, and they are printed using the HTYPE=1 option in the MODEL statement. However, following Diggle (1988) and Wolfinger (1993), you should not do this until you have selected a covariance structure.

8.2.2 Other Covariance Structures

The strategy here for selecting a covariance structure is to fit several structures and then compare them using various likelihood-based criteria. In addition to the previously-fitted unstructured (UN) model, the structures investigated in this fashion are denoted AR(1), ARH(1), CS, CSH, HF, FA(1), FA1(1), RC, RCQ, and I-I. Brief descriptions of each of these now follow, and further details can be found in the PROC MIXED documentation and in Wolfinger (1996).

- The AR(1) structure is the first order autoregressive structure. It has homogeneous variances and correlations that decline exponentially with distance. Although this structure is used almost exclusively with equally-spaced time series data, it still can be used for these data by making TMP a proxy for time and exploiting the fact that the data are approximately equally spaced in TMP. AR(1) has two unknown parameters: the variance and the lag-one correlation.

- The ARH(1) is a direct generalization of AR(1). It has the same correlation structure, but it has heterogeneous variances instead of homogeneous ones. For these data with seven repeated measurements, it has eight unknown parameters (seven variances and one correlation parameter).

- CS is the well-known compound symmetry structure. Like AR(1), it has two unknown parameters, one modeling a homogeneous variance and the other a correlation. But unlike AR(1), the correlation is assumed to remain constant.

- CSH is to CS what ARH(1) is to AR(1). That is, CSH has constant correlations but heterogeneous variances. Like ARH(1), it has eight unknown parameters for these data.

- HF is the "spherical contrast" structure discussed by Huynh and Feldt (1970). It is similar to CSH in that it has a different variance parameter at each repeated measurement, but the covariances are constructed by taking arithmetic rather than geometric means. Therefore, the correlations are not constant although there is still only one parameter modeling them. HF thus has eight unknown parameters in all.

FA(1) and FA1(1) are first-order factor analysis structures. They are constructed by taking the outer product of a vector of unknown factor loadings and adding a diagonal matrix of specific variances to it. The specific variances are all different in the standard FA(1) structure, producing a total of fourteen parameters. In the FA1(1) structure, they are the same, producing eight parameters.

The preceding seven structures are fit with PROC MIXED by making a simple change to the program used for the the basic UN model in the previous subsection. The MODEL statement is the same, and the TYPE= option of the REPEATED statement is changed to indicate the different covariance structure. For example, the ARH(1) model is fit with the following program:

```
proc mixed data=dial;
   class qb sub;
   model ufr = tmp|tmp|tmp|tmp qb|tmp|tmp|tmp|tmp;
   repeated / type=arh(1) subject=sub;
run;
```

The RC and RCQ models are random coefficient models as discussed in Chapter 7. They are fit with the following programs:

```
proc mixed data=dial ic;
   class qb sub;
   model ufr = tmp|tmp|tmp|tmp qb|tmp|tmp|tmp|tmp;
   random int tmp / subject=sub type=un;
run;

proc mixed data=dial ic;
   class qb sub;
   model ufr = tmp|tmp|tmp|tmp qb|tmp|tmp|tmp|tmp;
   random int tmp tmp*tmp / subject=sub type=un;
run;
```

In the first model (RC), the INT and TMP terms in the RANDOM statement model a random intercept and slope, respectively. The SUBJECT=SUB option is required to inform PROC MIXED of when new realizations of the random intercept and slopes are assumed to occur. The TYPE=UN option models an unstructured 2×2 covariance matrix for the random intercept and slope. This results in a **G** matrix which is 44×44 and block diagonal with twenty-two 2×2 blocks. **R** is assumed to equal a constant variance times the identity matrix; thus, this structure has four parameters in all.

The second model (RCQ) adds a third random coefficient, which is a quadratic term in TMP. The resulting **G** matrix from this model is 66×66 and block diagonal with twenty-two 3×3 blocks. **R** is again assumed to equal a constant variance times the identity matrix; thus, this structure has seven parameters in all. Among all of the linear and nonlinear covariance structures considered by Vonesh and Carter (1992), RCQ is the best fitting for a set of nonlinear least squares residuals, according to an adjusted R^2 criterion.

The final model is the independent increments (I-I) model (Louis, 1988), which assumes the observations form a random walk in time. Again, TMP is not a time variable, but the structure is included to see how well it fits. There is no I-I structure directly available in

PROC MIXED, but because all of its parameters enter the structure linearly, you can use the TYPE=LIN and LDATA= options as follows:

```
data ii;
   input parm row col1-col7;
   datalines;
1 1 1 1 1 1 1 1 1
1 2 1 1 1 1 1 1 1
1 3 1 1 1 1 1 1 1
1 4 1 1 1 1 1 1 1
1 5 1 1 1 1 1 1 1
1 6 1 1 1 1 1 1 1
1 7 1 1 1 1 1 1 1
2 2 0 1 1 1 1 1 1
2 3 0 1 1 1 1 1 1
2 4 0 1 1 1 1 1 1
2 5 0 1 1 1 1 1 1
2 6 0 1 1 1 1 1 1
2 7 0 1 1 1 1 1 1
3 3 0 0 1 1 1 1 1
3 4 0 0 1 1 1 1 1
3 5 0 0 1 1 1 1 1
3 6 0 0 1 1 1 1 1
3 7 0 0 1 1 1 1 1
4 4 0 0 0 1 1 1 1
4 5 0 0 0 1 1 1 1
4 6 0 0 0 1 1 1 1
4 7 0 0 0 1 1 1 1
5 5 0 0 0 0 1 1 1
5 6 0 0 0 0 1 1 1
5 7 0 0 0 0 1 1 1
6 6 0 0 0 0 0 1 1
6 7 0 0 0 0 0 1 1
7 7 0 0 0 0 0 0 1
run;

proc mixed data=dial ic;
   class qb sub;
   model ufr = tmp|tmp|tmp|tmp qb|tmp|tmp|tmp|tmp;
   repeated / type=lin(7) ldata=ii sub=sub r rcorr;
run;
```

The TYPE=LIN(7) option specifies a general linear structure that is of the form

$$\sum_{i=1}^{7} \theta_i \mathbf{A}_i$$

where the $\mathbf{A}_i$ are known matrices and the θ_i are unknown parameters. The LDATA= option specifies an auxiliary SAS data set containing the $\mathbf{A}_i$ matrices. This data set contains the PARM, ROW, and COL1-COL7 variables, which contain the indices, rows, and columns of all of the $\mathbf{A}_i$.

The I-I structure is of the general linear form, and is constructed by adding together $\mathbf{A}_i$, which have their lower $(8-i) \times (8-i)$ elements equal to 1 and the remaining elements equal to zero, with $i = 1, \ldots, 7$. These $\mathbf{A}_i$ are specified in the preceding data set.

8.2.3 Selecting a Covariance Structure

All of the preceding models are fit with separate runs of PROC MIXED. After each run, values for AIC_R, BIC_R −2 REML log likelihood values, and the number of parameters are cut and pasted from the "Model Fitting Information" table into a separate file. This process can be automated with the MAKE statement in PROC MIXED and the SAS macro facility, but this is not shown here.

This file is then used to create the following MODELS data set:

```
data models;
   length type$ 6;
   input type$ aic_r bic_r m2rll parms;
   model = _n_;
   datalines;
UN        -321.0  -361.2  586.1   28
AR(1)     -330.7  -333.6  657.5    2
ARH(1)    -314.9  -326.4  613.8    8
CS        -349.2  -352.0  694.3    2
CSH       -339.1  -350.6  662.2    8
HF        -341.7  -353.2  667.5    8
FA(1)     -333.8  -353.9  639.6   14
FA1(1)    -343.8  -355.3  671.6    8
RC        -339.1  -344.8  670.1    4
RCQ       -329.9  -340.0  645.8    7
I-I       -317.2  -327.3  620.4    7
run;
```

Not included in this comparison is the simple null model with homogeneous variances and zero covariances, which has $AIC_R = -370.6$, $BIC_R = -372.0$, and $-2l_R = 739.2$. All of the structures considered here fit dramatically better than this one, illustrating the strong need to account for some kind of heterogeneity and/or correlation in these data.

Program

A convenient way of investigating AIC_R and BIC_R for the models under consideration is to construct plots versus the number of parameters or versus each other. The following program does this and produces Figures 8.2, 8.3, and 8.4:

```
symbol1   color=black font=swiss value='UN     ' repeat=1;
symbol2   color=black font=swiss value='AR(1)  ' repeat=1;
symbol3   color=black font=swiss value='ARH(1)' repeat=1;
symbol4   color=black font=swiss value='CS     ' repeat=1;
symbol5   color=black font=swiss value='CSH    ' repeat=1;
symbol6   color=black font=swiss value='HF     ' repeat=1;
symbol7   color=black font=swiss value='FA(1)  ' repeat=1;
symbol8   color=black font=swiss value='FA1(1)' repeat=1;
symbol9   color=black font=swiss value='RC     ' repeat=1;
symbol10  color=black font=swiss value='RCQ    ' repeat=1;
symbol11  color=black font=swiss value='I-I    ' repeat=1;

proc gplot data=models;
   plot aic_r*parms=model / nolegend;
   plot bic_r*parms=model / nolegend;
   plot aic_r*bic_r=model / nolegend;
run;
```

The SYMBOL statements define features of the plots, and there is one for each model. The key specification is for VALUE=, which defines the plotting symbol to be the same as the model type. These symbol definitions are automatically incoporated into the PLOT statements from PROC GPLOT. Refer to *SAS/GRAPH Software: Reference* for further details about SYMBOL and PROC GPLOT.

Results

Figure 8.2 *AIC_R for High Flux Hemodialyzer Models*

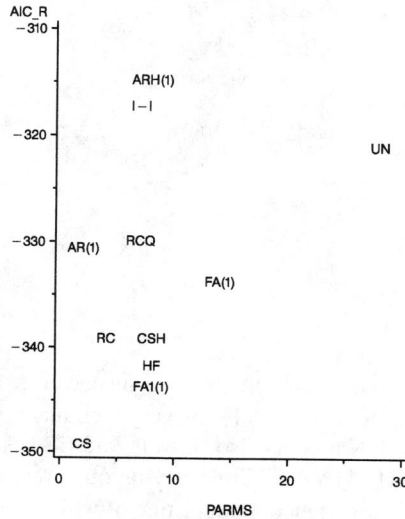

Figure 8.3 *BIC_R for High Flux Hemodialyzer Models*

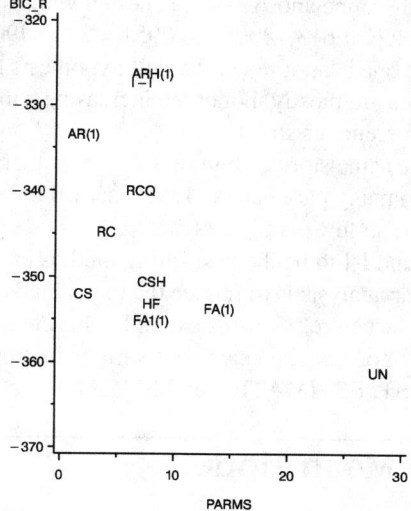

Figure 8.4 *AIC_R vs. BIC_R for High Flux Hemodialyzer Models*

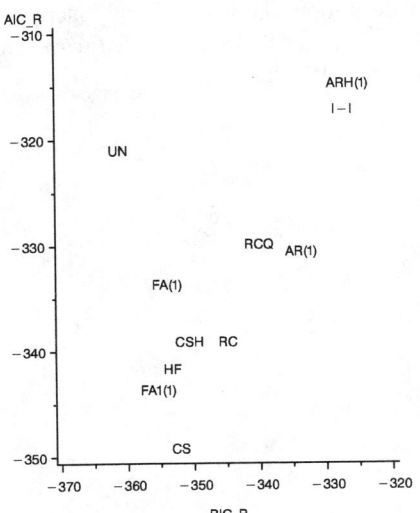

Interpretation

Figure 8.2 plots AIC_R versus model complexity. As suspected from inspection of the unstructured estimate, the heterogeneous AR(1) fits very well and is the best fitting according to AIC_R. The I-I and UN models also fit well, and CS fits the worst.

You can further compare ARH(1) and UN by carrying out a restricted likelihood ratio test. This test can compare two covariance models, one of which is nested within the other. It is constructed by subtracting values of −2 times the maximized restricted likelihoods and comparing this statistic with a χ^2-distribution with degrees of freedom equal to the difference in the number of covariance parameters in the two models. The restricted likelihood version of the test is valid provided the fixed effects component of the model remains constant. If nested mean models are also considered, you should switch to a regular likelihood ratio test by using the METHOD=ML option on the PROC MIXED statement to fit both models.

Here the mean models are the same and ARH(1) is nested within UN. The restricted likelihood ratio test has a χ^2 value of $613.7800 - 586.0951 = 27.6849$ with $28-8 = 20$ degrees of freedom and $p > 0.1$. Thus, one cannot reject the null hypothesis that the structure is ARH(1). Because the variances are mostly monotone increasing, similar results can be obtained for the independent increments structure.

Figure 8.3 tells basically the same story as Figure 8.2, except that UN is penalized much more under BIC_R for having so many parameters. Likewise, CS does comparatively better than under AIC_R because it has so few parameters.

Figure 8.4 shows ARH(1) and I-I to be the best fitting models under both AIC_R and BIC_R.

A final step in this particular analysis is to reduce the mean model under an ARH(1) assumption for the covariance structure. For this example, this entails dropping higher order terms from the quartic model. You can then carry out various inferences with the final model by using the CONTRAST, ESTIMATE, and LSMEANS statements.

8.2.4 Power-of-the-Mean Model

Another technique for handling within-subject heterogeneity like that present in the hemodialyzer data is to model it as a power of the mean.

Model

For this model the variance matrix $\mathbf{R}$ is assumed to be of the form

$$\mathbf{R} = \mathrm{diag}(\sigma^2 |x_i' \beta^*|^\theta)$$

where

x_i' is the ith row of the fixed-effects design matrix $\mathbf{X}$
β^* is a specified vector of fixed-effects parameters
θ is the power to be estimated.

Note that by itself this structure sets all covariances equal to zero. For the hemodialyzer data, there is strong evidence of within-subject correlation, and so something should be added to the model to account for it. Although it is possible to add a power-of-the-mean model to one of the REPEATED structures considered in the previous section, the approach for this section is to incorporate it into a random coefficients model.

Because the quadratic random coefficients model (RCQ) fits better than the linear one (RC) in Figure 8.4, it is taken as the base model. Recall that this model has a $\mathbf{G}$ matrix, which is 66×66 and a block diagonal with twenty-two 3×3 blocks. But instead of assuming $\mathbf{R}$ is equal to a constant variance times the identity matrix, $\mathbf{R}$ is here assumed to have the power-of-the-mean structure.

Program

In order to fit this combination of correlated random coefficients and power-of-the-mean models with PROC MIXED, you must first create a data set that contains estimates of the fixed-effects parameters. This is most easily accomplished by outputting them from an initial fit to the data as follows:

```
proc mixed data=dial;
   class qb sub;
   model ufr = tmp|tmp|tmp|tmp qb|tmp|tmp|tmp|tmp / s;
   random int tmp tmp*tmp / type=un sub=sub;
   make 'solutionf' out=sf;
run;

data cp;
   input est;
   datalines;
 2.24606822
-3.73117853
24.08025511
 0.68705846
-6.82952740
 2.17225966
 1
 0.0663507
run;
```

This program also creates a SAS data set WORK.CP that is used to provide a starting covariance parameter values for the full model. Its values are the covariance parameter estimates from the initial model along with a guess of 1 for θ. The estimated residual variance from the initial model fit is divided by 50 to provide an approximation to the new σ^2. You can now fit the combined model as follows:

```
proc mixed data=dial;
   class qb sub;
   model ufr = tmp|tmp|tmp|tmp qb|tmp|tmp|tmp|tmp / s;
   random int tmp tmp*tmp / type=un sub=sub;
   repeated / local=pom(sf);
   parms / pdata=cp;
   make 'solutionf' out=sf1;
   make 'covparms' out=cp1;
run;

proc compare brief data=sf compare=sf1;
   var est;
run;

data sf;
   set sf1;
run;

data cp;
   set cp1;
run;
```

The quadratic random coefficients are specified on the RANDOM statement and the power-of-the-mean model is specified using the SF data set on the REPEATED statement. The PARMS statement loads in the initial values for all of the covariance parameters as specified in the CP data set created earlier. The two MAKE statements convert tables printed by PROC MIXED into SAS data sets that are used in subsequent processing.

This program is designed to be submitted again and again until β^* in the SF data set equals $\hat{\beta}$ in the SF1 data set. The differences between the two data sets are printed by the call to PROC COMPARE. This iteration algorithm is not guaranteed to converge in general, but when it does, the resulting estimates maximize a restricted version of the pseudo-likelihood described in Chapter 3 of Carroll and Ruppert (1988). The PROC COMPARE call allows you to monitor differences, and the subsequent DATA steps update both the fixed-effects and covariance parameter estimates. The latter are saved to improve the stability of the algorithm and to speed convergence of PROC MIXED at each call through the PARMS statement.

Results

The fifth run of the preceding program produces Output 8.2.

Output 8.2 *Power of the Mean Results*

```
                        The MIXED Procedure

                    Class Level Information

        Class      Levels  Values

        QB             2  200 300
        SUB           22  1 2 3 4 5 6 7 8 9 10 11 12 13
                          14 15 16 17 18 19 20 21 22


                        Parameter Search

     COL1      COL2      COL3      COL4      COL5      COL6      COL7

   3.8360   -5.8353   28.2501    1.3778   -8.3312    2.6970    1.9785


                        Parameter Search

        COL8   Variance   REML_LL   -2REML_LL  Objective

      0.0020    0.0020   -307.322   614.6438   375.7198


                REML Estimation Iteration History

     Iteration  Evaluations     Objective     Criterion

             1            1   375.71981486   0.00000000

                Convergence criteria met.


           Covariance Parameter Estimates (REML)
```

Cov Parm		Ratio	Estimate	Std Error	Z	Pr > |Z|
INTERCEPT	UN(1,1)	1943.1053089	3.83604473	1.38820814	2.76	0.0057
	UN(2,1)	-2955.792315	-5.83527382	3.20270300	-1.82	**0.0685**
	UN(2,2)	14309.793129	28.25014490	10.96808693	2.58	0.0100
	UN(3,1)	697.89442480	1.37777104	0.95900894	1.44	0.1508
	UN(3,2)	-4220.075676	-8.33120006	3.38702078	-2.46	0.0139
	UN(3,3)	1366.1373415	2.69700460	1.09246313	2.47	0.0136
DIAG POM		1002.1987668	1.97852339	0.38351981	5.16	0.0001
Residual		1.00000000	0.00197418	0.00278965	0.71	0.4791

```
                    Model Fitting Information for UFR

          Description                      Value

          Observations                   140.0000
          Variance Estimate                0.0020
          Standard Deviation Estimate      0.0444
          REML Log Likelihood           -307.322
          Akaike's Information Criterion -315.322
          Schwarz's Bayesian Criterion  -326.792
          -2 REML Log Likelihood         614.6438
          PARMS Model LRT Chi-Square        0.0000
          PARMS Model LRT DF                7.0000
          PARMS Model LRT P-Value           1.0000


                     Solution for Fixed Effects
```

Parameter	Estimate	Std Error	DDF	T	Pr > |T|
INTERCEPT	-18.67360832	1.06515966	18	-17.53	0.0001
TMP	95.26030191	4.80718840	18	19.82	0.0001
TMP*TMP	-48.68023983	6.41623120	18	-7.59	0.0001
TMP*TMP*TMP	12.61426622	3.27171682	18	3.86	0.0012
TMP*TMP*TMP*TMP	-1.35667922	0.54091509	18	-2.51	0.0219
QB 200	1.99285871	1.41704443	76	1.41	0.1637
QB 300	0.00000000	.	.	.	.
TMP*QB 200	-3.45968953	6.40302704	76	-0.54	0.5906
TMP*QB 300	0.00000000	.	.	.	.
TMP*TMP*QB 200	0.13706117	8.48189473	76	0.02	0.9871
TMP*TMP*QB 300	0.00000000	.	.	.	.
TMP*TMP*TMP*QB 200	-1.54871746	4.30410209	76	-0.36	0.7200
TMP*TMP*TMP*QB 300	0.00000000	.	.	.	.
TMP*TMP*TMP*TMP*QB 200	0.38555065	0.70807275	76	0.54	0.5877
TMP*TMP*TMP*TMP*QB 300	0.00000000	.	.	.	.

```
                    Tests of Fixed Effects

Source                   NDF   DDF   Type III F   Pr > F

TMP                       1     18     853.48      0.0001
TMP*TMP                   1     18     131.39      0.0001
TMP*TMP*TMP               1     18      30.27      0.0001
TMP*TMP*TMP*TMP           1     18      10.81      0.0041
QB                        1     76       1.98      0.1637
TMP*QB                    1     76       0.29      0.5906
TMP*TMP*QB                1     76       0.00      0.9871
TMP*TMP*TMP*QB            1     76       0.13      0.7200
TMP*TMP*TMP*TMP*QB        1     76       0.30      0.5877


                    COMPARE Procedure
             Comparison of WORK.SF with WORK.SF1
                      (Method=EXACT)


            Value Comparison Results for Variables


          ||  Estimate
          ||    Base      Compare
    Obs   ||    EST         EST        Diff.       % Diff
  _____   ||  _____    _____     _____     _____
          ||
      1   ||  -18.67361  -18.67361   -4.404E-9   2.3583E-8
      2   ||   95.260302  95.260302   2.3074E-8   2.4223E-8
      3   ||  -48.68024  -48.68024   -3.405E-8   6.9943E-8
      4   ||   12.614266  12.614266   1.7393E-8   1.3788E-7
      5   ||   -1.356679  -1.356679  -2.813E-9   2.0733E-7
      6   ||    1.9928587  1.9928587  3.4921E-9   1.7523E-7
      8   ||   -3.459690  -3.459690  -1.762E-8    5.093E-7
     10   ||    .13706114  .13706117  2.495E-8   0.0000182
     12   ||   -1.548717  -1.548717  -1.243E-8   8.0257E-7
     14   ||    .38555065  .38555065  1.9795E-9   5.1341E-7
```

Interpretation

The PROC COMPARE results indicate that the estimates have converged. The final estimated power is 1.98, which is very close to a constant coefficient of variation model. Note also that the new value of AIC_R is -315.32, which is an improvement over the -329.9 value from the standard random coefficients model and is close to the value of -314.9 attained by the ARH(1) structure.

The NLINMIX macro discussed in Chapter 12 also allows you to specify a power-of-the-mean model, and it performs the iterations automatically. In fact, you can use it to specify an arbitrary positive function of the mean as a weight variable in conjunction with any of the aforementioned covariance structures. The final estimates are no longer maximum likelihood, but they do solve a set of pseudo-likelihood generalized estimating equations. NLINMIX also allows you to specify a nonlinear mean function like the one used by Vonesh and Carter (1992).

8.3 Example: Combining Between- and Within-Subject Heterogeneity

In this example both within- and between-subject heterogeneity play a role. The data are from Patel (1991) and represent the grip strengths (in mm Hg) of patients with rheumatoid arthritis undergoing two different treatments.

Model

The assumed fixed-effects model consists of 12 cell means (2 treatments by 2 genders by 3 measurement occasions), a baseline covariate, and its interaction with treatment, gender, and time. The SAS data set is in Data Set 8.2, "GRIP," in Appendix 4, "SAS Data Sets."

```
data grip;
   input subject x y1 y2 y3 trt sex$;
   array yy{3} y1-y3;
   do time = 1 to 3;
      t = time;
      y = yy{time};
      output;
   end;
   drop y1-y3;
   datalines;
...datalines...
run;
```

In contrast with the preceding example, some data are missing; that is, some patients are measured on less than three occasions. As long as the missingness is ignorable in the sense that the nonresponse mechanism is independent of the subject's unobserved response (Rubin, 1976), a restricted likelihood-based analysis is still appropriate. The following analyses are therefore based on an assumption of ignorable missingness.

Figures 8.5 and 8.6 plot the profiles of the females and males, respectively. No heterogeneity of variance is immediately apparent within either gender, and the amount of variability appears to be roughly the same for both genders.

Figure 8.5 *Grip Strength Data for Females*

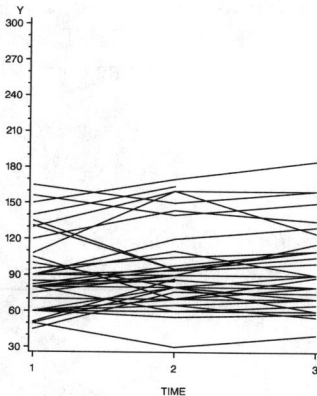

Figure 8.6 *Grip Strength Data for Males*

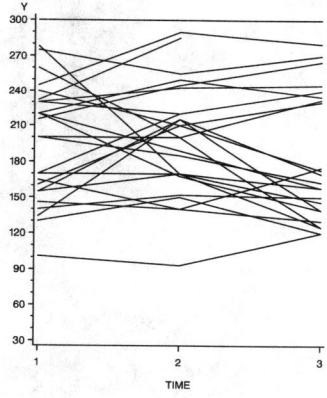

8.3.1 Basic Unstructured Covariance Model

The first model to consider is the same as the first one used with the previous example: blocks of **R** which have an unstructured form and therefore model completely general within-subject heterogeneity.

Program

The PROC MIXED program is as follows:

```
proc mixed data=grip;
   class subject trt sex time;
   model y = trt|sex|time x time*x sex*x trt*x;
   repeated / type=un subject=subject r rcorr;
run;
```

The MODEL statement specifies the 12 cell means involving TRT, SEX, and TIME. The bar operator (|) is used as a shorthand for all main effects and interactions between TRT, SEX, and TIME, and the lower order effects are included in order to carry out tests for whether the higher order terms are necessary. The mean model also includes different slopes of the covariate X for each of the three main effects.

The REPEATED statement requests the block-diagonal unstructured form for **R** with blocks corresponding to levels of the SUBJECT variable. The R and RCORR options request printouts of the first block of **R** and its corresponding correlation form.

The results are shown in Ouput 8.3.

Results

Output 8.3 *Grip Strength Results Using a Basic Unstructured Model*

```
                    The MIXED Procedure

                 Class Level Information

     Class      Levels  Values

     SUBJECT       67    1  2  3  4  5  6  7  8  9  10 13 15 17
                         18 19 20 21 22 23 24 25 26 27
                         28 29 30 31 34 35 36 37 38 39
                         40 41 42 43 44 45 46 47 48 49
                         50 51 52 53 54 55 56 57 58 59
                         61 62 63 64 65 67 70 71 72 73
                         74 75 76 79
     TRT            2    1  2
     SEX            2    F  M
     TIME           3    1  2  3


              REML Estimation Iteration History

     Iteration  Evaluations      Objective         Criterion

          0            1     1446.8231049
          1            2     1375.1884372       0.00000768
          2            1     1375.1830721       0.00000001

            Convergence criteria met.
```

```
                          R Matrix for SUBJECT 1

              Row         COL1          COL2          COL3

               1     638.86529394   337.34436171   311.93776233
               2     337.34436171   1003.9226800   939.04407161
               3     311.93776233   939.04407161   1382.6873028


                     R Correlation Matrix for SUBJECT 1

              Row         COL1          COL2          COL3

               1      1.00000000    0.42122940    0.33189546
               2      0.42122940    1.00000000    0.79702851
               3      0.33189546    0.79702851    1.00000000


                  Covariance Parameter Estimates (REML)

    Cov Parm          Estimate      Std Error      Z    Pr > |Z|

    DIAG UN(1,1)   638.86529394   116.90537922   5.46   0.0001
         UN(2,1)   337.34436171   112.19146725   3.01   0.0026
         UN(2,2)   1003.9226800   187.12174848   5.37   0.0001
         UN(3,1)   311.93776233   128.55972242   2.43   0.0152
         UN(3,2)   939.04407161   200.77377523   4.68   0.0001
         UN(3,3)   1382.6873028   265.50957832   5.21   0.0001
    Residual         1.00012128        .          .        .


                    Model Fitting Information for Y

         Description                          Value

         Observations                        189.0000
         Variance Estimate                     1.0001
         Standard Deviation Estimate           1.0001
         REML Log Likelihood                -845.649
         Akaike's Information Criterion     -851.649
         Schwarz's Bayesian Criterion       -861.091
         -2 REML Log Likelihood             1691.298
         Null Model LRT Chi-Square            71.6400
         Null Model LRT DF                     5.0000
         Null Model LRT P-Value                0.0000
```

```
                    Tests of Fixed Effects

        Source          NDF    DDF   Type III F   Pr > F

        TRT              1      60       0.13      0.7186
        SEX              1      60       2.54      0.1164
        TRT*SEX          1      60       0.78      0.3820
        TIME             2     112       1.53      0.2209
        TRT*TIME         2     112       0.59      0.5581
        SEX*TIME         2     112       1.94      0.1490
        TRT*SEX*TIME     2     112       0.14      0.8690
        X                1      60      97.73      0.0001
        X*TIME           2     112       0.84      0.4340
        X*SEX            1      60       0.04      0.8415
        X*TRT            1      60       0.09      0.7716
```

Interpretation

The blocks of **R** are 3×3 for this example. The estimated variances definitely appear to be increasing with time, but the covariances and correlations display no obvious pattern.

8.3.2 Incorporating Between-Subject Heterogeneity

As in the previous example, you can fit other structures by changing the TYPE= option on the REPEATED statement. Instead of fitting other structures, however, consider the two classification variables (TRT and GENDER) that may be used to model between-subject heterogeneity.

Program

The following program specifies separate unstructured estimates for each of the two levels of TRT:

```
proc mixed data=grip;
   class subject trt gender time;
   model y = trt|gender|time x time*x gender*x trt*x;
   repeated / type=un sub=subject group=trt r=1,2 rcorr=1,2;
run;
```

The GROUP= option on the REPEATED statement sets up the between-subject heterogeneity. Note also that the first 2 blocks of **R** and their corresponding correlations are requested with the R and RCORR options.

Results

This model produces $AIC_R = -852.8$ and $BIC_R = -871.7$, both of which are worse than the previous homogeneous model. However, using GROUP=GENDER instead of GROUP=TRT in the REPEATED statement produces Output 8.4.

Output 8.4 *Grip Strength Results Using Between-Subject Heterogeneity*

```
                         The MIXED Procedure

                     Class Level Information

       Class      Levels  Values

       SUBJECT        67  1  2  3  4  5  6  7  8  9 10 13 15 17
                          18 19 20 21 22 23 24 25 26 27
                          28 29 30 31 34 35 36 37 38 39
                          40 41 42 43 44 45 46 47 48 49
                          50 51 52 53 54 55 56 57 58 59
                          61 62 63 64 65 67 70 71 72 73
                          74 75 76 79
       TRT             2  1 2
       GENDER          2  F M
       TIME            3  1 2 3


                  REML Estimation Iteration History

      Iteration  Evaluations     Objective      Criterion

             0           1   1446.8231049
             1           2   1317.3964810    0.00076615
             2           1   1316.8105910    0.00007323
             3           1   1316.7589350    0.00000101
             4           1   1316.7582615    0.00000000

                    Convergence criteria met.

                    R Matrix for SUBJECT 1

       Row          COL1           COL2           COL3

         1  1065.7307907   668.92204926   598.46083728
         2   668.92204926  1957.7914096   1909.0772944
         3   598.46083728  1909.0772944   2782.1917871
```

```
                    R Correlation Matrix for SUBJECT 1

        Row           COL1            COL2            COL3

         1       1.00000000      0.46309335      0.34755092
         2       0.46309335      1.00000000      0.81798770
         3       0.34755092      0.81798770      1.00000000


                       R Matrix for SUBJECT 2

        Row           COL1            COL2            COL3

         1     319.92479563    83.34982134    105.32737084
         2      83.34982134   294.19656347    210.95552709
         3     105.32737084   210.95552709    275.75810311


                    R Correlation Matrix for SUBJECT 2

        Row           COL1            COL2            COL3

         1       1.00000000      0.27168266      0.35461177
         2       0.27168266      1.00000000      0.74064137
         3       0.35461177      0.74064137      1.00000000


                  Covariance Parameter Estimates (REML)
```

Cov Parm			Estimate	Std Error	Z	Pr > |Z|
DIAG UN(1,1)	GENDER	F	319.92479563	77.84897972	4.11	0.0001
UN(2,1)	GENDER	F	83.34982134	54.28745170	1.54	0.1247
UN(2,2)	GENDER	F	294.19656347	73.98411531	3.98	0.0001
UN(3,1)	GENDER	F	105.32737084	55.87958938	1.88	0.0594
UN(3,2)	GENDER	F	210.95552709	63.90281103	3.30	0.0010
UN(3,3)	GENDER	F	275.75810311	71.31268868	3.87	0.0001
DIAG UN(1,1)	GENDER	M	1065.7307907	297.07176715	3.59	0.0003
UN(2,1)	GENDER	M	668.92204926	314.40105296	2.13	0.0334
UN(2,2)	GENDER	M	1957.7914096	559.43409857	3.50	0.0005
UN(3,1)	GENDER	M	598.46083728	359.12947612	1.67	0.0956
UN(3,2)	GENDER	M	1909.0772944	612.49741484	3.12	0.0018
UN(3,3)	GENDER	M	2782.1917871	806.42669009	3.45	0.0006
Residual			1.00001544	.	.	.

```
                    Model Fitting Information for Y

            Description                       Value

            Observations                    189.0000
            Variance Estimate                 1.0000
            Standard Deviation Estimate       1.0000
            REML Log Likelihood            -816.437
            Akaike's Information Criterion  -828.437
            Schwarz's Bayesian Criterion    -847.322
            -2 REML Log Likelihood         1632.873
            Null Model LRT Chi-Square       130.0648
            Null Model LRT DF                11.0000
            Null Model LRT P-Value            0.0000


                    Tests of Fixed Effects

        Source          NDF   DDF   Type III F   Pr > F

        TRT               1    60       0.10     0.7562
        GENDER            1    60       1.40     0.2412
        TRT*GENDER        1    60       0.64     0.4253
        TIME              2   112       0.83     0.4382
        TRT*TIME          2   112       0.50     0.6089
        GENDER*TIME       2   112       2.19     0.1165
        TRT*GENDER*TIME   2   112       0.11     0.8943
        X                 1    60     147.73     0.0001
        X*TIME            2   112       0.38     0.6862
        X*GENDER          1    60       0.02     0.9022
        X*TRT             1    60       0.04     0.8403
```

Interpretation

Note that $AIC_R = -828.4$ and $BIC_R = -847.3$ indicate a considerable improvement over the homogeneous unstructured model. The estimates for the two different blocks of **R** reveal that the males are much more variable than the females, with the male variances being (1066, 1958, 2782) and the female variances (320, 294, 276). Furthermore, the male variances are increasing sharply over time while those for the females are slowly decreasing. The correlation patterns for the two genders are roughly the same.

The preceding statements are in apparent conflict with the observations made of figures 8.5 and 8.6 that they display no heterogeneity either within or between genders. The resolution of this conflict lies in the fact that the particular mean model used for these data, and primarily the covariate X, accounts for a significant portion of the variability, and it is the remaining variability that is modeled in the **R** matrix.

Figures 8.7 and 8.8 correspond to Figures 8.5 and 8.6, except they plot the ordinary least squares residuals after fitting the preceding mean model. They reflect the numerical results obtained from the REML analysis. These results show that both the mean and variance models account for variability in the data, and the general mixed model allows you the flexibility to choose which way to model it.

The programs to generate Figures 8.7 and 8.8 are as follows:

```
proc mixed data=grip;
   class subject trt gender time;
   model y = trt|gender|time x time*x gender*x trt*x / p;
   make 'predicted' out=p noprint;
   id time subject gender;
run;

symbol i=join c=black;
proc gplot data=p;
   where gender = 'F';
   plot resid*time=subject / nolegend hminor=0;
run;

proc gplot data=p;
   where gender = 'M';
   plot resid*time=subject / nolegend hminor=0;
run;
```

In this code the P option in the MODEL statement creates a table of predicted values and residuals. The MAKE statement requests that this table be converted to a data set named P, and the NOPRINT option suppresses the printing of the table with the PROC MIXED listing. The ID statement is necessary to include extra variables in the P data set.

The SYMBOL statement requests that the profiles be interpolated with a straight line and that their color be black. The two PROC GPLOT calls construct Figures 8.7 and 8.8 respectively, with the WHERE statements performing the appropriate subsetting of the P data set. Refer to *SAS/GRAPH Software: Reference* for further details about the SYMBOL statement and PROC GPLOT.

Figure 8.7 *Residuals from Grip Strength Data for Females*

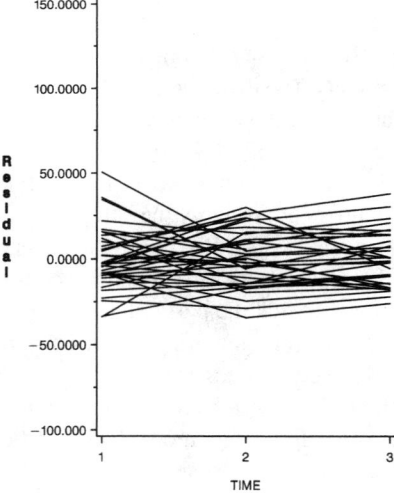

Figure 8.8 *Residuals from Grip Strength Data for Males*

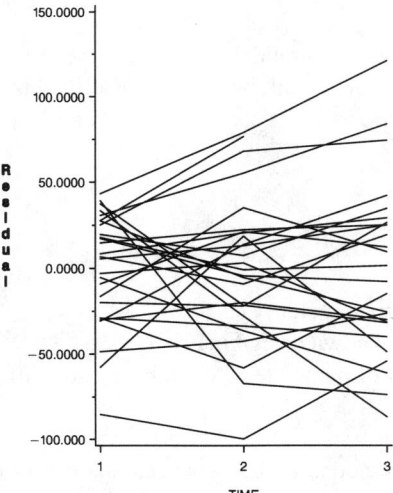

8.3.3 Heterogeneous Random Coefficients

As a more parsimonious alternative to the previous heterogeneous unstructured model, you can account for both between- and within-subject heterogeneity using a random coefficients model. Consider the the following two PROC MIXED specifications:

```
proc mixed data=grip;
   class subject trt gender time;
   model y = trt|gender|time x time*x gender*x trt*x;
   random int t / type=un sub=subject group=gender;
run;

proc mixed data=grip;
   class subject trt gender time;
   model y = trt|gender|time x time*x gender*x trt*x;
   random int t / type=un sub=subject group=gender;
   repeated / sub=subject group=gender;
run;
```

Both models fit separate unstructured parameters in **G** for the two genders via the GROUP= option in the RANDOM statements. However, they differ in that the first code models a common residual variance for the two genders, while the latter models separate estimates. The AIC_R values for the two models are -834.0 and -830.8, respectively, favoring the second specification for these data.

8.4 Example: Log-Linear Variance Models

In addition to the power-of-the-mean model discussed in Section 8.2.4, another type of diagonal heterogeneity is the log-linear variance model described by Harvey (1976) and Aitkin (1987) and related to the power-of-X model (Carroll and Ruppert, 1988). Here the variances are of the form

$$\mathbf{R} = \text{diag}[\sigma^2 \exp(\mathbf{u}_i'\mathbf{d})]$$

where
  σ^2 is an unknown scale parameter
  $\mathbf{u}_i$ is the ith row of some known design matrix
  $\mathbf{d}$ is an unknown vector of parameters, sometimes called **dispersion effects parameters**.

The $\mathbf{u}_i$'s provide flexibility in modeling the variances as a function of known experimental conditions.

These models appear to be applicable to industrial experiments where modeling and controlling variability is an important objective.

The pre-etch integrated circuit data from Phadke et al. (1983) provide an example. The widths of lines made by a photoresist-nanoline tool are measured in five different locations on silicon wafers, measurements being taken before an etching process. There are eight experimental factors for the experiment: Mask dimension, Viscosity, Spin speed, Bake temperature, Bake time, Aperture, Exposure, and Developing time. Refer to Wolfinger and Tobias (1995) for further details.

The experimental design is derived from an L_{18} orthogonal array and produces 33 measurements at each of the five locations for a total of 165 observations. Such designs are used to investigate many experimental factors with a relatively few number of experimental runs. You can construct the corresponding SAS data set as follows. The SAS data set is in Data Set 8.4, "PREETCH," in Appendix 4, "SAS Data Sets."

```
data preetch;
   input expt wafer mask viscos spin baketemp baketime aperture
         expos develop etch y1-y5;
   y = y1; loc = 'top'; output;
   y = y2; loc = 'cen'; output;
   y = y3; loc = 'bot'; output;
   y = y4; loc = 'lef'; output;
   y = y5; loc = 'rig'; output;
   drop y1-y5;
   datalines;
...datalines...
run;
```

8.4.1 Initial Model

With such limited data, a main-effects-only model is the most sensible. Because any of the experimental factors can be influencing the line-width response, a model is first fit with all of the factors included as both location (fixed) effects and dispersion effects.

Program

You can specify dispersion effects in PROC MIXED with the LOCAL=EXP option on the REPEATED statement as follows:

```
proc mixed data=preetch;
    class expt wafer mask viscos spin baketemp
        baketime aperture expos develop;
    model y = mask viscos spin baketemp
        baketime aperture expos develop;
    repeated / local=exp(mask viscos spin baketemp
        baketime aperture expos develop);
run;
```

The LOCAL=EXP option enables you to specify effects after it just as you would in the MODEL or RANDOM statements. PROC MIXED parses the effects in the same fashion and uses them to construct the u_i vectors and the corresponding **d** parameters to be estimated. This model thus lets you actually model the variance of the data as a function of experimental effects that may also be influencing the mean of the data. Note that the same effects are included in both the MODEL statement and as the argument to the LOCAL=EXP option.

Note also that wafer location is not included as an effect in the analysis in order to average over locations and model the response as a function of controllable factors. The output from this program is shown in Output 8.5.

Results

Output 8.5 *Initial Log-Linear Variance Model Results*

```
                    The MIXED Procedure

                Class Level Information

        Class      Levels  Values

        EXPT         18    1 2 3 4 5 6 7 8 9 10 11 12 13
                           14 15 16 17 18
        WAFER         2    1 2
        MASK          2    1 -1
        VISCOS        2    1 -1
        SPIN          3    0 1 -1
        BAKETEMP      2    1 -1
        BAKETIME      3    0 1 -1
        APERTURE      3    0 1 -1
        EXPOS         3    0 1 -1
        DEVELOP       3    0 1 -1
```

```
               REML Estimation Iteration History

        Iteration  Evaluations     Objective      Criterion

            0           1        -363.2704349
            1           2        -395.9819925     0.57034498
            2           6        -399.4416079     0.00786431
            3           1        -400.7220203     0.00059558
            4           1        -400.8465666     0.00000313
            5           1        -400.8471970     0.00000000


                   Convergence criteria met.


            Covariance Parameter Estimates (REML)
```

Cov Parm		Ratio	Estimate	Std Error	Z
EXP	MASK	-49.61849759	-0.65291564	0.14434368	-4.52
	VISCOS	-26.70811846	-0.35144450	0.18951846	-1.85
	SPIN 1	39.19795812	0.51579473	0.22142851	2.33
	2	-5.86688591	-0.07720068	0.21988201	-0.35
	BAKETEMP	-36.24873494	-0.47698675	0.16454498	-2.90
	BAKETIME 1	-6.30888915	-0.08301687	0.20488682	-0.41
	2	34.00375742	0.44744573	0.19785885	2.26
	APERTURE 1	11.66338470	0.15347515	0.18690492	0.82
	2	63.32771640	0.83331133	0.20006175	4.17
	EXPOS 1	17.30232847	0.22767640	0.19789807	1.15
	2	-12.77256744	-0.16807057	0.20834520	-0.81
	DEVELOP 1	4.98722279	0.06562544	0.20939355	0.31
	2	3.76953082	0.04960218	0.21737141	0.23
Residual		1.00000000	0.01315871	0.00218836	6.01

```
            Covariance Parameter Estimates (REML)
```

Cov Parm		Pr > |Z|
EXP	MASK	0.0001
	VISCOS	0.0637
	SPIN 1	0.0198
	2	0.7255
	BAKETEMP	0.0037
	BAKETIME 1	0.6853
	2	0.0237

```
           APERTURE 1          0.4116
                   2          0.0001
             EXPOS 1          0.2499
                   2          0.4198
           DEVELOP 1          0.7540
                   2          0.8195
      Residual               0.0001
```

Model Fitting Information for Y

Description	Value
Observations	165.0000
Variance Estimate	0.0132
Standard Deviation Estimate	0.1147
REML Log Likelihood	61.6639
Akaike's Information Criterion	47.6639
Schwarz's Bayesian Criterion	26.5429
-2 REML Log Likelihood	-123.328
Null Model LRT Chi-Square	37.5768
Null Model LRT DF	13.0000
Null Model LRT P-Value	0.0003

Solution for Fixed Effects

Parameter	Estimate	Std Error	DDF	T	Pr > |T|
INTERCEPT	2.49515657	0.02694980	19	92.59	0.0001
MASK 1	0.39500927	0.02634788	19	14.99	0.0001
MASK -1	0.00000000	.	.	.	.
VISCOS 1	-0.59504772	0.02987494	19	-19.92	0.0001
VISCOS -1	0.00000000	.	.	.	.
SPIN 0	0.26528530	0.02989443	19	8.87	0.0001
SPIN 1	0.55905776	0.02608501	19	21.43	0.0001
SPIN -1	0.00000000	.	.	.	.
BAKETEMP 1	0.05559104	0.02930057	19	1.90	0.0731
BAKETEMP -1	0.00000000	.	.	.	.
BAKETIME 0	-0.10269641	0.02525726	19	-4.07	0.0007
BAKETIME 1	0.08248821	0.02821828	19	2.92	0.0087
BAKETIME -1	0.00000000	.	.	.	.
APERTURE 0	0.01357576	0.02573886	19	0.53	0.6040
APERTURE 1	-0.02003877	0.03195118	19	-0.63	0.5380
APERTURE -1	0.00000000	.	.	.	.
EXPOS 0	-0.30570836	0.02858551	19	-10.69	0.0001

```
EXPOS 1        -0.39228494    0.02804322    19   -13.99    0.0001
EXPOS -1        0.00000000       .            .      .        .
DEVELOP 0      -0.00699286    0.03033840    19    -0.23    0.8202
DEVELOP 1       0.38986006    0.02632745    19    14.81    0.0001
DEVELOP -1      0.00000000       .            .      .        .


                    Tests of Fixed Effects


            Source       NDF   DDF   Type III F   Pr > F


            MASK          1     19     224.76     0.0001
            VISCOS        1     19     396.72     0.0001
            SPIN          2     19     230.02     0.0001
            BAKETEMP      1     19       3.60     0.0731
            BAKETIME      2     19      21.48     0.0001
            APERTURE      2     19       0.43     0.6577
            EXPOS         2     19     107.88     0.0001
            DEVELOP       2     19     158.40     0.0001
```

Interpretation

The key statistics to examine in such analyses are the *p*-values associated with each of the location and dispersion effects. Significant *p*-values are those that are likely to impact process mean and variability, respectively.

For the location effects, the "Tests of Fixed Effects" table reveals that MASK, VISCOS, SPIN, BAKETIME, EXPOS, and DEVELOP all appear significant. The analysis of dispersion effects in the "Covariance Parameter Estimates" table is more difficult because some of the effects are modeled by two parameters in **d** because they have three levels in the experiment. A conservative approach is to retain effects for which any of their associated parameters are significant. This approach declares MASK, SPIN, BAKETEMP, BAKETIME, and APERTURE as the significant dispersion effects.

Alternatively, you can compute likelihood ratio tests of the location and dispersion effects by fitting a series of reduced models, leaving out one effect in each. For these fits you should use standard maximum likelihood (with the METHOD=ML option on the PROC MIXED statement) for the location effect likelihood ratio tests because the restricted likelihood adjustment depends upon the location effects design matrix. Restricted likelihood ratio tests are appropriate for the dispersion effects.

8.4.2 Adding a Random Effect

A slightly more complicated model accounts for possible correlation that may exist between observations from the same wafer.

Program

You can accomplish this in PROC MIXED by adding a RANDOM statement as follows:

```
proc mixed data=preetch;
    class expt wafer mask viscos spin baketemp
        baketime aperture expos develop;
    model y = mask viscos spin baketemp
        baketime aperture expos develop / ddfm=bw;
    random int / sub=wafer(expt);
    repeated / local=exp(mask viscos spin baketemp
            baketime aperture expos develop)
            sub=wafer(expt);
run;
```

The SUB= option is used on both the RANDOM and REPEATED statements in order to speed computations. Also, the DDFM=BW option has been added to the MODEL statement so that the denominator degrees of freedom calculations match those performed in the previous analysis. (This option requests the between-within method for computing degrees of freedom.)

The results of this analysis are shown in Output 8.6.

Results

Output 8.6 *Log-Linear Variance Model with Random Effect Results*

```
                    The MIXED Procedure

                 Class Level Information

      Class      Levels  Values

      EXPT         18   1 2 3 4 5 6 7 8 9 10 11 12 13
                        14 15 16 17 18
      WAFER         2   1 2
      MASK          2   1 -1
      VISCOS        2   1 -1
      SPIN          3   0 1 -1
      BAKETEMP      2   1 -1
      BAKETIME      3   0 1 -1
      APERTURE      3   0 1 -1
      EXPOS         3   0 1 -1
      DEVELOP       3   0 1 -1
```

```
                REML Estimation Iteration History

     Iteration   Evaluations      Objective      Criterion

         0             1       -363.2704349
         1             2       -446.4261610     0.00769061
         2             1       -448.2543628     0.00012821
         3             1       -448.2835479     0.00000008
         4             1       -448.2835651     0.00000000

                   Convergence criteria met.


             Covariance Parameter Estimates (REML)

Cov Parm              Ratio      Estimate     Std Error        Z

INTERCEPT          1.77105025   0.01645825   0.00615560     2.67
EXP MASK         -51.17374322  -0.47555399   0.13260505    -3.59
    VISCOS       -12.72457319  -0.11824856   0.16035798    -0.74
    SPIN  1       29.02449272   0.26972256   0.18571437     1.45
          2      -15.35214772  -0.14266643   0.19491374    -0.73
    BAKETEMP       0.35826746   0.00332935   0.15457765     0.02
    BAKETIME 1   -15.29304350  -0.14211717   0.18889984    -0.75
          2       45.43763996   0.42224878   0.17451207     2.42
    APERTURE 1     2.48376827   0.02308148   0.18130553     0.13
          2       58.02086331   0.53918379   0.18542235     2.91
    EXPOS 1       19.16211933   0.17807222   0.19086257     0.93
          2      -44.31283319  -0.41179603   0.19630331    -2.10
    DEVELOP 1    -20.28656713  -0.18852164   0.18457629    -1.02
          2       11.21249222   0.10419690   0.19101813     0.55
Residual           1.00000000   0.00929293   0.00148336     6.26


             Covariance Parameter Estimates (REML)

Cov Parm           Pr > |Z|

INTERCEPT           0.0075
EXP MASK            0.0003
    VISCOS          0.4609
    SPIN  1         0.1464
          2         0.4642
    BAKETEMP        0.9828
```

```
              BAKETIME 1      0.4518
                       2      0.0155
              APERTURE 1      0.8987
                       2      0.0036
                 EXPOS 1      0.3508
                       2      0.0359
               DEVELOP 1      0.3071
                       2      0.5854
            Residual          0.0001


              Model Fitting Information for Y

          Description                      Value

          Observations                    165.0000
          Variance Estimate                 0.0093
          Standard Deviation Estimate       0.0964
          REML Log Likelihood              85.3821
          Akaike's Information Criterion   70.3821
          Schwarz's Bayesian Criterion     47.7525
          -2 REML Log Likelihood         -170.764


                   Tests of Fixed Effects

          Source      NDF   DDF   Type III F   Pr > F

          MASK         1    19       61.36     0.0001
          VISCOS       1    19       85.59     0.0001
          SPIN         2    19       37.19     0.0001
          BAKETEMP     1    19        1.21     0.2842
          BAKETIME     2    19        0.31     0.7373
          APERTURE     2    19        1.62     0.2235
          EXPOS        2    19       25.88     0.0001
          DEVELOP      2    19       13.30     0.0002
```

Interpretation

The large increase in AIC_R from to 47.7 to 70.4 as well as the other likelihood criteria and Wald test all indicate that the wafer variance component is highly significant. Its addition to the model has resulted in the removal of BAKETIME from the list of significant location effects, leaving MASK, VISCOS, SPIN, EXPOS, and DEVELOP. Also, the significant dispersion effects have changed from MASK, SPIN, BAKETEMP, BAKETIME, and APERTURE to MASK, BAKETIME, APERTURE, and EXPOS. Clearly the omission of an important variance parameter from your model can significantly influence statistical inference.

8.5 Summary

This chapter considers heterogeneous variance models; that is, models for which the variability of the data is assumed to change according to one or more factors. Assuming the data consist of repeated observations on a number of subjects, heterogeneity can be classified as either within-subject or between-subject. The first example, on high flux hemodialyzers, illustrates the wide variety of possible within-subject covariance structures and methods for selecting between them. The second example, on grip strengths, shows how between-subject heterogeneity can also play an important role in data modeling. The third and final example, on integrated circuits, highlights the log-linear variance model and how it allows you to directly model heterogeneity.

8.6 References

Aitkin, M. (1987), Modelling variance heterogeneity in normal regressing using GLIM, *Applied Statistics*, **36**, 332–339.

Box, G.E.P. (1950), Problems in the analysis of growth and wear curves, *Biometrics*, **6**, 362–389.

Bryk, A.S. and Raudenbush, S.W. (1992), *Hierarchical Linear Models*, Newbury Park, CA: Sage Publications, Inc.

Carroll, R.J. and Ruppert, D. (1988), *Transformation and Weighting in Regression*, London: Chapman and Hall.

Diggle, P.J. (1988), An approach to the analysis of repeated measurements, *Biometrics*, **44**, 959–971.

Goldstein, H. (1987), *Multilevel Models in Educational and Social Research*, New York: Oxford University Press.

Harvey, A.C. (1976), Estimating regression models with multiplicative heteroscedasticity, *Econometrica*, **44**, 461–465.

Huynh, H. and Feldt, L.S. (1970), Conditions under which mean square ratios in repeated measurements designs have exact F-distributions, *Journal of the American Statistical Association*, **65**, 1582–1589.

Louis, T.A. (1988), General methods for analysing repeated measures, *Statistics in Medicine*, 7, 29–45.

Patel, H.I. (1991), Analysis of incomplete data from a clinical trial with repeated measurements, *Biometrika*, **78**, 609–619.

Phadke, M.S., Kackar, R.N., Speeney, D.V., and Grieco, M.J. (1983), Off-line quality control for integrated circuit fabrication using experimental design, *Bell System Technical Journal*, **62**, 1273–1309.

Rubin, D.B. (1976), Inference and missing data, *Biometrika*, **63**, 581–592.

Vonesh, E.F. and Carter, R.L. (1992), Mixed-effects nonlinear regression for unbalanced repeated measures, *Biometrics*, **48**, 1–17.

Wolfinger, R.D. (1993), Covariance structure selection in general mixed models, *Communications in Statistics, Simulation and Computation*, **22**, 1079–1106.

Wolfinger, R.D. (1996), Heterogeneous variance covariance structures for repeated measures, *Journal of Agricultural, Biological, and Environmental Statistics*.

Wolfinger, R.D. and Tobias, R.D. (1995), Joint estimation of location, dispersion, and random effects, Cary, NC: SAS Institute Inc., unpublished manuscript.

Chapter 9 Spatial Variability

9.1 Introduction

Spatial variability, as the name implies, refers to variation among observations in space. Often, patterns exist in spatial variability; the goal of spatial statistics is to model and estimate these patterns. There are two main sets of methods: 1) those applicable to random locations, e.g., trees in a forest whose locations are random occurrences, and 2) those appropriate for fixed locations, e.g., a field study using a sampling design or a designed experiment. In a designed field study or experiment, small-scale dependence, that is, the relationship among observations in proximity to each other, is often of particular interest. Small-scale dependence can be positive or negative. PROC MIXED has several features that allow you to work with *positive* dependence. This chapter focuses on these methods.

9.2 Description

Positive, small-scale spatial dependence, or **positive spatial correlation**, refers to the tendency of observations closer together to be more alike than observations farther apart. For example, in a field survey to assess ground water contamination, several wells are drilled in the survey area and water quality measurements taken at each well. Typically, observations taken at wells in relatively close proximity are more highly correlated than those taken at more distant wells. In agronomic and horticultural experiments, adjacent experimental units have common fertility characteristics whereas more distant experimental units tend to be less alike. As the number of treatments increases, the potential importance of accounting for spatial variability in field experiments also increases. Cultivar evaluation trials, for example, often involve dozens or even hundreds of varieties. In many experiments, the most important objective is to find out if new treatments or varieties perform satisfactorily in marginal environments. In order to make realistic conclusions, these experiments must be conducted in fields with difficult growing conditions. Such fields typically exhibit a high degree of spatial heterogeneity. Failure to use statistical methods that account for spatial dependence can result in erroneous conclusions.

A good starting point for understanding spatial variability is to think of it as a multidimensional extension of repeated measures. In repeated measures, observations taken over time are correlated. In spatial statistics, observations are correlated in two spatial dimensions. As with repeated measures, most spatial procedures assume that the **errors**, i.e., the elements of **e** in the mixed model $\mathbf{y} = \mathbf{X}\boldsymbol{\beta} + \mathbf{Z}\mathbf{u} + \mathbf{e}$, are correlated. In principle, spatial correlation can be reflected in **G**, the covariance matrix of the random model effects, **u**, but this chapter considers only examples of **R**.

Statistical methods for spatial correlation can be divided into two basic groups, **characterization** and **adjustment**. Characterization involves estimating covariance parameters and making spatial maps. Adjustment involves removing the effects of spatial correlation to obtain more accurate estimates of, for example, treatment means or differences. PROC MIXED is particularly well-suited for **adjustment**.

PROC MIXED allows you to work with several different spatial correlation models. The purpose of this chapter is to demonstrate the use of PROC MIXED for characterization and for adjustment. Section 9.3 describes basic models for spatial variability. Section 9.4 integrates spatial models into the mixed model framework and describes the basic features of inference. Section 9.5 presents a characterization example. Section 9.6 presents two adjustment examples and section 9.7 contains a cautionary note about covariance estimation.

9.3 Spatial Correlation Models

Models for spatial correlation have their origins in statistical methods developed in geology for mining applications. Owing to this history, many important spatial models are called "geostatistical" models. Important references include Journel and Huijbregts (1978), Isaaks and Srivastava (1989), and Cressie (1991). While PROC MIXED uses geostatistical models, its approach differs from geostatistics, primarily for the sake of consistency with mixed model theory. Readers familiar with standard geostatistics will notice substantial differences in notation although the concepts are the same.

This section presents the basic spatial models used by PROC MIXED. Section 9.4 shows how these models are included in the mixed model. Also, Section 9.4 discusses key geostatistical concepts and their relationship to spatial mixed models.

9.3.1 Spatial Correlation Models Used in PROC MIXED

In the simplest spatial statistics problem, you have a set of observations whose physical location and response are known. Your primary objective is to estimate spatial correlation. The model is

$$y_i = \mu + e_i$$

where y_i is the ith observation and e_i is the corresponding error. Let s_i denote the physical location of y_i, where s_i is specified by two coordinates. For example, the coordinates could be latitude and longitude. Alternatively, the coordinates might be indices on a grid, such as north-south and east-west, or row and column dimensions respectively. For simplicity, we refer to the coordinates of s_i as the "row" and "column" coordinates. The specific meaning of "row" and "column" will depend on the particular data set.

In general, you can define spatial correlation models by letting

$\text{Var}(e_i) = \sigma_i^2$, and

$\text{Cov}(e_i, e_j) = \sigma_{ij}$

Typically, the covariance is assumed to be a function of the distance between the locations s_i and s_j. Let d_{ij} be the distance between s_i and s_j. The resulting models have the general form:

$\text{Cov}(e_i, e_j) = \sigma^2[f(d_{ij})]$

Models for which $f(d_{ij})$ is the same for all pairs of equally distant locations in a given direction, e.g., along the row, along the column, or diagonal, are called **stationary models**. If, in addition, $f(d_{ij})$ does not depend on the direction, then the model is said to be **isotropic**. The rest of this chapter focuses on working with isotropic models using PROC MIXED.

PROC MIXED allows you to work with the following models:

1. Spherical

$$f(d_{ij}) = [1 - 1.5(d_{ij}/\rho) + 0.5(d_{ij}/\rho)^3]1(d_{ij}<\rho)$$

2. Exponential

$$f(d_{ij}) = [\exp(-d_{ij}/\rho)]$$

3. Gaussian

$$f(d_{ij}) = [\exp(-d^2{}_{ij}/\rho^2)]$$

4. Linear

$$f(d_{ij}) = (1 - \rho d_{ij})1(\rho d_{ij}<2)$$

5. Linear Log

$$f(d_{ij}) = [1 - \rho\log(d_{ij})]1[\rho\log(d_{ij})<2]$$

6. Power

$$f(d_{ij}) = \rho^{d_{ij}}$$

The power function is a reparameterization of the exponential covariance model (2).

The function $1(d_{ij}<\rho)$, used in the spherical model, equals 1 when $d_{ij}<\rho$ and equals 0 otherwise. Similar $1(\bullet)$ functions used for the linear and linear log models equal 1 when the condition within the parenthesis holds and equal 0 otherwise. For readers familiar with geostatistics, the parameters σ^2 and ρ correspond to the **sill** and **range** respectively (see section 9.4.2).

9.3.2 Models with a Nugget Effect

In some applications, the covariance models given above do not adequately account for abrupt changes over relatively small distances. You can model these cases by adding an additional parameter. The resulting covariance models are

$$\mathrm{Var}(e_i) = \sigma^2 + \sigma_1^2$$

$$\mathrm{Cov}(e_i, e_j) = \sigma^2[f(d_{ij})]$$

where the $f(d_{ij})$ can be any of the six models given above. For these models, the parameters σ_1^2, $\sigma^2 + \sigma_1^2$, and ρ correspond to the geostatistics parameters **nugget**, **sill**, and **range**, respectively. Using geostatistics terminology, models with $\mathrm{Var}(e_i) = \sigma^2 + \sigma_1^2$ are called **models with a nugget effect** whereas models with $\mathrm{Var}(e_i) = \sigma^2$ are called **no nugget** models (see Section 9.4.2 for additional details).

9.4 Spatial Variability and Mixed Models

This section shows how the spatial variability models discussed in Section 9.3 are incorporated into mixed models. The underlying theory was discussed by Zimmerman and Harville (1991).

9.4.1 Integrating Spatial Variability into Mixed Models

You can apply the covariance models described above to mixed models in general. For example, in a field experiment with different treatments, a potentially useful model is

$$y_{ij} = \mu + \tau_i + e_{ij}$$

where the covariance structure of the e_{ij}'s follows one of the covariance models given above.
The general mixed model with spatial variability is

$$\mathbf{y} = \mathbf{X}\boldsymbol{\beta} + \mathbf{Z}\mathbf{u} + \mathbf{e}$$

where spatial covariance is modeled through $\mathbf{R} = \mathrm{Var}(\mathbf{e})$. Defining $\mathbf{F}$ as an $N \times N$ matrix whose ij^{th} element is $f(d_{ij})$, then $\mathbf{R}$ has one of two forms:

No nugget model: $\qquad \mathbf{R} = \sigma^2\mathbf{F}$

Model with nugget: $\qquad \mathbf{R} = \mathbf{I}\sigma_1^2 + \sigma^2\mathbf{F}$

As with other mixed models, PROC MIXED obtains estimates of the variance and covariance components of $\mathbf{R}$ and $\mathbf{G}$ using REML, and estimates of $\boldsymbol{\beta}$ and $\mathbf{u}$ from solutions to the mixed model equations.

Inference on estimates or contrasts involving predictable functions $\mathbf{K}'\boldsymbol{\beta} + \mathbf{M}'\mathbf{u}$ uses the same approach as has been described elsewhere in this book. That is, standard errors of $\mathbf{K}'\boldsymbol{\beta} + \mathbf{M}'(\mathbf{u}-\hat{\mathbf{u}})$ are computed as $\mathbf{L}'\mathbf{C}\mathbf{L}$, where $\mathbf{L}' = [\mathbf{K}'\ \mathbf{M}']$ and $\mathbf{C}$ is the generalized inverse of the left hand side of the mixed model equations using estimated $\mathbf{G}$ and $\mathbf{R}$. Test statistics for hypotheses use the F-approximation computed from the Wald statistic divided by the rank of $\mathbf{L}$. See Appendix 1 for details.

While competing covariance models cannot be tested directly, you can compare their model fitting criteria. In principle, the *best* model is the one whose Schwarz, Akaike, and Log REML Likelihood criteria are greatest.

You can use the likelihood ratio test to compare models if one is a subset of the other. For example, a model with no spatial correlation, that is with $\mathbf{R} = \mathbf{I}\sigma^2$, can be compared to any of the spatial models with no nugget effect, whose $\mathbf{R} = \sigma^2\mathbf{F}$, because $\mathbf{F}$ reduces to $\mathbf{I}$ if the spatial parameter $\rho=0$. Thus, comparing the -2 REML Log Likelihood for each model yields a likelihood ratio test for H_0: $\rho=0$ with 1 degree of freedom.

9.4.2 Geostatistics Related to PROC MIXED

This discussion refers to isotropic geostatistical models. Two main tools of geostatistics are the semivariogram and kriging.

The **semivariogram** is a standard statistical measure of spatial variability as a function of the distance between observations. It is defined as one-half the variance of the difference between two observations a given distance apart. In geostatistics, h is standard notation for distance. The **empirical semivariogram**, i.e., the estimated semivariogram, can be computed from the data using the formula

$$\gamma(h) = (1/2m)\Sigma(y_i - y_j)^2$$

where m is the number of pairs of observations a distance, h, apart. $\gamma(h)$ is estimated for all distances at which pairs of observations exist.

Figure 9.1 *Semivariogram*

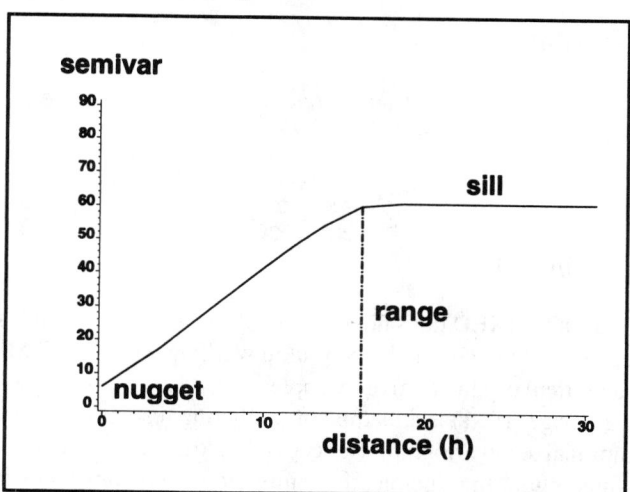

Figure 9.1 is an idealized graph of the semivariogram, an important tool in geostatistical modeling. The key features of the semivariogram are

- The **nugget**, defined as the intercept, i.e., the semivariogram at $h=0$. Standard geostatistical notation for the nugget is c_0.
- The **sill**, defined as the value of the semivariogram at the plateau reached for larger h. The sill corresponds to the variance of an observation. Standard geostatistical notation for the sill is $C(0)$.
- The **range**, defined as the value of h at which the semivariogram reaches the sill. For distances less than the range, observations are spatially correlated. The lower the semivariogram, the greater the correlation. For distances greater than or equal to the range, spatial correlation is effectively zero.

The semivariogram has a functional relationship to the **R** [Var(**e**)] matrix in the mixed model. Standard geostatistical notation for the covariance between two observations h units apart is $C(h)$. For **no nugget models**,

$$C(h) = C(0) - \gamma(h)$$

$$\gamma(0) = 0$$

Also, the semivariogram can be written in terms of the sill as

$$\gamma(h) = C(0)[1-f(h)]$$

where $f(\bullet)$ may be one of the functions of distance, e.g., spherical, given in Section 9.3.1. Thus, for these models, the sill, $C(0)$ corresponds to σ^2 as defined for **R** matrices in section 9.3.1. Also, since the semivariogram is equal to $C(0)[1-f(h)]$, then

$$C(h) = C(0)\{1 - [1-f(h)]\} = \sigma^2[f(h)]$$

The parameter ρ in the various functions $f(d_{ij})$ given in Section 9.3 corresponds to the range.

For models with a nugget effect, $C(0)$ is the variance of observations. The **partial sill**, denoted c_s, is the difference between the variance and the nugget, i.e., $c_s = C(0) - c_0$. The semivariance for such models is

$$Y(h) = c_s[1-f(h)]$$

Thus, the sill corresponds to $\sigma^2 + \sigma_1^2$ and the partial sill corresponds to σ^2. Relating these parameters to the covariance,

$$C(0) = \sigma^2 + \sigma_1^2$$

$$C(h) = \sigma^2[f(h)], \text{ for } h>0$$

While PROC MIXED does not compute the semivariogram *per se*, external estimates of the range, sill, and nugget can be helpful in working with PROC MIXED. Section 9.5 presents a particularly instructive example.

Kriging (Krige, 1951) is a method of predicting responses for unobserved locations based on the empirical semivariogram. Conceptually, kriging is similar to the method of best linear unbiased prediction. In principle, the semivariogram parameter estimates computed by PROC MIXED can be used for kriging. However, PROC MIXED was not developed with kriging in mind. No kriging examples are presented in this chapter.

The remaining sections of this chapter look at three PROC MIXED examples for spatial statistics.

9.5 Example: Estimating Spatial Covariance

This section presents a characterization example. Here, the objective is to find the most appropriate spatial model and estimate its covariance parameters.

The data for this example are from an agronomic uniformity trial, conducted on an 8 × 8 grid of plots. In a uniformity trial, a test crop is grown on a field with no experimental treatments applied. The response variable, in this case yield, is recorded. The idea is to characterize variability in the field in order to plan the design of experiments to be conducted on that field in the future. Traditionally, uniformity trials are used to decide how to block — e.g., whether to use a complete or incomplete block design or how to position the blocks. They may also be used to anticipate spatial variability.

The data are given in Appendix 4, Data Set 9.5. The variables ROW and COL locate the plots in the 8 × 8 grid. The field consisted of 4 quarters — the variable REP identifies each quarter field. Each quarter consisted of 4 "sub-quarters"— each identified by the variable BLOC. The response variable of interest was YIELD.

The researchers' primary objective was to use the information from these data to design a yield trial with 16 treatments. Specifically, they wanted to decide whether to conduct future experiments on the field as 1) a complete block design with 4 blocks (denoted REP in this example) 2) an incomplete block design with 16 blocks (denoted BLOC to avoid confusion with complete blocks), or 3) a completely random design with spatially correlated errors.

It is worth noting that, historically, blocking has acted as a simple model of spatial variation in field experiments. That is, blocking assumes that experimental units close together behave alike and can thus be grouped into reasonably homogeneous blocks. The existence of spatial correlation is implicit in blocking. While spatial covariance models are not necessarily alternatives to blocking in the design of experiments, they do provide an alternative to the standard ANOVA model for block designs as a way of accounting for field heterogeneity.

9.5.1 Estimating the No-Nugget Model

PROC MIXED allows you to analyze the data for any of the models mentioned above.

Program

For example, you can use the following program to fit a spherical covariance model:

```
proc mixed scoring=5;
   model yield= ;
   parms (0 to 10 by 2.5) (1 to 10 by 3);
   repeated / subject=intercept type=sp(sph)(row col);
   title 'no nugget - spherical covariance model';
run;
```

The SCORING option in the PROC MIXED command is not mandatory, but based on experience, we recommend using it in order to improve convergence and to get more reasonable estimators. The default method to compute covariance components in PROC MIXED is the Newton-Raphson algorithm. SCORING causes the Fisher scoring algorithm to be used instead. Jennerich and Sampson (1976) noted that the Fisher scoring algorithm is more robust to choice of starting values than Newton-Raphson. This seems to be particularly true when spatial covariance components are involved.

We also strongly recommend a parameter search using the PARMS option to get the REML procedure started in the vicinity of plausible values ρ and σ^2. These values are determined, for example, from previous experience or from an empirical semivariogram based on the residuals of an independent errors model. Otherwise, the REML procedure can converge to local maxima and provide grossly unreasonable estimates. The SUBJECT=INTERCEPT option treats all the observations in the data set as potentially correlated. You may need to change the SUBJECT= option depending on your data. For example, if an experiment were conducted at two locations, you would want to specify SUBJECT=LOCATION so that you do not try to compute correlations among observations at different locations.

The results of this program are given in Output 9.1.

Results

Output 9.1 *No Nugget - Spherical Covariance Model*

```
                              Parameter Search

      COL1       COL2    Variance   REML_LL   -2REML_LL  Objective
     0.0000     1.0000    3.1578    -127.694   255.3882   139.6020
     0.0000     4.0000    3.1578    -127.694   255.3882   139.6020
     0.0000     7.0000    3.1578    -127.694   255.3882   139.6020
     0.0000    10.0000    3.1578    -127.694   255.3882   139.6020
     2.5000     1.0000    3.0562    -113.925   227.8492   112.0630
     2.5000     4.0000    3.0562    -113.925   227.8492   112.0630
     2.5000     7.0000    3.0562    -113.925   227.8492   112.0630
     2.5000    10.0000    3.0562    -113.925   227.8492   112.0630
     5.0000     1.0000    6.6501    -118.169   236.3374   120.5511
     5.0000     4.0000    6.6501    -118.169   236.3374   120.5511
     5.0000     7.0000    6.6501    -118.169   236.3374   120.5511
     5.0000    10.0000    6.6501    -118.169   236.3374   120.5511
     7.5000     1.0000    9.6770    -117.569   235.1371   119.3509
     7.5000     4.0000    9.6770    -117.569   235.1371   119.3509
     7.5000     7.0000    9.6770    -117.569   235.1371   119.3509
     7.5000    10.0000    9.6770    -117.569   235.1371   119.3509
    10.0000     1.0000   13.0262    -117.963   235.9268   120.1405
    10.0000     4.0000   13.0262    -117.963   235.9268   120.1405
    10.0000     7.0000   13.0262    -117.963   235.9268   120.1405
    10.0000    10.0000   13.0262    -117.963   235.9268   120.1405


              Scoring stopped after iteration 5.
                 Convergence criteria met.

          Covariance Parameter Estimates (REML)

Cov Parm          Ratio      Estimate    Std Error     Z   Pr > |Z|

DIAG SP(SPH)   0.83173855   2.71209578  0.44624599   6.08   0.0001
Residual       1.00000000   3.26075517  0.65579410   4.97   0.0001


              Model Fitting Information for YIELD

       Description                      Value

       Observations                    64.0000
       Variance Estimate                3.2608
       Standard Deviation Estimate      1.8058
       REML Log Likelihood           -113.752
       Akaike's Information Criterion -115.752
       Schwarz's Bayesian Criterion  -117.895
       -2 REML Log Likelihood         227.5033
       PARMS Model LRT Chi-Square        0.3459
       PARMS Model LRT DF                1.0000
       PARMS Model LRT P-Value           0.5564
```

Interpretation

Key items are

- The estimated **range**, or ρ, is given in the "Covariance Parameter Estimates" table as DIAG SP(SPH). The estimated ρ is 2.712 with a standard error of 0.446.

- The estimated **sill**, or σ^2, also in the "Covariance Parameter Estimates" table, is given by the parameter "Residual." Here, the estimated σ^2 is 3.261 with a standard error of 0.656.

- The model fitting criteria are

REML Log Likelihood	-113.752
Akaike's Information Criterion	-115.752
Schwarz's Bayesian Criterion	-117.895
-2 REML Log Likelihood	227.5033

  These can be compared to corresponding criteria for other covariance models, such as exponential or Gaussian, or to alternative models, such as the complete block or incomplete block models mentioned above.

- The likelihood ratio test information is

PARMS Model LRT Chi-Square	0.3459
PARMS Model LRT DF	1.0000
PARMS Model LRT P-Value	0.5564

  Treat this output with care. The parameter tested is ρ, but the hypothesis actually tested here is H_0: $\rho = \rho_0$, where ρ_0 is the starting value of ρ from the search procedure initiated by the PARMS option. You can determine ρ_0 from the output: it is the value of ρ corresponding to the highest value of the REML log likelihood (REML_LL) in the "Parameter Search" table. In this case, $\rho_0 = 2.5$.

9.5.2 Likelihood-Ratio Test of Spatial Covariance

A more reasonable way to evaluate the model is to test H_0: $\rho = 0$. You can do this by computing a likelihood ratio statistic as the difference between the -2REML_LL given above (227.50) and the -2REML_LL obtained from the model for which $\rho = 0$, i.e., the independent errors model.

You can obtain the latter -2REML_LL using the program

```
proc mixed;
   model yield=;
   title 'zero covariance model - independent errors';
run;
```

The resulting -2REML_LL is 255.39. Thus, the likelihood ratio statistic is $255.39 - 227.50 = 27.89$. Because the spherical model has two covariance parameters (ρ and σ^2) whereas the independent errors model has one (σ^2), the resulting likelihood ratio test has one degree of freedom. Comparing 27.89 to $\chi^2_{(1)}$, H_0 is clearly rejected for any reasonable α. Thus, we can conclude that these data contain significant spatial variability.

9.5.3 Comparing Spatial Covariance Models

You can compare the spherical model to other models.

Program

For instance, you can estimate the parameters of the exponential model using the program:

```
proc mixed scoring=5;
   model yield= ;
   parms (0 to 10 by 2.5) (1 to 10 by 3);
   repeated / subject=intercept type=sp(exp)(row col);
   title 'no nugget - exponential covariance model';
run;
```

This program is identical to the program for the spherical model except TYPE=SP(EXP) replaces TYPE=SP(SPH) in the REPEATED statement. The same program using TYPE=SP(GAU) estimates the parameters of the Gaussian covariance model.

The results for the exponential and Gaussian models are given in Output 9.2.

Results

Output 9.2 *Results of Fitting Exponential and Gaussian Covariance Models*

```
                         no nugget - exponential covariance model


                   Covariance Parameter Estimates (REML)

   Cov Parm          Ratio      Estimate     Std Error      Z    Pr > |Z|

   DIAG SP(EXP)    0.43438498  1.75419519   0.89814309    1.95    0.0508
   Residual        1.00000000  4.03834219   1.66601133    2.42    0.0154


                    Model Fitting Information for YIELD

          Description                          Value

          Observations                        64.0000
          Variance Estimate                    4.0383
          Standard Deviation Estimate          2.0096
          REML Log Likelihood               -116.287
          Akaike's Information Criterion     -118.287
          Schwarz's Bayesian Criterion      -120.430
          -2 REML Log Likelihood             232.5740
          PARMS Model LRT Chi-Square            0.3480
          PARMS Model LRT DF                    1.0000
          PARMS Model LRT P-Value               0.5552



                     no nugget - gaussian covariance model
```

```
                    Covariance Parameter Estimates (REML)

Cov Parm              Ratio      Estimate    Std Error     Z   Pr > |Z|

DIAG SP(GAU)      0.00000000   0.00000000       .          .       .
Residual          1.00000000   3.15784641   0.56264664   5.61   0.0001
                    Model Fitting Information for YIELD

                   Description                 Value

                   Observations               64.0000
                   Variance Estimate           3.1578
                   Standard Deviation Estimate 1.7770
                   REML Log Likelihood      -127.694
                   Akaike's Information Criterion -129.694
                   Schwarz's Bayesian Criterion  -131.837
                   -2 REML Log Likelihood    255.3882
                   PARMS Model LRT Chi-Square   0.0000
                   PARMS Model LRT DF           1.0000
                   PARMS Model LRT P-Value      1.0000
```

Interpretation

You can use the model fitting information in Output 9.2 to decide whether either the exponential or Gaussian model fits the data better than the spherical. Here are the relevant results:

Gaussian

Akaike's Information Criterion	-129.694
Schwarz's Bayesian Criterion	-131.837
-2 REML Log Likelihood	255.388

Exponential

Akaike's Information Criterion	-118.287
Schwarz's Bayesian Criterion	-120.430
-2 REML Log Likelihood	232.574

Spherical

Akaike's Information Criterion	-115.752
Schwarz's Bayesian Criterion	-117.895
-2 REML Log Likelihood	227.503

Because all three models have two covariance parameters (ρ and σ^2), a likelihood ratio test is not possible. However, the fact that the spherical model has the highest Akaike and Schwarz statistics and the lowest -2REML_LL suggests that the spherical model is the best of the three.

9.5.4 Comparing Spatial Models to Nonspatial Models

You can also compare nonspatial models with spatial models. To complete the objectives of this uniformity trial, the complete block and incomplete block models must be evaluated.

Program

You can obtain the relevant model fitting information from the programs:

```
proc mixed;
   class rep;
   model yield= ;
   random rep;
   title 'complete block error model';
run;

proc mixed;
   class bloc;
   model yield= ;
   random bloc;
   title 'incomplete block error model';
run;
```

Selected results are given in Output 9.3.

Results

Output 9.3 *Results of Nonspatial Models for Yield Trial Data*

```
                              rcb error model


                 Covariance Parameter Estimates (REML)

   Cov Parm          Ratio        Estimate     Std Error        Z   Pr > |Z|

   REP          -0.00000000    -0.00000000          .           .         .
   Residual      1.00000000     3.15784641    0.56264664      5.61    0.0001


                   Model Fitting Information for YIELD

      Description                              Value

      Observations                           64.0000
      Variance Estimate                       3.1578
      Standard Deviation Estimate             1.7770
      REML Log Likelihood                  -127.694
      Akaike's Information Criterion       -129.694
      Schwarz's Bayesian Criterion         -131.837
      -2 REML Log Likelihood                255.3882


                       incomplete block error model


                 Covariance Parameter Estimates (REML)

    Cov Parm          Ratio        Estimate     Std Error        Z   Pr > |Z|

    BLOC          0.72590924    1.35532004    0.67211938      2.02    0.0437
    Residual      1.00000000    1.86706542    0.38111313      4.90    0.0001
```

```
            Model Fitting Information for YIELD

        Description                         Value

        Observations                        64.0000
        Variance Estimate                    1.8671
        Standard Deviation Estimate          1.3664
        REML Log Likelihood               -121.354
        Akaike's Information Criterion    -123.354
        Schwarz's Bayesian Criterion      -125.498
        -2 REML Log Likelihood             242.7089
```

Interpretation

The following points are relevant to the objective of the uniformity trial.

- The estimated REP variance component is 0 and the −2REML_LL is 255.39—the same as the independent errors model without blocking. This means that because of spatial variability there is as much variability among the plots *within* the proposed complete blocks as there is variability *among the blocks themselves*. Thus, a randomized complete block design is a poor choice for an experiment conducted in this field. The resulting information would be just as imprecise as a completely random design.

- The estimated BLOC variance is 1.355 and the −2REML_LL is 242.71. Thus, the incomplete block design would clearly do a better job controlling field heterogeneity than would a complete block design. However, the −2REML_LL is much higher than either the exponential or spherical covariance models. Thus, using the incomplete block model is less desirable than modeling spatial covariance directly. Section 9.6 further examines the consequences of using a blocked model versus a covariance model.

9.5.5 Estimating the Model with a Nugget Effect

You can estimate a model with a nugget effect by modifying the PARMS and REPEATED statements.

Program

For example, the following program allows you to estimate a spherical model with a nugget effect:

```
proc mixed scoring=50 convh=1e-06;
   model yield= ;
   parms (0 to 10 by 2.5) (1 to 10 by 3) (0.05 to 1.05 by 0.25);
   repeated / subject=intercept local type=sp(sph)(row col);
   title ' nugget effect - spherical covariance model';
run;
```

The REPEATED statement is identical to the REPEATED statement used to estimate the no-nugget spherical model given in section 9.5.1, except that the LOCAL option is added to the list of options. The LOCAL option adds the NUGGET parameter σ_1^2 to σ^2 and ρ used in the no-nugget model — i.e. it adds $\mathbf{I}\sigma_1^2$ to the covariance matrix so that the modified covariance matrix is now $\sigma^2\mathbf{F} + \mathbf{I}\sigma_1^2$, as defined in section 9.3.

If you use the PARMS statement, you must include some specification for σ_1^2. The value(s) are given last because that is the order in which PROC MIXED treats σ_1^2.

In this program, the PROC MIXED statement has been modified. SCORING=50 uses the scoring algorithm for all 50 iterations of the REML procedure. You could also modify the default limit of 50 iterations if necessary. The CONVH=1E-06 option reduces the convergence criterion from 10^{-8} to 10^{-6}. Options this extreme are not ordinarily necessary, but they can be used if the REML procedure does not otherwise converge. The iterations histories obtained using

```
proc mixed scoring=5;
```

and using

```
proc mixed scoring=50 convh=1e-06;
```

are given in Output 9.4.

Results of Iteration Using Different Convergence Criteria

Output 9.4 *Iteration Results Fitting Nugget Effect - Spherical Covariance Model*

---

using PROC MIXED SCORING=50 CONVH=1E-06;

REML Estimation Iteration History

Iteration	Evaluations	Objective	Criterion
1	3	112.81588923	0.03064546
2	2	111.73684461	0.00019468
3	1	111.73118137	0.00008045
4	1	111.72842874	0.00003120
5	1	111.72745586	0.00001258
6	1	111.72697691	0.00000513
7	1	111.72679072	0.00000230
8	1	111.72666511	0.00000119
9	1	111.72659435	0.00000076

Scoring did not stop.

Convergence criteria met.

using PROC MIXED SCORING=5;

REML Estimation Iteration History

Iteration	Evaluations	Objective	Criterion
1	3	112.81588923	0.03064546
2	2	111.73684461	0.00019468
3	1	111.73118137	0.00008045
4	1	111.72842874	0.00003120
5	1	111.72745586	0.00001258
6	1	111.72697691	0.00004664
7	1	111.72348648	0.00002892
8	1	111.72348367	0.00002890

```
          9          1  111.72348366    0.00002890
         10          1  111.72348366    0.00002890
         11          1  111.72348366    0.00002890
         12          1  111.72348366    0.00002890
          .          .  .               .

          .          .  .               .

          .          .  .               .

         50          1  111.72348365    0.00002890

          Scoring stopped after iteration 5.

                    Did not converge.
```

Interpretation

With SCORING=5, the CRITERION made progress to .00001258 by the fifth iteration, then regressed to .00004664 on the sixth iteration, when scoring ceased to be used. It then progressed to .00002890 on the eighth iteration and made no further progress. With SCORING=50 the CRITERION made steady progress until reaching the convergence criterion of 10^{-6} on the ninth iteration. The program

```
proc mixed scoring=50;
```

without the CONVH modification was also run. The CRITERION never got much lower than the .00000076 value given in Output 9.5. It never reached as low as 10^{-7}. Thus, the CONVH=1E-06 option was used to obtain convergence.

The parameter estimates and model fitting information are given in Output 9.5.

Results of Nugget-Effect Spherical Covariance Model Estimation

Output 9.5 *Nugget Effect - Spherical Covariance Model*

```
              Covariance Parameter Estimates (REML)

Cov Parm            Ratio      Estimate    Std Error      Z    Pr > |Z|

DIAG Diagonal   271.96327117   3.23565391  0.68560704   4.72    0.0001
     SP(SPH)    227.99646164   2.71256350  0.44487235   6.10    0.0001
Residual          1.00000000   0.01189739  0.11063921   0.11    0.9144


               Model Fitting Information for YIELD

              Description                         Value

              Observations                       64.0000
              Variance Estimate                   0.0119
              Standard Deviation Estimate         0.1091
              REML Log Likelihood              -113.756
              Akaike's Information Criterion    -116.756
              Schwarz's Bayesian Criterion     -119.971
              -2 REML Log Likelihood            227.5128
              PARMS Model LRT Chi-Square           5.9712
              PARMS Model LRT DF                   2.0000
              PARMS Model LRT P-Value              0.0505
```

Interpretation

Key results are as follows. First, from the "Covariance Parameter Estimates" table:

- The estimated **sill**, σ^2, appears as "DIAG Diagonal." The estimated σ^2 is 3.236 with a standard error of 0.686.

- The estimated **range**, ρ, appears as "SP(SPH)." The estimated ρ is 2.713 with a standard error of 0.445.

- The estimated **nugget**, σ_1^2 appears as "Residual." The estimated σ_1^2 is 0.012 with a standard error of 0.111.

Second, from the "Model Fitting Information" table

REML Log Likelihood	-113.756
Akaike's Information Criterion	-116.756
Schwarz's Bayesian Criterion	-119.971
-2 REML Log Likelihood	227.513

These values are almost indistinguishable from the model fitting statistics obtained for the no-nugget spherical model discussed in section 9.5.1. This is evidence that the nugget effect is zero. A formal likelihood ratio statistic to test $H_0{:}\sigma_1^2{=}0$ can be calculated from the difference between the -2REML_LL's of the nugget and no-nugget models. The test has one degree of freedom because the nugget model has three parameters and the no-nugget model has two. In this case, the result seems obvious by inspection — actually doing the calculations does not seem warranted.

Also in the model fitting table is the PARMS model likelihood ratio test:

PARMS Model LRT Chi-Square	5.9712
PARMS Model LRT DF	2.0000
PARMS Model LRT P-Value	0.0505

This output tests the joint hypothesis that $\sigma^2 = (\sigma^2)_0$ and $\rho = \rho_0$, where $(\sigma^2)_0$ and ρ_0 are the values of σ^2 and ρ, respectively, from the parameter search minimizing the REML log likelihood. These results are not very meaningful.

9.6 Examples: Using Spatial Covariance for Adjustment

PROC MIXED is especially useful for estimating regression and analysis of variance models when the assumption of independent errors is violated, as it is whenever spatial variability is present. Failure to account for correlated errors can result in severely distorted regression estimates or erroneous conclusions about treatment effects. In this section, we will present two examples showing how to used PROC MIXED to adjust for spatial correlation. The first is a regression example, and the second is an analysis of variance example.

9.6.1 A Regression Example

This example is from an environmental study. The investigator wanted to evaluate water drainage characteristics at a potential hazardous waste disposal site. The data are given in Appendix 4, Data Set 9.6.1. Thirty samples were taken at various locations in the site. Locations were classified by their north-south (NORTHING) and east-west (EASTING) coordinates. Water movement was measured by log-transmissivity (LOGT). The investigator suspected that a linear relationship existed between LOGT and the thickness of a layer of salt

(SALT), which was a geological feature of the area. Also, the LOGT of samples relatively close together were suspected to be more alike than those farther apart.

Spatial Covariance Model

You can describe the linear relationship between LOGT and SALT by the regression model

$$LOGT = \beta_0 + \beta_1 SALT + e$$

However, unlike standard regression, inference on this model must take spatial correlation among the errors into account.

Program

An example of an appropriate PROC MIXED program to analyze these data is

```
proc mixed scoring=50;
   model logt=salt/solution;
   parms (1 to 7 by 3) (2 to 17 by 5) (0.1 to 0.5 by 0.2);
   repeated / subject=intercept local
                type=sp(exp)(easting northing);
   title 'exponential covariance model';
run;
```

As discussed in section 9.5, while the SCORING and PARMS options are not mandatory, we strongly recommended using them. They serve two purposes: 1) they improve convergence, and 2) they improve the likelihood of obtaining reasonable estimates of the spatial covariance parameters. In this case, the choice of an exponential covariance model with a nonzero nugget effect and the range of starting values used in the PARMS statement are based on the investigators' prior experience. In the absence of clear-cut guidelines, you can use model comparisons like those presented in section 9.5.

The results of this analysis are given in Output 9.6.

Results

Output 9.6 *Regression Example with Exponential Covariance Model*

```
                  Covariance Parameter Estimates (REML)

Cov Parm              Ratio      Estimate     Std Error      Z   Pr > |Z|

DIAG Diagonal      61.40710164   2.52628996   2.53025476   1.00   0.3181
      SP(EXP)     280.32921652  11.53275217  13.82908989   0.83   0.4043
Residual            1.00000000   0.04114003   0.06345252   0.65   0.5168




                  Model Fitting Information for LOGT


             Description                        Value

             Observations                     30.0000
             Variance Estimate                 0.0411
```

```
      Standard Deviation Estimate          0.2028
      REML Log Likelihood                -39.3953
      Akaike's Information Criterion     -42.3953
      Schwarz's Bayesian Criterion       -44.3936
      -2 REML Log Likelihood              78.7906
      PARMS Model LRT Chi-Square           0.0052
      PARMS Model LRT DF                   2.0000
      PARMS Model LRT P-Value              0.9974



                Solution for Fixed Effects


      Parameter       Estimate      Std Error    DDF         T   Pr > |T|


      INTERCEPT     -5.09934562    0.89223492      0     -5.72        .
      SALT          -0.02116848    0.00622921     28     -3.40   0.0021



                Tests of Fixed Effects


      Source         NDF    DDF   Type III F   Pr > F


      SALT             1     28       11.55    0.0021
```

The key items are

- The "Covariance Parameter Estimates" table. The estimated **sill**, σ^2 (DIAG Diagonal), is 2.526 with a standard error of 2.530. The estimated **range**, ρ (DIAG SP(EXP)), is 11.533 with a standard error of 13.829. The estimated **nugget effect**, σ_1^2 (Residual), is 0.041 with a standard error of 0.063.

- The "Solutions for Fixed Effects" table. The estimated intercept, β_0 is -5.099 with a standard error of 0.892. The estimated slope, β_1, is -0.021 with a standard error of 0.006.

- The "Test of Fixed Effects" table. The F-value for the test of $H_0: \beta_1 = 0$ is 11.55, with a p-value of 0.0021.

- The "Model Fitting Information" table. The -2REML_LL, Akaike and Schwarz criteria can be used to compare the exponential covariance model with other alternatives.

As noted in Section 9.5, the likelihood ratio test information presented here must be treated with care. The statistics test the joint hypothesis that the sill and range, σ^2 and ρ, are equal to the starting values selected by the PARMS option parameter search. A more reasonable approach compares the -2REML_LL for this model with the corresponding -2REML_LL for the independent errors model. This tests $H_0: \rho=0$ and $\sigma_1^2=0$, which is interpreted as a test of the existence of spatial variability. This test is a χ^2 test with 2 degrees of freedom, corresponding to the 2 parameters tested. Fitting the independent errors model, the -2REML_LL is 94.07. The resulting likelihood ratio χ^2 value is $94.07-78.79=15.28$. Therefore, you conclude that significant spatial variability exists at this site.

Comparison with Independent Errors Model

A final point to consider is how much the regression estimates and conclusions about the effect of SALT thickness on LOGT are affected by accounting for spatial covariance among the errors. You can estimate the regression equation under the assumption of independent errors using several SAS procedures, for example, PROC REG, PROC GLM, as well as PROC MIXED. The PROC MIXED program is

```
proc mixed;
    model logt=salt/solution;
run;
```

This results in an estimated intercept, β_0 and slope, β_1, of -5.025 and -0.034, respectively. The F-value to test $H_0{:}\beta_1{=}0$ is 26.46 with a p-value of 0.0001. The magnitude of the slope estimate is roughly 50% greater and the F-value is over twice as large. While the general conclusions *for this particular data set* do not change, it is easy to see that they could be greatly affected in other data sets.

Different Covariance Models

Finally, you could try a different covariance model. For example, if you fit a spherical model with a nugget effect, the -2REML_LL is 79.49, which is only negligibly different from the exponential model. The estimated intercept and slope are -5.110 and -0.021, respectively. The F-value to test slope is 10.95 with a p-value of 0.0026. Again, these are only negligibly different from the results obtained using the exponential model. This is typical of spatially correlated data — the major impact on inference results from using a *reasonable* covariance model. The specific model used is not nearly as important, as long as it is "in the ballpark."

9.6.2 An Analysis of Variance Example

This example is from an agronomic yield trial reported by Stroup and Baenziger (1994). The investigator wanted to compare the mean yield of fifty-six varieties of wheat. A randomized complete block (RCB) design was used — all varieties were planted in each of four blocks. The data are given in Appendix 4, Data Set 9.6.2.

The variables in the data set are wheat variety (NAME), block (REP), field plot location by row (LAT) and column (LNG), and YIELD.

Models

The standard analysis of variance model for this experiment is

$$y_{ij} = \mu + r_i + \tau_j + e_{ij}$$

where r_i is the block (REP) effect, τ_j is the variety (NAME) effect, and the errors (e_{ij}) are iid normal. As a practical matter, however, 56 field plots per block may be too many to expect within-block homogeneity. In addition, after doing a standard ANOVA, the investigator was troubled by several results that did not make sense. These are discussed below.

An alternative model for these data is

$$y_{ij} = \mu + \tau_j + e_{ij}$$

where the errors are assumed to be spatially correlated. This model made biological sense to the investigator because the variability at the location did seem to consist of the sort of irregular fertility gradients that would be expected in a spatial correlation process.

The model was fit in two ways, one using REML covariance estimates (obtained as in sections 9.5 and 9.6.1) and the other using an empirical semivariogram to obtain a reasonable spatial covariance model. PROC MIXED does not compute semivariograms or use them in model-fitting. However, in many cases (these data are an example) using a semivariogram procedure external to PROC MIXED yields more reasonable covariance estimates than does the REML procedure. Semivariogram procedures are described in Journel and Huijbregts (1978) and Cressie (1991).

Figure 9.2 *Estimated Semivariogram*

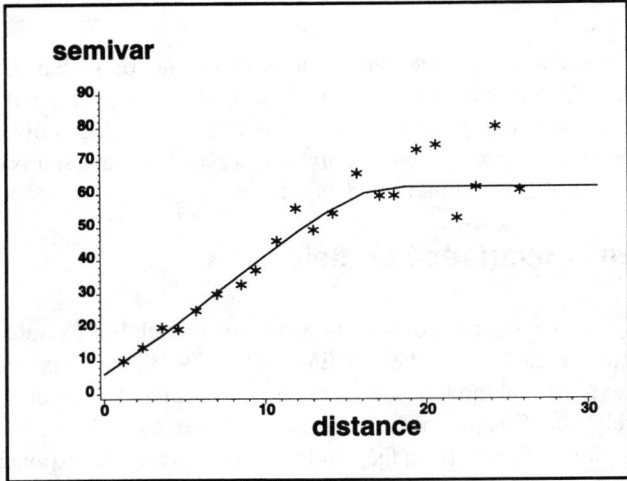

Figure 9.2 shows the estimated semivariogram for these data. The resulting spatial covariance model was spherical with a range, ρ, of 18.1 and a sill, σ^2, of 61.6.

Program

You can use these values to obtain appropriate estimates and test statistics for the ANOVA model with spatial correlation using the following program:

```
proc mixed noprofile;
   class name;
   model y=name;
   parms (61.6) (18.1)(1)/ noiter;
   repeated / subject=intercept type=sp(sph)(lat lng);
   lsmeans name;
   estimate 'arap v brul' name 1 -1 0;
   estimate 'arap v buck' name 1 0 -1 0;
   estimate 'arap v ks83' name 1 0 0 0 0 0 0 0 0 0 -1 0;
   estimate 'brul v ks83' name 0 1 0 0 0 0 0 0 0 0 -1 0;
run;
```

The ESTIMATE statements given here are just examples. The NOITER option in the PARMS statement prevents iteration. The NOPROFILE option in the PROC statement causes the residual variance to be included in the REML variance estimation procedure. Otherwise, PROC MIXED attempts to estimate a second error variance. The two options work together to force the values of σ^2 and ρ given in PARMS to be used in solving the mixed model equations.

Results

The covariance estimates, model fitting information, and test of fixed effects appear in Output 9.7(a). Output 9.7(b) contains the LSMEANS.

Output 9.7(a) *Analysis of Yield Trial Using Covariance Estimates from Semivariogram*

```
                    Covariance Parameter Estimates (Parms)

            Cov Parm              Ratio        Estimate

            DIAG Diagonal    61.600000000    61.60000000
                 SP(SPH)     18.100000000    18.10000000
            Residual          1.00000000      1.00000000


                    Model Fitting Information for Y

            Description                        Value

            Observations                     224.0000
            Variance Estimate                  0.0000
            Standard Deviation Estimate        0.0010
            REML Log Likelihood             -584.796
            Akaike's Information Criterion  -587.796
            Schwarz's Bayesian Criterion    -592.482
            -2 REML Log Likelihood          1169.592


                        Tests of Fixed Effects

            Source      NDF   DDF  Type III F  Pr > F

            NAME         55   168       6.09   0.0001


                       ESTIMATE Statement Results

Parameter               Estimate     Std Error   DDF      T  Pr > |T|

arap v brul            1.62784959    1.90045475  168   0.86   0.3929
arap v buck           -9.13236343    1.97477560  168  -4.62   0.0001
arap v ks83            0.43849704    1.92329483  168   0.23   0.8199
brul v ks83           -1.18935255    1.91970540  168  -0.62   0.5364
```

Output 9.7(b) *Least Squares Means for Yield Trial Data Using Semivariogram Estimates*

```
Level                LSMEAN      Std Error   DDF      T  Pr > |T|

NAME ARAPAHOE      28.21443538   2.77222759  168  10.18   0.0001
NAME BRULE         26.58658579   2.78520666  168   9.55   0.0001
NAME BUCKSKIN      37.34679881   2.82695769  168  13.21   0.0001
NAME CENTURA       27.05147945   2.80064257  168   9.66   0.0001
NAME CENTURK 78    26.81412320   2.80572202  168   9.56   0.0001
NAME CHEYENNE      26.96665613   2.78738312  168   9.67   0.0001
NAME CODY          22.03026461   2.78389605  168   7.91   0.0001
NAME COLT          26.58619459   2.77778862  168   9.57   0.0001
NAME GAGE          24.92977708   2.77405452  168   8.99   0.0001
NAME HOMESTEAD     22.41054487   2.78166410  168   8.06   0.0001
NAME KS831374      27.77593835   2.76850131  168  10.03   0.0001
NAME LANCER        25.55644815   2.78828911  168   9.17   0.0001
```

NAME	LANCOTA	21.99290607	2.80666947	168	7.84	0.0001
NAME	NE83404	24.89078940	2.77349482	168	8.97	0.0001
NAME	NE83406	26.94748528	2.79289146	168	9.65	0.0001
NAME	NE83407	25.50279804	2.79739219	168	9.12	0.0001
NAME	NE8343	23.14511136	2.77130237	168	8.35	0.0001
NAME	NE83498	29.03472884	2.79931696	168	10.37	0.0001
NAME	NE83T12	24.38248277	2.79915027	168	8.71	0.0001
NAME	NE84557	24.65803495	2.77662907	168	8.88	0.0001
NAME	NE85556	30.41972511	2.76812375	168	10.99	0.0001
NAME	NE85623	25.59011539	2.77081262	168	9.24	0.0001
NAME	NE86482	26.54448229	2.78094537	168	9.55	0.0001
NAME	NE86501	25.73317241	2.79336967	168	9.21	0.0001
NAME	NE86503	27.70064819	2.78623640	168	9.94	0.0001
NAME	NE86507	28.13470216	2.78998260	168	10.08	0.0001
NAME	NE86509	24.33302866	2.79336038	168	8.71	0.0001
NAME	NE86527	28.98786062	2.79014258	168	10.39	0.0001
NAME	NE86582	22.75046799	2.79755881	168	8.13	0.0001
NAME	NE86606	27.89905217	2.80165378	168	9.96	0.0001
NAME	NE86607	27.99270989	2.81069690	168	9.96	0.0001
NAME	NE86T666	15.86353322	2.83703366	168	5.59	0.0001
NAME	NE87403	20.66009819	2.79935722	168	7.38	0.0001
NAME	NE87408	24.96623381	2.79799319	168	8.92	0.0001
NAME	NE87409	27.64844719	2.78562305	168	9.93	0.0001
NAME	NE87446	23.33722888	2.77756544	168	8.40	0.0001
NAME	NE87451	25.16615860	2.78286481	168	9.04	0.0001
NAME	NE87457	25.36436030	2.79356477	168	9.08	0.0001
NAME	NE87463	24.73404924	2.80058497	168	8.83	0.0001
NAME	NE87499	23.86464646	2.79023373	168	8.55	0.0001
NAME	NE87512	22.91262237	2.79683859	168	8.19	0.0001
NAME	NE87513	22.35995212	2.80169847	168	7.98	0.0001
NAME	NE87522	20.79652260	2.78822127	168	7.46	0.0001
NAME	NE87612	26.83693111	2.83602362	168	9.46	0.0001
NAME	NE87613	27.60331349	2.79307285	168	9.88	0.0001
NAME	NE87615	24.40430445	2.77401605	168	8.80	0.0001
NAME	NE87619	29.18401903	2.78784516	168	10.47	0.0001
NAME	NE87627	18.12804158	2.82138044	168	6.43	0.0001
NAME	NORKAN	21.22304118	2.77187996	168	7.66	0.0001
NAME	REDLAND	29.09439350	2.77523735	168	10.48	0.0001
NAME	ROUGHRIDER	27.76525935	2.80800465	168	9.89	0.0001
NAME	SCOUT 66	28.77384929	2.78415329	168	10.33	0.0001
NAME	SIOUXLAND	26.49038269	2.79418347	168	9.48	0.0001
NAME	TAM 107	24.55920215	2.77834404	168	8.84	0.0001
NAME	TAM 200	19.22925349	2.77182946	168	6.94	0.0001
NAME	VONA	25.70623348	2.81524079	168	9.13	0.0001

Interpretation

The key results are

- The F-value for the hypothesis of equal variety (NAME) means is 6.09, with a *p*-value of 0.0001. In the standard RCB ANOVA, the F-value was 0.88.

- The -2REML_LL is 1169.59. In the RCB ANOVA, the -2REML_LL was 1217.70, indicating that the spatial covariance model is a far more accurate description of variability among the data.

- The standard errors for the LSMEANS are not constant. Their values depend on the particular field plots assigned to a given entry and their location relative to spatial gradients. Similar variation occurs in the standard errors for treatment differences as well.

The standard error of a mean using the RCB model is 3.86, whereas the standard errors for the spatial covariance model vary from 2.76 to 2.84. It is *not necessarily true* that a better fitting model will yield lower standard errors. This point is discussed further in the next subsection.

LSMEANS of RCB Analysis Compared with Spatial Covariance Model

One of the results that troubled the investigator was that the variety BUCKSKIN was known to be a superior performer. This was confirmed by observations in the field. BUCKSKIN performed noticeably better than the varieties in nearby plots. However, in the RCB analysis, BUCKSKIN had the 28th highest yield and certainly would not have been identified as a desirable variety. Using the spatial covariance model, BUCKSKIN's LSMEAN yield was almost 7 units higher than the second best yielding variety. Also, the varieties BRULE and KS831374 were known to be similar. Although not statistically significant, their yields differed by 1.95 in the RCB analysis. This difference was 1.12 in the spatial correlation model. These were two of several reasons why the spatial correlation model gave more plausible results to the investigator than the RCB ANOVA.

Output 9.8 contains the LSMEANS and ranking (1=highest yield, 56=lowest) for the RCB and spatial covariance (SPH) model.

Output 9.8 *Rankings of LSMEANS — RCB versus Spatial (SPH) Analysis*

OBS	LEVEL		RCB	RCB_RANK	SPH	SPH_RANK
1	NAME	NE86503	32.6500	1	27.7006	14
2	NAME	NE87619	31.2625	2	29.1840	3
3	NAME	NE86501	30.9375	3	25.7332	26
4	NAME	REDLAND	30.5000	4	29.0944	4
5	NAME	CENTURK 78	30.3000	5	26.8141	21
6	NAME	NE83498	30.1250	6	29.0347	5
7	NAME	SIOUXLAND	30.1125	7	26.4904	25
8	NAME	NE86606	29.7625	8	27.8991	11
9	NAME	ARAPAHOE	29.4375	9	28.2144	8
10	NAME	NE87613	29.4000	10	27.6033	16
11	NAME	NE86607	29.3250	11	27.9927	10
12	NAME	LANCER	28.5625	12	25.5564	29
13	NAME	TAM 107	28.4000	13	24.5592	38
14	NAME	CHEYENNE	28.0625	14	26.9667	18
15	NAME	NE87446	27.6750	15	23.3372	43
16	NAME	HOMESTEAD	27.6375	16	22.4105	47
17	NAME	SCOUT 66	27.5250	17	28.7738	7
18	NAME	NE83404	27.3875	18	24.8908	35
19	NAME	COLT	27.0000	19	26.5862	23
20	NAME	NE86509	26.8500	20	24.3330	41
21	NAME	NE87513	26.8125	21	22.3600	48
22	NAME	LANCOTA	26.5500	22	21.9929	50
23	NAME	NE85556	26.3875	23	30.4197	2
24	NAME	NE87408	26.3000	24	24.9662	33

25	NAME BRULE	26.0750	25	26.5866	22
26	NAME NE87463	25.9125	26	24.7340	36
27	NAME NE87615	25.6875	27	24.4043	39
28	NAME BUCKSKIN	25.5625	28	37.3468	1
29	NAME NE87403	25.1250	29	20.6601	53
30	NAME NE87522	25.0000	30	20.7965	52
31	NAME NE87451	24.6125	31	25.1662	32
32	NAME NE86582	24.5375	32	22.7505	46
33	NAME GAGE	24.5125	33	24.9298	34
34	NAME NORKAN	24.4125	34	21.2230	51
35	NAME NE86482	24.2875	35	26.5445	24
36	NAME NE83406	24.2750	36	26.9475	19
37	NAME KS831374	24.1250	37	27.7759	12
38	NAME NE87457	23.9125	38	25.3644	31
39	NAME NE86507	23.7875	39	28.1347	9
40	NAME VONA	23.6000	40	25.7062	27
41	NAME NE87512	23.2500	41	22.9126	45
42	NAME NE87627	23.2250	42	18.1280	55
43	NAME NE83407	22.6875	43	25.5028	30
44	NAME NE86527	22.0125	44	28.9879	6
45	NAME NE87612	21.8000	45	26.8369	20
46	NAME NE85623	21.7250	46	25.5901	28
47	NAME CENTURA	21.6500	47	27.0515	17
48	NAME NE83T12	21.5625	48	24.3825	40
49	NAME NE86T666	21.5375	49	15.8635	56
50	NAME NE87409	21.3750	50	27.6484	15
51	NAME TAM 200	21.2375	51	19.2293	54
52	NAME CODY	21.2125	52	22.0303	49
53	NAME ROUGHRIDER	21.1875	53	27.7653	13
54	NAME NE84557	20.5250	54	24.6580	37
55	NAME NE87499	20.4125	55	23.8646	42
56	NAME NE83432	19.7250	56	23.1451	44

Interpretation

The table is ranked by the order of preference that would have resulted from using the RCB ANOVA. The discrepancy between the two sets of rankings is striking. This illustrates the severely deceptive conclusions that can result from failing to account for spatial variability.

9.7 A Caution about Estimating Spatial Covariance

The yield trial example presented in Section 9.6.2 used estimates of σ^2 and ρ obtained from an empirical semivariogram. You can also estimate σ^2 and ρ using REML in PROC MIXED, as shown in the examples in sections 9.5 and 9.6.1.

Program

The program to analyze the data using the spherical covariance model with REML covariance estimates is

```
proc mixed;
   class name;
   model y=name;
   parms (0 to 20 by 5) (25 to 100 by 75);
   repeated / subject=intercept type=sp(sph)(lat lng);
   lsmeans name;
run;
```

However, the yield trial data illustrate a problem that may occur with REML.

Results

Outputs 9.9(a) and 9.9(b) contain the results of the REML analysis of the yield trial. Output 9.9(b) contains the LSMEANS, and Output 9.9(a) contains the rest of the analysis.

Output 9.9(a) *Analysis of Yield Trial Data*

```
                  Spherical Covariance Model - REML Estimates


                  Covariance Parameter Estimates (REML)

Cov Parm            Ratio        Estimate     Std Error      Z    Pr > |Z|

DIAG SP(SPH)      0.14021158   21.16149005   0.92521018   22.87   0.0001
Residual          1.00000000  150.92541169  17.01992515    8.87   0.0001


                  Model Fitting Information for Y

           Description                         Value

           Observations                       224.0000
           Variance Estimate                  150.9254
           Standard Deviation Estimate         12.2852
           REML Log Likelihood               -553.169
           Akaike's Information Criterion    -555.169
           Schwarz's Bayesian Criterion      -558.293
           -2 REML Log Likelihood            1106.339
           PARMS Model LRT Chi-Square           0.0333
           PARMS Model LRT DF                   1.0000
           PARMS Model LRT P-Value              0.8552


                  Tests of Fixed Effects

           Source       NDF   DDF   Type III F   Pr > F

           NAME          55   168        2.89    0.0001
```

```
                        ESTIMATE Statement Results

Parameter                 Estimate    Std Error    DDF        T   Pr > |T|


arap v brul              1.52931914   2.75230195   168     0.56    0.5792
arap v buck             -9.20954107   2.86256382   168    -3.22    0.0016
arap v ks83              0.19622627   2.78571656   168     0.07    0.9439
brul v ks83             -1.33309286   2.78862766   168    -0.48    0.6332
```

Output 9.9(b) *Least Squares Means of Yield Trial Data*

```
                  Spherical Covariance - REML Estimates

Level                    LSMEAN     Std Error    DDF        T   Pr > |T|


NAME ARAPAHOE          28.27773655  4.67396964   168     6.05    0.0001
NAME BRULE             26.74841741  4.68668161   168     5.71    0.0001
NAME BUCKSKIN          37.48727761  4.74268630   168     7.90    0.0001
NAME CENTURA           27.11064345  4.70432592   168     5.76    0.0001
NAME CENTURK 78        27.04161031  4.71778687   168     5.73    0.0001
NAME CHEYENNE          26.90345830  4.68809688   168     5.74    0.0001
NAME CODY              22.26288048  4.68753943   168     4.75    0.0001
NAME COLT              26.85081701  4.67298672   168     5.75    0.0001
NAME GAGE              25.09108427  4.67257768   168     5.37    0.0001
NAME HOMESTEAD         22.43362625  4.68017069   168     4.79    0.0001
NAME KS831374          28.08151028  4.65990343   168     6.03    0.0001
NAME LANCER            25.23166131  4.69461674   168     5.37    0.0001
NAME LANCOTA           22.28318664  4.71106000   168     4.73    0.0001
NAME NE83404           24.99612259  4.67261899   168     5.35    0.0001
NAME NE83406           26.78809670  4.69903261   168     5.70    0.0001
NAME NE83407           25.59675022  4.68697505   168     5.46    0.0001
NAME NE83432           23.33708906  4.66772927   168     5.00    0.0001
NAME NE83498           29.05399435  4.70008275   168     6.18    0.0001
NAME NE83T12           24.67771514  4.70966135   168     5.24    0.0001
NAME NE84557           24.47356833  4.67989071   168     5.23    0.0001
NAME NE85556           30.49696741  4.67208993   168     6.53    0.0001
NAME NE85623           25.91472495  4.67682539   168     5.54    0.0001
NAME NE86482           26.90764510  4.67810248   168     5.75    0.0001
NAME NE86501           25.91824612  4.68645123   168     5.53    0.0001
NAME NE86503           27.85815183  4.68287810   168     5.95    0.0001
NAME NE86507           28.21242810  4.69705162   168     6.01    0.0001
NAME NE86509           24.39492941  4.70660918   168     5.18    0.0001
NAME NE86527           29.26520690  4.69008374   168     6.24    0.0001
NAME NE86582           23.08995525  4.70894613   168     4.90    0.0001
NAME NE86606           27.68703259  4.72006768   168     5.87    0.0001
NAME NE86607           27.97833082  4.72290510   168     5.92    0.0001
NAME NE86T666          16.02137978  4.76040047   168     3.37    0.0009
NAME NE87403           20.83836806  4.71098509   168     4.42    0.0001
NAME NE87408           25.36067619  4.69832410   168     5.40    0.0001
NAME NE87409           27.84756263  4.68846536   168     5.94    0.0001
NAME NE87446           23.39487834  4.68266285   168     5.00    0.0001
NAME NE87451           25.34905368  4.68419122   168     5.41    0.0001
NAME NE87457           25.24308255  4.70442279   168     5.37    0.0001
NAME NE87463           24.74680745  4.71507004   168     5.25    0.0001
NAME NE87499           24.00374225  4.69691051   168     5.11    0.0001
NAME NE87512           23.16831968  4.69407257   168     4.94    0.0001
```

NAME NE87513	22.78791364	4.69983821	168	4.85	0.0001
NAME NE87522	20.91203557	4.68422505	168	4.46	0.0001
NAME NE87612	27.07252266	4.73591135	168	5.72	0.0001
NAME NE87613	27.70822709	4.68681920	168	5.91	0.0001
NAME NE87615	24.54404782	4.67635417	168	5.25	0.0001
NAME NE87619	29.46555792	4.69831069	168	6.27	0.0001
NAME NE87627	18.16921218	4.73743461	168	3.84	0.0002
NAME NORKAN	21.36461504	4.67260017	168	4.57	0.0001
NAME REDLAND	29.23342286	4.66867543	168	6.26	0.0001
NAME ROUGHRIDER	27.76502938	4.70758233	168	5.90	0.0001
NAME SCOUT 66	29.04862223	4.68735431	168	6.20	0.0001
NAME SIOUXLAND	26.61971090	4.69368273	168	5.67	0.0001
NAME TAM 107	24.38278344	4.68193904	168	5.21	0.0001
NAME TAM 200	19.53191060	4.66553381	168	4.19	0.0001
NAME VONA	25.63764541	4.71868364	168	5.43	0.0001

Interpretation

The key features of Output 9.9 are

- The -2REML_LL is 1106.34. This compares to 1169.59 for the models using the externally estimated σ^2 and ρ.

- The estimated σ^2 and ρ are 150.92 and 21.16, respectively, compared with 61.6 and 18.1 using the external estimates.

Superficially, REML seems to have produced a better-fitting model. However, the semivariograms shown in Figures 9.2 and 9.3 illustrate the problem.

Figure 9.3 *Semivariogram for All Pairs of Observations*

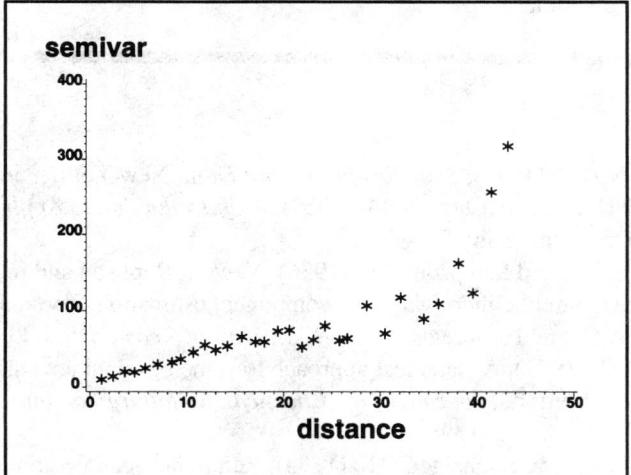

Figure 9.3 shows the semivariogram for *all* pairs of observations, regardless of distance. Figure 9.2 shows the semivariogram edited according to the following rationale. The *full* semivariogram (Figure 9.3) looks like the *text-book* illustration in Figure 9.1, discussed in section 9.2, except for the very high values at the longer distances. The accuracy of these values is highly suspect because they are computed from too few values. That is, there are many pairs of observations at relatively short distances, but few pairs far apart.

You can obtain accurate estimates of covariance at distances where information is ample, but past a critical distance, there are too few pairs for reliable estimation. Most spatial variability experts discount the information from the most distant pairs when estimating spatial covariance, recommending, instead, an edited semivariogram such as Figure 9.2. REML uses information similar to the full semivariogram, thus tending to give the more distant pairs too much weight. For data such as these, the resulting REML estimates, particularly of σ^2, are too high.

In this particular example, the overestimates of σ^2 and ρ have a negligible effect on the estimates of **LSMEANS** and differences, but the F-value for testing equal variety yields is reduced from 6.09 to 2.89, the standard errors of **LSMEANS** increase from a typical value of 2.8 to a typical value of 4.8, and the standard error of a difference increases from a typical value of 1.9 to a typical value of 2.8. Clearly, the covariance models estimated from the semivariogram procedure and from REML could lead to very different conclusions about variety effects.

With reasonable covariance estimates, PROC MIXED is an extremely useful tool for analyzing data with spatial variation. The main caution is that the REML procedure should be used with caution, especially with larger data sets. A reasonable procedure should involve fitting a semivariogram to the residuals of the model fit by REML in PROC MIXED and verifying that it appears reasonable. If it does not, covariance estimates from the semivariogram can be substituted. Also, starting values for REML can be obtained by fitting a semivariogram to the residuals of an independent errors model whose other components (i.e., the fixed and random effects) are the same as the spatial covariance model. In this way, you can take advantage of the most useful features of PROC MIXED for the analysis of spatial data without undue risk of poorly estimated covariance parameters.

9.8 Summary

This chapter shows how to analyze mixed models with spatial variability. PROC MIXED allows you to work with spatially correlated errors. Sections 9.3 and 9.4 described spatial correlation models and showed how you can include them in mixed models. Section 9.5 and 9.6 presented examples using PROC MIXED, showing how to write the needed programs and how to interpret the results. Section 9.7 gave some cautions regarding the reliability of REML estimation.

9.9 References

Cressie, N.A.C. (1991), *Statistics for Spatial Data*, New York: John Wiley & Sons, Inc.

Isaaks, E.H. and Srivastava, R.M. (1989), *An Introduction to Applied Geostatistics*, Oxford: Oxford University Press.

Jennerich, R.J. and Sampson, P.F. (1976), Newton-Raphson and related algorithms for maximum likelihood variance component estimation, *Technometrics*, **18**, 11–17.

Journel, A.G. and Huijbregts, C.J. (1978), *Mining Geostatistics*, London: Academic Press.

Krige, D.G. (1951), A statistical approach to some basic mine valuation problems on the Witswaterrand, *Journal of the Chemical, Metallurgical, and Mining Society of South Africa*, **52**, 119–139.

Stroup, W.W. and Baenziger, P.S. (1994), Removing spatial variation from wheat yield trials: a comparison of methods, *Crop Science*, **34**, 62–66.

Zimmerman, D.L. and Harville, D.A. (1991), A random field approach to the analysis of field-plot experiments and other spatial experiments, *Biometrics*, **47**, 223–239.

Chapter 10 Case Studies

10.1 Introduction

Case studies provide the reader with information that is not centered in a single previous chapter. The case studies in this chapter also provide additional descriptions of experiments and more detail on using the results from PROC MIXED than do most of the examples in the previous chapters. The case studies are from a limited set of areas of application to which mixed models can be used, but it is hoped that the information provided in the case studies enables you to understand and then use the advanced options available in PROC MIXED. When it is instructive to do so, the PROC MIXED results are compared to PROC GLM results.

The case study in Section 10.2 involves the use of a split-plot design for which it is desired to fit a response surface model to data from a corn milling experiment. In Section 10.3, a split-plot design is used for a line-source irrigation study where the levels of the whole-plot factor cannot be randomized and thus the whole-plot experimental units are correlated. Next, an incomplete Latin Square is used for the whole-plot treatments in a complex split-plot design in an agricultural experiment, as described in Section 10.4. A strip-split-split-plot design used to evaluate a reclamation study in the sand hills of Nebraska is described in Section 10.5. The next two examples involve the use of 2^3 factorial treatment structures in the semiconductor industry. The case study in Section 10.6 involves a split-plot design where the three-way interaction is the whole-plot effect, and the one in Section 10.7 involves incomplete blocks with balanced confounding. Section 10.8 consists of a case study involving product acceptability (like taste testing) in a cross-over design with repeated measures. The PROC MIXED code involves using more than one RANDOM statement and the REPEATED statement to fit the desired model. The analysis of multilocation experiments requires the use of mixed models. A multilocation experiment consisting of an on-farm-trial is the topic of Section 10.9. The example in Section 10.10 consists of applying a random coefficients model to data from a multicenter, randomized comparative trial of two compounds in HIV-infected patients.

10.2 Response Surface Experiment in a Split-Plot Design

10.2.1 Introduction

Many industrial applications involve the use of split-plot designs when carrying out experiments. The split-plot design occurs when one or more of the factors in the experiment are "hard to vary" and the researcher "restricts" the randomization of the run order by grouping sets of runs together based on the hard-to-vary factor or factors. The experiment described in this section has one hard-to-vary factor. The experiment consists of milling corn to determine the amount of grits that can be obtained from a one minute run of a grinding mill. The four factors are moisture content of the corn (A), roll gap (B), screen size (C) and roller speed (D). To prepare corn for the experiment, a batch of corn (30 Kg) has to be tempered to the desired moisture content. Thus it was decided to prepare a batch of corn to satisfy a specified moisture content, split the batch of corn into three parts (10 Kg each), and then carry out three runs involving the other three factors. The objective of the experiment is to build a response surface model to describe this milling process. The selected response surface model consists of the linear terms, quadratic terms, and cross product terms of the four factors. An optimal design selected from four factors at three levels with 30 runs was created using PROC OPTEX of the SAS System. The runs were grouped into sets of three runs where each set of three had the same level of moisture. The order of the three runs within a group was randomized and the order of the sets of three runs was randomized. The data along with the factor settings are displayed in Data Set 10.2.1 in Appendix 4, "SAS Data Sets." The three levels for each factor were equally spaced, so the coded values of -1, 0, and 1 are used in the analysis. There are four sets of runs at A=1, four sets of runs at A=-1 and two sets of runs at A=0. Because the three runs within a set were run together, the set of three runs or batch of corn becomes the experimental unit for the levels of A. The run or part of a batch of corn is the experimental unit for the levels of the other three factors.

The second order response surface model used to describe this data is

$$y_{ijk} = \beta_0 + \beta_1 a_i + \beta_2 b_{ijk} + \beta_3 c_{ijk} + \beta_4 d_{ijk} + \beta_5 a_i^2 + \beta_6 b_{ijk}^2 + \beta_7 c_{ijk}^2 + \beta_8 d_{ijk}^2$$
$$+ \beta_9 a_i b_{ijk} + \beta_{10} a_i c_{ijk} + \beta_{11} a_i d_{ijk} + \beta_{12} b_{ijk} c_{ijk} + \beta_{13} b_{ijk} d_{ijk} + \beta_{14} c_{ijk} d_{ijk}$$
$$+ s_{ij} + e_{ijk} \quad i=1,2,3, j=1,...,n_i, k=1,2,3$$

where

$s_{ij}, i=1,2,3, j=1,...,n_i$ denote the batch error terms with
distributions $s_{ij} \sim$ iid $N(0, \sigma_s^2)$

$e_{ijk}, i=1,2,3, j=1,...,n_i, k=1, 2, 3$ denote the run error terms within a batch with
distributions $e_{ij} \sim$ iid $N(0, \sigma_e^2)$

i is the index for the levels of A

j is the index for the batches within a level of A (which can go from 1 to 4 for A=−1
and A=1 and from 1 to 2 for A=0)

k denotes the run within the jth batch within the ith level of A.

We want to fit a regression model with the levels of A playing two roles.

First, we use the levels of A as quantitative in the regression model. Second, we use the levels of A as qualitative (a class variable) to extract the batch-to-batch error term. Because A plays two roles, we need to generate a second variable equivalent to A, in this case denoted by AA, so we can let one play the quantitative role and one play the qualitative role. Thus, the term BATCH(AA) is used to extract the batch-to-batch variation from the data.

10.2.2 Analysis Using PROC MIXED

Program

The program used to read the data and generate the variable AA is

```
data design;
   input batch a b c d y;
   aa=a;
run;
```

Using the above variables, the PROC MIXED program to fit the above model is

```
proc mixed; class batch aa;
   model y=a|b|c|d@2 a*a b*b c*c d*d /solution ;
   random batch(aa);
run;
```

The code A|B|C|D@2 generates the linear and cross product terms in the model and A*A B*B C*C D*D adds the quadratic terms in the model. The SOLUTION option requests that the least squares estimates of the coefficients in the response surface model be displayed along with their estimated standard errors, *t*-values testing the parameter is zero, and resulting significance level. The RANDOM BATCH(AA) enables PROC MIXED to compute the batch-to-batch variance component. By having the random effects in the RANDOM statement and the fixed effects in the MODEL, we can use A as a quantitative variable and a qualitative variable (AA) in the same model and extract all of the information about the parameters of the regression model and of the variance components.

Results are in Output 10.1.

Results

Output 10.1 *PROC MIXED for the Response Surface Model with a Split-Plot Design
without Approximate Degrees of Freedom*

```
                        The MIXED Procedure
                     Class Level Information
           Class     Levels  Values
           BATCH       10    1 2 3 4 5 6 7 8 9 10
           AA           3    0 1 -1
```

Covariance Parameter Estimates (REML)

Cov Parm	Ratio	Estimate	Std Error	Z	Pr > |Z|
BATCH(AA)	0.72361505	3.78529638	4.03472817	0.94	0.3482
Residual	1.00000000	5.23109131	2.58479270	2.02	0.0430

Solution for Fixed Effects

Parameter	Estimate	Std Error	DDF	T	Pr > |T|
INTERCEPT	493.06576241	2.08466820	7	236.52	0.0001
A	1.66269729	0.84710734	8	1.96	0.0853
B	1.51372410	0.53555318	8	2.83	0.0223
A*B	2.16854479	0.57280611	8	3.79	0.0053
C	2.70968649	0.56652308	8	4.78	0.0014
A*C	0.44578580	0.65658125	8	0.68	0.5163
B*C	0.35518688	0.59626643	8	0.60	0.5679
D	-0.06885040	0.49999003	8	-0.14	0.8939
A*D	-0.38134665	0.58482203	8	-0.65	0.5326
B*D	-1.69750500	0.64731569	8	-2.62	0.0305
C*D	2.63959285	0.59239740	8	4.46	0.0021
A*A	0.05377743	1.90458108	8	0.03	0.9782
B*B	2.50612461	1.32760400	8	1.89	0.0958
C*C	1.37258483	1.19650437	8	1.15	0.2845
D*D	0.51812469	1.26417055	8	0.41	0.6927

Tests of Fixed Effects

Source	NDF	DDF	Type III F	Pr > F
A	1	8	3.85	0.0853
B	1	8	7.99	0.0223
A*B	1	8	14.33	0.0053
C	1	8	22.88	0.0014
A*C	1	8	0.46	0.5163
B*C	1	8	0.35	0.5679
D	1	8	0.02	0.8939
A*D	1	8	0.43	0.5326
B*D	1	8	6.88	0.0305
C*D	1	8	19.85	0.0021
A*A	1	8	0.00	0.9782

B*B	1	8	3.56	0.0958
C*C	1	8	1.32	0.2845
D*D	1	8	0.17	0.6927

Interpretation

The estimated standard error of the estimated regression coefficient for A is larger than those for the other linear terms, and the estimated standard error of the regression coefficient for A*A is larger than those for the other quadratic terms. The larger estimated standard errors occur because the levels of A are assigned to the batch experimental unit while the other factors are assigned to the run-within-a-batch experimental unit. The estimate of the batch-to-batch variance component is 3.785, and the estimate of the run-to-run variance component is 5.231.

The information about the parameters of the regression model is coming from both between-batch comparisons and between-run-within-a-batch comparisons. PROC MIXED extracts the information from both parts of the model and computes combined estimates of the regression parameters. The degrees of freedom for the analysis in Output 10.1 all correspond to the run-to-run variance and not the batch-to-batch variance. The DDFM=SATTERTH option can be used to compute appropriate approximate degrees of freedom for each of the estimated standard errors.

Program—Including DDFM=SATTERTH

The PROC MIXED program with the DDFM=SATTERTH option is

```
proc mixed;
   class batch aa;
   model y=a|b|c|d@2 a*a b*b c*c d*d /solution ddfm=satterth;
   random batch(aa);
run;
```

The results of using PROC MIXED with the DDFM=SATTERTH option are in Output 10.2.

Results

Output 10.2 *PROC MIXED for the Response Surface Model with a Split-Plot Design with Approximate Degrees of Freedom*

```
                        The MIXED Procedure

                    Class Level Information

             Class     Levels  Values

             BATCH        10   1 2 3 4 5 6 7 8 9 10
             AA            3   0 1 -1

          Covariance Parameter Estimates (REML)
```

Cov Parm	Ratio	Estimate	Std Error	Z	Pr > |Z|
Batch(AA)	0.72361505	3.78529638	4.03472817	0.94	0.3482
Residual	1.00000000	5.23109131	2.58479270	2.02	0.0430

Solution for Fixed Effects

Parameter	Estimate	Std Error	DDF	T	Pr > |T|
INTERCEPT	493.06576241	2.08466820	8.84	236.52	0.0001
A	1.66269729	0.84710734	4.57	1.96	0.1123
B	1.51372410	0.53555318	11.1	2.83	0.0163
A*B	2.16854479	0.57280611	10.3	3.79	0.0034
C	2.70968649	0.56652308	13.7	4.78	0.0003
A*C	0.44578580	0.65658125	14.5	0.68	0.5078
B*C	0.35518688	0.59626643	11.8	0.60	0.5626
D	-0.06885040	0.49999003	9.29	-0.14	0.8934
A*D	-0.38134665	0.58482203	10.3	-0.65	0.5287
B*D	-1.69750500	0.64731569	13.5	-2.62	0.0206
C*D	2.63959285	0.59239740	10.6	4.46	0.0011
A*A	0.05377743	1.90458108	4.68	0.03	0.9786
B*B	2.50612461	1.32760400	13.9	1.89	0.0801
C*C	1.37258483	1.19650437	10.6	1.15	0.2765
D*D	0.51812469	1.26417055	12.5	0.41	0.6888

Tests of Fixed Effects

Source	NDF	DDF	Type III F	Pr > F
A	1	4.57	3.85	0.1123
B	1	11.1	7.99	0.0163
A*B	1	10.3	14.33	0.0034
C	1	13.7	22.88	0.0003
A*C	1	14.5	0.46	0.5078
B*C	1	11.8	0.35	0.5626
D	1	9.29	0.02	0.8934
A*D	1	10.3	0.43	0.5287
B*D	1	13.5	6.88	0.0206
C*D	1	10.6	19.85	0.0011
A*A	1	4.68	0.00	0.9786
B*B	1	13.9	3.56	0.0801
C*C	1	10.6	1.32	0.2765
D*D	1	12.5	0.17	0.6888

Interpretation

The approximate degrees of freedom provide another indication as to which estimates are based on the batch-to-batch variance. The denominator degrees of freedom associated with the estimates of the standard errors of the coefficients for A and A*A are smaller than the degrees of freedom associated with the estimated standard errors of the other estimates, indicating the information is coming from between the batches instead of within the batches.

10.2.3 Comparison with PROC GLM

PROC GLM extracts the within-block information about the effects in the model (except in very special conditions with class variables). By the inclusion of both A and AA in the model, a singularity is generated, and there is no within-batch information available for estimating the coefficients for A and A*A.

Program—PROC GLM

The PROC GLM program is

```
proc glm;
   class batch aa;
   model y= batch(aa) a|b|c|d@2 a*a b*b c*c d*d /solution;
   random batch(aa) /test;
run;
```

The results of fitting the above model are in Output 10.3.

Results

Output 10.3 *PROC GLM Results for the Response Surface Model in a Split-Plot Design*

```
                    General Linear Models Procedure
                       Class Level Information
             Class     Levels   Values
             BATCH        10     1 2 3 4 5 6 7 8 9 10
             AA            3      0 1 -1


             Number of observations in data set = 30
Dependent Variable: Y
                             Sum of        Mean
Source              DF       Squares       Square   F Value    Pr > F
Model               21      641.29667     30.53794    5.89     0.0073
Error                8       41.50333      5.18792
Corrected Total     29      682.80000

                  R-Square         C.V.       Root MSE       Y Mean
                  0.939216       0.458474      2.2777         496.8
Source              DF    Type III SS   Mean Square   F Value    Pr > F
BATCH(AA)            7      83.15412      11.87916      2.29     0.1343
A                    0       0.00000          .           .        .
B                    1      59.60561      59.60561     11.49     0.0095
A*B                  1      56.76339      56.76339     10.94     0.0107
C                    1     100.40388     100.40388     19.35     0.0023
A*C                  1       0.43642       0.43642      0.08     0.7792
B*C                  1       1.89759       1.89759      0.37     0.5621
D                    1       0.22628       0.22628      0.04     0.8398
A*D                  1       5.15844       5.15844      0.99     0.3479
B*D                  1      12.37829      12.37829      2.39     0.1610
C*D                  1      77.10367      77.10367     14.86     0.0048
A*A                  0       0.00000          .           .        .
B*B                  1      31.65842      31.65842      6.10     0.0387
C*C                  1       8.70150       8.70150      1.68     0.2314
D*D                  1       0.18051       0.18051      0.03     0.8567


                                  T for H0:    Pr > |T|   Std Error of
Parameter         Estimate      Parameter=0                 Estimate
INTERCEPT        491.0776350 B    179.20       0.0001     2.74044353
BATCH(AA) 4 0      4.1382762 B      1.72       0.1240     2.40800263
          6 0     -2.3046623 B     -0.89       0.4000     2.59261777
          1 1     -0.3175617 B     -0.12       0.9072     2.63914947
          2 1      2.6619284 B      0.92       0.3865     2.90620715
          8 1      5.9020880 B      2.24       0.0554     2.63490296
```

9	1	1.8908147	B	0.75	0.4723	2.50677759
3	-1	1.8008609	B	0.73	0.4842	2.45542252
5	-1	-1.5583385	B	-0.48	0.6421	3.22700551
7	-1	-2.9362114	B	-0.92	0.3855	3.19884592
10	-1	0.0000000	B	.	.	.
A		0.0000000	B	.	.	.
B		1.9655640		3.39	0.0095	0.57988257
A*B		2.0074229		3.31	0.0107	0.60687768
C		2.9568828		4.40	0.0023	0.67213316
A*C		0.2345614		0.29	0.7792	0.80872301
B*C		0.3988874		0.60	0.5621	0.65954643
D		-0.1078211		-0.21	0.8398	0.51626929
A*D		-0.6188687		-1.00	0.3479	0.62063465
B*D		-1.1571537		-1.54	0.1610	0.74913012
C*D		2.4305689	B	3.86	0.0048	0.63047354
A*A		0.0000000	B	.	.	.
B*B		3.8761610		2.47	0.0387	1.56911104
C*C		1.6620744		1.30	0.2314	1.28336408
D*D		0.2673105		0.19	0.8567	1.43304559

Interpretation

Results show that the TYPE III sum of squares for A and A*A are zero. The zero occurs because we have the BATCH(AA) term in the model, and that term removes all of the batch-to-batch information. That is, because all of the information about the coefficients of A and A*A comes from the batch-to-batch variability, there is no information remaining after adjusting for the batch-to-batch effects or BATCH(AA). PROC GLM extracts the within-block information about the regression parameters and does not include information from the between-batch part of the model as PROC MIXED does. The estimates of the parameters in Output 10.3 are somewhat different from those obtained by PROC MIXED, but for other than A and A*A, the magnitudes are similar. The combined estimates from PROC MIXED have smaller estimated standard errors than those obtained from PROC GLM. These smaller estimated standard errors are due in part because PROC MIXED is using more information to estimate the coefficients than PROC GLM uses. Finally, PROC GLM indicates that there is a colinearity between C*D and other parameters in the model. PROC MIXED has no problem handling that situation.

PROC MIXED enables us to fit a model with a variable taking on two roles as long as one role is in the MODEL statement and the other role is in the RANDOM statement. A non-mixed-models approach cannot fit such models. In order to properly fit response surface models with blocks or split plots, you must use a mixed models approach implemented as in PROC MIXED.

10.3 A Split-Plot Experiment with Correlated Whole Plots

10.3.1 Introduction

Experiments with correlated **errors** frequently occur. Common examples include repeated measures, discussed in Chapter 3, and spatially correlated experimental units, discussed in Chapter 9. In this example, a split-plot experiment was conducted in such a way that the **sub-plot errors** were independent but the **whole-plot experimental units** were correlated. This section 1) describes the design that led to this unusual situation, 2) presents the PROC MIXED program required to analyze the data, and 3) discusses the important differences between the analysis accounting for correlation and the standard, independent whole-plot analysis.

The purpose of this experiment was to compare the response to irrigation of three varieties of maize. A line-source irrigation system was used, similar to a system described in Johnson, et. al. (1983). In a line-source system, water emits from a linear source — essentially a long, straight pipe with regularly spaced nozzles. The amount of water reaching the ground decreases with increasing distance from the water source. In a standard line-source experiment, treatments are planted in long strips perpendicular to the line source. Within-a-strip measurements are taken at regularly spaced distances from the line source. Thus, distance corresponds to the amount of irrigation. The design is pictured in Figure 10.1.

Figure 10.1 *Display of the Line-Source Arrangement of Treatments and Irrigation Levels*

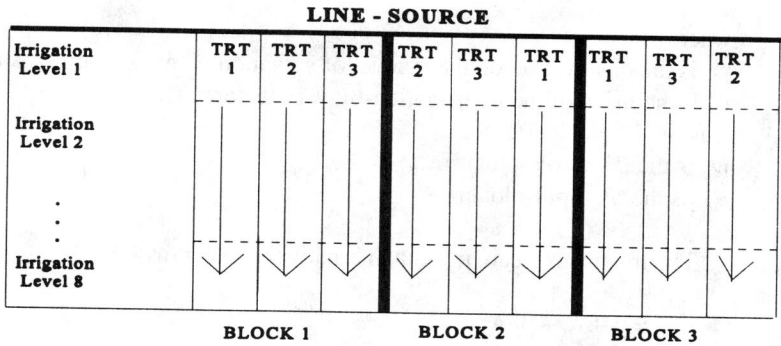

Because distance — and hence amount of irrigation — cannot be randomized, some correlation among the measurements at successive distances is possible. Thus, amount of irrigation behaves in the analysis like time in a repeated measures experiment. The analysis of this type of experiment using PROC MIXED is described in *SAS/STAT Software: Changes and Enhancements through Release 6.11* (1996).

The example considered here uses a different design. The strips perpendicular to the line-source were divided into plots corresponding to increasing distance, i.e. amount of irrigation. Each plot was divided into three sub-plots, each of which was randomly assigned to a maize variety, as displayed in Figure 10.2.

Figure 10.2 *Line-Source Layout Where Each Level of Irrigation Is Split into Three Sub-Plots within Each Block*

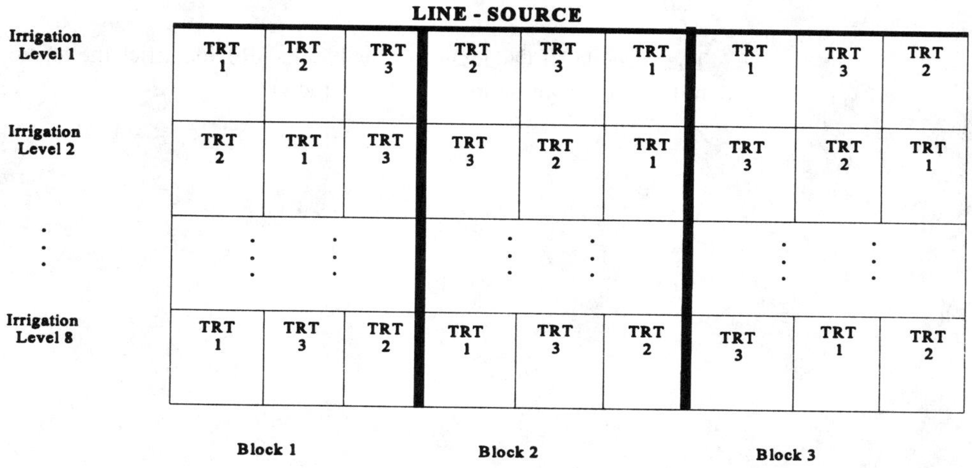

There is a crucial difference between this design and the standard line-source experiment. In the *standard* experiment, the treatments are applied in whole plots and the amounts of irrigation are divisions of the whole plot. In *this* example, the amounts of irrigation are whole plots, and the treatments are applied to subplots within each whole plot. The whole plots cannot be randomized because they are defined in terms of their distance from the line source. Thus, the analysis of this experiment must account for the possibility of correlation among whole plots. The data for this experiment are in Data Set 10.3.1 in Appendix 4, "SAS Data Sets."

A model for this experiment is

$$y_{ijk} = \mu_{ij} + r_k + w_{ik} + e_{ijk}$$

where
y_{ijk} is the observation on the ith level of irrigation, j^{th} maize variety, and k^{th} block
μ_{ij} is the mean of the ij^{th} irrigation-by-variety combination
r_k is the kth block effect
w_{ik} is the ik^{th} whole-plot effect
e_{ijk} is the ijk^{th} split-plot error.

The treatment mean, μ_{ik}, can alternatively be expressed as

$$\mu_{ij} = \mu + \alpha_i + \beta_j + \gamma_{ij}$$

where

μ is the intercept
α_i is the ith irrigation level effect
β_j is the jth variety effect
γ_{ij} is the ij^{th} irrigation-by-variety interaction effect.

The effects r_k, w_{ik}, and e_{ijk} are assumed to be random. The block effects and the split-plot errors are assumed to be normal and independent. Specifically, $r_k \sim$ iid $N(0,\sigma_B^2)$, and $e_{ijk} \sim$ iid $N(0,\sigma^2_e)$. The whole-plot errors are assumed to be normal but correlated within a block. Specifically,

$$\text{Var}(w_{ik}) = \sigma_W^2$$

$$\text{Cov}(w_{ik}, w_{i'k}) = \sigma_W^2\rho_{ii'}, \text{ where } i \neq i'$$

$$\text{Cov}(w_{ik}, w_{i'k'}) = 0, \text{ where } k \neq k'$$

The variable BLOC identifies the block, TRT identifies the maize variety, LEVEL identifies the irrigation level, and Y is the yield.

10.3.2 Analysis Using PROC MIXED

Program

The program required to analyze the data according to the model described above is

```
proc mixed;
   class bloc trt level;
   model y=level trt trt*level;
   random intercept /subject=bloc;
   random  level / subject=bloc type=ar(1);
   lsmeans trt/diff;
   lsmeans level trt*level;
   estimate 'lev 1 vs lev 2' level 1 -1 0;
   estimate 'lev 1 vs lev 8' level 1 0  0  0  0  0  0  -1;
   estimate 'trt 1 vs trt 2' trt 1 -1 0;
   estimate 'trt 1 v 2 given lev 1' trt 1 -1 0
trt*level 1 0 0 0 0 0 0 0 -1 0;
   estimate 'lev 1 v 2 given trt 1' level 1 -1 0 trt*level 1 -1 0;
   estimate 'lev 1 v 8 given trt 1' level 1 0 0 0 0 0 0 -1
                  trt*level    1 0 0 0 0 0 0 -1 0;
   contrast 'linear' level -7 -5 -3 -1 1 3 5 7;
   contrast 'quadratic' level 7 1 -3 -5 -5 -3 1 7;
   contrast 'other' level -7 5 7 3 -3 -7 -5 7,
                level 7 -13 -3 9 9 -3 -13 7,
                level -7 23 -17 -15 15 17 -23 7,
                level 1 -5 9 -5 -5 9 -5 1,
                level -1 7 -21 35 -35 21 -7 1;
   run;
```

The CLASS and MODEL statements in this program are identical to standard split-plot analyses. The RANDOM statements for block and whole-plot error are handled differently. Because the block effects are independent but the whole-plot errors are correlated, separate RANDOM statements are needed for each effect. The RANDOM INTERCEPT/SUBJECT=BLOCK statement defines the block effect. The second random statement defines the whole-plot error. The TYPE=AR(1) option defines the correlation — in this case a first-order autocorrelation structure — among whole plots. The SUBJECT=BLOC option defines the correlation as being among whole plots *within* a block. Although we use the AR(1) model in this example, you can use any of the correlation models described in the PROC MIXED documentation.

The ESTIMATE statements given in the program are examples of the statements you may want to use in practice. Other main-effect or simple-effect estimates can be defined. The method for constructing these statements was described in Chapter 2.

The LSMEANS TRT/DIFF statement causes PROC MIXED to estimate all possible differences between varieties and their associated standard errors and *t*-test statistics. The CONTRAST statements given in this example reflect the researcher's interest in testing the fit of a hypothesized quadratic relationship between irrigation level and yield.

Selected results from this analysis are given in Output 10.4.

Results

Output 10.4 *Analysis Using AR(1) Correlation among Whole-Plot Errors*

Covariance Parameter Estimates (REML)					
Cov Parm	Ratio	Estimate	Std Error	Z	Pr > |Z|
INTERCEPT	4.81385277	5.80840023	11.22178132	0.52	0.6047
LEVEL Diagonal	10.19135897	12.29690534	9.42816449	1.30	0.1921
AR(1)	0.60405402	0.72885227	0.21729351	3.35	0.0008
Residual	1.00000000	1.20660114	0.34494707	3.50	0.0005

Model Fitting Information for Y

Description	Value
Observations	72.0000
Variance Estimate	1.2066
Standard Deviation Estimate	1.0985
REML Log Likelihood	-116.388
Akaike's Information Criterion	-120.388
Schwarz's Bayesian Criterion	-124.131
-2 REML Log Likelihood	232.7763

Tests of Fixed Effects

Source	NDF	DDF	Type III F	Pr > F
LEVEL	7	21	2.21	0.0758
TRT	2	24	29.63	0.0001
TRT*LEVEL	14	24	1.58	0.1563

CONTRAST Statement Results

Source	NDF	DDF	F	Pr > F
linear	1	21	0.06	0.8133
quadratic	1	21	3.66	0.0695
other	5	21	2.24	0.0882

ESTIMATE Statement Results

Parameter	Estimate	Std Error	DDF	T	Pr > |T|
lev 1 vs lev 2	-1.84799144	1.39374820	21	-1.33	0.1991
lev 1 vs lev 8	-1.31196370	2.39845222	21	-0.55	0.5901
trt 1 vs trt 2	-1.08642821	0.34713956	24	-3.13	0.0046
trt 1 v 2 given lev	-2.28527159	0.97409910	24	-2.35	0.0276
lev 1 v 2 given trt	-1.34483034	1.60154970	24	-0.84	0.4094
lev 1 v 8 given trt	-1.31196370	2.39845222	21	-0.55	0.5901

Least Squares Means

Level	LSMEAN	Std Error	DDF	T	Pr > |T|
TRT 1	42.16118268	1.75590018	24	24.01	0.0001
TRT 2	43.24761088	1.75590018	24	24.63	0.0001
TRT 3	40.59013366	1.75590018	24	23.12	0.0001
LEVEL 1	39.66123228	2.15969891	21	18.36	0.0001
LEVEL 2	41.50922372	2.15966535	21	19.22	0.0001
LEVEL 3	44.15431234	2.15966521	21	20.44	0.0001
LEVEL 4	42.27879078	2.15966521	21	19.58	0.0001
LEVEL 5	41.96919488	2.15966521	21	19.43	0.0001
LEVEL 6	44.49249945	2.15966521	21	20.60	0.0001
LEVEL 7	40.95868980	2.15966535	21	18.97	0.0001
LEVEL 8	40.97319599	2.15969891	21	18.97	0.0001
TRT*LEVEL 1 1	39.68953154	2.23172334	24	17.78	0.0001
TRT*LEVEL 1 2	41.03436187	2.23110852	24	18.39	0.0001
TRT*LEVEL 1 3	44.26198242	2.23110362	24	19.84	0.0001
TRT*LEVEL 1 4	42.67332815	2.23110349	24	19.13	0.0001
TRT*LEVEL 1 5	42.79876242	2.23110349	24	19.18	0.0001
TRT*LEVEL 1 6	44.60817587	2.23110362	24	19.99	0.0001
TRT*LEVEL 1 7	41.54806656	2.23110852	24	18.62	0.0001
TRT*LEVEL 1 8	40.67525257	2.23172334	24	18.23	0.0001
TRT*LEVEL 2 1	41.97480312	2.23172334	24	18.81	0.0001
TRT*LEVEL 2 2	44.29772574	2.23110852	24	19.85	0.0001
TRT*LEVEL 2 3	45.07001883	2.23110362	24	20.20	0.0001
TRT*LEVEL 2 4	43.19154493	2.23110349	24	19.36	0.0001

TRT*LEVEL 2 5	42.59956900	2.23110349	24	19.09	0.0001
TRT*LEVEL 2 6	45.81096297	2.23110362	24	20.53	0.0001
TRT*LEVEL 2 7	40.78253431	2.23110852	24	18.28	0.0001
TRT*LEVEL 2 8	42.25372818	2.23172334	24	18.93	0.0001
TRT*LEVEL 3 1	37.31936219	2.23172334	24	16.72	0.0001
TRT*LEVEL 3 2	39.19558354	2.23110852	24	17.57	0.0001
TRT*LEVEL 3 3	43.13093577	2.23110362	24	19.33	0.0001
TRT*LEVEL 3 4	40.97149927	2.23110349	24	18.36	0.0001
TRT*LEVEL 3 5	40.50925324	2.23110349	24	18.16	0.0001
TRT*LEVEL 3 6	43.05835950	2.23110362	24	19.30	0.0001
TRT*LEVEL 3 7	40.54546855	2.23110852	24	18.17	0.0001
TRT*LEVEL 3 8	39.99060720	2.23172334	24	17.92	0.0001

Interpretation

Important items are

- Covariance Parameter Estimates

  The INTERCEPT corresponds to the block variance σ_B^2. The estimated block variance is 5.808.

  Under LEVEL, the "Diagonal" parameter is σ_W^2, and the AR(1) element is the autocorrelation parameter ρ. The estimates are 12.297 and 0.729, respectively. The significance level corresponding to testing that the autocorrelation parameter is zero or not is 0.0008, indicating there is a significant amount of autocorrelation among whole plots within the blocks.

  The "Residual" is the split-plot error variance, σ_e^2. Its estimate is 1.207. The value of -2 REML Log Likelihood is 232.7763.

- Tests of Fixed Effects

  The F-tests are for the main-effects of irrigation (LEVEL) and variety (TRT) and the irrigation-by-variety (LEVEL*TRT) interaction. These results show that there is no significant interaction between irrigation and variety (F=1.58, p-value=0.1563), there is a significant variety main effect (F=29.63, p-value<0.0001), and there is a moderately significant irrigation effect (F=2.21, p-value=0.0758).

- ESTIMATE Statement Results

  These give specific main-effect differences and simple-effect differences. The main thing to notice is that for the comparisons among LEVELS, which involve comparisons among correlated experimental units at varying distances apart, the standard error increases with distance. Thus, adjacent levels, e.g., LEVEL 1 and 2, are compared more precisely than levels farther apart, e.g., LEVEL 1 and 8. This is true of both LEVEL main effects and LEVEL simple effects holding TRT constant.

- CONTRAST Statement Results

  There is weak evidence of a quadratic relationship between LEVEL of irrigation and yield (F=3.66, p-value=0.0695) and of a more complex polynomial regression ("other," F-=2.24, p-value=0.0882). Looking at the pattern of the LSMEANS over LEVEL, it is difficult to see any biologically intelligible relationship between irrigation level and yield. However, the pattern may suggest problems in correctly adjusting the equipment. That is, the "hot spots" at LEVEL 3 and 6 (whose means are 44.15 and 44.49, whereas other means range between 39.66 and 42.28) indicate misaligned nozzles in the line-source irrigator. This is a problem of interest to the irrigation engineers.

- Differences of the Least Squares Means

  The estimated mean yield of variety (TRT) 1 is 1.086 units lower than variety (TRT) 2, with a standard error of 0.347. The difference between varieties 1 and 2 is statistically significant (t= −3.13, p-value=0.0046). Also, TRT 1 and 2 both have significantly higher yields than TRT 3.

10.3.3 Comparison with Standard Split-Plot ANOVA

The standard split-plot analysis assumes that the whole-plot errors are independent. How does the analysis assuming correlated whole-plot errors compare to the standard split-plot analysis? You can obtain the usual analysis using the method described in Chapter 2.

Program

For these data, the PROC MIXED statements are

```
proc mixed;
   class bloc trt level;
   model y=level trt trt*level;
   random bloc bloc*level;
run;
```

The LSMEANS, ESTIMATE, and CONTRAST statements are identical to those used in the previous section. The *only* difference is in the RANDOM statements.

The results of the analysis are given in Output 10.5.

Results

Output 10.5 *Standard Split-Plot Analysis*

Covariance Parameter Estimates (REML)					
Cov Parm	Ratio	Estimate	Std Error	Z	Pr > |Z|
BLOC	7.03332934	8.54105460	7.90939483	1.08	0.2802
BLOC*LEVEL	6.90668174	8.38725773	2.78295620	3.01	0.0026
Residual	1.00000000	1.21436864	0.34985562	3.47	0.0005

Model Fitting Information for Y	
Description	Value
Observations	72.0000
Variance Estimate	1.2144
Standard Deviation Estimate	1.1020
REML Log Likelihood	−121.254
Akaike's Information Criterion	−124.254

```
        Schwarz's Bayesian Criterion      -127.061
        -2 REML Log Likelihood             242.5085
```

Tests of Fixed Effects

Source	NDF	DDF	Type III F	Pr > F
LEVEL	7	21	1.18	0.3547
TRT	2	24	29.45	0.0001
TRT*LEVEL	14	24	1.49	0.1894

ESTIMATE Statement Results

Parameter	Estimate	Std Error	DDF	T	Pr > |T|
lev 1 vs lev 2	-1.84191652	2.11458918	21	-0.87	0.3936
lev 1 vs lev 8	-1.27664610	2.11458918	21	-0.60	0.5525
trt 1 vs trt 2	-1.08455467	0.34820460	24	-3.11	0.0047
trt 1 v 2 given lev	-2.24401321	0.97978593	24	-2.29	0.0311
lev 1 v 2 given trt	-1.45529732	2.26064655	24	-0.64	0.5258
lev 1 v 8 given trt	-1.27664610	2.11458918	21	-0.60	0.5525

CONTRAST Statement Results

Source	NDF	DDF	F	Pr > F
linear	1	21	0.12	0.7274
quadratic	1	21	4.31	0.0503
other	5	21	0.77	0.5838

Least Squares Means

Level	LSMEAN	Std Error	DDF	T	Pr > |T|
TRT 1	42.16225820	1.56689857	24	26.91	0.0001
TRT 2	43.24681287	1.56689857	24	27.60	0.0001
TRT 3	40.58920780	1.56689857	24	25.90	0.0001
LEVEL 1	39.67682193	2.09070117	21	18.98	0.0001
LEVEL 2	41.51873845	2.09070117	21	19.86	0.0001
LEVEL 3	44.14588424	2.09070117	21	21.12	0.0001
LEVEL 4	42.28680137	2.09070117	21	20.23	0.0001
LEVEL 5	41.98154466	2.09070117	21	20.08	0.0001
LEVEL 6	44.45632909	2.09070117	21	21.26	0.0001
LEVEL 7	40.97582254	2.09070117	21	19.60	0.0001
LEVEL 8	40.95346803	2.09070117	21	19.59	0.0001
TRT*LEVEL 1 1	39.69692131	2.16587739	24	18.33	0.0001
TRT*LEVEL 1 2	41.15221863	2.16587739	24	19.00	0.0001
TRT*LEVEL 1 3	44.22732170	2.16587739	24	20.42	0.0001
TRT*LEVEL 1 4	42.64828629	2.16587739	24	19.69	0.0001
TRT*LEVEL 1 5	42.89424355	2.16587739	24	19.80	0.0001
TRT*LEVEL 1 6	44.50141388	2.16587739	24	20.55	0.0001
TRT*LEVEL 1 7	41.55601686	2.16587739	24	19.19	0.0001
TRT*LEVEL 1 8	40.62164336	2.16587739	24	18.76	0.0001
TRT*LEVEL 2 1	41.94093452	2.16587739	24	19.36	0.0001
TRT*LEVEL 2 2	44.23886053	2.16587739	24	20.43	0.0001
TRT*LEVEL 2 3	45.05002056	2.16587739	24	20.80	0.0001
TRT*LEVEL 2 4	43.18288547	2.16587739	24	19.94	0.0001
TRT*LEVEL 2 5	42.61534324	2.16587739	24	19.68	0.0001
TRT*LEVEL 2 6	45.80119923	2.16587739	24	21.15	0.0001
TRT*LEVEL 2 7	40.85580220	2.16587739	24	18.86	0.0001
TRT*LEVEL 2 8	42.28945719	2.16587739	24	19.53	0.0001
TRT*LEVEL 3 1	37.39260998	2.16587739	24	17.26	0.0001
TRT*LEVEL 3 2	39.16513619	2.16587739	24	18.08	0.0001
TRT*LEVEL 3 3	43.16031047	2.16587739	24	19.93	0.0001

TRT*LEVEL 3 4	41.02923234	2.16587739	24	18.94	0.0001
TRT*LEVEL 3 5	40.43504718	2.16587739	24	18.67	0.0001
TRT*LEVEL 3 6	43.06637417	2.16587739	24	19.88	0.0001
TRT*LEVEL 3 7	40.51564856	2.16587739	24	18.71	0.0001
TRT*LEVEL 3 8	39.94930355	2.16587739	24	18.44	0.0001

```
                    Differences of Least Squares Means
Level 1    Level 2  Difference   Std Error   DDF   T      Pr > |T|
TRT 1      TRT 2    -1.08455467  0.34820460  24    -3.11  0.0047
TRT 1      TRT 3     1.57305039  0.34820460  24     4.52  0.0001
TRT 2      TRT 3     2.65760506  0.34820460  24     7.63  0.0001
```

Interpretation

The following is a summary of the major differences:

- Covariance Parameter Estimates

    Only the variance components, σ_B^2, σ_W^2, and σ_e^2 are estimated. For the block variance, the estimate of σ_B^2 is 8.541, compared with 5.808 in the previous analysis. For whole-plot error, the estimate of σ_W^2 is 8.387, compared with 12.297. For split-plot error, the estimate of σ^2 is 1.214, compared to 1.207. The value of −2REML Log Likelihood is 242.5085 as compared to 232.7762, indicating the model with the autocorrelated errors is fitting the data better than the usual split-plot model.

- Tests of Fixed Effects

    These results indicate no significant interaction between irrigation and variety (F=1.49, p-value=0.1894) and no significant level main effect (F=1.18, p-value=0.3547). There is a highly significant variety effect (F=29.45, p-value<0.0001). These results are similar for the split-plot effects (TRT and TRT*LEVEL) but different for the whole-plot main effect (LEVEL), which was marginally significant in the previous analysis. Because the main difference in the analyses is in the way whole-plot error is modelled, the greatest impact should be on the conclusions regarding the whole-plot treatment effect.

- ESTIMATE Statement Results

    The main difference here is in the standard errors of the irrigation LEVEL main effects and simple effects holding variety constant. In the correlated whole-plot model, the standard error of a difference depends on the distance between levels being compared. In the standard split-plot analysis, the standard errors are constant. Obviously, this can greatly affect the accuracy of interval estimation and hypothesis testing involving irrigation LEVEL.

- CONTRAST Statement Results

    These results indicate a significant quadratic effect (F=4.31, p-value=0.0503) and no evidence of lack of fit (for the lack-of-fit contrast "other," F=0.77). This result is in marked contrast to the previous results, which revealed evidence of lack of fit.

    If the results of the standard analysis contrasts are used, you may naively report a quadratic effect of irrigation. Biologically, this makes sense, so it may not occur to anyone to challenge the conclusion. However, the result is not consistent with the estimated LSMEANS, nor is it consistent with the conclusions the irrigation engineers ultimately draw. That is, in the analysis accounting for whole-plot correlation, the engineers were alerted to improperly adjusted equipment.

The LSMEANS in the two analyses are virtually identical, yet the CONTRAST results place them in an entirely different light. This is an example of the potential for rather serious misinterpretation that can result if the model assumptions do not closely reflect the actual design used to conduct the experiment.

- Differences of the Least Squares Means

  The differences estimated in this analysis are between varieties. These are split-plot effects, which are not expected to be greatly affected by changes in the whole-plot component of the model. In fact, these results are virtually identical to the results obtained in the correlated whole-plot analysis.

Finally, you can evaluate the need to account for correlation among the whole plots by testing the whole-plot correlation parameter. This example compares the AR(1) model to the independent whole-plot error model. Formally, it tests H_0: $\rho=0$ using a likelihood ratio test. You can calculate the likelihood ratio statistic by taking the difference between the -2 REML Log-Likelihood values in the two analyses. For the independent whole-plot errors model, the -2 REML Log-Likelihood is 242.5085. For the AR(1) model it is 232.7763. The resulting likelihood ratio χ^2 statistic is 242.5085 $-$ 232.7763 = 9.7322. Noting that the likelihood ratio statistic for this test has 1 d.f., we reject H_0 for any reasonable α-level and conclude that ρ is different from 0; i.e., there is statistically significant correlation among the whole plots.

10.4 A Complex Split Plot: Whole Plot Conducted As an Incomplete Latin Square

10.4.1 Introduction

This example presents the analysis of a split-plot experiment in which the whole plot has been set up as an incomplete Latin square. Such experiments are often desirable in view of the natural sources of variation among experimental units. However, using Latin squares and related designs as whole plots in split-plot experiments has been a traditional source of frustration for data analysts. The remainder of this section contains a description of the design and model. Section 10.4.2 contains a description of the main features of the analysis using PROC MIXED. Section 10.4.3 describes the difficulties this design presents using more traditional methods of analysis, e.g. PROC GLM.

The experiment was conducted to evaluate the performance of two varieties of a crop at five levels of nitrogen fertilization. The five levels of nitrogen were mechanically applied to relatively large plots. Each plot was split into two sub-plots. Each genotype was randomly assigned to a sub-plot. Because of substantial north-south and east-west gradients, row-column, or Latin-square-like, blocking was used. However, as only 15 whole-plots were available in a 5 x 3 grid, an incomplete Latin square was used. The layout of the experiment is given in Figure 10.3. The data are given in Data Set 10.4.1 of Appendix 4, "SAS Data Sets."

Figure 10.3 *Display of Randomization of Levels of Nitrogen to the Whole Plots and Levels of Genotype to the Sub-plots*

Figure 10.3

	Col 1	Col 2	Col 3	Col 4	Col 5
Row 1	G 1 Nit 1 ---- G 2	G 2 Nit 2 ---- G 1	G 2 Nit 5 ---- G 1	G 2 Nit 4 ---- G 1	G 1 Nit 3 ---- G 2
Row 2	G 1 Nit 2 ---- G 2	G 1 Nit 1 ---- G 2	G 1 Nit 3 ---- G 2	G 2 Nit 5 ---- G 1	G 1 Nit 4 ---- G 2
Row 3	G 2 Nit 3 ---- G 1	G 2 Nit 4 ---- G 1	G 1 Nit 1 ---- G 2	G 1 Nit 2 ---- G 2	G 2 Nit 5 ---- G 1

A model for the data is

$$y_{ijkl} = \mu_{ij} + c_k + r_l + w_{ikl} + e_{ijkl}$$

where

y_{ijkl} is the observation on the ith nitrogen (N) level, j^{th} genotype (G), k^{th} column (COL) and l^{th} row

μ_{ij} is the ij^{th} nitrogen-by-genotype mean

c_k is the kth column effect, assumed iid $N(0,\sigma_c^2)$

r_l is the lth row effect, assumed iid $N(0,\sigma_r^2)$

w_{ikl} is the ikl^{th} whole-plot error, assumed iid $N(0,\sigma_w^2)$

e_{ijkl} is the $ijkl^{th}$ split-plot error, assumed iid $N(0,\sigma_e^2)$.

You can describe the nitrogen-by-genotype mean in terms of treatment effects as

$$\mu_{ij} = \mu + N_i + G_j + NG_{ij}$$

where

μ is the intercept

N_i is the ith nitrogen level main effect

G_j is the jth genotype main effect

NG_{ij} is the ij^{th} nitrogen-by-genotype interaction.

The researcher was interested in 1) seeing if the nitrogen effect was similar for the two genotypes, 2) characterizing the effect of nitrogen on response (Y) — separately for each genotype or averaged over genotypes, depending on the similarity of response — and 3) determining an optimum nitrogen rate for each genotype.

10.4.2 Analysis Using PROC MIXED

Program

You can obtain the analysis for the model described above using the following PROC MIXED statements:

```
proc mixed;
   class row col n g;
   model y= n g n*g/ddfm=satterth;
   random row col row*col*n;
   lsmeans n g n*g;
run;
```

The levels of nitrogen are denoted by N and the levels of genotype are denoted by G. The fixed-effects part of the model consists of the two-way model for main effects for nitrogen and genotype and of the interaction of nitrogen and genotype. The design structure consists of a rectangular plot of land split into rows and columns. The rows are a blocking factor and thus a random effect, and the columns are a blocking factor and thus a random effect. The whole-plot error is included by using the term ROW*COL*N in the RANDOM statement. The LSMEANS statement is included to show how the genotypes respond to the levels of nitrogen.

The results of the estimates of the variance components and the tests for the fixed effects are in Output 10.6.

Results

Output 10.6 *Estimates of the Variance Components and Tests for the Fixed Effects*

```
                  Covariance Parameter Estimates (REML)

    Cov Parm          Ratio        Estimate      Std Error      Z   Pr > |Z|

    ROW            41.36515464    13.23733274    13.66442562   0.97   0.3327
    COL             2.72476097     0.87195534     1.31188502   0.66   0.5063
    ROW*COL*N       6.12043907     1.95861200     1.46782503   1.33   0.1821
    Residual        1.00000000     0.32001168     0.14311358   2.24   0.0253


                       Tests of Fixed Effects

          Source        NDF    DDF   Type III F   Pr > F

          N              4    4.94        3.56    0.0994
          G              1     10      222.33     0.0001
          N*G            4     10       15.99     0.0002
```

Interpretation

- Covariance Parameter Estimates

  The estimate of σ_r^2 is 13.24, the estimate of σ_c^2 is 0.87, the estimate of σ_w^2 is 1.96 and the estimate of σ_e^2 is 0.32. Thus, the estimate of the whole-plot variance component is 1.96, and the estimate of the sub-plot variance component is 0.32. The row-block variance component is much larger than any of the other variance components.

- Tests of Fixed Effects

   The nitrogen level-by-genotype (N*G) interaction is highly significant (F=15.99, p-value=0.0002) indicating the two genotypes did respond differently to the levels of nitrogen fertilizer.

   There is also a highly significant main effect of genotype (F=222.33, p-value<0.0001). We approach the interpretation of this effect with caution, pending developing a complete understanding of the form of the N*G interaction.

CONTRAST statements are used to investigate the form of the relationship of the response the genotypes have to the levels of the nitrogen fertilizer. Because the levels of nitrogen are equally spaced, orthogonal polynomial coefficients for five equally spaced levels are used in constructing the contrasts. The coefficients for the five levels denoted by 1, 2, 3, 4, and 5 for the linear trend are $-2 -1\ 0\ 1\ 2$, for the quadratic trend are $2 -1 -2 -1\ 2$, for the cubic trend are $-1\ 2\ 0 -2\ 1$, and for the quartic trend are $1 -4\ 6 -4\ 1$. The following CONTRAST statements are used to evaluate the respective trends for the main effect of nitrogen.

Program—CONTRAST Statements for Main Effects of N

```
contrast 'n lin' n -2 -1 0 1 2;
contrast 'n quad' n  2 -1 -2 -1 2;
contrast 'n cubic' n -1 2 0 -2 1;
contrast 'n quartic' n 1 -4 6 -4 1;
```

The following CONTRAST statements are used to check to see if the genotypes have equal linear trends (GXN LIN), have equal quadratic trends (GXN QUAD), have equal cubic trends (GXN CUBIC), and have equal quartic trends (GXN QUARTIC). The following CONTRAST statements are used to compare the above genotype trends.

Program—CONTRAST Statements to Compare Trends Across Genotypes

```
contrast 'g x n lin' n*g -2 2 -1 1 0 0 1 -1 2 -2;
contrast 'g x n quad' n*g  2 -2 -1 1 -2 2 -1 1 2 -2;
contrast 'g x n cubic' n*g -1 1 2 -2 0 0 -2 2 1 -1;
contrast 'g x n quartic' n*g 1 -1 -4 4 6 -6 -4 4 1 -1;
```

Results

The results of the above two sets of CONTRAST statements are in Output 10.7.

Output 10.7 *Results of CONTRAST Statements Investigating the Shape of the Genotype Curve*

	CONTRAST Statement Results				
Source		NDF	DDF	F	Pr > F
n lin		1	5.71	8.90	0.0261
n quad		1	4.38	4.87	0.0860
n cubic		1	4.36	0.05	0.8252
n quartic		1	5.69	0.33	0.5897

g x n lin	1	10	63.44	0.0001
g x n quad	1	10	0.20	0.6668
g x n cubic	1	10	0.17	0.6899
g x n quartic	1	10	0.17	0.6876

Interpretation

- Only the linear main-effect trend is significant at the 0.05 level. Because the levels of nitrogen were applied to the whole plots, the denominator degrees of freedom associated with these contrasts of the nitrogen levels correspond to the whole-plot error degrees of freedom. Because the design is not balanced (incomplete Latin square), the denominator degrees of freedom differ as each contrast involves a different set of weights of the nitrogen level means.

- The GXN LIN contrast is the only significant interaction (F=63.44, p-value<0.0001). This indicates the N*G interaction consists primarily of the large difference in the genotype linear trends across the levels of nitrogen. The interaction trend comparisons have 10 denominator degrees of freedom, the degrees of freedom associated with the sub-plot error.

The next step is to compute the estimates of the genotype-by-nitrogen means and plot them to provide a visual description of the results of the CONTRAST statements.

Results

The LSMEANS statement in the above PROC MIXED statements provide the estimates of the main-effects means and of the interaction or cell means that are displayed in Output 10.8.

Output 10.8 *Least Squares Means for the Main Effects and Cells*

	Least Squares Means				
Level	LSMEAN	Std Error	DDF	T	Pr > |T|
N 1	13.01770276	2.31385388	2.74	5.63	0.0141
N 2	15.26700368	2.31385388	2.74	6.60	0.0093
N 3	17.13374773	2.31385388	2.74	7.40	0.0069
N 4	16.74454586	2.31385388	2.74	7.24	0.0073
N 5	16.60366664	2.31385388	2.74	7.18	0.0075
G 1	17.29333333	2.17686554	2.16	7.94	0.0124
G 2	14.21333333	2.17686554	2.16	6.53	0.0186
N*G 1 1	13.46770276	2.32535052	2.8	5.79	0.0124
N*G 1 2	12.56770276	2.32535052	2.8	5.40	0.0148
N*G 2 1	16.18367034	2.32535052	2.8	6.96	0.0076
N*G 2 2	14.35033701	2.32535052	2.8	6.17	0.0105
N*G 3 1	18.55041440	2.32535052	2.8	7.98	0.0053
N*G 3 2	15.71708106	2.32535052	2.8	6.76	0.0082
N*G 4 1	18.94454586	2.32535052	2.8	8.15	0.0050
N*G 4 2	14.54454586	2.32535052	2.8	6.25	0.0101
N*G 5 1	19.32033330	2.32535052	2.8	8.31	0.0047
N*G 5 2	13.88699997	2.32535052	2.8	5.97	0.0114

Interpretation

- Figure 10.4 is a graph of the genotype LSMEANS as a function of the levels of nitrogen. From the list of LSMEANS in Output 10.8 or the graph, the means for genotype G1 increase for increasing levels of N, from 13.47 at N1 to 19.32 at N5. On the other hand the means for G2 increase slightly from N1 (12.57) to N3 (15.72) and decrease a little at N4 (14.54) and then at N5 (13.89).

Figure 10.4 *Plots of Genotype Means Across Levels of Nitrogen*

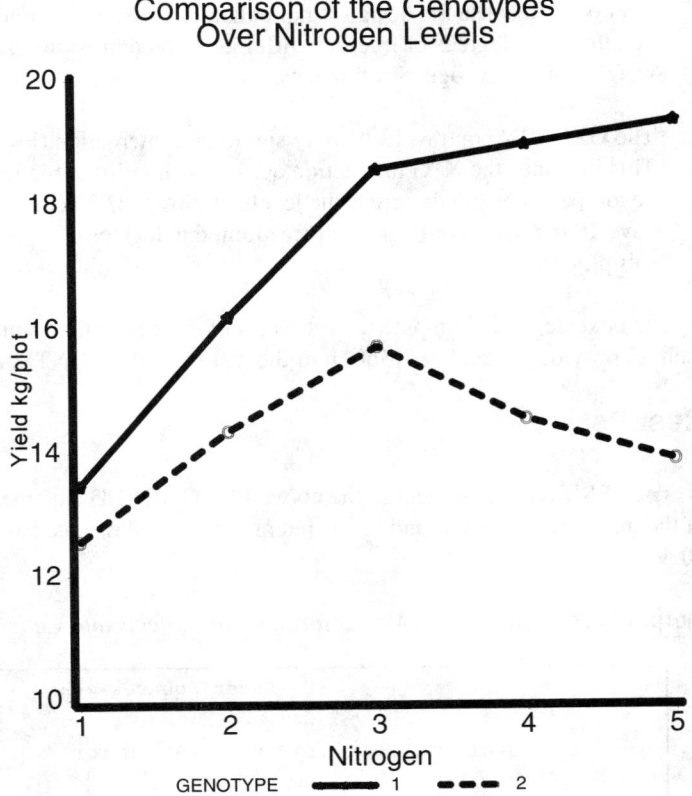

- The N*G least squares means also reveal that for every level of N, genotype G1 has a higher response than genotype G2. Thus, the main effect of G noted earlier can indeed be used to conclude that the difference between G1 and G2 is statistically significant.

Program—ESTIMATE Statements

In this experiment as in all split-plot experiments the standard errors of various main effects, simple effects, etc., consist of various linear combinations of the variance components. In this example the linear combination of the variance components is not simple because the design is unbalanced. However, PROC MIXED does compute the appropriate estimated standard errors and, using the DDFM=SATTERTH option, computes approximate degrees of freedom associated with each estimated standard error. You can compute the main-effect and simple-effect contrasts using the ESTIMATE statement. The coefficients are determined using the same methods discussed in Chapter 2. The following are examples of main-effect and simple-effect comparisons you can compute:

```
estimate 'n main eff mu1.-mu2.' n 1 -1 0 0 0;
estimate 'g main eff mu.1-mu.2' g 1 -1;
estimate 'mu11-mu12 same n' g 1 -1 n*g 1 -1 0 0 0 0 0 0 0 0;
estimate 'mu11-mu21 same g' n 1 -1 0 0 0 n*g 1 0 -1 0 0 0 0 0 0;
estimate 'mu11-mu22 diff n,g' n 1 -1 0 0 0 g 1 -1 n*g 1 0 0 -1 0 0 0 0 0;
```

The results of the ESTIMATE statements are in Output 10.9.

Results

Output 10.9 *Results of the ESTIMATE Statements for Selected Main-Effect and Cell Means Comparisons*

	ESTIMATE Statement Results					
Parameter	Estimate	Std Error	DDF	T	Pr > |T|
n main eff mu1.-mu2.	-2.24930091	1.22951664	4.74	-1.83	0.1300
g main eff mu.1-mu.2	3.08000000	0.20656288	10	14.91	0.0001
mu11-mu12 same n	0.90000000	0.46188865	10	1.95	0.0799
mu11-mu21 same g	-2.71596758	1.27215633	5.42	-2.13	0.0816
mu11-mu22 diff n,g	-0.88263425	1.27215633	5.42	-0.69	0.5164

Interpretation

The first ESTIMATE statement is a main-effect comparison between the first levels of nitrogen, i.e., n main eff mu1.-mu2. denotes $\bar{\mu}_{1\cdot} - \bar{\mu}_{2\cdot}$, indicating the second level of nitrogen has a 2.25 larger yield than the first nitrogen level, though this difference is not statistically significant at $\alpha=0.05$. The second ESTIMATE statement is a main-effect comparison between the two genotypes, i.e., g main eff mu.1-mu.2 denotes $\bar{\mu}_{\cdot 1} - \bar{\mu}_{\cdot 2}$, indicating that the first genotype outyields the second genotype by 3.08 kg/plot. The last three ESTIMATE statements estimate the simple effects $\mu_{11} - \mu_{12}$ (mu11-mu12 same n), $\mu_{11} - \mu_{21}$ (mu11-mu21 same g), and $\mu_{11} - \mu_{22}$ (mu11-mu22 diff n,g). The comparisons $\bar{\mu}_{\cdot 1} - \bar{\mu}_{\cdot 2}$ and $\mu_{11} - \mu_{12}$ are within-whole-plot comparisons, and thus the corresponding estimated standard errors have 10 degrees of freedom, the degrees of freedom associated with the sub-plot error. The other three comparisons involve between whole-plot information and thus have fewer degrees of freedom approximated by the Satterthwaite approximation.

To pursue the researcher's objectives, we need to separate the estimates of the regression between nitrogen levels and response for each genotype. The model for μ_{ij} to accomplish this separation is

$$\mu_{ij} = \mu + G_j + N(G)_{ij}$$

where $N(G)_{ij}$ is the ith nitrogen level nested within the jth genotype and the other parameters are defined as before. This model allows us to define orthogonal polynomial contrasts over the levels of N for each level of G. The linear, quadratic, cubic and quartic trends for each level of genotype across the levels of nitrogen are evaluated using the following PROC MIXED program.

Program—Nitrogen Levels Nested within the Levels of Genotype

```
proc mixed;
    class row col n g;
    model y= g n(g)/ ddfm=satterth;;
    random row col row*col*n;
    lsmeans n(g);

    contrast 'n lin for g1' n(g) -2 -1 0 1 2 0;
    contrast 'n quad for g1' n(g)  2 -1 -2 -1 2 0;
    contrast 'n cubic for g1' n(g) -1 2 0 -2 1 0;
    contrast 'n quartic for g1' n(g) 1 -4 6 -4 1 0;

    contrast 'n lin for g2' n(g) 0 0 0 0 0 -2 -1 0 1 2;
    contrast 'n quad for g2' n(g)  0 0 0 0 0 2 -1 -2 -1 2;
    contrast 'n cubic for g2' n(g) 0 0 0 0 0 -1 2 0 -2 1;
    contrast 'n quartic for g2' n(g) 0 0 0 0 0 1 -4 6 -4 1;
run;
```

The results of using the nested model to evaluate the orthogonal polynomial contrasts for each genotype are in Output 10.10.

Results

Output 10.10 *Tests for the Fixed Effects for Model with Nitrogen Levels Nested within Levels of Genotypes with CONTRAST Statements and Least Squares Means*

```
                     Tests of Fixed Effects

            Source      NDF   DDF   Type III F  Pr > F

            G           1     10    222.33      0.0001
            N(G)        8     6.3   9.78        0.0052


                   CONTRAST Statement Results

            Source              NDF   DDF      F    Pr > F

            n lin for g1        1     6.44   23.41  0.0024
            n quad for g1       1     5.04    4.06  0.0997
            n cubic for g1      1     5.02    0.01  0.9101
            n quartic for g1    1     6.42    0.20  0.6657
            n lin for g2        1     6.44    0.90  0.3776
            n quad for g2       1     5.04    5.05  0.0742
            n cubic for g2      1     5.02    0.11  0.7520
            n quartic for g2    1     6.42    0.43  0.5351


                      Least Squares Means

     Level         LSMEAN        Std Error    DDF      T    Pr > |T|

     N(G) 1 1    13.46770276    2.32535052    2.8    5.79   0.0124
     N(G) 2 1    16.18367034    2.32535052    2.8    6.96   0.0076
     N(G) 3 1    18.55041440    2.32535052    2.8    7.98   0.0053
     N(G) 4 1    18.94454586    2.32535052    2.8    8.15   0.0050
     N(G) 5 1    19.32033330    2.32535052    2.8    8.31   0.0047
     N(G) 1 2    12.56770276    2.32535052    2.8    5.40   0.0148
```

N(G)	2 2	14.35033701	2.32535052	2.8	6.17	0.0105
N(G)	3 2	15.71708106	2.32535052	2.8	6.76	0.0082
N(G)	4 2	14.54454586	2.32535052	2.8	6.25	0.0101
N(G)	5 2	13.88699997	2.32535052	2.8	5.97	0.0114

Interpretation

The estimates of the variance components are identical to those in Output 10.6 because the means of the model are just redescribed as nested instead of as cross classified. The least squares means have been listed as the levels of nitrogen within each level of genotype. The results of the CONTRAST statements indicate there is a significant linear trend across the levels of nitrogen for genotype G1 (p-value=0.0024) and possible quadratic trends across both genotypes (p-value=0.0997 for G1 and p-value=0.0742 for G2). Thus, genotype G1 has a significant linear response to nitrogen fertilizer whereas no statistically significant response to the level of nitrogen fertilizer is observed for G2 (at $\alpha = 0.05$).

Finally, the researcher wanted an estimate of the linear regression coefficient for G1. You can fit a model with different linear regression models for each level of genotype using the following PROC MIXED statements.

Program—Linear Regression Model for Each Genotype

To fit the regression model treating the levels of nitrogen as continuous and to compute the whole-plot error, which is a function of the categorical levels of nitrogen, construct a new variable, NLEV, which takes on the values of N. NLEV is included in the CLASS statement whereas N is not in the CLASS statement. The term N(G) in the MODEL statement generates the two different slopes, one for each genotype, and the term ROW*COL*NLEV generates the whole-plot error:

```
proc mixed;
   class row col nlev g;
   model y= g n(g)/solution ddfm=satterth;;
   random row col row*col*nlev;
run;
```

The results of fitting the linear regression models to each genotype are in Output 10.11.

Results

Output 10.11 *Results of Fitting a Linear Regression Model to the Levels of Nitrogen for Each Level of Genotype*

Covariance Parameter Estimates (REML)					
Cov Parm	Ratio	Estimate	Std Error	Z	Pr > |Z|
ROW	50.70456705	13.15133582	13.66344638	0.96	0.3358
COL	4.17765049	1.08356481	1.43166281	0.76	0.4491
ROW*COL*NLEV	9.32176966	2.41780436	1.33672747	1.81	0.0705
Residual	1.00000000	0.25937182	0.10173400	2.55	0.0108

```
                    Solution for Fixed Effects

    Parameter        Estimate     Std Error   DDF        T  Pr > |T|

    INTERCEPT      13.36120799    2.39370518   3.13    5.58    0.0101
    G 1            -0.41000000    0.43612613     13   -0.94    0.3643
    G 2             0.00000000         .          .      .         .
    N(G) 1          1.44737512    0.32503923   10.3    4.45    0.0012
    N(G) 2          0.28404178    0.32503923   10.3    0.87    0.4022


                     Tests of Fixed Effects

           Source      NDF    DDF   Type III F   Pr > F

           G             1     13         0.88   0.3643
           N(G)          2   10.9        42.83   0.0001
```

Interpretation

The main items of interest are the estimates of the linear regression coefficients. The estimates of the variance components have changed from those in Output 10.6 because here we are fitting only a linear response to the levels of nitrogen for each genotype. The results in Output 10.6 are obtained from a model with nitrogen cell means for each level of genotype.

- The SOLUTION option on the MODEL statement provides the estimates of the linear regression coefficients for each level of genotype. The line corresponding to N(G) 1 provides the estimate of the slope for nitrogen for G1, which is 1.447 with estimated standard error 0.325. The line corresponding to N(G) 2 provides the estimate of the slope for nitrogen for G2, which is 0.284 with estimated standard error 0.325. The slope for nitrogen for G1 is significantly different from zero (p-value=0.0012), whereas the slope for nitrogen for G2 is not significantly different from zero (p-value=0.4022).

Thus, genotype G1 has a significant linear response to nitrogen fertilizer levels, whereas there is no statistically significant response to nitrogen fertilizer for G2.

10.4.3 Problems Encountered with Using PROC GLM

We mentioned in the introduction that, traditionally, analysis of split-plot experiments with unbalanced whole-plot design structures has been a frustrating experience. We can illustrate this by looking at the PROC GLM statements you would have used to analyze this experiment prior to the introduction of PROC MIXED.

Program—PROC GLM

```
proc glm;
   class row col n g;
   model y=row col n row*col*n g n*g;
   random row col row*col*n/test;
   lsmeans n g n*g;
run;
```

The results of the above PROC GLM statements are in Output 10.12 and Output 10.13.

Results

Output 10.12 *Results of Using PROC GLM*

```
                    General Linear Models Procedure

Dependent Variable: Y
                          Sum of        Mean
Source              DF    Squares      Square   F Value    Pr > F
Model               19   491.83467    25.88604    80.89    0.0001
Error               10     3.20000     0.32000
Corrected Total     29   495.03467


                 R-Square       C.V.      Root MSE      Y Mean
                 0.993536     3.590894     0.5657       15.753


Source              DF   Type III SS  Mean Square  F Value    Pr > F

ROW                  2   273.21667    136.60833     426.90    0.0001
COL                  4    34.40139      8.60035      26.88    0.0001
N                    4    50.36139     12.59035      39.34    0.0001
ROW*COL*N            4    17.29527      4.32382      13.51    0.0005
G                    1    71.14800     71.14800     222.34    0.0001
N*G                  4    20.47200      5.11800      15.99    0.0002


Source       Type III Expected Mean Square

ROW          Var(Error) + 2 Var(ROW*COL*N) + 10 Var(ROW)
COL          Var(Error) + 2 Var(ROW*COL*N) + 5 Var(COL)
N            Var(Error) + 2 Var(ROW*COL*N) + Q(N,N*G)
ROW*COL*N    Var(Error) + 2 Var(ROW*COL*N)
G            Var(Error) + Q(G,N*G)
N*G          Var(Error) + Q(N*G)


          Tests of Hypotheses for Mixed Model Analysis of Variance

Source: ROW
Error: MS(ROW*COL*N)
                    Denominator  Denominator
  DF    Type III MS      DF          MS      F Value   Pr > F
   2   136.60833333       4     4.3238181818  31.5944   0.0035


Source: COL
Error: MS(ROW*COL*N)
                    Denominator  Denominator
  DF    Type III MS      DF          MS      F Value   Pr > F
   4   8.6003484848       4     4.3238181818   1.9891   0.2609


Source: N *
Error: MS(ROW*COL*N)
                    Denominator  Denominator
  DF    Type III MS      DF          MS      F Value   Pr > F
   4   12.590348485       4     4.3238181818   2.9119   0.1626
* - This test assumes one or more other fixed effects are zero.
```

```
Source: ROW*COL*N
Error: MS(Error)
                        Denominator   Denominator
  DF     Type III MS         DF            MS      F Value   Pr > F
   4     4.3238181818         10          0.32    13.5119    0.0005


Source: G *
Error: MS(Error)
                        Denominator   Denominator
  DF     Type III MS         DF            MS      F Value   Pr > F
   1        71.148            10          0.32   222.3375    0.0001
* - This test assumes one or more other fixed effects are zero.


Source: N*G
Error: MS(Error)
                        Denominator   Denominator
  DF     Type III MS         DF            MS      F Value   Pr > F
   4        5.118             10          0.32    15.9937    0.0002
```

Output 10.13 *Results of the LSMEANS Statement from PROC GLM*

```
Least Squares Means

N             Y
            LSMEAN

1       Non-est
2       Non-est
3       Non-est
4       Non-est
5       Non-est




G             Y
            LSMEAN

1    17.2933333
2    14.2133333




N   G         Y
            LSMEAN

1   1     Non-est
1   2     Non-est
2   1     Non-est
2   2     Non-est
3   1     Non-est
3   2     Non-est
4   1     Non-est
4   2     Non-est
5   1     Non-est
5   2     Non-est
```

Interpretation

The main problem evident in Output 10.13 is that the least squares means of N and N*G are deemed non-estimable. For reasons discussed in Chapter 2, the non-estimability is erroneous, an artifact of PROC GLM treating the whole-plot error component as if it were a fixed effect when diagnosing estimability. Most of the ESTIMATE and CONTRAST statements required to compute main effects and simple effects are similarly affected. For those that can be computed, only the estimates are correct. The estimated standard errors are mostly likely incorrect, often drastically so.

A final point about this example is worth considering. Much of the conventional wisdom regarding the design of experiments is linked to analysis based on the theory underlying PROC GLM or even more dated approaches. Until the introduction of PROC MIXED, a design like the one presented in this experiment—which is a very good design with the resources available—probably would have been avoided because of the inconvenience of the analysis. However, with PROC MIXED, highly efficient unbalanced designs can be analyzed as easily as any other design. In an era of vastly improved statistical software, and, more importantly, tighter research budgets, conventional wisdom for design needs to be rethought.

10.5 A Complex Strip-Split-Split-Plot Example

10.5.1 Introduction

This example considers a complex extension of the split-plot principles introduced in Chapter 2. The data are based on an experiment comparing methods of rangeland reclamation in the Sandhills area of Nebraska.

Three treatment factors were studied: irrigation (IR) at two levels (1=low, 2=high); erosion control (EC), two methods; and seed mixes (V), two types. The objective of the study was to evaluate the effect of these three factors on the restoration of grassland areas that had been damaged by previous abuse.

Irrigation was applied using a center-pivot irrigator. This is a long, straight unit mounted on wheels that rotates around a central point. The center point acts both as an anchor for the unit and as the water source. The nozzles on the unit can be adjusted to various water flow rates, allowing level of irrigation to be varied in concentric circles around the center.

The circle defined by the center-pivot was split in half. One side was managed using one erosion control method, and the other side was managed using the other method of erosion control. Within each irrigation level-by-erosion control sector, plots were assigned to the different seed mixes. Three center-pivot irrigation units were used in the experiment. Figure 10.5 shows the layout of the experiment for each location. The data are given in Data Set 10.5.1 in Appendix 4, "SAS Data Sets."

Figure 10.5 *Layout of One Center-Pivot Irrigation Unit with the Levels of Irrigation, Erosion Control, and Seed Mixes*

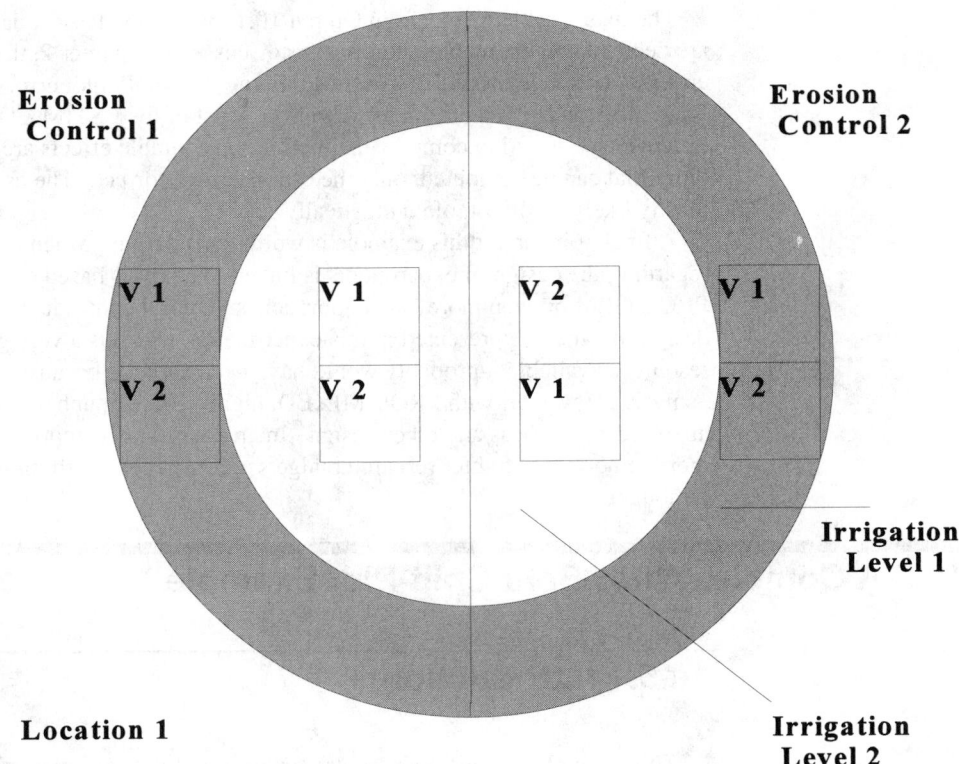

The design is a split block, also known as a strip plot, with respect to the irrigation and erosion control treatments. With respect to the seed mixes, the design is a split-split-plot. For lack of a better name, the overall design was called a "strip-split-split-plot." The fields, or locations (denoted LOC in the SAS data set), occupied by the center-pivot units were considered blocks. The experimental units with respect to irrigation were the concentric subdivision in each field, i.e., LOC*IR combinations. The experimental unit for erosion control was a half-field, i.e., the LOC*EC combination. The experimental unit for an irrigation-by-erosion control treatment combination was LOC*EC*IR. The experimental unit for seed mix was the sub-plot within LOC*EC*IR combinations. Thus, there are four different experimental units and hence four sources of random error in this experiment.

The model for this experiment is

$$y_{ijkl} = \mu_{ijk} + r_l + a_{il} + b_{jl} + c_{ijl} + e_{ijkl}$$

where

y_{ijkl} is the observation on the lth LOC ($l=1,...,L$), i^{th} EC level ($i=1,...,I$), j^{th} level of IR ($j=1,...,J$), and k^{th} level of V ($k=1,...,K$)

μ_{ijk} is the mean of the ijk^{th} EC, IR, V treatment combination

r_l is the lth LOC effect, assumed iid $N(0,\sigma_R^2)$

a_{il} is the il^{th} LOC*EC effect, assumed iid $N(0,\sigma_A^2)$

b_{jl} is the jl^{th} LOC*IR effect, assumed iid $N(0,\sigma_B^2)$

c_{ijl} is the ijl^{th} LOC*ED*IR effect, assumed iid $N(0,\sigma_C^2)$

e_{ijkl} is sub-plot error, assumed iid $N(0,\sigma_e^2)$.

In this experiment, $I=J=K=2$ and $L=3$. You can extend the methods presented in this example to any number of treatment levels and blocks — we give the general range of subscripts to make extension easier. Also, you can express μ_{ijk} in terms of specific main effects and interactions as

$$\mu_{ijk} = \mu + E_i + I_j + Ei_{ij} + V_k + VE_{ik} + VI_{jk} + VEI_{ijk}$$

where

μ is the intercept

E_i is the ith EC main effect

I_j is the jth IR main effect

Ei_{ij} is the ij^{th} EC*IR interaction

V_k is the kth V main effect

VE_{ik} is the ik^{th} V*EC interaction

VI_{jk} is the jk^{th} V*IR interaction

VEI_{ijk} is the ijk^{th} V*EC*IR interaction.

Traditionally, such experiments are analyzed using analysis of variance methods. The ANOVA for this experiment is shown in Table 10.1.

Table 10.1 *ANOVA for a Complex Strip-Split-Split-Plot Example*

Source	df	EMS
LOC	2	$\sigma_e^2 + K\sigma_C^2 + IK\sigma_B^2 + JK\sigma_A^2 + IJK\sigma_R^2$
EC	1	$\sigma_e^2 + K\sigma_C^2 + JK\sigma_A^2 + \phi_E$
LOC*EC = error a	2	$\sigma_e^2 + K\sigma_C^2 + JK\sigma_A^2$
IR	1	$\sigma_e^2 + K\sigma_C^2 + IK\sigma_B^2 + \phi_I$
LOC*IR = error b	2	$\sigma_e^2 + K\sigma_C^2 + IK\sigma_B^2$
EC*IR	1	$\sigma_e^2 + K\sigma_C^2 + \phi_{EI}$
LOC*EC*IR = error c	2	$\sigma_e^2 + K\sigma_C^2$
V	1	$\sigma_e^2 + \phi_V$
V*EC	1	$\sigma_e^2 + \phi_{VE}$
V*IR	1	$\sigma_e^2 + \phi_{VI}$
V*EC*IR	1	$\sigma_e^2 + \phi_{VEI}$
ERROR = error d	8	σ_e^2

The terms ϕ_E, ϕ_I, etc. represent the quadratic forms for the various fixed effects. These terms are described in more detail in Chapters 1 and 2.

10.5.2 Analysis Using PROC MIXED

Program

You can obtain the basic analysis consistent with the model described above using the following program:

```
proc mixed;
   class loc ec ir v;
   model y=ec ir  ec*ir  v v*ec v*ir v*ec*ir/ddfm=satterth;
   random loc loc*ec loc*ir loc*ec*ir;
   lsmeans ec ir ec*ir v v*ec v*ir v*ec*ir;
run;
```

The results appear in Output 10.14.

Results

Output 10.14 *Fixed Effects Test*

Tests of Fixed Effects

Source	NDF	DDF	Type III F	Pr > F
EC	1	2	42.51	0.0227
IR	1	2	0.47	0.5650
EC*IR	1	2	0.16	0.7305
V	1	8	45.34	0.0001
EC*V	1	8	2.68	0.1406
IR*V	1	8	13.50	0.0063
EC*IR*V	1	8	0.20	0.6674

Interpretation

The main results of interest are the significance of the various treatment effects. According to the "Tests of Fixed Effects" the V*IR interaction and the EC and V main effect are significant.

The following LSMEANS options help explain the significant effects.

Program—LSMEANS

```
lsmeans ec /diff;
lsmeans v*ir/slice=v diff;
lsmeans v*ir/slice=ir;
```

The EC/DIFF option shows the difference between the two erosion control means. The two V*IR statements using the SLICE option evaluate the simple effects of V given IR and vice versa. The V main effect is not evaluated because of the significant V*IR interaction. The results of the LSMEANS statements are given in Output 10.15.

Results

Output 10.15 *Results from LSMEANS Statements*

```
                   Least Squares Means

       Level            LSMEAN       Std Error   DDF        T  Pr > |T|

       EC 1           27.96666667   5.33719912  2.12     5.24   0.0305
       EC 2           39.86666667   5.33719912  2.12     7.47   0.0148
       IR 1           33.10000000   5.39273560  2.21     6.14   0.0200
       IR 2           34.73333333   5.39273560  2.21     6.44   0.0181
       EC*IR 1 1      27.45000000   5.52165560  2.42     4.97   0.0255
       EC*IR 1 2      28.48333333   5.52165560  2.42     5.16   0.0235
       EC*IR 2 1      38.75000000   5.52165560  2.42     7.02   0.0115
       EC*IR 2 2      40.98333333   5.52165560  2.42     7.42   0.0101
       V 1            31.27500000   5.27322410  2.02     5.93   0.0266
       V 2            36.55833333   5.27322410  2.02     6.93   0.0196
       EC*V 1 1       25.96666667   5.36595816  2.17     4.84   0.0342
       EC*V 1 2       29.96666667   5.36595816  2.17     5.58   0.0255
       EC*V 2 1       36.58333333   5.36595816  2.17     6.82   0.0169
       EC*V 2 2       43.15000000   5.36595816  2.17     8.04   0.0119
       IR*V 1 1       29.01666667   5.42120003  2.25     5.35   0.0255
       IR*V 1 2       37.18333333   5.42120003  2.25     6.86   0.0149
       IR*V 2 1       33.53333333   5.42120003  2.25     6.19   0.0187
       IR*V 2 2       35.93333333   5.42120003  2.25     6.63   0.0161
       EC*IR*V 1 1 1  23.83333333   5.57712341  2.52     4.27   0.0331
       EC*IR*V 1 1 2  31.06666667   5.57712341  2.52     5.57   0.0179
       EC*IR*V 1 2 1  28.10000000   5.57712341  2.52     5.04   0.0226
       EC*IR*V 1 2 2  28.86666667   5.57712341  2.52     5.18   0.0212
       EC*IR*V 2 1 1  34.20000000   5.57712341  2.52     6.13   0.0142
       EC*IR*V 2 1 2  43.30000000   5.57712341  2.52     7.76   0.0080
       EC*IR*V 2 2 1  38.96666667   5.57712341  2.52     6.99   0.0104
       EC*IR*V 2 2 2  43.00000000   5.57712341  2.52     7.71   0.0082

                 Differences of Least Squares Means

Level 1      Level 2     Difference    Std Error   DDF       T  Pr > |T|

EC 1         EC 2       -11.90000000   1.82505708    2    -6.52   0.0227
V 1          V 2         -5.28333333   0.78461774    8    -6.73   0.0001
IR*V 1 1     IR*V 1 2    -8.16666667   1.10961705    8    -7.36   0.0001
IR*V 1 1     IR*V 2 1    -4.51666667   2.51596293  2.45   -1.80   0.1909
IR*V 1 1     IR*V 2 2    -6.91666667   2.51596293  2.45   -2.75   0.0888
IR*V 1 2     IR*V 2 1     3.65000000   2.51596293  2.45    1.45   0.2619
IR*V 1 2     IR*V 2 2     1.25000000   2.51596293  2.45    0.50   0.6604
IR*V 2 1     IR*V 2 2    -2.40000000   1.10961705    8    -2.16   0.0625
```

```
                    Tests of Effect Slices

        Effect   Slice   NDF   DDF       F   Pr > F

        IR*V     V 1       1   2.45    3.22   0.1909
        IR*V     V 2       1   2.45    0.25   0.6604
        IR*V     IR 1      1     8    54.17   0.0001
        IR*V     IR 2      1     8     4.68   0.0625
```

Interpretation

The estimated mean response to EC1 is 11.9 units less than EC2, with a standard error of 1.825. Using the SLICE results, the significant IR*V interaction results from there being a highly significant seed mix effect at irrigation level IR1 (F=54.17, *p*-value<0.0001) but only a marginally significant V effect at IR2 (F=4.68, *p*-value=0.0625). Using the "Differences of Least Square Means" table, seed mix V1 has a mean response 8.17 units lower that V2 at IR1 but only 2.4 units lower at IR2. The standard error for these simple-effect differences is 1.10. Alternatively, you can characterize the V*IR interaction in terms of simple effects of irrigation for a given seed mix. For seed mix V1, IR1 is 4.52 units lower than IR2, whereas for V2, IR1 has a mean response 1.25 units *higher* than IR2. Neither of these simple effects is statistically significant, however, as the standard error is 2.52.

Program—ESTIMATE

As an alternative to the LSMEANS statements above, you can also obtain the main-effect and simple-effects estimates using the ESTIMATE statement. Respectively, the statements are written

```
estimate 'ec main eff' ec 1 -1;
estimate 'ir1 v ir2 | v1' ir 1 -1 v*ir 1 0 -1 0;
estimate 'ir1 v ir2 | v2' ir 1 -1 v*ir 0 1 0 -1;
estimate 'v1 v v2 | ir1' v 1 -1 v*ir 1 -1 0 0;
estimate 'v1 v v2 | ir2' v 1 -1 v*ir 0 0 1 -1;
```

The results of these statements are given in Output 10.16.

Results

Output 10.16 *Results from ESTIMATE Statements Equivalent to LSMEANS .../DIFF*

```
                      ESTIMATE Statement Results

   Parameter              Estimate     Std Error    DDF       T   Pr > |T|

   ec main eff         -11.90000000   1.82505708      2   -6.52    0.0227
   ir1 v ir2 | v1       -4.51666667   2.51596293   2.45   -1.80    0.1909
   ir1 v ir2 | v2        1.25000000   2.51596293   2.45    0.50    0.6604
   v1 v v2 | ir1        -8.16666667   1.10961705      8   -7.36    0.0001
   v1 v v2 | ir2        -2.40000000   1.10961705      8   -2.16    0.0625
```

Interpretation

The estimates and standard errors are identical to those obtained using the LSMEANS with the DIFF and SLICE options. The LSMEANS approach is easier, but may result in a very long output, particularly if the treatment factors have many levels. You may want to use the ESTIMATE approach when there are only a few simple-effects of interest and you want to limit the amount of output.

One important feature of a complex design such as this one is that the standard errors for various main effects and simple effects consist of different linear combinations of the variance components.

Program—ESTIMATE Statements

The following list of ESTIMATE statements is a sample of the main and simple effects of potential interest in this design:

```
estimate 'ir main eff' ir 1 -1;
estimate 'v  main eff' v 1 -1;

estimate 'e x i same e' ir 1 -1 ec*ir 1 -1 0 0;
estimate 'e x i same i' ec 1 -1 ec*ir 1 0 -1 0;
estimate 'e x i diff e,i' ec 1 -1 ir 1 -1 ec*ir 1 0 0 -1;
estimate 'v x e same e' v 1 -1 v*ec 1 -1 0 0;
estimate 'v x e diff e' ec 1 -1 v*ec 1 0 -1 0;
estimate 'v x e diff e,v' ec 1 -1 v 1 -1 v*ec 1 0 0 -1;
estimate 'v x e x i same e,i' v 1 -1 v*ec 1 -1 0 0 v*ir 1 -1 0 0
         v*ec*ir 1 -1 0 0 0 0 0 0;
estimate 'same e,v  diff i' ir 1 -1 ec*ir 1 -1 0 0 v*ir 1 0 -1 0
         v*ec*ir 1 0 -1 0 0 0 0 0;
estimate 'same e  diff v,i' ir 1 -1 v 1 -1 ec*ir 1 -1 0 0
         v*ec 1 -1 0 0 v*ir 1 0 0 -1 v*ec*ir 1 0 0 -1 0 0 0 0;
estimate 'same v, diff e,i' ec 1 -1 ir 1 -1 ec*ir 1 0 0 -1
         v*ec 1 0 -1 0 v*ir 1 0 -1 0 v*ec*ir 1 0 0 0 0 0 -1 0;
estimate 'diff e,i,v' ec 1 -1 ir 1 -1 v 1 -1 ec*ir 1 0 0 -1
         v*ec 1 0 0 -1 v*ir 1 0 0 -1 v*ec*ir 1 0 0 0 0 0 0 -1;
```

Most of these have unique standard errors. Table 10.2 contains a list of the estimates obtained by the above ESTIMATE statements and their associated variances.

Table 10.2 *Variance of Estimated Difference for Various Main Effects and Simple Effects*

Contrast Title	Comparison*	Variance
ec main eff	$\mu_{1\bullet\bullet} - \mu_{2\bullet\bullet}$ $\mu_{j\bullet\bullet} - \mu_{j'\bullet\bullet}$	$(2/JKL)(JK\sigma_A^2 + K\sigma_C^2 + \sigma_e^2)$
ir main eff	$\mu_{\bullet 1\bullet} - \mu_{\bullet 2\bullet}$ $\mu_{\bullet j\bullet} - \mu_{\bullet j'\bullet}$	$(2/IKL)(IK\sigma_B^2 + K\sigma_C^2 + \sigma_e^2)$
v main eff	$\mu_{\bullet\bullet 1} - \mu_{\bullet\bullet 2}$ $\mu_{\bullet\bullet k} - \mu_{\bullet\bullet k'}$	$(2/IJL)\sigma_e^2$
e x i same e	$\mu_{11\bullet} - \mu_{12\bullet}$ $\mu_{ij\bullet} - \mu_{ij'\bullet}$	$(2/KL)[K(\sigma_B^2 + \sigma_C^2) + \sigma_e^2]$
e x i same i	$\mu_{11\bullet} - \mu_{21\bullet}$ $\mu_{ij\bullet} - \mu_{i'j\bullet}$	$(2/KL)[K(\sigma_A^2 + \sigma_C^2) + \sigma_e^2]$
e x i diff e,i	$\mu_{11\bullet} - \mu_{22\bullet}$ $\mu_{ij\bullet} - \mu_{i'j'\bullet}$	$(2/KL)[K(\sigma_A^2 + \sigma_B^2 + \sigma_C^2) + \sigma_e^2]$

v x e same e	$\mu_{1\cdot1} - \mu_{1\cdot2}$ $\mu_{i\cdot k} - \mu_{i\cdot k'}$	$(2/JL)\sigma_e^2$
v x e diff e	$\mu_{1\cdot1} - \mu_{2\cdot1}$ $\mu_{i\cdot k} - \mu_{i'\cdot k}$	$(2/JL)(J\sigma_A^2 + \sigma_C^2 + \sigma_e^2)$
v x e diff e,v	$\mu_{1\cdot1} - \mu_{2\cdot2}$ $\mu_{i\cdot k} - \mu_{i'\cdot k'}$	$(2/JL)(J\sigma_A^2 + \sigma_C^2 + \sigma_e^2)$
v x e x i same e,i	$\mu_{111} - \mu_{112}$ $\mu_{ijk} - \mu_{ijk'}$	$(2/L)\sigma_e^2$
same e,v diff i	$\mu_{111} - \mu_{121}$ $\mu_{ijk} - \mu_{ij'k}$	$(2/L)(\sigma_A^2 + \sigma_C^2 + \sigma_e^2)$
same e diff v,i	$\mu_{111} - \mu_{122}$ $\mu_{ijk} - \mu_{ij'k'}$	$(2/L)(\sigma_A^2 + \sigma_C^2 + \sigma_e^2)$
same v diff e,i	$\mu_{111} - \mu_{221}$ $\mu_{ijk} - \mu_{i'j'k}$	$(2/L)(\sigma_A^2 + \sigma_B^2 + \sigma_C^2 + \sigma_e^2)$
diff e,v,i	$\mu_{111} - \mu_{222}$ $\mu_{ijk} - \mu_{i'j'k'}$	$(2/L)(\sigma_A^2 + \sigma_B^2 + \sigma_C^2 + \sigma_e^2)$

* First line is comparison shown in SAS example; second line is general form of comparison.

Results

PROC MIXED computes the standard errors by substituting the variance component estimates into each variance formula and taking the square root. Output 10.17 contains the variance component estimates and the results of the above list of ESTIMATE statements.

Output 10.17 *Variance Component Estimates and Standard Errors of Various Main- and Simple-Effect Estimates*

	Covariance Parameter Estimates (REML)				
Cov Parm	Ratio	Estimate	Std Error	Z	Pr > |Z|
LOC	21.08917090	77.89812500	83.12500781	0.94	0.3487
LOC*EC	0.41962775	1.55000000	6.06952660	0.26	0.7984
LOC*IR	1.38759165	5.12541667	9.23851225	0.55	0.5790
LOC*EC*IR	1.36598985	5.04562500	6.95408463	0.73	0.4681
Residual	1.00000000	3.69375000	1.84687500	2.00	0.0455

```
                        ESTIMATE Statement Results

    Parameter                  Estimate    Std Error   DDF        T    Pr > |T|


    v   main eff               -5.28333333  0.78461774    8    -6.73    0.0001
    ir main eff                -1.63333333  2.39049042    2    -0.68    0.5650
    e x i same e               -1.03333333  2.83053784  3.38    -0.37    0.7367
    e x i same i              -11.30000000  2.37241087  3.87    -4.76    0.0096
    e x i diff e,i            -13.53333333  3.00753683  3.74    -4.50    0.0126
    v x e same e               -4.00000000  1.10961705    8    -3.60    0.0069
    v x e diff e              -10.61666667  1.98656949  2.78    -5.34    0.0155
    v x e diff e,v            -17.18333333  1.98656949  2.78    -8.65    0.0043
    v x e x i same e,i         -7.23333333  1.56923548    8    -4.61    0.0017
    same e,v  diff i           -4.26666667  3.04026223  4.46    -1.40    0.2261
    same e  diff v,i           -5.03333333  3.04026223  4.46    -1.66    0.1658
    same v, diff e,i          -15.13333333  3.20570238  4.79    -4.72    0.0059
    diff e,i,v                -19.16666667  3.20570238  4.79    -5.98    0.0022
```

Interpretation

These results should emphasize the extreme care researchers and journal editors need to use to make sure that appropriate standard errors are used when reporting results from complex experiments. Single summary statistics to characterize variability, however tempting, should be avoided and emphatically discouraged.

10.6 2^3 Treatment Structure in a Split-Plot Design with the Three-way Interaction As the Whole-Plot Comparison

10.6.1 Introduction

When the number of treatments in the treatment structure is large, an incomplete block design structure is the most efficient way to carry out the experiment. When an incomplete block design is used, some information about the treatment comparisons is confounded with blocks. If the design is carried out in sets of blocks where within a set of blocks there is a complete replication of the treatment combinations, you can construct the blocks such that the same effect or effects are confounded with blocks within each replication. Such a design is of the split-plot type with the confounded effects consisting of the whole-plot comparisons and the other effects consisting of the sub-plot comparisons. The experiment described in this section consists of a 2^3 treatment structure with a design structure consisting of six sets or replications where there are two blocks of four experimental units within each set. The treatment combinations are assigned to the blocks by confounding the three-way interaction with blocks within each replication. The assignment of the treatment combinations to the two blocks within each replication is displayed in Tables 10.3 and 10.4. The symbols for the treatment combinations in Table 10.3 use the notation of Cochran and Cox (1957), and the symbols for the treatment combinations in Table 10.4 use the notation of Box, Hunter, and Hunter (1978).

Table 10.3 *Treatment Combinations Assigned to the Two Blocks within Each Replication to Confound the ABC Interaction Using the Notation of Cochran and Cox (1957)*

BLOCK 1	(0)[1]	ab	ac	ac
BLOCK 2	a	b	c	abc

[1]The presence of a letter indicates that factor at the high level and the absence of a letter indicates that factor at the low level.

Table 10.4 *Treatment Combinations Assigned to the Two Blocks within Each Replication to Confound the ABC Interaction Using the Notation of Box, Hunter, and Hunter (1978)*

BLOCK 1	- - -[1]	- + +	+ - +	+ + -
BLOCK 2	- - +	- + -	+ - -	+ + +

[1]The order of the "+" and "−" signs correspond to the levels of A, B, and C

The data in Data Set 10.6.1 in Appendix 4, "SAS Data Sets," are from an experiment studying the effect that three factors, pressure (A) at two levels, temperature (B) at two levels, and flow rate (C) at two levels have on the thickness (Y) of a silicon nitrate layer deposited on silicon wafers used in the manufacture of computer chips. Only four batches of wafers could be processed during a shift, so blocks of size four were needed to carry out the experiment. Two blocks of size four were run on consecutive days, or one complete replication of the set of treatment combinations could be obtained in two days. The measurement is the average thickness of the layer of Si_3N_4 deposited on all of the wafers in a batch (25 wafers are in a batch). The two blocks of four within each replication were determined using the arrangements in Table 10.3 or 10.4. Thus, the ABC interaction was confounded with blocks within each replication. Because there are six replications, information about the ABC interaction can be obtained from the data by averaging over the differences between the two blocks within each replication. The confounding of the ABC interaction with blocks within each replication means that the block or group of four batches is the experimental unit for the components of the ABC interaction. The batch within a block is the experimental unit for all other factorial effects. Hence, two error terms are required in the model used to describe the data, one for the blocks within a replication and one for the batches within a block. Because the pairs of consecutive days correspond to a replication, the model needs to contain a random effect for these pairs of days. The randomization scheme was to assign one of the two blocks to day one and then randomize the order of the runs within day one. During day 2, the other block of treatment combinations were run in random order. This randomization process was then repeated for the other five pairs of consecutive days or replications. In the data list of Data Set 10.6.1, the column titled REP corresponds to replication and the column titled BLK corresponds to block or day within a replication. The data are listed in nonrandomized order.

This data set can be analyzed in two ways. First, the analysis can be carried out by analyzing the means of the treatment combinations in the analysis of variance mode and second, the analysis can be carried out by using a regression model. A model used to describe the means of the data is

$$y_{ijkmn} = \mu + \alpha_k + \beta_m + \gamma_n + (\alpha\beta)_{km} + (\alpha\gamma)_{kn} + (\beta\gamma)_{mn} + (\alpha\beta\gamma)_{kmn}$$
$$+ r_i + a_{ij} + e_{ijkmn}$$

where

$i=1,2,...6$

$j=1,2$

$k=-1, +1$

$m=-1, +1$

$n=-1, +1$

$\gamma_i \sim$ iid N(0, σ^2_r)

$a_{ij} \sim$ iid N(0, σ^2_a)

$e_{ijkmn} \sim$ iid N(0, σ^2_e)

The indices denote levels as follows:

i=replication

j=block or day within a replication

k is the level of A

m is the level of B

n is the level of C

r_i denotes the replication effect

a_{ij} denotes the block or whole-plot error

e_{ijkmn} denotes the batch error term.

The regression model or response surface model is

$$y_{ijk} = \beta_0 + \beta_A A_k + \beta_B B_k + \beta_C C_k + \beta_{AB} A_k B_k + \beta_{AC} A_k C_k$$
$$+ \beta_{BC} B_k C_k + \beta_{ABC} A_k B_k C_k + r_i + a_{ij} + e_{ijkmn}$$

where

$i=1,2,...6$

$j=1,2$

$k=1,2,3,4$

$\gamma_i \sim$ iid N(0, σ^2_r)

$a_{ij} \sim$ iid N(0, σ^2_a)

$e_{ijkmn} \sim$ iid N(0, σ^2_e).

The indices denote levels as follows:

i=replication

j=block or day within a replication

k is the observation within a block

r_i denotes the replication effect

a_{ij} denotes the block or whole plot error

e_{ijkmn} denotes the batch error term.

10.6.2 Analysis Using PROC MIXED

Program—Input

The program used to read the data is

```
data fac_sp;
   input rep blk a b c y;
   abc=a*b*c;
run;
```

Because the ABC interaction and blocks are completely confounded, the variable ABC is computed to generate an indicator variable that has the value of -1 or +1 for those treatments corresponding to the linear combination used to compute the ABC interaction. The ABC interaction is a scalar multiple of the treatment combinations from Table 10.3 as $\{- a - b - c - abc + ab + ac + bc + (0)\}$. The ABC term is used in the PROC GLM comparison.

Program—Analysis of Variance Model

Using the above variables, the PROC MIXED program to fit the analysis of variance model is

```
proc mixed;
   class a b c rep blk;
   model y=a|b|c/ddfm=satterth;
   random rep blk(rep);
   lsmeans a*b b*c/pdiff;
   lsmeans a*b*c;
run;
```

By having A, B, and C in the CLASS statement, the model term A|B|C generates all of the main effects, the two-factor interactions, and the three-way interaction. The RANDOM statement contains the error terms for the model, REP for the replication variance component, and BLK(REP) for the block or group of four batches variance component. The DDFM=SATTERTH option is used to request that approximate degrees of freedom be computed for all fixed-effect tests.

The results of PROC MIXED are in Output 10.18.

Results

Output 10.18 *Results of PROC MIXED for Analyzing the Cell Means*

```
                    The MIXED Procedure
                  Class Level Information
                 Class    Levels  Values
                 A           2    1 -1
                 B           2    1 -1
                 C           2    1 -1
                 REP         6    1 2 3 4 5 6
                 BLK         2    1 2


             Covariance Parameter Estimates (REML)
Cov Parm          Ratio       Estimate      Std Error      Z   Pr > |Z|
REP            0.97319277    4.48750000    4.75265752    0.94   0.3451
BLK(REP)       0.86596386    3.99305556    3.26809323    1.22   0.2218
Residual       1.00000000    4.61111111    1.19058377    3.87   0.0001


                 Tests of Fixed Effects
          Source      NDF    DDF   Type III F   Pr > F
          A             1     30       26.10    0.0001
          B             1     30       24.74    0.0001
          A*B           1     30       18.51    0.0002
          C             1     30      115.66    0.0001
          A*C           1     30        1.46    0.2358
          B*C           1     30       26.10    0.0001
          A*B*C         1      5        0.10    0.7632
```

```
                                Least Squares Means
            Level                    LSMEAN       Std Error    DDF        T    Pr > |T|
            A*B  1  1            121.91666667     1.21034316   7.67    100.73    0.0001
            A*B  1 -1            121.50000000     1.21034316   7.67    100.38    0.0001
            A*B -1  1            127.75000000     1.21034316   7.67    105.55    0.0001
            A*B -1 -1            122.00000000     1.21034316   7.67    100.80    0.0001
            B*C  1  1            129.75000000     1.21034316   7.67    107.20    0.0001
            B*C  1 -1            119.91666667     1.21034316   7.67     99.08    0.0001
            B*C -1  1            123.50000000     1.21034316   7.67    102.04    0.0001
            B*C -1 -1            120.00000000     1.21034316   7.67     99.15    0.0001
            A*B*C  1  1  1       126.66666667     1.47714063   14.7     85.75    0.0001
            A*B*C  1  1 -1       117.16666667     1.47714063   14.7     79.32    0.0001
            A*B*C  1 -1  1       122.66666667     1.47714063   14.7     83.04    0.0001
            A*B*C  1 -1 -1       120.33333333     1.47714063   14.7     81.46    0.0001
            A*B*C -1  1  1       132.83333333     1.47714063   14.7     89.93    0.0001
            A*B*C -1  1 -1       122.66666667     1.47714063   14.7     83.04    0.0001
            A*B*C -1 -1  1       124.33333333     1.47714063   14.7     84.17    0.0001
            A*B*C -1 -1 -1       119.66666667     1.47714063   14.7     81.01    0.0001


                         Differences of Least Squares Means
Level 1        Level 2         Difference     Std Error    DDF        T    Pr > |T|
A*B  1  1      A*B  1 -1        0.41666667     0.87665188    30     0.48    0.6380
A*B  1  1      A*B -1  1       -5.83333333     0.87665188    30    -6.65    0.0001
A*B  1  1      A*B -1 -1       -0.08333333     0.87665188    30    -0.10    0.9249
A*B  1 -1      A*B -1  1       -6.25000000     0.87665188    30    -7.13    0.0001
A*B  1 -1      A*B -1 -1       -0.50000000     0.87665188    30    -0.57    0.5727
A*B -1  1      A*B -1 -1        5.75000000     0.87665188    30     6.56    0.0001
B*C  1  1      B*C  1 -1        9.83333333     0.87665188    30    11.22    0.0001
B*C  1  1      B*C -1  1        6.25000000     0.87665188    30     7.13    0.0001
B*C  1  1      B*C -1 -1        9.75000000     0.87665188    30    11.12    0.0001
B*C  1 -1      B*C -1  1       -3.58333333     0.87665188    30    -4.09    0.0003
B*C  1 -1      B*C -1 -1       -0.08333333     0.87665188    30    -0.10    0.9249
B*C -1  1      B*C -1 -1        3.50000000     0.87665188    30     3.99    0.0004
```

Interpretation

Because the ABC interaction is confounded with blocks in each replication, there are six estimates of the ABC effect, one from each replication. The variance of those six estimates has five degrees of freedom, which is the estimate of the block-to-block variance or whole-plot variance. The denominator degrees for the ABC F statistic is "5", those degrees of freedom for the whole-plot error. All other factorial effects have "30" denominator degrees of freedom indicating they are sub-plot comparisons.

- **LSMEANS**

  There is a significant A*B interaction and a significant B*C interaction. Thus, the two sets of interaction means are computed using the LSMEANS statement. The PDIFF option provides the pairwise comparison between the four interaction means within each set of four means. The mean corresponding to A=-1 and B=1 is significantly larger than the other three means, and they are not significantly different. The mean corresponding to B=1 and C=1 is significantly larger than the other three means. The mean corresponding to B=-1 and C=1 is significantly different from the means with B=1 and C=-1 or B=-1 and C=-1, but the last two means are not different. The LSMEANS statement is used to compute the A*B*C means or three-way cell means.

Program—Regression Model

The PROC MIXED program used to fit the regression model with the random effects is

```
proc mixed;
   class rep blk;
   model y=a|b|c/solution ddfm=satterth;
   random rep blk(rep);
run;
```

The term in the MODEL statement A|B|C generates a regression model with the linear terms, two-way cross product terms, and the three-way cross product term.

The results of the analysis are in Output 10.19.

Results

Output 10.19 *Results from PROC MIXED Analyzing the Regression Model*

```
                     The MIXED Procedure
                  Class Level Information
              Class     Levels   Values
              REP          6     1 2 3 4 5 6
              BLK          2     1 2
```

Covariance Parameter Estimates (REML)

Cov Parm	Ratio	Estimate	Std Error	Z	Pr > |Z|
REP	0.97319277	4.48750000	4.75265752	0.94	0.3451
BLK(REP)	0.86596386	3.99305556	3.26809323	1.22	0.2218
Residual	1.00000000	4.61111111	1.19058377	3.87	0.0001

Solution for Fixed Effects

Parameter	Estimate	Std Error	DDF	T	Pr > |T|
INTERCEPT	123.29166667	1.08477468	5	113.66	0.0001
A	-1.58333333	0.30994324	30	-5.11	0.0001
B	1.54166667	0.30994324	30	4.97	0.0001
A*B	-1.33333333	0.30994324	30	-4.30	0.0002
C	3.33333333	0.30994324	30	10.75	0.0001
A*C	-0.37500000	0.30994324	30	-1.21	0.2358
B*C	1.58333333	0.30994324	30	5.11	0.0001
A*B*C	0.20833333	0.65484307	5	0.32	0.7632

Tests of Fixed Effects

Source	NDF	DDF	Type III F	Pr > F
A	1	30	26.10	0.0001
B	1	30	24.74	0.0001
A*B	1	30	18.51	0.0002
C	1	30	115.66	0.0001
A*C	1	30	1.46	0.2358
B*C	1	30	26.10	0.0001
A*B*C	1	5	0.10	0.7632

The estimates of the variance components are identical to those obtained in Output 10.18 because the regression model has one parameter for each cell of data in the treatment structure. If a simpler regression model were used, the estimates of the variance components would change. The estimates of the regression coefficients are provided along with the estimated standard errors. The estimated standard error for β_{ABC} is 0.6548 and is based on "5" degrees of freedom, the degrees of freedom corresponding to the whole-plot error. As in the analysis of the means in Output 10.18, there are significant coefficients for A*B and B*C as well as significant linear coefficients.

10.6.3 Comparisons with PROC GLM

The analysis of the means using PROC GLM provides an appropriate analysis, but after some changing of the variables. The blocking structure is confounded with the ABC interaction, and it takes a new variable to separate the ABC effect and leave the whole-plot error intact. When you use A*B*C*REP as the whole plot error, all of the sub-plot error is combined with the whole-plot error, and the ERROR in the analysis is left with zero degrees of freedom. To get around this, you can compute a new indicator variable that indicates which blocks have the "–1" treatment combinations and the "+1" treatment combinations of the ABC interaction, as computed in the INPUT statements where ABC=A*B*C. Including ABC and ABC*REP in the model enables the whole-plot comparisons to be extracted and leaves the sub-plot error intact.

Program—Analysis of Variance Model

The PROC GLM statements needed to fit the model with the means is

```
proc glm;
   class rep blk abc;
   model y=rep abc abc*rep a|b|c@2/solution;
   contrast '111' intercept 1 abc 1 0 a 1 b 1 c 1 a*b 1 a*c 1 b*c 1;
   estimate '111' intercept 1 abc 1 0 a 1 b 1 c 1 a*b 1 a*c 1 b*c 1;
   random rep abc*rep/test;
   lsmeans a*b b*c/pdiff;
   lsmeans a*b*c;
run;
```

The terms ABC and ABC*REP provide the whole-plot analysis, and the term A|B|C@2 generates the main effects and the two-factor interactions (recall that ABC is extracting the ABC interaction and is not needed in this part of the definition of the model). The RANDOM statement identifies the random effects in the model and provides the expected mean squares for the TYPE III means squares.

The results are in Output 10.20.

Results

Output 10.20 *Results from PROC GLM Analyzing the Cell Means*

```
          General Linear Models Procedure
              Class Level Information
          Class    Levels     Values
          REP         6       1 2 3 4 5 6
          BLK         2       1 2
          A           2       1 -1
          B           2       1 -1
          C           2       1 -1
          ABC         2       1 -1
```

```
                   Number of observations in data set = 48
Dependent Variable: Y
                            Sum of        Mean
Source              DF      Squares      Square   F Value    Pr > F
Model               17    1367.5833     80.4461    17.45     0.0001
Error               30     138.3333      4.6111
Corrected Total     47    1505.9167


                    R-Square         C.V.      Root MSE     Y Mean
                    0.908140       1.741683     2.1473      123.29


Source       DF    Type III SS   Mean Square   F Value    Pr > F

REP           5    282.41667      56.48333      12.25      0.0001
ABC           1      2.08333       2.08333       0.45      0.5066
REP*ABC       5    102.91667      20.58333       4.46      0.0037
A             1    120.33333     120.33333      26.10      0.0001
B             1    114.08333     114.08333      24.74      0.0001
A*B           1     85.33333      85.33333      18.51      0.0002
C             1    533.33333     533.33333     115.66      0.0001
A*C           1      6.75000       6.75000       1.46      0.2358
B*C           1    120.33333     120.33333      26.10      0.0001


Contrast     DF    Contrast SS   Mean Square   F Value    Pr > F

111           1     96266.667    96266.667    20877.11     0.0001


                              T for H0:     Pr > |T|    Std Error of
Parameter    Estimate      Parameter=0                   Estimate

111         126.666667        144.49         0.0001      0.87665188


Source       Type III Expected Mean Square
REP          Var(Error) + 4 Var(REP*ABC) + 8 Var(REP)
ABC          Var(Error) + 4 Var(REP*ABC) + Q(ABC)
REP*ABC      Var(Error) + 4 Var(REP*ABC)
A            Var(Error) + Q(A,A*B,A*C)
B            Var(Error) + Q(B,A*B,B*C)
A*B          Var(Error) + Q(A*B)
C            Var(Error) + Q(C,A*C,B*C)
A*C          Var(Error) + Q(A*C)
B*C          Var(Error) + Q(B*C)


           Tests of Hypotheses for Mixed Model Analysis of Variance


Source: ABC
Error: MS(REP*ABC)
                    Denominator   Denominator
DF    Type III MS       DF            MS       F Value    Pr > F
 1   2.0833333333        5      20.583333333    0.1012    0.7632
```

Interpretation

The expected mean squares indicate that the REP*ABC term is the appropriate divisor for the ABC term and that computation is carried out by using the TEST option on the RANDOM statement. The appropriate test for the ABC interaction is provided with the abbreviated "Test of Hypotheses for Mixed Model Analysis of Variance". The other tests are not included as they are the same as provided by the TYPE III analysis. The results of the F-tests are identical to those provided by PROC MIXED.

LSMEANS are used to provide least squares estimates of the cell means for the A*B and B*C interactions as displayed in Output 10.21.

Output 10.21 *LSMEANS from the Cell Means Analysis of PROC GLM*

```
Contrast                    Contrast Expected Mean Square

111                         Var(Error) + Var(REP*ABC) + Var(REP)
                            + Q(INTERCEPT,ABC,A,B,A*B,C,A*C,B*C)



Least Squares Means


A     B              Y      Pr > |T| H0: LSMEAN(i)=LSMEAN(j)
                   LSMEAN   i/j    1       2       3       4


1     1      121.916667     1    .      0.6380  0.0001  0.9249
1    -1      121.500000     2  0.6380     .     0.0001  0.5727
-1    1      127.750000     3  0.0001  0.0001     .     0.0001
-1   -1      122.000000     4  0.9249  0.5727  0.0001     .



B     C              Y      Pr > |T| H0: LSMEAN(i)=LSMEAN(j)
                   LSMEAN   i/j    1       2       3       4


1     1      129.750000     1    .      0.0001  0.0001  0.0001
1    -1      119.916667     2  0.0001     .     0.0003  0.9249
-1    1      123.500000     3  0.0001  0.0003     .     0.0004
-1   -1      120.000000     4  0.0001  0.9249  0.0004     .
```

The PDIFF option is used to provide pairwise comparisons between the two sets of means. The conclusions are identical to those obtained by PROC MIXED. The STDERR option is not used as the estimated standard errors provided for the LSMEANS are not correct when there is more than one variance component in the model. The A*B*C LSMEANS are not available as the A*B*C term is not included in the model. Those LSMEANS can be computed by using ESTIMATE and CONTRAST statements.

The ESTIMATE and CONTRAST statements are included to demonstrate how you can extract or compute the "1 1 1" cell mean from the data. The CONTRAST statement is included to provide the appropriate estimate of the standard error. The "Expected Mean Square of the Contrast" in Output 10.21 indicates that the variance of the "1 1 1" cell mean is a scalar multiple of $\sigma^2_e + \sigma^2_{REP*ABC} + \sigma^2_{REP}$. The appropriate estimate of the standard error must be recomputed (see Chapter 28, Milliken and Johnson, 1984) by dividing the printed estimate of the standard error 0.87665 by the root mean square 2.14735 and then multiplying by the square of an estimate of $\sigma^2_e + \sigma^2_{REP*ABC} + \sigma^2_{REP}$, which is $4.6111 + 3.9904 + 4.4875 = 13.0917$. The new estimate of the standard error for the "1 1 1" cell mean is 1.74414. Because the model is balanced, the method of moments estimates of the variance components are identical to the REML estimates obtained by PROC MIXED. The estimate of the "1 1 1" cell mean and its estimated standard error from the above statements are identical to those obtained by PROC MIXED.

Program—Naive PROC GLM

Including random effects in a regression model for PROC GLM causes some difficulties when one of the effects is confounded with some of the blocking structure or random effects. The PROC GLM program that you might naively use is

```
proc glm;
   class rep blk;
   model y=rep blk(rep) a|b|c/solution;
   random rep blk(rep)/test;
run;
```

The results are in Output 10.22.

Results

Output 10.22 *Results from PROC GLM to Fit the Regression Model*

```
General Linear Models Procedure
Class Level Information
Class    Levels    Values
REP         6       1 2 3 4 5 6
BLK         2       1 2


Number of observations in data set = 48


Dependent Variable: Y
```

Source	DF	Sum of Squares	Mean Square	F Value	Pr > F
Model	17	1367.58333333	80.44607843	17.45	0.0001
Error	30	138.33333333	4.61111111		
Corrected Total	47	1505.91666667			

R-Square	C.V.	Root MSE	Y Mean
0.908140	1.741683	2.14734979	123.29166667

Source	DF	Type III SS	Mean Square	F Value	Pr > F
REP	5	282.41666667	56.48333333	12.25	0.0001
BLK(REP)	5	102.91666667	20.58333333	4.46	0.0037
A	1	120.33333333	120.33333333	26.10	0.0001
B	1	114.08333333	114.08333333	24.74	0.0001
A*B	1	85.33333333	85.33333333	18.51	0.0002
C	1	533.33333333	533.33333333	115.66	0.0001
A*C	1	6.75000000	6.75000000	1.46	0.2358
B*C	1	120.33333333	120.33333333	26.10	0.0001
A*B*C	0	0.00000000	.	.	.

Parameter	Estimate	T for H0: Parameter=0	Pr > |T|	Std Error of Estimate
A	-1.5833333	-5.11	0.0001	0.30994324
B	1.5416667	4.97	0.0001	0.30994324
A*B	-1.3333333	-4.30	0.0002	0.30994324
C	3.3333333	10.75	0.0001	0.30994324
A*C	-0.3750000	-1.21	0.2358	0.30994324
B*C	1.5833333	5.11	0.0001	0.30994324
A*B*C	0.0000000 B	.	.	.

```
Source          Type III Expected Mean Square

REP             Var(Error) + 4 Var(BLK(REP)) + 8 Var(REP)
BLK(REP)        Var(Error) + 4 Var(BLK(REP))
A               Var(Error) + Q(A)
B               Var(Error) + Q(B)
A*B             Var(Error) + Q(A*B)
C               Var(Error) + Q(C)
A*C             Var(Error) + Q(A*C)
B*C             Var(Error) + Q(B*C)
A*B*C           0
```

Interpretation

The quick examination of the results shows that there is no information available for estimating the coefficient of the A*B*C term in the regression model because the degrees of freedom associated with the sum of squares is 0, and the estimate is 0 with undefined estimated standard error. This analysis does not let you extract the information in the data about the coefficient for A*B*C. In fact, PROC GLM cannot fit a regression model to the data and provide information about the A*B*C coefficient. You can put ABC in the CLASS statement and then include ABC and REP*ABC in the MODEL statement to provide estimates of the regression coefficient for all of the linear and two-way cross product terms in the model. Doing that you get means or intercepts for the ABC levels, but at least you can see if there is a three-way interaction in the model.

Program—Whole-Plot Means and Sub-plot Regression

The PROC GLM program with ABC in the CLASS statement and REP*ABC in the MODEL statement is

```
proc glm;
   class rep blk abc;
   model y=rep abc abc*rep a|b|c@2/solution;
   contrast '111' intercept 1 abc 1 0 a 1 b 1 c 1 a*b 1 a*c 1 b*c 1;
   estimate '111' intercept 1 abc 1 0 a 1 b 1 c 1 a*b 1 a*c 1 b*c 1;
run;
```

The results of the above statements are in Output 10.23.

Results

Output 10.23 *Results of PROC GLM Fitting the Regression Model with an Indicator Variable for the ABC Interaction*

```
                General Linear Models Procedure
                   Class Level Information
              Class     Levels     Values
              REP          6       1 2 3 4 5 6
              BLK          2       1 2
              ABC          2       1 -1


           Number of observations in data set = 48

Dependent Variable: Y
                          Sum of          Mean
```

Source	DF	Squares	Square	F Value	Pr > F
Model	17	1367.5833	80.4461	17.45	0.0001
Error	30	138.3333	4.6111		
Corrected Total	47	1505.9167			

	R-Square	C.V.	Root MSE	Y Mean
	0.908140	1.741683	2.1473	123.29

Source	DF	Type III SS	Mean Square	F Value	Pr > F
REP	5	282.41667	56.48333	12.25	0.0001
ABC	1	2.08333	2.08333	0.45	0.5066
REP*ABC	5	102.91667	20.58333	4.46	0.0037
A	1	120.33333	120.33333	26.10	0.0001
B	1	114.08333	114.08333	24.74	0.0001
A*B	1	85.33333	85.33333	18.51	0.0002
C	1	533.33333	533.33333	115.66	0.0001
A*C	1	6.75000	6.75000	1.46	0.2358
B*C	1	120.33333	120.33333	26.10	0.0001

Source	Type III Expected Mean Square
REP	Var(Error) + 4 Var(REP*ABC) + 8 Var(REP)
ABC	Var(Error) + 4 Var(REP*ABC) + Q(ABC)
REP*ABC	Var(Error) + 4 Var(REP*ABC)
A	Var(Error) + Q(A)
B	Var(Error) + Q(B)
A*B	Var(Error) + Q(A*B)
C	Var(Error) + Q(C)
A*C	Var(Error) + Q(A*C)
B*C	Var(Error) + Q(B*C)

```
          Tests of Hypotheses for Mixed Model Analysis of Variance
```

Source: ABC
Error: MS(REP*ABC)

		Denominator	Denominator		
DF	Type III MS	DF	MS	F Value	Pr > F
1	2.0833333333	5	20.583333333	0.1012	0.7632

Contrast	DF	Contrast SS	Mean Square	F Value	Pr > F
111	1	96266.667	96266.667	20877.11	0.0001

		T for H0:	Pr > |T|	Std Error of
Parameter	Estimate	Parameter=0		Estimate
111	126.666667	144.49	0.0001	0.87665188

Interpretation

The results in Output 10.23 provide the same information about the ABC effect in the model as described for the analysis using the cells means analysis in Output 10.20. The estimates of the regression parameters are the same as obtained in Output 10.22 and the expected mean squares and resulting mixed models tests are identical to those in Output 10.20. The ESTIMATE and CONTRAST statements are used to provide predicted values for the regression model evaluated at A=1, B=1 and C=1. The expected mean square indicates that the estimated standard error needs to be recomputed as was done for the effect using the results in Output 10.20.

For regression models with random effects, such as replication and blocks with confounding, a mixed models procedure like PROC MIXED provides an appropriate analysis with little or no additional work. Using non-mixed models software like PROC GLM requires additional effort to extract the desired information from the data and in some cases it is impossible to obtain the information in the desired form.

10.7 2³ Treatment Structure in an Incomplete Block Design Structure with Balanced Confounding

10.7.1 Introduction

Incomplete block designs are useful when there are a large number of treatments or treatment combinations in the treatment structure and it is not possible to observe each of the treatments in a homogeneous period of time. When incomplete block designs are used, some of the information about the treatment effects is confounded with the blocks. One strategy is to confound one higher order interaction with the block effects and generate a split-plot design structure as described in section 10.6. The strategy in this section is to confound all interactions of the same order an equal number of times with blocks within some replication. So unlike the experiment in section 10.6 where the ABC interaction was confounded with blocks in all replications, different interactions are confounded with blocks in each of the replications. The following design involves a 2³ treatment structure in five replications of two blocks where the ABC interaction is confounded in replications one and two, the AB interaction is confounded in replication three, the AC interaction is confounded in replication four, and the BC interaction is confounded in replication five. The usual analysis extracts information from the design from the within-block comparisons (such as provided by PROC GLM). The mixed models analysis extracts information from the within-block comparisons and from the between-block comparisons and combines them into a common estimate. For the main effects, all information comes from the within-block comparisons, but for the interactions, some of the information comes from the within-block comparisons and some from the between-block comparisons. PROC MIXED provides estimates of the factorial effects that combines the intra- and the inter-block (within and between) information available for each effect into a common combined estimate. The example in this section demonstrates the combining process.

The data in Data Set 10.7.1 in Appendix 4, "SAS Data Sets," is like data from a photo resist coating experiment in the semiconductor industry. The experiment was to study the effect of developing time at two levels (A), developing temperature at two levels (B), and exposure at two levels (C) on the edge slope (EDGSLP) of silicon wafers. Groups of six wafers were subjected to a set of conditions and the edge slope was determined as the average from the set of six wafers. Four runs could be carried out during a shift, and thus blocks of size four were used in the design structure. During five consecutive days, two shifts each ran four runs so that a complete replication of the treatment combinations was observed during a day. The experiment was repeated for five days, thus providing five replications. The ABC interaction was confounded in replication one and two, and the AB, AC, and CB interactions were each confounded in replications three, four, and five respectively, generating a balanced confounded design.

The data are analyzed using the analysis of variance of the means and using the regression model. The analysis of variance model is

$$y_{ijkmn} = \mu + \alpha_k + \beta_m + \gamma_n + (\alpha\beta)_{km} + (\alpha\gamma)_{kn} + (\beta\gamma)_{mn} + (\alpha\beta\gamma)_{kmn}$$
$$+ r_i + a_{ij} + e_{ijkmn}$$

where

$i=1,2,...6$
$j=1,2$
$k=-1, +1$
$m=-1, +1$
$n=-1, +1$
$\gamma_i \sim$ iid $N(0, \sigma^2_r)$
$a_{ij} \sim$ iid $N(0, \sigma^2_a)$
$e_{ijkmn} \sim$ iid $N(0, \sigma^2_e)$.

The indices denote levels as follows:

i=replication or day
j=block or shift within a replication
k is the level of A
m is the level of B
n is the level of C
r_i denotes the replication effect
a_{ij} denotes the block
e_{ijkmn} denotes the error term corresponding to the group of six wafers.

The regression model is

$$y_{ijk} = \beta_0 + \beta_A A_k + \beta_B B_k + \beta_C C_k + \beta_{AB} A_k B_k + \beta_{AC} A_k C_k$$
$$+ \beta_{BC} B_k C_k + \beta_{ABC} A_k B_k C_k + r_i + a_{ij} + e_{ijkmn}$$

where

$i=1,2,...6$
$j=1,2$
$k=1,2,3,4$
$\gamma_i \sim$ iid $N(0, \sigma^2_r)$
$a_{ij} \sim$ iid $N(0, \sigma^2_a)$
$e_{ijkmn} \sim$ iid $N(0, \sigma^2_e)$.

The indices denote levels as follows:

i=replication or day
j=block or shift within a replication
k is the observation within a block
r_i denotes the replication effect
a_{ij} denotes the block
e_{ijkmn} denotes the error term corresponding to the group of six wafers.

10.7.2 Analysis Using PROC MIXED

Program—Input

The program to read in the data is

```
data two3;
   input rep blk a b c edslp;
   datalines;
```

The variable REP denotes the day or replication, BLK denotes the shift within a day or replication, A denotes the level of developing time, B denotes the level of developing temperature, and C denotes the level of exposure.

Program—Means Model

The PROC MIXED program to fit the model for analyzing the means of the treatment combinations is

```
proc mixed;
   class a b c rep blk;
   model edslp=a|b|c/ddfm=satterth;
   random rep blk(rep);
   lsmeans b c a*c b*c/pdiff;
   lsmeans a*b*c;
run;
```

The REP and BLK(REP) terms in the RANDOM statement provide the estimates of the variance components for day-to-day variation and shift-to-shift within a day variation respectively.

The results of the PROC MIXED are in Output 10.24.

Results

Output 10.24 *PROC MIXED Results for the Factorial Treatment Structure in a Balanced Confounded Design Structure for the Analysis of the Means*

```
                        The MIXED Procedure
                     Class Level Information
                   Class    Levels  Values
                   A          2     1 -1
                   B          2     1 -1
                   C          2     1 -1
                   REP        5     1 2 3 4 5
                   BLK        2     1 2


                Covariance Parameter Estimates (REML)

    Cov Parm          Ratio       Estimate     Std Error      Z    Pr > |Z|

    REP          2.34654726     0.08989142    0.13810432    0.65    0.5151
    BLK(REP)     4.36506415     0.16721667    0.11293995    1.48    0.1387
    Residual     1.00000000     0.03830795    0.01128321    3.40    0.0007



                        Tests of Fixed Effects

              Source      NDF    DDF   Type III F   Pr > F

              A            1    23.1        2.61    0.1198
              B            1    23.1       11.51    0.0025
              A*B          1    23.7        0.09    0.7624
              C            1    23.1       84.81    0.0001
              A*C          1    23.7        9.40    0.0054
              B*C          1    23.7        6.96    0.0145
              A*B*C        1    24.6        0.04    0.8479
```

```
                              Least Squares Means
          Level                 LSMEAN      Std Error   DDF        T   Pr > |T|

          B  1                5.00000000   0.19135137  4.22    26.13    0.0001
          B -1                4.79000000   0.19135137  4.22    25.03    0.0001
          C  1                5.18000000   0.19135137  4.22    27.07    0.0001
          C -1                4.61000000   0.19135137  4.22    24.09    0.0001
          A*C  1  1           5.12465534   0.19686080  4.72    26.03    0.0001
          A*C  1 -1           4.76534466   0.19686080  4.72    24.21    0.0001
          A*C -1  1           5.23534466   0.19686080  4.72    26.59    0.0001
          A*C -1 -1           4.45465534   0.19686080  4.72    22.63    0.0001
          B*C  1  1           5.37567339   0.19686080  4.72    27.31    0.0001
          B*C  1 -1           4.62432661   0.19686080  4.72    23.49    0.0001
          B*C -1  1           4.98432661   0.19686080  4.72    25.32    0.0001
          B*C -1 -1           4.59567339   0.19686080  4.72    23.34    0.0001
          A*B*C  1  1  1      5.32323057   0.20884123  5.94    25.49    0.0001
          A*B*C  1  1 -1      4.79778749   0.20884123  5.94    22.97    0.0001
          A*B*C  1 -1  1      4.92608011   0.20884123  5.94    23.59    0.0001
          A*B*C  1 -1 -1      4.73290184   0.20884123  5.94    22.66    0.0001
          A*B*C -1  1  1      5.42811622   0.20884123  5.94    25.99    0.0001
          A*B*C -1  1 -1      4.45086573   0.20884123  5.94    21.31    0.0001
          A*B*C -1 -1  1      5.04257311   0.20884123  5.94    24.15    0.0001
          A*B*C -1 -1 -1      4.45844495   0.20884123  5.94    21.35    0.0001
```

Interpretation

- **Variance Components**

    The shift variance component is about twice as large as the day variance component.

- **Fixed Effects and LSMEANS**

    There are significant A*C and B*C interactions. Thus the LSMEANS for those two-way interactions are computed and compared using the LSMEANS and PDIFF option. The LSMEANS are in Output 10.24 and the companions of the LSMEANS are in Output 10.25. The ABC LSMEANS are also computed and are in Output 10.24.

Output 10.25 *Comparison of LSMEANS from PROC MIXED for the Factorial Treatment Structure in a Balanced Confounded Design Structure for the Analysis of the Means*

```
                      Differences of Least Squares Means

    Level 1    Level 2      Difference    Std Error   DDF        T   Pr > |T|

    B  1       B -1         0.21000000   0.06189342  23.1     3.39    0.0025
    C  1       C -1         0.57000000   0.06189342  23.1     9.21    0.0001
    A*C  1  1  A*C  1 -1    0.35931068   0.09249490  23.4     3.88    0.0007
    A*C  1  1  A*C -1  1   -0.11068932   0.09249490  23.4    -1.20    0.2434
    A*C  1  1  A*C -1 -1    0.67000000   0.08753051  23.1     7.65    0.0001
    A*C  1 -1  A*C -1  1   -0.47000000   0.08753051  23.1    -5.37    0.0001
    A*C  1 -1  A*C -1 -1    0.31068932   0.09249490  23.4     3.36    0.0027
    A*C -1  1  A*C -1 -1    0.78068932   0.09249490  23.4     8.44    0.0001
    B*C  1  1  B*C  1 -1    0.75134679   0.09249490  23.4     8.12    0.0001
    B*C  1  1  B*C -1  1    0.39134679   0.09249490  23.4     4.23    0.0003
```

B*C 1 1	B*C -1 -1	0.78000000	0.08753051	23.1	8.91	0.0001
B*C 1 -1	B*C -1 1	-0.36000000	0.08753051	23.1	-4.11	0.0004
B*C 1 -1	B*C -1 -1	0.02865321	0.09249490	23.4	0.31	0.7595
B*C -1 1	B*C -1 -1	0.38865321	0.09249490	23.4	4.20	0.0003

Interpretation

Treatment combinations A=1 and C=1 and A=-1 and C=1 are not significantly different while all other comparisons are significantly different. Treatment combination A=-1 and C=-1 has the smallest mean edge slope. Treatment combinations B=1 and C=-1 and B=-1 and C=-1 are not significantly different, and they have the smaller mean edge slope values. All other means are significantly different. We can conclude that treatment combinations A=-1 B=1 and C=-1 and A=-1 B=-1 and C=-1 produce the smallest edge slopes.

Program—Regression Model

The PROC MIXED program to fit the regression model is

```
proc mixed;
   class rep blk;
   model edslp=a|b|c/solution ddfm=satterth;
   random rep blk(rep);
run;
```

Results

The results are in Output 10.26.

Output 10.26 *PROC MIXED Results for the Factorial Treatment Structure in a Balanced Confounded Design Structure for the Regression Model*

```
              The MIXED Procedure
            Class Level Information
          Class     Levels  Values


          REP          5   1 2 3 4 5
          BLK          2   1 2
```

```
         Covariance Parameter Estimates (REML)


Cov Parm          Ratio       Estimate      Std Error      Z   Pr > |Z|


REP            2.34761470    0.08992815    0.13815735    0.65    0.5151
BLK(REP)       4.36544142    0.16722337    0.11294784    1.48    0.1387
Residual       1.00000000    0.03830618    0.01128268    3.40    0.0007
```

```
              Solution for Fixed Effects


Parameter       Estimate      Std Error    DDF       T   Pr > |T|


INTERCEPT     4.89500000    0.18885344      4    25.92    0.0001
A             0.05000000    0.03094599   23.1     1.62    0.1198
B             0.10500000    0.03094599   23.1     3.39    0.0025
A*B           0.01050868    0.03436676   23.7     0.31    0.7624
C             0.28500000    0.03094599   23.1     9.21    0.0001
```

```
A*C        -0.10534423    0.03436676   23.7   -3.07   0.0054
B*C         0.09067314    0.03436676   23.7    2.64   0.0145
A*B*C      -0.00760725    0.03924874   24.6   -0.19   0.8479
```

```
                    Tests of Fixed Effects

          Source      NDF    DDF    Type III F    Pr > F

          A           1      23.1       2.61      0.1198
          B           1      23.1      11.51      0.0025
          A*B         1      23.7       0.09      0.7624
          C           1      23.1      84.82      0.0001
          A*C         1      23.7       9.40      0.0054
          B*C         1      23.7       6.96      0.0145
          A*B*C       1      24.6       0.04      0.8479
```

Interpretation

The term A|B|C generates the linear terms, the cross product terms for each pair, and the cross product of all three variables. Because a model is fit with the number of parameters equal to the number of cells in the treatment structure (in the regression or fixed effects part of the model), the estimates of the variance components are identical to those obtained from the analysis of the means. The analysis of the fixed effects indicates there are significant linear terms for B and C, and significant cross product terms for A*C and B*C. If the model is simplified by excluding nonsignificant terms the estimates of the variance components will change. You do not need to know the type of confounding in the design to carry out the analysis. PROC MIXED's estimation procedure extracts the available information about the regression coefficients and provides the combined estimates.

10.7.3 Analysis Using PROC GLM

Program—Means Model

The program to use PROC GLM to carry out the analysis of the means is

```
proc glm;
   class rep blk a b c;
   model edslp=rep blk(rep) a|b|c/solution;
   random rep blk(rep)/test;
   lsmeans b c a*c b*c/pdiff;
run;
```

The results are in Output 10.27.

Results

Output 10.27 *PROC GLM Results for the Factorial Treatment Structure in a Balanced Confounded Design Structure*

```
              General Linear Models Procedure
                  Class Level Information
            Class      Levels     Values
            REP             5      1 2 3 4 5
            BLK             2      1 2
```

```
                                  A        2   1 -1
                                  B        2   1 -1
                                  C        2   1 -1


                        Number of observations in data set = 40

Dependent Variable: EDSLP
                                    Sum of          Mean
Source                  DF        Squares         Square    F Value    Pr > F
Model                   16      14.756917       0.922307     24.05     0.0001
Error                   23       0.882083       0.038351
Corrected Total         39      15.639000


                        R-Square            C.V.       Root MSE    EDSLP Mean
                        0.943597        4.000720         0.1958        4.8950


Source           DF    Type III SS    Mean Square    F Value    Pr > F


REP               4      5.7065000      1.4266250      37.20     0.0001
BLK(REP)          5      3.0394167      0.6078833      15.85     0.0001
A                 1      0.1000000      0.1000000       2.61     0.1200
B                 1      0.4410000      0.4410000      11.50     0.0025
A*B               1      0.0012500      0.0012500       0.03     0.8583
C                 1      3.2490000      3.2490000      84.72     0.0001
A*C               1      0.3200000      0.3200000       8.34     0.0083
B*C               1      0.2450000      0.2450000       6.39     0.0188
A*B*C             1      0.0016667      0.0016667       0.04     0.8367



Source           Type III Expected Mean Square


REP              Var(Error) + 4 Var(BLK(REP)) + 8 Var(REP)
BLK(REP)         Var(Error) + 3.2 Var(BLK(REP))
A                Var(Error) + Q(A,A*B,A*C,A*B*C)
B                Var(Error) + Q(B,A*B,B*C,A*B*C)
A*B              Var(Error) + Q(A*B,A*B*C)
C                Var(Error) + Q(C,A*C,B*C,A*B*C)
A*C              Var(Error) + Q(A*C,A*B*C)
B*C              Var(Error) + Q(B*C,A*B*C)
A*B*C            Var(Error) + Q(A*B*C)
```

Interpretation

- **Analysis of Variance**

  The *F*-statistics for the main effects A, B, and C are quite similar to those provided by PROC MIXED in Output 10.24. The difference between the respective F-values is that PROC GLM used 3.8351449 as the estimate of the error while PROC MIXED used 3.830795110. But the other F-values provided by PROC GLM involve only the within-block comparisons; i.e., they are computed from only those blocks where the respective effects are not confounded. On the other hand, PROC MIXED extracts the between-block information about an effect and combines it with the within-block information that is used by PROC GLM. The expected mean squares indicate that the error for the model should be used as the denominator for all of the comparisons of the effects.

- **LSMEANS**

The LSMEANS and comparisons of the LSMEANS are in Output 10.28.

Output 10.28 *LSMEANS Results from PROC GLM for the Factorial Treatment Structure in a Balanced Confounded Design Structure Using the Analysis of the Means*

```
Least Squares Means


  B          EDSLP      Pr > |T| H0:
             LSMEAN    LSMEAN1=LSMEAN2
1         5.00000000        0.0025
-1        4.79000000


  C          EDSLP      Pr > |T| H0:
             LSMEAN    LSMEAN1=LSMEAN2


1         5.18000000        0.0001
-1        4.61000000


  A    C          EDSLP    Pr > |T|  H0: LSMEAN(i)=LSMEAN(j)
                  LSMEAN   i/j    1       2       3       4

1    1        5.13000000    1   .     0.0006  0.2929  0.0001
1    -1       4.76000000    2  0.0006  .      0.0001  0.0037
-1   1        5.23000000    3  0.2929 0.0001   .      0.0001
-1   -1       4.46000000    4  0.0001 0.0037  0.0001   .


  B    C          EDSLP    Pr > |T|  H0: LSMEAN(i)=LSMEAN(j)
                  LSMEAN   i/j    1       2       3       4

1    1        5.37250000    1   .     0.0001  0.0004  0.0001
1    -1       4.62750000    2  0.0001  .      0.0004  0.7098
-1   1        4.98750000    3  0.0004 0.0004   .      0.0003
-1   -1       4.59250000    4  0.0001 0.7098  0.0003   .
```

Interpretation

Again these means are computed from those blocks where the effects are not confounded whereas PROC MIXED uses information from all of the blocks.

Program—Regression Model

The program to fit the regression model using PROC GLM is

```
proc glm;
   class rep blk;
   model edslp=rep blk(rep) a|b|c/solution;
   random rep blk(rep)/test;
run;
```

The results are in Output 10.29.

Results

Output 10.29 *PROC GLM Results for the Factorial Treatment Structure in a Balanced Confounded Design Structure for the Regression Model*

```
                    General Linear Models Procedure
                        Class Level Information
                    Class    Levels    Values
                    REP         5      1 2 3 4 5
                    BLK         2      1 2
              Number of observations in data set = 40
Dependent Variable: EDSLP
```

Source	DF	Sum of Squares	Mean Square	F Value	Pr > F
Model	16	14.756917	0.922307	24.05	0.0001
Error	23	0.882083	0.038351		
Corrected Total	39	15.639000			

R-Square	C.V.	Root MSE	EDSLP Mean
0.943597	4.000720	0.1958	4.8950

Source	DF	Type III SS	Mean Square	F Value	Pr > F
REP	4	5.7065000	1.4266250	37.20	0.0001
BLK(REP)	5	3.0394167	0.6078833	15.85	0.0001
A	1	0.1000000	0.1000000	2.61	0.1200
B	1	0.4410000	0.4410000	11.50	0.0025
A*B	1	0.0012500	0.0012500	0.03	0.8583
C	1	3.2490000	3.2490000	84.72	0.0001
A*C	1	0.3200000	0.3200000	8.34	0.0083
B*C	1	0.2450000	0.2450000	6.39	0.0188
A*B*C	1	0.0016667	0.0016667	0.04	0.8367

Parameter			Estimate	T for H0: Parameter=0	Pr > |T|	Std Error of Estimate
INTERCEPT			4.862500000 B	46.82	0.0001	0.10385733
REP	1		-0.254166667 B	-1.71	0.0999	0.14823017
	2		0.070833333 B	0.48	0.6373	0.14823017
	3		0.406250000 B	2.77	0.0110	0.14687645
	4		0.137500000 B	0.94	0.3589	0.14687645
	5		0.000000000 B	.	.	.
BLK(REP)	1	1	-0.541666667 B	-3.39	0.0025	0.15989882
	2	1	0.000000000 B	.	.	.
	1	2	0.458333333 B	2.87	0.0087	0.15989882
	2	2	0.000000000 B	.	.	.
	1	3	-0.637500000 B	-4.12	0.0004	0.15482137
	2	3	0.000000000 B	.	.	.
	1	4	0.800000000 B	5.17	0.0001	0.15482137
	2	4	0.000000000 B	.	.	.
	1	5	-0.475000000 B	-3.07	0.0054	0.15482137
	2	5	0.000000000 B	.	.	.
A			0.050000000	1.61	0.1200	0.03096427
B			0.105000000	3.39	0.0025	0.03096427
A*B			0.006250000	0.18	0.8583	0.03461911
C			0.285000000	9.20	0.0001	0.03096427
A*C			-0.100000000	-2.89	0.0083	0.03461911
B*C			0.087500000	2.53	0.0188	0.03461911

```
A*B*C          -0.008333333     -0.21      0.8367     0.03997471

Source         Type III Expected Mean Square
REP            Var(Error) + 4 Var(BLK(REP)) + 8 Var(REP)
BLK(REP)       Var(Error) + 3.2 Var(BLK(REP))
A              Var(Error) + Q(A)
B              Var(Error) + Q(B)
A*B            Var(Error) + Q(A*B)
C              Var(Error) + Q(C)
A*C            Var(Error) + Q(A*C)
B*C            Var(Error) + Q(B*C)
A*B*C          Var(Error) + Q(A*B*C)
```

Interpretation

The estimates of the linear regression coefficients use information from all of the blocks, and they are the same as obtained by PROC MIXED (see Output 10.26). On the other hand, the estimates of the regression coefficients for the cross product terms are obtained using only information from those blocks where the effects are not confounded. On comparing the estimates of the coefficients of the cross products with those from PROC MIXED, we see that the estimates are a little different.

When the design involves confounding, either balanced as discussed in this example or partial or complete as discussed in section 10.5.3, PROC MIXED extracts all of the available information from the data whereas a non-mixed-models analysis does not.

10.8 Product Acceptability Study with Cross-over and Repeated Measures

10.8.1 Introduction

The data in Data Set 10.8.1 in Appendix 4, "SAS Data Sets," represent results from an experiment to evaluate the acceptability of four types of daily use products (such as tooth paste, facial soap, tissue, automobile, etc. The data are simulated). A person used three of the possible four products in a cross-over type of process and rated a given product after one week of use, two weeks of use, and three weeks of use. The four products were grouped into four blocks of size three forming a balanced incomplete block, as indicated in Table 10.5.

Table 10.5 *The Balanced Incomplete Block Used to Group the Four Products into Blocks of Size Three*

Block	PRODUCTS
1	1, 2, 3
2	1, 2, 4
3	1, 3, 4
4	2, 3, 4

The three products within each block were used in all six possible sequences, thus providing a cross-over design with the three products in each block, as shown in Table 10.6.

Table 10.6 *The Six Sequences of Three Products Used within Each Block*

BLOCK	Seq1	Seq2	Seq3	Seq4	Seq5	Seq6
1	1 2 3	1 3 2	2 1 3	2 3 1	3 2 1	3 1 2
2	1 2 4	1 4 2	2 1 4	2 4 1	4 2 1	4 1 2
3	1 3 4	1 4 3	3 1 4	3 4 1	4 3 1	4 1 3
4	2 3 4	2 4 3	3 2 4	3 4 2	4 3 2	4 2 3

There are twenty four total sequences, six from each of the four blocks. Twenty four women were selected from a group of college age women residing in a university town. The women were randomly assigned to the twenty four sequences providing one woman per sequence. Each woman used the three products in the designated sequence and rated the acceptability of the products at the end of one week, two weeks, and three weeks of exposure. The acceptability scale is from 0 to 7 with 0 being unacceptable and 7 extremely acceptable. Using a product means that the woman used the product daily for the seven days prior to providing an acceptability rating.

This particular data structure has several very interesting features. First, the woman uses the three specified products in a given sequence. Each product is used for three weeks with a one-week interval of using a control product. Thus, the woman's time in the experiment consists of three four-week periods, and she uses a different product within each period. The experimental unit for product is one four-week interval. Each woman is repeatedly measured three times as she uses three products in the three four-week intervals, thus providing a repeated measures aspect to the experiment. Second, each woman rates each product three times (one week apart) providing another level of repeated measures to the experiment.

The researcher was interested in evaluating the acceptability of products and as well as determining if the acceptability changes over time with use. The treatment structure is a three-way with levels of products (four levels) crossed with levels of time (three levels measured weekly within a product). A third factor is the period (with three levels) in which the products were used where period 1, 2 and 3 correspond to the first four weeks, second four weeks, and the third four weeks, respectively.

The design structure consists of (1) the blocks of three treatments, (2) the women within each block where the three treatments were observed in the six sequences, (3) the four weeks of time a product was used, and (4) the one-week time intervals between acceptability ratings. A model to describe the data is

$$y_{ijkmn} = \mu_{mn} + \rho_k + \lambda_{t_{k-1}} + b_i + w_{j(i)} + p_{k(ij)} + e_{ijkmn}$$

where

μ_{mn} is the expected mean acceptability rating for the mth product after the nth week of exposure

ρ_k is the effect of the kth period or set of four weeks

$\lambda_{t_{k-1}}$ is the carry-over effect of the t_{k-1} treatment occurring in the previous four week period prior to the current four week period ($\lambda_{t_{k-1}}$ does not occur in the model when k=1)

b_i is the random block effect assumed to be independgently distributed as $N(0, \sigma_b^2)$

$w_{j(i)}$ is the random effect for the variation in the women participating in the study assumed to be independently distributed as $N(0, \sigma_w^2)$

$p_{k(ij)}$ is the random effect corresponding to the four-week time intervals or periods with assumed distribution

$$
\begin{pmatrix} p_{1(ij)} \\ p_{2(ij)} \\ p_{3(ij)} \end{pmatrix} \sim \text{iid N} \left(\mathbf{0}, \begin{bmatrix} a_{11} & a_{12} & a_{13} \\ a_{12} & a_{22} & a_{23} \\ a_{13} & a_{23} & a_{33} \end{bmatrix} \right)
$$

e_{ijkmn} is the random effect of the one-week time intervals within a product or period with assumed distribution

$$
\begin{pmatrix} e_{ijkm1} \\ e_{ijkm2} \\ e_{ijkm3} \end{pmatrix} \sim \text{iid N} \left(\mathbf{0}, \begin{bmatrix} r_{11} & r_{12} & r_{13} \\ r_{12} & r_{22} & r_{23} \\ r_{13} & r_{23} & r_{33} \end{bmatrix} \right)
$$

Let matrices $\mathbf{R}^*$ and $\mathbf{A}$ be defined by

$$
\mathbf{R}^* = \begin{bmatrix} r_{11} & r_{12} & r_{13} \\ r_{12} & r_{22} & r_{23} \\ r_{13} & r_{23} & r_{33} \end{bmatrix} \quad \text{and} \quad \mathbf{A} = \begin{bmatrix} a_{11} & a_{12} & a_{13} \\ a_{12} & a_{22} & a_{23} \\ a_{13} & a_{23} & a_{33} \end{bmatrix}
$$

The covariance matrix of the vector of data is

$$
\text{Var}(\mathbf{y}) = \sigma_b^2 \, \mathbf{I}_4 \otimes \mathbf{J}_6 \otimes \mathbf{J}_3 \otimes \mathbf{J}_3 \ + \ \sigma_w^2 \, \mathbf{I}_4 \otimes \mathbf{I}_6 \otimes \mathbf{J}_3 \otimes \mathbf{J}_3 \ + \ \mathbf{I}_4 \otimes \mathbf{I}_6 \otimes \mathbf{A} \otimes \mathbf{J}_3 \ + \ \mathbf{I}_4 \otimes \mathbf{I}_6 \otimes \mathbf{I}_3 \otimes \mathbf{R}
$$

where $\mathbf{A} \otimes \mathbf{B}$ denotes the Kronecker product of the matrices $\mathbf{A}$ and $\mathbf{B}$.

The analysis is carried out with simplifying assumptions on $\mathbf{A}$ and $\mathbf{R}^*$. The independent errors assumptions are $\mathbf{A} = \sigma_p^2 \, \mathbf{I}$ and $\mathbf{R} = \sigma_e^2 \, \mathbf{I}$. The first order autoregressive error structure assumptions are

$$
\mathbf{A} = \sigma_p^2 \begin{pmatrix} 1 & \rho_a & \rho_a^2 \\ \rho_a & 1 & \rho_a \\ \rho_a^2 & \rho_a & 1 \end{pmatrix} \quad \text{and} \quad \mathbf{R} = \sigma_e^2 \begin{pmatrix} 1 & \rho_e & \rho_e^2 \\ \rho_e & 1 & \rho_e \\ \rho_e^2 & \rho_e & 1 \end{pmatrix}
$$

The analysis of the data set is carried out in three parts. The first analysis uses the independent errors model for both the $p_{k(ij)}$ and the e_{ijkmn}. The second analysis uses the independent errors model for the $p_{k(ij)}$ and the first order autoregressive errors model for the e_{ijkmn}. The third analysis uses the first order autoregressive errors model for both the $p_{k(ij)}$ and the e_{ijkmn}.

10.8.2 INPUT Statement and Variable Definition

The DATA step and INPUT statements follow where BLK is the block number, SEQ is the sequence number from Table 10.8.2, PERSON is the identification code assigned to each woman in the study, PERIOD corresponds to the four-weeks interval, PROD denotes the product, PRIORPRD denotes the product used in the previous four weeks (has a value of zero for data from first four weeks and thus can take on the values 0, 1, 2, 3, or 4), TIME is the one-week interval within a use of a product, and Li is one if the ith product is the prior product and zero if the ith product is not the prior product. The variables L1, L2, L3, and L4 are used to enable the $\lambda_{t_{k-1}}$ to be included in the model.

```
data prior;
    input  BLK  SEQ  PERSON  PERIOD  PROD  PRIORPRD TIME  Y  L1  L2  L3
           L4;
datalines;
```

10.8.3 Independent Errors Model

Program—Including PRIORPRD

The program for fitting the independent errors model to the data and to determine if the carry-over effects are different is

```
proc mixed data=prior;
    class blk person seq prod period time PRIORPRD;
    model y=prod period time time*prod priorprd/ddfm=satterth;
    random blk person(blk) period*person(blk);
    lsmeans prod time*prod;
run;
```

The MODEL option DDFM=SATTERTH is used to provide approximations to the denominator degrees of freedom for all of the tests and comparisons. The independent errors model is specified without using additional options in the RANDOM statement and without including a REPEATED statement.

The results are in Output 10.30 including the estimates of the variance components and the tests for the fixed effects.

Results

Output 10.30 *Results of Fitting the Independent Errors Model to the Acceptable Data Using the PRIORPRD Class Variable*

```
                      Covariance Parameter Estimates (REML)

Cov Parm                   Ratio     Estimate     Std Error      Z   Pr > |Z|
BLK                   5.06774957   0.49822375   0.46206005    1.08    0.2809
PERSON(BLK)           3.22558463   0.31711568   0.12165942    2.61    0.0091
PERSON*PERIOD(BLK)    1.57564511   0.15490580   0.04219378    3.67    0.0002
Residual              1.00000000   0.09831262   0.01192216    8.25    0.0001



                   Model Fitting Information for Y


             Description                        Value

             Observations                    216.0000
             Variance Estimate                 0.0983
             Standard Deviation Estimate       0.3135
             REML Log Likelihood             -155.502
             Akaike's Information Criterion   -159.502
             Schwarz's Bayesian Criterion    -166.088
             -2 REML Log Likelihood           311.0033
```

```
                    Tests of Fixed Effects


        Source      NDF   DDF   Type III F   Pr > F


        PROD         3    40.9      4.42     0.0088

        PERIOD       1    39.9      0.05     0.8254

        TIME         2    136      29.38     0.0001

        PROD*TIME    6    136      15.01     0.0001

        PRIORPRD     3    43.4      4.68     0.0064
```

Interpretation

There is a significant *F*-ratio for PRIORPRD indicating the carry over effects are not equal. Fortunately, this model allows for the estimation of the PROD effects in the presence of unequal carry over effects. Unfortunately, using PRIORPRD provides a model that is overparameterized and the PROD and PROD*TIME LSMEANS are not estimable. You can use ESTIMATE statements to compute and compare the LSMEANS from the estimable function information available from PROC MIXED.

Program—Including Li Terms

But it is easier to carry out the analysis using a model with the Li values instead of the PRIORPRD values as in the following program:

```
proc mixed data=prior;
   class blk person seq prod period time PRIORPRD;
   model y=prod period time time*prod L1 L2 L3 L4/ ddfm=satterth;
   random blk person(blk) prod*person (blk);
   lsmeans prod time*prod/pdiff;
run;
```

Results

The estimates of the variance components are identical to those in Output 10.30 obtained using the PRIORPRD, but now the LSMEANS are estimable. The tests for the Fixed Effects part of the model are in Output 10.31. The results for PROD, PERIOD, TIME, and PROD*TIME are identical to those in Output 10.30.

Output 10.31 *Type III F-Statistics for the Fixed Effects from the Independent Errors Model to the Acceptable Data Using the Li's As Variables*

```
                    Tests of Fixed Effects


        Source      NDF   DDF   Type III F   Pr > F


        PROD         3    40.9      4.42     0.0088

        PERIOD       1    39.9      0.05     0.8254

        TIME         2    136      29.38     0.0001

        PROD*TIME    6    136      15.01     0.0001

        L1           0     .         .        .

        L2           0     .         .        .

        L3           0     .         .        .

        L4           0     .         .        .
```

Interpretation

The Type III *F*-statistics for L1, L2, L3, and L4 are zero because there is a dependency or colinearity between the levels of PERIOD and the Li's. The LSMEANS for PROD*TIME are in Output 10.32. Because there is a significant PROD*TIME interaction, only the PROD means are compared within each TIME. (The LSMEANS statement in PROC MIXED computes comparisons among all pairs of means, and the output has been edited to contain only the comparisons among levels of PROD within each level of TIME).

Output 10.32 *LSMEANS and Some Comparisons from Fitting the Independent Errors Model to the Acceptable Data*

```
                                 Least Squares Means

Level                    LSMEAN      Std Error    DDF        T   Pr > |T|


PROD*TIME 1 1         3.91114240    0.39338248   3.59     9.94     0.0010
PROD*TIME 1 2         3.63336462    0.39338248   3.59     9.24     0.0013
PROD*TIME 1 3         2.85558685    0.39338248   3.59     7.26     0.0029
PROD*TIME 2 1         4.03190234    0.39338248   3.59    10.25     0.0009
PROD*TIME 2 2         3.69856901    0.39338248   3.59     9.40     0.0012
PROD*TIME 2 3         3.47634679    0.39338248   3.59     8.84     0.0015
PROD*TIME 3 1         3.81121937    0.39338248   3.59     9.69     0.0011
PROD*TIME 3 2         3.70010826    0.39338248   3.59     9.41     0.0012
PROD*TIME 3 3         3.64455270    0.39338248   3.59     9.26     0.0012
PROD*TIME 4 1         3.91240255    0.39338248   3.59     9.95     0.0010
PROD*TIME 4 2         4.19018033    0.39338248   3.59    10.65     0.0008
PROD*TIME 4 3         4.13462478    0.39338248   3.59    10.51     0.0008



                           Differences of Least Squares Means


Level 1           Level 2         Difference    Std Error    DDF       T   Pr > |T|


PROD*TIME 1 1    PROD*TIME 1 2     0.27777778   0.10451615   136     2.66    0.0088
PROD*TIME 1 1    PROD*TIME 1 3     1.05555556   0.10451615   136    10.10    0.0001
PROD*TIME 1 2    PROD*TIME 1 3     0.77777778   0.10451615   136     7.44    0.0001
PROD*TIME 1 1    PROD*TIME 2 1    -0.12075994   0.18948182   63.1   -0.64    0.5262
PROD*TIME 1 1    PROD*TIME 3 1     0.09992303   0.18948182   63.1    0.53    0.5998
PROD*TIME 1 1    PROD*TIME 4 1    -0.00126015   0.18948182   63.1   -0.01    0.9947
PROD*TIME 1 2    PROD*TIME 2 2    -0.06520439   0.18948182   63.1   -0.34    0.7319
PROD*TIME 1 2    PROD*TIME 3 2    -0.06674363   0.18948182   63.1   -0.35    0.7258
PROD*TIME 1 2    PROD*TIME 4 2    -0.55681571   0.18948182   63.1   -2.94    0.0046
PROD*TIME 1 3    PROD*TIME 2 3    -0.62075994   0.18948182   63.1   -3.28    0.0017
PROD*TIME 1 3    PROD*TIME 3 3    -0.78896585   0.18948182   63.1   -4.16    0.0001
PROD*TIME 1 3    PROD*TIME 4 3    -1.27903793   0.18948182   63.1   -6.75    0.0001
PROD*TIME 2 1    PROD*TIME 3 1     0.22068298   0.18948182   63.1    1.16    0.2485
PROD*TIME 2 1    PROD*TIME 4 1     0.11949979   0.18948182   63.1    0.63    0.5305
PROD*TIME 2 2    PROD*TIME 3 2    -0.00153925   0.18948182   63.1   -0.01    0.9935
PROD*TIME 2 2    PROD*TIME 4 2    -0.49161132   0.18948182   63.1   -2.59    0.0118
PROD*TIME 2 3    PROD*TIME 3 3    -0.16820591   0.18948182   63.1   -0.89    0.3781
PROD*TIME 2 3    PROD*TIME 4 3    -0.65827799   0.18948182   63.1   -3.47    0.0009
PROD*TIME 3 1    PROD*TIME 4 1    -0.10118319   0.18948182   63.1   -0.53    0.5952
PROD*TIME 3 2    PROD*TIME 4 2    -0.49007208   0.18948182   63.1   -2.59    0.0120
PROD*TIME 3 3    PROD*TIME 4 3    -0.49007208   0.18948182   63.1   -2.59    0.0120
```

Interpretation

The standard errors of the differences between pairs of PROD means at a common level of TIME are all identical, and the Satterthwaite approximation to the associated degrees of freedom is 63.1. Also included in Output 10.32 are comparisons among the levels of TIME for PROD 1. The standard errors of the differences between pairs of TIME means for PROD 1 are based on the residual variance and are based on 136 degrees of freedom. There are no significant differences among the levels of PROD at TIME = 1. Level 4 of PROD is significantly more acceptable than the other three levels of PROD at TIME = 2. At TIME = 3, level 1 of PROD is significantly less acceptable than the other three levels, levels 2 and 3 are not different, and level 4 of PROD is significantly more acceptable than the other three levels. A graph of these LSMEANS is in Figure 10.6. The acceptability of PROD 1 decreases over TIME, and the acceptability of PROD 4 increases over TIME.

Figure 10.6 *Plot of Product Means across Time*

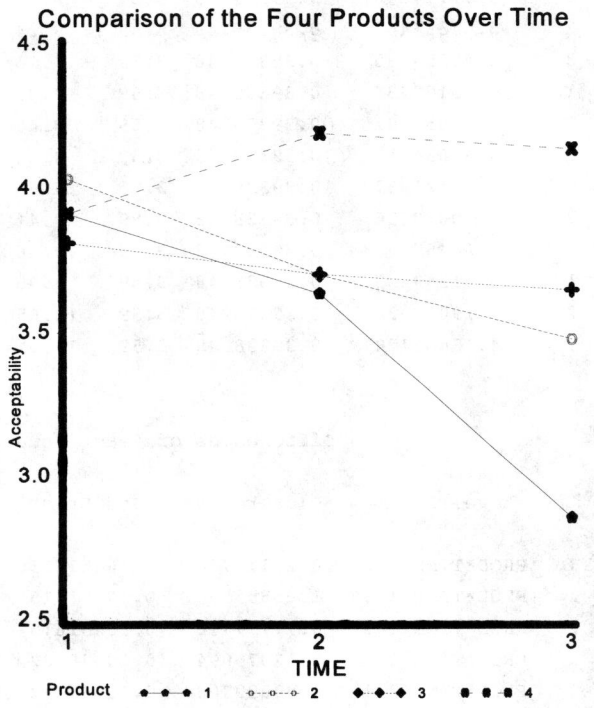

For comparison purposes, the data are reanalyzed using more general models to describe the repeated measures parts of the model.

10.8.4 Autoregressive Errors for the Time Interval Part of the Model

Program—Autoregressive Errors

The program to fit a model where $\mathbf{R}^*$ satisfies the autoregressive error structure and $\mathbf{A}$ still has the independent errors structure is as follows:

```
proc mixed data=prior;
    class blk person seq prod period time priorprd;
    model y=prod period time time*prod priorprd/ ddfm=satterth;
    random blk person(blk) period(person blk);
    repeated time/subject=period*person(blk) type=ar(1);
    parms (0.49973234) (0.31497310) (0.13799768) (0.20127984)
        (0.111540430);
run;
```

The REPEATED statement is used to specify a first-order autoregressive error structure for the three measurements made after one, two, and three weeks of use within a product or period for each person. The option TYPE = AR(1) specifies the covariance structure for the three observations common to a person within a PERIOD, specified as SUBJECT=PERIOD*PERSON*BLK. The PARMS statement is used to provide starting values (obtained from a previous run) to speed the computations.

The results of using the above statements to analyze the acceptability data are in Output 10.33.

Results

Output 10.33 *Results of Fitting the Autoregressive Time Errors and Independent Period Errors Model to the Acceptable Data Using the PRIORPRD Class Variable*

```
                    Covariance Parameter Estimates (REML)
```

Cov Parm	Ratio	Estimate	Std Error	Z	Pr > |Z|
BLK	4.33022677	0.49972796	0.46297873	1.08	0.2804
PERSON(BLK)	2.72927249	0.31497052	0.12097797	2.60	0.0092
PERIOD(BLK*PERSON)	1.19576900	0.13799721	0.04737498	2.91	0.0036
TIME AR(1)	1.74412882	0.20128044	0.19538700	1.03	0.3029
Residual	1.00000000	0.11540457	0.02686052	4.30	0.0001

```
              Model Fitting Information for Y
```

Description	Value
Observations	216.0000
Variance Estimate	0.1154
Standard Deviation Estimate	0.3397
REML Log Likelihood	-154.923
Akaike's Information Criterion	-159.923
Schwarz's Bayesian Criterion	-168.156
-2 REML Log Likelihood	309.8451
PARMS Model LRT Chi-Square	0.0171
PARMS Model LRT DF	4.0000
PARMS Model LRT P-Value	1.0000

```
                    Tests of Fixed Effects


         Source        NDF    DDF   Type III F   Pr > F


         PROD           3      0       4.41         .
         PERIOD         1     0.03     0.05       0.9686
         TIME           2     4.58    26.52       0.0030
         PROD*TIME      6     4.58    13.67       0.0078
         PRIORPRD       3      0       4.71         .
```

Interpretation

The estimate of the AR(1) parameter is 0.20. A test of whether the AR(1) covariance matrix more adequately describes the data than the independent errors model can be obtained by comparing the values of "-2 REML log Likelihood". The test statistic is $u = 311.0033 - 309.7517 = 1.2516$, which, under the hypothesis that the independent errors model fits the data, is asymptotically distributed as a central chi-square random variable based on 1 degree of freedom. (Degrees of freedom correspond to the difference between the number of parameters in the covariance structure of the models. In this case the independent errors model has 4 parameters and the autoregressive model has 5 parameters, giving a difference of 1.) The significance level of the test is 0.3173, indicating there is not sufficient evidence to not use the independent errors model compared to the autoregressive errors model. The Z-score corresponding to the AR(1) parameter has an associated significance level of 0.3029. For this data set the two test statistics are very similar in their results. The Type III F-values for the fixed effects part of the model are somewhat smaller than the corresponding values for the independent errors model.

Program—AR(1) Time Errors and the Li Terms

The program for fitting the model with the Li's to provide for the estimation of the LSMEANS is as follows:

```
proc mixed data=prior;
    class blk person seq prod period time priorprd;
    model y=prod period time time*prod L1 L2 L3 L4/ ddfm=satterth;
    random blk person(blk) period*person (blk);
    repeated time/subject=period*person(blk) type=ar(1);
    parms (0.49973234) (0.31497310) (0.13799768) (0.20127984)
          (0.111540430);
    lsmeans prod time*prod/pdiff;
run;
```

Results

The estimates of the variance components and model fitting information are the same as in Output 10.34 and the tests of the fixed effects are in Output 10.35.

Output 10.34 *Type III F-Statistics for the Fixed Effects from the Independent Errors Model to the Acceptable Data Using the Li's As Variables*

```
                    Tests of Fixed Effects


         Source        NDF    DDF   Type III F   Pr > F


         PROD           3      0       4.41         .
         PERIOD         1     0.03     0.05       0.9686
         TIME           2     4.58    26.52       0.0030
```

```
       PROD*TIME       6    4.58        13.67   0.0078
       L1              0     .              .        .
       L2              0     .              .        .
       L3              0     .              .        .
       L4              0     .              .        .
```

Output 10.35 *LSMEANS and Some Comparisons from Fitting the Autoregressive Errors for the Time Intervals and Independent Errors for the Periods Model to the Acceptable Data*

Least Squares Means

Level	LSMEAN	Std Error	DDF	T	Pr > |T|
PROD*TIME 1 1	3.91208040	0.39375649	1619	9.94	0.0001
PROD*TIME 1 2	3.63430262	0.39375649	3185	9.23	0.0001
PROD*TIME 1 3	2.85652484	0.39375649	685	7.25	0.0001
PROD*TIME 2 1	4.03388826	0.39375649	1640	10.24	0.0001
PROD*TIME 2 2	3.70055492	0.39375649	3295	9.40	0.0001
PROD*TIME 2 3	3.47833270	0.39375649	650	8.83	0.0001
PROD*TIME 3 1	3.80805036	0.39375649	3E26	9.67	1.0000
PROD*TIME 3 2	3.69693925	0.39375649	3E26	9.39	1.0000
PROD*TIME 3 3	3.64138369	0.39375649	3E26	9.25	1.0000
PROD*TIME 4 1	3.91264765	0.39375649	651	9.94	0.0001
PROD*TIME 4 2	4.19042543	0.39375649	1313	10.64	0.0001
PROD*TIME 4 3	4.13486987	0.39375649	352	10.50	0.0001

Differences of Least Squares Means

Level 1	Level 2	Difference	Std Error	DDF	T	Pr > |T|
PROD*TIME 1 1	PROD*TIME 1 2	0.27777778	0.10120161	3E31	2.74	1.0000
PROD*TIME 1 1	PROD*TIME 1 3	1.05555556	0.11091994	3795	9.52	0.0001
PROD*TIME 1 2	PROD*TIME 1 3	0.77777778	0.10120161	3333	7.69	0.0001
PROD*TIME 1 1	PROD*TIME 2 1	-0.12180786	0.18951829	37E7	-0.64	0.5204
PROD*TIME 1 1	PROD*TIME 3 1	0.10403004	0.18951829	16E4	0.55	0.5831
PROD*TIME 1 1	PROD*TIME 4 1	-0.00056725	0.18951829	146	-0.00	0.9976
PROD*TIME 1 2	PROD*TIME 2 2	-0.06625230	0.18951829	61E4	-0.35	0.7267
PROD*TIME 1 2	PROD*TIME 3 2	-0.06263663	0.18951829	61E4	-0.33	0.7410
PROD*TIME 1 2	PROD*TIME 4 2	-0.55612281	0.18951829	283	-2.93	0.0036
PROD*TIME 1 3	PROD*TIME 2 3	-0.62180786	0.18951829	61E4	-3.28	0.0010
PROD*TIME 1 3	PROD*TIME 3 3	-0.78485885	0.18951829	26E3	-4.14	0.0001
PROD*TIME 1 3	PROD*TIME 4 3	-1.27834503	0.18951829	32.3	-6.75	0.0001
PROD*TIME 2 1	PROD*TIME 3 1	0.22583789	0.18951829	29E4	1.19	0.2334
PROD*TIME 2 1	PROD*TIME 4 1	0.12124060	0.18951829	151	0.64	0.5233
PROD*TIME 2 2	PROD*TIME 3 2	0.00361567	0.18951829	2E35	0.02	1.0000
PROD*TIME 2 2	PROD*TIME 4 2	-0.48987051	0.18951829	295	-2.58	0.0102
PROD*TIME 2 3	PROD*TIME 3 3	-0.16305099	0.18951829	29E4	-0.86	0.3896
PROD*TIME 2 3	PROD*TIME 4 3	-0.65653717	0.18951829	29.8	-3.46	0.0016
PROD*TIME 3 1	PROD*TIME 4 1	-0.10459729	0.18951829	378	-0.55	0.5813
PROD*TIME 3 2	PROD*TIME 4 2	-0.49348618	0.18951829	650	-2.60	0.0094
PROD*TIME 3 3	PROD*TIME 4 3	-0.49348618	0.18951829	58.7	-2.60	0.0117

Interpretation

Again the Type III *F*-statistics for the Li's are zero as there is a colinearity between the Li's and the levels of PERIOD. The LSMEANS and comparisons of the means are in Output 10.35.

There are slight differences between the LSMEANS in Outputs 10.32 and 10.35 as well as between their estimated standard errors, which are due to the different model specifications. The conclusions are identical for both models. The main impact of the autoregressive error structure for the time intervals is seen in the estimated standard errors for the difference between two TIME means at the same level of PROD. The estimated standard error for the difference between two means one time period apart is 0.1012 and two time periods apart is 0.1109. The estimated standard errors of the differences of pairs of PROD means at the same level of TIME is 0.189518 for the autoregressive errors model compared to 0.189481 for the independent errors model. The approximate degrees of freedom are not meaningful using this form of the covariance matrix. A good strategy is to use the approximate degrees of freedom from the independent errors model in order to adjust for the different degrees of freedom associated with the various sizes of experimental units.

10.8.5 Autoregressive Errors for the Time Interval and Period Parts of the Model

Program—AR(1) Error Structure for the Time Interval and Period Parts of the Model

The program specifying autoregressive errors for both the time intervals and the periods part of the model is as follows:

```
proc mixed data=prior;
   class blk person seq prod period time priorprd;
   model y=prod period time time*prod priorprd/ddfm=satterth;
   random blk person(blk);
   random period/type=ar(1) subject=person(blk);
   repeated time/subject=period*person(blk) type=ar(1);
   parms (0.50079619) (0.32416655) (0.18092665) (-0.0558346)
         (0.20127984) (0.11540430);
run;
```

The REPEATED statement is the same as in the previous program, but the RANDOM statement has been split into two parts. The first RANDOM statement specifies the blocks, and the persons within the blocks are independent effects with respective variance components (this is a reasonable assumption unless the women in the study are all genetically or socially related). The second RANDOM statement specifies the error structure for the PERIOD errors or the four week time interval errors. The term PERIOD(PERSON*BLK) term has been modeled with the TYPE=AR(1) and the SUBJECT=PERSON(BLK), as the three periods are assumed to be dependent within a person and independent between persons.

The results of fitting the model to the acceptability data are in Output 10.36.

Results

Output 10.36 *Results of Fitting the Autoregressive Time Errors and Independent Period Errors Model to the Acceptable Data Using the PRIORPRD Class Variable*

```
                    Covariance Parameter Estimates (REML)

Cov Parm              Ratio      Estimate    Std Error      z   Pr > |z|

BLK                4.33057382   0.50417922   0.46681871   1.08   0.2801
PERSON(BLK)        2.80433542   0.32648968   0.12488933   2.61   0.0089
PERIOD Diagonal    1.08241336   0.12601802   0.05460446   2.31   0.0210
        AR(1)     -1.16884951  -0.13608119   0.42900356  -0.32   0.7511
TIME AR(1)         1.80239016   0.20984001   0.19906299   1.05   0.2918
Residual           1.00000000   0.11642319   0.02786973   4.18   0.0001



               Model Fitting Information for Y

       Description                         Value

       Observations                      216.0000
       Variance Estimate                   0.1164
       Standard Deviation Estimate         0.3412
       REML Log Likelihood              -154.876
       Akaike's Information Criterion   -160.876
       Schwarz's Bayesian Criterion     -170.756
       -2 REML Log Likelihood            309.7517
       PARMS Model LRT Chi-Square          0.8558
       PARMS Model LRT DF                  5.0000
       PARMS Model LRT P-Value             0.9733



                  Tests of Fixed Effects

       Source    NDF   DDF   Type III F   Pr > F
       PROD       3    0        4.59       .
       PERIOD     1    0.03     0.04       0.9728
       TIME       2    3.77    26.41       0.0061
       PROD*TIME  6    3.77    13.61       0.0148
       PRIORTRT   3    0        4.54       .
```

Interpretation

The variance component part of the model now has two parameters for the PERIOD part of the error structure, AR(1) for the correlation coefficient and PERIOD diagonal for the variance. The value of the -2 REML log likelihood is a very small improvement over the model with autoregressive errors for the time intervals and independent period errors.

Program—Add the Li's

The program to fit a model with Li's to provide LSMEANS is as follows:

```
proc mixed data=prior;
    class blk person seq prod period time priorprd;
    model y=prod period time time*prod L1 L2 L3 L4/ddfm=satterth;
    random blk person(blk);
    random period/type=ar(1) subject=person(blk);
    repeated time/subject=period*person*blk type=ar(1);
    parms (0.50079619) (0.32416655) (0.18092665) (-0.0558346) (0.20127984)
          (0.11540430);
    lsmeans prod time*prod/pdiff;
run;
```

The estimates of the variance components and the model fitting information are the same as the previous model with the **PRIORPRD** class variable. The tests for the fixed effects part of the model are in Output 10.37.

Results

Output 10.37 *Type III F-Statistics for the Fixed Effects from the Independent Errors Model to the Acceptable Data Using the Li's As Variables*

Tests of Fixed Effects				
Source	NDF	DDF	Type III F	Pr > F
PROD	3	0	4.59	.
PERIOD	1	0.03	0.04	0.9728
TIME	2	3.77	26.41	0.0061
PROD*TIME	6	3.77	13.61	0.0148
L1	0	.	.	.
L2	0	.	.	.
L3	0	.	.	.
L4	0	.	.	.

The LSMEANS and comparisons among the LSMEANS are in Output 10.38.

Output 10.38 *LSMEANS and Some Comparisons from Fitting the Autoregressive Errors for the Time Intervals and Independent Errors for the Periods Model to the Acceptable Data*

Least Squares Means					
Level	LSMEAN	Std Error	DDF	T	Pr > |T|
PROD*TIME 1 1	3.91120432	0.39476904	0	9.91	0.9999
PROD*TIME 1 2	3.63342655	0.39476904	0	9.20	0.9999
PROD*TIME 1 3	2.85564877	0.39476904	0	7.23	0.9999
PROD*TIME 2 1	4.03699455	0.39476904	0	10.23	0.9999
PROD*TIME 2 2	3.70366121	0.39476904	0	9.38	0.9999
PROD*TIME 2 3	3.48143899	0.39476904	0	8.82	0.9999
PROD*TIME 3 1	3.80496602	0.39476904	0	9.64	0.9999
PROD*TIME 3 2	3.69385491	0.39476904	0	9.36	0.9999
PROD*TIME 3 3	3.63829935	0.39476904	0	9.22	0.9999
PROD*TIME 4 1	3.91350178	0.39476904	0	9.91	0.9999
PROD*TIME 4 2	4.19127955	0.39476904	0	10.62	0.9999

```
PROD*TIME 4 3      4.13572400    0.39476904     0   10.48    0.9999
                     Differences of Least Squares Means


Level 1            Level 2          Difference  Std Error  DDF   T    Pr > |T|


PROD*TIME 1 1 PROD*TIME 1 2   0.27777778 0.10110113 0.55   2.75 0.3597
PROD*TIME 1 1 PROD*TIME 1 3   1.05555556 0.11120389 6.62   9.49 0.0001
PROD*TIME 1 2 PROD*TIME 1 3   0.77777778 0.10110113 0.55   7.69 0.2065
PROD*TIME 1 1 PROD*TIME 2 1  -0.12579022 0.18706703 0.04  -0.67 0.9309
PROD*TIME 1 1 PROD*TIME 3 1   0.10623830 0.18706703 0.04   0.57 0.9345
PROD*TIME 1 1 PROD*TIME 4 1  -0.00229745 0.18706703 0.04  -0.01 0.9977
PROD*TIME 1 2 PROD*TIME 2 2  -0.07023467 0.18706703 0.03  -0.38 0.9585
PROD*TIME 1 2 PROD*TIME 3 2  -0.06042836 0.18706703 0.03  -0.32 0.9609
PROD*TIME 1 2 PROD*TIME 4 2  -0.55785301 0.18706703 0.03  -2.98 0.9080
PROD*TIME 1 3 PROD*TIME 2 3  -0.62579022 0.18706703 0.04  -3.35 0.8783
PROD*TIME 1 3 PROD*TIME 3 3  -0.78265059 0.18706703 0.04  -4.18 0.8668
PROD*TIME 1 3 PROD*TIME 4 3  -1.28007523 0.18706703 0.04  -6.84 0.8578
PROD*TIME 2 1 PROD*TIME 3 1   0.23202853 0.18706703 0.04   1.24 0.9111
PROD*TIME 2 1 PROD*TIME 4 1   0.12349277 0.18706703 0.04   0.66 0.9316
PROD*TIME 2 2 PROD*TIME 3 2   0.00980631 0.18706703 0.03   0.05 0.9916
PROD*TIME 2 2 PROD*TIME 4 2  -0.48761834 0.18706703 0.03  -2.61 0.9103
PROD*TIME 2 3 PROD*TIME 3 3  -0.15686036 0.18706703 0.04  -0.84 0.9239
PROD*TIME 2 3 PROD*TIME 4 3  -0.65428500 0.18706703 0.04  -3.50 0.8771
PROD*TIME 3 1 PROD*TIME 4 1  -0.10853576 0.18706703 0.04  -0.58 0.9340
PROD*TIME 3 2 PROD*TIME 4 2  -0.49742464 0.18706703 0.03  -2.66 0.9067
PROD*TIME 3 3 PROD*TIME 4 3  -0.49742464 0.18706703 0.04  -2.66 0.8823
```

Interpretation

The values of the LSMEANS are a little different from the two previous analyses. The major effect is that the estimated standard errors of the difference between pairs of PROD means at the same level of TIME are a little smaller than the other two models. The estimated standard errors of the difference between two TIME means for the same level of PROD are about the same as those for the previous model.

10.8.6 Conclusions

The acceptability data were analyzed using three specifications of the error structure, and the results were compared. The major differences in the analyses are in the magnitudes of the Type III F-values and in the estimated standard errors. The values of the LSMEANS were affected least. The likelihood ratio test for comparing the models indicates that the independent errors model is adequate to describe the data as compared to models involving autoregressive error structures.

10.9 An On-Farm Trial

10.9.1 Introduction

The standard setting for agricultural research is in field plot, feed lot, or laboratory experimentation. However, once promising treatments are developed, interest shifts from basic research to technology transfer. That is, do treatments that perform well under the often idealized conditions of the experiment station also perform well under conditions actually encountered at the farms where the treatments are ultimately used? To answer this question, experiments need to be done by farmers on their fields.

Such an experiment is called an "on-farm trial." In an on-farm trial, an experiment to compare two or more treatments is conducted at each of several farms. The farms represent a random sample from the population of farms where the treatments are of potential interest. On-farm trials are often used in developing countries, where the level of technology at agricultural research facilities often far exceeds what is available to the average farmer. Under such circumstances, monitoring the applicability of experimenters' findings to farmers' resources is crucial. On-farm trials are also used in developed countries, especially when farming practices or environmental conditions vary widely.

In this example, two treatments were compared at each of seven farms. In the actual data set on which this example is based, there were 21 farms—a more realistic number —but to keep the example manageable, we use seven. The data from the seven farms are in Data Set 10.9.1 of Appendix 4, "SAS Data Sets."

The model for this experiment is

$$y_{ijk} = \mu + F_i + R(F)_{ij} + \tau_k + FT_{ik} + e_{ijk}$$

where

y_{ijk} is the observation on the jth block at the ith farm for the kth treatment
μ is the intercept
F_i is the effect of the ith farm
$R(F)_{ij}$ is the ij^{th} block within farm effect
τ_k is the effect of the kth treatment
FT_{ik} is the ik^{th} farm-by-treatment interaction effect
e_{ijk} is random error.

Because the farms are a random sample, the effects F_i, $R(F)_{ij}$, FT_{ik}, and e_{ijk} are all assumed random. Specifically

$F_i \sim \text{iidN}(0, \sigma_F^2)$
$R(F)_{ij} \sim \text{iidN}(0, \sigma_R^2)$
$FT_{ik} \sim \text{iidN}(0, \sigma_{FT}^2)$
$e_{ijk} \sim \text{iidN}(0, \sigma_e^2).$

The researchers primary objectives were to

- compare the mean response of the two treatments
- see if treatment differences were consistent across farms, or if there were specific farms that seemed to favor one treatment or the other.

Because farms are random, the latter objective calls for BLUPs of the treatment response at each farm. The next section presents a PROC MIXED analysis of the data.

10.9.2 Analysis Using PROC MIXED

Program

You can implement the basic analysis of the on-farm trial using the following PROC MIXED statements:

```
proc mixed;
   class farm rep trt;
   model y=trt/ddfm=satterth;
   random farm rep(farm) farm*trt;
run;
```

The results of this analysis are given in Output 10.39.

Results

Output 10.39 *Estimates of the Variance Components and the Test for the Fixed Effects*

```
              Covariance Parameter Estimates (REML)


Cov Parm          Ratio       Estimate     Std Error      Z    Pr > |Z|


FARM           0.42703117    5.34105241   30.14601364    0.18   0.8594
REP(FARM)      0.58072086    7.26331177    8.86024874    0.82   0.4124
FARM*TRT       4.16341122   52.07347635   35.49311194    1.47   0.1423
Residual       1.00000000   12.50740644    7.34667728    1.70   0.0887




                    Tests of Fixed Effects


          Source      NDF   DDF   Type III F   Pr > F


          TRT          1    5.76       2.11    0.1984
```

Interpretation

The main result of the analysis is that the TRT F-value is 2.11 with a *p*-value of 0.1984, indicating no statistically significant evidence of a difference among treatments averaged across all farms. The variance component estimates are also given.

One variance component estimate of particular interest is the farm-by-treatment (FARM*TRT) variance, σ_{FT}^2, which, at 52.07, appears to be quite substantial. This may indicate that averaging the treatment effect over all farms is deceptive — farm-specific effect may exist. You can examine this by testing H_0: $\sigma_{FT}^2 = 0$. Because of the relatively few degrees of freedom for the FARM*TRT effect (6), the Z-test given in the output is not reliable. You should use the likelihood-ratio test, instead. You need the -2 REML Log Likelihood statistic computed with the above model (165.46), which is given in Output 10.40.

Output 10.40 *Model Fitting for the Full Model*

```
                 Model Fitting Information for Y


            Description                      Value

            Observations                     26.0000
            Variance Estimate                12.5074
            Standard Deviation Estimate       3.5366
            REML Log Likelihood             -82.7308
            Akaike's Information Criterion   -86.7308
            Schwarz's Bayesian Criterion    -89.0869
            -2 REML Log Likelihood          165.4615
```

You also need to compute the -2 REML Log Likelihood for the reduced model, dropping FARM*TRT.

Program—Fit Reduced Model

The needed PROC MIXED statements are

```
proc mixed;
    class farm rep trt;
    model y=trt;
    random farm rep(farm);
run;
```

The "Model Fitting Information" for the reduced model is given in Output 10.41.

Results

Output 10.41 *Estimates of the Variance Components and Model Fitting Information for the Reduced Model*

```
Covariance Parameter Estimates (REML)

   Cov Parm          Ratio        Estimate      Std Error      Z    Pr > |Z|


   FARM           0.52651394    24.24538122   23.31690296    1.04    0.2984
   REP(FARM)     -0.00000000    -0.00000000        .          .        .
   Residual       1.00000000    46.04888722   15.54316590    2.96    0.0031



                 Model Fitting Information for Y


            Description                      Value

            Observations                     26.0000
            Variance Estimate                46.0489
            Standard Deviation Estimate       6.7859
            REML Log Likelihood             -85.7180
            Akaike's Information Criterion   -88.7180
            Schwarz's Bayesian Criterion    -90.4851
            -2 REML Log Likelihood          171.4361
```

Interpretation

The -2 REML Log Likelihood is 171.44. The resulting likelihood-ratio χ^2 statistic is $171.44 - 165.46 = 5.98$. The χ^2 statistic has 1 degree of freedom. The hypothesis that $\sigma^2_{FT}=0$ is thus rejected for any reasonable α-level.

Because there is significant FARM*TRT variation, we now address the researcher's second objective. You can use the ESTIMATE statement to compute treatment BLUPs for each farm and then compute farm-specific treatment differences.

ESTIMATE Statements for Treatment BLUPs

The needed PROC MIXED statements are

```
estimate 'farm 1 trt 1 blup' intercept 1 trt 1 0 |
  farm 1 0 0 0 0 0 0 farm*trt 1 0  0 0  0 0  0 0  0 0  0 0  0 0;
estimate 'farm 1 trt 2 blup' intercept 1 trt 0 1 |
  farm 1 0 0 0 0 0 0 farm*trt 0 1  0 0  0 0  0 0  0 0  0 0  0 0;

estimate 'farm 2 trt 1 blup' intercept 1 trt 1 0 |
  farm 0 1 0 0 0 0 0 farm*trt 0 0  1 0  0 0  0 0  0 0  0 0  0 0;
estimate 'farm 2 trt 2 blup' intercept 1 trt 0 1 |
  farm 0 1 0 0 0 0 0 farm*trt 0 0  0 1  0 0  0 0  0 0  0 0  0 0;

estimate 'farm 3 trt 1 blup' intercept 1 trt 1 0 |
  farm 0 0 1 0 0 0 0 farm*trt 0 0  0 0  1 0  0 0  0 0  0 0  0 0;
estimate 'farm 3 trt 2 blup' intercept 1 trt 0 1 |
  farm 0 0 1 0 0 0 0 farm*trt 0 0  0 0  0 1  0 0  0 0  0 0  0 0;

estimate 'farm 4 trt 1 blup' intercept 1 trt 1 0 |
  farm 0 0 0 1 0 0 0 farm*trt 0 0  0 0  0 0  1 0  0 0  0 0  0 0;
estimate 'farm 4 trt 2 blup' intercept 1 trt 0 1 |
  farm 0 0 0 1 0 0 0 farm*trt 0 0  0 0  0 0  0 1  0 0  0 0  0 0;

estimate 'farm 5 trt 1 blup' intercept 1 trt 1 0 |
  farm 0 0 0 0 1 0 0 farm*trt 0 0  0 0  0 0  0 0  1 0  0 0  0 0;
estimate 'farm 5 trt 2 blup' intercept 1 trt 0 1 |
  farm 0 0 0 0 1 0 0 farm*trt 0 0  0 0  0 0  0 0  0 1  0 0  0 0;

estimate 'farm 6 trt 1 blup' intercept 1 trt 1 0 |
  farm 0 0 0 0 0 1 0 farm*trt 0 0  0 0  0 0  0 0  0 0  1 0  0 0;
estimate 'farm 6 trt 2 blup' intercept 1 trt 0 1 |
  farm 0 0 0 0 0 1 0 farm*trt 0 0  0 0  0 0  0 0  0 0  0 1  0 0;

estimate 'farm 7 trt 1 blup' intercept 1 trt 1 0 |
  farm 0 0 0 0 0 0 1 farm*trt 0 0  0 0  0 0  0 0  0 0  0 0  1 0;
estimate 'farm 7 trt 2 blup' intercept 1 trt 0 1 |
  farm 0 0 0 0 0 0 1 farm*trt 0 0  0 0  0 0  0 0  0 0  0 0  0 1;


estimate 'farm 1 trt diff' trt 1 -1 |
  farm*trt 1 -1   0 0   0 0   0 0   0 0   0 0   0 0;
estimate 'farm 2 trt diff' trt 1 -1 |
  farm*trt 0 0   1 -1   0 0   0 0   0 0   0 0   0 0;
estimate 'farm 3 trt diff' trt 1 -1 |
  farm*trt 0 0   0 0   1 -1   0 0   0 0   0 0   0 0;
estimate 'farm 4 trt diff' trt 1 -1 |
  farm*trt 0 0   0 0   0 0   1 -1   0 0   0 0   0 0;
estimate 'farm 5 trt diff' trt 1 -1 |
  farm*trt 0 0   0 0   0 0   0 0   1 -1   0 0   0 0;
estimate 'farm 6 trt diff' trt 1 -1 |
  farm*trt 0 0   0 0   0 0   0 0   0 0   1 -1   0 0;
estimate 'farm 7 trt diff' trt 1 -1 |
  farm*trt 0 0   0 0   0 0   0 0   0 0   0 0   1 -1;
```

The first set of ESTIMATE statements, e.g., "farm 1 trt 1 blup," compute the treatment BLUPs for each farm. The second group of statements, e.g., "farm 1 trt diff," compute the BLUPs of the treatment differences for each farm.

The results are given in Output 10.42.

Output 10.42 *BLUPs for Each Treatment at Each Farm*

```
                         ESTIMATE Statement Results


    Parameter                Estimate    Std Error   DDF        T   Pr > |T|


    farm 1 trt 1 blup      43.51285495   2.44587504  12.9   17.79   0.0001
    farm 1 trt 2 blup      54.72859166   2.44587504  12.9   22.38   0.0001
    farm 2 trt 1 blup      44.60320720   2.92890586  14.4   15.23   0.0001
    farm 2 trt 2 blup      53.32617806   2.92890586  14.4   18.21   0.0001
    farm 3 trt 1 blup      41.06690050   2.92890586  14.4   14.02   0.0001
    farm 3 trt 2 blup      41.35307817   2.92890586  14.4   14.12   0.0001
    farm 4 trt 1 blup      33.75138637   2.92890586  14.4   11.52   0.0001
    farm 4 trt 2 blup      52.74135424   2.92890586  14.4   18.01   0.0001
    farm 5 trt 1 blup      46.35576606   3.89370618  18.2   11.91   0.0001
    farm 5 trt 2 blup      39.29319916   3.89370618  18.2   10.09   0.0001
    farm 6 trt 1 blup      46.54537122   3.89370618  18.2   11.95   0.0001
    farm 6 trt 2 blup      59.72167688   3.89370618  18.2   15.34   0.0001
    farm 7 trt 1 blup      41.20865487   2.92890586  14.4   14.07   0.0001
    farm 7 trt 2 blup      37.87906403   2.92890586  14.4   12.93   0.0001


    farm 1 trt diff      -11.21573671    2.79532502   6.71  -4.01   0.0056
    farm 2 trt diff       -8.72297086    3.37080840   7.16  -2.59   0.0354
    farm 3 trt diff       -0.28617767    3.37080840   7.16  -0.08   0.9347
    farm 4 trt diff      -18.98996787    3.37080840   7.16  -5.63   0.0007
    farm 5 trt diff        7.06256690    4.56174958   8.49   1.55   0.1580
    farm 6 trt diff      -13.17630566    4.56174958   8.49  -2.89   0.0190
    farm 7 trt diff        3.32959084    3.37080840   7.16   0.99   0.3555
```

These results suggest that the difference between treatments 1 and 2 is positive at farms 5 and 7, whereas it is negative at the other farms. The negative difference is substantial at all farms except farm 3, where the difference is close to zero. Also, for farms 1, 2, 4, and 6, the difference between the treatment BLUPs is statistically significant, whereas for farms 3, 5, and 7, the difference is not statistically significant.

Clearly these results suggest something different than the overall F-test for treatments. Instead of concluding no significant difference among treatments averaged over all farms, the researcher concluded that there was evidence to conclude that treatment 2 had a higher response than treatment 1 at farms 1, 2, 4, and 6 — and, by implication, farms in the target population with similar characteristics to these farms. On the other hand, no clear evidence favored either treatment at the other farms, although there was some indication that treatment 1 might be preferable at farms 5 and 7 and of similar farms in the population.

The differences in the two sets of farms led the researcher to collect additional information. As a result, the researcher was able to identify several characteristics of the two groups that indicated that treatment 1 was indeed preferable for one group and treatment 2 for the other. Outcomes like this occur frequently in on-farm trials — that is, subpopulations that are not anticipated or identifiable prior to the study are discovered during data analysis. On-farm researchers refer to the sets of farms where different treatments appear to be better suited as **recommendation domains**. Here, farms 5 and 7 belong to the recommendation domain where treatment 1 seems preferable. Farms 1, 2, 4, and 6 belong to the recommendation domain where treatment 2 seems preferable. Farm 3 is a question mark.

As a result of the study, the researcher wanted to test the difference between the treatment responses at farms 5 and 7 (those where treatment 1 had the higher response) versus the other farms. The specific hypotheses the researcher wanted to look at were

- Is there a difference between treatment effect for farms 5 and 7 versus the others?
- Are the treatment effects similar for farms 5 and 7?
- Are the treatment effects similar for the farms other than 5 and 7?

Each of these hypotheses can be defined as a FARM*TRT interaction.

Contrasts

You can test these hypotheses using the following CONTRAST statements. Note that these contrasts are defined on BLUPs because the FARM*TRT effect is random.

```
contrast 'farm 5&7 v oth x trt'
    | farm*trt 2 -2   2 -2  2 -2  2 -2  -5 5  2 -2  -5 5;
contrast 'farm 5 v 7 x trt'
    | farm*trt 0 0   0 0  0 0  0 0  1 -1   0 0  -1 1;
contrast 'oth farms x trt'
    | farm*trt 1 -1  -1 1   0 0   0 0   0 0   0 0   0 0,
    | farm*trt 1 -1   0 0  -1 1   0 0   0 0   0 0   0 0,
    | farm*trt 1 -1   0 0   0 0  -1 1   0 0   0 0   0 0,
    | farm*trt 1 -1   0 0   0 0   0 0   0 0  -1 1   0 0;
```

The results of these contrasts appear in Output 10.43.

Results

Output 10.43 *Results of the CONTRAST Statements*

```
                        CONTRAST Statement Results

            Source                 NDF   DDF       F  Pr > F

            farm 5&7 v oth x trt     1  8.29   23.83  0.0011
            farm 5 v 7 x trt         1   8.4    0.44  0.5236
            oth farms x trt          4  7.63    4.12  0.0447
```

Interpretation

They indicate that the difference in treatment effect between farms 5 and 7 on one hand and the other ('farm 5&7 v oth x trt') is statistically significant (F=23.83, *p*-value=0.0011), and there is some difference in the treatment effect among the farms other than 5 and 7 ('oth farms x trt', F=4.12, *p*-value=0.0447). You can drop farm 3 from this contrast, that is, run the CONTRAST

```
contrast 'among (1,2,4,6) x trt'
    | farm*trt 1 -1  -1 1   0 0   0 0   0 0   0 0   0 0,
    | farm*trt 1 -1   0 0   0 0  -1 1   0 0   0 0   0 0,
    | farm*trt 1 -1   0 0   0 0   0 0   0 0  -1 1   0 0;
```

and the result is no longer significant, suggesting a possible difference between farm 3 and farms 1, 2, 4, and 6. In this case, farm 3's characteristics were not appreciably different from farms 1, 2, 4, and 6, whereas they were quite different from farms 5 and 7. The researcher was thus reluctant to make much of the significant 'oth farms x trt' contrast.

After the fact, contrasts like the one just discussed must be interpreted with extra caution. First, you must consider the cautions normally associated with *all a posteriori* comparisons

— the effective α-rate is inflated. In addition, the distribution theory for comparing BLUPs is highly approximate and not completely understood. Results such as these should *never* be interpreted without some kind of external corroborating evidence. In this case, the researcher was careful to gather additional information about the relevant characteristics of the farms once there was some indication that the farms represented different subpopulations. Only then was it acceptable to discuss the differences in BLUPs.

10.9.3 A Brief Comment on PROC GLM for On-Farm Trials

Program—PROC GLM

Prior to the introduction of PROC MIXED, researchers analyzed on-farm trials with traditional ANOVA tools, e.g., those available in PROC GLM. You could use the following PROC GLM program to obtain the ANOVA, estimates of FARM*TRT means, and the contrasts discussed above:

```
proc glm;
    class farm rep trt;
    model y=farm rep(farm) trt farm*trt;

    random farm rep(farm) farm*trt / test;
    lsmeans farm*trt / stderr;
    contrast 'site 5&7 v oth x trt'
        farm*trt 2 -2  2 -2  2 -2  2 -2  -5 5  2 -2  -5 5;
    contrast 'farm 5 v 7 x trt'
        farm*trt 0 0  0 0  0 0  0 0  1 -1  0 0  -1 1;
    contrast 'oth sites x trt'
        farm*trt 1 -1  -1 1  0 0  0 0  0 0  0 0  0 0,
        farm*trt 1 -1  0 0  -1 1  0 0  0 0  0 0  0 0,
        farm*trt 1 -1  0 0  0 0  -1 1  0 0  0 0  0 0,
        farm*trt 1 -1  0 0  0 0  0 0  0 0  -1 1  0 0;
run;
```

The results are given in Output 10.44 and Output 10.45.

Results

Output 10.44 *PROC GLM Results for the On-Farm Trials*

Source	DF	Sum of Squares	Mean Square	F Value	Pr > F
Model	19	1835.970321	96.630017	7.87	0.0086
Error	6	73.680833	12.280139		
Corrected Total	25	1909.651154			

Source	DF	Type III SS	Mean Square	F Value	Pr > F
FARM	6	789.3086538	131.5514423	10.71	0.0055
REP(FARM)	6	156.4675000	26.0779167	2.12	0.1907
TRT	1	194.7508013	194.7508013	15.86	0.0073
FARM*TRT	6	584.8553205	97.4758868	7.94	0.0118

```
Source          Type III Expected Mean Square

FARM            Var(Error) + 1.8205 Var(FARM*TRT) + 2 Var(REP(FARM))
                + 3.641 Var(FARM)

REP(FARM)       Var(Error) + 2 Var(REP(FARM))

TRT             Var(Error) + 1.6154 Var(FARM*TRT) + Q(TRT)

FARM*TRT        Var(Error) + 1.8205 Var(FARM*TRT)

                Tests of Hypotheses for Mixed Model Analysis of Variance


Source: FARM
Error: MS(REP(FARM)) + MS(FARM*TRT) - MS(Error)


                        Denominator   Denominator
     DF     Type III MS         DF            MS      F Value    Pr > F
      6    131.55144231       7.19   111.27366453       1.1822    0.4089

Source: REP(FARM)
Error: MS(Error)

                        Denominator   Denominator
     DF     Type III MS         DF            MS      F Value    Pr > F
      6    26.077916667          6   12.280138889       2.1236    0.1907

Source: TRT
Error: 0.8873*MS(FARM*TRT) + 0.1127*MS(Error)


                        Denominator   Denominator
     DF     Type III MS         DF            MS      F Value    Pr > F
      1    194.75080128       6.19   87.876365866       2.2162    0.1856

Source: FARM*TRT
Error: MS(Error)

                        Denominator   Denominator
     DF     Type III MS         DF            MS      F Value    Pr > F
      6    97.475886752          6   12.280138889       7.9377    0.0118
```

Output 10.45 *LSMEANS and CONTRASTS from PROC GLM*

```
                    Least Squares Means


          FARM    TRT          Y      Std Err    Pr > |T|
                            LSMEAN     LSMEAN    H0:LSMEAN=0


            1      1     43.8333333   2.0232102     0.0001
            1      2     55.4666667   2.0232102     0.0001
            2      1     45.2000000   2.4779164     0.0001
            2      2     54.2500000   2.4779164     0.0001
            3      1     40.5000000   2.4779164     0.0001
            3      2     40.1000000   2.4779164     0.0001
            4      1     32.5000000   2.4779164     0.0001
            4      2     53.0500000   2.4779164     0.0001
            5      1     46.8000000   3.5043029     0.0001
```

5	2	36.6000000	3.5043029	0.0001
6	1	49.0000000	3.5043029	0.0001
6	2	63.9000000	3.5043029	0.0001
7	1	40.5000000	2.4779164	0.0001
7	2	36.0500000	2.4779164	0.0001

Contrast	DF	Contrast SS	Mean Square	F Value	Pr > F
site 5&7 v oth x trt	1	349.3540643	349.3540643	28.45	0.0018
farm 5 v 7 x trt	1	11.0208333	11.0208333	0.90	0.3800
oth sites x trt	4	233.0096667	58.2524167	4.74	0.0455

Interpretation

Several points of comparison between the PROC GLM and PROC MIXED results are

- the analysis of variance

    The two analyses produce similar results for the main effect of TRT. The F for PROC GLM is 2.22 and for PROC MIXED it is 2.11. For the FARM*TRT interaction, PROC GLM gives an F of 7.9377 with a p-value of 0.0118. The likelihood-ratio χ^2 of 5.98 has a similar p-value of 0.0145, for FARM*TRT using PROC MIXED.

- the FARM*TRT LSMEANS in PROC GLM versus BLUPs in PROC MIXED

    The PROC GLM estimates are obtained using methods appropriate for *fixed* FARM*TRT effects. These tend to overestimate differences between treatments at specific farms relative to the BLUPs computed by PROC MIXED. For example, for farm 1, PROC GLM obtains a mean difference of 43.83 − 55.47 = −11.64, whereas the BLUP of the difference is −11.21. In general, the discrepancy between PROC GLM and PROC MIXED is small, but it can be important. For example, you get a positive difference between treatment 1 and 2 at farm 3 using PROC GLM, but a negative difference using PROC MIXED. There is no theory to support PROC GLM's computational approach, whereas PROC MIXED is consistent with general linear model theory.

- the contrasts

    The F-values for the three contrasts defined in Section 10.9.2 all are higher in magnitude with PROC GLM. In general, the tests PROC GLM computes are less conservative than the corresponding tests using PROC MIXED.

The differences between the two sets of results appear to be fairly minor in this example. However, in cases where conclusions are borderline, failure to use the appropriate methodology can result in inaccurate inference. If the farms are a random sample of a larger target population, we strongly recommend the use of the procedures described in Section 10.9.2 using PROC MIXED. These methods are consistent with underlying linear model theory and are therefore more appropriate.

10.10 Random Coefficients Modeling of an AIDS Trial

The data for this example are the result of a clinical trial for AIDS patients comparing two drugs, ddI and ddC (Abrams, Goldman, Launer, et al. (1994) and Fleming, Neaton,

Goldman, et al. (1995); see also Lange, Carlin, and Gelfand (1992)). The study was a multicenter, randomized, open label comparative trial of ddI to ddC in HIV infected patients which were intolerant to or had failed ZDV therapy. Participants were men and women, aged 15-67, who had either advanced to AIDS or had a CD4 lymphocyte count less than or equal to 300. The primary objective of the study was to determine which monotherapy was better in this patient population. Some key features of the data are as follows:

- repeated measures on CD4 counts and several explanatories
- 467 subjects at 5 visits: baseline, 2, 6, 12, and 18 months, with a lot of missing values
- values well below the normal range of 22–31 on the square root scale.

Figure 10.7 provides profile plots of the longitudinal measurements.

Figure 10.7 *CD4 Data*

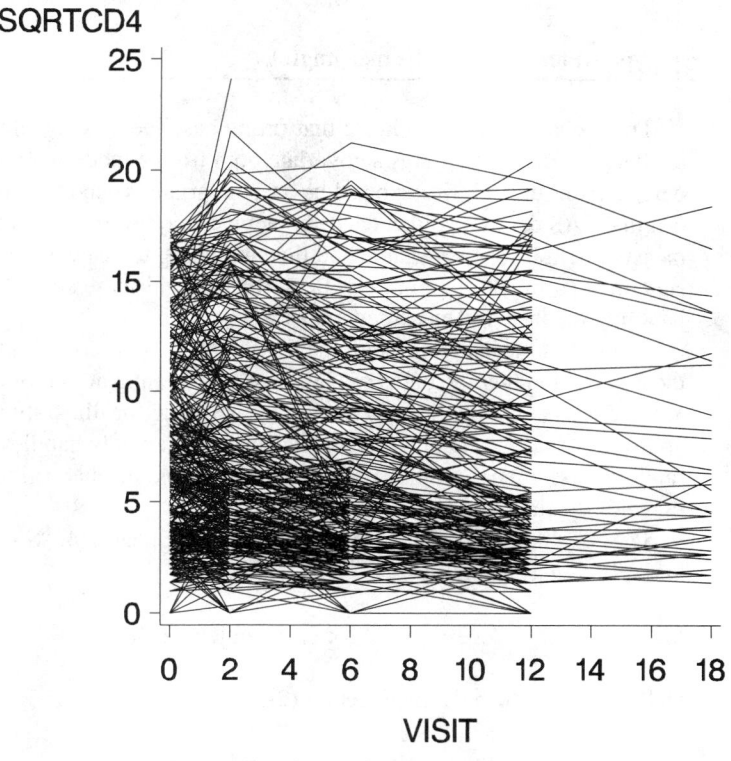

Scientific theory suggests an initial increase in the CD4 counts over the first few months and then a linear decline (in the square root scale) from there. The population mean of the responses is therefore modeled as a piecewise linear model with a join point at 2 months. This mean model is a "hockey stick" because it has one short line and one long one. The objectives for this case study analysis are as follows:

1. Fit a random coefficients model using a "hockey stick" population curve for SQRTCD4 with baseline as a dependent variable.
2. Compute estimates and standard errors for various linear combinations.
3. Compute and plot predicted values.

The first objective involves using the baseline measurement as a dependent variable; however, you can also use baseline as a covariate. Some pros and cons of each approach are shown in Table 10.7.

Table 10.7 *Pros and Cons of Using Baseline as a Dependent Variable or as a Covariate*

Baseline as Dependent	Baseline as Covariate
models baseline to first measurement	starts with first measurement
unconditional prediction	conditional prediction
must account for no treatment effect at baseline	treatment effect straightforward
account for covariance structure at baseline	covariance structure easier to model
Type III tests may not be meaningful	Type III tests straightforward

These characteristics indicate that fitting baseline as a dependent variable can be more challenging than fitting it as a covariate both from a modeling and an interpretation perspective. Indeed, fitting baseline as a covariate is accomplished by just reformulating the original SAS data set so that each subject has one fewer observation and the baseline measurement is a new variable and then including this new variable in the MODEL statement as an additional fixed effect. Instead, this case study focuses on techniques for handling the baseline measurement as a dependent variable.

The use of the standard random coefficients model (see Chapter 7) for these data relies on the assumption that the data are Gaussian and missing at random. Although these assumptions could be violated here, they are made for illustration purposes. A likelihood approach to fitting the random coefficients model nicely handles unequal spacing and random missingness. It also provides a reasonable mechanism for prediction beyond the range of the data.

The SAS data set CD4 is Data Set 10.10 in Appendix 4, "SAS DATA Sets." The key variables are as follows:

SEQ   a 3-digit ID for each subject (1-467)

UNIT   the clinical center (2-18)

RANDGRP   the treatment group (1=ddI, 2=ddC)

STRATUM   a time-invariant variable used to stratify the subjects (1=ZDV failure, 2=ZDV intolerant)

CD4   the CD4 count

VISIT   the month at which the CD4 count was measured (0=baseline, 2=2 months, 6=6 months, 12=12 months, 18=18 months)

SQRTCD4   the square-root of the CD4 count

NOTBASE   a dummy variable indicating if the measurement is baseline (0=baseline, 1=not baseline)

VISITM2   equals max(0,VISIT-2)

Program

The initial random coefficients model is set up in PROC MIXED as follows:

```
proc mixed data=cd4;
   class randgrp stratum unit seq;
   model sqrtcd4 = stratum unit
         notbase notbase*randgrp notbase*stratum
         visitm2 visitm2*randgrp visitm2*stratum  / ddfm=res;
   random int notbase visitm2 / type=un sub=seq g gcorr;
run;
```

The MODEL statement specifies the mean model for the data. STRATUM and UNIT are both considered main fixed effects, but note that the treatment variable RANDGRP is only included in interaction terms to account for the fact that it does not affect the baseline measurements.

NOTBASE and VISITM2 are the variables used to specify the piecewise linear "hockey stick" mean model. NOTBASE is effectively a new intercept starting at 2 months, and VISITM2 models a linear slope from there. Both NOTBASE and VISITM2 interact with RANDGRP and STRATUM to provide different "hockey sticks" for these classifications. The DDFM=RES option is used to speed computing time because of the large $\mathbf{Z}$ matrix (see below).

The RANDOM statement models three random coefficients using the following three effects: INT (an overall intercept), NOTBASE (a random jump at 2 months), and VISITM2 (a random slope starting at 2 months). Thus, each subject has a random starting point for its hockey stick, a random location for the bend in the stick, and a random angle for the stick. TYPE=UN models a full 3×3 covariance matrix for the random coefficients, and SUB=SEQ identifies the subjects. The G and GCORR options request a printout of the $\mathbf{G}$ matrix and its correlations.

In general mixed model notation, $\mathbf{X}$ is 1408×29 (overparameterized form). $\mathbf{Z}$ is 1408×1401 and is block diagonal with 467 blocks having dimensions $n_i \times 3$, where n_i is the number of observations for the ith subject. $\mathbf{G}$ is 1401×1401 and is block diagonal with 467 3×3 unstructured blocks. $\mathbf{R} = \sigma^2 \mathbf{I}_{1408}$.

Output 10.46 is a partial listing of the results for this initial model.

Results

Output 10.46 *Results for "Hockey Stick" Random Coefficients Model*

```
             REML Estimation Iteration History


    Iteration  Evaluations      Objective       Criterion


          0             1   5795.2472144
          1             4   4490.6679503              .
          2             1   4487.5580254      0.00008866
          3             1   4487.3485061      0.00000072
          4             1   4487.3468859      0.00000000


             Convergence criteria met.



                        G Matrix


Parameter    Subject   Row        COL1           COL2           COL3


INTERCEPT    SEQ 1       1    17.75684892    1.51322465    -0.33597058
```

```
NOTBASE    SEQ 1    2     1.51322465    0.25080292    0.07110720
VISITM2    SEQ 1    3    -0.33597058    0.07110720    0.02799909
```

```
                    G Correlation Matrix

Parameter    Subject    Row       COL1          COL2          COL3

INTERCEPT    SEQ 1       1     1.00000000    0.71705779   -0.47648186
NOTBASE      SEQ 1       2     0.71705779    1.00000000    0.84854599
VISITM2      SEQ 1       3    -0.47648186    0.84854599    1.00000000
```

```
              Covariance Parameter Estimates (REML)

Cov Parm                 Ratio       Estimate    Std Error        Z

INTERCEPT UN(1,1)     5.92851063    17.75684892   1.41310660    12.57
          UN(2,1)     0.50522300     1.51322465   0.62949488     2.40
          UN(2,2)     0.08373602     0.25080292   0.66848542     0.38
          UN(3,1)    -0.11217109    -0.33597058   0.07868704    -4.27
          UN(3,2)     0.02374069     0.07110720   0.05315647     1.34
          UN(3,3)     0.00934810     0.02799909   0.00997566     2.81
Residual              1.00000000     2.99516186   0.27437493    10.92
```

```
          Model Fitting Information for SQRTCD4

          Description                        Value

          Observations                     1408.000
          Variance Estimate                   2.9952
          Standard Deviation Estimate         1.7307
          REML Log Likelihood             -3516.40
          Akaike's Information Criterion  -3523.40
          Schwarz's Bayesian Criterion    -3541.72
          -2 REML Log Likelihood           7032.807
          Null Model LRT Chi-Square         1307.900
          Null Model LRT DF                   6.0000
          Null Model LRT P-Value              0.0000
```

```
                    Tests of Fixed Effects

          Source             NDF    DDF   Type III F   Pr > F

          STRATUM              1    1385      32.02     0.0001
          UNIT                15    1385       1.52     0.0914
          NOTBASE              1    1385       4.32     0.0379
          NOTBASE*RANDGRP      1    1385       7.40     0.0066
          NOTBASE*STRATUM      1    1385       4.22     0.0402
          VISITM2              1    1385      63.38     0.0001
          VISITM2*RANDGRP      1    1385       0.62     0.4300
          VISITM2*STRATUM      1    1385       0.24     0.6214
```

Interpretation

The REML algorithm converges successfully after 4 iterations. The "G Matrix" table reveals that there is some additional variability of the 2-month random effect beyond that modeled by the random intercept, with the variance estimate of this 2-month jump equalling 0.25. The "G Correlation Matrix" table reveals that the 2-month jump is positively correlated with the random intercept (0.72), and that the random slope is negatively correlated with the random intercept (−0.48) and positively correlated with the 2-month jump (0.85).

The residual variance estimate equals 3.00, and the minimized value of −2 REML log Likelihood equals 7032.8.

The "Tests of Fixed Effects" table reveals some evidence for significant treatment effect (the NOTBASE*RANDGRP effect has a *p*-value of 0.0066). Also, UNIT and the interactions involving VISITM2 do not appear to contribute much to the model. Before deleting them from the model, consider an enhancement to the variance-covariance model.

Program

The enhancement involves modeling heterogeneous residual variance groups, a topic discussed further in Chapter 8. The PROC MIXED program for this model is as follows:

```
proc mixed data=cd4;
   class randgrp stratum unit seq visit;
   model sqrtcd4 = stratum unit
         notbase notbase*randgrp notbase*stratum
         visitm2 visitm2*randgrp visitm2*stratum / ddfm=res;
   random int notbase visitm2 / type=un sub=seq;
   repeated visit / sub=seq group=randgrp*stratum;
run;
```

Note the addition of the REPEATED statement, whose purpose is to model **R** with 4 different variance components down its diagonal via the GROUP= option. These variance components correspond to the different combinations of treatment and stratum.

Abbreviated output from this model is displayed in Output 10.47.

Results

Output 10.47 *Results for "Hockey Stick" Heterogeneous Model*

```
              Covariance Parameter Estimates (REML)

Cov Parm                         Estimate      Std Error       Z

INTERCEPT UN(1,1)               18.47078220    1.43356930    12.88
          UN(2,1)                0.79266549    0.50810858     1.56
          UN(2,2)                0.00000000        .            .
          UN(3,1)               -0.35668230    0.07400877    -4.82
          UN(3,2)                0.13651467    0.03496885     3.90
          UN(3,3)                0.02144277    0.00764280     2.81
VISIT  RANDGRP*STRATUM 1 1       1.49431244    0.19398926     7.70
VISIT  RANDGRP*STRATUM 1 2       4.34739155    0.37583497    11.57
VISIT  RANDGRP*STRATUM 2 1       2.30205097    0.27031764     8.52
VISIT  RANDGRP*STRATUM 2 2       2.99787127    0.29013381    10.33
Residual                         1.00000009        .            .
```

```
            Model Fitting Information for SQRTCD4

       Description                           Value

       Observations                        1408.000
       Variance Estimate                      1.0000
       Standard Deviation Estimate            1.0000
       REML Log Likelihood                 -3493.11
       Akaike's Information Criterion      -3503.11
       Schwarz's Bayesian Criterion        -3529.28
       -2 REML Log Likelihood              6986.228
       Null Model LRT Chi-Square           1354.479
       Null Model LRT DF                      9.0000
       Null Model LRT P-Value                 0.0000



                   Tests of Fixed Effects


       Source           NDF   DDF  Type III F  Pr > F


       STRATUM            1  1385     31.65    0.0001
       UNIT              15  1385      1.56    0.0784
       NOTBASE            1  1385      5.90    0.0152
       NOTBASE*RANDGRP    1  1385      7.98    0.0048
       NOTBASE*STRATUM    1  1385      5.75    0.0167
       VISITM2            1  1385     78.47    0.0001
       VISITM2*RANDGRP    1  1385      0.36    0.5483
       VISITM2*STRATUM    1  1385      0.38    0.5390
```

Interpretation

The enhanced residual variance model results in a substantially better fit to the data: the difference in -2 REML log likelihoods equals $7032.8 - 6986.2 = 46.6$ on 3 degrees of freedom. There are definite differences in the residual variance component estimates for the four groups, with those for stratum 2 being smaller than the average value of 3.00 obtained in the previous model. Furthermore, the estimated **G** matrix for the enhanced model now has a zero estimate for the variance of the 2-month jumps. The fixed-effects tests change a little as a result of this different variance-covariance model.

Program

Before presenting the final model for this analysis, some additional code is required to set up for predicted values:

```
data cd4x;
    input seq randgrp stratum sqrtcd4 visit notbase;
    if (visit ne 0) then visitm2 = visit - 2;
    else visitm2 = 0;
    datalines;
```

```
1000 1 1 .  0 0
1000 1 1 .  2 1
1000 1 1 .  6 1
1000 1 1 . 12 1
1000 1 1 . 18 1
1001 1 2 .  0 0
1001 1 2 .  2 1
1001 1 2 .  6 1
1001 1 2 . 12 1
1001 1 2 . 18 1
1002 2 1 .  0 0
1002 2 1 .  2 1
1002 2 1 .  6 1
1002 2 1 . 12 1
1002 2 1 . 18 1
1003 2 2 .  0 0
1003 2 2 .  2 1
1003 2 2 .  6 1
1003 2 2 . 12 1
1003 2 2 . 18 1
run;

proc append base=cd4 data=cd4x;
run;
```

The resulting new CD4 data set allows population predictions to be constructed across the range of the data.

The final reduced "hockey stick" heterogeneous model is as follows, along with some relevant inferential statements:

```
proc mixed data=cd4;
    class randgrp stratum visit seq;
    model sqrtcd4 = stratum
        notbase notbase*randgrp notbase*stratum
        visitm2 / s ddfm=res p;
    random int notbase visitm2 / type=un sub=seq g gcorr;
    repeated visit / sub=seq group=randgrp*stratum;
    estimate 'ddI 2 - base s 2' notbase 1 notbase*randgrp 1 0
            visitm2 0 / cl;
    estimate 'ddC 2 - base s 2' notbase 1 notbase*randgrp 0 1
            visitm2 0;
    estimate 'ddI 6 - base s 2' notbase 1 notbase*randgrp 1 0
            visitm2 4;
    estimate 'ddC 6 - base s 2' notbase 1 notbase*randgrp 0 1
            visitm2 4;
    estimate 'ddI - ddC s 2' notbase*randgrp 1 -1;
    estimate 'ddI 24 s 1' int 1 stratum 1 0 notbase 1
            notbase*randgrp 1 0 notbase*stratum 1 0 visitm2 22;
    estimate 'ddC 24 s 1' int 1 stratum 1 0 notbase 1
            notbase*randgrp 0 1 notbase*stratum 1 0 visitm2 22;
    estimate 'ddI 24 s 2' int 1 notbase 1 notbase*randgrp 1 0
            visitm2 22;
    estimate 'ddC 24 s 2' int 1 notbase 1 notbase*randgrp 0 1
            visitm2 22;
    make 'predicted' out=p noprint;
    id visit seq;
run;
```

The S option in the MODEL statement requests a table of the fixed-effects parameter estimates. The P option in the MODEL statement requests a table of predicted values, which is converted to a SAS data set named P with the MAKE statement. The ID statement adds additional variables to this data set.

The ESTIMATE statements set up various interesting linear combinations of the fixed-effects parameter estimates. The first four construct differences with baseline for both treatments and the second stratum, and the fifth computes the overall treatment difference for the second stratum. The final four statements compute mean estimates at 24 months. The CL option in the first ESTIMATE statement requests confidence limits for all of the estimates.

Partial output from this model is in Output 10.48.

Results

Output 10.48 *Results for Reduced "Hockey Stick" Heterogeneous Model*

```
                    REML Estimation Iteration History


          Iteration  Evaluations    Objective     Criterion


              0            1      5829.0610551
              1            4      5020.5219605    1.03907624
              2            3      4942.5424433    0.73753172
              3            1      4899.2717164        .
              4            1      4890.7966036   33.83228172
              5            1      4862.8478126    1.59863199
              6            1      4703.9980990    0.15104343
              7            1      4610.1342200    0.17177558
              8            1      4523.9953672    6.75682410
              9            1      4474.7128097    0.06098045
             10            1      4455.9097684        .
             11            1      4450.2456949    0.00031480
             12            1      4449.4819118    0.00000906
             13            1      4449.4611964    0.00000002
             14            1      4449.4611593    0.00000000


                    Convergence criteria met.



                      G Correlation Matrix


Parameter   Subject   Row      COL1          COL2          COL3


INTERCEPT    SEQ 1     1    1.00000000    0.11976896   -0.44510691
NOTBASE      SEQ 1     2    0.11976896    1.00000000    0.54515995
VISITM2      SEQ 1     3   -0.44510691    0.54515995    1.00000000



              Covariance Parameter Estimates (REML)


Cov Parm                       Estimate     Std Error      Z


INTERCEPT UN(1,1)             18.72828464   1.41305539   13.25
          UN(2,1)              0.51729219   0.57769803    0.90
          UN(2,2)              0.99605944   0.55270878    1.80
          UN(3,1)             -0.32716332   0.07550525   -4.33
          UN(3,2)              0.09240976   0.04667678    1.98
          UN(3,3)              0.02884713   0.00856177    3.37
VISIT   RANDGRP*STRATUM 1 1    1.12462528   0.23722402    4.74
VISIT   RANDGRP*STRATUM 1 2    4.05470661   0.40194663   10.09
VISIT   RANDGRP*STRATUM 2 1    1.93194209   0.32916583    5.87
VISIT   RANDGRP*STRATUM 2 2    2.72791350   0.31249781    8.73
Residual                      1.00000011        .          .
```

Solution for Fixed Effects

Parameter	Estimate	Std Error	DDF	T
INTERCEPT	8.05888060	0.27298645	1402	29.52
STRATUM 1	-2.47774705	0.42852221	1402	-5.78
STRATUM 2	0.00000000	.	.	.
NOTBASE	-0.30765778	0.19027412	1402	-1.62
NOTBASE*RANDGRP 1	0.59042656	0.22264512	1402	2.65
NOTBASE*RANDGRP 2	0.00000000	.	.	.
NOTBASE*STRATUM 1	-0.50265038	0.22867633	1402	-2.20
NOTBASE*STRATUM 2	0.00000000	.	.	.
VISITM2	-0.15107413	0.01671108	1402	-9.04

Tests of Fixed Effects

Source	NDF	DDF	Type III F	Pr > F
STRATUM	1	1402	33.43	0.0001
NOTBASE	1	1402	5.18	0.0230
NOTBASE*RANDGRP	1	1402	7.03	0.0081
NOTBASE*STRATUM	1	1402	4.83	0.0281
VISITM2	1	1402	81.73	0.0001

ESTIMATE Statement Results

Parameter	Estimate	Std Error	DDF	T
ddI 2 - base s 2	0.03144359	0.16188280	1402	0.19
ddC 2 - base s 2	-0.55898297	0.15956048	1402	-3.50
ddI 6 - base s 2	-0.57285292	0.16655848	1402	-3.44
ddC 6 - base s 2	-1.16327948	0.16239718	1402	-7.16
ddI - ddC s 2	0.59042656	0.22264512	1402	2.65
ddI 24 s 1	2.03762114	0.47881930	1402	4.26
ddC 24 s 1	1.44719458	0.47447080	1402	3.05
ddI 24 s 2	3.52781985	0.39209716	1402	9.00
ddC 24 s 2	2.93739329	0.38633159	1402	7.60

ESTIMATE Statement Results

Pr > |T|	Alpha	Lower	Upper
0.8460	0.05	-0.2861	0.3490
0.0005	0.05	-0.8720	-0.2460
0.0006	0.05	-0.8996	-0.2461
0.0001	0.05	-1.4818	-0.8447
0.0081	0.05	0.1537	1.0272
0.0001	0.05	1.0983	2.9769
0.0023	0.05	0.5164	2.3779
0.0001	0.05	2.7587	4.2970
0.0001	0.05	2.1795	3.6952

Interpretation

The REML algorithm has more difficulty with this model, requiring 14 iterations to achieve convergence. The variance of the 2-month jump is positive again, but still small as compared to the variance of the random intercept. Also, the correlations involving the 2-month jump have dropped considerably from the initial analysis in Output 10.46. The four combinations of treatment and stratum continue to exhibit heterogeneity in their residual variances.

The "Solution for Fixed Effects" table lists estimates of the mixed-model β vector. The order and form of these estimates is important for formulating the ESTIMATE statements shown previously.

All fixed effects have p-values less than 0.05, and the p-value for treatments (NOTBASE*RANDGRP) equals 0.0081.

The first two rows of the "ESTIMATE Statement Results" table reveals that in stratum 2, the ddI treatment exhibits a slight increase from baseline at 2 months (0.03), which is not significantly different from zero, but the ddC treatment exhibits a significant decrease from baseline (-0.56). The corresponding 6 month estimates are both significantly below baseline.

The "ddI - ddC s 2" estimate has the same p-value as the NOTBASE*RANGRP test; both are testing the same null hypothesis of no difference in treatments. The estimate reveals that ddC patients have significantly lower counts than the ddI patients. The 24-month mean predictions are on the same order of magnitude, with the ddI patients who are ZDV intolerant having the largest predicted mean at 24 months.

Finally, you can plot the predicted values with the following program:

```
title 'Predicted Values for CD4 Data';
symbol1 i=join c=green w=1 r=467;
symbol2 i=join c=black w=4 r=4;
proc gplot data=p;
   plot pred*visit=seq / nolegend
         vaxis=0 to 25 by 5 vminor=0
         haxis=0 to 18 by 2 hminor=0;
run;
```

Figure 10.7, displayed previously, shows these predictions, with the population "hockey sticks" in bold. Note that predictions are available for all subjects at all time periods, even if a subject has only a few observations. For example, the sixth subject has only a baseline measurement, but a full, predicted, individual "hockey stick" is available based on that single measurement.

The predicted profiles are all essentially a weighted average between the original data profiles and the appropriate population curve, with the weights determined by the method of empirical Bayes. The predicted profiles for most subjects follow the basic pattern of the population curves. Several curves drop below zero and are truncated in Figure 10.8. On the other hand, a few exceptional subjects buck the trend and exhibit significant growth and good recovery potential.

10.8 *Predicted Values for CD4 date*

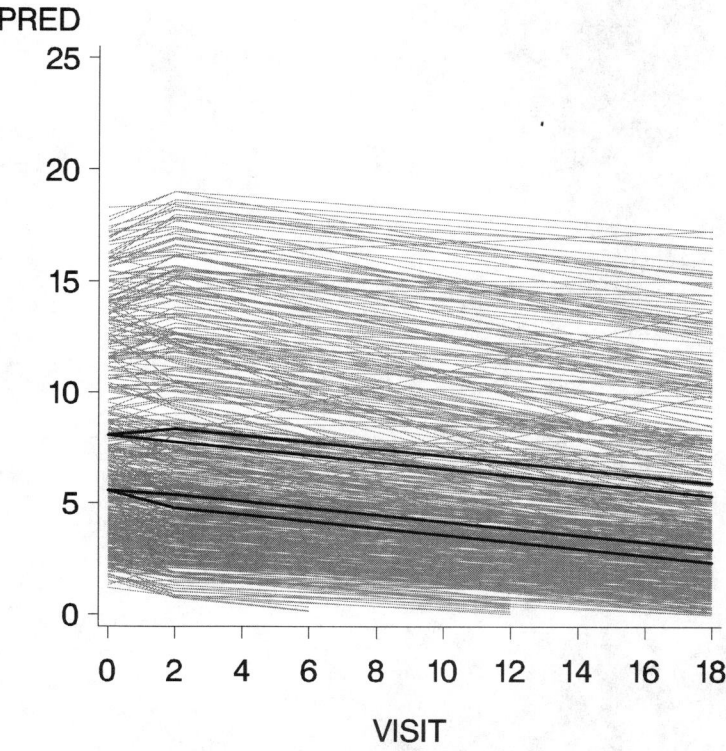

PRED

VISIT

10.11 References

Abrams D., Goldman A., Launer C., et al. (1994), A comparative trial of Didanosine or Zalcitabine after treatment with Zidovudine in patients with Human Immunodeficiency Virus Infection, *NEJM*, **330**, 657–662.

Box, G.E.P., Hunter, W.G., and Hunter, J.S. (1978), *Statistics for Experimenters*, New York: John Wiley & Sons, Inc., 653 pp.

Cochran, W.G. and Cox, G.M. (1957), *Experimental Designs, Second Edition*, New York: John Wiley & Sons, Inc.

Fleming T., Neaton J., Goldman A., et al. (1995), Insights from monitoring the CPCRA Didanosine/Zalcitabine Trial. *JAIDS*, **10**(Suppl. 2), S9–S18.

Johnson, D.E., Chaudhuri, U.N., and Kanemasu, E.T. (1983), Statistical analysis of line-source sprinkler irrigation experiments and other non-randomized experiments using multivariate methods, *J. Amer. Soil Sci. Soc.*, **47**, 309–312.

Lange, N., Carlin, B.P, and Gelfand, A.E. (1992), Hierarchical Bayes Models for the progression of HIV infection using longitudinal CD4 T-Cell numbers (with discussion). *JASA*, 87, 615–632.

Milliken, G.A.and Johnson, D.E. (1994), *Analysis of Messy Data, Volume 1: Designed Experiments*, London: Chapman Hall

SAS Institute Inc. (1996), *SAS/STAT Software: Changes and Enhancements through Release 6.11*, Cary, NC: SAS Institute Inc.

Chapter **11 Generalized Linear Mixed Models**

11.1 Introduction

The mixed models discussed in the previous nine chapters have two features in common. First, the errors are assumed to be normally distributed. Second, the response variable is equated directly to a linear combination of fixed and random effects. However, in many practical situations, the response variable of interest may not have a normal distribution. In other cases, there may be restrictions on the range of allowable values for predictable functions that direct modeling of the response variable cannot address. Nonnormality has traditionally been handled using various data transformations in conjunction with standard linear model methods. The more commonly used transformations are discussed in introductory statistical methods texts such as Steel and Torrie (1980) and Snedecor and Cochran (1989). Box and Cox (1964) discuss transformations in considerable depth.

Nelder and Wedderburn (1972) present a comprehensive alternative — the **generalized linear model**. The basic idea is to estimate the parameters of a linear model using maximum likelihood based on the distribution of the data. Originally developed for members of the exponential family of distributions, generalized linear models have been extended to a much broader range of applications by the use of **quasi-likelihood**, described in Section 11.4. McCullagh and Nelder's (1989) text contains a complete discussion of the theory and application of the generalized linear model.

In practice, generalized linear model estimation strongly resembles generalized least squares, the fixed-effects component of the mixed model procedure. In the 1980's a number of articles extended the generalized linear model to various special-purpose mixed model applications. Breslow and Clayton (1993) present a unifying approach tying together the underlying principles of the **generalized linear mixed model**. Wolfinger and O'Connell (1993) develop a refinement of the Breslow-Clayton procedure for estimating mixed model effects. Wolfinger and O'Connell's method explicitly accounts for dispersion parameters in the estimation of generalized linear mixed models (see Section 11.4 for more detail). GLIMMIX is a SAS macro that implements the Wolfinger-O'Connell procedure. Appendix 2 contains the documentation for the GLIMMIX macro.

Using the GLIMMIX macro, PROC MIXED allows you to work with a number of generalized linear mixed models. The purpose of this chapter is to introduce the basic concepts of the generalized linear mixed model and to show how to use GLIMMIX in conjunction with PROC MIXED. Section 11.2 presents two examples illustrating when generalized linear mixed models are of interest. Section 11.3 is an introduction to generalized linear models. Section 11.4 shows how random effects are incorporated to form generalized linear **mixed** models. Sections 11.5 and 11.6 present the GLIMMIX program statements and associated output for the two examples described in Section 11.2.

11.2 Two Examples to Illustrate When Generalized Linear Mixed Models Are Needed

As mentioned above, many practical applications call for mixed model methods, but the assumptions of the standard mixed linear model are violated. This section presents two common examples to illustrate when generalized linear mixed models are needed.

11.2.1 Example: Binomial Data

Beitler and Landis (1985) discuss data from a clinical trial involving 2 drug treatments and 8 clinics. The 8 clinics represented a sample from a larger target population. At the jth clinic ($j=1,2,...,8$), n_{1j} subjects were randomly assigned to receive treatment 1, and n_{2j} subjects were randomly assigned to treatment 2. Each subject was classified as having a "favorable" or "unfavorable" response to the treatment. The number of "favorable" responses to the ith treatment at the jth clinic was denoted y_{ij}, and the proportion of "favorable" responses for the ij^{th} treatment-clinic combination was denoted $p_{ij} = y_{ij}/n_{ij}$.

The objective of the trial was to determine the effect of treatment and clinic on the probability of a "favorable" response. A possible linear model for this trial is

$$p_{ij} = \mu + \tau_i + c_j + (\tau c)_{ij} + e_{ij} \tag{11.1}$$

where

μ is the overall mean
τ_i is the ith treatment effect
c_j is the jth clinic effect
$(\tau c)_{ij}$ is the ij^{th} treatment-by-clinic interaction
e_{ij} is error.

Because clinics were sampled from the population, c_j and $(\tau c)_{ij}$ are considered random effects.

There are three serious problems with model 11.1. First, if you use conventional linear model methods, including the mixed model methods discussed so far in this book, then the estimates of $(\tau c)_{ij}$ and e_{ij} are confounded. Confounding occurs because there is only one p_{ij} per clinic-treatment combination. This precludes evaluating the clinic-by-treatment interaction, which, if it exists, is of interest. Second, the data are binomial, implying that a number of standard mixed model assumptions, e.g., normality and homogeneity of variance, are violated. Finally, although the probability of a favorable response clearly must be between 0 and 1, predicted probabilities using the above model are not similarly restricted. A predicted probability that is negative or greater than one is entirely possible.

Beitler and Landis (1985) present a procedure for analyzing these data that addresses the confounding of $(\tau c)_{ij}$ and e_{ij} and the normality issues. Their method anticipates the generalized linear mixed model, although they did not develop their approach within that framework. Also, their model did not address the need for restrictions on predicted probabilities. Section 11.5 presents a generalized linear mixed model for these data and shows how to use the GLIMMIX macro and PROC MIXED for the analysis.

11.2.2 An Example with Count Data

A split-plot experiment was conducted to compare various treatments for improving damaged rangeland. The whole-plot treatments were various management methods. They were applied in randomized complete blocks. Each whole-plot was split into 4 split-plots; the split-plot treatments were different seed mixes. The response variable of interest was botanical composition, measured by the number of plants of various species present in a given plot.

This experiment is similar to the split-plot experiments described in Chapter 2. The model is

$$y_{ijk} = \mu + R_i + \tau_j + (R\tau)_{ij} + \delta_k + (\tau\delta)_{jk} + e_{ijk} \tag{11.2}$$

where

y_{ijk} is the number of plants of a given species in the ijk^{th} block-management method-seed mix combination
μ is the overall mean or intercept
R_i is the ith block effect
τ_j is the jth management method effect
$(R\tau)_{ij}$ is the whole-plot error (equivalent to the block-management interaction)
δ_k is the effect of the kth seed mix
$(\tau\delta)_{jk}$ is the management-seed mix interaction
e_{ijk} is the split-plot error.

The whole-plot errors, $(R\tau)_{ij}$ are clearly random effects. The block effects, R_i, are typically considered random as well.

Plausible assumptions are

- $R_i \sim \mathrm{NI}(0,\sigma_R^2)$ and

- $(R\tau)_{ij} \sim \mathrm{NI}(0,\sigma_{RM}^2)$.

In a standard split-plot model, you would also assume that $e_{ijk} \sim \mathrm{NI}(0,\sigma^2)$. However, because the ijk^{th} observation is a count, the e_{ijk}'s are not normally distributed. Moreover, a count cannot be negative, but negative predicted counts from the above model are possible.

Traditionally, counts have been presumed to follow a Poisson distribution. However, the Poisson distribution assumes that the mean and variance are equal. Recent work in a number of disciplines suggests that count data are typically **overdispersed**, that is, the variance is larger — often considerably larger — than the mean. Alternatives to the Poisson, such as the negative binomial distribution, often provide better models of variation among the counts and hence of the errors in a linear model.

The question is how to simultaneously take into account the random model effects and the nonnormally distributed errors. For count data, the standard approach is to analyze the square root of y_{ijk}, or the square root of $y_{ijk} + 1$ if zeros are prevalent. See, for example, Snedecor and Cochran (1989). However, transforming the data may be counterproductive. For example, a transformation can distort the distribution of the random model effects or the linearity of the model. More importantly, transforming the data still leaves open the possibility of negative predicted counts. Consequently, inference from a mixed model using transformed data is highly suspect.

Section 11.6 shows how to construct a generalized linear mixed model that is consistent with the data from this experiment and how to use the GLIMMIX macro to do the analysis.

11.3 Generalized Linear Model Background

Generalized linear models are extensions of fixed-effects linear models to cases where standard linear model assumptions are violated. This section presents an introduction to generalized linear models.

A complete introduction to the generalized linear model, with all the theoretical development and technical details, is a book in itself — beyond the scope of this text. The goal of this section is to present the *main ideas* so that 1) the methods presented in sections 11.5 and 11.6 make sense and 2) the available options in the GLIMMIX macro have an adequate context. References containing additional detail are provided throughout this section.

This section reviews fixed-effects models. Section 11.4 shows how random effects are incorporated to produce **generalized linear *mixed* models**.

11.3.1 Fixed-Effects Generalized Linear Models

Standard linear models are defined in terms of the observations *per se*. For example, the fixed-effects linear model, assuming normal errors, is

$$\mathbf{y} = \mathbf{X}\boldsymbol{\beta} + \mathbf{e}.$$

Another way to present this model, which is helpful in making the transition to generalized linear models, is in terms of $E(\mathbf{y})$, the expected values of the observations. For example, in the standard linear model, $E(\mathbf{y}) = \mathbf{X}\boldsymbol{\beta}$. In other words, $\mathbf{X}\boldsymbol{\beta}$ is a linear model of $E(\mathbf{y})$. The main functions of $\mathbf{X}\boldsymbol{\beta}$ are to provide, for example, predicted $E(\mathbf{y})$ for given $\mathbf{X}$, as in regression analysis, or comparisons among the $E(\mathbf{y})$ for various $\mathbf{X}$, as in analysis of variance where functions of the $E(\mathbf{y})$ typically represent treatment means.

Standard linear model methods, that is, models that apply least squares procedures to direct models of $\mathbf{y}$, are based on the assumption of normal errors. Standard methods include ordinary least squares, generalized least squares, and the mixed model equations. As noted in Section 11.1, although linear models are extremely useful for nonnormal data as well as for normal data, standard methods do not necessarily produce usable results. Problems include inefficient or inaccurate estimates, estimates outside the range of permissible values, misleading p-values in hypothesis tests, etc.

The main idea of the **generalized** linear model is to use a likelihood-based procedure to fit $\mathbf{X}\boldsymbol{\beta}$ to a function of $E(\mathbf{y})$ — not necessarily $E(\mathbf{y})$ itself — suggested by the distribution of the observations.

The generalized linear model is developed as follows. An observation, $\mathbf{y}$, is described as an additive function of **systematic** and **random** components. The systematic component corresponds to $E(\mathbf{y})$; the random component corresponds to error. Denote $E(\mathbf{y})$ by $\boldsymbol{\mu}$ and error by $\mathbf{e}$. Then an observation is

$$\mathbf{y} = \boldsymbol{\mu} + \mathbf{e}$$

In a fixed effects generalized linear model $\mathrm{Var}(\mathbf{y}) = \mathrm{Var}(\mathbf{e})$. Denote $\mathrm{Var}(\mathbf{e})$ by $\mathbf{R}$ for consistency with mixed model notation used elsewhere in this book.

The basic form of the generalized linear model is

$$\eta = \mathbf{X}\boldsymbol{\beta}$$

where $\eta = g[\boldsymbol{\mu}]$. Nelder and Wedderburn (1972) called $g(\boldsymbol{\mu})$ the **link function** because it links the linear model to the mean of **y**. The nomenclature stuck. Criteria for selecting an appropriate link function for a given data set vary. Link functions may follow directly from the form of the probability distribution or from some physical or biological model of μ. Various link function strategies are discussed below.

Nelder and Wedderburn (1972) showed that the maximum likelihood estimates for β can be obtained by iteratively solving

$$\mathbf{X'WX}\boldsymbol{\beta} = \mathbf{X'Wy}*$$

where

$$\mathbf{W} = \mathbf{D'R}^{-1}\mathbf{D}$$
$$\mathbf{y}* = \hat{\eta} + (y - \hat{\mu})\mathbf{D}^{-1}$$
$$\mathbf{D} = [\partial\mu/\partial\eta]$$
$$\mathbf{R} = \text{Var}(\mathbf{e})$$
$$\boldsymbol{\mu} = E(\mathbf{y}).$$

In practice, estimates of **D** and **R** are used in place of **D** and **R**. For standard linear models, $\eta = E(\mathbf{y}) = \mu$, and hence $\mathbf{D} = \mathbf{I}$. Consequently, the solution for β reduces to generalized least squares. That is, $\mathbf{X'R^{-1}X}\boldsymbol{\beta} = \mathbf{X'R^{-1}y}$.

11.3.2 Probability Distributions

The essential elements for estimating β in the generalized linear model are

- the **link function**, which determines η and **D**, and

- the **probability distribution**, which determines the mean and variance, $\boldsymbol{\mu}$ and **R**.

You can better understand the process for choosing a link function and the structure of the mean and variance by examining the probability distribution, or, more specifically, the likelihood function. Consider three distributions, the normal, Poisson, and binomial. These are among the most widely used and familiar probability distributions. The essential features of generalized linear models are present in at least one of the three distributions.

Binomial

For the binomial with n trials and a success probability of π, the familiar form of the probability distribution function is

$$f(y) = \binom{n}{y} \pi^y (1-\pi)^{n-y}$$

The log likelihood function is thus

$$l(\pi;y) = y \log\left(\frac{\pi}{1-\pi}\right) + n \log(1-\pi) + \log\binom{n}{y}$$

A sample proportion, y/n, thus has a log likelihood function of

$$l(\pi;y) = ny \log\left(\frac{\pi}{1-\pi}\right) + n \log(1-\pi) + \log\binom{n}{ny}$$

The mean of y/n is π and the variance is $\pi(1-\pi)/n$.

Poisson

For the Poisson, the probability distribution is

$$f(y) = \frac{\lambda^y e^{-\lambda}}{y!}$$

The log likelihood function is thus

$$l(\lambda;y) = y \log(\lambda) - \lambda - \log(y!)$$

The mean and the variance of the Poisson are both equal to λ.

Normal

For the normal, the probability density function is

$$f(y) = \left(\frac{1}{\sqrt{2\pi\sigma^2}}\right) \exp\left[-\frac{1}{2\sigma^2}(y - \mu)^2\right]$$

and thus the log likelihood function is

$$l(\mu,\sigma^2;y) = \left(-\frac{1}{2\sigma^2}\right)(y - \mu)^2 - \left(\frac{1}{2}\right)\log(2\pi\sigma^2)$$

or

$$l(\mu,\sigma^2;y) = \left[\frac{y\mu - \left(\frac{\mu^2}{2}\right)}{\sigma^2}\right] - \left[\left(\frac{y^2}{2\sigma^2}\right) + \left(\frac{1}{2}\right)\log(2\pi\sigma^2)\right]$$

where μ is the mean and σ^2 is the variance.

Common Features

The log likelihood functions for these three distributions have a common form,

$$l(\theta,\phi;y) = \frac{y\theta - b(\theta)}{a(\phi)} + c(y,\phi)$$

where

θ is the natural parameter
ϕ is a scale parameter.

You can see that θ is a function of the mean. Denote this function as $\theta(\mu)$. Also, you can express the variance as a function of the mean and $a(\phi)$. Specifically,

$$\text{Var}(y) = V(\mu)a(\phi)$$

where $V(\mu)$ denotes the **variance function** — the function of the mean involved in $\text{Var}(y)$. For the three distributions, the various functions can be summarized as shown in Table 11.1.

Table 11.1 *Functions for the Three Distributions*

	Sample Proportion (Binomial / n)	Poisson	Normal
Mean	π	λ	μ
$\theta(\mu)$	$\log[\pi/(1-\pi)]$	$\log(\lambda)$	μ
$a(\phi)$	$1/n$	1	σ^2
$V(\mu)$	$\pi(1-\pi)$	λ	1
$\text{Var}(y)$	$[\pi(1-\pi)]/n$	λ	σ^2

The Exponential Family of Distributions

A distribution whose log likelihood has the general form

$$l(\theta,\phi;y) = \frac{y\theta - b(\theta)}{a(\phi)} + c(y,\phi)$$

is said to be a member of the **exponential family of distributions**. The generalized linear model can be applied to any data whose distribution belongs to the exponential family.

If $y_1, y_2,..., y_n$ is a random sample from a distribution in the exponential family, then the log likelihood of y_i is

$$l(\theta_i,\phi_i;y_i) = \frac{y_i\theta_i - b(\theta_i)}{a(\phi_i)} + c(y_i,\phi_i)$$

and the joint log likelihood of $y_1, y_2, ..., y_n$ is

$$l(\theta, \phi; y_1, y_2, ..., y_n) = \sum \left[\frac{y_i \theta_i - b(\theta_i)}{a(\phi_i)} + c(y_i, \phi_i) \right]$$

You can write the joint log likelihood in matrix form as

$$l(\theta, \phi; \mathbf{y}) = \mathbf{y}' \mathbf{A}^{-1} \theta - (\mathbf{b}_\theta^{1/2})' \mathbf{A}^{-1} \mathbf{b}_\theta^{1/2} + \mathbf{1}' \mathbf{c}$$

where

> $\mathbf{A}$ is a diagonal matrix whose i^{th} diagonal element is $a(\phi_i)$
> θ is a vector whose i^{th} element is θ_i
> $\mathbf{b}_\theta$ is a vector whose i^{th} element is $b(\theta_i)$
> $\mathbf{c}$ is a vector whose i^{th} element is $c(y_i, \phi_i)$
> $\mathbf{1}$ is an n-dimensional vector of ones.

The notation $\mathbf{b}_\theta^{1/2}$ denotes a vector whose elements are the square roots of the corresponding elements of $\mathbf{b}_\theta$.

11.3.3 Link Functions and Variance Structure

The general form of the log-likelihood function reveals some of the basic considerations in the generalized linear model.

Link Functions

First, the observations are linear with respect to the **natural parameter**, θ. For normally distributed data, $\theta = \mu$. Because the likelihood is linear in μ, it is reasonable to fit a model directly to μ, or equivalently to y.

On the other hand, for Poisson data the observations are linear in $\theta = \log(\lambda)$. Thus, fitting a linear model to $\log(\lambda)$ is more reasonable than fitting a model directly to λ (or y). Fitting a model to $\log(\lambda)$ gives rise to the **log-linear model**.

Following the strategy of using θ as a guideline, you fit a linear model to $\log[\pi/(1-\pi)]$ for binomial data. Fitting a regression model to $\log[\pi/(1-\pi)]$, or **logit**, gives rise to **logistic regression**.

In each of these examples, $\theta(\mu)$, the function that relates μ to the natural parameter, is used as the link function. Link functions equal to $\theta(\mu)$ are called **canonical link functions**. This is a common method of choosing the link function, but not the only way. An alternative is discussed in the example in Section 11.5.

Variance Structure

You can describe the structure the variance-covariance matrix of the observations, or equivalently the errors, in terms of the scale parameter and variance function. Specifically,

$$\text{Var}(\mathbf{e}) = \mathbf{R} = \mathbf{R}_\mu^{1/2} \mathbf{A} \mathbf{R}_\mu^{1/2}$$

where

> $\mathbf{R}_u$ is a diagonal matrix whose i^{th} diagonal element is $V(\mu_i)$, the variance function for the ith observation

$R_\mu^{1/2}$ is a diagonal matrix of square roots of the corresponding elements of R_μ

A is the scale parameter matrix defined earlier.

The three example distributions, normal, binomial/n (sample proportion), and Poisson, R_μ and **A** are shown in Table 11.2.

Table 11.2 *Three Example Distributions*

Distribution	R_μ	A
Normal	I	$I\sigma^2$
Binomial/n	$\text{diag}[\pi_i(1-\pi_i)]$	$\text{diag}(1/n_i)$
Poisson	$\text{diag}(\lambda_i)$	I

11.3.4 Predicting Means from the Inverse Link Function

The **inverse link function** *is* defined as $h(\eta) = \mu$. You use the inverse link to obtain predicted values of μ from the estimated β vector. While there are complex generalized linear models for which the relationship between η and μ is not one-to-one, the examples considered here assume that a one-to-one relationship between η and μ does exist. Thus $h(\eta) = g^{-1}(\eta)$. Because η is estimated by $X\beta$, you obtain predicted μ as

$$\hat{\mu} = h(X\hat{\beta})$$

For the normal distribution, $h(X\beta) = X\beta$, since $\eta = \mu$. For the Poisson distribution using the canonical link, $\eta = \log(\lambda)$ and hence $\lambda = h(X\beta) = \exp(X\beta)$. For the binomial, $\eta = \log[\pi/(1-\pi)]$ and hence $\pi = h(X\beta) = \exp(X\beta)/[1+\exp(X\beta)]$.

11.3.5 Deviance

The **deviance** is defined as

$$D(\hat{\mu}y) = 2[l(y;y) - l(\hat{\mu}y)]$$

where

$l(y;y)$ is the value of the log likelihood for which θ is expressed as a function of y

$l(\hat{\mu}y)$ is the value of the log likelihood where θ is expressed as a function of $\hat{\mu}$.

The deviance is a generalization of the SS(error) in analysis of variance and the likelihood ratio χ^2 in contingency tables. The deviance is equal to SS(error) for normal errors, and the likelihood ratio χ^2 is equal to the deviance for Poisson errors.

You can use the deviance for two purposes: to evaluate **goodness of fit** and to test hypotheses.

Goodness of Fit

Deviance is a function of θ and ϕ. For many distributions ϕ is known. When ϕ is known, the deviance is approximately distributed χ^2 with n-p degrees of freedom, where n is the number of observations and p is the number of independent parameters in β. You can use the deviance as a χ^2 statistic to test the goodness of fit of the model.

Hypothesis Testing

If β is partitioned into two vectors β_1 and β_2 so that the model can be written $\mathbf{X}\beta = \mathbf{X}_1\beta_1 + \mathbf{X}_2\beta_2$, you can use the difference between the deviance of the full model and the deviance of the model fitting $\mathbf{X}_1\beta_1$ alone as a likelihood ratio statistic to test H_0: β_2=0. The likelihood ratio statistic is approximately distributed as a χ^2 with p-p_1 degrees of freedom, where p_1 is the number of independent parameters in β_1.

When ϕ is not known, you can estimate it and use it to compute the **scaled deviance**, defined as

$$D^*(\hat{\mu}\mathbf{y}) = D(\hat{\mu}\mathbf{y})/\hat{\phi}$$

You can use the scaled difference to test hypotheses. For example, in testing H_0:β_2=0 with a normal errors model, the difference between the deviance of the model $\mathbf{X}\beta$ and the deviance of $\mathbf{X}_1\beta_1$ is $SS(\beta_2|\beta_1)$. The estimate of ϕ is $\hat{\alpha}$, i.e., MS(error). The resulting scaled deviance, adjusting for the degrees of freedom for $SS(\beta_2|\beta_1)$, is

$$F = \frac{MS(\beta_1 \mid \beta_2)}{MSE}$$

The F-ratio is distributed F with p-p_1 numerator degrees of freedom and n-p denominator degrees of freedom.

11.3.6 Inference Using Estimable Functions

In addition to the deviance, you can use estimable functions of β for inference in the generalized linear model. The basic result is

$$\text{Var}(\hat{\beta}) = (\mathbf{X'WX})^{-1}$$

It follows that

- the variance of an estimable function $\mathbf{K'}\beta$ is
  $\text{Var}(\mathbf{K'}\hat{\beta}) = \mathbf{K'(X'WX)^{-1}K}$, and

- the Wald statistic for H_0: $\mathbf{K'}\beta = \mathbf{K'}\beta_0$ is
  $(\mathbf{K'}\hat{\beta}) - \mathbf{K'}\beta_0)'[\mathbf{K'(X'WX)^{-1}K}]^{-1}(\mathbf{K'}\hat{\beta} - \mathbf{K'}\beta_0)$.

Using the Wald Statistic for χ^2 tests

Recall that $\mathbf{W} = \mathbf{D'(R_\mu^{1/2}AR_\mu^{1/2})^{-1}D}$. If $\mathbf{A}$ is known (e.g., as it is for the Poisson or binomial distribution) then the Wald statistic is approximately distributed χ_v^2, where v=rank($\mathbf{K}$).

F-tests

When **A** depends on an unknown scale parameter ϕ (e.g., as it does for the normal distribution), then **W** depends on an estimate of **A**. In such cases, the Wald statistic divided by rank(**K**) has an approximate $F_{(v1, v2)}$ distribution where $v_1 = \text{rank}(\mathbf{K})$ and v_2 is the degrees of freedom associated with the estimate of ϕ. You can use $F = \text{Wald}/\text{rank}(\mathbf{K})$ to test H_0: $\mathbf{K}'\beta = 0$.

Relation Between Inference Using Generalized Linear Models versus Standard Linear Models

In the standard linear model with normal errors, the observation vector, **y**, has a normal distribution with mean $\mathbf{X}\beta$ and variance $\mathbf{I}\sigma^2$. The log likelihood function of this model can be written as

$$l(\beta, \sigma^2; \mathbf{y}) = \left(\frac{\mathbf{y}'\mathbf{X}\beta - \frac{1}{2}\beta'\mathbf{X}'\mathbf{X}\beta}{\sigma^2} \right) - \left[\frac{\mathbf{y}'\mathbf{y}}{2\sigma^2} + \frac{n}{2}\log(2\pi\sigma^2) \right]$$

The natural parameter for this model is $\mathbf{X}\beta$ and the scale parameter is σ^2. Using the canonical link, the generalized linear model is

$$\eta = \mathbf{X}\beta$$

which corresponds to the standard linear model. A link function with $\mu = \eta$ is called an **identity link**. The F-ratios used in the analysis of variance are identical to the Wald/rank(**K**) F-statistics defined above.

11.4 Incorporating Random Effects into Generalized Linear Models

The fixed-effects generalized linear models discussed in Section 11.3 are based on the **likelihood function**. Generalized linear mixed models use **quasi-likelihood**, an extension of likelihood methods. This section introduces quasi-likelihood and shows how it is used to accommodate random effects in generalized linear models. The resulting extension is the **generalized linear mixed model**.

11.4.1 Quasi-Likelihood

Quasi-likelihood was introduced by Wedderburn (1974) and discussed in detail by McCullagh (1981) and McCullagh and Nelder (1989).

Following Wedderburn (1974), the **quasi-likelihood function** is defined as follows. Suppose y_i $(i=1,...,n)$ is a set of observations with expectation $E(y_i) = \mu_i$ and variance $V(y_i) \propto V(\mu_i)$, where $V(\mu)$ is some known function. Also, suppose that μ_i is a function of a set of parameters $\beta_1,...,\beta_p$. For example, $\mu_i = h(\eta_i)$ where $\eta_i = \Sigma X_{ij}\beta_j$ and $h(\eta)$ is the **inverse link function** of a generalized linear model. The **quasi-likelihood function** $Q(\mu_i, y_i)$ is defined by the relation

$$\frac{\partial Q(\mu_i, y_i)}{\partial \mu_i} = \frac{y_i - \mu_i}{V(\mu_i)}$$

McCullagh (1981) called $Q(\mu_i, y_i)$ the "log quasi-likelihood" function. This inconsistency in nomenclature follows subsequent publications by various authors. For the purposes of this discussion, refer to $Q(\mu_i, y_i)$ as the **quasi-likelihood function**.

The log-likelihood function is a special case of the quasi-likelihood function. Wedderburn showed that you can use *any function* $Q(\mu_i, y_i)$ that satisfies the above definition as a basis for defining a generalized linear model and obtaining estimates of the β_j using the procedures described in Section 11.3. In other words, quasi-likelihood allows you to apply generalized linear model to *any response variable* whose mean and variance can be described, not merely to response variables whose distribution belongs to the exponential family. Indeed, it is not necessary to be able to fully specify the distribution of the response variable at all.

To see the implications in practical terms, consider the exponential family log-likelihoods discussed in Section 11.3.2. The generalized least squares equations used to estimate the parameters of the generalized linear model are determined by the log-likelihood

$$\left[\frac{y_i \theta_i - b(\theta_i)}{a(\phi_i)} \right] + c(y_i, \phi_i)$$

More precisely, the estimating equations are determined by

$$Q(\mu_i, y_i) = \left[\frac{y_i \theta_i - b(\theta_i)}{a(\phi_i)} \right]$$

The function $c(y_i, \phi_i)$ is not involved. Even for the exponential family, specifying the full likelihood is unnecessary. $Q(\mu_i, y_i)$ is the **quasi-likelihood function**. You can see that μ_i is involved in the right-hand side of the equation through the mean function θ_i.

The main practical consequence of quasi-likelihood is that you can apply the theory and methods for generalized linear models to any random variable for which you can write $Q(\mu_i, y_i)$. In other words, you can use generalized linear models if you know

- the mean (μ),

- the mean function, $\theta(\mu)$, used in the generalized linear model,

- the variance function, $\text{Var}(\mu)$, and

- the scale parameter, $a(\phi)$.

This extends generalized linear models to data whose distribution is not in the exponential family and may not even have an exact description.

11.4.2 Generalized Linear Mixed Models

In the normal errors mixed model

$$\mathbf{y} = \mathbf{X}\boldsymbol{\beta} + \mathbf{Z}\mathbf{u} + \mathbf{e}$$

the conditional mean of the observations given the random model effects is

$$E(\mathbf{y}|\mathbf{u}) = \mathbf{X}\boldsymbol{\beta} + \mathbf{Z}\mathbf{u}$$

and the conditional variance is

$$\text{Var}(\mathbf{y}\,|\,\mathbf{u}) = \mathbf{R} = \text{Var}(\mathbf{e})$$

The observations are described as

$$\mathbf{y} = \boldsymbol{\mu} + \mathbf{e}$$

where $\boldsymbol{\mu}$ denotes the **conditional mean**, $E(\mathbf{y}\,|\,\mathbf{u})$. As in the conventional mixed model, the random model effects $\mathbf{u}$ are assumed to be distributed MVN(0,$\mathbf{G}$).

In the generalized linear mixed model, the **conditional distribution** of $\mathbf{y}\,|\,\mathbf{u}$ plays the same role as the distribution of $\mathbf{y}$ in the fixed effects generalized linear model. That is, the **conditional quasi-likelihood** of an observation, $\mathbf{y}_i\,|\,\mathbf{u}_i$ is

$$Q(\mu_i, y_i \,|\, u_i) = \left[\frac{y_i \theta_i - b(\theta_i)}{a(\phi_i)} \right]$$

The **joint quasi-likelihood** of the observations, y, is the sum of the quasi-likelihood of $y\,|\,u$ and u. In matrix terms, the joint quasi-likelihood is

$$Q(\boldsymbol{\mu},\mathbf{u};\mathbf{y}) = [\mathbf{y}'\mathbf{A}^{-1}\boldsymbol{\theta} - (\mathbf{b}_\theta^{\frac{1}{2}})'\mathbf{A}^{-1}\mathbf{b}_\theta^{\frac{1}{2}}] + \tfrac{1}{2}\mathbf{u}'\mathbf{G}^{-1}\mathbf{u}$$

where

$\mathbf{A}$ is the matrix of $a(\phi_i)$'s
$\boldsymbol{\theta}$ is the vector of $\theta(\boldsymbol{\mu}_i)$'s
$\mathbf{b}_\theta$ is the vector of $b(\theta_i)$'s defined previously.

You apply the same basic strategies for fitting a generalized linear model to $E(\mathbf{y})$ in a fixed-effects model to fitting a mixed model to $E(\mathbf{y}\,|\,\mathbf{u})$. That is, the form of the conditional quasi-likelihood determines the **variance structure** and contains the natural parameter. The conditional mean function $\theta(\boldsymbol{\mu})$ can be used as a **canonical link**, or some other function of μ can be used.

The generalized linear mixed model is

$$\boldsymbol{\eta} = \mathbf{X}\boldsymbol{\beta} + \mathbf{Z}\mathbf{u}$$

where $\boldsymbol{\eta}$ is the link function $g(\boldsymbol{\mu})$ and $\boldsymbol{\mu}$ is the conditional mean.

11.4.3 Estimation and Inference

Generalized Mixed Model Equations

Breslow and Clayton (1993) and Wolfinger and O'Connell (1993) show that solutions for β and $\mathbf{u}$ can be obtained from $\mathbf{Q}(\boldsymbol{\mu},\mathbf{u};\mathbf{y})$ by iteratively solving the equations

$$\begin{bmatrix} \mathbf{X}'\mathbf{W}\mathbf{X} & \mathbf{X}'\mathbf{W}\mathbf{Z} \\ \mathbf{Z}'\mathbf{W}\mathbf{X} & \mathbf{Z}'\mathbf{W}\mathbf{Z} + \mathbf{G}^{-1} \end{bmatrix} \begin{bmatrix} \boldsymbol{\beta} \\ \mathbf{u} \end{bmatrix} = \begin{bmatrix} \mathbf{X}'\mathbf{W}\mathbf{y}^* \\ \mathbf{Z}'\mathbf{W}\mathbf{y}^* \end{bmatrix}$$

Where $\mathbf{W}$ and $\mathbf{y}^*$ are defined as in the solution equations for the fixed effects generalized linear model given above. That is,

$$\mathbf{W} = \mathbf{D'R^{-1}D}$$
$$\mathbf{y}^* = \hat{\boldsymbol{\eta}} + (\mathbf{y} - \hat{\boldsymbol{\mu}})\mathbf{D}^{-1}$$
$$\mathbf{D} = [\partial\boldsymbol{\mu}/\partial\boldsymbol{\eta}]$$
$$\mathbf{R} = \mathrm{Var}(\mathbf{e}) = (\mathbf{R}_{\mu}^{\frac{1}{2}}\mathbf{A}\mathbf{R}_{\mu}^{\frac{1}{2}}).$$

Breslow-Clayton and Wolfinger-O'Connell procedures are similar in that they both use the generalized mixed model equations. However, the Breslow-Clayton procedure, which they called **penalized quasi-likelihood** (PQL), assumes that the scale parameter $\phi=1$. The Wolfinger-O'Connell procedures, which they called **pseudo-likelihood** (PL) or **restricted pseudo-likelihood** (REPL), assumes ϕ is unknown. PL obtains a maximum-likelihood-like estimate of ϕ; REPL obtains a REML-like estimate of ϕ. PQL is a special case of PL when $\phi=1$. See Wolfinger and O'Connell (1993) for details.

The PL and REPL procedures have important advantages. These are discussed below in this section and illustrated in the example presented in Section 11.6.

Predictable Functions

As in standard mixed models, the primary tool of inference is the predictable function, $\mathbf{K'\beta} + \mathbf{M'u}$. The logic leading from the objectives of a particular study to the selection of predictable functions that address those objectives is identical to standard mixed models. Letting $\mathbf{L'} = [\mathbf{K'}\ \mathbf{M'}]$, the prediction error variance of a predictable function is

$$\mathrm{Var}[\mathbf{K'}\hat{\boldsymbol{\beta}} + \mathbf{M'}(\hat{\mathbf{u}} - \mathbf{u})] = \mathbf{L'CL}$$

where

$$\mathbf{C} = \begin{bmatrix} \mathbf{X'WX} & \mathbf{X'WZ} \\ \mathbf{Z'WX} & \mathbf{Z'WZ} + \mathbf{G^{-1}} \end{bmatrix}^{-}$$

You should beware that relatively little research has been done on the small-sample properties of inference statistics for the generalized linear mixed model. The test-statistics are basically reasonable-looking extensions of standard tests for mixed models and generalized linear models. More work is needed to either validate these procedures or develop needed corrections or alternatives.

Wald Statistics

This caution in mind, hypotheses about predictable functions can be tested using Wald Statistics or F-statistics.

The basic form of the Wald Statistic is

$$(\mathbf{L'}\hat{\boldsymbol{\alpha}})'(\mathbf{L'CL})^{-1}(\mathbf{L'}\hat{\boldsymbol{\alpha}})$$

where $\hat{\boldsymbol{\alpha}}' = [\hat{\boldsymbol{\beta}}\ (\hat{\mathbf{u}} - \mathbf{u})']$.

The Wald statistic is approximately distributed χ_v^2, where $v = \mathrm{rank}(\mathbf{L})$. When the conditional variance, $\mathbf{R}$, depends on a known scale parameter (i.e., $\mathbf{A}$ is known) then the χ^2 test may be used.

F-Tests

If **R** depends on an unknown scale parameter, the Wald statistic divided by rank(**L**) is preferable.

$$F = \text{Wald}/\text{rank}(\mathbf{L})$$

is approximately distributed $F_{(v1,v2)}$, where $v_1 = \text{rank}(\mathbf{L})$ and $v_2 =$ the degrees of freedom used to estimate **L'CL**. In simple cases, v_2 corresponds to the degrees of freedom required to estimate ϕ (e.g., σ^2 in normal errors models). In more complex cases, you must approximate v_2, e.g., using a Satterthwaite-type procedure.

You can see that the PQL procedure discussed above is appropriate when the scale parameter ϕ is known. When ϕ is unknown (as in the normal errors case) or when nominal assumptions about ϕ are violated (as in the example in Section 11.6), you should use a procedure capable of estimating ϕ, e.g., the PL and REPL procedures.

Alternatively, generalized linear mixed models may be evaluated using the deviance or scaled deviance statistics, as described earlier in this section.

You can analyze generalized linear mixed models using the GLIMMIX macro. The variance function, $\mathbf{R}_\mu$, forms a WEIGHT and the linear predictor, **y***, replaces **y** in the mixed model equations. These are then utilized in PROC MIXED to obtain PL or REPL estimates, depending on whether you specify ML or REML covariance component estimation. Documentation for the GLIMMIX macro appears in Appendix 2.

The next two sections consider two specific examples of generalized linear mixed models.

11.5 Example: Mixed Model with Binomial Errors

Section 11.2.1 described an experiment involving two treatments conducted at 8 randomly sampled clinics. The data, which appeared in Beitler and Landis (1985), are given in Data Set 11.5 in Appendix 4. At the jth CLINIC ($j=1,2,...,8$), n_{ij} subjects were assigned to the ith treatment (TRT) (I=1,2). At the ij^{th} treatment-clinic combination, y_{ij} subjects responded favorably and the remaining $n_{ij} - y_{ij}$ did not. The number of patients for the ij^{th} CLINIC by TRT combinations is denoted NIJ in the data set; the number of favorable responses y_{ij} is denoted FAV. The response variable of interest was the proportion of favorable responses, $p_{ij} = y_{ij}/n_{ij}$, or FAV/NIJ.

The distribution of the y_{ij} is binomial(n_{ij}, π_{ij}), where π_{ij} is the probability of a subject at the ij^{th} CLINIC by TRT having a favorable response. Thus p_{ij} is distributed binomial/n_{ij}. Thus, the conditional quasi-likelihood given the jth clinic has the binomial/n form as given in Section 11.3. It has the following features as shown in Table 11.3.

Table 11.3 *Features of Conditional Quasi-Likelihood*

Expression	Function	Value
Conditional mean	μ_{ij}	π_{ij}
natural parameter	$\theta(\mu_{ij})$	$\log[\pi_{ij}/(1-\pi_{ij})]$
variance function	$V(\mu_{ij})$	$\pi_{ij}(1-\pi_{ij})$
scale parameter	$a(\phi_{ij})$	$1/n_{ij}$

11.5.1 Analysis of Binomial Data Using Logit (Canonical) Link

Model

Using the canonical link, a generalized linear mixed model for these data is

$$\eta_{ij} = \log[\pi_{ij}/(1-\pi_{ij})] = m + \tau_i + c_j + (\tau c)_{ij}$$

where

m is the intercept
τ_i is the effect of the ith TRT
c_j is the effect of the jth CLINIC
$(\tau c)_{ij}$ is the ij^{th} TRT*CLINIC interaction effect.

Because the clinics are a random sample, the CLINIC and TRT*CLINIC effects are random. The assummptions are

- the vector of clinic effects, $\mathbf{c} = [c_1,...,c_8]'$ is distributed $N(0, \mathbf{I}\sigma_C^2)$, and
- the vector of TRT*CLINIC effects, $(\tau c) = [(\tau c)_{11},...,(\tau c)_{28}]'$ is distributed $N(0, \mathbf{I}\sigma_{TC}^2)$.

Thus, the random effects vector is $\mathbf{u}' = [\mathbf{c}' \ (\tau c)']$. Its variance-covariance matrix, $\mathbf{G} = Var(\mathbf{u})$, is

$$\mathbf{G} = \begin{bmatrix} \mathbf{I}\sigma_C^2 & 0 \\ 0 & \mathbf{I}\sigma_{TC}^2 \end{bmatrix}$$

The generalized mixed model equations for this model are

$$\begin{bmatrix} \mathbf{X'WX} & \mathbf{X'WZ} \\ \mathbf{Z'WX} & \mathbf{Z'WZ + G^{-1}} \end{bmatrix} \begin{bmatrix} \beta \\ \mathbf{u} \end{bmatrix} = \begin{bmatrix} \mathbf{X'Wy^*} \\ \mathbf{Z'Wy^*} \end{bmatrix}$$

where

$\beta = [m, \tau_1, \tau_2]'$
$\mathbf{W} = \mathbf{D}'(\mathbf{R}_\mu^{\frac{1}{2}} \mathbf{A} \mathbf{R}_\mu^{\frac{1}{2}})^{-1}\mathbf{D}$
$\mathbf{D} = [\partial \mu / \partial \eta] = diag[\pi_{ij}(1-\pi_{ij})]$
$\mathbf{R}_\mu = diag[\pi_{ij}(1-\pi_{ij})]$
$\mathbf{A} = diag[1/n_{ij}]$
$\mathbf{y}^* = \hat{\eta} + (\mathbf{y} - \hat{\mu})\mathbf{D}^{-1}$
$\hat{\eta} = \mathbf{X}\hat{\beta} + \mathbf{Z}\hat{\mathbf{u}}$
$\hat{\mu} = \exp(\mathbf{X}\hat{\beta} + \mathbf{Z}\hat{\mathbf{u}})/[1+\exp(\mathbf{X}\hat{\beta} + \mathbf{Z}\hat{\mathbf{u}})]$.

You obtain $\hat{\mu}$ from the inverse of the link function.
You can fit this model with the GLIMMIX macro using the following program statements.

Program

```
%include 'glimmix.sas';
%glimmix(data=a,
         procopt=method=reml,
         stmts=%str(
              class clinic trt;
              model fav/nij=trt/solution;
              random clinic trt*clinic/solution;
              estimate 'lsm trt 1' intercept 1 trt 1 0;
              estimate 'trt diff' trt 1 -1;
              estimate 'trt 1 clinic 1 BLUP' intercept 1 trt 1 0
                       | clinic 1 0;
              estimate 'trt 1 clinic 6 BLUP' intercept 1 trt 1 0
                       | clinic 0 0 0 0 0 1 0;),
              error=binomial,
              link=logit);
     run;
```

The %INCLUDE statement identifies the name of the file containing the GLIMMIX macro and its location. The GLIMMIX macro is not part of the standard PROC MIXED package. It is available in Appendix 2 and in SAS Online Samples. The %GLIMMIX command initiates the procedure. All commands within the parentheses specify the various characteristics of the procedure. These include the usual commands used in PROC MIXED and some additional commands to define the error distribution, link function and other options for the generalized linear model. You put the PROC MIXED statements within the parentheses beginning with the STMTS=%STR statement.

PROC MIXED Statements

The DATA, CLASS, RANDOM, LSMEANS, and ESTIMATE statements are usual PROC MIXED statements. Because this program uses a macro, these statements are included within the parenthesis just after the STMTS=%STR statement. Each statement is separated by a semicolon, as in any other SAS program.

MODEL Statement for Binomial Data

The MODEL statement for most generalized linear models is similar to standard PROC MIXED model statements, i.e. response variable = list of fixed model effects. *The binomial is unique in that you must give the response variable as a ratio of two.* The numerator variable is the number of "successes" (y_{ij}), and the denominator is the total number of observations (n_{ij}) for a given fixed-by-random effect combination. Here, FAV gives the number of favorable responses and NIJ gives the total number of subjects observed at the ij^{th} clinic-treatment combination. Thus the response variable, the sample proportion, is FAV/NIJ. This syntax is also used in PROC GENMOD and PROC LOGISTIC.

The ERROR, LINK, and PROCOPT statements specify the error distribution, the link function, and the variance component estimation procedure, respectively. If you specify METHOD=REML, you get REML variance component estimates. REML estimates produce REPL estimation of the generalized linear mixed model. METHOD=ML obtains ML variance estimates and hence PL estimation of the model. Further details regarding statement options available in the GLIMMIX macro are given in Appendix 2.

Alternative Estimation of Binomial Models Using 0's and 1's

When the response variable is y_{ij}/n_{ij}, e.g., FAV/NIJ, convergence of the PL and REPL algorithms is a problem in some data sets such as Data Set 11.5.

You get more consistent convergence by re-expressing the data so that each factor-combination (e.g., CLINIC*TRT for these data) consists of y_{ij} 1's and $n_{ij} - y_{ij}$ 0's and then using the 0–1 variable as the response. You can do this as follows.

Program

```
data new;
   set a;
   do i=1 to fav;
      y=1;
      output;
   end;
   do i=1 to unfav;
      y=0;
      output;
   end;

%include 'glimmix.sas';
%glimmix(data=new,
   procopt=method=reml ,
   stmts=%str(
         class clinic trt;
         model y=trt/solution;
         random clinic clinic*trt/solution;
         lsmeans trt;
         estimate 'lsm trt 1' intercept 1 trt 1 0/cl;
         estimate 'trt diff' trt 1 -1;
         estimate 'trt 1 clinic 1 blup' intercept 1 trt 1 0
                  | clinic 1 0;
         estimate 'trt 1 clinic 6 blup' intercept 1 trt 1 0
                  | clinic 0 0 0 0 0 1 0; ),
         error=binomial,
         link=logit);
   run;
```

The covariance estimates, test statistics, and ESTIMATE results are shown in Output 11.1. Other results follow.

Results

Output 11.1 *Binomial Example — LOGIT Link*

```
                    Covariance Parameter Estimates

                    Cov Parm          Estimate

                    CLINIC          2.03177163
                    CLINIC*TRT      0.08132250




                     Tests of Fixed Effects

           Source    NDF    DDF    Type III F    Pr > F

           TRT        1      7         5.13       0.0579
```

```
                              ESTIMATE Statement Results

Parameter                Estimate    Std Error    DDF         T    Pr > |T|

CNTL LSMEAN               -1.1778       0.5683      7     -2.07      0.0769
TRT DIFF                  -0.7596       0.3354      7     -2.27      0.0579
TRT 1 CLINIC 1 BLUP       -1.2919       0.3622      7     -3.57      0.0091
TRT 1 CLINIC 6 BLUP       -2.8238       0.7372      7     -3.83      0.0065


Alpha       Lower        Upper         Mu      LowerMu      UpperMu

0.05      -2.5216       0.1659       0.2354     0.0744       0.5414
0.05      -1.5526       0.0334       0.3187     0.1747       0.5083
0.05      -2.1483      -0.4356       0.2155     0.1045       0.3928
0.05      -4.5670      -1.0807       0.0560     0.0103       0.2534


                             Least Squares Means

Level        LSMEAN     Std Error    DDF         T    Pr > |T|      Mu

TRT cntl     -1.1778      0.5683       7     -2.07      0.0769    0.2354
TRT drug     -0.4182      0.5628       7     -0.74      0.4816    0.3969
```

Interpretation

The main features are

1. **The variance component (covariance parameter) estimates**

   The covariance parameters CLINIC and TRT*CLINIC are the estimates of σ_C^2 (2.032) and σ_{TC}^2 (0.0813), respectively. These variance components are interpreted like any other variance component in a mixed model except that they are estimated in terms of the scale determined by the link function. Here, we are estimating the variance of CLINIC effects and TRT*CLINIC effects measured on the "logit scale."

   When the link function is a model of the mean that has a real-world basis, you can interpret the variance components with respect to that model (for example, see the alternative analysis of these data using the **probit** model given below). When you use the **canonical link** and do not frame it in real-world terms, the meaning of the variance components is more elusive. The random effects act linearly on η, and thus indirectly on the conditional mean through the model given by the inverse link, $h(\eta)$.

2. **Tests of Fixed Effects**

   This is the $F = \text{Wald}/\text{rank}(\mathbf{K})$ statistic described in Section 11.4. It tests H_0: $\tau_1 = \tau_2$. You interpret it like any other F-statistic. Here, $F=5.13$ with a p-value of 0.0579. There is marginal evidence (depending on the α-level you deem appropriate) of a difference in the probability of a favorable output between the **CNTL** and **TRT** drugs.

3. **ESTIMATE Statement Results**

The ESTIMATE option provides you with the following:

- **Parameter estimates** computed by applying the the generalized mixed model solutions to the various predictable functions. Estimates are defined on the **link function** scale. **Mu** uses the inverse link to express the estimate on the original scale. Here, **estimates** are logits, **Mu's** are sample proportions, *except where the predictable function is a difference.* An example below shows how **estimate** and **mu** are obtained, and when you can validly interpret **mu**.

- **Standard error.** The GLIMMIX macro computes the standard errors using the formula $(L'CL)^{-1}$ given in section 11.4.

- **T-test (DDF, T, Pr > |T|).** The *t*-tests result from *t*=(estimate)/(std error). DDF are determined using containment rules described in Chapters 1 and 2.

- **Confidence Limits**. The terms **lower** and **upper** are confidence limits for the **estimate**. They use the link function scale. Here they are logits. **LowerMu** and **UpperMu** are confidence limits for **mu**. They use the original scale (in this case, the sample proportion).

4. **Least Squares Means**

   LSMEANs are obtained using estimable functions for treatment means, e.g., $m + \tau_i$ for these data. The ESTIMATE 'CNTL LSMEAN' shows the coefficients used for the "TRT CNTL" LSMEAN. You can see that they produce the same results. The LSMEAN is expressed in terms of the link function — the logit in this example. **Mu** uses the inverse link to express the least squares mean in terms of the original scale (here, the sample proportion).

Example: How Estimates and Mu's Are Obtained

This example show how the solution vectors for the fixed and random effects are used to obtain the logit **estimate** and the sample proportion **mu** for these data.
Output 11.2 gives the solution vectors.

Output 11.2 *Solution Vectors for Binomial Data, Logit Model*

Parameter Estimates					
Parameter	Estimate	Std Error	DDF	T	Pr > |T|
INTERCEPT	-0.4182	0.5628	7	-0.74	0.4816
TRT cntl	-0.7596	0.3354	7	-2.27	0.0579
TRT drug	0.0000	.	.	.	.

Random Effects Estimates					
Parameter	Estimate	SE Pred	DDF	T	Pr > |T|
CLINIC 1	-0.1141	0.6023	257	-0.19	0.8499
CLINIC 2	1.7877	0.6208	257	2.88	0.0043
CLINIC 3	0.9538	0.6243	257	1.53	0.1278
CLINIC 4	-1.3181	0.7101	257	-1.86	0.0646
CLINIC 5	-0.6280	0.6725	257	-0.93	0.3512

CLINIC 6	-1.6460	0.8078	257	-2.04	0.0426
CLINIC 7	-0.7320	0.7768	257	-0.94	0.3470
CLINIC 8	1.6967	0.7324	257	2.32	0.0213
CLINIC*TRT 1 cntl	0.1131	0.2630	257	0.43	0.6674
CLINIC*TRT 1 drug	-0.1177	0.2627	257	-0.45	0.6545
CLINIC*TRT 2 cntl	0.0679	0.2668	257	0.25	0.7995
CLINIC*TRT 2 drug	0.0037	0.2678	257	0.01	0.9890
CLINIC*TRT 3 cntl	-0.0894	0.2674	257	-0.33	0.7384
CLINIC*TRT 3 drug	0.1276	0.2674	257	0.48	0.6337
CLINIC*TRT 4 cntl	-0.0233	0.2769	257	-0.08	0.9330
CLINIC*TRT 4 drug	-0.0294	0.2759	257	-0.11	0.9151
CLINIC*TRT 5 cntl	-0.1319	0.2753	257	-0.48	0.6322
CLINIC*TRT 5 drug	0.1068	0.2738	257	0.39	0.6968
CLINIC*TRT 6 cntl	-0.0468	0.2808	257	-0.17	0.8677
CLINIC*TRT 6 drug	-0.0190	0.2795	257	-0.07	0.9457
CLINIC*TRT 7 cntl	-0.0129	0.2788	257	-0.05	0.9631
CLINIC*TRT 7 drug	-0.0164	0.2790	257	-0.06	0.9533
CLINIC*TRT 8 cntl	0.1234	0.2770	257	0.45	0.6563
CLINIC*TRT 8 drug	-0.0555	0.2777	257	-0.20	0.8417

Interpretation

As in conventional mixed models, the solutions themselves have no intrinsic meaning because they are based on a generalized inverse. However, **linear predictors**, that is, estimates of predictable functions $\mathbf{K}'\beta + \mathbf{M}'\mathbf{u}$ obtained from the solution vectors of β and $\mathbf{u}$, *do* have meaning.

You can use the elements of the solution vector to obtain best linear unbiased predictors. For example, consider the ESTIMATE statement "TRT 1 CLINIC 1." This is the **broad** inference space BLUP for the CNTL treatment at clinic 1. It is defined as

$$\text{BLUP(trt 1, clinic 1)} = m + \tau_1 + c_1$$

That is,

$$\mathbf{K}' = [1\ 1\ 0] \text{ and } \mathbf{M}' = [1\ 0\ ...\ 0]$$

Using the elements of the solution vector,

$$\begin{aligned}\text{BLUP(trt 1, clinic 1)} &= -0.4182 - 0.7596 - 0.1141\\ &= -1.2919\end{aligned}$$

The linear predictor is computed on the *logit* scale. You can convert it to a predicted probability by applying the inverse link function. Here

$$\hat{\pi}_{11} = \exp(-1.2919)/[1+\exp(-1.2919)] = 0.2155$$

You can calculate BLUPs for all TRT*CLINIC combinations using the appropriate m, τ_i, and c_j estimates.

You can calculate the narrow inference space BLUP by adding (τc_{ij}). For example, the narrow space BLUP for treatment 1, clinic 1 is $m + \tau_1 + c_1 + (\tau c_{ij})$.

You can compute least squares means for TRT using the estimable function $m + \tau_i$. For example, for TRT CNTL, the linear predictor, the estimate of $\eta_i = m + \tau_i$ is $-0.4182 - 0.7596 = -1.1778$. The corresponding MU is $h(\eta)$, which in this case is

$$\mathbf{MU} = \exp(-1.1778)/[1 + \exp(-1.1778)] = 0.2354$$

The **standard errors** are computed on the logit scale. The output gives the estimate converted to **mu**, but does not give the converted standard error. You can get an approximate standard error using the **Delta method**, which involves a Taylor series approximation of $h(\eta)$. See Bishop, Fienberg, and Holland (1975) for details. The formula is

$$s.e.[\mathbf{h}(\eta)] = \sqrt{\left[\frac{\partial h(\eta)}{\partial \eta}\right]^2 \mathbf{K'(X'WX)^-K}}$$

For example, the LSMEAN TRT cntl has a standard error of 0.5683. This is computed from

$$\sqrt{\mathbf{K'(X'WX)^-K}}$$

Note that $\mathbf{K'(X'WX)^-K = L'CL}$ when the vector **m** contains all zeroes, as it does in here. The derivative, $\partial[\mathbf{h}(\eta)]/\partial \eta$, was obtained in forming the **D** matrix used in the estimating equation. For the logit link, $\partial[\mathbf{h}(\eta)]/\partial \eta = \pi(1-\pi)$, which is estimated by $\mathbf{MU}(1-\mathbf{MU})$. The resulting standard error for TRT CNTL is

$$\sqrt{\pi(1-\pi)\ \mathbf{K'(X'WX)^-K}} = \sqrt{[0.2354(1-0.2354)]^2(0.5683)^2} = 0.102$$

Applying a similar set of calculations, the standard error for TRT DRUG is 0.135.

Caution - How to Correctly Determine a Treatment Difference

The difference between predicted probabilities should be calculated as the difference between inverse links — i.e., MU values — NOT as the inverse link of the estimable function for a difference. For example, for CNTL and DRUG, the difference between the predicted probabilities is

$$MU_{CNTL} - MU_{DRUG} = 0.397 - 0.235 = 0.162$$

On the other hand, if you work with the estimable function for a difference (given in Output 11.1 as TRT DIFF) using the model parameters, $\tau_1 - \tau_2 = -0.7596 - 0 = -0.7596$. Applying the inverse link to $\tau_1 - \tau_2$ yields

$$\exp(-0.7596)/[1+\exp(-0.7596)] = 0.3187$$

which clearly is nonsense. The reason for this discrepancy is that the inverse link is nonlinear.

The standard error and t-statistics given with TRT DIFF *are valid*. Only the results associated with **Mu** (**Mu**, **LowerMu** and **UpperMu**) are invalid.

You can use standard error for the difference for the logit scale, but the transformation to the difference between predicted *probabilities* is not straightforward. A simple approach used in fixed effects generalized linear models is to let the variance of the difference equal the sum of the variance of the means. However, the variance of the means in a mixed model involves variance components which are NOT part of the variance of a difference, so the approximation cannot be used in mixed models.

Model-fitting Statistics

The model fitting statistics are given as **GLIMMIX Model Statistics**. Output 11.3 provides the results for this example.

Output 11.3 *Model Fitting Statistics for the Binomial Data, Logit Model*

```
GLIMMIX Model Statistics


Description                          Value


Deviance                           275.3750
Scaled Deviance                    295.7677
Pearson Chi-Square                 245.4188
Scaled Pearson Chi-Square          263.5930
Extra-Dispersion Scale               0.9311
```

The GLIMMIX model statistics include

- **The extra-dispersion parameter**

  In many generalized linear models, the observed conditional variance of the errors, $V(e|u)$, may differ from theory. For example, in this example, the conditional error variance should be determined by the binomial distribution, i.e., $[\pi_{ij}(1-\pi_{ij})]/n_{ij}$. The GLIMMIX macro allows for the possibility that the conditional error variance is actually $\phi[\pi_{ij}(1-\pi_{ij})]/n_{ij}$, where ϕ is called the **extra-dispersion parameter**. You assume $\phi>0$. Ideally, $\phi=1$, indicating that the variance is consistent with the assumed distribution. If ϕ is substantially less than 1, the distribution of the conditional errors is said to be **underdispersed**. If ϕ is substantially greater than 1, the distribution is **overdispersed**. Serious underdispersion can result in inflated standard errors and deflated test statistics. Overdispersion can result in unrealistically large test statistics and small standard errors. Interpreting ϕ is part art, part science.

  If you conclude ϕ is substantially different from 1, you should adjust the deviance by dividing it by $\hat{\phi}$. You should also adjust standard errors and test statistics. The GLIMMIX macro automatically adjusts for $\hat{\phi}$.

  Here, the estimated extra-dispersion is $\hat{\phi}=0.9311$, very close to 1. Thus, the data provide no evidence of over- or under-dispersion.

- **Deviance**

  The deviance was defined in Section 11.3. For generalized linear models, deviance is the difference between **quasi-likelihood** for the full data and quasi-likelihood under the model. Because the binomial distribution has a known scale parameter $\mathbf{a}(\phi)$, i.e., $1/n_{ij}$, the deviance can be interpreted as a lack-of-fit statistic for the *conditional model given the random effects*, i.e., the fixed component of the model.

  Using the logit mixed model, the deviance is approximately distributed χ^2 with N-p degrees of freedom, where N is the number of observation proportions (8 clinics $\times$ 2 treatments = 16) and p is the number of independent fixed effects parameters (2). Thus, the degrees of freedom are 14.

  When you re-express the data in terms of 0's and 1's to get convergence, you also change the degrees of freedom. The number of observations in the data actually computed is the sum of NIJ for all CLINIC*TRT combinations, which is 273. The computed deviance should be evaluated against $273-2=271$ degrees of freedom.

The computed deviance is 275.375. Relative to $\chi^2_{(271)}$ there is no evidence of lack of fit.

Computing the Deviance Using the Original Model

If you want to compute the deviance that is consistent with the logit mixed model, you can use the original GLIMMIX program with variance component estimates obtained from the $0 - 1$ data.

Program

```
%glimmix(data=a,
    stmts=%str(
        class clinic trt;
        model fav/nij=trt/solution;
        random clinic trt*clinic/solution;
        repeated;
        parms (2.032) (0.0813) (1.0)(1.0)/noiter;
        error=binomial,
        link=logit);
    run;
```

The PARMS statement gives the variance components and the NOITER option prevents iteration. Thus, the GLIMMIX macro solves the generalized mixed model equations for the variance components given. The resulting deviance output is shown in Output 11.4.

Results

Output 11.4 *Deviance Using Original Model*

GLIMMIX Model Statistics	
Description	Value
Deviance	8.1426
Scaled Deviance	8.6487
Pearson Chi-Square	6.0313
Scaled Pearson Chi-Square	6.4062
Extra-Dispersion Scale	0.9415

Interpretation

The deviance is 8.1426. Relative to $\chi^2_{(14)}$ there is no evidence of lack of fit of the conditional model.

11.5.2 Alternative Link Functions

Previous sections have only considered canonical link functions. In many generalized linear models, the link function may be suggested by something other than the natural parameter. Often, the link function represents a physical or biological model of the mean. For example, binomial responses are often assumed to be observable manifestations of unobservable underlying, continuous processes. Imagine there is a continuous (normally distributed) variable. When it is below a certain **threshold**, the observable response is unfavorable. When the unobservable process is at or above the threshold, a favorable response is observed. The probability of a favorable response can be determined from the normal c.d.f.

Model Using Probit Link

Assume that $\mathbf{X\beta} + \mathbf{Zu}$ is a generalized linear mixed model of the underlying process. Then the probability, π, is

$$\pi = \Phi(\mathbf{X\beta} + \mathbf{Zu})$$

Thus, the link function is

$$\eta = \Phi^{-1}(\mathbf{\mu})$$

where $\Phi(\eta)$ is the normal c.d.f. evaluated at η. The link function, $\eta = \Phi^{-1}(\mu)$, is called the **probit link**. Probit analysis is based on a generalized linear model using the probit link.

You can fit a generalized linear mixed model for the treatment-clinic example using the probit link function instead of the logit link. The model, $m + \tau_i + c_j + (\tau c_{ij})$, remains the same. The variance function and scale parameter, used in $\mathbf{R}_\mu$ and $\mathbf{A}$, remain the same. $\mathbf{D}$ and η are different, reflecting the different link function.

Program for Analysis Using Probit Link

You can obtain an analysis of the probit mixed model using the following GLIMMIX statements:

```
%glimmix(data=new,
         procopt=method=reml,
         stmts=%str(
             class clinic trt;
             model y=trt/solution;
             random clinic trt*clinic/solution;
             estimate 'lsm trt 1' intercept 1 trt 1 0;
             estimate 'trt diff' trt 1 -1;
             estimate 'trt 1 clinic 1 BLUP' intercept 1 trt 1 0
                     | clinic 1 0;
             estimate 'trt 1 clinic 6 BLUP' intercept 1 trt 1 0
                     | clinic 0 0 0 0 0 1 0;),
             error=binomial,
             link=probit);
    run;
```

This program is similar to the previous analysis, but with the following changes: A different data set, NEW, is used instead of A. The NEW data set is an expanded version of A in which all of the values of Y are 0s and 1s. This data set is used to improve the stability of GLIMMIX. Also, LINK=PROBIT is used instead of LINK=LOGIT. The results from this analysis are given in Output 11.5.

Results

Output 11.5 *Binomial Example - PROBIT Link*

```
 Covariance Parameter Estimates

Cov Parm          Estimate

CLINIC           0.72727366
CLINIC*TRT       0.02623896

GLIMMIX Model Statistics

Description                      Value

Deviance                      275.1875
Scaled Deviance               293.8288
Pearson Chi-Square            246.8220
Scaled Pearson Chi-Square     263.5418
Extra-Dispersion Scale          0.9366


Tests of Fixed Effects

Source    NDF    DDF    Type III F    Pr > F

TRT        1      7        5.55       0.0506

ESTIMATE Statement Results

Parameter            Estimate    Std Error    DDF        T    Pr > |T|

CNTL LSMEAN           -0.7076      0.3360       7     -2.11     0.0732
TRT DIFF              -0.4562      0.1936       7     -2.36     0.0506
TRT 1 CLINIC 1 BLUP   -0.7870      0.2110       7     -3.73     0.0074
TRT 1 CLINIC 6 BLUP   -1.6946      0.3974       7     -4.26     0.0037


Alpha        Lower        Upper         Mu      LowerMu      UpperMu

0.05       -1.5022       0.0869       0.2396     0.0665       0.5346
0.05       -0.9140       0.0015       0.3241     0.1804       0.5006
0.05       -1.2859      -0.2881       0.2156     0.0992       0.3866
0.05       -2.6343      -0.7548       0.0451     0.0042       0.2252


Least Squares Means

Level        LSMEAN     Std Error    DDF        T    Pr > |T|      Mu

TRT cntl     -0.7076      0.3360       7     -2.11     0.0732     0.2396
TRT drug     -0.2514      0.3341       7     -0.75     0.4764     0.4008
```

Interpretation

The major features of the analysis are similar to the analysis using the logit link. The main differences reflect the different link function. The main points are

- The variance component estimates of σ_C^2 (CLINIC – 0.727) and σ_{TC}^2 (TRT*CLINIC – 0.0262) are similar, relatively, to those obtained using the logit link. The difference in magnitude results from the use of a different link. In the probit model, the variance components have an interpretation. They reflect the variance of the CLINIC and TRT*CLINIC effects on the underlying, normally-distributed threshold process described above.

- The deviance is 275.19. With 271 degrees of freedom, you conclude there is no evidence of lack-of-fit. You can use the variance components and re-fit the model using the sample proportion FAV/NIJ instead of the 0-1 data. The resulting deviance is then based on 14 degrees of freedom. The method for doing so and the interpretation are the same as shown in the section 11.5.1 for the logit model.

- The extra-dispersion parameter estimate is 0.9366. This is similar to the estimate of ϕ for the logit-link. There is no evidence of underdispersion for the probit model.

- The *F*-statistic to test the equality of treatment effects is 5.55. This is similar to the *F*-value obtained using the logit link. In this case, you would reach the same conclusion about treatments. Clearly, given the *right* set of data, it is possible to reach different conclusions. McCullagh and Nelder (1989) discuss procedures you can use to check the adequacy of the model assumptions you have made, including your choice of link function. We strongly recommend you use their procedures when fitting any generalized linear model.

- The **estimates** and **least squares means** are expressed on the probit scale. These are obtained in the same way as shown in Section 11.5.1, except that you use the solutions fitting the probit model. These are given in Output 11.6.

Results - Fixed and Random Effect Solutions for Probit Model

Output 11.6 *Solution for Probit Model*

			Parameter Estimates			
Parameter	Estimate	Std Error	DDF	T	Pr > |T|
INTERCEPT	-0.2514	0.3341	7	-0.75	0.4764
TRT cntl	-0.4562	0.1936	7	-2.36	0.0506
TRT drug	0.0000	.	.	.	.

			Random Effects Estimates			
Parameter	Estimate	SE Pred	DDF	T	Pr > |T|
CLINIC 1	-0.0794	0.3573	257	-0.22	0.8244
CLINIC 2	1.0868	0.3677	257	2.96	0.0034
CLINIC 3	0.5768	0.3728	257	1.55	0.1230
CLINIC 4	-0.7745	0.4063	257	-1.91	0.0577

CLINIC 5	-0.4024	0.3962	257	-1.02	0.3108
CLINIC 6	-0.9869	0.4552	257	-2.17	0.0311
CLINIC 7	-0.4415	0.4513	257	-0.98	0.3288
CLINIC 8	1.0211	0.4363	257	2.34	0.0200
CLINIC*TRT 1 cntl	0.0632	0.1501	257	0.42	0.6739
CLINIC*TRT 1 drug	-0.0661	0.1500	257	-0.44	0.6599
CLINIC*TRT 2 cntl	0.0379	0.1521	257	0.25	0.8037
CLINIC*TRT 2 drug	0.0013	0.1526	257	0.01	0.9929
CLINIC*TRT 3 cntl	-0.0508	0.1529	257	-0.33	0.7400
CLINIC*TRT 3 drug	0.0716	0.1529	257	0.47	0.6400
CLINIC*TRT 4 cntl	-0.0090	0.1566	257	-0.06	0.9541
CLINIC*TRT 4 drug	-0.0189	0.1562	257	-0.12	0.9037
CLINIC*TRT 5 cntl	-0.0753	0.1563	257	-0.48	0.6302
CLINIC*TRT 5 drug	0.0608	0.1556	257	0.39	0.6963
CLINIC*TRT 6 cntl	-0.0265	0.1590	257	-0.17	0.8676
CLINIC*TRT 6 drug	-0.0091	0.1584	257	-0.06	0.9544
CLINIC*TRT 7 cntl	-0.0061	0.1583	257	-0.04	0.9692
CLINIC*TRT 7 drug	-0.0098	0.1586	257	-0.06	0.9507
CLINIC*TRT 8 cntl	0.0667	0.1578	257	0.42	0.6728
CLINIC*TRT 8 drug	-0.0299	0.1581	257	-0.19	0.8502

Interpretation

The broad space BLUP of the CNTL treatment for clinic 1, $m + \tau_1 + c_1$, has a linear predictor of

$$\hat{\eta}_{11} = -0.2514 - 0.4562 - 0.0794 = -0.7870$$

Applying the inverse link,

$$\hat{\pi}_{11} = \Phi(-0.7870) = 0.2156$$

You can obtain other BLUPs in a similar fashion. Again, the only difference between the procedure used here and the one used in the logit model is the inverse link function. As for the logit model, the inverse link is not meaningful when applied to differences. The **Mu** values for TRT 1 LSMEAN and TRT 1 CLINIC 1 BLUP are valid, but the **Mu** for TRT DIFF is not.

Model and Program Using Identity Link

You can also fit the **identity link**, i.e., $\eta = \pi$, to these data, as Beitler and Landis did. The only change in the GLIMMIX program is to change the LINK = command. For the identity link, you use LINK=IDENTITY. The rest of the program is identical to the programs shown above for the logit and probit links. Because GLIMMIX has great difficulty converging for this analysis, we fix the variance components using the NOITER option in the PARMS statement. The results are displayed in Output 11.7 and are not intended to be definitive, but rather are used for illustration purposes.

Results

Output 11.7 *Binomial Example - IDENTITY Link*

```
                        Covariance Parameter Estimates

                        Cov Parm              Estimate

                        CLINIC              0.15925685
                        CLINIC*TRT          0.00955541

                        GLIMMIX Model Statistics

             Description                        Value

             Deviance                          0.0928
             Scaled Deviance                   1.1649
             Pearson Chi-Square                0.0923
             Scaled Pearson Chi-Square         1.1587
             Extra-Dispersion Scale            0.0796

                        Tests of Fixed Effects

             Source      NDF      DDF     Type III F     Pr > F

             TRT          1        7         5.53        0.0509

                        ESTIMATE Statement Results
```

Parameter	Estimate	Std Error	DDF	T	Pr > |T|
LSM TRT 1	0.2924	0.1455	7	2.01	0.0844
TRT DIFF	-0.1200	0.0510	7	-2.35	0.0509
TRT 1 CLINIC 1 BLUP	0.2300	0.0743	7	3.10	0.0174
TRT 1 CLINIC 6 BLUP	-0.0044	0.0735	7	-0.06	0.9540

```
Mu
0.2924
-0.1200
0.2300
-0.0044
```

```
                        Least Squares Means
```

Level	LSMEAN	Std Error	DDF	T	Pr > |T|	Mu
TRT cntl	0.2924	0.1455	7	2.01	0.0844	0.2924
TRT drug	0.4124	0.1458	7	2.83	0.0254	0.4124

Interpretation

Most of the features of Output 11.7 are analogous to the output for the logit and probit models. Two aspects of the output deserve special attention:

- The extra-dispersion parameter estimate is 0.0796. This is substantially less than 1. This is evidence of serious **underdispersion**.

The extra-dispersion parameter *could* indicate that the data are not binomial. However, neither the logit and probit links showed evidence of underdispersion. The other explanation for the low extra-dispersion is that the identity link function does not fit these data as well as either the logit or the probit. This is typical of binomial data.

- The identity link does not guarantee reasonable predicted values — in this case probabilities.

In the logit and probit models, once the linear predictor of $\mathbf{K'\beta + M'u}$ was calculated, it was converted to a predicted probability using the inverse link function. The logit and probit inverse links guarantee that the corresponding predicted probabilities are between 0 and 1.

When the identity link is used, the linear predictor of $\mathbf{K'\beta + M'u}$ is equal to the predicted probability. There is no guarantee that $\mathbf{K'\beta + M'u}$ is between 0 and 1. For example, for the CNTL treatment at clinic 6, the broad space BLUP is

$$m + \tau_1 + c_6$$

You can obtain this BLUP from the solutions, given in Output 11.8.

Output 11.8 *Solution for Identity Link Model*

```
                              Parameter Estimates

Parameter        Estimate     Std Error     DDF         T     Pr > |T|


INTERCEPT          0.4124       0.1458        7        2.83     0.0254
TRT cntl          -0.1200       0.0510        7       -2.35     0.0509
TRT drug           0.0000          .          .          .         .



                            Random Effects Estimates

Parameter             Estimate      SE Pred    DDF          T     Pr > |T|


CLINIC 1             -0.0625        0.1555       0       -0.40        .
CLINIC 2              0.3793        0.1556       0        2.44        .
CLINIC 3              0.1947        0.1560       0        1.25        .
CLINIC 4             -0.2522        0.1554       0       -1.62        .
CLINIC 5             -0.1761        0.1555       0       -1.13        .
CLINIC 6             -0.2968        0.1553       0       -1.91        .
CLINIC 7             -0.1890        0.1569       0       -1.21        .
CLINIC 8              0.4027        0.1574       0        2.56        .
CLINIC*TRT 1 cntl     0.0386        0.0739       0        0.52        .
CLINIC*TRT 1 drug    -0.0423        0.0739       0       -0.57        .
CLINIC*TRT 2 cntl     0.0150        0.0742       0        0.20        .
CLINIC*TRT 2 drug     0.0078        0.0742       0        0.11        .
CLINIC*TRT 3 cntl    -0.1076        0.0749       0       -1.44        .
CLINIC*TRT 3 drug     0.1193        0.0749       0        1.59        .
CLINIC*TRT 4 cntl     0.0181        0.0738       0        0.25        .
CLINIC*TRT 4 drug    -0.0333        0.0738       0       -0.45        .
CLINIC*TRT 5 cntl    -0.1156        0.0740       0       -1.56        .
CLINIC*TRT 5 drug     0.1050        0.0742       0        1.42        .
```

```
CLINIC*TRT 6 cntl      0.0054       0.0735      0       0.07      .
CLINIC*TRT 6 drug     -0.0232       0.0736      0      -0.32      .
CLINIC*TRT 7 cntl      0.0071       0.0764      0       0.09      .
CLINIC*TRT 7 drug     -0.0184       0.0766      0      -0.24      .
CLINIC*TRT 8 cntl      0.1391       0.0772      0       1.80      .
CLINIC*TRT 8 drug     -0.1149       0.0774      0      -1.49      .
```

Using the estimates in Output 11.8, the resulting BLUP is

$$\hat{\eta}_{16} = 0.4124 - 0.1200 - 0.2968 = -0.0044$$

Thus, the predicted probability is $\hat{\pi}_{11} = -0.0044$, outside the allowable bounds for a probability. At the very least, using the identity link for binomial data can leave you with some very awkward problems in interpretation!

11.6 Example: A Mixed Model with Count Data

Section 11.2.2 described a split-plot experiment with different management methods as the whole-plot treatment factor and different seed mixes as the split-plot treatment factor. The whole-plots were arranged in randomized complete blocks. Botanical composition was measured, expressed as the number of plants of a given species per split-plot experimental unit.

The data for this example are given in Appendix 4, Data Set 11.6. The variables are TRT (management method — 7 types), BLK (4 blocks), MIX (seed mix — 4 types) and COUNT (the number of plants of the species of interest).

Model

Model 11.2 can be modified to accommodate the classical assumption that COUNT's have a Poisson distribution. The resulting generalized linear mixed model for these data is

$$\eta_{ijk} = \log(\lambda_{ijk}) = m + r_i + \tau_j + (r\tau)_{ij} + \delta_k + (\tau\delta)_{ik}$$

where λ_{ijk} is the conditional mean count given the random effects
  m is the intercept
  r_i is the BLK effect
  τ_j is the TRT effect
  $(r\tau)_{ij}$ is the BLK*TRT (whole-plot error) effect
  δ_k is the MIX effect
  $(\tau\delta)_{ik}$ is the TRT*MIX interaction.

Assumptions for the model are

- BLK and BLK*TRT are random effects

- $r_i \sim NI(0, \sigma_R^2)$

- $(r\tau)_i \sim NI(0, \sigma_{RT}^2)$

As in Section 11.5, you need to determine the various terms needed to work with the model assuming Poisson errors. These are summarized in Table 11.4.

Table 11.4

Expression	Function	Value
Conditional mean	μ_{ijk}	λ_{ijk}
natural parameter	$\theta(\mu_{ijk})$	$\log(\lambda_{ijk})$
variance function	$V(\mu_{ijk})$	λ_{ijk}
scale parameter	$a(\phi_{ijk})$	1
inverse link	$h(\eta_{iik})$	$\exp(\eta_{iik})$

Program to Analyze Count Data

You can obtain an analysis of this model with the GLIMMIX macro using the program

```
%include 'glimmix.sas';
%glimmix(data=a,
    procopt=method=reml,
    stmts=%str(
        class trt blk mix;
        model  y=trt mix trt*mix;
        random blk blk*trt;
        lsmeans trt mix;),
    error=poisson,
    link=log);
run;
```

The program is similar to the GLIMMIX programs used in Section 11.5. The most important change is that you use the ERROR=POISSON and LINK=LOG commands to reflect the model assumptions.

The results of the GLIMMIX analysis are given in Output 11.9.

Results

Output 11.9 *Example with Counts — Default Analysis*

```
              Covariance Parameter Estimates
              Cov
              Parm          Estimate


              BLK           0.00000000
              TRT*BLK       0.04761342


              GLIMMIX Model Statistics


       Description                        Value

       Deviance                        753.7934
       Scaled Deviance                  82.4237
       Pearson Chi-Square              701.0413
       Scaled Pearson Chi-Square        76.6555
       Extra-Dispersion Scale            9.1454
```

```
                          Tests of Fixed Effects

                 Source       NDF     DDF    Type III F    Pr > F

                 TRT           6       18          3.65    0.0150
                 MIX           3       63          1.62    0.1940
                 TRT*MIX      18       63          1.12    0.3559


                          Least Squares Means

Level     LSMEAN     Std Error     DDF       T     Pr > |T|          Mu

TRT 1     2.5894       0.2394       18    10.81     0.0001      13.3216
TRT 2     3.0363       0.2008       18    15.12     0.0001      20.8271
TRT 3     2.9237       0.2068       18    14.13     0.0001      18.6094
TRT 4     3.1836       0.1905       18    16.71     0.0001      24.1336
TRT 5     3.5038       0.1716       18    20.42     0.0001      33.2406
TRT 6     3.3866       0.1803       18    18.79     0.0001      29.5641
TRT 7     3.7092       0.1637       18    22.66     0.0001      40.8209
MIX 1     3.3584       0.1203       63    27.91     0.0001      28.7436
MIX 2     3.2638       0.1270       63    25.71     0.0001      26.1488
MIX 3     3.1456       0.1269       63    24.78     0.0001      23.2332
MIX 4     2.9936       0.1393       63    21.48     0.0001      19.9572
```

Interpretation

Most aspects of interpretation are similar to those discussed in the binomial example in Section 11.5. The main feature of Output 11.9 is that the BLK variance component estimate is zero. You can go ahead and interpret the output, or you can re-fit the model by dropping BLK. If you do, the GLIMMIX program is

```
%include 'glimmix.sas';
%glimmix(data=a,
   procopt=method=reml,
   stmts=%str(
        class trt blk mix;
        model  y=trt mix trt*mix;
        random blk*trt;
        lsmeans trt mix;),
        error=poisson,
        link=log);
run;
```

The results are given in Output 11.10.

Output 11.10 *Analysis of Count Data Dropping BLK*

```
              Covariance Parameter Estimates

     Cov
     Parm            Estimate


     TRT*BLK          0.04763161
                GLIMMIX Model Statistics


     Description                         Value


     Deviance                          753.7577
     Scaled Deviance                    82.4228
     Pearson Chi-Square                701.0055
     Scaled Pearson Chi-Square          76.6544
     Extra-Dispersion Scale              9.1450



                Tests of Fixed Effects


     Source     NDF     DDF    Type III F    Pr > F


       TRT       6       21        3.65      0.0122
       MIX       3       63        1.62      0.1940
     TRT*MIX    18       63        1.12      0.3558
```

Interpretation

You can see that none of the results change from Output 11.9 to 11.10, except the DDF for TRT changes from 18 to 21. The BLK*TRT variance component, the model statistics, and tests of fixed effects are identical. The LSMEANS are also unaffected although these are only shown in Output 11.9. The major results are

- The BLK*TRT variance component (σ_{RT}^2) estimate is 0.0476. The reflects the variances of the whole-plot errors on the link function (LOG) scale.

- The deviance is 753.76. The degrees of freedom are the number of observations (112) minus the number of independent fixed-effects parameters (28), or 84. There is evidence of lack of fit. For these data, the lack of fit results from overdispersion, discussed below.

- The extra-dispersion parameter estimate is 9.145. This is compelling evidence of **overdispersion**.

  Recall from Section 11.2 that in the Poisson distribution the mean and variance are equal, but empirical count data typically have a variance greater than the mean. This characteristic is called **overdispersion**.

  Failing to account for overdispersion can result in inflated test statistics. A simple method to account for overdispersion adjusts the variance by the scale parameter so that the conditional variance is $\phi\lambda$, rather than λ. The scale parameter ϕ in this context is called the **overdispersion parameter**. See McCullagh and Nelder (1989) for details. The GLIMMIX macro uses this adjustment.

- The *F*-statistics are automatically adjusted for overdispersion. In this case, the main effect of TRT is statistically significant (*F*=3.65, *p*-value 0.0122), but the MIX and TRT*MIX effects are not.

- The least squares means are computed in terms of relevant estimable functions of the fixed effects. For example, the least squares mean of TRT 1 is

$$m + \tau_1 + \delta_. + (\tau\delta)_{1.}$$

As in the binomial example, least squares means (and other estimates) are calculated on the link function scale (in this case, the log). The η_{ijk} are converted back to the COUNT scale (λ_{ijk}) using the inverse link, in this case $\exp(\eta_{ijk})$.

Failing to Account for Overdispersion

To see what happens if you do NOT account for overdispersion, you can override the automatic estimate of the extra-dispersion parameter ϕ.

You override the overdispersion adjustment by setting $\phi=1$. Use the program

```
%include 'glimmix.sas';
%glimmix(data=a,
   procopt=method=reml,
   stmts=%str(
        class trt blk mix;
        model  y=trt mix trt*mix;
        random blk*trt;
        parms (1) (1) / eqcons=2;
        lsmeans trt mix;),
     error=poisson,
     link=log);
run;
```

The PARMS (1) (1) / EQCONS=2 statement sets and holds ϕ at 1.

Selected results are given in Output 11.11.

Output 11.11 *GLMM with No Adjustment for Overdispersion*

Covariance Parameter Estimates	
Cov Parm	Estimate
TRT*BLK	0.14934349

GLIMMIX Model Statistics	
Description	Value
Deviance	622.9275
Scaled Deviance	622.9275
Pearson Chi-Square	584.7615
Scaled Pearson Chi-Square	584.7615
Extra-Dispersion Scale	1.0000

```
                        Tests of Fixed Effects

            Source      NDF     DDF    Type III F    Pr > F

            TRT          6       21        3.55      0.0139
            MIX          3       63       14.80      0.0001
            TRT*MIX     18       63       10.24      0.0001


                        Least Squares Means

Level       LSMEAN    Std Error    DDF        T    Pr > |T|         Mu

TRT 1       2.5818     0.2058       21    12.54     0.0001     13.2208
TRT 2       2.9464     0.2026       21    14.54     0.0001     19.0379
TRT 3       2.8884     0.2024       21    14.27     0.0001     17.9653
TRT 4       3.1459     0.2005       21    15.69     0.0001     23.2395
TRT 5       3.4740     0.1984       21    17.51     0.0001     32.2667
TRT 6       3.3030     0.2000       21    16.52     0.0001     27.1929
TRT 7       3.6993     0.1975       21    18.73     0.0001     40.4196
MIX 1       3.3165     0.0822       63    40.32     0.0001     27.5629
MIX 2       3.2219     0.0833       63    38.66     0.0001     25.0747
MIX 3       3.1036     0.0833       63    37.25     0.0001     22.2788
MIX 4       2.9516     0.0855       63    34.54     0.0001     19.1374
```

You can see that test statistics are inflated. For example, F for TRT*MIX is 10.24, whereas it is only 1.12 when you account for overdispersion. Failing to account for overdispersion can result in serious misinterpretation of the data.

Failing to Account for Whole-Plot Error

The main advantages of the generalized linear mixed model are that you can account for the distribution of the count data using the appropriate generalized linear model and that you can account for the split-plot nature of the experiment by fitting the BLK*TRT random effect and by computing F-statistics and standard errors accordingly. Conventional generalized linear model programs (e.g., PROC GENMOD) do not provide for random effects, and conventional mixed models do not provide for nonnormal errors.

You can obtain a conventional generalized linear model analysis to evaluate the effect of failing to account for whole-plot error (BLK*TRT) by deleting the RANDOM statement from the GLIMMIX program:

```
%include 'glimmix.sas';
%glimmix(data=a,
    procopt=method=reml,
    stmts=%str(
        class trt blk mix;
        model  y=trt mix trt*mix;
        lsmeans trt mix;),
        error=poisson,
        link=log);
run;
```

The results are given in Output 11.12.

Output 11.12 *Generalized Linear Model Analysis Ignoring Whole-Plot Error*

```
                          GLIMMIX Model Statistics

                     Description                        Value

                     Deviance                         928.1706
                     Scaled Deviance                  928.1706
                     Pearson Chi-Square               885.7419
                     Scaled Pearson Chi-Square        885.7419
                     Dispersion Scale                   1.0000

                            Tests of Fixed Effects

                  Source     NDF    DDF    Type III F    Pr > F

                  TRT          6     84       4.75        0.0003
                  MIX          3     84       1.40        0.2475
                  TRT*MIX     18     84       0.97        0.5001

                            Least Squares Means
```

Level	LSMEAN	Std Error	DDF	T	Pr > |T|	Mu
TRT 1	2.5899	0.2288	84	11.32	0.0001	13.3288
TRT 2	3.0454	0.1805	84	16.87	0.0001	21.0187
TRT 3	2.9271	0.1885	84	15.53	0.0001	18.6741
TRT 4	3.1889	0.1674	84	19.04	0.0001	24.2616
TRT 5	3.5104	0.1419	84	24.75	0.0001	33.4630
TRT 6	3.4017	0.1533	84	22.19	0.0001	30.0153
TRT 7	3.7123	0.1309	84	28.36	0.0001	40.9495
MIX 1	3.3646	0.1213	84	27.74	0.0001	28.9224
MIX 2	3.2700	0.1289	84	25.37	0.0001	26.3115
MIX 3	3.1518	0.1288	84	24.46	0.0001	23.3778
MIX 4	2.9998	0.1429	84	21.00	0.0001	20.0814

You can see that the resulting *F*-statistics are different. The whole-plot effect (TRT for these data) is particularly affected. In this case, the conclusion is not affected. You conclude that TRT effects are significant in both analyses. It is easy to see, however, that for the *right data* you can easily reach erroneous conclusions if you do not account for whole-plot error.

11.7 Summary

This chapter shows how to use the GLIMMIX macro to analyze **generalized linear mixed models**. The generalized linear mixed model is an extension of the mixed model to accommodate nonnormal errors. Section 11.2 presents two examples illustrating the need for such models. Section 11.3 gives an introduction to generalized linear models — fixed-effects nonnormal error linear models. Section 11.4 shows how random effects are incorporated to produce generalized linear mixed models. Sections 11.5 and 11.6 present analysis of the two examples discussed in Section 11.2 using the GLIMMIX macro. Section 11.5 is a binomial example, Section 11.6 is a Poisson example. Sections 11.5 and 11.6 focus on the required SAS programs and interpretation of the output.

11.8 References

Bishop, Y.M.M., Fienberg, S.E., and Holland, P.W. (1975), *Discrete Multivariate Analysis*, Cambridge, MA: MIT Press.

Beitler, P.J. and Landis, J.R. (1985), A mixed-effects model for categorical data, *Biometrics*, **41**, 991–1000.

Breslow, N.R. and Clayton, D.G. (1993). Approximate inference in generalized linear mixed models, *Journal of the American Statistical Association,* **88**, 9–25.

Box, G.E.P. and Cox, D.R. (1964), An analysis of transformations, *Journal of the Royal Statistical Society* B, **26**, 211–252.

McCullagh, P. (1983), Quasi-likelihood function, *Ann. Statist*, **11**, 59–67.

McCullagh, P. and Nelder, J.A. (1989), *Generalized Linear Models*, 2nd Edition, New York: Chapman and Hall.

Nelder, J.A. and Wedderburn, R.W.M. (1972), Generalised linear models, *Journal of the Royal Statistical Society* A, **135**, 370–384.

Snedecor, G.W. and Cochran, W.G. (1989), *Statistical Methods, 8th Edition*, Ames, IA: Iowa State University Press.

Steel, R.D.G. and Torrie, J.H. (1980), *Principles and Procedures of Statistics, 2nd Edition*, New York: McGraw-Hill, Inc.

Wedderburn, R.W.M. (1974), Quasilikelihood methods, generalised linear models, and the Gauss-Newton method, *Biometrika*, **61**, 439–447.

Wolfinger, R. and O'Connell, M. (1993), Generalized linear models: a pseudo-likelihood approach, *J. Statist. Comput. Simul.*, **48**, 233–243.

Chapter **12** **Nonlinear Mixed Models**

12.1 Introduction

In Chapters 1 through 10, the models have all been **linear**, with the response variable modeled directly by linear combinations of fixed and random effects. The resulting models have a common form

$$\mathbf{y} = \mathbf{X}\boldsymbol{\beta} + \mathbf{Zu} + \mathbf{e} \tag{12.1}$$

In Chapter 11, linear combinations of fixed and random effects were used to model the **link function** of the mean of a nonnormal response variable. The resulting generalized linear mixed model is

$$E(y|u) = g^{-1}(X\beta + Zu) \tag{12.2}$$

However, not all data can be adequately characterized by linear models. Many applications require **nonlinear models**.

Traditional nonlinear models have the general form

$$y = f(X,\beta) + \mathbf{e} \tag{12.3}$$

where $f(X,\beta)$ is a nonlinear function of known constants (X) and unknown parameters (β). Such nonlinear models are **fixed-effects models**. As is the case for other models, nonlinear models must also be able to accommodate random effects.

For example, suppose your experimental data are in the form of repeated measurements on response and explanatory variables from several subjects, and you would like to fit a model to them that simultaneously accounts for their overall mean structure as well as their variability both between and within subjects. Suppose further that the mean model you have in mind is nonlinear in its parameters, in contrast to mixed models considered in previous chapters. This situation calls for a nonlinear mixed model.

For example, suppose you are a botanist studying growth patterns in the orange tree data from Draper and Smith (1981, p. 524) and Lindstrom and Bates (1990). Figure 12.1 plots these data, which are trunk circumferences of five orange trees measured at seven time points. The curves display a mildly nonlinear trend along with a marked increase in variability over time.

One analysis strategy is to fit a higher order polynomial trend along with a heterogeneous variance-covariance structure like those discussed in Chapter 8. However, your experience as a botanist indicates that the logistic growth model $y = \beta_1/(1 + \beta_2 e^{\beta_3 x})$ is more interpretable and appropriate. Furthermore, you want to account for both intersubject variability and intrasubject correlation and heterogeneity.

The primary questions that arise are "How should I construct an appropriate nonlinear mixed model?" and "How should I fit it to the data?" Several different answers have been proposed to this question, and new ones are appearing in the literature. Rather than discuss all of the possibilities, this chapter focuses on three general methods that you can currently use in the SAS System with the NLINMIX macro. The macro is listed in Appendix 3 and is also available through SAS Online Samples by anonymous ftp (ftp.sas.com), on the world wide web (http://www.sas.com/), in the SAS supplemental library, or from the SAS Technical Support Division.

The next section introduces the three NLINMIX methods and the following section provides the theoretical details behind them. Sections 12.4 and 12.5 contain two examples illustrating the methods, and the chapter concludes with further information about the NLINMIX macro.

Figure 12.1 *Orange Tree Data*

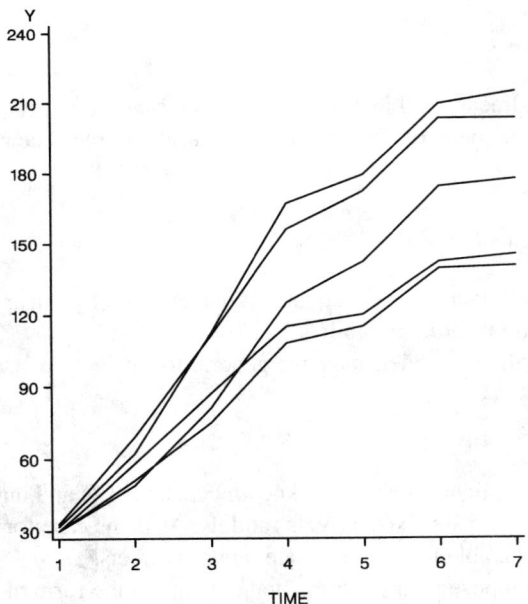

12.2 Three General Methods Available in the NLINMIX Macro

The three methods available in the NLINMIX macro all use the same basic algorithm, which is to iterate between the following two steps until the parameter estimates converge:

1. Create pseudo-data, usually modified residuals computed from the original data and the assumed model evaluated at current estimates of the parameters.
2. Call PROC MIXED using the pseudo-data and obtain new estimates of the parameters.

The three methods differ in how they create the pseudo-data and in their PROC MIXED specifications. Table 12.1 outlines the major differences. The next section provides the theoretical details behind the methods.

Table 12.1 *Three Methods Available in the NLINMIX Macro*

Method	Name	Pseudo-data	PROC MIXED Statement Used
1	Approximate first-order	residuals+fixed	RANDOM
2	Approximate second-order	residuals+fixed+random	RANDOM
3	Marginal structures	residuals+fixed	REPEATED

Method 1 results in estimates similar to those from the first-order method described in Beal and Sheiner (1982) and Sheiner and Beal (1985), as it is based on a Taylor series expansion around zero, which is the expected value of the random effects. Method 2 produces the estimates of Lindstrom and Bates (1990) although using a different algorithm from the one they describe. It is based on a Taylor series expansion around the empirical BLUPs of the random effects (see Chapter 6). Method 3 has close ties with the population-averaged generalized estimating equation (GEE) approach of Zeger, Liang, and Albert (1988) and is based on a marginal approximation to the nonlinear mixed model.

None of the three methods is clearly superior to the others for all data analytic situations, and Table 12.2 provides a comparison of some of the advantages and disadvantages of each.

Table 12.2 *Advantages and Disadvantages of the Three Methods*

Method	Advantages	Disadvantages
1	Both subject-specific and population-averaged inference, more robust to model misspecification, converges quickly	Approximation may be inaccurate
2	More accurate approximation, subject-specific inference, weights can depend on random effects	Sensitive to model misspecification, sometimes converges slowly or not at all
3	Population-averaged inference, wide variety of covariance structures helps prevent model misspecification, converges quickly	Can be difficult to interpret and to compute predictions

Because all three methods are implemented through calls to PROC MIXED, they accommodate unbalanced and randomly missing data quite well. The statistics produced by the final call to PROC MIXED are asymptotically valid provided that you have correctly specified the first and second moments. These include the approximate standard errors for the estimates of β and θ, the former being model-based as opposed to the "empirical sandwich" estimator commonly associated with GEE (Liang and Zeger, 1986). The weight matrix $\mathbf{W}_i$ provides a nice mechanism for modeling heterogeneity, especially the type which varies with a power of the mean function (Carroll and Ruppert, 1988; Davidian and Giltinan, 1993). Also, the EBLUPs from the final PROC MIXED call from Methods 1 and 2 are empirical estimates of the random effects.

An option available to you with all three methods is the use of either maximum likelihood (ML) or restricted maximum likelihood (REML) in the PROC MIXED calls. For Method 1, the use of ML is closer to Sheiner and Beal's first-order method than is REML, but it is not exactly the same because of a difference in their estimating equations. ML criteria also appear to be better suited for comparing different models than are criteria based on REML because the approximate fixed-effects design matrices depend upon the fixed-effects parameter estimates and thus change from fit to fit. REML is attractive because of its bias adjustments, and also because it is based on an orthogonality between β and θ that is also present in the form of the estimating equations solved by the three methods. Of course, the differences between ML and REML are slight whenever there are only a few fixed-effects parameters, which is often the case with many nonlinear mixed models.

Together the three methods offer you a flexible set of nonlinear methods that can accommodate a wide range of correlation and heterogeneity scenarios.

12.3 Theoretical Details for the Three Methods

To fix notation and assumptions, write the jth $(j = 1,\ldots,t_i)$ observation on the ith $(i = 1,\ldots,s)$ subject as

$$\mathbf{y}_{ij} = f(\mathbf{x}_{ij}, \beta, \mathbf{u}_i) + \mathbf{e}_{ij}$$

where

f is some nonlinear function

$\mathbf{x}_{ij}$ is a known vector of covariates

β is an unknown vector of fixed-effect parameters

$\mathbf{u}_i$ is a vector of unknown random-effect parameters

$\mathbf{e}_{ij}$ are unknown random errors.

The $\mathbf{u}_i$ are assumed to be independent vectors with zero mean and variance-covariance matrix $\mathbf{G}$. The $\mathbf{e}_{ij}$, $j = 1,\ldots,t_i$ form a multivariate random vector with zero mean and conditional (on $\mathbf{u}_i$) variance-covariance matrix

$$\mathbf{W}_i(x_i,\beta,\mathbf{u}_i)^{-1/2}\mathbf{R}_i(\varphi)\mathbf{W}_i(x_i,\beta,\mathbf{u}_i)^{-1/2}$$

where

$\mathbf{X_i}$ is the vector of covariate values x_{ij}, $j=1,\ldots,t_i$

$\mathbf{W_i}$ is a $t_i \times t_i$ diagonal weight matrix that may depend on $\mathbf{x}_i$, as well as β and $\mathbf{u}_i$

$\mathbf{R}_i$ is a $t_i \times t_i$ variance-covariance matrix depending on a vector of unknown parameters ϕ.

To begin distinguishing the three methods of Table 12.1 assume that for Methods 1 and 2 $\mathbf{R}_i(\phi)=\sigma^2\mathbf{I}_{t_i}$, where $\mathbf{I}_{t_i}$ is the $t_i \times t_i$ identity matrix and that the $\mathbf{u}_i$ establish correlations for these methods. In contrast, assume that in Method 3 the $\mathbf{u}_i$ are not present, and thus $\mathbf{R}_i(\phi)$ models all correlations for Method 3.

All three methods are implemented by iterative calls to PROC MIXED on pseudo-data, and Table 12.3 provides the form of the pseudo-data for all three methods.

Table 12.3 *Pseudo-data for the Three Nonlinear Mixed Model Methods*

Method	Pseudo-data y_{ij}^*
1	$y_{ij}-f(x_{ij},\beta,0)+\tilde{X}_{ij}(\beta,0)^T\beta$
2	$y_{ij}-f(x_{ij},\beta,\hat{\mathbf{u}}_i)+\tilde{X}_{ij}(\beta,\hat{\mathbf{u}}_i)^T\beta+\tilde{Z}_{ij}(\beta,\hat{\mathbf{u}}_i)^T\hat{\mathbf{u}}_i$
3	$y_{ij}-f(x_{ij},\beta)+\tilde{X}_{ij}(\beta)^T\beta$

For Method 1,

$$\tilde{X}_{ij}(\beta,0) = \frac{\partial f(x_{ij},\beta,\mathbf{u}_i)}{\partial\beta^T}(\beta,0)$$

where $\hat{\beta}$ is the current estimate of the fixed effects-parameters. Method 1 is therefore carried out by a Taylor series expansion of f about $\mathbf{u}_i = 0$.

For Method 2,

$$\tilde{\mathbf{X}}_{ij}(\hat{\beta},\hat{\mathbf{u}}_i) = \frac{\partial f(x_{ij},\beta,\mathbf{u}_i)}{\partial\beta^T}(\hat{\beta},\hat{\mathbf{u}}_i)$$

$$\tilde{\mathbf{Z}}_{ij}(\hat{\beta},\hat{\mathbf{u}}_i) = \frac{\partial f(x_{ij},\beta,\mathbf{u}_i)}{\partial\mathbf{u}_i^T}(\hat{\beta},\hat{\mathbf{u}}_i)$$

and the expansion is now about $\mathbf{u}_i = \hat{\mathbf{u}}_i$, the current EBLUP.

For Method 3, as noted above, the dependence on $\mathbf{u}_i$ is dropped, and the pseudodata are a mechanism for taking Gauss-Newton optimization steps. The notation $\tilde{\mathbf{X}}_{ij}$ reflects the fact that these vectors form the rows of the fixed-effects design matrices for each call to PROC MIXED in all three methods.

The specification of the linear mixed model fitted at each PROC MIXED step is completed with a covariance structure. Define θ to be the vector of unknown variance-covariance parameters, which are those in $(\mathbf{G}, \sigma^2)$ for Methods 1 and 2 and ϕ for Method 3. Table 12.4 displays the form of this structure for each of the three methods. For Methods 1 and 2, $\tilde{\mathbf{Z}}_i$ is the matrix with rows $\tilde{\mathbf{Z}}_{ij}$, and this matrix is passed to the RANDOM statement in PROC MIXED. For Method 3, the covariance structure in $\mathbf{R}_i(\phi)$ is passed to the TYPE= option of the REPEATED statement in PROC MIXED. For all three methods, the elements of the diagonal matrix $\mathbf{W}_i$ are used as a WEIGHT variable in PROC MIXED. Note that for Method 2 the weights in $\mathbf{W}_i$ can depend on the current estimates of the random effects, but not for Method 1.

Table 12.4 *Covariance Structure for the Three Nonlinear Mixed Model Methods*

Method	$\mathbf{V}_i(\beta, \theta)$
1	$\tilde{\mathbf{Z}}_i(\hat{\beta}, 0)\mathbf{G}\tilde{\mathbf{Z}}_i(\hat{\beta}, 0)^T + \sigma^2 \mathbf{W}_i^{-1}(\mathbf{x}_i, \hat{\beta}, 0)$
2	$\tilde{\mathbf{Z}}_i(\hat{\beta}, \hat{\mathbf{u}}_i)\mathbf{G}\tilde{\mathbf{Z}}_i(\hat{\beta}, \hat{\mathbf{u}}_i)^T + \sigma^2 \mathbf{W}_i^{-1}(\mathbf{x}_i, \hat{\beta}, \hat{\mathbf{u}}_i)$
3	$\mathbf{W}_i(\mathbf{x}_i, \beta)^{-1/2}\mathbf{R}_i(\varphi)\mathbf{W}_i(\mathbf{x}_i, \beta)^{-1/2}$

The final estimates $\hat{\beta}$ and $\hat{\theta}$ for all three methods solve a set of generalized estimating equations (GEE) that can be written as follows:

$$\sum_{i=1}^{s} \tilde{X}_i^T V_i(\hat{\beta}, \hat{\theta})^{-1}(y_i^* - \tilde{X}_i\hat{\beta}) = 0$$

$$\sum_{i=1}^{s} \frac{\partial l(y_i^*, x_i, \beta, \theta)}{\partial\theta}(\hat{\beta}, \hat{\theta}) = 0$$

Here $\tilde{\mathbf{X}}_i$ is the matrix with rows $\tilde{\mathbf{X}}_{ij}$ and l is the standard linear mixed model likelihood or restricted likelihood from Chapter 6.

The estimates from Method 1 are similar to those from the first-order method of Beal and Sheiner (1982) and Sheiner and Beal (1985). The methods are generally different, though, because Beal and Sheiner maximize the extended least squares objective function and because its estimating equations for β involve an extra derivative term whenever $\mathbf{V}_i$ depends on β. Method 1 is also closely related to the techniques of Hirst, Zerbe, Boyle, and Wilkening (1991) and Vonesh and Carter (1992), as well as to the marginal quasi-likelihood method of Breslow and Clayton (1993).

Method 2 produces the estimates of Lindstrom and Bates (1990) although it uses a different algorithm from the one they describe (refer to Wolfinger (1993) for details). Method 2 is also very similar to the penalized quasi-likelihood approach for generalized linear mixed models (Breslow and Clayton, 1993), and in fact, NLINMIX can be used to produce the estimates from the GLIMMIX macro discussed in Chapter 11.

When the random-effects parameters enter the model linearly and their design matrix does not depend upon the fixed-effects parameters, then Methods 1 and 2 are equivalent and produce the maximum likelihood estimates of Gumpertz and Pantula (1992) or their restricted maximum likelihood counterparts.

Method 3 generalizes the multivariate nonlinear model of Gennings, Chinchilli, and Carter (1989) to consider parameterized covariance structures. Method 3 has close ties with the population-averaged GEE approach of Zeger, Liang, and Albert (1988).

All three of the methods simultaneously solve GEE for both mean and variance-covariance parameters similar to the GEE2 methodology of Prentice and Zhao (1991).

The NLINMIX macro, listed in Appendix 3, implements all three methods. NLINMIX iteratively creates pseudo-data and calls PROC MIXED until consecutive parameter estimates do not differ by some specified criterion, which by default is $1e$-8. The next two sections provide examples to illustrate its use.

12.4 Example: Logistic Growth Curve

As a first example of NLINMIX, consider the orange tree data described in the introduction. The following program creates the data set listed in Data Set 12.4, "TREE" in Appendix 4, "SAS Data Sets."

```
data tree;
   input tree time x y;
   datalines;
...datalines...
run;
```

Model

Consider the following logistic random coefficient model for the jth ($j = 1,\ldots,7$) observation on the ith ($i = 1,\ldots,5$) tree:

$$y_{ij} = \frac{\beta_1 + u_{i1}}{1 + (\beta_2 + u_{i2})\exp^{\beta_3 x_{ij}}} + e_{ij}$$

The three fixed-effect parameters to be estimated are $\beta_1, \beta_2, \beta_3$. The two random-effect parameters are u_{i1}, u_{i2}, differing from the specification of Lindstrom and Bates (1990) because of the inclusion of u_{i2}. The parameters u_{i1}, u_{i2} are assumed to be the ith independent realization from a multivariate distribution with mean zero and 2×2 unstructured covariance matrix **G**. The residual errors e_{ij} are assumed to be independent and identically distributed random variables with mean zero and variance σ^2.

Program for Method 1

To implement Method 1, the mean function is approximated with a first-order multivariate Taylor series expansion about $u_{i1} = u_{i2}, = 0$, producing the approximate model

$$y_{ij} \cong \frac{\beta_1}{1 + \beta_2 e^{\beta_3 x_{ij}}} + \frac{1}{1 + \beta_2 e^{\beta_3 x_{ij}}} u_{i1} + \frac{-\beta_1 e^{\beta_3 x_{ij}}}{(1 + \beta_2 e^{\beta_3 x_{ij}})^2} u_{i2} + e_{ij}$$

Note that the approximation is exact in u_{i1} because it enters the model linearly. The NLINMIX program to implement Method 1 for this model is as follows:

```
%nlinmix(data=tree,
    response=y,
    subject=tree,
    model=%str(
        num = b1+u1;
        e = exp(b3*x);
        den = 1 + (b2+u2)*e;
        pred = num/den;
    ),
    derivs=%str(
        d_b1 = 1/den;
        d_b2 = -num/den/den*e;
        d_b3 = -num/den/den*b2*x*e;
        d_u1 = d_b1;
        d_u2 = d_b2;
    ),
    parms=%str(b1=150 b2=10 b3=-.001),
    random=u1 u2,
    type=un,
    expand=zero
)
```

A description of the syntax of the macro is as follows:

- The DATA= argument specifies the SAS data set to use for the analysis, which in this case is TREE. The RESPONSE= argument specifies the variable within the SAS data set which contains the response data y_{ij}. Here this variable is Y. The SUBJECT= argument specifies the subject effect, which for this example is represented by the variable TREE.

- The MODEL= statement is an important part of the code as it defines the nonlinear mean function. DATA step code is used to specify the model. Because there are multiple statements ending with semicolons, the entire argument is enclosed with the %STR() macro. The variables B1, B2, and B3 represent the fixed-effects parameters in this model specification, and they correspond to β_1, β_2, β_3 in the logistic model. U1 and U2 are the random-effects parameters corresponding to u_{i1}, u_{i2}. The auxiliary variables NUM, E, and DEN make the MODEL= statement easier, and the final predicted value must be assigned to the PRED variable.

- The DERIVS= argument specifies the derivatives of the model with respect to the fixed- and random-effects parameters. You must assign the derivatives to variables created by adding the 'D_' prefix to each of their names. You can reuse auxiliary variables created in the MODEL= statement to speed coding. If you omit DERIVS=, NLINMIX computes the derivatives using finite difference methods.

- The fixed-effects parameters and their starting values are listed in the PARMS= argument. Our starting values for this problem are $\beta_1 = 150$, $\beta_2 = 10$, and $\beta_3 = -.001$. As with most nonlinear optimization problems, good starting values are important to ensure convergence of the algorithm. They should be selected from prior knowledge or a preliminary nonlinear least squares analysis.

- U1 and U2 are indicated as random-effects parameters in the RANDOM= argument, and the TYPE=UN option models their 2×2 covariance matrix **G** as unstructured with three parameters to be estimated. The EXPAND=ZERO argument requests a Method 1 analysis which employs a first-order Taylor series expansion around $u_{i1} = 0$ and $u_{i2} = 0$. NLINMIX therefore sets U1 and U2 equal to zero throughout the iterations for this analysis.

Results for Method 1

The macro prints the following results in Output 12.1 to the SAS log.

Output 12.1 *SAS Log for Method 1*

```
                        The NLINMIX Macro

        Data Set                  : WORK.TREE
        Response                  : Y
        Subject                   : TREE
        Fixed Effects Parameters  : B1 B2 B3
        Random Effects Parameters : U1 U2
        Covariance Type           : UN
        Expansion Point           : ZERO
        Optimization Method       : REML



                        Dimensions

            Observations              : 35
            Subjects                  : 5
            Maximum Obs per Subject   : 7
            Fixed Effects Parameters  : 3
            Random Effects per Subject : 2


Calling PROC NLIN to initialize.
Iteratively calling PROC MIXED.
   PROC MIXED call 0

iteration = 0
convergence criterion = .
B1=192.68759424 B2=7.8565635269 B3=-0.002828585 COVP1=1578.8089538
  COVP2=32.943539974 COVP3=1.2060351372 COVP4=57.969860508
   PROC MIXED call 1
```

```
iteration = 1
convergence criterion = 7.5400689E-9
B1=192.68759206 B2=7.8565637192 B3=-0.002828585 COVP1=1578.8089419
  COVP2=32.943539726 COVP3=1.2060351281 COVP4=57.969860071
Convergence criteria met.
NOTE: Numeric values have been converted to character
      values at the places given by: (Line):(Column).
      2466:50
NOTE: The data set WORK._NLINMIX has 35 observations and 24
      variables.
NOTE: The DATA statement used 0:00:00.1 real 0:00:00.10 cpu.
   PROC MIXED call 2
NOTE: The data set WORK._SOLN has 3 observations and 9 variables.
NOTE: The data set WORK._COV has 4 observations and 9 variables.
NOTE: The data set WORK._SOLNR has 10 observations and 3 variables.
NOTE: The data set WORK._FIT has 10 observations and 2 variables.
```

Interpretation for Method 1

The macro first prints some basic information about your model specification as well as some relevant dimensions. It then calls PROC NLIN one time to obtain initial estimates of the fixed effects parameters. NLINMIX uses these, along with 0's for the random effects parameters, to create the first pseudodata set according to the details of the previous section.

The iterative phase begins after the initial call to PROC MIXED, and only one iteration is required in order to drop below the default convergence criterion of $1e$-8.

Several data sets are available for your use after the macro terminates. WORK._NLINMIX, the primary working data set, has all of your original data plus parameter estimates, derivatives, and the pseudo-data values in a variable named _RESID. WORK._SOLN contains the fixed-effects parameter estimates along with their estimated standard errors and approximate confidence limits. WORK._COV and WORK._SOLNR have the same quantities for the covariance parameters and the EBLUPs, respectively. Finally, WORK._FIT has the basic model fitting information, which can be useful in comparing different models.

NLINMIX also prints the results from the final PROC MIXED call to SAS output. The results are in Output 12.2.

Output 12.2 *Results for Method 1*

```
                 The MIXED Procedure


              Class Level Information


      Class      Levels  Values


      _SUBJECT      5    1 2 3 4 5
```

```
                         Parameter Search

         COL1       COL2       COL3       COL4   Variance    REML_LL

     1578.809    32.9435     1.2060    57.9699    57.9699   -134.221


                         Parameter Search

                    -2REML_LL   Objective

                     268.4416    209.6295


                  REML Estimation Iteration History

         Iteration  Evaluations      Objective      Criterion

             1           1      209.62949853      0.00000000

                    Convergence criteria met.


                 Covariance Parameter Estimates (REML)

     Cov Parm              Ratio        Estimate      Std Error        Z

     D_U1 UN(1,1)    27.23499660   1578.8089412   1154.0249245     1.37
          UN(2,1)     0.56828738     32.94353971    37.21791064     0.89
          UN(2,2)     0.02080452      1.20603513     1.75794426     0.69
     Residual         1.00000000     57.96986005    16.73445715     3.46


                 Covariance Parameter Estimates (REML)

                    Pr > |Z|   Alpha     Lower      Upper

                      0.1713    0.05   -683.038   3840.656
                      0.3761    0.05    -40.0022   105.8893
                      0.4927    0.05     -2.2395     4.6515
                      0.0005    0.05     25.1709    90.7688


                  Model Fitting Information for _RESID

            Description                          Value

            Observations                        35.0000
            Variance Estimate                   57.9699
            Standard Deviation Estimate          7.6138
```

```
REML Log Likelihood                 -134.221
Akaike's Information Criterion      -138.221
Schwarz's Bayesian Criterion        -141.152
-2 REML Log Likelihood               268.4416
PARMS Model LRT Chi-Square             0.0000
PARMS Model LRT DF                     3.0000
PARMS Model LRT P-Value                1.0000
```

Solution for Fixed Effects

Parameter	Estimate	Std Error	DDF	T	Pr > |T|	Alpha
D_B1	192.68759194	18.95397306	24	10.17	0.0001	0.05
D_B2	7.85656373	0.93202830	24	8.43	0.0001	0.05
D_B3	-0.00282858	0.00021235	24	-13.32	0.0001	0.05

Solution for Fixed Effects

Lower	Upper
153.5685	231.8067
5.9330	9.7802
-0.0033	-0.0024

Tests of Fixed Effects

Source	NDF	DDF	Type III F	Pr > F
D_B1	1	24	103.35	0.0001
D_B2	1	24	71.06	0.0001
D_B3	1	24	177.44	0.0001

Interpretation for Method 1

The "Class Levels" table provides the levels of the created _SUBJECT variable. The "Parameter Search" table is printed because the covariance parameter values from the previous iteration are read into PROC MIXED as starting values. The "REML Estimation Iteration History" table reveals that only one step is required to attain convergence from this initial value.

The data from the next four tables, beginning with the "Covariance Parameter Estimates" table, made the four data sets mentioned at the end of the SAS log listing above. The estimate for $\mathbf{G}$ is

$$\hat{\mathbf{G}} = \begin{bmatrix} 1578.81 & 32.94 \\ 32.94 & 1.21 \end{bmatrix}$$

and $\hat{\sigma}^2 = 57.97$. As mentioned by Lindstrom and Bates (1990), it appears that nearly all of the intersubject variability occurs in the $\mathbf{u}_{i1}$ parameters.

The estimates for the fixed-effects parameters are $\hat{\beta}_1 = 192.69$, $\hat{\beta}_2 = 7.85$, and $\hat{\beta}_3 = -.0028$. Because they each have 1 degree of freedom, the squares of their t-statistics equal the F-statistics in the "Tests of Fixed Effects" table.

Program for Method 2

The Method 1 estimates are quite close to the Lindstrom and Bates estimates of 191.185, 8.153, and $-.0029$. You can use the following program to duplicate these latter results using Method 2:

```
%nlinmix(data=tree,
    response=y,
    subject=tree,
    model=%str(
        num = b1+u1;
        e = exp(b3*x);
        den = 1 + b2*e;
        pred = num/den;
    ),
    derivs=%str(
    d_b1 = 1/den;
        d_b2 = -num/den/den*e;
        d_b3 = -num/den/den*b2*x*e;
        d_u1 = d_b1;
    ),
    parms=%str(b1=150 b2=10 b3=-.001),
    random=u1,
    expand=eblup
)
```

Note that only 1 random-effect parameter is now specified and EXPAND=EBLUP. This produces a Method 2 analysis that converges in 6 iterations.

Program for Method 3

As an example of a Method 3 analysis, consider an $\mathbf{R}(\phi)$ which has the compound symmetry structure and a diagonal weight matrix $\mathbf{W}_i(\mathbf{x}_i, \beta)$ which has elements that are a power of the mean function. Recall the assumed variance-covariance matrix is then $\mathbf{W}_i(\mathbf{x}_i, \beta)^{-1/2} \mathbf{R}_i(\phi) \mathbf{W}_i(\mathbf{x}_i, \beta)^{-1/2}$.

The initial power is chosen as -2, which is a constant coefficient-of-variation model. The NLINMIX program is as follows:

```
%nlinmix(data=tree,
    method=ml,
    response=y,
    subject=tree,
    model=%str(
        num = b1;
        e = exp(b3*x);
        den = 1 + b2*e;
        pred = num/den;
    ),
    derivs=%str(
        d_b1 = 1/den;
        d_b2 = -num/den/den*e;
        d_b3 = -num/den/den*b2*x*e;
```

```
    ),
    parms=%str(b1=200 b2=7.6 b3=-.0025),
    rtype=cs,
    weight=1/pred**2;
)
```

METHOD=ML is used here instead of the default METHOD=REML to facilitate a later comparison between different power models. Note that U1 and U2 have been removed from the MODEL= statement because this is a Method 3 analysis. Likewise, D_U1 and D_U2 are absent from the DERIVS= argument. Improved starting values from the previous analysis are specified in the PARMS= argument. No RANDOM= is given as in the previous analysis; rather, the RTYPE= argument requests that $\mathbf{R}(\phi)$ have the compound symmetry structure. Finally, the WEIGHT= argument sets up $\mathbf{W}_i(\mathbf{x}_i, \beta)$.

Results for Method 3

The SAS log from this program is shown in Output 12.3.

Output 12.3 *SAS Log for Method 3*

```
                        The NLINMIX Macro

        Data Set                    : WORK.TREE
        Response                    : Y
        Subject                     : TREE
        Fixed Effects Parameters    : B1 B2 B3
        REPEATED Covariance Type    : CS
        Weight                      : 1/PRED**2;
        Optimization Method         : ML


                         Dimensions


            Observations              : 35
            Subjects                  : 5
            Maximum Obs per Subject   : 7
            Fixed Effects Parameters  : 3

Calling PROC NLIN to initialize.

WARNING: Step size shows no improvement.
WARNING: PROC NLIN failed to converge.

WARNING: PROC NLIN failed to converge.

Iteratively calling PROC MIXED.
   PROC MIXED call 0
iteration = 0
convergence criterion = .
B1=198.83116797 B2=7.6370658532 B3=-0.002668541
   PROC MIXED call 1
```

```
iteration = 1
convergence criterion = 5.8002889E-7
B1=198.83340291 B2=7.6370684823 B3=-0.002668498
   PROC MIXED call 2


iteration = 2
convergence criterion = 3.0241946E-8
B1=198.83328758 B2=7.6370683959 B3=-0.0026685
   PROC MIXED call 3


iteration = 3
convergence criterion = 1.5757283E-9
B1=198.83329359 B2=7.6370684005 B3=-0.0026685
Convergence criteria met.
NOTE: Numeric values have been converted to character
      values at the places given by: (Line):(Column).
      3736:50
NOTE: The data set WORK._NLINMIX has 35 observations and 21
      variables.
NOTE: The DATA statement used 0:00:01.0 real 0:00:00.10 cpu.
   PROC MIXED call 4
NOTE: The data set WORK._SOLN has 3 observations and 9 variables.
NOTE: The data set WORK._COV has 2 observations and 9 variables.
NOTE: The data set WORK._FIT has 10 observations and 2 variables.
```

Note that the initial call to PROC NLIN did not converge for this particular model but that the macro is still able to iterate to convergence in just 3 steps.

The final PROC MIXED results are shown in Output 12.4.

Output 12.4 *Results for Method 3*

```
                    The MIXED Procedure

                 Class Level Information

          Class      Levels  Values

          _SUBJECT        5  1 2 3 4 5



              ML Estimation Iteration History

      Iteration Evaluations    Objective    Criterion

              0           1   230.90418958
              1           1   204.61942104   0.00000000

                 Convergence criteria met.
```

```
                  Covariance Parameter Estimates (MLE)

     Cov Parm          Ratio      Estimate     Std Error        Z


     DIAG CS         2.15047335   0.01837532   0.01239761     1.48
     Residual        1.00000000   0.00854478   0.00220625     3.87


                  Covariance Parameter Estimates (MLE)


                   Pr > |Z|   Alpha     Lower      Upper


                    0.1383    0.05    -0.0059     0.0427
                    0.0001    0.05     0.0042     0.0129



                  Model Fitting Information for _RESID
                            Weighted by _W


              Description                            Value


              Observations                         35.0000
              Variance Estimate                     0.0085
              Standard Deviation Estimate           0.0924
              Log Likelihood                      -134.473
              Akaike's Information Criterion       -136.473
              Schwarz's Bayesian Criterion        -138.028
              -2 Log Likelihood                    268.9451
              Null Model LRT Chi-Square             26.2848
              Null Model LRT DF                      1.0000
              Null Model LRT P-Value                 0.0000
                     Solution for Fixed Effects

Parameter     Estimate      Std Error     DDF       T   Pr > |T|   Alpha


D_B1       198.83329329   15.90382966    27    12.50    0.0001    0.05
D_B2         7.63706840    0.45455903    27    16.80    0.0001    0.05
D_B3        -0.00266850    0.00016579    27   -16.10    0.0001    0.05



                    Solution for Fixed Effects


                         Lower      Upper


                       166.2013   231.4653
                         6.7044     8.5697
                        -0.0030    -0.0023
```

```
                       Tests of Fixed Effects
            Source    NDF    DDF    Type III F    Pr > F
            D_B1       1      27       156.31     0.0001
            D_B2       1      27       282.28     0.0001
            D_B3       1      27       259.07     0.0001
```

Interpretation for Method 3

The estimate of the common correlation assumed in $\mathbf{R}(\phi)$ is obtained from values in the "Covariance Parameter Estimates" table:

$$\hat{\phi} = 0.01837532/(0.01837532+0.00854478)$$
$$= 0.68$$

The fixed-effects parameter estimates are $\hat{\beta}_1=198.83$, $\hat{\beta}_2=7.64$, and $\hat{\beta}_3=-.0027$. These values, along with their estimated standard errors and approximate confidence limits, are listed in the "Solution for Fixed Effects" table.

Program to Compare Powers

An interesting exercise is to fit models with different powers to see which one minimizes the approximate -2 Log Likelihood. For this model with a power of -2, its value is 268.9451. Values for other models are listed in the following data set:

```
data pom;
   input power m2ll;
   datalines;
-4      275.4207
-3.5    269.8219
-3      266.9001
-2.75   266.4461
-2.5    266.6548
-2.25   267.5017
-2      268.9451
-1      279.5383
 0      295.2636
run;
```

You can fit a quadratic curve through these points with the following program:

```
proc glm data=pom;
   model m2ll = power power*power;
run;
```

This program produces an optimal power estimate of $-22.0336041/4.1773302/2 = -2.637$.

Comparing the Three Methods

Table 12.5 summarizes the three previous analyses by presenting estimates for β_1, β_2, and β_3 and their approximate standard errors. Note that $\hat{\beta}_1$ and $\hat{\beta}_3$ from Method 3 are somewhat larger than the Method 1 and 2 estimates, whereas $\hat{\beta}_2$ is smaller. The standard errors from Method 3 are uniformly smaller. This illustrates that the choice of covariance model and analysis method can impact inferences on fixed effects.

Table 12.5 *Estimates of* β_1, β_2, β_3 *and their Estimated Standard Errors from the Logistic Model*

Method	$\hat{\beta}_1$ (SE)	$\hat{\beta}_2$ (SE)	$\hat{\beta}_3$ (SE)
1	192.69 (18.95)	7.86 (0.93)	-0.00283 (0.00021)
2	191.19 (17.12)	8.15 (0.89)	-0.00290 (0.00023)
3	198.83 (15.90)	7.64 (0.45)	-0.00267 (0.00017)

12.5 Example: One-Compartment Pharmacokinetic Model

For a more complex example, consider the phenobarbital data from Grasela and Donn (1985), which are also analyzed by Davidian and Gallant (1993). These are routine clinical data collected from 59 newborn infants treated with phenobarbital during the first 16 days after birth.

Data Set 12.5, "PHENO," in Appendix 4 lists the data, which are processed with the following statements:

```
data pheno;
   input indiv time dose weight apgar conc;
   retain cursub .;
   if cursub ne indiv then do;
      newsub = 1;
      cursub = indiv;
   end;
   else newsub = 0;
   if (apgar < 5) then apgarlow = 1;
   else apgarlow = 0;
   tlag = lag(time);
   if (newsub=1) then tlag = 0;
   drop apgar cursub;
   datalines;
...datalines...
run;
```

Table 12.6 describes the variables in the PHENO data set. Note that each time point represents either a dose administration or a concentration measurement.

Table 12.6 *Description of PHENO Data Set*

Variable	Description
INDIV	subject
NEWSUB	equals 1 if the current observation is from a new subject, 0 otherwise
TLAG	the previous time value of (if NEWSUB=0) or 0.0 (if NEWSUB=1)
DOSE	dose amount (in μg/kg)
WEIGHT	birthweight (in kg)
APGARLOW	equals 1 if 5-minute Apgar score is less than 5, 0 otherwise
CONC	plasma concentration of phenobarbital (in μg/kg)

You can use the following program to reproduce Figure 12.2, which graphs the subject profiles:

```
symbol i=join r=100;
proc gplot data=pheno;
   plot conc*time=indiv / nolegend;
run;
```

Subject 50 is a potential outlier because of its larger values, but it is retained in the analysis for comparison purposes.

Figure 12.2 *Phenobarbital Data*

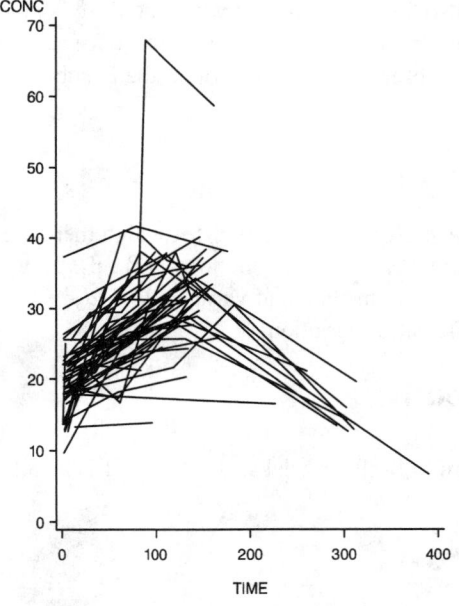

Model

The proposed pharmacokinetic model for mean phenobarbital concentration is a one-compartment open model with intravenous bolus administration and first-order elimination. The mean concentration for subject i at time t due to a single dose d_{ij} given at time $t_{ij} < t$ is modeled as

$$(d_{ij}/v_i)\exp[-(t-t_{ij})c_i/v_i]$$

Here c_i is the total clearance of phenobarbital in (liter/hour)/kg and v_i is the apparent volume of distribution of phenobarbital in liter/kg. The specific models for c_i and v_i in terms of fixed- and random-effects parameters are as follows:

$$c_i = \beta_1 w_i \exp(u_{1i})$$

$$v_i = \beta_2 w_i (1 + \beta_3 \delta_i) \exp(u_{2i})$$

where

β_1, β_2, and β_3 are the fixed-effects parameters to be estimated
u_{1i} and u_{2i} are the ith subject's random effects having mean 0 and variance-covariance matrix to be estimated
w_i is the ith subject's birth weight
δ_i equals 1 if the ith subject's 5-minute Apgar score is less than 5 and 0 otherwise.

Because each subject receives multiple doses, the concentration at any particular time is computed as the sum of the contributions from all doses received prior to that time. For computational purposes, it is convenient to write this sum recursively as

$$f(d_{ij}, t_{ij}, c_i, v_i) = d_{ij}/v_i + f(d_{i,j-1}, t_{i,j-1}, c_i, v_i)\exp[-(t_{ij}-t_{i,j-1})c_i/v_i]$$

where $f(d_{ij}, t_{ij}, c_i, v_i)$ is the concentration for subject i immediately after receiving dose d_{ij} at time t_{ij}. This expression also holds for times at which no dose is given if one simply sets $d_{ij} = 0$ for these times. This fact is exploited in the NLINMIX specification.

Letting y_{ik} denote the kth observed concentration of the ith subject, the complete stochastic model is

$$y_{ik} = f(d_{ik}, t_{ik}, c_i, v_i) + e_{ik}$$

where the d_{ik} and t_{ik} are the subset of the d_{ij} and t_{ij} for which there are observed measurements. Note here that c_i and v_i are functions of β_1, β_2, β_3, $\mathbf{u}_{1i}$, $\mathbf{u}_{2i}$. Finally, e_{ik} are unobserved Gaussian errors with mean 0 and variance $[\sigma f(d_{ik}, t_{ik}, c_i, v_i)]^2$, implying that the data have a constant coefficient of variation.

Program for Method 1

The NLINMIX program to fit this model with Method 1 is as follows:

```
%nlinmix(data=pheno,
    response=conc,
    subject=indiv,
    model=%str(
```

```
            clear = beta1*weight*exp(u1);
            vol = beta2*weight*(1+beta3*apgarlow)*exp(u2);
            eterm = exp(-(time-tlag)*clear/vol);
            pred = dose/vol + plag[call]*eterm;
            plag[call] = pred;
            call = call + 1;
        ),
        modinit=%str(
            array plag{11} _temporary_;
            if (newsub=1) then do call = 1 to 11;
               plag[call] = 0;
            end;
            call = 1;
        ),
        parms=%str(beta1=.01 beta2=1 beta3=.1),
        random=u1 u2,
        expand=zero,
        weight=1/pred**2
    )
  run;
```

The heart of the code is the MODEL= statement. Note that the CLEAR, VOL, and ETERM variables are all based directly on the theoretical model. The computation of the PRED variable uses the recursion relation, but some special coding discussed below is required in order to implement it correctly.

Because no derivatives are specified, NLINMIX computes them numerically. In order for NLINMIX to carry out the finite differencing correctly for each observation, however, it must retain two previous values of PRED for each of the fixed and random effect parameters. This results in 10 values to save, and these, plus the original prediction, make 11. Therefore, the array PLAG is created under the MODINIT= option with 11 elements. The MODINIT= option is called only once at the beginning of the DATA step processing for each observation, and is available for applications like this one.

The _TEMPORARY_ variables are used in PLAG because they are automatically retained and are not saved as a part of the data. The NEWSUB variable is used to initialize them to 0 for each new subject, and the CALL variable is used to index evaluations of the model. NLINMIX uses the first element of PLAG to save the actual prediction, and the other 10 those from numerical differentiation.

The PLAG array is unnecessary if you specify your own derivatives with the DERIVS= option; however, you would have to use the RETAIN statement to keep track of the previous value of PRED.

The PARMS= option specifies initial values for the fixed effects parameters, and RANDOM=U1 U2 specifies the two random effects. By default their covariance structure is simple variance components. EXPAND=ZERO requests the Method 1 expansion around 0, and the WEIGHT= option specifies a constant coefficient of variation, weighting by the reciprocal of the squared prediction.

Results

The SAS log from this program is shown in Output 12.5.

Output 12.5 *SAS Log for Method 1*

```
                      The NLINMIX Macro


              Data Set                : WORK.PHENO
              Response                : CONC
              Subject                 : INDIV
              Fixed Effects Parameters : BETA1 BETA2 BETA3
              Random Effects Parameters : U1 U2
              Covariance Type         : SIMPLE
              Expansion Point         : ZERO
              Weight                  : 1/PRED**2
              Optimization Method     : REML



                        Dimensions


              Observations            : 744
              Subjects                : 59
              Maximum Obs per Subject  : 20
              Fixed Effects Parameters : 3
              Random Effects per Subject : 2

Calling PROC NLIN to initialize.



WARNING: Step size shows no improvement.
WARNING: PROC NLIN failed to converge.


WARNING: PROC NLIN failed to converge.

Iteratively calling PROC MIXED.
   PROC MIXED call 0

iteration = 0
convergence criterion = .
BETA1=0.0047991795 BETA2=0.950986376 BETA3=0.218640263
   PROC MIXED call 1

iteration = 1
convergence criterion = 0.0034932327
BETA1=0.0046568331 BETA2=0.9672754424 BETA3=0.1436106997
   PROC MIXED call 2

iteration = 2
convergence criterion = 0.0000837881
BETA1=0.0046537704 BETA2=0.967261143 BETA3=0.1471039324
   PROC MIXED call 3
```

```
iteration = 3
convergence criterion = 5.1481435E-7
BETA1=0.0046538742 BETA2=0.967252209 BETA3=0.1471877205
   PROC MIXED call 4


iteration = 4
convergence criterion = 1.8306643E-8
BETA1=0.0046538758 BETA2=0.9672523113 BETA3=0.1471881928
   PROC MIXED call 5


iteration = 5
convergence criterion = 1.131183E-10
BETA1=0.0046538759 BETA2=0.9672523122 BETA3=0.147188194
Convergence criteria met.
NOTE: Numeric values have been converted to character
      values at the places given by: (Line):(Column).
      5751:50
NOTE: Missing values were generated as a result of performing an
      operation on missing values.
      Each place is given by: (Number of times) at (Line):(Column).
      589 at 5751:72
NOTE: The data set WORK._NLINMIX has 744 observations and 33
      variables.
NOTE: The DATA statement used 0:00:01.0 real 0:00:00.60 cpu.
   PROC MIXED call 6
NOTE: The data set WORK._SOLN has 3 observations and 9 variables.
NOTE: The data set WORK._COV has 3 observations and 9 variables.
NOTE: The data set WORK._SOLNR has 118 observations and 3 variables.
NOTE: The data set WORK._FIT has 10 observations and 2 variables.
```

The NLINMIX macro first echoes several specifications and then prints the dimensions of the problem. The calculations begin with an initial call to PROC NLIN; however, it fails to converge. This may be caused by inaccuracies due to numerical differentiation, but nonetheless, the final estimates of β_1, β_2, and β_3 serve as reasonable starting values for the PROC MIXED iterations.

The NLINMIX macro requires 5 calls to PROC MIXED to drop below the convergence tolerance of $1e$-8. All notes are suppressed during these iterations, but they are enabled again before a final call to PROC MIXED.

The WORK._NLINMIX data set is used as input for the sixth and final call to PROC MIXED, and four data sets are output as a result. The WORK._SOLN data set contains the fixed-effects parameter estimates and the WORK._COV data set those for the variance-covariance parameters. The WORK._SOLNR data set contains the EBLUPs of the random-effects parameters, and the WORK._FIT data set contains model fitting information. NLINMIX creates these data sets with the MAKE statement (see Appendix 3).

The output from the final call to PROC MIXED is shown in Output 12.6.

Output 12.6 *Results for Method 1*

```
                         The MIXED Procedure

                      Class Level Information

          Class     Levels  Values

          _SUBJECT      59  1 2 3 4 5 6 7 8 9 10 11 12 13
                            14 15 16 17 18 19 20 21 22 23
                            24 25 26 27 28 29 30 31 32 33
                            34 35 36 37 38 39 40 41 42 43
                            44 45 46 47 48 49 50 51 52 53
                            54 55 56 57 58 59
NOTE: 589 observations are not included because of missing values.

                         Parameter Search

      COL1       COL2        COL3  Variance   REML_LL   -2REML_LL

    0.0457     0.0283      0.0108    0.0108  -442.910    885.8209

                         Parameter Search

                           Objective

                            606.4636

                   REML Estimation Iteration History

         Iteration  Evaluations    Objective    Criterion

              1            1       606.4636    0.00000000

                    Convergence criteria met.

                Covariance Parameter Estimates (REML)

       Cov Parm       Ratio      Estimate     Std Error       Z

       D_U1       4.23755422   0.04566781   0.02121079     2.15
       D_U2       2.62332638   0.02827140   0.00698674     4.05
       Residual   1.00000000   0.01077693   0.00193095     5.58
```

Covariance Parameter Estimates (REML)

Pr > |Z|	Alpha	Lower	Upper
0.0313	0.05	0.0041	0.0872
0.0001	0.05	0.0146	0.0420
0.0001	0.05	0.0070	0.0146

Model Fitting Information for _RESID
Weighted by _W

Description	Value
Observations	155.0000
Variance Estimate	0.0108
Standard Deviation Estimate	0.1038
REML Log Likelihood	-442.910
Akaike's Information Criterion	-445.910
Schwarz's Bayesian Criterion	-450.446
-2 REML Log Likelihood	885.8209
PARMS Model LRT Chi-Square	0.0000
PARMS Model LRT DF	2.0000
PARMS Model LRT P-Value	1.0000

Solution for Fixed Effects

Parameter	Estimate	Std Error	DDF	T	Pr > |T|	Alpha
D_BETA1	0.00465388	0.00021953	45	21.20	0.0001	0.05
D_BETA2	0.96725231	0.02702044	45	35.80	0.0001	0.05
D_BETA3	0.14718819	0.07649945	45	1.92	0.0607	0.05

Solution for Fixed Effects

Lower	Upper
0.0042	0.0051
0.9128	1.0217
-0.0069	0.3013

Tests of Fixed Effects

Source	NDF	DDF	Type III F	Pr > F
D_BETA1	1	45	449.40	0.0001
D_BETA2	1	45	1281.43	0.0001
D_BETA3	1	45	3.70	0.0607

Interpretation for Method 1

The approximate REML estimates of the variances of u_{1i} and u_{2i} are 0.0457 and 0.0283, respectively. The covariance between them is assumed to equal 0 for this model, but you can estimate it by re-running the NLINMIX macro with the TYPE=UN option. (Doing this results in a covariance estimate of 0.0140, with the variance estimates changing to 0.0433 and 0.0242.) The estimate of σ^2 is 0.0108. Recall that you must multiply it by the estimated mean to obtain an estimate of the variance of e_{ik}.

The estimates of the fixed effects β_1, β_2, and β_3 are 0.0047, 0.9673, and 0.1472, respectively. These values and their estimated standard errors agree fairly well with the first-order method estimates reported by Grasela and Donn (1985) and Davidian and Gallant (1993), but they are not exactly the same. The "Solution for Random Effects" table is omitted because of its length of 118 rows. It contains 2 EBLUPs for each subject, and you can do a scatter plot of them with the following program:

```
data _solnr;
   set _solnr;
   sub = substr(subject,10) + 0;
run;

proc transpose data=_solnr out=eblup;
   var est;
   by sub;
   id parm;
run;

proc gplot data=eblup;
   plot d_u1*d_u2;
run;
```

SAS/INSIGHT is a useful tool for performing more extensive analyses of the EBLUPs and residuals.

Results for Method 2

To perform a Method 2 analysis of these data, use the EXPAND=EBLUP option. Table 12.7 displays the results from this model using METHOD=ML and TYPE=UN. Convergence is slower for this model, requiring 17 iterations. The estimates are close both to those obtained previously and to the normal effects maximum likelihood estimates in Table 2 of Davidian and Gallant (1993) computed using Gauss-Hermite quadrature.

Table 12.7 *Results from NLINMIX Using METHOD=ML, EXPAND=EBLUP, and TYPE=UN*

Parameter	Estimate	Standard Error
β_1	0.0048	0.0002
β_2	0.9769	0.0257
β_3	0.1349	0.0748
$var(u_{1i})$	0.0402	0.0180
$cov(u_{1i}, u_{2i})$	0.0202	0.00910
$var(u_{2i})$	0.230	0.0068
σ^2	0.0129	0.0022

12.6 Common Errors and Convergence Problems

Although NLINMIX attempts to recover from errors when possible, you may encounter cases where it exits abnormally. Because of its great flexibility, the SAS macro language is not always clear about precisely what makes it abend (exit abnormally). The following is a brief list of possible causes:

- there are missing variables in the input data set
- the input data set is not sorted by subject
- a syntax error appears in the NLINMIX specification in the form of missing or extra commas or semicolons.

If NLINMIX fails to converge, double check your MODEL= and DERIVS= (if you have any) specifications. Please be aware that the methods in the NLINMIX macro are not guaranteed to converge even when the specification is correct. Models which do not reasonably explain a data set are often difficult to fit to that data. Data with outliers can also cause problems.

If you feel that your model should be converging but isn't, the following suggestions may help:

- Rescale the data and model so that all parameters are of the same order of magnitude. This can improve the stability of the algorithms.

- If the convergence criterion appears to be descending nicely, you may only need to increase the maximum number of iterations using the MAXIT= option.

- Try different starting values, possibly those from EXPAND=ZERO if you are using EXPAND=EBLUP.

- Skip the initial PROC NLIN step by using OPTIONS=SKIPNLIN.

- If you are not specifying your own derivatives, use the TOL= option, which may help in computing them more accurately.

- The PROC MIXED itself is not converging, try the RIDGE= option. This option allows you to change the minimum initial ridge value applied to Hessian matrices, which are not positive definite. The default is 0.3125, and lowering it to 1e-3 or 1e-6 often works well.

- If you are using EXPAND=EBLUP, the GAUSS=, MAXSUBIT=, FRACTION=, and SUBCONV= options request NLINMIX to take extra Gauss-Newton steps within each iteration. Using these can help you achieve and speed convergence. They are documented as a part of the header portion of the macro (see Appendix 3).

12.7 Summary

This chapter considers mixed models for which the fixed and random effects enter nonlinearly. Standard likelihood approaches are much more difficult to implement in this situation than with the linear mixed models considered in previous chapters. Hence, three approximation methods are discussed, which work by iteratively fitting linear mixed models to pseudo-data. Using the NLINMIX macro, the methods are applied to two examples, one a straightforward logistic model and the other a more complex model from pharmacokinetics. Tips for troubleshooting the NLINMIX macro are also provided.

12.8 References

Beal, S.L. and Sheiner, L.B. (1982), Estimating population kinetics, *CRC Crit. Rev. Biomed. Eng.*, **8**, 195–222.

Beal, S.L. and Sheiner, L.B. (1988), Heteroskedastic nonlinear regression, *Technometrics*, **30**, 327–338.

Breslow, N.E. and Clayton, D.G. (1993), Approximate inference in generalized linear mixed models, *Journal of the American Statistical Association*, **88**, 9–25.

Carroll, R.J. and Ruppert, D. (1988), *Transformation and Weighting in Regression.*, London: Chapman and Hall.

Davidian, M. and Gallant, R.A. (1993), The nonlinear mixed effects model with a smooth random effects density, *Biometrika*, **80**, 475–488.

Davidian, M. and Giltinan, D. (1993), Some general estimation methods for nonlinear mixed effects models, *Journal of Biopharmaceutical Statistics*, **3**, 23–55.

Draper, N.R., and Smith, H. (1981), *Applied Regression Analysis, Second Edition*, New York: John Wiley & Sons, Inc.

Gennings, C., Chinchilli, V.M., and Carter, W.H. (1989), Response surface analysis with correlated data: a nonlinear model approach,. *Journal of the American Statistical Association*, **84**, 805–809.

Grasela, T.H., Jr. and Donn, S.M. (1985), Neonatal population pharmacokinetics for phenobarbital derived from routine clinical data, *Dev. Pharmacol. Ther*, **8**, 374–383.

Gumpertz, M.L. and Pantula, S.G. (1992), Nonlinear regression with variance components, *Journal of the American Statistical Association*, **87**, 201–209.

Hirst, K., Zerbe, G.O., Boyle, D.W., Wilkening, R.B. (1991), On nonlinear random effects models for repeated measurements, *Communications in Statistics Simulation*, **20**, 463–478.

Lindstrom, M.J. and Bates, D.M. (1990), Nonlinear mixed effects models for repeated measures data, *Biometrics,* **46**, 673–687.

Prentice, R.L. and Zhao, L.P. (1991), Estimating equations for parameters in means and covariances of multivariate discrete and continuous responses, *Biometrics*, **47**, 825–839.

Sheiner, L.B. and Beal, S.L. (1985), Pharmacokinetic parameter estimates from several least squares procedures: Superiority of extended least squares, *Journal of Pharmacokinetics and Biopharmaceutics,* **13**, 185–201.

Vonesh, E.F. (1995), A note on the use of Laplace's approximation for nonlinear mixed-effects models, Unpublished manuscript.

Vonesh, E.F. and Carter, R.L. (1992), Mixed-effects nonlinear regression for unbalanced repeated measures, *Biometrics*, **48**, 1–17.

Wolfinger, R.D. (1993), Laplace's approximation for nonlinear mixed models, *Biometrika*, **80**, 791-795.

Zeger, S.L., Liang, K.Y., and Albert, P.S. (1988), Models for longitudinal data: a generalized estimating equation approach, *Biometrics*, **44**, 1049–1060.

Appendix 1: **Mixed Models Theory**

Introduction

This appendix provides an overview of a modern approach to general linear mixed models. This approach simplifies and unifies many common statistical analyses, including those involving repeated measures, random effects, and random coefficients. The basic assumption is that the data are linearly related to unobserved multivariate normal random variables. Extensions to nonlinear and nonnormal situations are possible but are not discussed here.

Matrix Notation

Suppose you observe n data points $y_1, \ldots, y_n$ and you want to explain them using n values for each of p explanatory variables $x_{11}, \ldots, x_{1p}, x_{21}, \ldots, x_{2p}, \ldots, x_{n1}, \ldots, x_{np}$. The x_{ij} values may be either regression-type continuous variables or dummy variables indicating class membership. The standard linear model for this setup is

$$y_i = \sum_{j=1}^{p} x_{ij}\beta_j + e_i \qquad i = 1, \ldots, n$$

where $\beta_1, \ldots, \beta_p$ are unknown **fixed-effects parameters** to be estimated and $e_1, \ldots, e_n$ are unknown independent and identically distributed normal (Gaussian) random variables with mean 0 and variance σ^2.

The above equations can be written simultaneously using vectors and a matrix as follows:

$$
\begin{bmatrix} y_1 \\ y_2 \\ \vdots \\ y_n \end{bmatrix} = \begin{bmatrix} x_{11} & x_{12} & \cdots & x_{1p} \\ x_{21} & x_{22} & \cdots & x_{2p} \\ \vdots & \vdots & & \vdots \\ x_{n1} & x_{n2} & \cdots & x_{np} \end{bmatrix} \begin{bmatrix} \beta_1 \\ \beta_2 \\ \vdots \\ \beta_p \end{bmatrix} + \begin{bmatrix} e_1 \\ e_2 \\ \vdots \\ e_n \end{bmatrix}
$$

For convenience, simplicity, and extendability, we write this entire system as

$$\mathbf{y} = \mathbf{X}\beta + \mathbf{e}$$

where $\mathbf{y}$ denotes the vector of observed y_i's, $\mathbf{X}$ is the known matrix of x_{ij}'s, β is the unknown fixed-effects parameter vector, and $\mathbf{e}$ is the unobserved vector of independent and identically distributed Gaussian random errors.

In addition to denoting data, random variables, and explanatory variables in the preceding fashion, the subsequent development makes use of basic matrix operators such as transpose ($'$), inverse ($^{-1}$), generalized inverse ($^-$), determinant ($|\cdot|$), and matrix multiplication. Refer to Searle (1982) for details on these and other matrix techniques.

Formulation of the Mixed Model

The previous general linear model is certainly a useful one (Searle, 1971), and it is the one fitted by the GLM procedure. However, many times the distributional assumption about $\mathbf{e}$ is too restrictive. The mixed model extends the general linear model by allowing a more flexible specification of the covariance matrix of $\mathbf{e}$. In other words, it allows for both correlation and heterogeneous variances although you still assume normality.

The mixed model is written as

$$\mathbf{y} = \mathbf{X}\beta + \mathbf{Z}\mathbf{u} + \mathbf{e}$$

where everything is the same as in the general linear model except for the addition of the known design matrix, $\mathbf{Z}$, and the vector of unknown **random-effects parameters**, $\mathbf{u}$. $\mathbf{Z}$ can contain either continuous or dummy variables, just like $\mathbf{X}$. The name **mixed model** comes from the fact that the model contains both fixed-effects parameters, β, and random-effects parameters, $\mathbf{u}$. Refer to Henderson (1990) and Searle, Casella, and McCulloch (1992) for historical developments of the mixed model.

A key assumption in the foregoing analysis is that $\mathbf{u}$ and $\mathbf{e}$ are normally distributed with

$$
E\begin{bmatrix} \mathbf{u} \\ \mathbf{e} \end{bmatrix} = \begin{bmatrix} 0 \\ 0 \end{bmatrix}
$$

$$
\mathrm{Var}\begin{bmatrix} \mathbf{u} \\ \mathbf{e} \end{bmatrix} = \begin{bmatrix} \mathbf{G} & 0 \\ 0 & \mathbf{R} \end{bmatrix}
$$

The variance of $\mathbf{y}$ is therefore $\mathbf{V} = \mathbf{ZGZ'} + \mathbf{R}$. You can model $\mathbf{V}$ by setting up the random-effects design matrix $\mathbf{Z}$ and by specifying covariance structures for $\mathbf{G}$ and $\mathbf{R}$.

Note that this is a general specification of the mixed model, in contrast to many texts and articles that discuss only simple random effects. Simple random effects are a special case of the general specification with $\mathbf{Z}$ containing dummy variables, $\mathbf{G}$ containing variance components in a diagonal structure, and $\mathbf{R} = \sigma^2 \mathbf{I}_n$, where $\mathbf{I}_n$ denotes the $n \times n$ identity matrix. The general linear model is a further special case with $\mathbf{Z} = \mathbf{0}$ and $\mathbf{R} = \sigma^2 \mathbf{I}_n$.

The following two examples illustrate the most common formulations of the general linear mixed model.

Example: Growth Curve with Compound Symmetry

Suppose you have 3 growth curve measurements for s individuals, and you want to fit an overall linear trend in time. Your $\mathbf{X}$ matrix is as follows:

$$\mathbf{X} = \begin{bmatrix} 1 & 1 \\ 1 & 2 \\ 1 & 3 \\ \vdots & \vdots \\ 1 & 1 \\ 1 & 2 \\ 1 & 3 \end{bmatrix}$$

The first column (coded entirely with 1s) fits an intercept, and the second column (coded with times of 1,2,3) fits a slope. Here $n = 3s$ and $p = 2$.

Suppose further that you want to introduce a common correlation among the observations from a single individual, that correlation being the same for all individuals. One way of setting this up in the general mixed model is to eliminate the $\mathbf{Z}$ and $\mathbf{G}$ matrices and let the $\mathbf{R}$ matrix be block diagonal with blocks corresponding to the individuals, each block having the *compound-symmetry* structure. This structure has two unknown parameters, one modeling a common covariance and the other a residual variance. The form for $\mathbf{R}$ is then as follows:

$$\mathbf{R} = \begin{bmatrix} \sigma_1^2 + \sigma^2 & \sigma_1 & \sigma_1 & & & & \\ \sigma_1^2 & \sigma_1^2 + \sigma^2 & \sigma_1 & & & & \\ \sigma_1^2 & \sigma_1^2 & \sigma_1^2 + \sigma^2 & & & & \\ & & & \ddots & & & \\ & & & & \sigma_1^2 + \sigma^2 & \sigma_1^2 & \sigma_1^2 \\ & & & & \sigma_1^2 & \sigma_1^2 + \sigma^2 & \sigma_1^2 \\ & & & & \sigma_1^2 & \sigma_1^2 & \sigma_1^2 + \sigma^2 \end{bmatrix}$$

The PROC MIXED program to fit this model is the following:

```
proc mixed;
   class indiv;
   model y = time;
   repeated / type=cs subject=indiv;
run;
```

Here INDIV is a classification variable indexing individuals. The MODEL statement fits a straight line for TIME; the intercept is fit by default just as in PROC GLM. The REPEATED statement models the $\mathbf{R}$ matrix: TYPE=CS specifies the compound symmetry structure and SUBJECT=INDIV specifies the blocks of $\mathbf{R}$.

An alternative way of specifying the common intra-individual correlation is to let

$$\mathbf{Z} = \begin{bmatrix} 1 & & \\ 1 & & \\ 1 & & \\ & 1 & \\ & 1 & \\ & 1 & \\ & & \ddots & \\ & & & 1 \\ & & & 1 \\ & & & 1 \end{bmatrix}$$

$$\mathbf{G} = \begin{bmatrix} \sigma_1^2 & & & \\ & \sigma_1^2 & & \\ & & \ddots & \\ & & & \sigma_1^2 \end{bmatrix}$$

and $\mathbf{R} = \sigma^2 \mathbf{I}_n$. $\mathbf{Z}$ has $3s$ rows and s columns, and $\mathbf{G}$ is $s \times s$.
You can set up this model in PROC MIXED in 2 different but equivalent ways:

```
proc mixed;
   class indiv;
   model y = time;
   random indiv;
run;

proc mixed;
   class indiv;
   model y = time;
   random intercept / subject=indiv;
run;
```

Both of these specifications fit the same model as the previous one using the REPEATED statement; however, the RANDOM specifications constrain the correlation to be positive whereas the REPEATED specification leaves the correlation unconstrained.

Example: Split-Plot Design

The split-plot design involves two experimental treatment factors, **A** and **B**, and two different sizes of experimental units to which they are applied (refer to Winer 1971, Snedecor and Cochran 1980, Milliken and Johnson 1992). The levels of **A** are randomly assigned to the larger size of experimental unit, called **whole plots**, whereas the levels of **B** are assigned to the smaller size of experimental unit, the **subplots**. The subplots are assumed to be nested within the whole plots so that a whole plot consists of a cluster of subplots and a level of **A** is applied to the entire cluster.

Such an arrangement is often necessary by nature of the experiment, the classical example being the application of fertilizer to large plots of land, and different crop varieties planted in subdivisions of the large plots. For this example fertilizer is the whole plot factor **A** and variety the subplot factor **B**.

The first example is a split-plot design for which the whole plots are arranged in a randomized block design. The appropriate PROC MIXED program is as follows:

```
proc mixed;
   class a b block;
   model y = a|b;
   random block a*block;
run;
```

Here

$$\mathbf{R} = \sigma^2 \mathbf{I}_{24}$$

and **X**, **Z**, and **G** have the following form:

$$
\mathbf{X} = \begin{bmatrix}
1 & 1 & & 1 & & 1 & & & & & & \\
1 & 1 & & & 1 & & 1 & & & & & \\
1 & & 1 & 1 & & & & 1 & & & & \\
1 & & 1 & 1 & & & & & 1 & & & \\
1 & & & 1 & 1 & & & & & 1 & & \\
1 & & & 1 & 1 & & & & & & 1 & \\
\vdots & & \vdots & & \vdots & & & & \vdots & & & \\
1 & 1 & & 1 & & 1 & & & & & & \\
1 & 1 & & & 1 & & 1 & & & & & \\
1 & & 1 & 1 & & & & 1 & & & & \\
1 & & 1 & 1 & & & & & 1 & & & \\
1 & & & 1 & 1 & & & & & 1 & & \\
1 & & & 1 & 1 & & & & & & 1 &
\end{bmatrix}
$$

$$
\mathbf{Z} =
\begin{bmatrix}
1 & & 1 & & & \\
1 & & 1 & & & \\
1 & & & 1 & & \\
1 & & & 1 & & \\
1 & & & & 1 & \\
1 & & & & 1 & \\
& 1 & & & & 1 \\
& 1 & & & & 1 \\
& 1 & & & & & 1 \\
& 1 & & & & & 1 \\
& 1 & & & & & & 1 \\
& 1 & & & & & & 1 \\
& & 1 & & & & & & 1 \\
& & 1 & & & & & & 1 \\
& & 1 & & & & & & & 1 \\
& & 1 & & & & & & & 1 \\
& & 1 & & & & & & & & 1 \\
& & 1 & & & & & & & & 1 \\
& & & 1 & & & & & & & & 1 \\
& & & 1 & & & & & & & & 1 \\
& & & 1 & & & & & & & & & 1 \\
& & & 1 & & & & & & & & & 1 \\
& & & 1 & & & & & & & & & & 1 \\
& & & 1 & & & & & & & & & & 1 \\
\end{bmatrix}
$$

$$
\mathbf{G} =
\begin{bmatrix}
\sigma_B^2 & & & & & & & \\
& \sigma_B^2 & & & & & & \\
& & \sigma_B^2 & & & & & \\
& & & \sigma_B^2 & & & & \\
& & & & \sigma_{AB}^2 & & & \\
& & & & & \sigma_{AB}^2 & & \\
& & & & & & \ddots & \\
& & & & & & & \sigma_{AB}^2
\end{bmatrix}
$$

where σ_B^2 is the variance component for BLOCK and σ_{AB}^2 is the variance component for A*BLOCK. Changing the RANDOM statement to

```
random int a / subject=block;
```

fits the same model, but with **Z** and **G** sorted differently:

$$
\mathbf{Z} = \begin{bmatrix}
1 & 1 & & & & & & & & & & \\
1 & 1 & & & & & & & & & & \\
1 & & 1 & & & & & & & & & \\
1 & & 1 & & & & & & & & & \\
1 & & & 1 & & & & & & & & \\
1 & & & 1 & & & & & & & & \\
& & & & 1 & 1 & & & & & & \\
& & & & 1 & 1 & & & & & & \\
& & & & 1 & & 1 & & & & & \\
& & & & 1 & & 1 & & & & & \\
& & & & 1 & & & 1 & & & & \\
& & & & 1 & & & 1 & & & & \\
& & & & & & & & 1 & 1 & & \\
& & & & & & & & 1 & 1 & & \\
& & & & & & & & 1 & & 1 & \\
& & & & & & & & 1 & & 1 & \\
& & & & & & & & 1 & & & 1 \\
& & & & & & & & 1 & & & 1 \\
& & & & & & & & & & & & 1 & 1 \\
& & & & & & & & & & & & 1 & 1 \\
& & & & & & & & & & & & 1 & & 1 \\
& & & & & & & & & & & & 1 & & 1 \\
& & & & & & & & & & & & 1 & & & 1 \\
& & & & & & & & & & & & 1 & & & 1
\end{bmatrix}
$$

$$
\mathbf{G} = \begin{bmatrix}
\sigma_B^2 & & & & & & & & \\
& \sigma_{AB}^2 & & & & & & & \\
& & \sigma_{AB}^2 & & & & & & \\
& & & \sigma_{AB}^2 & & & & & \\
& & & & \ddots & & & & \\
& & & & & \sigma_B^2 & & & \\
& & & & & & \sigma_{AB}^2 & & \\
& & & & & & & \sigma_{AB}^2 & \\
& & & & & & & & \sigma_{AB}^2
\end{bmatrix}
$$

Estimating G and R in the Mixed Model

Estimation is more difficult in the mixed model than in the general linear model. Not only do you have β as in the general linear model, but you have unknown parameters in $\mathbf{u}$, $\mathbf{G}$, and $\mathbf{R}$ as well. Least-squares is no longer the best method. **Generalized least-squares (GLS)** is more appropriate, minimizing

$$(y - \mathbf{X}\beta)' \mathbf{V}^{-1}(y - \mathbf{X}\beta)$$

However, GLS requires knowledge of $\mathbf{V}$ and, therefore, knowledge of $\mathbf{G}$ and $\mathbf{R}$. Lacking such information, one approach is to use **estimated** GLS, in which you insert some reasonable estimate for $\mathbf{V}$ into the minimization problem. The goal thus becomes finding a reasonable estimate of $\mathbf{G}$ and $\mathbf{R}$.

In many situations, the best approach is to use **likelihood-based** methods, exploiting the assumption that $\mathbf{u}$ and $\mathbf{e}$ are normally distributed (Hartley and Rao 1967, Patterson and Thompson 1971, Harville 1977, Laird and Ware 1982, Jennrich and Schluchter 1986). PROC MIXED implements two likelihood-based methods: **maximum likelihood** (ML) and **restricted/residual maximum likelihood** (REML). PROC MIXED constructs an objective function associated with ML or REML and maximizes it over all unknown parameters. Using a little calculus, it is possible to reduce this maximization problem to one over only the parameters in $\mathbf{G}$ and $\mathbf{R}$. The corresponding log likelihood functions are as follows:

$$ML: \quad l(\mathbf{G},\mathbf{R}) = -\frac{1}{2}\log|\mathbf{V}| - \frac{1}{2}\mathbf{r}'\mathbf{V}^{-1}\mathbf{r} - \frac{n}{2}\log 2\pi$$

$$REML: \quad l_R(\mathbf{G},\mathbf{R}) = -\frac{1}{2}\log|\mathbf{V}| - \frac{1}{2}\log|\mathbf{X}'\mathbf{V}^{-1}\mathbf{X}|$$
$$- \frac{1}{2}\mathbf{r}'\mathbf{V}^{-1}\mathbf{r} - \frac{n-p}{2}\log 2\pi$$

where $\mathbf{r} = \mathbf{y} - \mathbf{X}(\mathbf{X}'\mathbf{V}^{-1}\mathbf{X})^{-}\mathbf{X}'\mathbf{V}^{-1}\mathbf{y}$ and p is the rank of $\mathbf{X}$. PROC MIXED minimizes -2 times these functions using a ridge-stabilized Newton-Raphson algorithm. Lindstrom and Bates (1988) provide reasons for preferring Newton-Raphson to the Expectation-Maximum (EM) algorithm described in Dempster, Laird, and Rubin (1977) and Laird, Lange, and Stram (1987), as well as analytical details for implementing a QR-decomposition approach to the problem. Wolfinger, Tobias, and Sall (1994) present the sweep-based algorithms that are implemented in PROC MIXED.

One advantage of using the Newton-Raphson algorithm is that the second derivative matrix of the objective function evaluated at the optima is available upon completion. Denoting this matrix $\mathbf{H}$, the asymptotic theory of maximum likelihood (refer to Serfling 1980) shows that $2\mathbf{H}^{-1}$ is an asymptotic variance-covariance matrix of the estimated parameters of $\mathbf{G}$ and $\mathbf{R}$. Thus, tests and confidence intervals based on asymptotic normality can be obtained. However, these can be unreliable in small samples, especially for parameters such as variance components whose small-sample sampling distributions tend to be skewed to the right.

Instead of ML or REML, you can use the noniterative MIVQUE0 method to estimate $\mathbf{G}$ and $\mathbf{R}$ (Rao 1972, LaMotte 1973, Wolfinger, Tobias, and Sall 1994). However, Swallow and Monahan (1984) present simulation evidence favoring REML and ML over MIVQUE0. MIVQUE0 is recommended primarily for large data sets or for situations when the iterative REML and ML procedures fail to converge.

Estimating β and u in the Mixed Model

ML, REML, or MIVQUE0 provide estimates of $\mathbf{G}$ and $\mathbf{R}$, which are denoted $\hat{\mathbf{G}}$ and $\hat{\mathbf{R}}$. To obtain estimates of β and $\mathbf{u}$, the standard method is to solve the **mixed model equations** (Henderson, 1984):

$$
\begin{bmatrix} \mathbf{X}'\hat{\mathbf{R}}^{-1}\mathbf{X} & \mathbf{X}'\hat{\mathbf{R}}^{-1}\mathbf{Z} \\ \mathbf{Z}'\hat{\mathbf{R}}^{-1}\mathbf{X} & \mathbf{Z}'\hat{\mathbf{R}}^{-1}\mathbf{Z}+\hat{\mathbf{G}}^{-1} \end{bmatrix} \begin{bmatrix} \hat{\beta} \\ \hat{\mathbf{u}} \end{bmatrix} = \begin{bmatrix} \mathbf{X}'\hat{\mathbf{R}}^{-1}\mathbf{y} \\ \mathbf{Z}'\hat{\mathbf{R}}^{-1}\mathbf{y} \end{bmatrix}
$$

The solutions can also be written as

$$
\hat{\beta} = (\mathbf{X}'\hat{\mathbf{V}}^{-1}\mathbf{X})^{-}\mathbf{X}'\hat{\mathbf{V}}^{-1}\mathbf{y}
$$
$$
\hat{\mathbf{u}} = \hat{\mathbf{G}}\mathbf{Z}'\hat{\mathbf{V}}^{-1}(\mathbf{y}-\mathbf{X}\hat{\beta})
$$

and have connections with empirical Bayes estimators (Laird and Ware 1982).

Note that the mixed model equations are extended normal equations, and the above expression assumes that $\hat{\mathbf{G}}$ is nonsingular. For the extreme case when the eigenvalues of $\hat{\mathbf{G}}$ are very large, $\hat{\mathbf{G}}^{-1}$ contributes very little to the equations and $\hat{\mathbf{u}}$ is close to what it would be if $\mathbf{u}$ actually contained fixed-effects parameters. On the other hand, when the eigenvalues of $\hat{\mathbf{G}}$ are very small, $\hat{\mathbf{G}}^{-1}$ dominates the equations and $\hat{\mathbf{u}}$ is close to $\mathbf{0}$. If $\hat{\mathbf{G}}$ is singular, then the equations must be modified (Henderson 1984), and the elements of $\hat{\mathbf{u}}$ corresponding to the singular portion of $\hat{\mathbf{G}}$ equal $\mathbf{0}$. An example of this situation is when a variance component estimate falls on the boundary constraint of $\mathbf{0}$. For intermediate cases, $\hat{\mathbf{G}}^{-1}$ can be viewed as shrinking the fixed-effects estimates of $\mathbf{u}$ towards $\mathbf{0}$ (Robinson 1991).

Chapter 6 shows how this shrinkage works for simple mixed models.

Model Selection

The previous section on estimation assumes the specification of a mixed model in terms of **X**, **Z**, **G**, and **R**. Even though **X** and **Z** have known elements, their specific form and construction is flexible, and several possibilities may present themselves for a particular data set. Likewise, several different covariance structures for **G** and **R** might be reasonable.

Space does not permit a thorough discussion of model selection, but a few brief comments and references are in order. First, subject matter considerations and objectives should certainly be foremost in the analyst's mind when selecting a model. Interested readers are referred to Diggle (1988) and Lindsey (1993).

Second, when the data themselves are looked to for guidance, many of the graphical methods and diagnostics appropriate for the general linear model extend to the mixed model setting as well (Christensen, Pearson, and Johnson 1992).

Finally, a likelihood-based approach to the mixed model provides several statistical measures for model adequacy as well. The most common of these are the likelihood ratio test and Akaike's and Schwarz's criteria (Bozdogan 1987, Wolfinger 1993).

Statistical Properties

If **G** and **R** are known, $\hat{\beta}$ is the **best linear unbiased estimator** (BLUE) of β and $\hat{u}$ is the **best linear unbiased predictor** (BLUP) of **u** (Searle 1971, Harville 1988, 1990, Robinson 1991, McLean, Sanders, and Stroup 1991). Here **best** means minimum mean squared error. The covariance matrix of $\hat{\beta}$ and $\hat{u}$ is

$$C = \begin{bmatrix} X'R^{-1}X & X'R^{-1}Z \\ Z'R^{-1}X & Z'R^{-1}Z+G^{-1} \end{bmatrix}^{-}$$

where $^{-}$ to denote a generalized inverse (refer to Searle 1971).

However, **G** and **R** are usually unknown and are estimated using one of the aforementioned methods. These estimates, $\hat{G}$ and $\hat{R}$, are therefore simply substituted into the preceding expression to obtain

$$\hat{C} = \begin{bmatrix} X'\hat{R}^{-1}X & X'\hat{R}^{-1}Z \\ Z'\hat{R}^{-1}X & Z'\hat{R}^{-1}Z+\hat{G}^{-1} \end{bmatrix}^{-}$$

as the approximate variance-covariance matrix of $\hat{\beta}$ and $\hat{u}$. In this case, the BLUE and BLUP acronyms no longer apply, but the word **empirical** is often added to indicate such an approximation. The appropriate acronyms thus become **EBLUE** and **EBLUP**.

Henderson (1984) and McLean and Sanders (1988) show that $\hat{\mathbf{C}}$ can also be written as

$$\hat{\mathbf{C}} = \begin{bmatrix} \hat{\mathbf{C}}_{11} & \hat{\mathbf{C}}_{21}' \\ \hat{\mathbf{C}}_{21} & \hat{\mathbf{C}}_{22} \end{bmatrix}$$

where

$$\hat{\mathbf{C}}_{11} = (\mathbf{X}'\mathbf{V}^{-1}\mathbf{X})^-$$
$$\hat{\mathbf{C}}_{21} = -\mathbf{G}\mathbf{Z}'\mathbf{V}^{-1}\mathbf{X}\hat{\mathbf{C}}_{11}$$
$$\hat{\mathbf{C}}_{22} = (\mathbf{Z}'\mathbf{R}^{-1}\mathbf{Z}+\hat{\mathbf{G}}^{-1})^{-1} - \hat{\mathbf{C}}_{21}\mathbf{X}'\mathbf{V}^{-1}\mathbf{Z}\hat{\mathbf{G}}$$

Note that $\hat{\mathbf{C}}_{11}$ is the familiar formula for the estimated variance-covariance matrix of the GLS estimate of β.

As a cautionary note, $\hat{\mathbf{C}}$ tends to underestimate the true sampling variability of $\hat{\beta}$ and $\hat{\mathbf{u}}$ because no account is made for the uncertainty in estimating $\mathbf{G}$ and $\mathbf{R}$. Although inflation factors have been proposed (Kackar and Harville 1984, Kass and Steffey 1989, Prasad and Rao 1990), they tend to be small for data sets that are fairly well balanced. PROC MIXED does not currently compute any inflation factors, but rather accounts for the downward bias by using the approximate t- and F-statistics described subsequently.

Inference and Test Statistics

For inferences concerning the covariance parameters in your model, you can use likelihood-based statistics. One common such statistic is the **Wald Z**, which is computed as the parameter estimate divided by its asymptotic standard error. The asymptotic standard errors are computed from the inverse of the second derivative matrix of the likelihood with respect to each of the covariance parameters. The Wald Z is valid for large samples, but it can be unreliable for small data sets and for parameters such as variance components that are known to have a skewed or bounded sampling distribution.

A better alternative is the likelihood ratio χ^2. This statistic compares two covariance models, one a special case of the other. To compute it, you must run PROC MIXED twice, once for each of the two models, and then subtract the corresponding values of -2 times the log likelihoods. You can use either ML or REML to construct this statistic, which tests if the full model is necessary beyond the reduced model. Several examples of the likelihood ratio test are given throughout this book. See Chapters 2, 3, 8, and 9.

As long as the reduced model does not occur on the boundary of the covariance parameter space, the χ^2-statistic computed in this fashion has a large-sample sampling distribution which is χ^2 with degrees of freedom equal to the difference in the number of covariance parameters between the two models. If the reduced model does occur on the boundary of the covariance parameter space, you must make adjustments to the asymptotic distribution (Self and Liang 1987). A common example of this is when you are testing that a variance component equals its lower boundary constraint of 0.

For inferences concerning the fixed- and random-effects parameters in the mixed model, consider estimable linear combinations of the following form:

$$\mathbf{L}\begin{bmatrix} \beta \\ \mathbf{u} \end{bmatrix}$$

Functions of this form are called predictable functions if the β-portion satisfies the estimability requirement (Searle 1971). Chapter 6 gives examples of the logic underlying the construction of predictable functions. Such a formulation in terms of a general **L** matrix encompasses a wide variety of common inferential procedures such as those employed with Type I and III tests and least squares means. The CONTRAST and ESTIMATE statements in PROC MIXED allow you to specify your own **L** matrices. Typically inference on fixed effects is the focus, and in this case the **u** portion of **L** is assumed to contain all 0s.

Statistical inferences are obtained by testing the hypothesis

$$H:\mathbf{L}\begin{bmatrix}\beta\\\mathbf{u}\end{bmatrix} = \mathbf{0}$$

or by constructing point and/or interval estimates.

When **L** consists of a single row, a general t-statistic can be constructed as follows:

$$t = \frac{\mathbf{L}\begin{bmatrix}\hat{\beta}\\\mathbf{u}\end{bmatrix}}{\sqrt{\mathbf{L}\hat{\mathbf{C}}\mathbf{L}'}}$$

See McLean and Sanders (1988), and Stroup (1989) for details. Under the assumed normality of **u** and **e**, t has an exact t-distribution only for data exhibiting certain types of balance and for some special unbalanced cases. In general, t is only approximately t-distributed, and its degrees of freedom must be estimated. See the DDFM= option in the MODEL statement for a description of the various degrees of freedom methods available in PROC MIXED.

Letting $\hat{\nu}$ be the approximate degrees of freedom, the associated confidence interval is the following:

$$\mathbf{L}\begin{bmatrix}\hat{\beta}\\\mathbf{u}\end{bmatrix} \pm t_{\hat{\nu},\alpha/2}\sqrt{\mathbf{L}\hat{\mathbf{C}}\mathbf{L}'}$$

where $t_{\hat{\nu},\alpha/2}$ is the $(1-\alpha/2)100^{th}$ percentile of the $t_{\hat{\nu}}$-distribution.

When the rank of **L** is greater than 1, PROC MIXED constructs the following general F-statistic:

$$F = \frac{\begin{bmatrix}\hat{\beta}\\\mathbf{u}\end{bmatrix}'\mathbf{L}'(\mathbf{L}'\hat{\mathbf{C}}\mathbf{L})^{-1}\mathbf{L}\begin{bmatrix}\hat{\beta}\\\mathbf{u}\end{bmatrix}}{\text{rank}(\mathbf{L})}$$

Analogous to t, F in general has an approximate F-distribution, with rank(**L**) numerator degrees of freedom and $\hat{\nu}$ denominator degrees of freedom.

The t- and F-statistics allow you to make inferences about your fixed effects that account for the variance-covariance model you select. An alternative is the χ^2-statistic associated with the likelihood ratio test. This statistic compares two fixed-effects models, one a special case of the other. It is computed just as when comparing different covariance models. You should use ML and not REML here, however, because the penalty term associated with restricted likelihoods depends upon the fixed-effects specification.

References

Akaike, H. (1974), A new look at the statistical model identification, *IEEE Transaction on Automatic Control*, AC-19, 716–723.

Bozdogan, H. (1987), Model selection and Akaike's information criterion (AIC): the general theory and its analytical extensions, *Psychometrika*, **52**, 345–370.

Christensen, R., Pearson, L.M., and Johnson, W. (1992), Case-deletion diagnostics for mixed models, *Technometrics*, **34**, 38–45.

Dempster, A.P., Laird, N.M., and Rubin, D.B. (1977), Maximum likelihood from incomplete data via the EM algorithm, Ser. B., **39**, 1–38.

Diggle, P.J. (1988), An approach to the analysis of repeated measurements, *Biometrics*, **44**, 959–971.

Hartley, H.O., and Rao, J.N.K. (1967), Maximum-likelihood estimation for the mixed analysis of variance model, *Biometrika*, **54**, 93–108.

Harville, D. A. (1977), Maximum likelihood approaches to variance component estimation and to related problems, *Journal of the American Statistical Association*, **72**, 320–338.

Harville, D. A. (1988), Mixed-model Methodology: theoretical justifications and future directions, *Proceedings of the Statistical Computing Section*, New Orleans: American Statistical Association, 41–49.

Harville, D. A. (1990), BLUP (best linear unbiased prediction), and beyond, in *Advances in Statistical Methods for Genetic Improvement of Livestock*, New York: Springer-Verlag, 239–276.

Henderson, C. R. (1984), *Applications of Linear Models in Animal Breeding*, University of Guelph.

Henderson, C. R. (1990), Statistical method in animal improvement: historical overview, in *Advances in Statistical Methods for Genetic Improvement of Livestock*, Springer-Verlag, 1–14.

Jennrich, R. I. and Schluchter, M. D. (1986), Unbalanced repeated-measures models with structured covariance matrices, *Biometrics*, **42**, 805–820.

Kackar, R.N. and Harville, D. A. (1984), Approximations for standard errors of estimators of fixed and random effects in mixed linear models, *Journal of the American Statistical Association*, **79**, 853–862.

Kass, R.E. and Steffey, D. (1989), Approximate Bayesian inference in conditionally independent hierarchical models (parametric empirical Bayes models), *Journal of the American Statistical Association*, **84**, 717–726.

Laird, N.M., Lange, N., and Stram, D. (1987), Maximum likelihood computations with repeated measures: application of the EM algorithm, *Journal of the American Statistical Association*, **82**, 97–105.

Laird, N.M. and Ware, J.H. (1982), Random-effects models for longitudinal data, *Biometrics*, **38**, 963–974.

LaMotte, L.R. (1973), Quadratic estimation of variance components, *Biometrics*, **29**, 311–330.

Liang, K.Y. and Zeger, S.L. (1986), Longitudinal data analysis using generalized linear models, *Biometrika*, **73**, 13–22.

Lindsey, J.K. (1993), *Models for Repeated Measurements*, Oxford: Clarendon Press.

Lindstrom, M.J. and Bates, D.M. (1988), Newton-Raphson and EM algorithms for linear mixed-effects models for repeated-measures data, *Journal of the American Statistical Association*, **83**, 1014–1022.

McLean, R.A. and Sanders, W.L. (1988), Approximating degrees of freedom for standard errors in mixed linear models, *Proceedings of the Statistical Computing Section*, New Orleans: American Statistical Association, 50–59.

McLean, R.A., Sanders, W.L., and Stroup, W.W. (1991), A unified approach to mixed linear models, *The American Statistician*, **45**, 54–64.

Milliken, G.A. and Johnson, D.E. (1992), *Analysis of Messy Data, Volume 1: Designed Experiments*, New York: Chapman and Hall.

Patterson, H.D. and Thompson, R. (1974), Recovery of inter-block information when block sizes are unequal, *Biometrika*, **58**, 545–554.

Prasad, N.G.N. and Rao, J.N.K. (1990), The estimation of mean squared error of small-area estimators, *Journal of the American Statistical Association*, **85**, 163–171.

Rao, C.R. (1972), Estimation of variance and covariance components in linear models, *Journal of the American Statistical Association*, **67**, 112–115.

Robinson, G.K. (1991), That BLUP is a good thing: the estimation of random effects, *Statistical Science*, **6**, 15–51.

SAS Institute Inc. (1996), *SAS/STAT Software: Changes and Enhancements through Release 6.11*, Cary, NC: SAS Institute Inc.

Searle, S. R. (1971), *Linear Models*, New York: John Wiley & Sons, Inc.

Searle, S.R. (1982), *Matrix Algebra Useful for Statistics*, New York: John Wiley & Sons, Inc.

Searle, S. R., Casella, G., and McCulloch, C. E. (1992), *Variance Components*, New York: John Wiley & Sons, Inc.

Self, S.G. and Liang, K.Y. (1987), Asymptotic properties of maximum likelihood estimators and likelihood ratio tests under nonstandard conditions, *Journal of the American Statistical Association*, **82**, 605–610.

Serfling, R.J. (1980), *Approximation Theorems of Mathematical Statistics*, New York: John Wiley & Sons, Inc.

Snedecor, G.W. and Cochran, W.G. (1980), *Statistical Methods*, Ames: The Iowa State University Press.

Stroup, W.W. (1989), Predictable functions and prediction space in the mixed model procedure, in *Applications of Mixed Models in Agriculture and Related Disciplines*, Southern Cooperative Series Bulletin No. 343, Baton Rouge: Louisiana Agricultural Experiment Station, 39–48.

Swallow, W.H. and Monahan, J.F. (1984), Monte Carlo comparison of ANOVA, MIVQUE, REML, and ML estimators of variance components. *Technometrics*, 26, 47–57.

Winer, B.J. (1971), *Statistical Principles in Experimental Design*, Second Edition, New York: McGraw-Hill, Inc.

Wolfinger, R.D. (1993), Covariance structure selection in general mixed models, *Communications in Statistics Simulation and Computation*, **22**(4), 1079–1106.

Wolfinger, R.D., Tobias, R.D., and Sall, J. (1994), Computing Gaussian likelihoods and their derivatives for general linear mixed models, *SIAM Journal on Scientific Computing*, **15**(6), 1294–1310.

Appendix **2 GLIMMIX Macro**

```
/*-------------------------------------------------------------*/
/* TITLE                                                       */
/* -----                                                       */
/* GLIMMIX: a SAS macro for fitting generalized linear mixed   */
/* models using PROC MIXED and the Output Delivery System (ODS).*/
/* Requires SAS/STAT release 6.08 or later.                    */
/*                                                             */
/* SUPPORT                                                     */
/* -------                                                     */
/* Russ Wolfinger, SAS Institute Inc.  The original version was */
/* written by Jason Brown, formerly of SAS Institute Inc.      */
/* Please send email to sasrdw@unx.sas.com with any suggestions */
/* or corrections.                                             */
/*                                                             */
/* HISTORY                                                     */
/* -------                                                     */
/* initial coding                                01Jun92  jbb  */
/* a few changes and additions                   09Oct92  rdw  */
/* corrections from Dale McLerran, FHCRC          16Feb94  rdw  */
/* suggestions from David Murray, U. Minnesota    21Sep95  rdw  */
/* suggestions from Ken Goldberg, Wyeth-Ayerst    27Oct95  rdw  */
/*                                                             */
/* DESCRIPTION                                                 */
/* -----------                                                 */
/* The macro uses iteratively reweighted likelihoods to fit the */
/* model; refer to Wolfinger, R. and O'Connell, M., 1993,      */
/* ``Generalized Linear Mixed Models:  A Pseudo-Likelihood     */
/* Approach,'' Journal of Statistical Computation and          */
/* Simulation, 48.                                             */
/*                                                             */
/* By default, GLIMMIX uses restricted/residual psuedo         */
/* likelihood (REPL) to find the parameter estimates of the    */
/* generalized linear mixed model you specify.  The macro calls */
/* PROC MIXED iteratively until convergence, which is decided  */
/* using the relative deviation of the variance/covariance     */
/* parameter estimates. An extra-dispersion scale parameter is */
/* estimated by default.                                       */
/*                                                             */
/* There are a few macros at the beginning; all are used in the */
/* main macro, GLIMMIX.  This macro will work on any type of   */
/* model with the error distributions and link functions given */
/* in the ERRLINK macro.  In addition, you can specify your    */
/* own error and/or link functions.  In order to do this, you  */
/* must specify error=user and/or link=user in conjunction with */
/* the errvar=, errdev=, linku=, linkud=, and linkui= options. */
/*                                                             */
/* The relevant information is saved using the MAKE statement  */
/* of PROC MIXED, which is a part of ODS.                      */
/*                                                             */
/* The following are reserved variable names and should not be */
/* used in your input SAS data set:                            */
/*                                                             */
/*    _col, _deta, _eta, _pred, _mu, _var, _offset, _orig, _w, _wght, */
/*    _y, _z                                                   */
/*                                                             */
/* SYNTAX                                                      */
/* ------                                                      */
/* Syntax for the macro is similar to that of PROC MIXED.      */
/* There are other options that are macro-specific, however.   */
/*                                                             */
/* %glimmix(data=,                                             */
/*     procopt=,                                               */
```

```
/*      stmts=,                                                          */
/*      weight=,                                                         */
/*      freq=,                                                           */
/*      error=,                                                          */
/*      errvar=,                                                         */
/*      errdev=,                                                         */
/*      link=,                                                           */
/*      linkn=,                                                          */
/*      linknd=,                                                         */
/*      linkni=,                                                         */
/*      linku=,                                                          */
/*      linkud=,                                                         */
/*      linkui=,                                                         */
/*      approx=,                                                         */
/*      cf=,                                                             */
/*      offset=,                                                         */
/*      output=,                                                         */
/*      title=,                                                          */
/*      options=                                                         */
/*   )                                                                   */
/*                                                                       */
/*   where                                                               */
/*                                                                       */
/*   data     specifies the data set you are using.                     */
/*                                                                       */
/*   procopt  specifies options appropriate for a PROC                   */
/*            MIXED statement.  Refer to the PROC MIXED                  */
/*            documentation for more information.                        */
/*                                                                       */
/*   stmts    specifies PROC MIXED statements for the analysis,          */
/*            separated by semicolons and listed as a single            */
/*            argument to the %str() macro function.  Statements         */
/*            may include any of the following:  CLASS, MODEL,           */
/*            RANDOM, REPEATED, PARMS, ID, CONTRAST, ESTIMATE,           */
/*            and LSMEANS.  Syntax and options for each                  */
/*            statement are exactly as in the PROC MIXED                 */
/*            documentation.                                             */
/*                                                                       */
/*   weight   specifies a weighting variable for the analysis           */
/*            This allows you to construct your own weights             */
/*            which can modify or replace the ones constructed           */
/*            by GLIMMIX.                                                */
/*                                                                       */
/*   freq     specifies a frequency variable for the analysis.          */
/*            It replicates observations with the number of              */
/*            replicates being equal to the value of the FREQ           */
/*            variable.                                                  */
/*                                                                       */
/*   error    specifies the error distribution. Valid types are:        */
/*                                                                       */
/*                binomial|b, normal|n, poisson|p, gamma|g,             */
/*                invgaussian|ig, and user|u                            */
/*                                                                       */
/*            When you specify error=user, you must also provide        */
/*            the errvar= and errdev= options.  The default             */
/*            error distribution is binomial.                            */
/*                                                                       */
/*   errvar   specifies the user-defined variance function.  It         */
/*            must be expressed as a function the argument "mu"          */
/*            (see examples).                                            */
/*                                                                       */
/*   errdev   specifies the user-defined deviance function.  It         */
/*            must be expressed as a function the arguments              */
/*            "_y", which is the response variable, and "mu",           */
/*            which is the mean.  You are allowed to use "_wght"         */
/*            also, which corresponds to the denominator of a            */
/*            binomial response.  Typical deviance functions are         */
/*            as follows:                                                */
```

```
/*                                                            */
/*            normal         (_y-mu)**2                       */
/*            poisson        2*_y*log(_y/mu);                 */
/*            binomial       2*_wght*(_y*log(_y/mu)+          */
/*                           (1-_y)*log((1-_y)/(1-mu)))       */
/*            gamma          -2*log(_y/mu)                     */
/*            invgaussian    (((_y-mu)**2)/(_y*mu*mu))        */
/*                                                            */
/*            The default deviance is binomial.               */
/*                                                            */
/*  link      specifies the link function. Valid types are    */
/*                                                            */
/*                logit, probit, cloglog, loglog, identity,   */
/*                power(), log, exp, reciprocal, nlin, and user. */
/*                (warning: nlin has not been tested)          */
/*                                                            */
/*                When you specify link=nlin, you must also provide */
/*                the linkn=, linknd=, and linkni= options.  When */
/*                you specify link=user, you must also provide the */
/*                ulink=, dulink=, and iulink= options.  The default */
/*                link is different for each error distribution and */
/*                is as follows:                               */
/*                                                            */
/*                     Distribution      Default Link          */
/*                     ------------      ------------          */
/*                     Binomial          Logit                 */
/*                     Poisson           Log                   */
/*                     Normal            Identity              */
/*                     Gamma             Reciprocal            */
/*                     Invgaussian       Power(-2)             */
/*                                                            */
/*  linkn     specifies the nonlinear link function.  It must be */
/*            enclosed in %str() and assign a value to "mu" by  */
/*            using parameters "b1" - "bk" (see examples).     */
/*                                                            */
/*  linknd    specifies the derivative of the nonlinear link   */
/*            function.                                        */
/*                                                            */
/*  linkni    specifies the initial values for the nonlinear   */
/*            link function.                                   */
/*                                                            */
/*  linku     specifies the user-defined link function.  It must */
/*            be expressed as a function with the argument "mu". */
/*                                                            */
/*  linkud    specifies the derivative of the user-defined link */
/*            function with respect to mu.  It must be expressed */
/*            as a function with argument "mu".  For an        */
/*            approximation, use the formula                   */
/*                                                            */
/*                    (u(mu+h)-u(mu-h))/(2*h)                  */
/*                                                            */
/*            where u() is the link and h is a small number.   */
/*                                                            */
/*  linkui    specifies the inverse of the user-defined link.  */
/*            It must be expressed as a function with argument  */
/*            "eta".                                           */
/*                                                            */
/*  approx    specifies the values used to approximate the     */
/*            derivative of the link function. It has a default */
/*            of 0.0001.                                       */
/*                                                            */
/*  cf        specifies the correction factor added to the data */
/*            in order to avoid singularities in the initial   */
/*            iteration.  By default this is set to 0.5.       */
/*                                                            */
/*  converge  sets the convergence criterion for the GLIMMIX   */
/*            macro.  This is not the convergence criteria used */
/*            for each internal PROC MIXED call, but rather the */
```

```
/*              criterion used to assess convergence of the entire */
/*              macro algorithm.  By default this is set to 1E-8.  */
/*                                                                 */
/* maxit        specifies the maximum number of iterations for the */
/*              GLIMMIX macro to converge.  By default this is set */
/*              to 20.                                             */
/*                                                                 */
/* offset       specifies the offset variable.  It has a default  */
/*              of 0.                                             */
/*                                                                 */
/* output       specifies that an output dataset is desired. The  */
/*              following options are available with this         */
/*              argument:                                         */
/*                                                                 */
/*   OUT=filename       specifiles the output data set name.      */
/*                      If none is given, then a default name     */
/*                      of _OUTFILE is used.                      */
/*                                                                 */
/*   XBETA=varname      creates a variable named varname and      */
/*                      sets it equal to the predicted mean,      */
/*                      mu.                                       */
/*                                                                 */
/*   PRED=varname       creates a variable named varname and      */
/*                      sets it equal to the linear predictor,    */
/*                      eta.                                      */
/*                                                                 */
/*   RESCHI=varname     sets the Pearson or Chi-Square            */
/*                      residual, defined as:                     */
/*                                                                 */
/*                         (Y-mu)/sqrt(phi*V(mu))                 */
/*                                                                 */
/*                      to varname, where phi is the estimate     */
/*                      of scale and V(mu) is the variance        */
/*                      function evaluated at mu, the predicted   */
/*                      mean, and Y is the response value.        */
/*                                                                 */
/*   RESRAW=varname     sets the raw residual, Y-mu to varname.   */
/*                                                                 */
/*   Make sure you do not insert any spaces around the equal      */
/*   signs when using these output options.                       */
/*                                                                 */
/* title        specifies a title that is printed with the output */
/*              tables.                                           */
/*                                                                 */
/* options      specifies GLIMMIX macro options separated by      */
/*              spaces:                                           */
/*                                                                 */
/*   INITIAL=values  sets initial values for the parameter        */
/*                   estimates in the model. The intercept        */
/*                   term is initialized with the INTERCEPT       */
/*                   option below.  The values are assigned       */
/*                   to the the variables in the model            */
/*                   statement in the same order that they        */
/*                   appear in the MODEL statement.  ALL          */
/*                   variable levels must be specified, even      */
/*                   if they are not estimable (e.g., some        */
/*                   class variable levels).  Be sure to note     */
/*                   the order of the variables and levels as     */
/*                   they can change with the ORDER= option.      */
/*                                                                 */
/*   INTERCEPT=value initializes the intercept to value. If       */
/*                   the NOINT option is also specifed, then      */
/*                   the intercept is not estimated, but an       */
/*                   intercept term of value is added to the      */
/*                   model.                                      */
/*                                                                 */
/*   MIXPRINTALL     prints all PROC MIXED runs.                  */
/*                                                                 */
```

```
/*      MIXPRINTLAST      prints the final PROC MIXED run.          */
/*                                                                  */
/*      MQL               computes MQL estimates (see Breslow and   */
/*                        Clayton, 1993, JASA, 9-25).  The default  */
/*                        is PQL with an extra-dispersion           */
/*                        parameter.   Requires Release 6.11.       */
/*                                                                  */
/*      NOINT             specifies that the intercept is not to    */
/*                        be estimated. If the INTERCEPT= option    */
/*                        is also specified, then the intercept     */
/*                        is not estimated, but an intercept term   */
/*                        of value is added to the model.           */
/*                                                                  */
/*      NOPRINT           suppresses all printing.                  */
/*                                                                  */
/*      NOITPRINT         suppresses printing of the iteration      */
/*                        history.                                  */
/*                                                                  */
/*      PRINTDATA         prints the pseudo data after each         */
/*                        iteration.                                */
/*                                                                  */
/*                                                                  */
/* OUTPUT                                                           */
/* ------                                                           */
/* The output from this macro is a printout of selected tables     */
/* from the final iteration of PROC MIXED.  All of these tables    */
/* are stored in data sets whose names begin with an               */
/* underscore; you can scan the macro code to find the name of     */
/* the data set you wish to use.                                   */
/*                                                                  */
/*                                                                  */
/* EXAMPLE SYNTAX                                                   */
/* --------------                                                  */
/* 1) Both of the following examples specifiy the same             */
/*    analysis:  logistic regression, no random effects            */
/*                                                                  */
/*    %glimmix(data=ingots,                                        */
/*       stmts=%str(                                               */
/*          class soak;                                            */
/*          model nready/ntotal=soak heat;                        */
/*       )                                                         */
/*    )                                                            */
/*                                                                  */
/*    %glimmix(data=ingots,                                        */
/*       stmts=%str(                                               */
/*          class soak;                                            */
/*          model nready/ntotal=soak heat;                        */
/*       ),                                                        */
/*       error=user,errvar=mu*(1-mu),                              */
/*       errdev=2*_wght*(_y*log(_y/mu) +                           */
/*              (1-_y)*log((1-_y)/(1-mu))),                        */
/*       link=user,linku=log(mu/(1-mu)),                          */
/*       linkud=1/(mu*(1-mu)),linkui=exp(eta)/(1+exp(eta))        */
/*    )                                                            */
/*                                                                  */
/*    Here _wght corresponds to ntotal and _y to nready/ntotal.    */
/*                                                                  */
/* 2) This example uses the random, lsmeans, and options           */
/*    arguments:                                                    */
/*                                                                  */
/*    %glimmix(data=salaman1,                                      */
/*       stmts=%str(                                               */
/*          class fpop fnum mpop mnum;                             */
/*          model y = fpop|mpop;                                   */
/*          random fpop*fnum mpop*mnum;                            */
/*          lsmeans fpop|mpop / cl;                                */
/*       ),                                                        */
/*       options=mixprintlast                                      */
```

```
/*      )                                                       */
/*                                                              */
/* 3) This example uses the procopt, random, and offset        */
/*    arguments:                                                */
/*                                                              */
/*    %glimmix(data=ship,                                       */
/*       procopt=order=data,                                    */
/*       stmts=%str(                                            */
/*          class type year period;                            */
/*          model y=type;                                       */
/*          random year period;                                */
/*       ),                                                     */
/*       error=poisson,link=log,offset=service                 */
/*    )                                                         */
/*                                                              */
/* 4) This example uses the repeated argument:                 */
/*                                                              */
/*    %glimmix(data=salaman1,                                   */
/*       stmts=%str(                                            */
/*          class fpop fnum mpop mnum;                          */
/*          model y = fpop|mpop;                                */
/*          repeated / type=ar(1) sub=fpop*fnum;                */
/*          lsmeans fpop|mpop / cl;                             */
/*       )                                                      */
/*    )                                                         */
/*                                                              */
/* DISCLAIMER                                                   */
/* ----------                                                  */
/*                                                              */
/* THIS INFORMATION IS PROVIDED BY SAS INSTITUTE INC. AS A      */
/* SERVICE TO ITS USERS.  IT IS PROVIDED "AS IS".  THERE ARE NO */
/* WARRANTIES, EXPRESSED OR IMPLIED, AS TO MERCHANTABILITY OR   */
/* FITNESS FOR A PARTICULAR PURPOSE REGARDING THE ACCURACY OF   */
/* THE MATERIALS OR CODE CONTAINED HEREIN.                      */
/*                                                              */
/*-------------------------------------------------------------*/



/*-------------------------------------------------------------*/
/*                                                             */
/*    %mvarlst                                                 */
/*    Make a variable list from the class list, model          */
/*    specification, and random specification.                 */
/*                                                             */
/*-------------------------------------------------------------*/
%macro mvarlst;
%let varlst =;
%let mdllst = &mdlspec;

/*---get response variable---*/
%if %index(&response,/) %then
   %let varlst = %scan(&response,1,/) %scan(&response,2,/) &varlst;
%else %let varlst = &response &varlst;

/*---get fixed effects---*/
%if %index(&mdllst,@) %then %do;
   %let j = 1;
   %let mdl = &mdllst;
   %let mdllst=;
   %do %while(%length(%scan(&mdl,&j,' ')));
      %let var=%scan(&mdl,&j,' ');
      %if %index(&var,@) %then %do;
         %let b = %eval(%index(&var,@)-1);
         %let mdllst = &mdllst %substr(%quote(&var),1,&b);
      %end;
      %else %let mdllst = &mdllst &var;
```

```
            %let j = %eval(&j+1);
        %end;
    %end;

    %let iv = 1;
    %do %while (%length(%scan(&mdllst,&iv)));
        %let varlst = &varlst %scan(&mdllst,&iv);
        %let iv = %eval(&iv + 1);
    %end;

    /*---get random effects---*/
    %let iv = 1;
    %do %while (%length(%scan(&rndlst,&iv)));
        %let temp = %scan(&rndlst,&iv);
        %if &temp ne INT and &temp ne INTERCEPT %then
            %let varlst = &varlst &temp;
        %let iv = %eval(&iv + 1);
    %end;

    %let varlst = &varlst &class &id &freq &weight;
%mend mvarlst;


    /*-------------------------------------------------------------*/
    /*                                                             */
    /*     %trimlst                                                */
    /*     Get rid of repetitions in a list                        */
    /*                                                             */
    /*-------------------------------------------------------------*/
%macro trimlst(name,lst);
  %let i1 = 1;
  %let tname =;
  %do %while (%length(%scan(&lst,&i1,%str( ))));
     %let first = %scan(&lst,&i1,%str( ));
     %let i2 = %eval(&i1 + 1);
     %do %while (%length(%scan(&lst,&i2,%str( ))));
        %let next = %scan(&lst,&i2,%str( ));
        %if %quote(&first) = %quote(&next) %then %let i2=10000;
        %else %let i2 = %eval(&i2 + 1);
     %end;
     %if (&i2<10000) %then %let tname = &tname &first;
     %let i1 = %eval(&i1 + 1);
  %end;
  %let &name = &tname;
%mend trimlst;


    /*-------------------------------------------------------------*/
    /*                                                             */
    /*     %errlink                                                */
    /*     Create macro variables that contain the link, invlink,  */
    /*     derivative, and the variance funtion for the following  */
    /*     error distributions and link functions:                 */
    /*                                                             */
    /*     error distn: normal, binomial, poisson, gamma, and      */
    /*                  inverse gaussian                           */
    /*     link func:   logit, probit, complementary log-log,      */
    /*                  log-log, identity, power(), log, exp, and   */
    /*                  reciprocal.                                 */
    /*                                                             */
    /*     The user-defined specification is given by leaving the  */
    /*     error distribution field blank and then giving the link,*/
    /*     the derivative of the link, the inverse link, and the   */
    /*      variance function.  The parameters for each are:       */
    /*                                                             */
    /*          mu:   variance function, link, and the derivative  */
    /*                of the link                                  */
    /*          eta:   inverse link;                               */
```

```
/*                                                                    */
/*--------------------------------------------------------------*/
%macro errlink;

/*---error distributions: set variance and deviance functions---*/
%let exit = 0;
%if %length(&error)=0 %then %do;
   %if %length(&errvar) and %length(&errdev) %then %let error=USER;
   %else %let error=BINOMIAL;
%end;
%if %length(&linkn) and %length(&link)=0 %then %let link=NLIN;
%if %length(&linku) and %length(&link)=0 %then %let link=USER;
%if &error=BINOMIAL or &error=B %then %do;
   %let errorfn=BINOMIAL;
   %let varform=mu*(1-mu);
   %let devform=_wght*2*(_y*log(_y/mu) + (1-_y)*log((1-_y)/(1-mu)));
   %if %length(&link)=0 %then %let link=LOGIT;
%end;
%else %if &error=POISSON or &error=P %then %do;
   %let errorfn=POISSON;
   %let varform=mu;
   %let devform=_wght*2*_y*log(_y/mu);
   %if %length(&link)=0 %then %let link=LOG;
%end;
%else %if &error=NORMAL or &error=N %then %do;
   %let errorfn=NORMAL;
   %let varform=1;
   %let devform=_wght*(_y-mu)**2;
   %if %length(&link)=0 %then %let link=IDENTITY;
%end;
%else %if &error=GAMMA or &error=G %then %do;
   %let errorfn=GAMMA;
   %let varform=mu**2;
   %let devform=_wght*-2*log(_y/mu);
   %if %length(&link)=0 %then %let link=RECIPROCAL;
%end;
%else %if &error=INVGAUSSIAN or &error=IG %then %do;
   %let errorfn=INVERSE GAUSSIAN;
   %let varform=mu**3;
   %let devform=_wght*(((_y-mu)**2)/(_y*mu*mu));
   %if %length(&link)=0 %then %let link=INVGAUSSIAN;
%end;
%else %if &error=USER or &error=U %then %do;
   %let errorfn=USER-DEFINED;
   %if %length(&errvar) %then %let varform=&errvar;
   %else %let exit = 1;
   %if %length(&errdev) %then %let devform=&errdev;
   %else %let exit = 1;
   %if %length(&link)=0 %then %let link=LOGIT;
%end;

/*---truncate link function, so we can match if a power link---*/
%if %length(&link)>5 %then %let trlink=%substr(&link,1,5);
%else %let trlink=&link;

/*---link functions; set eta, mu, and derivative formulas---*/
%if &trlink=LOGIT %then %do;
   %let linkfn=LOGIT;
   %let etaform=log(mu/(1-mu));
   %let detaform=1/(mu*(1-mu));
   %let muform=exp(eta)/(1+exp(eta));
%end;
%else %if &trlink=PROBI %then %do;
   %let linkfn=PROBIT;
   %let etaform=probit(mu);
   %let detaform=(probit(mu+&approx)-probit(mu-&approx))/
      (2*&approx);
   %let muform=probnorm(eta);
```

```
   %end;
   %else %if &trlink=CLOGL %then %do;
      %let linkfn=COMPLEMENTARY LOG LOG;
      %let etaform=log(-log(1-mu));
      %let detaform=-1/((1-mu)*log(1-mu));
      %let muform=1-exp(-exp(eta));
   %end;
   %else %if &trlink=LOGLO %then %do;
      %let linkfn=LOG LOG;
      %let etaform=-log(-log(mu));
      %let detaform=-1/(mu*log(mu));
      %let muform=exp(-exp(-eta));
   %end;
   %else %if &trlink=IDENT %then %do;
      %let linkfn=IDENTITY;
      %let etaform=mu;
      %let detaform=1;
      %let muform=eta;
   %end;
   %else %if &trlink=LOG %then %do;
      %let linkfn=LOG;
      %let etaform=log(mu);
      %let detaform=1/mu;
      %let muform=exp(eta);
   %end;
   %else %if &trlink=EXP %then %do;
      %let linkfn=EXPONENTIAL;
      %let etaform=exp(mu);
      %let detaform=exp(mu);
      %let muform=log(eta);
   %end;
   %else %if &trlink=RECIP %then %do;
      %let linkfn=INVERSE;
      %let etaform=1/mu;
      %let detaform=-1/mu**2;
      %let muform=1/eta;
   %end;
   %else %if &trlink=POWER %then %do;
      %let linklen = %eval(%length(&link)-7);
      %let expon=%substr(&link,7,&linklen);
      %let linkfn=POWER(&expon);
      %let etaform=mu**(&expon);
      %let detaform=((mu+&approx)**(&expon)-(mu-&approx)**(&expon))/
         (2*&approx);
      %let muform=eta**(1/(&expon));
   %end;
   %else %if &trlink=INVGA %then %do;
      %let linkfn=POWER(-2);
      %let etaform=mu**(-2);
      %let detaform=-2*mu**(-3);
      %let muform=eta**(-1/2);
   %end;
   %else %if &trlink=BOXCO %then %do;
      %let linkfn=BOX-COX;
      %let linklen = %eval(%length(&link)-8);
      %let expon=%substr(&link,8,&linklen);
      %let etaform=(mu**(&expon)-1)/(&expon);
      %let detaform=mu**((&expon)-1);
      %let muform=((&expon)*eta + 1)**(1/(&expon));
   %end;
   %else %if &trlink=USER %then %do;
      %let linkfn=USER-DEFINED;
      %if %length(&linku) %then %let etaform=&linku;
      %else %let exit = 1;
      %if %length(&linkud) %then  %let detaform=&linkud;
      %else %let exit = 1;
      %if %length(&linkui) %then %let muform=&linkui;
      %else %let exit = 1;
```

```
        %end;
        %else %if &trlink=NLIN %then %do;
           %let linkfn=NONLINEAR;
           %if %length(&linkn) %then %let nlinform=&linkn;
           %else %let exit = 1;
           %if %length(&linknd) %then %let nlinder=&linknd;
           %else %let exit = 1;
        %end;

        %if %index(&options,DEBUG) %then %do;
           %put options = &options;
           %put intopt = &intopt;
           %put varlst = &varlst;
           %put error = &errorfn;
           %put variance = &varform;
           %put deviance = &devform;
           %put link:  eta = &etaform;
           %put dlink:  deta = &detaform;
           %put invlink:  mu = &muform;
        %end;

     %mend errlink;




     /*-------------------------------------------------------------*/
     /*                                                             */
     /*     %init                                                   */
     /*     Sets the initial values for the iterations.             */
     /*                                                             */
     /*-------------------------------------------------------------*/
     %macro init;

      %if %index(&options,DEBUG) %then %put Initializing.;
      %else %do;
         options nonotes nodate nonumber;
      %end;
      title &title;

      /*---turn off printing to log and output---*/
      %global _print_;
      %if not %index(&options,MIXPRINTALL) %then %let _print_ = off;

      /*---override offset if NOINT and INTERCEPT= options---*/
      %if %index(&options,NOINT) and %index(&options,INTERCEPT) %then
         %do;
         %let i = %index(&options,INTERCEPT);
         %let offset = %scan(%substr(&options,&i),2,'=' ' ');
      %end;

      %let off = &offset;

      %if %index(&intopt,NLIN) %then %do;
         /*---determine number of parameters---*/
         %let nb = 0;
         %let i = 1;
         %do %while(%index(&linkni,B&i));
            %let nb = %eval(&nb + 1);
            %let i = %eval(&i + 1);
            %end;
         %let nu = 0;
         %let ns = 0;
         %let nus = 0;
         %let varlst = &varlst one x mu;
      %end;

      data _ds;
         set &data;
```

```
          /*---move away from parameter space boundary for the binomial
             error situation---*/
      %if %index(&response,/) %then %do;
          mu = (%scan(&response,1,/) + &cf)/(%scan(&response,2,/) +
             2*&cf);
          _wght = %scan(&response,2,/) ;
      %end;
      %else %if &error=BINOMIAL %then %do;
          mu = (&response + &cf)/(1 + 2*&cf);
          _wght = 1;
      %end;
      %else %do;
          mu = &response + &cf;
          _wght = 1;
      %end;
      %if %length(&weight) %then %do;
          _wght = &weight * _wght;
      %end;
      _y      = &response;
      var     = &varform;
      _offset = &off;
      %if %index(&intopt,NLIN) %then %do;
          array b{&nb} b1-b&nb;
          array db{&nb} db1-db&nb;
          one = 1;
          %do i = 1 %to &nb;
              %let idx = %index(&linkni,B&i);
              b&i = %scan(%substr(&linkni,&idx),2,'=' ' ');
          %end;
          &nlinform
          _z = _y - mu;
          &nlinder
          do i = 1 to &nb;
              _z = _z + db{i}*b{i};
          end;
          _w = _wght / var;
      %end;
      %else %do;
          eta  = &etaform ;
          deta = &detaform ;
          _w   = _wght /((deta**2)*(var));
          _z   = (_y-mu)*deta + eta - _offset;
      %end;
      %if %length(&freq) %then %do;
          do i = 1 to &freq;
              if i=1 then _orig='y';
              else _orig='n';
              output;
          end;
      %end;
      %else %do;
          _orig='y';
      %end;
      /*
      keep _y _z _w _offset _wght _orig &varlst;
      */
run;

%if %index(&options,PRINTDATA) %then %do;
   proc print;
   run;
%end;

%let iter = 0;

%mend init;
```

```
/*----------------------------------------------------------------*/
/*                                                                */
/*     %mixed                                                     */
/*     Calculate the predicted values and parameter estimates.    */
/*     If there is no RANDOM statement, then it uses maximum       */
/*     likelihood to find the parameter estimates, otherwise it   */
/*     uses REML, the default for PROC MIXED.                     */
/*                                                                */
/*----------------------------------------------------------------*/
%macro mixed;

%if %index(&options,DEBUG) %then %put Calling PROC MIXED.;

%let mivque0 = 0;

%again:

/*---get rid of predicted data set---*/
proc datasets lib=work nolist;
   delete _pred;
run;

/*---use mivque0 if did not converge the first time---*/
%if (&mivque0 = 1) %then %do;
   /*---save the original method---*/
   %let procopt0 = &procopt;
   %let procopt = &procopt METHOD=MIVQUE0;
%end;

proc mixed data=_ds &procopt;
   %if %length(&class) %then %do;
      class &class ;
      %if not %index(&procopt,NOCLPRINT) %then %do;
         make 'classlevels' out=_class;
      %end;
   %end;
   model _z = &mdlspec &mdlopt;
   %if %length(%scan(&mdlspec,1)) %then %do;
      make 'tests' out=_tests;
   %end;
   make 'solutionf' out=_soln;
   %if %index(&options,MQL) %then %do;
      make 'predmeans' out=_pred noprint;
   %end;
   %else %do;
      make 'predicted' out=_pred;
   %end;
   make 'fitting' out=_fitted;
   weight _w;
   %if %length(&spec) %then %do;
      %unquote(&spec)
      %if %index(&intopt,COVMOD) %then %do;
         make 'covparms' out=_cov;
         %if %index(&intopt,SOLNR) %then %do;
            make 'solutionr' out=_solnr;
         %end;
      %end;
      %if %index(&spec,ESTIMATE) %then %do;
         make 'estimate' out=_est;
      %end;
      %if %index(&spec,CONTRAST) %then %do;
         make 'contrast' out=_con;
      %end;
      %if %index(&spec,LSMEANS) %then %do;
         make 'lsmeans' out=_lsm;
         %if %index(&spec,DIFF) or %index(&spec,ADJUST) %then %do;
            make 'diffs' out=_diff;
```

```
                    %end;
                    %if %index(&spec,SLICE) %then %do;
                       make 'slices' out=_slice;
                    %end;
                %end;
            %end;
        %if %length(&parmspec) and (&mivque0 = 0) %then %do;
            parms &parmspec &parmopt ;
        %end;
        %if %index(&procopt,INFO) %then %do;
            make 'model' out=_model;
            make 'dimensions' out=_dim;
        %end;
        id _y _offset _wght _orig &varlst;
    run;

    /*---check for convergence, if not, then run again
            with method=mivque0---*/
    %if (&mivque0 = 1) %then %do;
        %let procopt = &procopt0;
        %let mivque0 = 0;
    %end;
    %else %do;
        %let there = no;
        data _null_;
            set _pred;
            call symput('there','yes');
        run;
        %if ("&there" = "no") %then %do;
            %put Computing MIVQUE0 estimates in iteration &iter because;
            %put %str(   )PROC MIXED did not converge.;
            %let mivque0 = 1;
            %goto again;
        %end;
    %end;

    /*---merge in new estimates of b and u---*/
    %if %index(&intopt,NLIN) %then %do;
        proc transpose data=_soln out=beta;
            var est;
        run;
        data beta;
            set beta;
            array b{&nb} b1-b&nb;
            array col{&nb} col1-col&nb;
            do i = 1 to &nb;
                b{i} = col{i};
                end;
            one = 1;
            keep one b1-b&nb;
        run;
        %if %index(&intopt,SOLNR) %then %do;
            proc sort data=u;
                by parm;
            data u;
                set u;
                keep est;
            proc transpose data=u out=blup;
                var est;
            run;
            data blup;
                set blup;
                array u{&nus} u1-u&nus;
                array col{&nus} col1-col&nus;
                do i = 1 to &nus;
                    u{i} = col{i};
                    end;
                one = 1;
```

```
              keep one u1-u&nus;
          run;
      %end;
      data _ds;
          set _ds;
          drop b1-b&nb;
      run;
      data _ds;
          merge _ds beta;
          by one;
      run;
      %end;

%mend mixed;

  /*------------------------------------------------------------*/
  /*                                                            */
  /*     %newdata                                               */
  /*     Create the new data set with the updated values        */
  /*                                                            */
  /*------------------------------------------------------------*/
%macro newdata;
  /*---save previous parameter estimates---*/
  data _oldsoln;
    set _soln;
    keep parm est;
  run;

  /*---save previous estimates of covariance matrix---*/
  %if %index(&intopt,COVMOD) %then %do;
     data _oldcov;
         set _cov;
         keep covparm est;
     run;
  %end;

  %if %index(&options,DEBUG) %then %put Creating new pseudo data.;

  /*---make new data set---*/
  data _ds;
     %if %index(&intopt,NLIN) %then %do;
         set _ds;
         array b{&nb} b1-b&nb;
         array db{&nb} db1-db&nb;
         /*
         array u{&nu,&ns} u1-u&nus;
         array du{&nu,&ns} du1-du&nus;
         array _r{&nu} _r1-_r&nu;
         */
         &nlinform
         _z = _y - mu;
         &nlinder
         do i = 1 to &nb;
             _z = _z + db{i}*b{i};
         end;
         /*
         do i = 1 to &nu;
            _r{i} = du{i,subject};
            _z = _z + _r{i}*u{i,subject};
            end;
         end;
         */
         var = &varform;
         _w = _wght / var;
         /*
         keep _y _z _w _offset _wght _orig &varlst db1-db&nb one x;
         */
         %end;
```

```
      %else %do;
         set _pred;
         eta = pred + _offset;
         mu = &muform;
         deta = &detaform;
         var = &varform;
         _w = _wght /((deta**2)*(var));
         _z = (_y - mu)*deta + eta - _offset;
         /*
         keep _y _z _w _offset _wght _orig &varlst;
         */
         %end;
      run;

   %if %index(&options,PRINTDATA) %then %do;
      proc print;
      run;
   %end;

%mend newdata;


   /*------------------------------------------------------------*/
   /*                                                            */
   /*      %compare                                              */
   /*      Compare the last two parameter estimates to check for */
   /*      convergence if no random components, else compare     */
   /*      estimates of covariance matrix.                       */
   /*                                                            */
   /*------------------------------------------------------------*/
%macro compare;
/*---Use relative difference of parameter estimates or
      covariance matrix as a measure of convergence---*/
%if %index(&intopt,COVMOD) %then %let type=cov;
%else %let type=soln;

/*---save convergence information in conv and crit---*/
data _compare;
   merge _old&type(rename=(est=oldest)) _&type end=last;
   retain crit 0;
   denom = (abs(oldest) + abs(est))/2;
   if (denom > &converge) then do;
      reldiff = abs(oldest - est) / denom;
      crit = max(crit,reldiff);
   end;
   output;
   if last then do;
      call symput('crit',left(crit));
      if (crit<&converge) then conv = 1;
      else conv = 0;
      call symput('conv',conv);
   end;
run;

%if %index(&options,DEBUG) %then %do;
   proc print data=_compare;
   run;
%end;

%mend compare;


   /*------------------------------------------------------------*/
   /*                                                            */
   /*      %iterate                                              */
   /*      Iteration process                                     */
   /*                                                            */
   /*------------------------------------------------------------*/
```

```sas
%macro iterate;

%let conv = 0;
%let iter = 1;

/*---start at different spot?---*/
%if (%index(&options,INITIAL) or (%index(&options,INTERCEPT) and
   %index(&options,NOINT)=0 )) %then %do;
   %if %index(&options,INTERCEPT) and %index(&options,NOINT)=0
      %then %do;
      %let i = %index(&options,INTERCEPT);
      %let intstart = %scan(%substr(&options,&i),2,'=' ' ');
      data _intcpt;
         set _soln;
         if parm = 'INTERCEPT';
         est = &intstart;
      run;
   %end;

   data _parms;
      set _soln;
      if parm ne 'INTERCEPT';
   run;
   %if %index(&options,INITIAL) %then %do;
      /*---get number of parameters---*/
      data _null_;
         if 0 then set _parms nobs=count;
         call symput('nobs',left(put(count,8.)));
         stop;
      run;

      %let i  = %index(&options,INITIAL);
      %let ix = 2;
      data _parmst;
         set _parms;
         %do %until (&ix > %eval(&nobs + 1));
            est=%scan(%substr(&options,&i),&ix,'=' ' ');
            if _n_ = %eval(&ix-1) then output;
            %let ix = %eval(&ix + 1);
         %end;
      run;
      data _parms;
         merge _parms _parmst;
      run;
   %end;
   data _soln;
      set _intcpt _parms;
   run;
%end;

%do %while(&iter <= &maxit);
   %newdata
   %mixed
   %compare
   %if not %index(&options,NOITPRINT) %then %do;
      %if (&iter=1) %then %do;
         %put %str(    ) GLIMMIX Iteration History;
         %put;
         %put Iteration    Convergence criterion;
      %end;
      %if (&iter<10) %then
         %put %str(    ) &iter           &crit;
      %else %if (&iter<100) %then
         %put %str(  ) &iter           &crit;
      %else
         %put %str( ) &iter           &crit;
   %end;
   %let iter = %eval(&iter+1);
```

```
        %if (&conv=1) %then %let iter=%eval(&maxit+1);
    %end;

%mend iterate;


    /*-------------------------------------------------------------*/
    /*                                                             */
    /*     %compile                                                */
    /*     Compile the macro results.                              */
    /*                                                             */
    /*-------------------------------------------------------------*/
%macro compile;

    /*---get variance estimate---*/
    data _null_;
        set _fitted;
        if descr='Variance Estimate' then call symput('xdisp',value);
    run;

    /*---calculate deviance and Pearson Chi-Squared---*/
    %if %index(&intopt,NLIN) %then %do;
        data _pred;
            set _pred;
            one = 1;
        run;
        data _pred;
            merge _pred beta;
            by one;
        run;
    %end;

    data _stats;
        set _pred end=last;
        retain deviance 0 pearson 0 nn 0;
        if ((_y ne .) and (pred ne .)) then do;
            _y  = _y + 1e-10*(_y=0) - 1e-10*(_y=1);
            eta = pred + _offset;
            %if %index(&intopt,NLIN) %then %do;
                &nlinform;
            %end;
            %else %do;
                mu = &muform;
            %end;
            deviance + &devform;
            pearson  + _wght * ((_y-mu)**2/(&varform));
            nn + 1;
        end;
        if last;
        if last then do;
            call symput('deviance',deviance);
            call symput('n',nn);
        end;
        keep deviance pearson;
    run;

    /*---get scale parameter---*/
    %gscale

    data _stats;
        length descript $35;
        set _stats;
        descript = 'Deviance';
        value = deviance; output;
        descript = 'Scaled Deviance';
        value = deviance / &scale; output;
        descript = 'Pearson Chi-Square';
        value = pearson; output;
```

```
                    descript = 'Scaled Pearson Chi-Square';
                    value = pearson / &scale; output;
                    %if %index(&intopt,COVMOD) %then %do;
                        descript = 'Extra-Dispersion Scale';
                    %end;
                    %else %do;
                        descript = 'Dispersion Scale';
                    %end;
                    value = &scale;
                    output;
                    keep descript value;
                    label descript = 'Description' value = 'Value';
                run;

                /*---ESTIMATE statement results---*/
                %if %index(&spec,ESTIMATE) %then %do;
                    data _est;
                        set _est;
                        %if not %index(&intopt,NLIN) %then %do;
                            eta = est;
                            mu = &muform;
                            label mu = 'Mu';
                            drop eta;
                            %if %index(&intopt,ESTCL) %then %do;
                                %mulu;
                            %end;
                        %end;
                    run;
                %end;

                /*---least squares means---*/
                %if %index(&spec,LSMEANS) %then %do;
                    data _lsm;
                        set _lsm;
                        %if not %index(&intopt,NLIN) %then %do;
                            eta = lsmean;
                            mu = &muform;
                            label mu = 'Mu';
                            %if %index(&intopt,LSMCL) %then %do;
                                %mulu;
                            %end;
                            drop eta;
                        %end;
                    run;
                %end;

            %mend compile;

            %macro mulu;
              eta = lower;
              lowermu = &muform;
              eta = upper;
              uppermu = &muform;
              label lowermu = 'LowerMu' uppermu = 'UpperMu';
            %mend mulu;




                /*-------------------------------------------------------------*/
                /*                                                             */
                /*     %gscale                                                 */
                /*     Calculate scale parameter.                              */
                /*                                                             */
                /*-------------------------------------------------------------*/
            %macro gscale;
            %if %index(&intopt,COVMOD) %then %do;
                %let scale = &xdisp;
            %end;
```

```
   %else %if &error=BINOMIAL or &error=B &error=POISSON or &error=P or
      &error=USER %then %do;
      %let scale = 1;
   %end;
   %else %if &error=NORMAL or &error=N or &error=INVGAUSSIAN or
      &error=IG %then %do;
      data _null_;
         scale = &deviance / &n;
         call symput('scale',scale);
      run;
   %end;
   %else %if &error=GAMMA or &error=G %then %do;
      data _null_;
         dev = &deviance;
         n   = &n;
         mid = n/dev;
         lo  = 0.2;
         hi  = mid + 5;
         fl  = -2*n*(digamma(lo)-log(lo))   ;
         fm  = -2*n*(digamma(mid)-log(mid)) ;
         fh  = -2*n*(digamma(hi)-log(hi))   ;
         do until (abs(fh-fl)<1e-5);
             if fm < dev then do; hi=mid; mid=(hi+lo)/2; end;
             else do; lo = mid; mid=(hi+lo)/2;
         end;
         fl  = -2*n*(digamma(lo)-log(lo))   ;
         fm  = -2*n*(digamma(mid)-log(mid)) ;
         fh  = -2*n*(digamma(hi)-log(hi))   ;
         end;
         call symput('scale',1/mid);
      run;
   %end;
   %else %do;
      %let scale = 1;
   %end;

%mend gscale;

   /*-----------------------------------------------------------------*/
   /*                                                                 */
   /*     %printout                                                   */
   /*     Print out the macro results.                                */
   /*                                                                 */
   /*-----------------------------------------------------------------*/
%macro printout;
%if %length(&title) %then %let titlen = title2;
%else %let titlen = title1;

%if %index(&procopt,INFO) %then %do;
   &titlen 'GLIMMIX Model Information';
   proc print data=_model noobs label;
   run;
%end;

%if %length(&class) and not %index(&procopt,NOCLPRINT) %then %do;
   &titlen 'Class Level Information';
   proc print data=_class noobs label;
   run;
%end;

%if %index(&procopt,INFO) %then %do;
   &titlen 'Dimensions';
   proc print data=_dim noobs label;
   run;
%end;

%if %index(&intopt,COVMOD) %then %do;
   &titlen 'Covariance Parameter Estimates';
```

```
      proc print data=_cov noobs label;
         var covparm est;
         where covparm ne 'Residual';
      run;
%end;

&titlen 'GLIMMIX Model Statistics';
proc print data=_stats noobs label;
   format value 10.4;
run;

%if %index(&intopt,SOLNF) %then %do;
   &titlen 'Parameter Estimates';
   proc print data=_soln noobs label;
      format est 10.4 se 10.4;
   run;
%end;

%if %index(&intopt,SOLNR) %then %do;
   &titlen 'Random Effects Estimates';
   proc print data=_solnr noobs label;
      format est 10.4 se_pred 10.4;
   run;
%end;

%if %length(%scan(&mdlspec,1)) %then %do;
   &titlen 'Tests of Fixed Effects';
   proc print data=_tests noobs label;
   run;
%end;

%if %index(&spec,CONTRAST) %then %do;
   &titlen 'CONTRAST Statement Results';
   proc print data=_con noobs label;
   run;
%end;

%if %index(&spec,ESTIMATE) %then %do;
   &titlen 'ESTIMATE Statement Results';
   proc print data=_est noobs label;
      format est 10.4 se 10.4;
      %if not %index(&intopt,NLIN) %then %do;
         format mu 10.4;
         %if %index(&intopt,ESTCL) %then %do;
            format lower 10.4 upper 10.4 lowermu 10.4 uppermu 10.4;
         %end;
      %end;
   run;
%end;

%if %index(&spec,LSMEANS) %then %do;
   &titlen 'Least Squares Means';
   proc print data=_lsm noobs label;
      format lsmean 10.4 se 10.4;
      %if not %index(&intopt,NLIN) %then %do;
         format mu 10.4;
         %if %index(&intopt,LSMCL) %then %do;
            format lower 10.4 upper 10.4 lowermu 10.4 uppermu 10.4;
         %end;
      %end;
   run;

   %if %index(&spec,DIFF) or %index(&spec,ADJUST) %then %do;
      &titlen 'Differences of Least Squares Means';
      proc print data=_diff noobs label;
         format diff 10.4 se 10.4;
      run;
   %end;
```

```
      %if %index(&spec,SLICE) %then %do;
          &titlen 'Tests of Effect Slices';
          proc print data=_slice noobs label;
          run;
      %end;

  %end;

%mend printout;



  /*-------------------------------------------------------------*/
  /*                                                             */
  /*      %outinfo                                               */
  /*      Make an output data set.                               */
  /*                                                             */
  /*-------------------------------------------------------------*/
%macro outinfo(output);
%if %index(&output,OUT) %then %do;
    %let i = %index(&output,OUT);
    %let outfile = %scan(%substr(&output,&i),2,'=' ' ');
%end;
%else %do;
    %let outfile = _OUTFILE;
%end;

  data &outfile;
     set _pred;
     eta = pred + _offset;
     mu = &muform;
     deta = &detaform;
     var = &varform;
     _w = _wght /((deta**2)*(var));
     _z = (_y - mu)*deta + eta - _offset;
     %let keeplst = &varlst;
     %if %index(&output,XBETA=) %then %do;
         %let i = %index(&output,XBETA=);
         %let muvar = %scan(%substr(&output,&i),2,'=' ' ');
         &muvar = mu;
         %let keeplst = &keeplst &muvar ;
     %end;
     %if %index(&output,PRED=) %then %do;
         %let i = %index(&output,PRED=);
         %let etavar = %scan(%substr(&output,&i),2,'=' ' ');
         &etavar = eta;
         %let keeplst = &keeplst &etavar ;
     %end;
     %if %index(&output,RESCHI=) %then %do;
         %let i = %index(&output,RESCHI=);
         %let chires = %scan(%substr(&output,&i),2,'=' ' ');
         &chires = (_y-mu)/sqrt(&scale * var);
         %let keeplst = &keeplst &chires ;
     %end;
     %if %index(&output,RESRAW=) %then %do;
         %let i = %index(&output,RESRAW=);
         %let rawres = %scan(%substr(&output,&i),2,'=' ' ');
         &rawres = _y - mu;
         %let keeplst = &keeplst &rawres ;
     %end;
     if _orig='y';
     keep &keeplst;
  run;

%mend outinfo;

  /*-------------------------------------------------------------*/
```

```
/*                                                                    */
/*      %glimmix                                                      */
/*      Put it all together                                          */
/*                                                                    */
/*--------------------------------------------------------------------*/
/*---set default values of error, approx, and offset---*/
%macro glimmix(data=,procopt=,stmts=,weight=,freq=,
    error=BINOMIAL,errvar=,errdev=,link=,linku=,linkud=,linkui=,
    linkn=,linknd=,linkni=,approx=0.0001,cf=0.5,converge=1e-8,
    maxit=20,offset=0,output=,title=,options=);

/*---default data set---*/
%if %bquote(&data)= %then %let data=&syslast;

/*---change to uppercase---*/
%let data      = %qupcase(&data);
%let procopt   = %qupcase(&procopt);
%let weight    = %qupcase(&weight);
%let freq      = %qupcase(&freq);
%let stmts     = %qupcase(&stmts);
%let error     = %qupcase(&error);
%let errvar    = %qupcase(&errvar);
%let errdev    = %qupcase(&errdev);
%let link      = %qupcase(&link);
%let linkn     = %qupcase(&linkn);
%let linknd    = %qupcase(&linknd);
%let linkni    = %qupcase(&linkni);
%let linku     = %qupcase(&linku);
%let linkud    = %qupcase(&linkud);
%let linkui    = %qupcase(&linkui);
%let offset    = %qupcase(&offset);
%let output    = %qupcase(&output);
%let options   = %qupcase(&options);

/*---loop through statements and extract information---*/
%let spec = ;
%let class = ;
%let parms = ;
%let id = ;
%let rndlst = ;
%let intopt = ;
%let iv = 1;
%do %while (%length(%scan(&stmts,&iv,;)));

    %let stmt = %qscan(&stmts,&iv,%str(;));
    %let first = %qscan(&stmt,1);
    %let fn = %eval(%index(&stmt,&first) + %length(&first));

    /*---check RANDOM options and extract random effects list---*/
    %if %index(&first,RANDOM) or %index(&first,REPEATED) %then %do;
        %let intopt = &intopt COVMOD;
    %end;
    %if %index(&first,RANDOM) %then %do;
        %let i = %index(&stmt,/);
        %if (&i = 0) %then %let i = %length(&stmt);
        %else %do;
            %let rndopt = / %qscan(&stmt,2,/);
            %if %index(&rndopt,%str( S )) or %index(&rndopt,SOLUTION) or
                %index(&rndopt,CL) or %index(&rndopt,ALPHA) %then %do;
                %let intopt = &intopt SOLNR;
            %end;
        %end;
        %let rndlst = %substr(&stmt,&fn,%eval(&i-&fn+1));
    %end;

    /*---check ESTIMATE and LSMEANS options---*/
    %if %index(&first,ESTIMATE) and
        (%index(&stmt,CL) or %index(&stmt,ALPHA)) %then %do;
```

```
                %let intopt = &intopt ESTCL;
            %end;
        %if %index(&first,LSMEANS) %then %do;
            %if %index(&stmt,CL) or %index(&stmt,ALPHA) %then %do;
                %let intopt = &intopt LSMCL;
            %end;
            /*---change OM to OM=&data to avoid weights---*/
            %if %index(&stmt,OM) %then %do;
                %let i = %eval(%index(&stmt,OM) + 2);
                %if not %index(%scan(%substr(&stmt,&i),1),=) %then %do;
                    %let stmtnew = %substr(&stmt,1,%eval(&i-1)) = &data
                        %substr(&stmt,&i);
                    %let stmt = &stmtnew;
                %end;
            %end;
        %end;
    %end;

    /*---save statements---*/
    %if %index(&first,CLASS) %then %do;
        %let class = %qsubstr(&stmt,&fn);
    %end;
    %else %if %index(&first,MODEL) %then %do;
        %let model = %qsubstr(&stmt,&fn);
    %end;
    %else %if %index(&first,ID) %then %do;
        %let id = %qsubstr(&stmt,&fn);
    %end;
    %else %if %index(&first,PARMS) %then %do;
        %let parms = %qsubstr(&stmt,&fn);
    %end;
    %else %let spec = &spec &stmt %str(;) ;

    %let iv = %eval(&iv + 1);
%end;

/*---get response, model specification, and model options---*/
%let response = %scan(&model,1,=);
%let eqidx = %eval(%index(&model,=)+1);
%if (&eqidx > %length(&model)) %then %let mdl = %str();
%else %let mdl = %str( ) %qsubstr(&model,&eqidx);
%if %index(&mdl,/) %then %do;
    %let mdlspec = %qscan(&mdl,1,/);
    %let mdlopt = / %qscan(&mdl,2,/);
    %if %index(&mdlopt,%str( S )) or %index(&mdlopt,SOLUTION) or
        %index(&mdlopt,CL) or %index(&mdlopt,ALPHA) %then %do;
        %let intopt = &intopt SOLNF;
    %end;
    %if %index(&options,MQL) %then %do;
        %let mdlopt = &mdlopt S PM;
    %end;
    %else %do;
        %let mdlopt = &mdlopt S P;
    %end;
    %if %index(&mdlopt,NOINT) and %index(&options,NOINT)=0 %then
        %do;
        %let options = &options NOINT;
    %end;
    %if %index(&mdlopt,NOINT)=0 and %index(&options,NOINT) %then
        %do;
        %let mdlopt = &mdlopt NOINT;
    %end;
%end;
%else %do;
    %let mdlspec = &mdl;
    %if %index(&options,MQL) %then %do;
        %let mdlopt  = / S PM;
    %end;
    %else %do;
```

```
                    %let mdlopt  = / S P;
              %end;
              %if %index(&options,NOINT) %then %let mdlopt = &mdlopt NOINT;
      %end;
      /*---add an @ sign if it is missing---*/
      %if %index(&mdlspec,|) %then %do;
          %let mdl=&mdlspec;
          %let mdlspec=;
          %let i=1;
          %do %while(%length(%scan(&mdl,&i,' ')));
              %let mdlterm = %scan(&mdl,&i,' ');
              %if %index(&mdlterm,|) and %index(&mdlterm,@)=0 %then %do;
                  %let j=1;
                  %do %while(%length(%scan(&mdlterm,&j,|)));
                   %let j = %eval(&j+1);
                  %end;
                  %let atvalue = %eval(&j-1);
                  %let mdlterm = &mdlterm.@&atvalue;
              %end;
              %let mdlspec = &mdlspec &mdlterm;
              %let i = %eval(&i+1);
          %end;
      %end;


      /*---get parms specification, and parms options---*/
      %if %index(&parms,/) %then %do;
          %let parmspec = %scan(&parms,1,/);
          %let parmopt  = / %scan(&parms,2,/);
      %end;
      %else %do;
          %let parmspec = %qupcase(&parms);
          %let parmopt  = ;
      %end;

      %if %length(&linkn) %then %let intopt = &intopt NLIN;

      /*---create local variables---*/
      %local varlst errorfn linkfn varform devform etaform muform
         detaform nlinform nlinder deviance scale n nb nu ns nus
         crit conv cf intopt iter exit;

      /*---get variable list and trim it---*/
      %mvarlst
      %trimlst(varlst,&varlst);

      /*---set error and link function macro variables---*/
      %errlink

      /*---print header---*/
      %if not %index(&options,NOPRINT) %then %do;
          %if %index(&data,.)=0 %then %let data=WORK.&data;
          %put;
          %put %str(        ) The GLIMMIX Macro;
          %put;
          %put Data Set             : &data;
          %put Error Distribution : &errorfn;
          %put Link Function        : &linkfn;
          %put Response Variable  : &response;
          %if %length(&weight) %then
             %put Weight                : &weight;
          %if %length(&freq) %then
             %put Frequency             : &freq;
          %put;
          %put;
      %end;

      /*---initialize iteration starting values---*/
      %init
```

```
/*---run first estimates for convergence tests---*/
%mixed

/*---iterate until convergence---*/
%iterate

/*---turn the printing back on---*/
%let _print_ = on;

/*---final PROC MIXED run---*/
%if %index(&options,MIXPRINTLAST) %then %do;
   %put;
   %put Output from last PROC MIXED run:;
   %put;
   %mixed
%end;

/*---stop if did not converge---*/
%if &conv ne 1 %then %do;
   %put GLIMMIX did not converge.;
%end;
/*---otherwise compile and print results---*/
%else %do;
   %compile
   %if not %index(&options,NOPRINT) %then %do;
      %printout
   %end;
   /*---create output data set---*/
   %if %length(&output) %then %do;
      %outinfo(%quote(&output));
   %end;
%end;

/*---turn back on the notes, dates, and page numbers---*/
options notes date number;
/*---clear the title---*/
title;

%mend glimmix;
```

Appendix 3 NLINMIX Macro

```
/*------------------------------------------------------------*/
/* TITLE                                                      */
/* -----                                                      */
/* NLINMIX: a SAS macro for fitting nonlinear mixed models    */
/* using PROC NLIN and PROC MIXED. Requires SAS/STAT Release  */
/* 6.08 or later.                                             */
/*                                                            */
/* SUPPORT                                                    */
/* -------                                                    */
/* Russ Wolfinger (sasrdw@unx.sas.com)                        */
/* Please send email with any suggestions or corrections.     */
/*                                                            */
/* HISTORY                                                    */
/* -------                                                    */
/* initial coding                                 01Jun92 rdw */
/* revision                                       21Oct92 rdw */
/* removed PROC NLIN from iterations and revised  08Mar94 rdw */
/* changed syntax to include random effects                   */
/*     explicitly, added numerical derivatives and           */
/*     optional Gauss-Newton steps                19Dec94 rdw */
/* added rtype=                                   09Feb95 rdw */
/* changed tech= to expand=                       13Feb95 rdw */
/*                                                            */
/* DESCRIPTION                                                */
/* -----------                                                */
/* Available estimation methods are as follows, all of which  */
/* are implemented via iterative calls to PROC MIXED using    */
/* appropriately constructed pseudo data:                     */
/*                                                            */
/*     1. Expanding the nonlinear function about random effects */
/*        parameters set equal to zero, which is similar to Sheiner */
/*        and Beal's first-order method (NONMEM User's Guide,  */
/*        University of California, San Francisco).  This method is */
/*        the default for random effects specifications, and uses */
/*        the RANDOM statement in PROC MIXED.                 */
/*                                                            */
/*     2. Expanding the nonlinear function about random effects */
/*        parameters set equal to their current empirical best */
/*        linear unbiased predictor (EBLUP), which is Lindstrom and */
/*        Bates' approximate second-order method (Lindstrom and */
/*        Bates, 1990, Biometrics 46, 673-687).              */
/*          The method is implemented using an intitial call to */
/*        PROC NLIN and then iterative calls to PROC MIXED.  This */
/*        differs from Lindstrom and Bates' implementation, in */
/*        which pseudo data is constructed and iterative calls are */
/*        made alternately to PROC MIXED and PROC NLIN.  This */
/*        macro's implementation requires much less time and space */
/*        for larger problems, and it works because solving the */
/*        mixed-model equations in PROC MIXED is equivalent to */
/*        taking the first Gauss-Newton step in PROC NLIN     */
/*        (Wolfinger, 1993, Biometrika 80, 791-795).  Use     */
/*        EXPAND=EBLUP to implement this method, which uses    */
/*        the RANDOM statement in PROC MIXED.                 */
/*                                                            */
/*     3. Iteratively fitting a covariance structure outside of */
/*        the nonlinear function.  This is a second-order     */
/*        generalized estimating equation approach (Prentice and */
/*        Zhao, 1991, Biometrics 47, 825-839).  Use RTYPE= or */
/*        ROPT= to implement this method, which uses the REPEATED */
/*        statement in PROC MIXED.                            */
/*                                                            */
/*                                                            */
```

```
/* SYNTAX                                                              */
/* ------                                                             */
/* %nlinmix(                                                          */
/*    data=,                                                          */
/*    response=,                                                      */
/*    subject=,                                                       */
/*    model=,                                                         */
/*    derivs=,                                                        */
/*    tol=,                                                           */
/*    parms=,                                                         */
/*    covparms=,                                                      */
/*    random=,                                                        */
/*    ranopt=,                                                        */
/*    type=,                                                          */
/*    rtype=,                                                         */
/*    reffect=,                                                       */
/*    rsub=,                                                          */
/*    ropt=,                                                          */
/*    weight=,                                                        */
/*    add=,                                                           */
/*    method=,                                                        */
/*    expand=,                                                        */
/*    converge=,                                                      */
/*    subconv=,                                                       */
/*    maxit=,                                                         */
/*    maxsubit=,                                                      */
/*    gauss=,                                                         */
/*    fraction=,                                                      */
/*    procopt=,                                                       */
/*    modopt=,                                                        */
/*    options=                                                        */
/* )                                                                  */
/*                                                                    */
/* where                                                              */
/*                                                                    */
/*  data      specifies the analysis data set; default=last          */
/*            created; it must be sorted by subject                   */
/*                                                                    */
/*  response  specifies the response variable, default=y             */
/*                                                                    */
/*  subject   specifies the subject variable, default=subject        */
/*                                                                    */
/*  model     specifies the nonlinear mixed model in terms of         */
/*            parameters of your choice; the fixed-effects            */
/*            parameters are listed in the PARMS= argument            */
/*            and the random-effects in the RANDOM= argument;         */
/*            the final value of the model should be assigned to      */
/*            a variable named PRED, which is the predicted           */
/*            value for that observation; you may use multiple        */
/*            statements and auxiliary variables; the names of        */
/*            fixed and random effects parameters should be           */
/*            unique and should not exceed 6 characters in            */
/*            length; you should enclose the entire                   */
/*            specification with the %str() macro (see example        */
/*            syntax below)                                           */
/*                                                                    */
/*  modinit   specifies modeling statements to be called only         */
/*            once at the beginning of the modeling step; this        */
/*            option is usually used in conjunction with              */
/*            initializing recursively defined models which           */
/*            are to be differentiated numerically; this code         */
/*            should have no references to the fixed- or random-      */
/*            effects parameters                                      */
/*                                                                    */
/*  derivs    specifies the derivatives of the predicted value        */
/*            in the preceding model specification with respect       */
/*            to the fixed- and random-effects parameters; the        */
/*            derivatives are specified using the same parameter      */
```

```
/*              names but with d_ appended beforehand; you        */
/*              may use multiple statements, auxiliary variables, */
/*              and variables defined in the model specification, */
/*              and you should enclose the entire specification   */
/*              with the %str() macro (see example syntax below); */
/*              if you do not specify this argument, derivatives  */
/*              are computed numerically using central differences */
/*              with width tol*(1+abs(parm)), where tol is from   */
/*              the TOL= argument                                 */
/*                                                                */
/* tol          specifies the tolerance for numerical derivatives; */
/*              default=1e-5, and the width is computed as        */
/*              tol*(1+abs(parm)), where parm is the parameter    */
/*              being differentiated                              */
/*                                                                */
/* parms        specifies the starting values of the fixed-effects */
/*              parameters in the form %str(b1=value b2=value ... */
/*              bN=value)                                         */
/*                                                                */
/* covparms     specifies the starting values of the covariance  */
/*              parameters for each PROC MIXED call; the argument */
/*              must be in the form of a PROC MIXED PARMS         */
/*              statement, omitting the PARMS keyword and the     */
/*              final semicolon                                   */
/*                                                                */
/* random       specifies which variables in the model specifica- */
/*              tion are to be considered random effects          */
/*              parameters having zero mean and variance-         */
/*              covariance to be estimated                        */
/*                                                                */
/* ranopt       specifies options to be included on PROC MIXED's  */
/*              RANDOM statement                                  */
/*                                                                */
/* type         specifies the covariance structure for the       */
/*              variance matrix of the random effects, default=vc */
/*              (variance components), and the most common        */
/*              alternative is type=un (unstructured), see the    */
/*              PROC MIXED documentation for other possible types */
/*                                                                */
/* rtype        specifies the covariance structure for the       */
/*              variance matrix of the residual errors, the       */
/*              default is sigma^2 times the identity matrix;     */
/*              this is used to set up a REPEATED statement in    */
/*              the PROC MIXED calls; refer to the PROC MIXED     */
/*              documentation for possible types                  */
/*                                                                */
/* reffect      specifies the effect for the REPEATED statement,  */
/*              the default is no effect                          */
/*                                                                */
/* rsub         specifies the subject effect for the REPEATED     */
/*              statement, the default is the SUBJECT= variable   */
/*                                                                */
/* ropt         specifies options for the REPEATED statement,     */
/*              refer to the PROC MIXED documentation for details */
/*                                                                */
/* weight       specifies the weight expression, which may use    */
/*              auxiliary variables defined in the model and      */
/*              derivs specifications                             */
/*                                                                */
/* add          specifies additional PROC MIXED statements to be  */
/*              included with each call; they are typically       */
/*              CONTRAST, ESTIMATE, LSMEANS, or MAKE statements,  */
/*              and you should end them with semicolons and       */
/*              enclose the entire argument with %str()           */
/*                                                                */
/* method       specifies the PROC MIXED optimization method,     */
/*              default=REML                                      */
/*                                                                */
```

```
/*    expand    specifies the Taylor series expansion point,        */
/*              default=ZERO (Method 1 above), EBLUP specifies       */
/*              the current EBLUPs (Method 2 above)                  */
/*                                                                    */
/*    converge specifies the convergence criterion for the macro,   */
/*              default=1e-8                                          */
/*                                                                    */
/*    subconv  specifies the convergence criterion for the Gauss-   */
/*              Newton iterations, default=1e-12                      */
/*                                                                    */
/*    maxit     specifies the maximum number of iterations for the  */
/*              macro to converge, default=20                        */
/*                                                                    */
/*    maxsubit specifies the maximum number of Gauss-Newton steps   */
/*              in a suiteration, default=10                          */
/*                                                                    */
/*    gauss     specifies the number of iterations for which to     */
/*              perform Gauss-Newton subiterations, default=0        */
/*                                                                    */
/*    fraction specifies the multiplier by which to step-shorten    */
/*              when Gauss-Newton fails to improve the objective     */
/*              function, default=0.9                                */
/*                                                                    */
/*    procopt  specifies options for the PROC MIXED statement       */
/*                                                                    */
/*    modopt   specifies options for the MODEL statement in each    */
/*              PROC MIXED call                                       */
/*                                                                    */
/*    options  specifies nlinmix macro options:                     */
/*                                                                    */
/*       noclass            removes the subject effect from          */
/*                          the CLASS statement (Release 6.10        */
/*                          and later)                               */
/*                                                                    */
/*       noprev             does not use previous values as          */
/*                          starting values for the next             */
/*                          iteration                                */
/*                                                                    */
/*       noprint            suppresses all printing                  */
/*                                                                    */
/*       printall           prints all PROC NLIN and MIXED          */
/*                          steps; the final PROC MIXED step         */
/*                          is printed by default                    */
/*                                                                    */
/*       printfirst         prints the first PROC NLIN and          */
/*                          MIXED runs                               */
/*                                                                    */
/*       skipnlin           skips the initial PROC NLIN call        */
/*                                                                    */
/*                                                                    */
/* EXAMPLE SYNTAX                                                    */
/* --------------                                                   */
/*                                                                    */
/* %nlinmix(data=tree,                                               */
/*    response=y,                                                    */
/*    subject=tree,                                                  */
/*    model=%str(                                                    */
/*       num = b1+u1;                                                */
/*       e = exp(b3*x);                                              */
/*       den = 1 + b2*e;                                             */
/*       pred = num/den;                                             */
/*    ),                                                             */
/*    derivs=%str(                                                   */
/*       d_b1 = 1/den;                                               */
/*       d_b2 = -num/den/den*e;                                      */
/*       d_b3 = -num/den/den*b2*x*e;                                 */
/*       d_u1 = d_b1;                                                */
/*    ),                                                             */
```

```
/*      parms=%str(b1=150 b2=10 b3=-.001)                           */
/*      random=u1                                                   */
/* )                                                                */
/*                                                                  */
/*                                                                  */
/* DISCLAIMER                                                       */
/* ----------                                                       */
/*                                                                  */
/* THIS INFORMATION IS PROVIDED BY SAS INSTITUTE INC. AS A          */
/* SERVICE TO ITS USERS.  IT IS PROVIDED "AS IS".  THERE ARE NO     */
/* WARRANTIES, EXPRESSED OR IMPLIED, AS TO MERCHANTABILITY OR       */
/* FITNESS FOR A PARTICULAR PURPOSE REGARDING THE ACCURACY OF       */
/* THE MATERIALS OR CODE CONTAINED HEREIN.                          */
/*                                                                  */
/*----------------------------------------------------------------*/


/*----------------------------------------------------------------*/
/*                                                                  */
/*     %init                                                        */
/*     Sets the initial values for the iterations.                 */
/*                                                                  */
/*----------------------------------------------------------------*/
%macro init;

 /*---determine number of parameters---*/
%let another = 1;
%let nb = 0;
%let pos = 1;
%let prevpos = 1;
%let _error = 0;
%let fixed = ;
%let d_fixed = ;
%let d_fixedn = ;
%do %while(&another = 1);
   %let effect = %scan(&parms,&pos,' ' =);
   %if %length(&effect) %then %do;
      %let fixed = &fixed &effect;
      %let d_fixed = &d_fixed D_&effect;
      %let d_fixedn = &d_fixedn der.&effect;
      %let nb = %eval(&nb + 1);
      %let pos = %eval(&pos + 2);
   %end;
   %else %let another = 0;
%end;

%let another = 1;
%let nu = 0;
%let d_random = ;
%do %while(&another = 1);
   %let effect = %scan(&random,%eval(&nu+1),' ');
   %if %length(&effect) %then %do;
      %let d_random = &d_random D_&effect;
      %let nu = %eval(&nu + 1);
   %end;
   %else %let another = 0;
%end;

%if %length(&rtype) | %length(&reffect) | %length(&ropt) %then
   %let nr = 1;
%else %let nr = 0;

%if %index(&options,DEBUG) %then %do;
   %put model = &mod;
   %put derivatives = &der;
   %put fixed = &fixed;
   %put d_fixed = &d_fixed;
   %put random = &random;
```

```
        %put d_random = &d_random;
        %if (&nr = 1) %then
            %put repeated = &reffect / TYPE=&rtype SUB=&rsub &ropt;
    %end;

    %if not %index (&expand,EBLUP) | (&switch > 0) %then
        %let expand = ZERO;
    %if (&expand = ZERO) %then %do;
        %let savegau = &gauss;
        %let gauss = 0;
    %end;

    /*---number of subjects and maximum observations per subject---*/
    data _nlinmix;
        retain _cursub . _cursub1 0 _curobs 1 _maxobs 1;
        set %unquote(&data);
        if _cursub ne %unquote(&subject) then do;
            _cursub = %unquote(&subject);
            _cursub1 = _cursub1 + 1;
            call symput('ns',left(_cursub1));
            _maxobs = max(_maxobs,_curobs);
            call symput('nos',left(_maxobs));
            _curobs = 1;
        end;
        else do;
            _curobs = _curobs + 1;
        end;
        _subject = _cursub1;
        drop _cursub _cursub1 _curobs _maxobs;
        _one = 1;
    run;

    /*---number of observations and random effects---*/
    data _null_;
        set _nlinmix nobs=count;
        call symput('no',left(put(count,8.)));
        nus = &nu*&ns;
        call symput('nus',left(nus));
    run;

    /*---starting values for b and u---*/
    data _nlinmix;
        set _nlinmix;
        %let idx = 1;
        %if %index(&options,SKIPNLIN) %then %do;
            %do i = 1 %to &nb;
                %scan(&parms,&idx,' ' =) =
                    %scan(&parms,%eval(&idx+1),' ' =);
                %let idx = %eval(&idx + 2);
            %end;
        %end;
        %do i = 1 %to &nu;
            %scan(&random,&i,' ') = 0;
        %end;
    run;

    %mend init;

    /*-------------------------------------------------------*/
    /*                                                       */
    /*    %numder                                            */
    /*    numerical derivatives                              */
    /*                                                       */
    /*-------------------------------------------------------*/
    %macro numder;

        do _i = 1 to &nb;
            _b0 = _b{_i};
```

```
            _tol = &tol*(1+abs(_b0));
            _b{_i} = _b0 - _tol;
            &mod
            _predl = pred;
            _b{_i} = _b0 + _tol;
            &mod
            _predu = pred;
            _db{_i} = (_predu - _predl)/2/_tol;
            _b{_i} = _b0;
         end;
      %if (&nu) %then %do;
         do i = 1 to &nu;
            _u0 = _u{i};
            _tol = &tol*(1+abs(_u0));
            _u{i} = _u0 - _tol;
            &mod
            _predl = pred;
            _u{i} = _u0 + _tol;
            &mod
            _predu = pred;
            _du{i} = (_predu - _predl)/2/_tol;
            _u{i} = _u0;
         end;
      %end;

%mend numder;


   /*--------------------------------------------------------*/
   /*                                                        */
   /*    %nlin                                               */
   /*    PROC NLIN call                                      */
   /*                                                        */
   /*--------------------------------------------------------*/
%macro nlin;

%if (not %index(&options,NOPRINT)) & ((&nu) | (&nr)) %then %do;
   %put Calling PROC NLIN to initialize.;
%end;

proc nlin data=_nlinmix &_printn_;
   array _b{&nb} &fixed;
   array _db{&nb} &d_fixed;
   array _derb{&nb} &d_fixedn;

   /*---set starting values---*/
   parms %unquote(&parms);
   /*---compute the nonlinear function and its derivatives---*/
   &modinit
   &mod
   model %unquote(&response) = pred;
   %if %length(&weight) ne 0 %then %do;
      _weight_ = %unquote(&weight);
   %end;
   %if %length(&der) %then %do;
      &der
   %end;
   %else %do;
      %if (&nu) %then %do;
         array _u{&nu} &random;
         array _du{&nu} &d_random;
      %end;
      %numder
   %end;
   do i = 1 to &nb;
      _derb{i} = _db{i};
   end;
```

```
        output out=_nlinmix parms=&fixed;
run;

%mend nlin;


  /*------------------------------------------------------------*/
  /*                                                            */
  /*    %resder                                                 */
  /*    construct residuals and derivatives                     */
  /*                                                            */
  /*------------------------------------------------------------*/
%macro resder;

data _nlinmix;
   set _nlinmix end=_last;
   %if (&nb) %then %do;
      array _b{&nb} &fixed;
      array _db{&nb} &d_fixed;
   %end;
   %if (&nu) %then %do;
      array _u{&nu} &random;
      array _du{&nu} &d_random;
   %end;
   retain _rss 0;
   &modinit
   &mod
   _resid = %unquote(&response) - pred;
   %if %index(&options,DEBUG) %then %do;
      _residy = _resid;
   %end;
   %if %length(&weight) %then %do;
      _w = %unquote(&weight);
      if (_resid ne .) then _rss = _rss + _resid*_resid*_w;
   %end;
   %else %do;
      if (_resid ne .) then _rss = _rss + _resid*_resid;
   %end;
   %if %length(&der) %then %do;
      &der
   %end;
   %else %do;
      %numder
   %end;
   if (_resid ne .) then do;
      %if (&nb) %then %do;
         do _i = 1 to &nb;
            _resid = _resid + _db{_i}*_b{_i};
         end;
      %end;
      %if (&nu) & (&expand=EBLUP) %then %do;
         do _i = 1 to &nu;
            _resid = _resid + _du{_i}*_u{_i};
         end;
      %end;
   end;
   if _last then call symput('rss',left(_rss));
   drop _rss;
   if (_error_ = 1) then do;
      call symput('_error',left(_error_));
      stop;
   end;
run;

%if %index(&options,DEBUG) %then %do;
   proc print data=_nlinmix(obs=30);
   run;
   proc means data=_nlinmix uss;
```

```
            var _residy;
        run;
%end;


%if %index(&options,PLOT) %then %do;
    symbol i=join r=500 c=black;
    proc gplot data=_nlinmix;
        plot &response*pred=_subject / nolegend;
        plot _resid*(&d_fixed)=_subject / nolegend;
%end;


%mend resder;

    /*----------------------------------------------------------*/
    /*                                                          */
    /*    %mixed                                                */
    /*    PROC MIXED step                                       */
    /*                                                          */
    /*----------------------------------------------------------*/
%macro mixed;

%let ncall = %eval(&ncall + 1);
%if not %index(&options,NOPRINT) %then
    %put %str(    )PROC MIXED call &ncall;


proc mixed data=_nlinmix method=%unquote(&method)
    %unquote(&procopt) %if (&hold>0) %then %do; noprofile %end; cl;
    %if not %index(&options,NOCLASS) %then %do;
        class _subject;
    %end;
    %if (&nb) %then %do;
        model _resid = &d_fixed / s cl noint %unquote(&modopt);
    %end;
    %else %do;
        model _resid = / noint %unquote(&modopt);
    %end;
    %if (&nu) %then %do;
        random &d_random / type=%unquote(&type) sub=_subject
            %if (&expand=EBLUP) %then %do; s %end;
            %if (&gauss>0) %then %do; gci %end; &ranopt ;
        %if (&hold>0) %then
            %str(parms / pdata=_covsave noiter;) ;
        %else %if %length(&covparms) %then
            %str(parms %unquote(&covparms);) ;
        %else %if (&ncall>0) & not %index(&options,NOPREV) %then
            %str(parms / pdata=_covsave;) ;
    %end;
    %if %length(&weight) %then %str(weight _w;);
    %if (&nr) %then %do;
        %if %length(&rtype) %then
            %str(repeated &reffect / type=&rtype sub=&rsub &ropt;);
        %else %str(repeated &reffect / sub=&rsub &ropt;);
    %end;
    %if %length(&add) %then %do;
        %unquote(&add)
    %end;
    %if (&nb) %then %do;
        make 'solutionf' out=_soln;
    %end;
    %if (&nu) | (&nr) %then %do;
        make 'covparms' out=_cov;
        %if (&nu) & (&expand=EBLUP) %then %do;
            make 'solutionr' out=_solnr(keep=parm subject est);
        %end;
        %if (&nu) & (&gauss>0) %then %do;
            make 'gci' out=_gci;
        %end;
    %end;
```

```
                             make 'fitting' out=_fit;
                  run;

                    /*---check for convergence---*/
                  %let there = 0;
                  data _null_;
                     set _fit;
                     call symput('there',1);
                  run;
                  %if (&there = 0) %then %do;
                     %if not %index(&options,NOPRINT) %then
                          %put PROC MIXED did not converge.;
                     %let _error = 1;
                  %end;

                  %mend mixed;

                    /*-------------------------------------------------------------*/
                    /*                                                             */
                    /*    %merge                                                   */
                    /*    merge in new estimates of b and u                        */
                    /*                                                             */
                    /*-------------------------------------------------------------*/
                  %macro merge;

                    /*---drop variables for subsequent merge---*/
                  data _nlinmix;
                     set _nlinmix;
                     drop pred;
                     %if (&nb) %then %do;
                        drop &fixed;
                     %end;
                     %if (&nu) & (&expand=EBLUP) %then %do;
                        drop &random;
                     %end;
                  run;

                    /*---merge in b---*/
                  %if (&nb) %then %do;
                     proc transpose data=saveb out=_beta;
                        var est;
                     run;

                     data _beta;
                        set _beta;
                        array _b{&nb} &fixed;
                        %do i = 1 %to &nb;
                           _b{&i} = col&i;
                        %end;
                        _one = 1;
                        keep _one &fixed;
                     run;

                     data _nlinmix;
                        merge _nlinmix _beta;
                        by _one;
                     run;
                  %end;

                    /*---merge in u---*/
                  %if (&nu) & (&expand=EBLUP) %then %do i=1 %to &nu;

                     %let effect = %scan(&random,&i,' ');
                     %let d_effect = %scan(&d_random,&i,' ');

                     data _eblup;
                        set saveu;
                        pp = "&d_effect";
```

```
               if (parm = pp);
               %if %index(&options,NOCLASS) %then %do;
                  _subject = subject;
               %end;
               %else %do;
                  _subject = substr(subject,9);
               %end;
               _sub = 0;
               _sub = _sub + _subject;
               &effect = est;
               keep _sub &effect;
            run;

            data _eblup;
               set _eblup;
               _subject = _sub;
               keep _subject &effect;
            run;

            data _nlinmix;
               merge _nlinmix _eblup;
               by _subject;
            run;

      %end;

      %mend merge;

      /*----------------------------------------------------------*/
      /*                                                          */
      /*    %uquad                                                */
      /*    compute u'inv(G)u                                     */
      /*                                                          */
      /*----------------------------------------------------------*/
      %macro uquad;

      %if not (&nu) | not (&expand=EBLUP) %then %let uq = 0;
      %else %do;

         data _eblup;
            set saveu;
            %if %index(&options,NOCLASS) %then %do;
               _subject = subject;
            %end;
            %else %do;
               _subject = substr(subject,9);
            %end;
            _sub = 0;
            _sub = _sub + _subject;
            keep est _sub;
         run;

         proc transpose data=_eblup out=_eb;
            var est;
            by _sub;
         run;

         data _eb;
            set _eb end=_last;
            array col{&nu} col1-col&nu;
            array us{&nu} us1-us&nu;
            retain uq 0;

            /*---compute InvChol(G)*u---*/
            %do i = 1 %to &nu;
               us{&i} = 0;
                  %do j = 1 %to &i;
                     us{&i} = us{&i} + &&gci&i&j*col{&j};
```

```
                %end;
            %end;

            /*---accumulate sum of squares---*/
            do i = 1 to &nu;
                uq = uq + us{i}*us{i};
            end;
            output;
            if _last then call symput("uq",left(uq));
        run;
    %end;

%mend uquad;


    /*-------------------------------------------------------*/
    /*                                                       */
    /*      %iterate                                         */
    /*      Iteration process                                */
    /*                                                       */
    /*-------------------------------------------------------*/
%macro iterate;

    /*---initial data set for iterinfo---*/
    data _beta;
        set _nlinmix(obs=1);
        %if (&nb) %then %do;
            keep &fixed;
        %end;
    run;

    /*---intitial data sets for Gauss-Newton---*/
    %if (&gauss > 0) %then %do;
        %if (&nb) %then %do;
            data oldb;
                set _beta;
                array _b{&nb} &fixed;
                %do i = 1 %to &nb;
                    oldest = _b{&i};
                    output;
                %end;
                keep oldest;
            run;
        %end;
        %if (&nu) & (&expand=EBLUP) %then %do;
            data oldu;
                oldest = 0;
                %do i = 1 %to &nus;
                    output;
                %end;
            run;
        %end;
    %end;

    /*---initial macro variables---*/
    %let crit = .;
    %let conv = 0;
    %let hold = 0;
    %let ni = 0;
    %let ncall = -1;

    /*---iterate until convergence---*/
    %do %while(&ni <= &maxit);

        %if (&ni = 0) and not %index(&options,NOPRINT) %then
            %put Iteratively calling PROC MIXED.;

        %if (&switch > 0) and (&ni = &switch) %then %do;
```

```
        %let expand = EBLUP;
        %let gauss = &savegau;
        %let ni = 0;
        %let switch = 0;
        %put Switching from EXPAND=ZERO to EXPAND=EBLUP;
    %end;

    /*---save estimates---*/
    %if (&ni ne 0) and ((&nu) | (&nr)) %then %do;
        data _covold;
            set _covsave;
            estold = est;
            keep estold;
        run;
    %end;
    %if (&ni ne 0) and (&nb) %then %do;
        data _solnold;
            set saveb;
            estold = est;
            keep estold;
        run;
    %end;

    /*---set up pseudo data and compute first step---*/
    %resder
    %if (&_error = 1) %then %goto finish;
    %mixed
    %if (&_error = 1) %then %goto finish;

    %if (&nu) | (&nr) %then %do;
        data _covsave;
            set _cov;
        run;
    %end;

    /*---check for convergence---*/
    %if (&ni ne 0) %then %do;
        %let crit = 0;
        %if (&nu) | (&nr) %then %do;
            data _null_;
                merge _cov _covold end=last;
                retain cr &crit;
                crit = abs(est-estold)/
                    max(abs(estold),max(abs(est),1));
                cr = max(cr,crit);
                if last then do;
                    call symput('crit',left(cr));
                end;
            run;
        %end;
        %if (&nb) %then %do;
            data _null_;
                merge _soln _solnold end=last;
                retain cr &crit;
                crit = abs(est-estold)/
                    max(abs(estold),max(abs(est),1));
                cr = max(cr,crit);
                if last then do;
                    call symput('crit',left(cr));
                end;
            run;
        %end;
        data _null_;
            cr = &crit;
            if (cr < &converge) then call symput('conv',left(1));
        run;
    %end;
    %else %if %index(&options,PRINTFIRST) %then %let _print_ = off;
```

```
%if not %index(&options,NOPRINT) %then %do;
   %put %str(    );
   %put iteration = &ni;
   %put convergence criterion = &crit;
   %getbc;
   %put &bstr &cstr;
%end;
%if (&conv = 1) %then %do;
   %let maxit = -1;
   %let gauss = -1;
%end;
%else %let ni = %eval(&ni + 1);

/*---if no Gauss-Newton, just merge in new estimates and
     loop back (this is equivalent to taking 1 G-N step)---*/
%if (&ni > &gauss) %then %do;
   /*---save step---*/
   %if (&nb) %then %do;
      data saveb;
         set _soln;
      run;
   %end;
   %if (&nu) & (&expand=EBLUP) %then %do;
      data saveu;
         set _solnr;
      run;
   %end;
   %merge;
%end;
/*---Gauss-Newton steps---*/
%else %do;
   /*---get residual variance estimate---*/
   data _null_;
      set _fit;
      if (descr = 'Variance Estimate') then
         call symput('resid',left(value));
   run;
   /*---load elements of InvChol(G) into macro variables---*/
   %if (&nu) %then %do;
      data _null_;
         set _gci;
         array col{&nu} col1-col&nu;
         %do i = 1 %to &nu;
            %do j = 1 %to &i;
               %local gci&i&j;
               if (row = &i) then
                  call symput("gci&i&j",left(col{&j}));
            %end;
         %end;
      run;
   %end;

   /*---compute quadratic form of random effects---*/
   %if (&ni > 1) %then %uquad;
   %else %let uq = 0;
   /*---compute initial objective function---*/
   data _null_;
      obj = &rss/&resid + &uq;
      call symput('oldobj',left(obj));
   run;
   %if not %index(&options,NOPRINT) %then %do;
      %put %str(    );
      %put %str(    )subiteration = 0;
      %put %str(    )Gauss-Newton starting objective = &oldobj;
      %put %str(    )rss=&rss  resid=&resid  uq=&uq;
      %getbc;
      %put %str(    )&bstr &cstr;
   %end;
```

```
           /*---save step---*/
           %if (&nb) %then %do;
              data bestb;
                 set _soln;
              run;
           %end;
           %if (&nu) & (&expand=EBLUP) %then %do;
              data bestu;
                 set _solnr;
              run;
           %end;

           /*---Gauss-Newton loop---*/
           %let hold = 1;
           %let nsi = 1;
           %do %while(&nsi <= &maxsubit);
             /*---save step---*/
             %if (&nb) %then %do;
                data saveb;
                   set _soln;
                run;
             %end;
             %if (&nu) & (&expand=EBLUP) %then %do;
                data saveu;
                   set _solnr;
                run;
             %end;
             /*---merge in new estimates of b and u---*/
             %merge;
             /*---update pseudo data---*/
             %resder;
             /*---compute u`*inv(G)*u---*/
             %uquad;
             /*---check to see if objective has improved---*/
             %let better = 0;
             %let sconv = 0;
             data _null_;
                obj = &rss/&resid + &uq;
                reldiff = (&oldobj - obj)/
                   max(&oldobj,max(obj,1));
                if (reldiff > 0) then call symput('better',left(1));
                if (abs(reldiff) < &subconv) then
                   call symput('sconv',left(1));
                call symput('obj',left(obj));
                call symput('reldiff',left(reldiff));
             run;
             %if not %index(&options,NOPRINT) %then %do;
                %put %str(    );
                %put %str(    )subiteration = &nsi;
                %put %str(    )old objective = &oldobj;
                %put %str(    )new objective = &obj;
                %put %str(    )relative diff = &reldiff;
                %put %str(    )subconverged  = &sconv;
                %put %str(    )better = &better;
                %put %str(    )rss=&rss  resid=&resid  uq=&uq;
                %getbc;
                %put %str(    )&bstr &cstr;
             %end;

             /*---stop looping if objectives are within tolerance---*/
             %if (&sconv = 1) %then %let nsi = &maxsubit;

             /*---if better, update saves and take another step---*/
             %if (&better = 1) %then %do;
                %if (&nb) %then %do;
                   data bestb;
                      set saveb;
                   run;
```

```
                    data oldb;
                        set saveb;
                        oldest = est;
                        keep oldest;
                    run;
                %end;
                %if (&nu) & (&expand=EBLUP) %then %do;
                    data bestu;
                        set saveu;
                    run;
                    data oldu;
                        set saveu;
                        oldest = est;
                        keep oldest;
                    run;
                %end;
                %let oldobj = &obj;
                /*---compute new iterate, holding variance
                        parameters fixed---*/
                %if (&nsi < &maxsubit) %then %mixed;
            %end;
            /*---if not better, step shorten---*/
            %else %if (&nsi < &maxsubit) %then %do;
                %put %str(    )step-shortening with fraction &fraction;
                %if (&nb) %then %do;
                    data _soln;
                        merge saveb oldb;
                        est = &fraction*est+(1-&fraction)*oldest;
                        drop oldest;
                    run;
                %end;
                %if (&nu) & (&expand=EBLUP) %then %do;
                    data _solnr;
                        merge saveu oldu;
                        est = &fraction*est+(1-&fraction)*oldest;
                        drop oldest;
                    run;
                %end;
            %end;
            /*---increment counter---*/
            %let nsi = %eval(&nsi + 1);
        %end;

        /*---merge in best parameters---*/
        %if (&nb) %then %do;
            data saveb;
                set bestb;
            run;
        %end;
        %if (&nu) & (&expand=EBLUP) %then %do;
            data saveu;
                set bestu;
            run;
        %end;
        %merge
        %let hold = 0;
    %end;
    /*---get rid of fitting data set---*/
    %if (&there = 1) %then %do;
        proc datasets lib=work nolist;
            delete _fit;
        run;
    %end;
%end;

/*---turn on printing and options---*/
%finish:
%let _print_ = on;
```

```
%let _printn_ = ;
%let niter = &ni;
options notes number;
%if not %index(&options,NOPRINT) %then %do;
   %if (&conv = 1) %then %do;
      %put NLINMIX convergence criteria met.;
      /*---compute final results---*/
      %resder
      %if (&expand = ZERO) %then %let expand = EBLUP;
      %mixed
   %end;
   %else %put NLINMIX did not converge.;
%end;

%mend iterate;




/*-------------------------------------------------------------*/
/*                                                             */
/*     %baseinfo                                               */
/*     Print basic information about the macro                 */
/*                                                             */
/*-------------------------------------------------------------*/
%macro baseinfo;

%if %index(&data,.)=0 %then %let data=WORK.&data;
%put;
%put %str(                        The NLINMIX Macro);
%put;
%put %str(        Data Set                    : &data);
%put %str(        Response                    : &response);
%put %str(        Subject                     : &subject);
%if (&nb) %then
%put %str(        Fixed Effects Parameters    : &fixed);
%if (&nu) %then %do;
%put %str(        Random Effects Parameters   : &random);
%put %str(        Covariance Type             : &type);
%put %str(        Expansion Point             : &expand);
%end;
%if %length(&reffect) %then
%put %str(        REPEATED Effect             : &rtype);
%if %length(&rtype) %then
%put %str(        REPEATED Covariance Type    : &rtype);
%if %length(&ropt) %then
%put %str(        REPEATED Options            : &ropt);
%if %length(&weight) %then
%put %str(        Weight                      : &weight);
%put %str(        Optimization Method         : &method);
%put;
%put;
%put %str(                        Dimensions);
%put;
%put %str(            Observations            : &no);
%put %str(            Subjects                : &ns);
%put %str(            Maximum Obs per Subject : &nos);
%put %str(            Fixed Effects Parameters : &nb);
%if (&nu) %then
%put %str(            Random Effects per Subject : &nu);
%put;

%mend baseinfo;


/*-------------------------------------------------------------*/
/*                                                             */
/*     %getbc                                                  */
/*     load current estimate of b into macro variables         */
/*                                                             */
```

```
        /*-----------------------------------------------------------*/
        %macro getbc;

        %let bstr = ;
        %let cstr = ;

        %if (&nb) %then %do;
           data _beta;
              set _beta;
              %do i = 1 %to &nb;
                 call symput("bb&i",left(%scan(&fixed,&i,' ')));
              %end;
           run;

           %do i = 1 %to &nb;
              %let bstr = &bstr %scan(&fixed,&i,' ')=&&bb&i;
           %end;
        %end;

        %if (&nu) or (&nr) %then %do;
           data _null_;
              set _cov nobs=count;
              call symput('ncov',left(put(count,8.)));
           run;

           data _null_;
              set _cov;
              %do i = 1 %to &ncov;
                 if (_n_ = &i) then do;
                    call symput("cc&i",left(est));
                 end;
              %end;
           run;

           %do i = 1 %to &ncov;
              %let cstr = &cstr COVP&i=&&cc&i;
           %end;
        %end;


        %mend getbc;

        /*-----------------------------------------------------------*/
        /*                                                           */
        /*     %nlinmix()                                            */
        /*     the main macro                                        */
        /*                                                           */
        /*-----------------------------------------------------------*/
        %macro nlinmix(data=,response=y,subject=subject,modinit=,model=,
           derivs=,tol=1e-5,parms=,covparms=,random=,ranopt=,type=simple,
           rtype=,reffect=,rsub=_SUBJECT,ropt=,weight=,add=,method=reml,
           expand=ZERO,converge=1e-8,subconv=1e-12,maxit=20,maxsubit=10,
           switch=0,gauss=0,fraction=0.5,procopt=,modopt=,options=);

        /*---check for mandatories---*/
        %if %bquote(&model)= %then %let missing = MODEL=;
        %else %let missing =;
        %if %length(&missing) %then %do;
           %put ERROR: The NLINMIX &missing argument is not present.;
        %end;
        %else %do;
           /*---default data set---*/
           %if %bquote(&data)= %then %let data=&syslast;

           /*---change variables to quoted uppercase---*/
           %let data     = %qupcase(&data);
           %let response = %qupcase(&response);
           %let subject  = %qupcase(&subject);
```

```
%let modinit  = %qupcase(&modinit);
%let mod      = %qupcase(&model);
%let der      = %qupcase(&derivs);
%let parms    = %qupcase(&parms);
%let covparms = %qupcase(&covparms);
%let random   = %qupcase(&random);
%let type     = %qupcase(&type);
%let rtype    = %qupcase(&rtype);
%let reffect  = %qupcase(&reffect);
%let rsub     = %qupcase(&rsub);
%let ropt     = %qupcase(&ropt);
%let weight   = %qupcase(&weight);
%let add      = %qupcase(&add);
%let method   = %qupcase(&method);
%let expand   = %qupcase(&expand);
%let procopt  = %qupcase(&procopt);
%let modopt   = %qupcase(&modopt);
%let options  = %qupcase(&options);

/*---turn off options and printing---*/
title;
options nospool nonotes nodate nonumber;
%local nb nu ns nos no nus ni ncall nr fixed d_fixed d_fixedn
   d_random crit hold rss resid uq bstr cstr there savegau
     _error;

/*---initialize---*/
%init
%global _print_ _printn_;
%if %index(&options,PRINTALL) or %index(&options,PRINTFIRST)
   %then %do;
    %let _print_ = on;
    %let _printn_ = ;
%end;
%else %do;
   %let _print_ = off;
   %let _printn_ = noprint;
%end;

/*---print basic macro information---*/
%if not %index(&options,NOPRINT) %then %baseinfo;

/*---run PROC NLIN to get initial estimates---*/
%if (&nb) & not %index(&options,SKIPNLIN) %then %do;
   %if not (&nu) & not (&nr) %then %let _printn_ = ;
   %nlin;
%end;

/*---iterate PROC MIXED calls until convergence---*/
   %iterate;
%end;

%mend nlinmix;
```

Appendix **4** **SAS® Data Sets**

Data Set 1.2.4 BOND

```
Chapter 1: Randomized Block Designs
RCBD Data

data bond;
   input ingot metal $ pres;
   datalines;
1 n 67.0
1 i 71.9
1 c 72.2
2 n 67.5
2 i 68.8
2 c 66.4
3 n 76.0
3 i 82.6
3 c 74.5
4 n 72.7
4 i 78.1
4 c 67.3
5 n 73.1
5 i 74.2
5 c 73.2
6 n 65.8
6 i 70.8
6 c 68.7
7 n 75.6
7 i 84.9
7 c 69.0
;
```

Data from a table of Exercise 13.36, p. 619, of Mendenhall, M., Wackerly, D.D., and Scheaffer, R.L., *Mathematical Statistics*. Copyright © 1990 by Wadsworth Publishing Company. Reproduced with permission.

Data Set 1.5.1 PBIB

```
Chapter 1: Randomized Block Designs
Data from Incomplete Block Design

data pbib;
   array trt{4} trt1-trt4;
   array y{4} y1-y4;
   input blk trt1 y1 trt2 y2 trt3 y3 trt4 y4;
   do i=1 to 4;
      response=y{i};
      treat=trt{i};
      output;
   end;
   keep blk response treat;
   datalines;
 1 15 2.4   9 2.5   1 2.6  13 2.0
 2  5 2.7   7 2.8   8 2.4   1 2.7
 3 10 2.6   1 2.8  14 2.4   2 2.4
 4 15 3.4  11 3.1   2 2.1   3 2.3
 5  6 4.1  15 3.3   4 3.3   7 2.9
 6 12 3.4   4 3.2   3 2.8   1 3.0
 7 12 3.2  14 2.5  15 2.4   8 2.6
 8  6 2.3   3 2.3  14 2.4   5 2.7
 9  5 2.8   4 2.8   2 2.6  13 2.5
10 10 2.5  12 2.7  13 2.8   6 2.6
11  9 2.6   7 2.6  10 2.3   3 2.4
```

```
12   8 2.7    6 2.7    2 2.5    9 2.6
13   5 3.0    9 3.6   11 3.2   12 3.2
14   7 3.0   13 2.8   14 2.4   11 2.5
15  10 2.4    4 2.5    8 3.2   11 3.1
;
```

Data from Cochran, W.G. and Cox, M.G., *Experimental Designs*, p. 456.
Copyright © 1957 by John Wiley & Sons, Inc. Reprinted by permission of
John Wiley & Sons, Inc.

Data Set 2.2(a) Data from Cultivar-Inoculation Trial

```
Chapter 2: Common Mixed Models
Data from Cultivar_Inoculation Trial

data a;
   input block cult $ inoc $ drywt;
   datalines;
1 a con 27.4
1 a dea 29.7
1 a liv 34.5
1 b con 29.4
1 b dea 32.5
1 b liv 34.4
2 a con 28.9
2 a dea 28.7
2 a liv 33.4
2 b con 28.7
2 b dea 32.4
2 b liv 36.4
3 a con 28.6
3 a dea 29.7
3 a liv 32.9
3 b con 27.2
3 b dea 29.1
3 b liv 32.6
4 a con 26.7
4 a dea 28.9
4 a liv 31.8
4 b con 26.8
4 b dea 28.6
4 b liv 30.7
;
```

Data from Littell, R.C., Freund, R.J., and Spector P.C., *SAS System for
Linear Models, Third Edition*. Copyright © 1991 by SAS Institute Inc.,
Cary, NC, USA. Reproduced with permission.

Data Set 2.2(b) Data from Semiconductor Example

```
Chapter 2: Common Mixed Models
Data from Semiconductor Example

data b;
   input resista et wafer pos;
   datalines;
5.22 1 1 1
5.61 1 1 2
6.11 1 1 3
6.33 1 1 4
6.13 1 2 1
6.14 1 2 2
```

```
5.60 1 2 3
5.91 1 2 4
5.49 1 3 1
4.60 1 3 2
4.95 1 3 3
5.42 1 3 4
5.78 2 1 1
6.52 2 1 2
5.90 2 1 3
5.67 2 1 4
5.77 2 2 1
6.23 2 2 2
5.57 2 2 3
5.96 2 2 4
6.43 2 3 1
5.81 2 3 2
5.83 2 3 3
6.12 2 3 4
5.66 3 1 1
6.25 3 1 2
5.46 3 1 3
5.08 3 1 4
6.53 3 2 1
6.50 3 2 2
6.23 3 2 3
6.84 3 2 4
6.22 3 3 1
6.29 3 3 2
5.63 3 3 3
6.36 3 3 4
6.75 4 1 1
6.97 4 1 2
6.02 4 1 3
6.88 4 1 4
6.22 4 2 1
6.54 4 2 2
6.12 4 2 3
6.61 4 2 4
6.05 4 3 1
6.15 4 3 2
5.55 4 3 3
6.13 4 3 4
;
```

Data from Littell, R.C., Freund, R.J., and Spector P.C., *SAS System for Linear Models, Third Edition.* Copyright © 1991 by SAS Institute Inc., Cary, NC, USA. Reproduced with permission.

Data Set 2.8.1 Multilocation Trial

```
Chapter 2: Common Mixed Models
Data from Multilocation Trial

data mltloc;
   input obs loc block trt adg fe;
   datalines;
    3     A     1     3     3.16454     7.1041
    4     A     1     4     3.12500     6.6847
    6     A     1     2     3.15944     6.8338
    7     A     1     1     3.25000     6.5254
    9     A     2     2     2.71301     8.2505
   10     A     2     1     3.20281     7.5922
   12     A     2     3     3.02423     7.3894
   16     A     2     4     2.87245     7.4604
   19     A     3     1     2.68878     8.2785
```

20	A	3	2	2.86862	7.9470
21	A	3	3	2.89923	7.9739
22	A	3	4	3.02806	8.4331
25	B	1	3	2.18131	6.6691
27	B	1	4	2.51914	5.6281
28	B	1	2	1.88739	7.0723
31	B	1	1	2.34685	6.0295
33	B	2	4	2.45608	5.6195
35	B	2	1	2.25225	6.3978
36	B	2	3	2.23649	6.1799
40	B	2	2	2.47523	5.9985
41	B	3	2	1.94200	7.2975
44	B	3	3	2.43243	6.4350
47	B	3	4	2.30180	6.3339
48	B	3	1	2.53378	6.1564
50	C	1	4	2.96014	7.5110
51	C	1	2	3.23551	7.4762
54	C	1	3	3.24638	7.2063
56	C	1	1	3.04710	7.6389
58	C	2	3	3.26449	7.5466
59	C	2	2	2.71377	9.0895
61	C	2	1	3.06522	7.8723
62	C	2	4	2.71739	8.2318
66	C	3	4	3.03623	7.9426
67	C	3	3	3.10507	8.4608
69	C	3	1	3.16304	8.5549
70	C	3	2	3.02899	8.5038
74	D	1	1	2.49164	9.5758
77	D	1	3	2.51833	9.5121
79	D	1	2	2.35631	10.3264
80	D	1	4	2.30331	9.7715
81	D	2	3	2.72688	9.5628
83	D	2	2	2.59512	9.9414
85	D	2	1	2.56516	9.3887
88	D	2	4	2.91523	8.3158
89	D	3	3	2.57943	10.4416
90	D	3	4	2.98159	8.7710
93	D	3	2	2.35370	11.0148
94	D	3	1	2.21953	11.2417
99	E	1	3	2.84158	8.7886
100	E	1	4	2.65264	8.6946
102	E	1	2	2.47112	9.7143
103	E	1	1	2.89769	9.2401
105	E	2	2	2.57343	9.5353
106	E	2	1	2.99752	8.7538
110	E	2	4	2.95380	8.8210
112	E	2	3	3.08663	8.9427
114	E	3	1	2.72525	9.4308
115	E	3	2	2.75825	9.7721
116	E	3	3	3.08333	8.9010
117	E	3	4	3.12129	8.4852
122	F	1	1	3.20600	6.3983
123	F	1	2	2.89500	6.6569
125	F	1	4	3.36900	6.0821
126	F	1	3	3.12000	6.5349
130	F	2	2	3.19300	6.6729
131	F	2	1	3.29800	6.5488
133	F	2	4	3.09700	6.6598
135	F	2	3	3.38500	6.2998
139	F	3	3	3.44900	6.2849
140	F	3	2	3.05000	6.9957
141	F	3	1	3.43500	6.7302
143	F	3	4	3.60600	6.3827
145	G	1	2	2.58669	8.1394
147	G	1	1	3.17892	7.0972
148	G	1	4	2.95284	7.3140
151	G	1	3	3.17924	6.9430
154	G	2	4	2.62344	7.5150

155	G	2	3	2.64286	8.0237
157	G	2	1	3.12760	7.3169
160	G	2	2	2.54993	8.1957
163	G	3	4	2.58322	7.9687
164	G	3	3	2.84813	7.9284
166	G	3	2	2.69279	8.5303
167	G	3	1	3.14424	7.3564
169	H	1	3	3.39974	6.5945
173	H	1	2	3.12370	6.7530
175	H	1	4	3.17969	6.4279
176	H	1	1	3.70052	6.4830
177	H	2	2	2.95192	7.3809
179	H	2	3	3.44661	6.7929
182	H	2	4	3.28906	6.4807
184	H	2	1	3.37500	6.8139
188	H	3	4	3.65104	6.3068
190	H	3	1	3.27734	7.4789
191	H	3	3	3.42708	6.9327
192	H	3	2	3.04818	7.7264
193	I	1	2	2.22105	8.4243
196	I	1	1	3.15526	6.7119
197	I	1	4	2.40263	7.7486
198	I	1	3	3.00000	6.9215
203	I	2	1	2.29079	8.8861
204	I	2	4	2.25395	8.6850
205	I	2	3	2.60526	8.4150
208	I	2	2	2.34737	8.7866
209	I	3	2	2.50505	8.5975
212	I	3	1	2.31316	8.9267
213	I	3	4	2.42105	8.7750
214	I	3	3	2.74211	8.1599
;

Data Set 3.2(a) WEIGHTS

```
Chapter 3: Analysis of Repeated Measures Data
Strength Data Set in Multivariate Form

data weights;
    input subj program $  s1 s2 s3 s4 s5 s6 s7;
    datalines;
 1     CONT     85     85     86     85     87     86     87
 2     CONT     80     79     79     78     78     79     78
 3     CONT     78     77     77     77     76     76     77
 4     CONT     84     84     85     84     83     84     85
 5     CONT     80     81     80     80     79     79     80
 6     CONT     76     78     77     78     78     77     74
 7     CONT     79     79     80     79     80     79     81
 8     CONT     76     76     76     75     75     74     74
 9     CONT     77     78     78     80     80     81     80
10     CONT     79     79     79     79     77     78     79
11     CONT     81     81     80     80     80     81     82
12     CONT     77     76     77     78     77     77     77
13     CONT     82     83     83     83     84     83     83
14     CONT     84     84     83     82     81     79     78
15     CONT     79     81     81     82     82     82     80
16     CONT     79     79     78     77     77     78     78
17     CONT     83     82     83     85     84     83     82
18     CONT     78     78     79     79     78     77     77
19     CONT     80     80     79     79     80     80     80
20     CONT     78     79     80     81     80     79     80
 1     RI       79     79     79     80     80     78     80
 2     RI       83     83     85     85     86     87     87
 3     RI       81     83     82     82     83     83     82
 4     RI       81     81     81     82     82     83     81
```

5	RI	80	81	82	82	82	84	86
6	RI	76	76	76	76	76	76	75
7	RI	81	84	83	83	85	85	85
8	RI	77	78	79	79	81	82	81
9	RI	84	85	87	89	88	85	86
10	RI	74	75	78	78	79	78	78
11	RI	76	77	77	77	77	76	76
12	RI	84	84	86	85	86	86	86
13	RI	79	80	79	80	80	82	82
14	RI	78	78	77	76	75	75	76
15	RI	78	80	77	77	75	75	75
16	RI	84	85	85	85	85	83	82
1	WI	84	85	84	83	83	83	84
2	WI	74	75	75	76	75	76	76
3	WI	83	84	82	81	83	83	82
4	WI	86	87	87	87	87	87	86
5	WI	82	83	84	85	84	85	86
6	WI	79	80	79	79	80	79	80
7	WI	79	79	79	81	81	83	83
8	WI	87	89	91	90	91	92	92
9	WI	81	81	81	82	82	83	83
10	WI	82	82	82	84	86	85	87
11	WI	79	79	80	81	81	81	81
12	WI	79	80	81	82	83	82	82
13	WI	83	84	84	84	84	83	83
14	WI	81	81	82	84	83	82	85
15	WI	78	78	79	79	78	79	79
16	WI	83	82	82	84	84	83	84
17	WI	80	79	79	81	80	80	80
18	WI	80	82	82	82	81	81	81
19	WI	85	86	87	86	86	86	86
20	WI	77	78	80	81	82	82	82
21	WI	80	81	80	81	81	82	83

;

Data Set 3.2(b) WEIGHT2

Chapter 3: Analysis of Repeated Measures Data
Strength Data Set in Univariate Form

```
data weight2; set weights;
  time=1; strength=s1; output;
  time=2; strength=s2; output;
  time=3; strength=s3; output;
  time=4; strength=s4; output;
  time=5; strength=s5; output;
  time=6; strength=s6; output;
  time=7; strength=s7; output;
keep subj program time strength;
run;

proc sort data=weight2; by program time;
run;

proc print data=weight2;
title2 'Output 3.2  Strength Data Set in Univariate Form';
run;
```

Data Set 3.2(c) AVG

Chapter 3: Analysis of Repeated Measures Data
Strength Means by Time and Program

```
proc means data=weight2 noprint; by program time; var strength;
   output out=avg mean=strength;
run;

proc print data=avg;
title2 'Output 3.3  Strength Means by Time and Program';
run;
```

Data from Littell, R.C., Freund, R.J., and Spector P.C., *SAS System for Linear Models, Third Edition*. Copyright © 1991 by SAS Institute Inc., Cary, NC, USA. Reproduced with permission.

Data Set 3.4(a) WTSMISS

Chapter 3: Analysis of Repeated Measures Data
Strength Data Set with Missing Values

```
data wtsmiss;
   input subj program $  s1 s2 s3 s4 s5 s6 s7;
   u1=ranuni(54321); if u1<.15 then s1=.;
   u2=ranuni(65432); if u2<.15 then s2=.;
   u3=ranuni(76543); if u3<.15 then s3=.;
   u4=ranuni(87654); if u4<.15 then s4=.;
   u5=ranuni(98765); if u5<.15 then s5=.;
   u6=ranuni(09876); if u6<.15 then s6=.;
   u7=ranuni(10987); if u7<.15 then s7=.;
   datalines;
```

subj	program	s1	s2	s3	s4	s5	s6	s7
1	CONT	85	85	86	85	87	86	87
2	CONT	80	79	79	78	78	79	78
3	CONT	78	77	77	77	76	76	77
4	CONT	84	84	85	84	83	84	85
5	CONT	80	81	80	80	79	79	80
6	CONT	76	78	77	78	78	77	74
7	CONT	79	79	80	79	80	79	81
8	CONT	76	76	76	75	75	74	74
9	CONT	77	78	78	80	80	81	80
10	CONT	79	79	79	79	77	78	79
11	CONT	81	81	80	80	80	81	82
12	CONT	77	76	77	78	77	77	77
13	CONT	82	83	83	83	84	83	83
14	CONT	84	84	83	82	81	79	78
15	CONT	79	81	81	82	82	82	80
16	CONT	79	79	78	77	77	78	78
17	CONT	83	82	83	85	84	83	82
18	CONT	78	78	79	79	78	77	77
19	CONT	80	80	79	79	80	80	80
20	CONT	78	79	80	81	80	79	80
1	RI	79	79	79	80	80	78	80
2	RI	83	83	85	85	86	87	87
3	RI	81	83	82	82	83	83	82
4	RI	81	81	81	82	82	83	81
5	RI	80	81	82	82	82	84	86
6	RI	76	76	76	76	76	76	75
7	RI	81	84	83	83	85	85	85
8	RI	77	78	79	79	81	82	81
9	RI	84	85	87	89	88	85	86
10	RI	74	75	78	78	79	78	78
11	RI	76	77	77	77	77	76	76

```
12      RI      84      84      86      85      86      86      86
13      RI      79      80      79      80      80      82      82
14      RI      78      78      77      76      75      75      76
15      RI      78      80      77      77      75      75      75
16      RI      84      85      85      85      85      83      82
 1      WI      84      85      84      83      83      83      84
 2      WI      74      75      75      76      75      76      76
 3      WI      83      84      82      81      83      83      82
 4      WI      86      87      87      87      87      87      86
 5      WI      82      83      84      85      84      85      86
 6      WI      79      80      79      79      80      79      80
 7      WI      79      79      79      81      81      83      83
 8      WI      87      89      91      90      91      92      92
 9      WI      81      81      81      82      82      83      83
10      WI      82      82      82      84      86      85      87
11      WI      79      79      80      81      81      81      81
12      WI      79      80      81      82      83      82      82
13      WI      83      84      84      84      84      83      83
14      WI      81      81      82      84      83      82      85
15      WI      78      78      79      79      78      79      79
16      WI      83      82      82      84      84      83      84
17      WI      80      79      79      81      80      80      80
18      WI      80      82      82      82      81      81      81
19      WI      85      86      87      86      86      86      86
20      WI      77      78      80      81      82      82      82
21      WI      80      81      80      81      81      82      83
;

proc print data=wtsmiss; var subj program s1-s7;
title1 'Chapter 3  Analysis of Repeated Measures Data';
title2 'Strength Data Set with Missing Values';
run;
```

Data Set 3.4(b) WT2MISS

Chapter 3: Analysis of Repeated Measure Data
Strength Data Set with Missing Values in Univariate Form

```
data wt2miss; set wtsmiss;
  time=1; t=time; strength=s1; output;
  time=2; t=time; strength=s2; output;
  time=3; t=time; strength=s3; output;
  time=4; t=time; strength=s4; output;
  time=5; t=time; strength=s5; output;
  time=6; t=time; strength=s6; output;
  time=7; t=time; strength=s7; output;
  keep subj program time t strength;

proc sort data=wt2miss; by program time;
run;

proc means data=wt2miss noprint; by program time; var strength;
  output out=avgmiss mean=strength;
run;

proc print data=avgmiss;
title2 'Means by Time and Program with Missing Values';

run;
```

```
proc plot data=avgmiss;
   plot strength*time=program;
title3 'Output 3.16  Plot of Strength Means over Time for Each Program';
title4 'with Missing Values';
run;
```

Data from Littell, R.C., Freund, R.J., and Spector P.C., *SAS System for Linear Models, Third Edition*. Copyright © 1991 by SAS Institute Inc., Cary, NC, USA. Reproduced with permission.

Data Set 3.5 HR

Chapter 3: Analysis of Repeated Measures
Unequally Spaced Repeated Measures

```
data hr;
   input patient drug$ basehr hr1 hr5 hr15 hr30 hr1h;
   array hra{5} hr1 hr5 hr15 hr30 hr1h;
   do i = 1 to 5;
      if (i = 1) then hours = 1/60;
      else if (i = 2) then hours = 5/60;
      else if (i = 3) then hours = 15/60;
      else if (i = 4) then hours = 30/60;
      else hours = 1;
      hours1 = hours;
      hr = hra{i};
      output;
   end;
   drop i hr1 hr5 hr15 hr30 hr1h;
   datalines;
201 p   92  76  84  88  96  84
202 b   54  58  60  60  60  64
203 p   84  86  82  84  86  82
204 a   72  72  68  68  78  72
205 b   80  84  84  96  92  72
206 p   68  72  68  68  64  62
207 a  100 104 100  92  92  68
208 a   60  60  58  56  50  56
209 a   88 104  88  88  78  84
210 b   92  82  82  76  82  80
211 b   88  80  84  80  80  78
212 p  102  86  86  96  86  88
214 a   84  92 100  88  88  80
215 b  104 100  96  88  92  84
216 a   92  80  72  64  68  64
217 p   92  88  84  76  88  84
218 a   72  84  78  80  80  76
219 b   72 100  92  84  88  80
220 p   80  80  80  78  80  78
221 p   72  68  76  72  72  68
222 b   88  88  98  98  96  88
223 b   88  88  96  88  88  80
224 p   88  78  84  64  68  64
232 a   78  72  72  78  80  68
;
```

Data Set 3.6 DEMAND

Chapter 3: Analysis of Repeated Measures
Doubly Repeated Measures

```
data demand;
    input state$ year d y rd rt rs;
    logd = log(d);
    logy = log(y);
    logrd = log(rd);
    logrt = log(rt);
    logrs = log(rs);
    datalines;
CA  1949   533   1347   0.343   1.114   2.905
CA  1950   603   1464   0.364   1.162   2.935
CA  1951   669   1608   0.367   1.493   3.093
CA  1952   651   1636   0.369   1.567   3.073
CA  1953   609   1669   0.410   1.594   3.357
CA  1954   634   1716   0.499   1.609   3.295
CA  1955   665   1779   0.496   1.637   3.451
CA  1956   676   1878   0.533   1.757   3.539
CA  1957   642   1963   0.630   2.641   3.930
CA  1958   678   2034   0.667   2.641   3.982
CA  1959   714   2164   0.664   2.648   4.047
DC  1949   854   1603   0.261   0.676   2.803
DC  1950  1013   1773   0.267   0.662   2.877
DC  1951  1185   2017   0.266   0.677   3.006
DC  1952  1076   1921   0.267   0.729   2.975
DC  1953  1004   1856   0.287   0.883   3.035
DC  1954  1044   1868   0.308   1.500   3.083
DC  1955  1067   1931   0.318   1.504   3.177
DC  1956  1062   1951   0.322   1.598   3.250
DC  1957  1120   2085   0.346   2.231   3.368
DC  1958  1196   2144   0.360   2.100   3.457
DC  1959  1168   2167   0.418   2.342   3.727
FL  1949   408   1024   0.354   0.909   2.314
FL  1950   433   1007   0.342   0.957   2.327
FL  1951   469   1068   0.335   1.002   2.428
FL  1952   470   1068   0.328   1.052   2.577
FL  1953   464   1138   0.354   1.118   2.625
FL  1954   465   1137   0.374   1.268   2.871
FL  1955   545   1306   0.378   1.339   2.882
FL  1956   567   1339   0.399   1.486   3.032
FL  1957   531   1383   0.447   2.420   3.338
FL  1958   533   1409   0.498   2.453   3.353
FL  1959   522   1457   0.523   2.489   3.575
IL  1949   843   1465   0.143   0.852   2.504
IL  1950   860   1468   0.146   0.847   2.448
IL  1951   887   1555   0.147   0.936   2.449
IL  1952   914   1648   0.144   1.059   2.568
IL  1953   909   1711   0.150   1.091   2.703
IL  1954   928   1775   0.164   1.130   2.748
IL  1955   939   1815   0.172   1.141   2.778
IL  1956   944   1915   0.183   1.354   2.932
IL  1957   899   1980   0.203   1.628   3.155
IL  1958   919   2001   0.214   1.737   3.402
IL  1959   874   2035   0.231   2.054   3.497
NY  1949  1370   1492   0.112   0.687   2.099
NY  1950  1405   1515   0.119   0.724   2.082
NY  1951  1409   1566   0.119   0.795   2.218
NY  1952  1421   1659   0.120   1.050   2.435
NY  1953  1395   1744   0.134   1.241   2.477
NY  1954  1415   1802   0.145   1.346   2.540
NY  1955  1431   1808   0.146   1.406   2.655
NY  1956  1416   1916   0.168   1.754   2.774
NY  1957  1443   2074   0.189   2.231   2.957
```

```
NY   1958   1453   2120   0.192   2.360   3.073
NY   1959   1417   2197   0.203   2.521   3.223
TX   1949    573    995   0.149   0.839   2.755
TX   1950    634   1052   0.147   0.836   2.740
TX   1951    679   1154   0.148   0.812   2.819
TX   1952    668   1176   0.147   1.070   2.880
TX   1953    666   1228   0.160   1.170   3.082
TX   1954    708   1285   0.182   1.328   3.093
TX   1955    722   1335   0.191   1.368   3.071
TX   1956    708   1358   0.208   1.544   3.068
TX   1957    675   1416   0.250   2.121   3.487
TX   1958    716   1457   0.278   2.241   3.413
TX   1959    703   1520   0.303   2.435   3.671
WA   1949    418   1146   0.358   0.937   2.068
WA   1950    501   1324   0.361   0.973   2.229
WA   1951    525   1433   0.365   1.039   2.367
WA   1952    519   1481   0.381   1.305   2.553
WA   1953    500   1531   0.414   1.342   2.848
WA   1954    537   1602   0.481   1.348   2.865
WA   1955    545   1649   0.529   1.770   2.907
WA   1956    525   1656   0.587   1.779   3.011
WA   1957    494   1711   0.681   2.313   3.252
WA   1958    521   1754   0.716   2.302   3.306
WA   1959    515   1809   0.730   2.495   3.507
;
```

Data from Feige, E.L., *The Demand for Liquid Assets: A Temporal Cross-Section Analysis*. Copyright © 1964 by Prentice-Hall, Englewood Cliffs, NJ. Reproduced with permission.

Data Set 4.2 Mississippi River

```
Chapter 4: Random Effects Models
Data for an Example of a One-way Random Effects Treatment Structure

data e_2_2;
    input influent y;
    if influent=3 or influent=5 then type=1;
    else if influent=6 then type=3;
    else type=2;
    datalines;
1        21
1        27
1        29
1        17
1        19
1        12
1        29
1        20
1        20
2        21
2        11
2        18
2         9
2        13
2        23
2         2
3        20
3        19
3        20
3        11
3        14
4        14
4        24
4        30
```

```
                              4         21
                              4         31
                              4         27
                              5          7
                              5         15
                              5         18
                              5          4
                              5         28
                              6         41
                              6         42
                              6         35
                              6         34
                              6         30
                              ;
```

Data Set 4.4 Semiconductor

```
Chapter 4: Random Effects Models
Data for a Three-level Nested Design Structure

data e_2_4;
    input sor lot wafer site y;
    datalines;
1       1       1       1       2006
1       1       1       2       1999
1       1       1       3       2007
1       1       2       1       1980
1       1       2       2       1988
1       1       2       3       1982
1       1       3       1       2000
1       1       3       2       1998
1       1       3       3       2007
1       2       1       1       1991
1       2       1       2       1990
1       2       1       3       1988
1       2       2       1       1987
1       2       2       2       1989
1       2       2       3       1988
1       2       3       1       1985
1       2       3       2       1983
1       2       3       3       1989
1       3       1       1       2000
1       3       1       2       2004
1       3       1       3       2004
1       3       2       1       2001
1       3       2       2       1996
1       3       2       3       2004
1       3       3       1       1999
1       3       3       2       2000
1       3       3       3       2002
1       4       1       1       1997
1       4       1       2       1994
1       4       1       3       1996
1       4       2       1       1996
1       4       2       2       2000
1       4       2       3       2002
1       4       3       1       1987
1       4       3       2       1990
1       4       3       3       1995
2       5       1       1       2013
2       5       1       2       2004
2       5       1       3       2009
2       5       2       1       2023
```

```
2        5        2        2        2018
2        5        2        3        2010
2        5        3        1        2020
2        5        3        2        2023
2        5        3        3        2015
2        6        1        1        2032
2        6        1        2        2036
2        6        1        3        2030
2        6        2        1        2018
2        6        2        2        2022
2        6        2        3        2026
2        6        3        1        2009
2        6        3        2        2010
2        6        3        3        2011
2        7        1        1        1984
2        7        1        2        1993
2        7        1        3        1993
2        7        2        1        1992
2        7        2        2        1992
2        7        2        3        1990
2        7        3        1        1996
2        7        3        2        1993
2        7        3        3        1987
2        8        1        1        1996
2        8        1        2        1989
2        8        1        3        1996
2        8        2        1        1997
2        8        2        2        1993
2        8        2        3        1996
2        8        3        1        1990
2        8        3        2        1989
2        8        3        3        1992
;
```

Data Set 4.5 Genetics

```
Chapter 4: Random Effects Models
Data for a Two-way Random Effects Treatment Structure for Estimating
Heritability

data ex2_5;
    input loc block fam y;
    datalines;
1        1        1        268
1        2        1        279
1        3        1        261
1        1        2        242
1        2        2        261
1        3        2        258
1        1        3        242
1        2        3        245
1        3        3        234
1        1        4        225
1        2        4        231
1        3        4        219
1        1        5        236
1        2        5        260
1        3        5        248
2        1        1        238
2        2        1        220
2        3        1        243
2        1        2        215
2        2        2        192
2        3        2        226
2        1        3        198
```

```
2        2        3        151
2        3        3        191
2        1        4        195
2        2        4        182
2        3        4        202
2        1        5        201
2        2        5        161
2        3        5        196
3        1        1        221
3        2        1        216
3        3        1        224
3        1        2        208
3        2        2        197
3        3        2        201
3        1        3        186
3        2        3        173
3        3        3        161
3        1        4        207
3        2        4        183
3        3        4        186
3        1        5        200
3        2        5        207
3        3        5        190
4        1        1        194
4        2        1        194
4        3        1        197
4        1        2        203
4        2        2        191
4        3        2        204
4        1        3        177
4        2        3        170
4        3        3        180
4        1        4        180
4        2        4        195
4        3        4        193
4        1        5        199
4        2        5        183
4        3        5        208
;
```

Data Set 5.3 Average Daily Gain

```
Chapter 5: Analysis of Covariance
Data for an Example of a One-way Treatment Structure in a Randomized
Complete Blocks Design

data rcb;
   input id blk trt adg iwt;
   datalines;
 1       1        0      1.03      338
 2       1       10      1.54      477
 3       1       20      1.82      444
 4       1       30      1.86      370
 5       2        0      1.31      403
 6       2       10      2.16      451
 7       2       20      2.13      450
 8       2       30      2.23      393
 9       3        0      1.59      394
10       3       10      2.53      499
11       3       20      2.33      482
12       3       30      1.80      317
13       4        0      2.09      499
14       4       10      2.20      411
15       4       20      2.21      391
16       4       30      2.82      396
```

```
17      5       0       1.66    371
18      5      10       2.30    418
19      5      20       2.65    486
20      5      30       2.18    333
21      6       0       1.42    395
22      6      10       1.93    325
23      6      20       1.58    316
24      6      30       1.49    311
25      7       0       1.41    414
26      7      10       1.65    313
27      7      20       1.08    309
28      7      30       1.34    323
29      8       0       0.18    315
30      8      10       0.64    376
31      8      20       0.76    308
32      8      30       0.70    439
;
```

Data Set 5.4 Balanced Incomplete Block

```
Chapter 5: Analysis of Covariance
Data for an Example of a One-way Treatment Structure in a Balanced
Incomplete Block Design Structure

data bib;
   input   id blk trt y x grp;
   datalines;
 1      1       1      31      20      13
 2      1       2      29      18      24
 3      1       3      31      11      13
 4      2       1      29      37      13
 5      2       2      34      37      24
 6      2       4      33      39      24
 7      3       1      31      29      13
 8      3       3      28      12      13
 9      3       4      34      31      24
10      4       2      39      37      24
11      4       3      35      29      13
12      4       4      32      28      24
13      5       1      33      12      13
14      5       2      35      19      24
15      5       3      38      16      13
16      6       1      35      31      13
17      6       2      31      13      24
18      6       4      42      39      24
19      7       1      42      38      13
20      7       3      43      30      13
21      7       4      42      25      24
22      8       2      27      13      24
23      8       3      37      39      13
24      8       4      29      21      24
;
```

Data Set 5.5 Unbalanced Incomplete Block

```
Chapter 5: Analysis of Covariance
Data for an Example of a One-way Treatment Structure in an Unbalanced
Incomplete Block Design Structure

data incblk;
    input id blk trt y x;
    datalines;
  1      1      1      0.62      0.078
  2      1      2      0.91      0.010
  3      2      1      0.41      0.032
  4      2      2      0.48      0.050
  5      3      1      0.41      0.000
  6      3      2      0.49      0.015
  7      4      1      0.26      0.010
  8      4      2      0.28      0.016
  9      5      1      0.29      0.053
 10      5      2      0.37      0.069
 11      6      1      0.73      0.007
 12      6      2      0.72      0.062
 13      7      3      0.33      0.036
 14      7      4      0.31      0.068
 15      8      3      0.18      0.068
 16      8      4      0.18      0.057
 17      9      3      0.19      0.077
 18      9      4      0.25      0.090
 19     10      3      0.28      0.023
 20     10      4      0.32      0.039
 21     11      3      0.33      0.017
 22     11      4      0.27      0.062
 23     12      3      0.24      0.058
 24     12      4      0.23      0.082
 ;
```

Data Set 5.6 Teaching Methods I

```
Chapter 5: Analysis of Covariance
Data for an Example of a Split-Plot Design with the Covariate Measured on
the Large Size Experimental Unit or Whole Plot

data splitpt;
    input id met teacher gen $ student score y_ex;
    datalines;
  1      1      1      f      1      15      11
  2      1      1      f      2      17      11
  3      1      1      f      3      16      11
  4      1      1      f      4      16      11
  5      1      1      m      1      17      11
  6      1      1      m      2      16      11
  7      1      1      m      3      17      11
  8      1      1      m      4      17      11
  9      1      2      f      1      18      8
 10      1      2      f      2      17      8
 11      1      2      f      3      17      8
 12      1      2      f      4      16      8
 13      1      2      m      1      16      8
 14      1      2      m      2      17      8
 15      1      2      m      3      18      8
 16      1      2      m      4      17      8
 17      1      3      f      1      15      9
 18      1      3      f      2      15      9
 19      1      3      f      3      15      9
```

20	1	3	f	4	16	9
21	1	3	m	1	15	9
22	1	3	m	2	15	9
23	1	3	m	3	15	9
24	1	3	m	4	16	9
25	1	4	f	1	16	17
26	1	4	f	2	17	17
27	1	4	f	3	16	17
28	1	4	f	4	15	17
29	1	4	m	1	14	17
30	1	4	m	2	17	17
31	1	4	m	3	17	17
32	1	4	m	4	16	17
33	2	1	f	1	21	6
34	2	1	f	2	22	6
35	2	1	f	3	22	6
36	2	1	f	4	21	6
37	2	1	m	1	20	6
38	2	1	m	2	20	6
39	2	1	m	3	21	6
40	2	1	m	4	22	6
41	2	2	f	1	21	11
42	2	2	f	2	20	11
43	2	2	f	3	20	11
44	2	2	f	4	21	11
45	2	2	m	1	18	11
46	2	2	m	2	19	11
47	2	2	m	3	20	11
48	2	2	m	4	19	11
49	2	3	f	1	23	13
50	2	3	f	2	23	13
51	2	3	f	3	24	13
52	2	3	f	4	23	13
53	2	3	m	1	21	13
54	2	3	m	2	20	13
55	2	3	m	3	21	13
56	2	3	m	4	22	13
57	2	4	f	1	23	18
58	2	4	f	2	22	18
59	2	4	f	3	22	18
60	2	4	f	4	22	18
61	2	4	m	1	19	18
62	2	4	m	2	19	18
63	2	4	m	3	19	18
64	2	4	m	4	20	18
65	3	1	f	1	33	8
66	3	1	f	2	31	8
67	3	1	f	3	31	8
68	3	1	f	4	32	8
69	3	1	m	1	27	8
70	3	1	m	2	28	8
71	3	1	m	3	27	8
72	3	1	m	4	27	8
73	3	2	f	1	28	18
74	3	2	f	2	27	18
75	3	2	f	3	27	18
76	3	2	f	4	29	18
77	3	2	m	1	23	18
78	3	2	m	2	23	18
79	3	2	m	3	24	18
80	3	2	m	4	23	18
81	3	3	f	1	30	12
82	3	3	f	2	29	12
83	3	3	f	3	29	12
84	3	3	f	4	30	12
85	3	3	m	1	25	12
86	3	3	m	2	25	12
87	3	3	m	3	26	12

```
88   3      3      m      4      24     12
89   3      4      f      1      28     6
90   3      4      f      2      27     6
91   3      4      f      3      28     6
92   3      4      f      4      30     6
93   3      4      m      1      25     6
94   3      4      m      2      25     6
95   3      4      m      3      22     6
96   3      4      m      4      25     6
;
```

Data Set 5.7 Teaching Methods II

```
Chapter 5: Analysis of Covariance
Data for an Example of a Split-Plot Design with the Covariate Measured on
the Small Size Experimental Unit or Subplot

data splitpt;
   input id met teacher gen $ iq score;
   datalines;
  1     1      1      f      89     54
  2     1      1      f     105     55
  3     1      1      f     108     54
  4     1      1      f     116     64
  5     1      1      m      95     59
  6     1      1      m     103     58
  7     1      1      m      91     42
  8     1      1      m      82     48
  9     1      2      f      83     48
 10     1      2      f     103     56
 11     1      2      f     123     67
 12     1      2      f     103     54
 13     1      2      m     118     65
 14     1      2      m     101     65
 15     1      2      m     101     50
 16     1      2      m      82     55
 17     1      3      f     115     71
 18     1      3      f      91     66
 19     1      3      f     109     69
 20     1      3      f      85     59
 21     1      3      m      98     76
 22     1      3      m      84     64
 23     1      3      m      91     63
 24     1      3      m     110     74
 25     1      4      f     120     75
 26     1      4      f      98     60
 27     1      4      f      99     64
 28     1      4      f      91     59
 29     1      4      m      80     55
 30     1      4      m     112     70
 31     1      4      m     105     63
 32     1      4      m      94     62
 33     2      1      f      97     67
 34     2      1      f     105     74
 35     2      1      f     120     78
 36     2      1      f      92     69
 37     2      1      m      91     67
 38     2      1      m      96     64
 39     2      1      m      95     65
 40     2      1      m      84     52
 41     2      2      f     105     73
 42     2      2      f     110     78
 43     2      2      f      98     75
 44     2      2      f      92     65
 45     2      2      m     104     75
```

```
46    2    2    m    105    78
47    2    2    m     82    58
48    2    2    m    109    75
49    2    3    f    141    97
50    2    3    f    107    68
51    2    3    f    116    82
52    2    3    f    105    86
53    2    3    m     93    71
54    2    3    m    113    82
55    2    3    m     92    72
56    2    3    m    115    77
57    2    4    f    112    74
58    2    4    f     96    76
59    2    4    f    103    78
60    2    4    f    105    77
61    2    4    m    111    75
62    2    4    m    121    86
63    2    4    m     87    68
64    2    4    m     90    74
65    3    1    f     87    71
66    3    1    f     78    71
67    3    1    f    117    85
68    3    1    f    108    87
69    3    1    m     92    65
70    3    1    m    111    72
71    3    1    m    126    85
72    3    1    m    123    78
73    3    2    f    126    91
74    3    2    f    112    80
75    3    2    f    108    75
76    3    2    f     92    65
77    3    2    m     95    73
78    3    2    m    109    73
79    3    2    m    115    78
80    3    2    m    115    71
81    3    3    f    102    82
82    3    3    f     96    72
83    3    3    f    113    87
84    3    3    f    127    91
85    3    3    m    112    85
86    3    3    m     96    68
87    3    3    m    114    86
88    3    3    m    101    78
89    3    4    f     95    86
90    3    4    f    105    91
91    3    4    f     95    81
92    3    4    f    102    85
93    3    4    m     80    68
94    3    4    m     97    81
95    3    4    m    114    89
96    3    4    m    100    87
;

proc means data=splitpt; var y_ex;
run;
```

Data Set 5.8 Wafer Types

```
Chapter 5: Analysis of Covariance
Data for an Example of a Complex Strip Plot
Design with the Covariate Measured on an Intermediate Size Experimental
Unit

data lots;
    input id grp temp type $ wafer site delta thick;
    datalines;
```

id	grp	temp	type	wafer	site	delta	thick
1	1	900	A	1	1	291	1919
2	1	900	A	1	2	295	1919
3	1	900	A	1	3	294	1919
4	1	900	A	2	1	318	2113
5	1	900	A	2	2	315	2113
6	1	900	A	2	3	315	2113
7	1	900	B	1	1	349	1965
8	1	900	B	1	2	348	1965
9	1	900	B	1	3	345	1965
10	1	900	B	2	1	332	1829
11	1	900	B	2	2	334	1829
12	1	900	B	2	3	331	1829
13	1	1000	A	1	1	319	2098
14	1	1000	A	1	2	315	2098
15	1	1000	A	1	3	321	2098
16	1	1000	A	2	1	290	1823
17	1	1000	A	2	2	289	1823
18	1	1000	A	2	3	292	1823
19	1	1000	B	1	1	358	2059
20	1	1000	B	1	2	357	2059
21	1	1000	B	1	3	362	2059
22	1	1000	B	2	1	365	2145
23	1	1000	B	2	2	367	2145
24	1	1000	B	2	3	367	2145
25	1	1100	A	1	1	264	1846
26	1	1100	A	1	2	266	1846
27	1	1100	A	1	3	268	1846
28	1	1100	A	2	1	276	2028
29	1	1100	A	2	2	280	2028
30	1	1100	A	2	3	278	2028
31	1	1100	B	1	1	352	2086
32	1	1100	B	1	2	353	2086
33	1	1100	B	1	3	350	2086
34	1	1100	B	2	1	330	1899
35	1	1100	B	2	2	330	1899
36	1	1100	B	2	3	334	1899
37	2	900	A	1	1	306	1841
38	2	900	A	1	2	302	1841
39	2	900	A	1	3	305	1841
40	2	900	A	2	1	342	2170
41	2	900	A	2	2	341	2170
42	2	900	A	2	3	336	2170
43	2	900	B	1	1	342	1981
44	2	900	B	1	2	341	1981
45	2	900	B	1	3	340	1981
46	2	900	B	2	1	366	2190
47	2	900	B	2	2	363	2190
48	2	900	B	2	3	361	2190
49	2	1000	A	1	1	299	1915
50	2	1000	A	1	2	296	1915
51	2	1000	A	1	3	297	1915
52	2	1000	A	2	1	329	2161
53	2	1000	A	2	2	330	2161
54	2	1000	A	2	3	332	2161
55	2	1000	B	1	1	348	2072
56	2	1000	B	1	2	346	2072

57	2	1000	B	1	3	346	2072
58	2	1000	B	2	1	350	2082
59	2	1000	B	2	2	346	2082
60	2	1000	B	2	3	347	2082
61	2	1100	A	1	1	285	1854
62	2	1100	A	1	2	292	1854
63	2	1100	A	1	3	289	1854
64	2	1100	A	2	1	306	2046
65	2	1100	A	2	2	303	2046
66	2	1100	A	2	3	304	2046
67	2	1100	B	1	1	357	2062
68	2	1100	B	1	2	360	2062
69	2	1100	B	1	3	359	2062
70	2	1100	B	2	1	361	2055
71	2	1100	B	2	2	361	2055
72	2	1100	B	2	3	360	2055
73	3	900	A	1	1	318	2019
74	3	900	A	1	2	323	2019
75	3	900	A	1	3	323	2019
76	3	900	A	2	1	307	1872
77	3	900	A	2	2	308	1872
78	3	900	A	2	3	308	1872
79	3	900	B	1	1	372	2182
80	3	900	B	1	2	371	2182
81	3	900	B	1	3	370	2182
82	3	900	B	2	1	348	1973
83	3	900	B	2	2	349	1973
84	3	900	B	2	3	352	1973
85	3	1000	A	1	1	264	1828
86	3	1000	A	1	2	265	1828
87	3	1000	A	1	3	265	1828
88	3	1000	A	2	1	274	1827
89	3	1000	A	2	2	268	1827
90	3	1000	A	2	3	275	1827
91	3	1000	B	1	1	332	2109
92	3	1000	B	1	2	337	2109
93	3	1000	B	1	3	335	2109
94	3	1000	B	2	1	322	2003
95	3	1000	B	2	2	326	2003
96	3	1000	B	2	3	321	2003
97	3	1100	A	1	1	273	1925
98	3	1100	A	1	2	275	1925
99	3	1100	A	1	3	276	1925
100	3	1100	A	2	1	276	1942
101	3	1100	A	2	2	273	1942
102	3	1100	A	2	3	273	1942
103	3	1100	B	1	1	333	1893
104	3	1100	B	1	2	332	1893
105	3	1100	B	1	3	332	1893
106	3	1100	B	2	1	349	2170
107	3	1100	B	2	2	350	2170
108	3	1100	B	2	3	352	2170
109	4	900	A	1	1	295	1862
110	4	900	A	1	2	297	1862
111	4	900	A	1	3	296	1862
112	4	900	A	2	1	326	2149
113	4	900	A	2	2	326	2149
114	4	900	A	2	3	328	2149
115	4	900	B	1	1	322	1888
116	4	900	B	1	2	325	1888
117	4	900	B	1	3	327	1888
118	4	900	B	2	1	335	1998
119	4	900	B	2	2	332	1998
120	4	900	B	2	3	334	1998
121	4	1000	A	1	1	258	1815
122	4	1000	A	1	2	260	1815
123	4	1000	A	1	3	260	1815
124	4	1000	A	2	1	280	1981

125	4	1000	A	2	2	276	1981
126	4	1000	A	2	3	278	1981
127	4	1000	B	1	1	319	2012
128	4	1000	B	1	2	322	2012
129	4	1000	B	1	3	317	2012
130	4	1000	B	2	1	311	1892
131	4	1000	B	2	2	313	1892
132	4	1000	B	2	3	313	1892
133	4	1100	A	1	1	282	2083
134	4	1100	A	1	2	282	2083
135	4	1100	A	1	3	279	2083
136	4	1100	A	2	1	271	2036
137	4	1100	A	2	2	271	2036
138	4	1100	A	2	3	270	2036
139	4	1100	B	1	1	335	2174
140	4	1100	B	1	2	339	2174
141	4	1100	B	1	3	338	2174
142	4	1100	B	2	1	304	1802
143	4	1100	B	2	2	303	1802
144	4	1100	B	2	3	303	1802

;

Data Set 6.4 Animal Breeding

```
Chapter 6: Best Linear Unbiased Prediction
Data for Obtaining BLUPs in a Random Effects Model

data;
    input sire dam adg;
    datalines;
1 1 2.24
1 1 1.85
1 2 2.05
1 2 2.41
2 1 1.99
2 1 1.93
2 2 2.72
2 2 2.32
3 1 2.33
3 1 2.68
3 2 2.69
3 2 2.71
4 1 2.42
4 1 2.01
4 2 1.86
4 2 1.79
5 1 2.82
5 1 2.64
5 2 2.58
5 2 2.56
;
```

Data Set 6.5 Machine Operator

```
Chapter 6: Best Linear Unbiased Prediction
Data for a Two-Factor Mixed Model

data;
    input machine operator y;
    datalines;
1 1 51.43
1 1 51.28
1 2 50.93
1 2 50.75
1 3 50.47
1 3 50.83
2 1 51.91
2 1 52.43
2 2 52.26
2 2 52.33
2 3 51.58
2 3 51.23
;
```

From McLean, R.A., Sanders, W.L., and Stroup, W.W. (1991). A unified approach to mixed linear models, *American Statistician*, **45**, 54-64. Copyright © 1991 by the American Statistical Association. Reproduced with permission.

Data Set 7.2 Winter Wheat

```
Chapter 7: Random Coefficient Models
Data for One-way Random Effects Treatment Structure in a Completely
Randomized Design Structure

*random sample of wheat varieties, measure moisture content in plot
before planting--determine the yield of the plots;

data wheat;
    input id variety yield moist;
    datalines;
```

id	variety	yield	moist
1	1	41	10
2	1	69	57
3	1	53	32
4	1	66	52
5	1	64	47
6	1	64	48
7	2	49	30
8	2	44	21
9	2	44	20
10	2	46	26
11	2	57	44
12	2	42	19
13	3	69	50
14	3	62	40
15	3	50	23
16	3	76	58
17	3	48	21
18	3	55	30
19	4	48	22
20	4	60	40
21	4	45	17
22	4	47	21
23	4	62	44
24	4	43	13

25	5	65	49
26	5	63	44
27	5	71	57
28	5	68	51
29	5	52	27
30	5	68	52
31	6	76	55
32	6	46	11
33	6	45	11
34	6	67	43
35	6	65	38
36	6	79	60
37	7	35	17
38	7	37	20
39	7	30	11
40	7	30	10
41	7	57	48
42	7	49	36
43	8	75	57
44	8	64	41
45	8	46	15
46	8	54	28
47	8	52	23
48	8	52	23
49	9	51	26
50	9	63	44
51	9	42	13
52	9	61	40
53	9	67	48
54	9	69	53
55	10	60	37
56	10	73	58
57	10	66	44
58	10	71	53
59	10	67	48
60	10	74	59

;

Data Set 8.2 DIAL

```
Chapter 8: Heterogeneous Variance Models
Within-Subject Heterogeneity

data dial;
    input sub qb tmp ufr index;
    tmp = tmp/100;
    ufr = ufr/100;
    datalines;
1 200   24.0    64.5 1
1 200   50.5 2011.5 2
1 200   99.5 3846.0 3
1 200  148.5 4498.5 4
1 200  202.0 5176.5 5
1 200  249.5 4657.5 6
1 200  297.0 4081.5 7
2 200   24.0  372.0 1
2 200   54.0 1888.5 2
2 200   99.5 3469.5 3
2 200  147.5 4030.5 4
2 200  200.0 4447.5 5
2 200  250.0 4243.5 6
2 200  301.0 4465.5 7
3 200   24.5  298.5 1
3 200   48.0 1770.0 2
3 200  101.0 3529.5 3
```

```
 3 200 150.5 4195.5 4
 3 200 200.0 4761.0 5
 3 200 251.5 4473.0 6
 3 200 297.0 4603.5 7
 4 200  25.5  393.0 1
 4 200  49.5 1983.0 2
 4 200  99.5 4042.5 3
 4 200 148.0 5226.0 4
 4 200 199.5 4939.5 5
 4 200 249.0 4597.5 6
 4 200 303.0 4191.0 7
 5 200  25.5  321.0 1
 5 200  51.5 1770.0 2
 5 200 100.0 3249.0 3
 5 200 150.5 4233.0 4
 5 200 202.0 4573.5 5
 5 200 249.0 4785.0 6
 5 200 301.0 4804.5 7
 6 200  26.0  366.0 1
 6 200  50.0 1695.0 2
 6 200 102.0 3609.0 3
 6 200 149.0 4263.0 4
 6 200 199.0 4647.0 5
 6 200 248.0 4627.5 6
 6 200 299.5 4398.0 7
 7 200  30.5  982.5 1
 7 200  50.5 2163.0 2
 7 200  98.0 4227.0 3
 7 200 150.5 5028.0 4
 7 200 200.5 4551.0 5
 7 200 250.5 4425.0 6
 7 200 299.0 4230.0 7
 8 200  30.5  948.0 1
 8 200  50.5 2175.0 2
 8 200  99.5 3723.0 3
 8 200 150.0 4443.0 4
 8 200 199.0 4216.5 5
 8 200 248.0 4306.5 6
 8 200 300.0 3661.5 7
 9 200  25.0  156.0 1
 9 200  49.5 1665.0 2
 9 200 100.0 3453.0 3
 9 200 150.0 4381.5 4
 9 200 196.5 4849.5 5
 9 200 248.5 4752.0 6
 9 200 298.0 4164.0 7
10 200  23.5  123.0 1
10 200  50.5 1537.5 2
10 200 102.0 3283.5 3
10 200 147.5 3783.0 4
10 200 197.0 4059.0 5
10 200 248.0 3255.0 6
10 200 300.0 3430.5 7
11 300  25.5  388.5 1
11 300  50.0 1915.5 2
11 300  98.0 3765.0 3
11 300 149.0 4789.5 4
11 300 201.5 5449.5 5
11 300 251.0 5317.5 6
11 300 298.0 5935.5 7
12 300  28.0  571.5 1
12 300  50.5 2050.5 2
12 300 100.0 3940.5 3
12 300 149.0 5010.0 4
12 300 200.0 5515.5 5
12 300 250.5 6118.5 6
12 300 302.0 5071.5 7
13 300  35.5 1041.0 1
```

```
13 300   48.0 1932.0 2
13 300  102.5 4377.0 3
13 300  150.0 5122.5 4
13 300  199.0 5809.5 5
13 300  250.0 5409.0 6
13 300  300.5 6201.0 7
14 300   23.5  360.0 1
14 300   48.0 2049.0 2
14 300  101.0 4188.0 3
14 300  149.0 4999.5 4
14 300  199.0 5767.5 5
14 300  248.0 6247.5 6
14 300  300.5 6214.5 7
15 300   26.0  189.0 1
15 300   51.5 1851.0 2
15 300   97.0 3721.5 3
15 300  150.5 5235.0 4
15 300  199.0 6091.5 5
15 300  250.0 6298.5 6
15 300  299.5 6477.0 7
16 300   23.5  117.0 1
16 300   48.5 1768.5 2
16 300  102.5 3970.5 3
16 300  151.5 5268.0 4
16 300  199.0 6180.0 5
16 300  251.0 6148.5 6
16 300  302.0 6142.5 7
17 300   28.5  150.0 1
17 300   52.0 1540.5 2
17 300  100.5 3252.0 3
17 300  150.0 4243.5 4
17 300  198.5 4857.0 5
17 300  249.0 5368.5 6
17 300  299.5 5365.5 7
18 300   29.5  642.0 1
18 300   51.5 2025.0 2
18 300  101.0 4305.0 3
18 300  148.0 5811.0 4
18 300  200.0 6199.5 5
18 300  248.0 6091.5 6
18 300  300.5 6360.0 7
19 300   29.0  405.0 1
19 300   49.5 1659.0 2
19 300  101.5 4051.5 3
19 300  152.0 5284.5 4
19 300  202.0 6043.5 5
19 300  250.0 6483.0 6
19 300  297.5 6382.5 7
20 300   40.0 1093.5 1
20 300   47.0 1347.0 2
20 300  101.0 3535.5 3
20 300  151.5 4534.5 4
20 300  198.0 4944.0 5
20 300  251.0 5362.5 6
20 300  300.0 5643.0 7
21 200   25.0      . 1
21 200   50.0      . 2
21 200  100.0      . 3
21 200  150.0      . 4
21 200  200.0      . 5
21 200  250.0      . 6
21 200  300.0      . 7
22 300   25.0      . 1
22 300   50.0      . 2
22 300  100.0      . 3
22 300  150.0      . 4
```

```
22 300 200.0    .  5
22 300 250.0    .  6
22 300 300.0    .  7
;
```

Data from Vonesh, E.F. and Carter, R.L. (1992), Mixed-effects nonlinear regression for unbalanced repeated measures, *Biometrics*, 1-17. Copyright © 1992, The International Biometric Society. Reproduced with permission.

Data Set 8.3 GRIP

```
Chapter 8: Heterogeneous Variance Models
Combining Between- and Within-Subject Heterogeneity

data grip;
   input subject x y1 y2 y3 trt sex$;
   array yy{3} y1-y3;
   do time = 1 to 3;
      t = time;
      y = yy{time};
      output;
   end;
   drop y1-y3;
   datalines;
26 175 161 210 230 1 M
27 165 215 245 265 1 M
29 175 134 215 139 1 M
34 178 165 140 175 1 M
35 220 220 189 158 1 M
38  90 146 140 130 1 M
42 300 300 300 300 1 M
44 238 278 170 158 1 M
54 200 230 220 240 1 M
57 130 155 170 125 1 M
74 215 230 243 245 1 M
76 207 220   .   . 1 M
79 225 220 250 235 1 M
 1 120 130 150 120 2 M
25 300 300 300 300 2 M
28 179 232 285   . 2 M
31 209 260 200 125 2 M
36 200 200 200 232 2 M
39 300 300 300 300 2 M
41 200 245 290 280 2 M
43 172 170 170 146 2 M
45 158 140 152 150 2 M
47 150 220 168 139 2 M
53 135 155 215 170 2 M
56  75 170 220 240 2 M
58 150 200 185 163 2 M
61 155 101  93 120 2 M
73 190 240 210 173 2 M
75 265 275 255 270 2 M
 2  80  80  86  80 1 F
 4  64  80  80  70 1 F
 5  40  60   .   . 1 F
 8  40  50  30  40 1 F
 9  70  90 110  90 1 F
15  70  80  95 110 1 F
18  70  80  86   . 1 F
19  70  60  70  80 1 F
21  50  80  90  90 1 F
24  40  60  60  65 1 F
40 140 156 140 150 1 F
46 110  82  98 110 1 F
```

```
48 180 165 150 160 1 F
50 155 150 170 185 1 F
52  55 105  70  88 1 F
59  95  90  90 116 1 F
63  90 135  95   . 1 F
64 145 140 164   . 1 F
70  34  51  87   . 1 F
 3  60  80  60  60 2 F
 6  50  70  70  70 2 F
 7  80  75  90  90 2 F
10  80 100  80  90 2 F
13  80  60  65  70 2 F
17  58  50  80  80 2 F
20  60  60  80  60 2 F
22  80  90 120 130 2 F
23  60  90  94 100 2 F
30  75 131  95 105 2 F
37 150 108 160 160 2 F
49  55  60  65  55 2 F
51 130 130 160 125 2 F
55 115  95 105 110 2 F
62 135 120 144 135 2 F
65  60  85  85   . 2 F
67  40  45  76  75 2 F
71 104 107   .   . 2 F
72  60  60  55  58 2 F
;
```

Data from Patel, H.I. (1991), Analysis of incomplete data from a clinical trial with repeated measurements, *Biometrika*, **78**, 609-619. Copyright © 1991, Biometrika Trust. Reproduced with permission.

Data Set 8.4.1 PREETCH

Chapter 8: Heterogeneous Variance Models
Log-Linear Variance Models

```
data preetch;
   input expt wafer mask viscos spin baketemp baketime aperture
         expos develop etch y1-y5;
   y = y1; loc = 'top'; output;
   y = y2; loc = 'cen'; output;
   y = y3; loc = 'bot'; output;
   y = y4; loc = 'lef'; output;
   y = y5; loc = 'rig'; output;
   drop y1-y5;
   datalines;
 1 1 -1 -1 -1 -1 -1 -1 -1 -1 -1 2.43 2.52 2.63 2.52 2.5
 1 2 -1 -1 -1 -1 -1 -1 -1 -1 -1 2.36 2.5  2.62 2.43 2.49
 2 1 -1 -1  0 -1  0  0  0  0  0 2.76 2.66 2.74 2.6  2.53
 2 2 -1 -1  0 -1  0  0  0  0  0 2.66 2.73 2.95 2.57 2.64
 3 1 -1 -1  1 -1  1  1  1  1  1 2.82 2.71 2.78 2.55 2.36
 3 2 -1 -1  1 -1  1  1  1  1  1 2.76 2.67 2.9  2.62 2.43
 4 1 -1  1 -1 -1 -1  0  0  1  1 2.02 2.06 2.21 1.98 2.13
 4 2 -1  1 -1 -1 -1  0  0  1  1 1.85 1.66 2.07 1.81 1.83
 5 1 -1  1  0 -1  0  1  1 -1 -1 1.87 1.78 2.07 1.8  1.83
 6 1 -1  1  1 -1  1 -1 -1  0  0 2.51 2.56 2.55 2.45 2.53
 6 2 -1  1  1 -1  1 -1 -1  0  0 2.68 2.6  2.85 2.55 2.56
 7 1 -1 -1 -1  1  0 -1  1  0  1 1.99 1.99 2.11 1.99 2.0
 7 2 -1 -1 -1  1  0 -1  1  0  1 1.96 2.2  2.04 2.01 2.03
 8 1 -1 -1  0  1  1  0 -1  1 -1 3.15 3.44 3.67 3.09 3.06
 8 2 -1 -1  0  1  1  0 -1  1 -1 3.27 3.29 3.49 3.02 3.19
 9 1 -1 -1  1  1 -1  1  0 -1  0 3.0  2.91 3.07 2.66 2.74
 9 2 -1 -1  1  1 -1  1  0 -1  0 2.73 2.79 3.0  2.69 2.7
10 1  1 -1 -1 -1  1  1  0  0 -1 2.69 2.5  2.51 2.46 2.4
```

```
10 2  1 -1 -1 -1  1  1  0  0 -1 2.75  2.73  2.75  2.78  3.03
11 1  1 -1  0 -1 -1 -1  1  1  0 3.2   3.19  3.32  3.2   3.15
11 2  1 -1  0 -1 -1 -1  1  1  0 3.07  3.14  3.14  3.13  3.12
12 1  1 -1  1 -1  0  0 -1 -1  1 3.21  3.32  3.33  3.23  3.10
12 2  1 -1  1 -1  0  0 -1 -1  1 3.48  3.44  3.49  3.25  3.38
13 1  1  1 -1 -1  0  1 -1  1  0 2.6   2.56  2.62  2.55  2.56
13 2  1  1 -1 -1  0  1 -1  1  0 2.53  2.49  2.79  2.5   2.56
14 1  1  1  0 -1  1 -1  0 -1  1 2.18  2.2   2.45  2.22  2.32
14 2  1  1  0 -1  1 -1  0 -1  1 2.33  2.2   2.41  2.37  2.38
15 1  1  1  1 -1 -1  0  1  0 -1 2.45  2.50  2.51  2.43  2.43
16 1  1 -1 -1  1  1  0  1 -1  0 2.67  2.53  2.72  2.7   2.6
16 2  1 -1 -1  1  1  0  1 -1  0 2.76  2.67  2.73  2.69  2.6
17 1  1 -1  0  1 -1  1 -1  0  1 3.31  3.3   3.44  3.12  3.14
17 2  1 -1  0  1 -1  1 -1  0  1 3.12  2.97  3.18  3.03  2.95
18 1  1 -1  1  1  0 -1  0  1 -1 3.46  3.49  3.5   3.45  3.57
;
```

Data from Phadke, M.S., Kackar, R.N., Speeney, D.V., and Grieco, M.J. (1983), Off-line quality control for integrated circuit fabrication using experimental design, *Bell System Technical Journal*, **62**, 1273-1309. Copyright © 1983. Reproduced with permission.

Data Set 9.5 Agronomic Uniformity Trial

Chapter 9: Spatial Variability
Data for Estimating Spatial Covariance

```
data spatvar;
   input rep bloc row col yield;
   datalines;
1      4      1      1      10.5411
1      4      1      2       8.5806
1      2      1      3      11.2790
1      2      1      4      12.4344
1      4      2      1      10.3416
1      4      2      2      11.3103
1      2      2      3       9.0282
1      2      2      4       9.7985
1      3      3      1      10.4939
1      3      3      2      11.2576
1      1      3      3       7.3720
1      1      3      4       6.0833
1      3      4      1       9.8869
1      3      4      2       8.2849
1      1      4      3       7.2836
1      1      4      4       8.0018
2      7      5      1      10.3349
2      7      5      2       9.9135
2      6      5      3       8.1662
2      6      5      4      10.7679
2      7      6      1      12.1580
2      7      6      2      11.0230
2      6      6      3       9.2912
2      6      6      4       9.1392
2      5      7      1      13.1097
2      5      7      2      10.0121
2      8      7      3       8.2482
2      8      7      4       7.3975
2      5      8      1      11.0226
2      5      8      2      10.7690
2      8      8      3       6.2206
2      8      8      4       6.5696
3     12      1      5      11.1944
3     12      1      6       7.9737
3     11      1      7       5.8400
```

```
3      11      1      8      6.9580
3      12      2      5     10.2561
3      12      2      6      9.8180
3      11      2      7     10.3009
3      11      2      8      7.4719
3       9      3      5     10.1148
3       9      3      6      9.6252
3      10      3      7      8.7800
3      10      3      8     11.2786
3       9      4      5      7.9548
3       9      4      6      6.1100
3      10      4      7      8.6507
3      10      4      8      9.2237
4      16      5      5     10.3129
4      16      5      6      7.3161
4      13      5      7      8.6394
4      13      5      8      7.8669
4      16      6      5      9.0250
4      16      6      6      7.2483
4      13      6      7     10.0104
4      13      6      8     10.0473
4      14      7      5      7.0507
4      14      7      6     11.1225
4      15      7      7     12.0253
4      15      7      8     10.4298
4      14      8      5      7.3220
4      14      8      6     10.5104
4      15      8      7     12.6808
4      15      8      8     10.4482
;
```

Data Set 9.6.1 Water Drainage Characteristics

```
Chapter 9: Spatial Variability
Data for Example Using Spatial Covariance for Adjustment

data a;
   input easting northing logt salt xxx $;
   if logt=1e31 or logt<-10 then delete;
   if salt=1e31 then delete;
   datalines;
 16.442  18.128  -6.02895   28.6     H-1
 15.670  18.095  -6.20046   26.9     H-2b1
 16.748  17.339  -5.60886   -0.6     H-3b1
 15.399  14.927  -5.99598    0       H-4b
 19.891  21.245  -7.01145   1E31     H-5b
 13.613  21.452  -4.44995   -0.6     H-6b
 11.143  11.092  -2.81246  -37.1     H-7b1
 11.702      0   -5.05465  -19.9     H-8b
 17.008   4.705  -3.90188    0       H-9b
 25.994   8.917  -7.12337    0       H-10b
 18.365  15.574  -4.50570   1E31   H-11b1
 20.042  11.896  -6.71319  100.3     H-12
  15.36  16.798  -6.48422   1E31     H-14
 18.334  18.303  -6.88042   1E31     H-15
 16.388  18.656  -6.11491   32.8     H-16
 18.737  13.957  -6.63614   64.6     H-17
 15.283   19.61  -5.77751   27.4     H-18
 18.222  16.777  -4.92707   1E31     DOE-1
 16.702  21.738  -4.01908   1E31     DOE-2
 15.357  16.785   1E+31     24.3     P-1
 18.335  18.292   1E+31     31.1     P-2
 15.818  18.342   1E+31     29.9     P-3
 17.954  16.763   1E+31     31.7     P-4
 16.703  19.984   1E+31     29.6     P-5
```

```
13.628   17.528    1E+31      -0.5     P-6
15.327   14.922    1E+31      20.7     P-7
16.849   14.911    1E+31      33.2     P-8
18.375   15.569    1E+31      31.4     P-9
20.106   17.647    1E+31       114     P-10
20.035   19.901    1E+31      30.5     P-11
13.475   19.896    1E+31      -0.9     P-12
13.55    21.473    1E+31      -1.2     P-13
12.103   18.42    -3.55706    -2.4     P-14
13.643   15.191   -7.03535      25     P-15
15.714   13.765    1E+31      28.6     P-16
16.945   13.91    -5.96847    34.4     P-17
21.386   16.794  -10.1233    132.2     P-18
20.7     18.862    1E+31     69.36     P-19
21.551   20.212    1E+31      30.8     P-20
19.917   21.293    1E+31      30.2     P-21
16.81    22.919    1E+31         0     WIPP-11
16.729   19.968   -6.96847    29.9     WIPP-12
15.663   20.691   -4.12962       0     WIPP-13
16.754   19.623   -6.49134    30.3     WIPP-18
16.758   19.226   -6.19031       0     WIPP-19
16.762   18.763   -6.57053    29.9     WIPP-21
16.758   19.097   -6.40026    29.8     WIPP-22
 9.404   20.472   -3.54116   -10.7     WIPP-25
 7.033   17.606   -2.91359    -3.3     WIPP-26
 7.445   29.523   -3.36921     -28     WIPP-27
14.285   31.124   -4.6839    -17.7     WIPP-28
     0   15.138   -2.96847   -32.9     WIPP-29
16.74    26.145   -6.60227       0     WIPP-30
12.649   20.463    1E+31     1E31      WIPP-33
17.353   21.586    1E+31     1E31      WIPP-34
21.239   25.452    1E+31      -0.1     ERDA-6
16.715   18.402   -6.29637    26.7     ERDA-9
 9.704    6.959    1E+31     -15.2     ERDA-10
16.21    14.493   -6.52131    1E31     C-B1
17.972    3.898   -4.33500    1E31     ENGLE
 9.481    5.903   -3.25842    1E31     USGS-1
 8.86     6.331    1E+31     1E31      USGS-4
 8.898    6.332    1E+31     1E31      USGS-8
11.721   15.321   -5.68971    1E31     D-268
24.145   25.825   -6.55349    18.7     AEC-7
20.544   22.886    1E+31         0     AEC-8
14.714   17.053    1E+31      -0.3     B-25
16.736   18.524    1E+31     1E31      EX. SHAFT
10.48    26.499    1E+31     1E31      FFG-107
 2.258    8.668    1E+31     1E31      FFG-153
 4.878    9.65     1E+31     1E31      FFG-165
 7.234    5.137    1E+31     1E31      FFG-181
 6.9     -0.971    1E+31     1E31      FFG-188*
32.296   33.411    1E+31     1E31      FFG-225*
23.873   33.47     1E+31     1E31      FFG-236
30.198   25.776    1E+31     1E31      FFG-244*
-4.458   28.01     1E+31     1E31      FFG-426*
-1.181   21.666    1E+31     1E31      1 DANF
 4.331   25.36     1E+31     1E31      1 DUNC
;
```

Used with permission of Sandia Laboratories.

Data Set 9.6.2 Wheat Yield

```
Chapter 9: Spatial Variability
Data from an Agronomic Yield Trial Analysis of Variance Example

data wheat;
    input name entry plot rawyld rep loc nloc y lat lng;
    datalines;
LANCER       1  1101  585  1      4  29.25  4.3 19.2
BRULE        2  1102  631  1      4  31.55  4.3 20.4
REDLAND      3  1103  701  1      4  35.05  4.3 21.6
CODY         4  1104  602  1      4  30.10  4.3 22.8
ARAPAHOE     5  1105  661  1      4  33.05  4.3 24.0
NE83404      6  1106  605  1      4  30.25  4.3 25.2
NE83406      7  1107  704  1      4  35.20  4.3 26.4
NE83407      8  1108  388  1      4  19.40  8.6  1.2
CENTURA      9  1109  487  1      4  24.35  8.6  2.4
SCOUT 66    10  1110  511  1      4  25.55  8.6  3.6
COLT        11  1111  502  1      4  25.10  8.6  4.8
NE83498     12  1112  492  1      4  24.60  8.6  6.0
NE84557     13  1113  509  1      4  25.45  8.6  7.2
NE83432     14  1114  268  1      4  13.40  8.6  8.4
NE85556     15  1115  633  1      4  31.65  8.6  9.6
NE85623     16  1116  513  1      4  25.65  8.6 10.8
CENTURK 78  17  1117  632  1      4  31.60  8.6 12.0
NORKAN      18  1118  446  1      4  22.30  8.6 13.2
KS831374    19  1119  684  1      4  34.20  8.6 14.4
TAM 200     20  1120  422  1      4  21.10  8.6 15.6
NE86482     21  1121  560  1      4  28.00  8.6 16.8
HOMESTEAD   22  1122  566  1      4  28.30  8.6 18.0
LANCOTA     23  1123  514  1      4  25.70  8.6 19.2
NE86501     24  1124  635  1      4  31.75  8.6 20.4
NE86503     25  1125  840  1      4  42.00  8.6 21.6
NE86507     26  1126  618  1      4  30.90  8.6 22.8
NE86509     27  1127  658  1      4  32.90  8.6 24.0
TAM 107     28  1128  481  1      4  24.05  8.6 25.2
CHEYENNE    29  1129  564  1      4  28.20  8.6 26.4
BUCKSKIN    30  1130  597  1      4  29.85 12.9  1.2
NE86527     31  1131  580  1      4  29.00 12.9  2.4
NE86582     32  1132  418  1      4  20.90 12.9  3.6
NE86606     33  1133  526  1      4  26.30 12.9  4.8
NE86607     34  1134  517  1      4  25.85 12.9  6.0
ROUGHRIDER  35  1135  479  1      4  23.95 12.9  7.2
VONA        36  1136  506  1      4  25.30 12.9  8.4
SIOUXLAND   37  1137  542  1      4  27.10 12.9  9.6
GAGE        38  1138  513  1      4  25.65 12.9 10.8
NE83T12     39  1139  504  1      4  25.20 12.9 12.0
NE86T666    40  1140  368  1      4  18.40 12.9 13.2
NE87403     41  1141  437  1      4  21.85 12.9 14.4
NE87408     42  1142  540  1      4  27.00 12.9 15.6
NE87409     43  1143  631  1      4  31.55 12.9 16.8
NE87446     44  1144  610  1      4  30.50 12.9 18.0
NE87451     45  1145  639  1      4  31.95 12.9 19.2
NE87457     46  1146  611  1      4  30.55 12.9 20.4
NE87463     47  1147  545  1      4  27.25 12.9 21.6
NE87499     48  1148  598  1      4  29.90 12.9 22.8
NE87512     49  1149  656  1      4  32.80 12.9 24.0
NE87513     50  1150  557  1      4  27.85 12.9 25.2
NE87522     51  1151  486  1      4  24.30 12.9 26.4
NE87612     52  1152  563  1      4  28.15 17.2  1.2
NE87613     53  1153  539  1      4  26.95 17.2  2.4
NE87615     54  1154  502  1      4  25.10 17.2  3.6
NE87619     55  1155  605  1      4  30.25 17.2  4.8
NE87627     56  1156  403  1      4  20.15 17.2  6.0
CENTURA      9  2101  556  2      4  27.80 17.2  8.4
NE85623     16  2102  569  2      4  28.45 17.2  9.6
```

CODY	4	2103	455	2	4	22.75	17.2	10.8
NE86582	32	2104	534	2	4	26.70	17.2	12.0
NE87408	42	2105	513	2	4	25.65	17.2	13.2
NE87451	45	2106	549	2	4	27.45	17.2	14.4
NE83432	14	2107	620	2	4	31.00	17.2	15.6
CENTURK 78	17	2108	498	2	4	24.90	17.2	16.8
NE83T12	39	2109	513	2	4	25.65	17.2	18.0
NE87409	43	2110	648	2	4	32.40	17.2	19.2
NE87513	50	2111	624	2	4	31.20	17.2	20.4
NE87627	56	2112	552	2	4	27.60	17.2	21.6
ARAPAHOE	5	2113	693	2	4	34.65	17.2	22.8
LANCER	1	2114	570	2	4	28.50	17.2	24.0
TAM 107	28	2115	589	2	4	29.45	17.2	25.2
REDLAND	3	2116	611	2	4	30.55	17.2	26.4
VONA	36	2117	536	2	4	26.80	21.5	1.2
NE87463	47	2118	477	2	4	23.85	21.5	2.4
NE86507	26	2119	548	2	4	27.40	21.5	3.6
BUCKSKIN	30	2120	602	2	4	30.10	21.5	4.8
ROUGHRIDER	35	2121	495	2	4	24.75	21.5	6.0
NE86527	31	2122	507	2	4	25.35	21.5	7.2
SCOUT 66	10	2123	520	2	4	26.00	21.5	8.4
NE86509	27	2124	500	2	4	25.00	21.5	9.6
NE86606	33	2125	587	2	4	29.35	21.5	10.8
NE84557	13	2126	572	2	4	28.60	21.5	12.0
KS831374	19	2127	534	2	4	26.70	21.5	13.2
GAGE	38	2128	505	2	4	25.25	21.5	14.4
NE87619	55	2129	675	2	4	33.75	21.5	15.6
NE87499	48	2130	446	2	4	22.30	21.5	16.8
CHEYENNE	29	2131	561	2	4	28.05	21.5	18.0
NE86607	34	2132	691	2	4	34.55	21.5	19.2
NE83498	12	2133	748	2	4	37.40	21.5	20.4
NE83404	6	2134	580	2	4	29.00	21.5	21.6
NE87446	44	2135	624	2	4	31.20	21.5	22.8
SIOUXLAND	37	2136	742	2	4	37.10	21.5	24.0
HOMESTEAD	22	2137	590	2	4	29.50	21.5	25.2
NE86501	24	2138	627	2	4	31.35	21.5	26.4
NE87512	49	2139	404	2	4	20.20	25.8	1.2
NE83407	8	2140	528	2	4	26.40	25.8	2.4
NE87403	41	2141	513	2	4	25.65	25.8	3.6
NE87457	46	2142	638	2	4	31.90	25.8	4.8
NE83406	7	2143	621	2	4	31.05	25.8	6.0
COLT	11	2144	615	2	4	30.75	25.8	7.2
NE87522	51	2145	543	2	4	27.15	25.8	8.4
NORKAN	18	2146	606	2	4	30.30	25.8	9.6
NE87615	54	2147	634	2	4	31.70	25.8	10.8
NE85556	15	2148	610	2	4	30.50	25.8	12.0
TAM 200	20	2149	487	2	4	24.35	25.8	13.2
LANCOTA	23	2150	522	2	4	26.10	25.8	14.4
NE86503	25	2151	599	2	4	29.95	25.8	15.6
NE86482	21	2152	656	2	4	32.80	25.8	16.8
BRULE	2	2153	563	2	4	28.15	25.8	18.0
NE87612	52	2154	654	2	4	32.70	25.8	19.2
NE87613	53	2155	738	2	4	36.90	25.8	20.4
NE86T666	40	2156	368	2	4	18.40	25.8	21.6
NE86607	34	3101	623	3	4	31.15	25.8	24.0
LANCOTA	23	3102	539	3	4	26.95	25.8	25.2
NE87513	50	3103	616	3	4	30.80	25.8	26.4
NE87408	42	3104	438	3	4	21.90	30.1	1.2
NE83407	8	3105	592	3	4	29.60	30.1	2.4
NORKAN	18	3106	485	3	4	24.25	30.1	3.6
REDLAND	3	3107	542	3	4	27.10	30.1	4.8
KS831374	19	3108	421	3	4	21.05	30.1	6.0
COLT	11	3109	479	3	4	23.95	30.1	7.2
NE86527	31	3110	546	3	4	27.30	30.1	8.4
VONA	36	3111	600	3	4	30.00	30.1	9.6
TAM 107	28	3112	690	3	4	34.50	30.1	10.8
CENTURK 78	17	3113	662	3	4	33.10	30.1	12.0
NE87627	56	3114	564	3	4	28.20	30.1	13.2

NE86T666	40	3115	516	3	4	25.80	30.1	14.4
NE87615	54	3116	679	3	4	33.95	30.1	15.6
NE86501	24	3117	607	3	4	30.35	30.1	16.8
NE87522	51	3118	378	3	4	18.90	30.1	18.0
CHEYENNE	29	3119	678	3	4	33.90	30.1	19.2
SIOUXLAND	37	3120	675	3	4	33.75	30.1	20.4
NE87451	45	3121	679	3	4	33.95	30.1	21.6
GAGE	38	3122	500	3	4	25.00	30.1	22.8
LANCER	1	3123	562	3	4	28.10	30.1	24.0
NE87446	44	3124	500	3	4	25.00	30.1	25.2
NE86482	21	3125	606	3	4	30.30	30.1	26.4
CODY	4	3126	337	3	4	16.85	34.4	1.2
NE87612	52	3127	342	3	4	17.10	34.4	2.4
NE87457	46	3128	191	3	4	9.55	34.4	3.6
NE84557	13	3129	30	3	4	1.50	34.4	4.8
NE83T12	39	3130	255	3	4	12.75	34.4	6.0
NE86507	26	3131	443	3	4	22.15	34.4	7.2
TAM 200	20	3132	384	3	4	19.20	34.4	8.4
NE87613	53	3133	471	3	4	23.55	34.4	9.6
ARAPAHOE	5	3134	501	3	4	25.05	34.4	10.8
SCOUT 66	10	3135	665	3	4	33.25	34.4	12.0
NE87403	41	3136	480	3	4	24.00	34.4	13.2
NE85623	16	3137	635	3	4	31.75	34.4	14.4
NE86509	27	3138	481	3	4	24.05	34.4	15.6
NE85556	15	3139	769	3	4	38.45	34.4	16.8
HOMESTEAD	22	3140	517	3	4	25.85	34.4	18.0
NE83404	6	3141	656	3	4	32.80	34.4	19.2
NE86503	25	3142	702	3	4	35.10	34.4	20.4
NE86582	32	3143	621	3	4	31.05	34.4	21.6
NE87619	55	3144	663	3	4	33.15	34.4	22.8
NE87463	47	3145	580	3	4	29.00	34.4	24.0
NE86606	33	3146	643	3	4	32.15	34.4	25.2
BRULE	2	3147	818	3	4	40.90	34.4	26.4
BUCKSKIN	30	3148	360	3	4	18.00	38.7	1.2
NE83406	7	3149	43	3	4	2.15	38.7	2.4
NE87409	43	3150	75	3	4	3.75	38.7	3.6
NE87499	48	3151	59	3	4	2.95	38.7	4.8
CENTURA	9	3152	174	3	4	8.70	38.7	6.0
NE83432	14	3153	221	3	4	11.05	38.7	7.2
NE87512	49	3154	247	3	4	12.35	38.7	8.4
ROUGHRIDER	35	3155	449	3	4	22.45	38.7	9.6
NE83498	12	3156	538	3	4	26.90	38.7	10.8
NE86T666	40	4101	471	4	4	23.55	38.7	13.2
NE87403	41	4102	580	4	4	29.00	38.7	14.4
NE87512	49	4103	553	4	4	27.65	38.7	15.6
NE87446	44	4104	480	4	4	24.00	38.7	16.8
CENTURA	9	4105	515	4	4	25.75	38.7	18.0
NE86503	25	4106	471	4	4	23.55	38.7	19.2
NE87408	42	4107	613	4	4	30.65	38.7	20.4
COLT	11	4108	564	4	4	28.20	38.7	21.6
LANCER	1	4109	568	4	4	28.40	38.7	22.8
NE83406	7	4110	574	4	4	28.70	38.7	24.0
NE86607	34	4111	515	4	4	25.75	38.7	25.2
SIOUXLAND	37	4112	450	4	4	22.50	38.7	26.4
NE87612	52	4113	185	4	4	9.25	43.0	1.2
BUCKSKIN	30	4114	486	4	4	24.30	43.0	2.4
NE85556	15	4115	99	4	4	4.95	43.0	3.6
BRULE	2	4116	74	4	4	3.70	43.0	4.8
NE86507	26	4117	294	4	4	14.70	43.0	6.0
ROUGHRIDER	35	4118	272	4	4	13.60	43.0	7.2
VONA	36	4119	246	4	4	12.30	43.0	8.4
NE83404	6	4120	350	4	4	17.50	43.0	9.6
CODY	4	4121	303	4	4	15.15	43.0	10.8
NE87463	47	4122	471	4	4	23.55	43.0	12.0
NE86582	32	4123	390	4	4	19.50	43.0	13.2
NE87499	48	4124	530	4	4	26.50	43.0	14.4
NORKAN	18	4125	416	4	4	20.80	43.0	15.6
SCOUT 66	10	4126	506	4	4	25.30	43.0	16.8

```
NE87513        50   4127   348   4         4   17.40  43.0  18.0
NE83T12        39   4128   453   4         4   22.65  43.0  19.2
CENTURK 78     17   4129   632   4         4   31.60  43.0  20.4
NE87627        56   4130   339   4         4   16.95  43.0  21.6
NE86606        33   4131   625   4         4   31.25  43.0  22.8
NE87457        46   4132   473   4         4   23.65  43.0  24.0
NE86509        27   4133   509   4         4   25.45  43.0  25.2
LANCOTA        23   4134   549   4         4   27.45  43.0  26.4
KS831374       19   4135   291   4         4   14.55  47.3   1.2
NE86482        21   4136   121   4         4    6.05  47.3   2.4
NE85623        16   4137    21   4         4    1.05  47.3   3.6
NE86527        31   4138   128   4         4    6.40  47.3   4.8
NE87451        45   4139   102   4         4    5.10  47.3   6.0
NE87409        43   4140   356   4         4   17.80  47.3   7.2
GAGE           38   4141   443   4         4   22.15  47.3   8.4
NE83407         8   4142   307   4         4   15.35  47.3   9.6
NE87615        54   4143   240   4         4   12.00  47.3  10.8
ARAPAHOE        5   4144   500   4         4   25.00  47.3  12.0
CHEYENNE       29   4145   442   4         4   22.10  47.3  13.2
REDLAND         3   4146   586   4         4   29.30  47.3  14.4
NE83432        14   4147   469   4         4   23.45  47.3  15.6
NE87619        55   4148   558   4         4   27.90  47.3  16.8
NE83498        12   4149   632   4         4   31.60  47.3  18.0
NE87613        53   4150   604   4         4   30.20  47.3  19.2
NE86501        24   4151   606   4         4   30.30  47.3  20.4
TAM 200        20   4152   406   4         4   20.30  47.3  21.6
NE87522        51   4153   593   4         4   29.65  47.3  22.8
NE84557        13   4154   531   4         4   26.55  47.3  24.0
TAM 107        28   4155   512   4         4   25.60  47.3  25.2
HOMESTEAD      22   4156   538   4         4   26.90  47.3  26.4
```

Data from Stroup, W.W. and Baenziger, P.S. (1994), Removing spatial variation from wheat yield trials: a comparison of methods, *Crop Science*, **34**, 62-66. Copyright © 1994. Reproduced with permission.

Data Set 10.2.1 DESIGN

```
Chapter 10: Case Studies
Data for the Response Surface Model with the Split-Plot

data design;
   input batch a b c d y aa;
   datalines;
1    1    1    1    1   505    1
1    1   -1   -1   -1   493    1
1    1   -1    1   -1   491    1
2    1    1   -1    0   498    1
2    1    1   -1   -1   504    1
2    1   -1    1    0   500    1
3   -1    0   -1   -1   494   -1
3   -1    0    1    0   498   -1
3   -1   -1    0    1   498   -1
4    0   -1   -1    0   496    0
4    0    0    1    1   503    0
4    0   -1    0   -1   496    0
5   -1   -1    1    1   503   -1
5   -1    1    1   -1   495   -1
5   -1   -1    1   -1   494   -1
6    0    0    0    0   486    0
6    0    1    1   -1   501    0
6    0    1   -1    1   490    0
7   -1    1    0    0   494   -1
7   -1    1    1    1   497   -1
7   -1   -1    1   -1   492   -1
8    1   -1    1    1   503    1
```

```
  8      1      0      0     -1    499     1
  8      1      0     -1      1    493     1
  9      1      1      1     -1    505     1
  9      1      1      0      1    500     1
  9      1     -1     -1      1    490     1
 10     -1     -1     -1      1    494    -1
 10     -1      1     -1     -1    497    -1
 10     -1     -1     -1     -1    495    -1
  ;
```

Data Set 10.3.1 Response of Maize to Irrigation

```
Chapter 10: Case Studies
Data for Correlated Whole-Plot Case Study

data maize;
   input xobs bloc trt level y;
   datalines;
   1      1      1      1     43
   2      1      2      1     45
   3      1      1      2     41
   4      1      2      2     45
   5      1      1      3     46
   6      1      2      3     46
   7      1      1      4     46
   8      1      2      4     46
   9      1      1      5     45
  10      1      2      5     45
  11      1      1      6     50
  12      1      2      6     51
  13      1      1      7     49
  14      1      2      7     47
  15      1      1      8     46
  16      1      2      8     49
  17      2      1      1     39
  18      2      2      1     44
  19      2      3      1     39
  20      2      1      2     43
  21      2      2      2     47
  22      2      3      2     42
  23      2      1      3     47
  24      2      2      3     49
  25      2      3      3     45
  26      2      1      4     40
  27      2      2      4     42
  28      2      3      4     40
  29      2      1      5     38
  30      2      2      5     39
  31      2      3      5     37
  32      2      1      6     43
  33      2      2      6     45
  34      2      3      6     42
  35      2      1      7     36
  36      2      2      7     36
  37      2      3      7     36
  38      2      1      8     39
  39      2      2      8     40
  40      2      3      8     39
  41      3      2      1     34
  42      3      3      1     31
  43      3      2      2     38
  44      3      3      2     34
  45      3      2      3     37
  46      3      3      3     36
```

47	3	2	4	39
48	3	3	4	37
49	3	2	5	43
50	3	3	5	42
51	3	2	6	43
52	3	3	6	41
53	3	2	7	40
54	3	3	7	39
55	3	2	8	39
56	3	3	8	37
57	4	1	1	44
58	4	3	1	39
59	4	1	2	45
60	4	3	2	41
61	4	1	3	47
62	4	3	3	47
63	4	1	4	46
64	4	3	4	43
65	4	1	5	45
66	4	3	5	40
67	4	1	6	43
68	4	3	6	41
69	4	1	7	41
70	4	3	7	40
71	4	1	8	40
72	4	3	8	38
;				

Data Set 10.4.1 Complex Split-Plot

```
Chapter 10: Case Studies
Data for a Complex Split-Plot: Whole Plot Conducted as an Incomplete
Latin Square

data complex;
   input row col n g y;
   datalines;
1      1      1      1      20.1
1      1      1      2      20.4
2      1      2      1      16.2
2      1      2      2      14.0
3      1      3      1      16.2
3      1      3      2      12.6
1      2      2      1      18.1
1      2      2      2      16.7
2      2      1      1      10.3
2      2      1      2       8.1
3      2      4      1      15.1
3      2      4      2      10.5
1      3      5      1      23.1
1      3      5      2      18.1
2      3      3      1      17.8
2      3      3      2      16.1
3      3      1      1       9.8
3      3      1      2       9.0
1      4      4      1      22.0
1      4      4      2      18.0
2      4      5      1      18.1
2      4      5      2      12.9
3      4      2      1      14.0
3      4      2      2      12.1
```

```
1     5     3     1     22.7
1     5     3     2     19.5
2     5     4     1     18.9
2     5     4     2     14.3
3     5     5     1     17.0
3     5     5     2     10.9
;
```

Data Set 10.5.1 Methods of Rangeland Reclamation

```
Chapter 10: Case Studies
Data for Strip-Split-Split Plot Experiment

data range;
   input loc ec ir v y;
   datalines;
1     1     1     1     30.0
1     1     1     2     40.9
1     1     2     1     38.9
1     1     2     2     38.2
1     2     1     1     41.8
1     2     1     2     52.2
1     2     2     1     54.8
1     2     2     2     58.2
2     1     1     1     20.5
2     1     1     2     26.9
2     1     2     1     21.4
2     1     2     2     25.1
2     2     1     1     26.4
2     2     1     2     36.7
2     2     2     1     28.9
2     2     2     2     35.9
3     1     1     1     21.0
3     1     1     2     25.4
3     1     2     1     24.0
3     1     2     2     23.3
3     2     1     1     34.4
3     2     1     2     41.0
3     2     2     1     33.2
3     2     2     2     34.9
;
```

Data Set 10.6.1 FAC_SP

```
Chapter 10: Case Studies
Data for the Factorial Experiment Run as a Split-Plot

data fac-sp;
   input rep blk a b c y;
   datalines;
1     1    -1    -1    -1    117
1     1    -1     1     1    130
1     1     1    -1     1    122
1     1     1     1    -1    113
1     2    -1    -1     1    123
1     2    -1     1    -1    121
1     2     1    -1    -1    122
1     2     1     1     1    125
2     1    -1    -1    -1    127
2     1    -1     1     1    137
```

```
2      1      1     -1      1     131
2      1      1      1     -1     122
2      2     -1     -1      1     128
2      2     -1      1     -1     124
2      2      1     -1     -1     124
2      2      1      1      1     130
3      1     -1     -1     -1     114
3      1     -1      1      1     132
3      1      1     -1      1     121
3      1      1      1     -1     116
3      2     -1     -1      1     125
3      2     -1      1     -1     124
3      2      1     -1     -1     122
3      2      1      1      1     129
4      1     -1     -1     -1     118
4      1     -1      1      1     132
4      1      1     -1      1     120
4      1      1      1     -1     117
4      2     -1     -1      1     120
4      2     -1      1     -1     118
4      2      1     -1     -1     113
4      2      1      1      1     122
5      1     -1     -1     -1     120
5      1     -1      1      1     132
5      1      1     -1      1     118
5      1      1      1     -1     120
5      2     -1     -1      1     127
5      2     -1      1     -1     127
5      2      1     -1     -1     118
5      2      1      1      1     130
6      1     -1     -1     -1     122
6      1     -1      1      1     134
6      1      1     -1      1     124
6      1      1      1     -1     115
6      2     -1     -1      1     123
6      2     -1      1     -1     122
6      2      1     -1     -1     123
6      2      1      1      1     124
;
```

Data Set 10.7.1 Photo Resist Coating Experiment

```
Chapter 10: Case Studies
Data for 2³ Treatment Structure in an Incomplete Block Design Structure
with Balanced Confounding

data resist;
   input rep blk a b c edslp;
   datalines;
1      1     -1     -1     -1      3.6
1      1     -1      1      1      4.5
1      1      1     -1      1      4.2
1      1      1      1     -1      4.0
1      2     -1     -1      1      5.1
1      2     -1      1     -1      3.9
1      2      1     -1     -1      4.5
1      2      1      1      1      4.9
2      1     -1     -1     -1      5.2
2      1     -1      1      1      5.9
2      1      1     -1      1      5.3
2      1      1      1     -1      5.2
2      2     -1     -1      1      5.2
2      2     -1      1     -1      4.6
2      2      1     -1     -1      4.7
```

```
2       2       1       1       1       5.2
3       1      -1       1      -1       4.3
3       1      -1       1       1       5.1
3       1       1      -1      -1       4.5
3       1       1      -1       1       4.6
3       2      -1      -1      -1       4.8
3       2      -1      -1       1       5.2
3       2       1       1      -1       5.2
3       2       1       1       1       5.9
4       1      -1      -1       1       5.9
4       1      -1       1       1       6.4
4       1       1      -1      -1       5.7
4       1       1       1      -1       5.6
4       2      -1      -1      -1       4.3
4       2      -1       1      -1       4.4
4       2       1      -1       1       5.3
4       2       1       1       1       5.6
5       1      -1      -1       1       4.3
5       1      -1       1      -1       4.2
5       1       1      -1       1       4.3
5       1       1       1      -1       4.4
5       2      -1      -1      -1       4.5
5       2      -1       1       1       5.5
5       2       1      -1      -1       4.6
5       2       1       1       1       5.2
;
```

Data Set 10.8.1 Product Acceptability Study

```
Chapter 10: Case Studies
Data for Product Acceptability Study with Cross-over and Repeated
Measures

data prior;
    input blk seq t1 t2 t3 person y11 y12 y13 y21 y22 y23 y31 y32 y33;
    array yy{3,3} y11-y13 y21-y23 y31-y33;
    array tt{3} t1-t3;
    array ll{4} l1-l4;
    do period = 1 to 3;
        prod = tt{period};
        do i = 1 to 4;
            ll{i} = 0;
        end;
        if (period = 1) then priorprd = 0;
        else do;
            priorprd = tt{period - 1};
            ll{priorprd} = 1;
        end;
        do time = 1 to 3;
            y = yy{period,time};
            output;
        end;
    end;
    drop i t1-t3 y11-y13 y21-y23 y31-y33;
    datalines;
1    1    1    2    3    101    5    4    3    5    5    5    5    4    4
1    2    1    3    2    102    4    4    3    6    6    6    5    5    4
1    3    2    1    3    103    5    4    4    5    5    4    5    5    5
1    4    2    3    1    104    4    4    4    4    4    4    4    4    4
1    5    3    2    1    105    5    5    5    5    5    5    6    6    5
1    6    3    1    2    106    6    5    5    6    6    5    7    6    6
2    1    1    2    4    201    3    2    1    3    3    3    2    3    3
2    2    1    4    2    202    4    4    3    4    5    5    4    3    3
2    3    2    1    4    203    4    3    3    3    3    2    4    5    5
```

2	4	2	4	1	204	4	4	3	4	4	4	3	3	2
2	5	4	2	1	205	4	4	4	3	3	2	4	3	3
2	6	4	1	2	206	4	4	4	3	3	2	4	4	4
3	1	1	3	4	301	4	4	3	5	5	5	4	5	5
3	2	1	4	3	302	3	3	3	4	4	4	3	4	3
3	3	3	1	4	303	4	4	4	4	4	3	4	4	4
3	4	3	4	1	304	3	2	2	3	3	3	3	2	2
3	5	4	3	1	305	2	2	2	2	2	2	2	2	1
3	6	4	1	3	306	4	4	4	4	3	2	4	4	4
4	1	2	3	4	401	3	3	3	3	3	3	4	4	4
4	2	2	4	3	402	3	2	2	4	4	4	3	3	3
4	3	3	2	4	403	4	4	4	5	5	4	4	4	4
4	4	3	4	2	404	2	2	2	3	3	3	4	4	3
4	5	4	3	2	405	4	4	4	4	4	4	4	4	4
4	6	4	2	3	406	3	4	3	4	3	4	3	3	3

```
;
```

y11, y12, and y13 are acceptability scores for the product in period 1
y21, y22, and y23 are acceptability scores for the product in period 2
y31, y32, and y33 are acceptability scores for the product in period 3
T1, T2, and T3 are the three treatments used in the sequences

Data Set 10.9.1 On-Farm Trial

```
Chapter 10: Case Studies
Data for On-Farm Trial

data farm;
   input farm rep trt y;
   datalines;
1        1        1        49.7
1        1        2        56.2
1        2        1        41.0
1        2        2        52.8
1        3        1        40.8
1        3        2        57.4
2        1        1        42.9
2        1        2        55.9
2        2        1        47.5
2        2        2        52.6
3        1        1        41.8
3        1        2        46.9
3        2        1        39.2
3        2        2        33.3
4        1        1        31.5
4        1        2        51.6
4        2        1        33.5
4        2        2        54.5
5        1        1        46.8
5        1        2        36.6
6        1        1        49.0
6        1        2        63.9
7        1        1        43.2
7        1        2        40.2
7        2        1        37.8
7        2        2        31.9
;
```

Data Set 10.10 CD4

Chapter 11: Case Studies
Data for a Complex Split-Plot: Whole Plot Conducted as an Incomplete
Latin Square

```
data cd4;
   input randgrp stratum unit @@;
   seq = _n_;
   do visit = 0,2,6,12,18;
      input cd4 @@;
      sqrtcd4 = sqrt(cd4);
      if visit ne 0 then notbase = 1;
      else notbase = 0;
      if visit ne 0 then visitm2 = visit - 2;
      else visitm2 = 0;
      output;
   end;
   datalines;
2    2    2    114      .       71      89       .
1    2    2    40       .       66      21      25
1    2    3    12      13       38       .       .
2    1    3    15      21        7       3       .
1    1    3    53      74       74      45       .
2    1    3    21       .        .       .       .
2    2    3    46      29       20      10       .
1    2    5    12       1        0       .       .
2    1    5     0      33        .       .       .
1    2    5    147    180      111      56       .
2    2    5    47       .        .       .       .
1    2    5    185    262      177      91     138
2    2    5     6      16        6       .       .
1    2    5     4       8        .       .       .
1    1    5    138     97       83      79       .
2    2    5     3       1       26       .       .
2    2    5    43      24       25      25       .
2    2    5    32      29        9       7       .
1    2    5     9       .        .       .       .
2    1    6    363    364      270     279       .
1    2    6    52      29       11       .       .
1    2    6     3       3        2       4       .
1    2    6    15       .        .       .       .
2    2    6    197    255        .     235     206
2    1    6     5       .        .       .       .
1    2    6    295    394      411     291     185
2    2    6    17       .        5       2       3
1    1    6    285      .        .       .       .
1    1    6    21       .        .       .       .
2    2    6    33       .       19       .       .
2    2    6    83     112       31       .       .
1    2    6     3       .        1       .       .
1    1    6    60      43        .       .      12
2    2    6     1       .        2       .       7
1    2    6    157    101       51      47      40
2    2    6     0       .        1       .       .
2    2    6    15       9        5       .       .
1    2    6    280    233        .       .       .
2    2    6    100      .       61      20       .
1    2    6    263    204        .       .       .
2    2    6    22      11        .       2       .
2    2    6    69       .        .       .       .
2    2    6    272      .        .       .       .
1    2    6    21      29       12       .       .
2    1    6     3       .        .       .       .
1    2    6    39      24        7       .       .
2    1    6    16      13        .       .       .
```

2	1	6	1	2	.	.	.
1	2	6	1	.	.	.	.
1	2	6	190	207	147	16	.
1	2	6	9	20	.	.	.
2	2	6	2	0	.	.	.
2	1	6	13	.	.	.	.
2	1	7	111	187	130	81	.
2	2	7	6	10	23	4	.
2	1	7	48	53	13	20	.
1	2	7	11	32	10	.	.
1	2	7	6	3	3	.	.
2	2	7	130	27	33	.	.
2	1	7	8	.	5	1	.
2	2	7	154	177	.	.	.
2	2	7	271	250	125	169	.
2	1	7	194	307	142	99	.
1	2	7	32	31	6	.	.
1	1	7	15	.	.	.	.
1	1	7	50	.	21	.	.
1	1	7	17	.	6	.	.
1	1	7	192	78	33	11	.
2	1	7	5	.	.	.	.
1	2	7	46	61	79	.	.
2	2	7	4	5	.	.	.
2	2	7	226	187	190	187	.
1	2	7	1	.	.	.	.
1	2	7	21	37	4	8	.
1	1	7	110	66	58	.	.
2	2	7	19	19	16	10	.
2	1	7	14	1	2	.	.
1	2	7	52	137	104	130	.
2	2	7	21	31	32	8	.
2	2	8	120	300	220	272	.
1	2	8	5	5	.	.	.
1	1	8	42	34	15	.	7
1	1	8	50	50	.	.	.
2	2	8	64	15	.	.	.
1	2	8	15	54	45	25	.
1	2	8	242	390	264	332	.
2	1	8	39	2	24	.	.
2	1	8	8	30	3	.	.
2	1	8	4	11	2	21	19
1	2	8	199	203	286	255	183
2	2	8	65	51	46	5	37
1	1	8	45	48	60	61	42
2	2	8	291	314	453	382	273
1	2	8	39	30	21	16	.
2	2	8	115	90	139	141	.
2	2	8	224	.	363	262	.
1	1	8	40	16	.	.	.
2	1	8	40	26	36	.	.
2	2	8	24	.	3	.	.
2	1	8	21	35	28	.	.
1	1	8	176	198	98	22	.
1	1	8	6	2	.	.	.
2	2	8	13	162	.	42	.
2	1	8	15	20	20	.	.
2	2	8	11	5	.	.	.
1	2	8	275	415	284	308	.
1	1	8	50	72	36	.	.
2	1	8	2	.	.	.	.
2	1	8	61	.	.	.	.
1	1	8	274	265	.	.	.
1	1	8	28	42	16	.	.
2	2	8	41	30	.	.	.
1	1	8	54	.	.	.	.
1	2	8	4	4	2	.	.
2	1	8	54	21	.	.	.

2	1	8	29	21	.	.	.
1	1	8	100	.	14	29	.
2	1	8	10	.	.	.	.
1	2	8	156	.	39	.	.
1	2	8	0	.	.	.	.
1	2	8	59	43	61	25	.
2	2	8	6	4	.	.	.
2	2	8	71	.	.	6	.
1	2	8	27	8	13	18	.
2	2	9	15	3	3	4	.
2	2	9	63	30	22	4	.
1	2	9	25	163	113	59	.
1	1	9	14	.	.	.	.
2	2	9	21	15	5	.	.
2	2	9	197	154	135	110	31
1	2	9	130	582	.	.	.
2	2	9	16	37	10	8	.
2	1	9	37	26	0	8	.
1	2	9	10	12	9	.	.
2	2	9	50	40	20	10	.
2	2	9	109	42	18	.	.
1	2	9	89	19	43	9	6
1	2	9	52	15	26	.	.
2	2	9	42	23	30	11	15
1	1	9	7	.	1	.	.
1	2	9	10	0	5	.	.
1	2	9	232	221	166	141	.
2	1	9	117	17	.	55	.
1	2	9	288	268	150	298	.
2	2	9	168	226	129	144	.
2	1	9	169	149	93	45	.
2	2	9	12	16	0	.	.
1	2	9	126	246	153	140	.
1	2	9	136	112	.	86	.
2	2	9	1	3	0	0	.
1	2	9	91	37	.	.	.
2	2	9	280	.	319	.	.
2	2	9	160	115	57	69	.
1	2	9	46	31	8	10	.
1	2	9	5	3	3	7	.
1	1	9	0	.	.	.	.
1	2	10	246	333	.	232	177
1	2	10	224	.	204	141	.
1	2	10	240	360	.	310	.
2	2	10	198	172	.	286	.
2	1	10	66	89	81	18	.
1	1	10	40	15	34	5	.
1	1	10	10	30	.	.	.
1	1	10	30	.	.	.	.
2	2	10	120	160	120	130	80
2	1	10	50	.	20	10	.
1	2	10	47	110	63	20	.
2	1	10	20	10	20	.	.
2	2	10	30	40	95	50	.
2	2	10	80	50	60	10	.
2	1	10	30	4	40	10	.
1	1	10	76	110	.	.	.
2	2	10	250	.	210	220	.
2	2	10	30	40	40	320	.
2	1	10	100	40	.	.	.
2	1	10	140	105	.	89	.
2	1	10	20	20	10	20	.
2	2	10	270	290	220	240	.
1	1	10	40	20	30	.	.
2	2	10	190	90	130	80	.
1	1	10	40	.	.	.	.
1	2	10	40	80	20	20	.
2	2	10	70	40	30	0	.

1	2	10	180	260	160	180	·
1	1	10	0	·	60	70	·
2	2	10	190	280	130	200	·
2	2	10	270	370	360	350	·
1	2	10	7	4	6	287	·
1	2	10	370	·	·	·	·
2	2	10	24	3	11	7	·
1	2	10	144	237	242	119	·
1	1	10	13	27	·	19	·
1	2	10	104	174	194	·	·
2	1	10	25	0	9	23	·
1	2	10	110	250	170	80	·
1	2	10	20	·	·	·	·
2	2	10	130	·	·	·	·
1	2	10	160	230	300	200	·
1	2	10	190	300	150	240	·
2	2	10	20	10	0	4	·
1	1	10	5	0	·	·	·
2	1	11	59	·	·	·	·
1	1	11	5	14	5	·	·
1	2	11	28	·	46	·	·
1	1	12	6	5	·	·	·
2	2	12	107	126	72	14	·
1	1	12	23	·	·	·	·
2	1	12	4	5	4	9	·
1	1	12	32	39	46	30	34
1	2	12	143	154	264	176	·
2	1	12	14	8	·	·	·
2	2	12	273	383	263	369	·
1	1	12	72	20	9	·	·
2	2	12	77	19	·	·	·
1	2	12	95	234	216	98	·
2	1	12	94	53	29	5	·
1	2	12	165	·	35	·	·
1	2	12	6	18	·	·	·
2	2	12	281	207	160	71	62
2	2	12	17	10	·	·	·
1	2	12	7	15	11	·	·
1	2	12	109	92	85	·	68
2	2	12	222	136	·	179	·
1	2	12	6	10	8	5	11
2	2	12	10	8	3	·	·
1	2	12	21	17	8	·	·
1	2	12	10	·	·	·	·
2	1	12	0	21	·	·	·
2	2	12	13	·	·	·	·
2	2	12	14	·	·	·	·
1	2	12	9	·	10	30	·
1	2	12	11	7	14	16	·
2	1	12	53	27	·	·	·
2	2	12	131	129	122	66	·
1	1	12	3	7	·	·	·
1	2	12	216	249	14	139	·
1	1	12	8	7	·	·	·
1	2	12	37	30	21	16	·
2	2	12	200	·	203	209	·
2	2	12	32	57	13	7	·
2	2	12	67	40	32	54	·
2	2	12	235	·	134	53	·
2	2	12	43	55	·	·	·
1	2	12	35	19	11	·	·
1	2	12	228	235	29	294	·
1	2	12	109	124	88	·	·
1	1	12	11	·	·	·	·
2	2	12	82	·	·	·	·
2	1	12	112	9	5	·	·
1	2	12	181	110	·	·	·
2	1	12	76	18	11	7	·

2	1	12	152	168	144	68	.
2	1	12	7	8	5	2	.
2	2	12	230	253	17	170	.
2	1	13	2	3	2	4	.
2	1	13	1	2	1	1	.
2	2	13	9	22	8	11	.
2	2	13	281	300	368	202	130
1	2	13	5	.	.	.	.
2	2	13	12	35	34	14	14
2	2	13	277	84	.	.	.
1	1	13	4	3	1	1	.
2	1	13	2	2	2	2	.
1	2	13	254	284	291	204	.
2	2	13	51	75	78	.	.
1	1	13	6	2	1	.	.
1	2	13	19	27	34	12	.
2	2	13	16	10	3	4	.
1	2	13	2	6	1	1	.
1	2	13	8	12	4	.	.
2	1	14	17	4	7	.	.
1	2	14	11	8	.	5	.
1	2	14	41	52	30	1	.
1	1	14	54	39	23	14	19
1	1	14	16	.	10	2	4
1	2	14	70	35	49	26	.
1	1	14	10	.	.	.	.
2	2	14	10	10	4	.	.
1	1	14	8	9	6	9	.
2	2	14	12	.	6	.	.
2	1	14	10	8	3	7	.
1	2	14	17	3	1	.	.
1	1	14	15	5	1	1	.
1	1	14	31	26	27	12	.
1	2	14	40	9	.	.	.
1	2	14	44	30	.	.	.
2	1	14	40	6	.	.	.
1	1	14	12	.	.	.	.
1	1	14	80	35	47	3	.
1	2	14	99	200	152	191	.
2	1	14	8	.	.	5	.
2	2	14	3	.	.	.	.
2	2	14	34	34	36	13	.
1	2	14	60	33	37	14	.
2	2	14	38	17	12	55	.
2	1	14	31	22	10	.	.
2	1	14	34	13	9	.	.
1	1	14	11	11	3	.	.
1	1	14	77	51	37	.	.
1	2	14	9	21	.	.	.
1	2	14	122	112	77	72	.
2	2	14	273	129	163	154	.
2	1	14	81	52	26	.	.
1	1	14	10	7	14	10	.
2	1	14	4	.	6	.	.
2	1	14	35	.	11	4	.
2	2	14	65	58	22	15	.
2	1	14	7	4	6	.	.
2	2	14	180	238	171	65	.
2	1	14	4	8	3	.	.
2	2	14	93	142	.	15	.
2	2	14	297	122	89	40	.
2	2	14	300	330	290	270	340
2	2	15	13	10	.	.	.
1	1	15	8	15	17	12	8
2	1	15	3	3	8	6	3
1	1	15	7	9	2	.	.
1	1	15	273	152	65	38	21
1	2	15	137	121	146	138	.

2	2	15	42	.	.	.	.
1	1	15	8	.	.	.	.
2	2	15	62	.	.	.	.
1	2	15	3	4	3	4	.
2	1	15	13	7	3	.	.
2	1	15	37	17	20	1	.
2	1	15	6	3	1	.	.
1	2	15	128	.	24	15	.
1	2	15	64	28	.	.	.
1	1	15	2	.	.	.	.
1	2	15	125	147	203	113	.
2	1	15	18	30	22	.	.
2	2	15	21	.	8	7	.
2	2	15	47	56	.	.	.
1	2	15	5	5	4	.	.
2	1	15	11	12	8	.	.
2	2	15	184	138	37	.	.
1	1	15	12	.	.	.	.
2	1	15	7	10	9	4	.
1	2	15	40	29	28	20	.
2	2	15	100	145	88	45	.
1	2	15	113	116	173	126	.
1	2	15	74	56	29	27	.
2	2	15	161	176	.	30	.
2	2	15	5	.	.	.	.
2	2	15	31	24	31	.	.
1	1	15	233	269	182	71	.
1	2	15	63	71	16	16	.
1	1	15	247	289	219	.	.
1	1	15	10	20	.	.	.
2	2	15	291	367	323	267	.
2	2	15	30	41	22	16	.
2	2	15	5	.	.	.	.
1	2	15	108	475	284	151	.
1	2	15	13	15	.	.	.
1	2	15	341	.	.	.	.
1	1	15	6	6	.	.	.
2	1	15	7	12	9	0	.
1	2	16	23	54	.	.	.
1	1	16	27	33	18	5	12
1	2	16	52	48	84	63	20
1	1	16	0	.	15	.	.
2	1	16	0	.	.	.	.
2	2	16	4	10	0	.	.
1	2	16	14	.	.	0	.
2	2	16	48	143	.	.	.
2	2	16	49	77	.	90	.
2	2	16	5	2	.	.	.
1	2	16	63	110	55	26	.
2	1	16	6	0	.	5	.
2	1	16	8	0	.	.	.
2	1	16	10	.	7	.	.
2	2	16	237	306	286	276	.
1	2	16	66	70	.	.	.
2	1	16	155	104	.	184	.
1	2	16	281	.	.	.	.
1	1	16	0	.	.	.	.
2	2	16	201	238	240	418	.
1	1	16	6	0	.	.	.
1	2	17	20	12	12	.	.
2	2	17	27	20	11	.	.
2	2	17	110	57	41	.	.
2	1	17	37	40	.	.	.
2	2	17	3	5	1	.	.
1	2	17	176	207	383	161	.
2	1	17	217	90	97	9	.
2	1	17	84	39	.	.	.
2	2	17	22	14	6	.	.

2	1	17	8	29	16	7	.
1	2	17	80	51	.	.	.
2	1	17	224	194	125	.	.
1	2	17	13	19	.	3	2
2	2	17	96	53	.	.	.
2	1	17	10	17	9	.	.
1	2	17	30	.	.	.	.
2	2	17	57	55	.	11	.
1	1	17	2	3	11	.	.
2	2	17	19	.	.	.	.
1	2	17	39	14	16	.	.
1	2	17	288	323	357	369	.
2	1	17	15	11	3	.	.
1	2	17	43	13	.	.	.
1	1	17	14	14	10	.	.
1	2	17	125	.	.	.	.
1	1	17	7	7	3	11	.
1	2	17	14	9	10	7	.
1	1	17	2	8	.	.	.
2	2	17	11	7	8	0	.
2	2	17	5	7	.	.	.
1	1	17	46	47	35	25	.
2	2	17	3	2	.	.	.
2	2	17	132	90	60	23	.
1	1	17	84	57	54	.	.
1	1	17	26	.	.	.	.
1	2	17	239	200	89	51	.
2	2	17	4	.	.	.	.
2	2	17	29	23	35	.	.
1	2	17	21	113	5	.	.
1	2	17	166	.	.	.	.
1	2	17	273	87	359	285	.
2	2	17	181	.	.	.	.
1	2	17	2	4	2	0	.
2	1	17	28	43	28	28	.
2	2	17	70	60	66	49	.
1	2	17	76	105	40	.	.
2	2	17	78	.	.	.	.
1	2	18	75	132	.	.	.
2	1	18	36	.	.	.	.
2	2	18	12	6	16	13	.
2	1	18	40	.	28	.	.
2	2	18	16	50	17	5	.
2	1	18	5	.	.	.	.
1	1	18	3	12	.	.	.
1	1	18	56	45	9	8	.
2	2	18	66	78	50	32	.
2	2	18	65	96	60	91	.
1	2	18	272	240	234	98	.
2	1	18	60	24	90	76	.
1	2	18	105	272	375	150	.
1	2	18	36	32	42	.	.
2	1	18	24	4	.	.	.
2	1	18	300	270	143	160	.
2	2	18	20	18	10	.	.
2	2	18	13	14	6	7	7
1	2	18	42	20	30	18	.
2	2	18	27	42	6	6	.
1	1	18	7	9	21	.	.
1	2	18	70	63	30	.	.
1	2	18	159	73	.	.	.
1	1	18	14	16	5	.	.
1	1	18	138	140	154	120	126
1	2	18	169	144	84	.	.
2	1	18	40	36	.	10	.
1	1	18	40	.	.	.	.
1	2	18	24	15	5	5	3
2	2	18	21	12	24	102	.

```
2   2   18     6      24      .      .      .
2   1   18    10      20     14      3      .
1   2   18   190     136      .      .      .
1   2   18   220     400    240      .      .
1   1   18   247     300    220    242      .
1   1   18     9      30     10      .      .
1   1   18     3      21      .      .      .
1   2   18     7      10      6      7      .
2   2   18    24       .      .      .      .
1   1   18    10       6     12      .      .
2   2   18     9      10      .      .      .
2   1   18    30       5      .      .      .
run;
```

Data Set 11.5 NEW

Chapter 11: Generalized Linear Mixed Models
Data for Example of Mixed Model with Binomial Errors

```
data clin;
   input clinic trt $ fav unfav;
   nij=fav+unfav;
   if fav=0 then fav=0.1/nij;
   datalines;
1 drug 11 25
1 cntl 10 27
2 drug 16 4
2 cntl 22 10
3 drug 14 5
3 cntl 7 12
4 drug 2 14
4 cntl 1 16
5 drug 6 11
5 cntl 0 12
6 drug 1 10
6 cntl 0 10
7 drug 1 4
7 cntl 1 8
8 drug 4 2
8 cntl 6 1
;
```

Beitler, P.J. and Landis, J.R. (1985), A mixed-effects model for categorical data, *Biometrics*, **41**, 991-1000. Copyright © 1985 by The International Biometric Society. Reproduced with permission.

Data Set 11.6 A

Chapter 11: Generalized Linear Mixed Models
Data for a Mixed Model with Count Data

```
data a;
   input trt blk mix count;
   y=count&1;
   datalines;
1 1 1 24
1 1 2 12
1 1 3 8
1 1 4 13
1 2 1 9
1 2 2 9
1 2 3 9
```

```
1 2 4 18
1 3 1 12
1 3 2 8
1 3 3 44
1 3 4 0
1 4 1 8
1 4 2 12
1 4 3 25
1 4 4 0
2 1 1 11
2 1 2 32
2 1 3 12
2 1 4 22
2 2 1 41
2 2 2 15
2 2 3 39
2 2 4 38
2 3 1 30
2 3 2 11
2 3 3 5
2 3 4 50
2 4 1 11
2 4 2 0
2 4 3 7
2 4 4 10
3 1 1 0
3 1 2 0
3 1 3 19
3 1 4 25
3 2 1 33
3 2 2 14
3 2 3 20
3 2 4 30
3 3 1 46
3 3 2 31
3 3 3 5
3 3 4 7
3 4 1 8
3 4 2 25
3 4 3 19
3 4 4 3
4 1 1 19
4 1 2 50
4 1 3 20
4 1 4 7
4 2 1 13
4 2 2 42
4 2 3 37
4 2 4 6
4 3 1 10
4 3 2 9
4 3 3 10
4 3 4 24
4 4 1 24
4 4 2 34
4 4 3 35
4 4 4 45
5 1 1 19
5 1 2 48
5 1 3 50
5 1 4 34
5 2 1 0
5 2 2 36
5 2 3 24
5 2 4 24
5 3 1 40
5 3 2 40
5 3 3 14
```

```
5 3 4 18
5 4 1 99
5 4 2 39
5 4 3 21
5 4 4 25
6 1 1 115
6 1 2 38
6 1 3 16
6 1 4 34
6 2 1 52
6 2 2 55
6 2 3 17
6 2 4 18
6 3 1 37
6 3 2 19
6 3 3 44
6 3 4 10
6 4 1 10
6 4 2 11
6 4 3 14
6 4 4 13
7 1 1 46
7 1 2 45
7 1 3 37
7 1 4 13
7 2 1 30
7 2 2 96
7 2 3 41
7 2 4 37
7 3 1 59
7 3 2 34
7 3 3 28
7 3 4 20
7 4 1 84
7 4 2 56
7 4 3 26
7 4 4 27
;
```

Data Set 12.4 Tree

```
Chapter 12: Nonlinear Mixed Models
Logistic Growth Curve

data tree;
   input tree time x y;
   datalines;
1 1  118    30
1 2  484    58
1 3  664    87
1 4 1004   115
1 5 1231   120
1 6 1372   142
1 7 1582   145
2 1  118    33
2 2  484    69
2 3  664   111
2 4 1004   156
2 5 1231   172
2 6 1372   203
2 7 1582   203
3 1  118    30
3 2  484    51
3 3  664    75
3 4 1004   108
```

```
3 5 1231  115
3 6 1372  139
3 7 1582  140
4 1  118   32
4 2  484   62
4 3  664  112
4 4 1004  167
4 5 1231  179
4 6 1372  209
4 7 1582  214
5 1  118   30
5 2  484   49
5 3  664   81
5 4 1004  125
5 5 1231  142
5 6 1372  174
5 7 1582  177
;
```

From Draper, N.R., and Smith, H. (1981), *Applied Regression Analysis.*
Copyright © 1981 by John Wiley & Sons, Inc. Reprinted by permission of
John Wiley & Sons, Inc.

Data Set 12.5 PHENO

Chapter 12: Nonlinear Mixed Models
A One-Compartment Pharmokinetic Model

```
data pheno;
   input indiv time dose weight apgar conc;
   retain cursub .;
   if cursub ne indiv then do;
      newsub = 1;
      cursub = indiv;
   end;
   else newsub = 0;
   if (apgar < 5) then apgarlow = 1;
   else apgarlow = 0;
   tlag = lag(time);
   if (newsub=1) then tlag = 0;
   drop apgar cursub;
   datalines;
1    0.    25.0    1.4    7    .
1    2.0    0.0    1.4    7    17.3
1   12.5    3.5    1.4    7    .
1   24.5    3.5    1.4    7    .
1   37.0    3.5    1.4    7    .
1   48.0    3.5    1.4    7    .
1   60.5    3.5    1.4    7    .
1   72.5    3.5    1.4    7    .
1   85.3    3.5    1.4    7    .
1   96.5    3.5    1.4    7    .
1  108.5    3.5    1.4    7    .
1  112.5    0.0    1.4    7    31.0
2    0.    15.0    1.5    9    .
2    2.0    0.0    1.5    9    9.7
2    4.0    3.8    1.5    9    .
2   16.0    3.8    1.5    9    .
2   27.8    3.8    1.5    9    .
2   40.0    3.8    1.5    9    .
2   52.0    3.8    1.5    9    .
2   63.5    0.0    1.5    9    24.6
2   64.0    3.8    1.5    9    .
2   76.0    3.8    1.5    9    .
```

2	88.0	3.8	1.5	9	.
2	100.0	3.8	1.5	9	.
2	112.0	3.8	1.5	9	.
2	124.0	3.8	1.5	9	.
2	135.5	0.0	1.5	9	33.0
3	0.	30.0	1.5	6	.
3	1.5	0.0	1.5	6	18.0
3	11.5	3.7	1.5	6	.
3	23.5	3.7	1.5	6	.
3	35.5	3.7	1.5	6	.
3	47.5	3.7	1.5	6	.
3	59.3	3.7	1.5	6	.
3	73.0	3.7	1.5	6	.
3	83.5	0.0	1.5	6	23.8
3	84.0	3.7	1.5	6	.
3	96.5	3.7	1.5	6	.
3	108.5	3.7	1.5	6	.
3	120.0	3.7	1.5	6	.
3	132.0	3.7	1.5	6	.
3	134.3	0.0	1.5	6	24.3
4	0.	18.6	0.9	6	.
4	1.8	0.0	0.9	6	20.8
4	12.0	2.3	0.9	6	.
4	24.3	2.3	0.9	6	.
4	35.8	2.3	0.9	6	.
4	48.1	2.3	0.9	6	.
4	59.3	0.0	0.9	6	23.9
4	59.8	2.3	0.9	6	.
4	71.8	2.3	0.9	6	.
4	83.8	2.3	0.9	6	.
4	95.8	2.3	0.9	6	.
4	107.8	2.3	0.9	6	.
4	119.8	2.3	0.9	6	.
4	130.8	0.0	0.9	6	31.7
5	0.	27.0	1.4	7	.
5	2.0	0.0	1.4	7	14.2
5	12.0	3.4	1.4	7	.
5	24.0	3.4	1.4	7	.
5	36.0	3.4	1.4	7	.
5	48.0	3.4	1.4	7	.
5	59.5	0.0	1.4	7	18.2
5	60.0	3.4	1.4	7	.
5	72.0	3.4	1.4	7	.
5	84.0	3.4	1.4	7	.
5	96.0	3.4	1.4	7	.
5	108.0	3.4	1.4	7	.
5	120.0	3.4	1.4	7	.
5	132.0	0.0	1.4	7	20.3
6	0.	24.0	1.2	5	.
6	1.8	0.0	1.2	5	19.0
6	11.8	3.0	1.2	5	.
6	23.8	3.0	1.2	5	.
6	35.8	3.0	1.2	5	.
6	47.8	3.0	1.2	5	.
6	59.3	0.0	1.2	5	17.3
6	59.8	3.0	1.2	5	.
6	71.8	3.0	1.2	5	.
6	83.8	3.0	1.2	5	.
6	95.8	3.0	1.2	5	.
6	107.8	3.0	1.2	5	.
6	120.1	3.0	1.2	5	.
6	131.8	3.0	1.2	5	.
6	142.8	0.0	1.2	5	32.5
7	0.	19.0	1.0	5	.
7	2.0	0.0	1.0	5	17.9
7	11.3	2.4	1.0	5	.
7	23.3	2.4	1.0	5	.
7	36.5	2.4	1.0	5	.

7	48.2	2.4	1.0	5	.
7	60.3	2.4	1.0	5	.
7	73.8	0.0	1.0	5	23.4
7	75.8	2.4	1.0	5	.
7	84.3	2.4	1.0	5	.
7	96.3	2.4	1.0	5	.
7	108.3	2.4	1.0	5	.
7	120.3	2.4	1.0	5	.
7	132.3	2.4	1.0	5	.
7	144.5	2.4	1.0	5	.
7	165.3	0.0	1.0	5	25.8
8	0.	24.0	1.2	7	.
8	1.7	0.0	1.2	7	25.8
8	11.8	3.0	1.2	7	.
8	23.7	3.0	1.2	7	.
8	35.7	3.0	1.2	7	.
8	47.7	3.0	1.2	7	.
8	59.7	3.0	1.2	7	.
8	71.7	3.0	1.2	7	.
8	73.7	0.0	1.2	7	34.2
8	83.7	3.0	1.2	7	.
8	95.7	3.0	1.2	7	.
8	107.7	3.0	1.2	7	.
8	119.7	3.0	1.2	7	.
8	131.7	3.0	1.2	7	.
8	143.7	3.0	1.2	7	.
8	146.7	0.0	1.2	7	36.1
9	0.	27.0	1.4	8	.
9	1.1	0.0	1.4	8	22.1
9	11.1	3.2	1.4	8	.
9	22.3	3.2	1.4	8	.
9	34.6	3.2	1.4	8	.
9	46.6	3.2	1.4	8	.
9	58.7	3.2	1.4	8	.
9	70.9	3.2	1.4	8	.
9	82.7	0.0	1.4	8	29.2
9	83.2	3.2	1.4	8	.
9	94.6	3.2	1.4	8	.
9	106.6	3.2	1.4	8	.
9	118.6	3.2	1.4	8	.
9	130.6	3.2	1.4	8	.
9	142.1	0.0	1.4	8	34.2
9	142.6	3.2	1.4	8	.
9	312.6	0.0	1.4	8	19.6
10	0.	27.0	1.4	7	.
10	1.2	0.0	1.4	7	19.9
10	11.2	3.5	1.4	7	.
10	23.2	3.5	1.4	7	.
10	35.3	3.5	1.4	7	.
10	47.2	3.5	1.4	7	.
10	59.2	3.5	1.4	7	.
10	70.7	0.0	1.4	7	23.4
10	71.2	3.5	1.4	7	.
10	83.2	3.5	1.4	7	.
10	95.2	3.5	1.4	7	.
10	107.2	3.5	1.4	7	.
10	119.2	3.5	1.4	7	.
10	131.2	3.5	1.4	7	.
10	142.2	0.0	1.4	7	30.9
11	0.	24.0	1.2	7	.
11	11.5	24.0	1.2	7	.
11	23.5	3.0	1.2	7	.
11	35.5	3.0	1.2	7	.
11	47.5	3.0	1.2	7	.
11	57.5	0.0	1.2	7	24.3
12	0.	26.0	1.3	6	.
12	2.0	0.0	1.3	6	17.0
12	12.0	3.3	1.3	6	.

12	13.0	5.0	1.3	6	.
12	24.5	3.3	1.3	6	.
12	36.0	3.3	1.3	6	.
12	48.5	3.3	1.3	6	.
12	60.0	3.3	1.3	6	.
12	72.0	3.3	1.3	6	.
12	84.0	3.3	1.3	6	.
12	96.0	3.3	1.3	6	.
12	108.0	3.3	1.3	6	.
12	120.0	3.3	1.3	6	.
12	132.2	0.0	1.3	6	34.1
12	132.5	3.3	1.3	6	.
12	302.5	0.0	1.3	6	16.0
13	0.	11.0	1.1	6	.
13	12.0	11.0	1.1	6	.
13	25.0	2.8	1.1	6	.
13	36.5	0.0	1.1	6	24.1
13	37.0	2.8	1.1	6	.
13	49.0	2.8	1.1	6	.
13	61.0	2.8	1.1	6	.
13	74.0	2.8	1.1	6	.
13	85.0	2.8	1.1	6	.
13	98.0	2.8	1.1	6	.
13	110.0	2.8	1.1	6	.
13	121.3	2.8	1.1	6	.
13	134.0	2.8	1.1	6	.
13	145.0	2.8	1.1	6	.
13	157.0	2.8	1.1	6	.
13	169.0	0.0	1.1	6	38.2
14	0.	22.0	1.1	7	.
14	2.3	0.0	1.1	7	25.6
14	11.8	2.8	1.1	7	.
14	23.8	2.8	1.1	7	.
14	35.8	2.8	1.1	7	.
14	47.8	2.8	1.1	7	.
14	59.3	0.0	1.1	7	25.6
14	59.8	2.8	1.1	7	.
14	71.8	2.8	1.1	7	.
14	83.8	2.8	1.1	7	.
14	95.8	2.8	1.1	7	.
14	107.3	2.8	1.1	7	.
14	119.8	2.8	1.1	7	.
14	131.5	0.0	1.1	7	25.7
14	131.8	2.8	1.1	7	.
14	143.8	2.8	1.1	7	.
14	303.3	0.0	1.1	7	14.3
15	0.	26.0	1.3	7	.
15	12.2	3.3	1.3	7	.
15	22.2	0.0	1.3	7	19.3
15	24.2	3.3	1.3	7	.
15	36.2	3.3	1.3	7	.
15	47.8	3.3	1.3	7	.
15	70.2	3.3	1.3	7	.
15	85.6	3.3	1.3	7	.
15	96.2	3.3	1.3	7	.
15	108.2	3.3	1.3	7	.
15	120.2	3.3	1.3	7	.
15	132.2	3.3	1.3	7	.
15	143.7	3.3	1.3	7	.
15	145.7	0.0	1.3	7	29.7
16	0.	12.0	1.2	9	.
16	9.0	12.0	1.2	9	.
16	12.0	0.0	1.2	9	17.3
16	15.4	4.0	1.2	9	.
16	21.3	3.0	1.2	9	.
16	33.0	3.0	1.2	9	.
16	45.0	3.0	1.2	9	.
16	56.0	0.0	1.2	9	26.8

16	57.0	3.0	1.2	9	.
16	69.0	3.0	1.2	9	.
16	81.0	3.0	1.2	9	.
16	93.0	3.0	1.2	9	.
16	105.0	3.0	1.2	9	.
16	117.0	3.0	1.2	9	.
16	129.5	3.0	1.2	9	.
16	141.5	3.0	1.2	9	.
16	**152.8**	**3.0**	**1.2**	**9**	.
16	153.5	0.0	1.2	9	38.4
17	0.	22.0	1.1	5	.
17	12.0	2.8	1.1	5	.
17	24.0	2.8	1.1	5	.
17	32.0	0.0	1.1	5	21.3
17	35.5	2.8	1.1	5	.
17	48.0	2.8	1.1	5	.
17	60.0	2.8	1.1	5	.
17	72.0	0.0	1.1	5	28.8
17	72.3	2.8	1.1	5	.
17	84.3	2.8	1.1	5	.
17	95.8	2.8	1.1	5	.
17	108.0	2.8	1.1	5	.
17	120.0	2.8	1.1	5	.
17	132.0	2.8	1.1	5	.
17	144.0	2.8	1.1	5	.
17	155.0	0.0	1.1	5	34.9
18	0.	20.0	1.0	5	.
18	2.8	0.0	1.0	5	21.9
18	11.8	20.0	1.0	5	.
18	23.8	2.5	1.0	5	.
18	35.8	2.5	1.0	5	.
18	48.1	2.5	1.0	5	.
18	59.3	2.5	1.0	5	.
18	71.3	0.0	1.0	5	25.9
18	71.8	2.5	1.0	5	.
18	82.8	2.5	1.0	5	.
18	95.8	2.5	1.0	5	.
18	107.8	2.5	1.0	5	.
18	119.8	2.5	1.0	5	.
18	131.8	2.5	1.0	5	.
18	143.8	0.0	1.0	5	28.9
18	389.8	0.0	1.0	5	6.7
19	0.	10.0	1.0	1	.
19	4.0	10.0	1.0	1	.
19	9.5	0.0	1.0	1	18.9
19	13.0	2.5	1.0	1	.
19	24.0	2.5	1.0	1	.
19	35.9	3.0	1.0	1	.
19	48.0	3.0	1.0	1	.
19	59.9	3.0	1.0	1	.
19	72.0	3.0	1.0	1	.
19	83.5	0.0	1.0	1	23.2
19	84.3	3.0	1.0	1	.
19	96.0	3.0	1.0	1	.
19	108.3	3.0	1.0	1	.
19	120.0	3.0	1.0	1	.
19	132.0	3.0	1.0	1	.
19	144.0	3.0	1.0	1	.
19	158.0	0.0	1.0	1	32.9
20	0.	24.0	1.2	6	.
20	2.0	0.0	1.2	6	23.1
20	12.0	3.0	1.2	6	.
20	24.0	3.0	1.2	6	.
20	36.0	3.0	1.2	6	.
20	48.0	3.0	1.2	6	.
20	60.5	3.0	1.2	6	.
20	62.5	0.0	1.2	6	27.8
20	72.0	3.0	1.2	6	.

20	84.0	3.0	1.2	6	.
20	95.5	3.0	1.2	6	.
20	108.0	3.0	1.2	6	.
20	120.0	3.0	1.2	6	.
20	132.0	3.0	1.2	6	.
20	134.0	0.0	1.2	6	34.0
21	0.	17.5	1.8	7	.
21	4.2	17.5	1.8	7	.
21	8.3	0.0	1.8	7	21.1
21	15.8	4.5	1.8	7	.
21	28.0	4.5	1.8	7	.
21	39.8	4.5	1.8	7	.
21	51.8	4.5	1.8	7	.
21	63.8	4.5	1.8	7	.
21	76.8	4.5	1.8	7	.
21	88.3	4.5	1.8	7	.
21	100.8	4.5	1.8	7	.
21	112.3	0.0	1.8	7	29.1
21	112.8	4.5	1.8	7	.
21	124.3	4.5	1.8	7	.
21	136.3	4.5	1.8	7	.
21	148.8	4.5	1.8	7	.
21	260.6	0.0	1.8	7	21.1
22	0.	15.0	1.5	8	.
22	4.0	15.0	1.5	8	.
22	6.0	0.0	1.5	8	21.8
22	16.0	4.0	1.5	8	.
22	28.0	4.0	1.5	8	.
22	40.0	4.0	1.5	8	.
22	51.0	0.0	1.5	8	25.0
23	0.	60.0	3.1	3	.
23	11.0	0.0	3.1	3	22.3
23	11.5	7.5	3.1	3	.
23	24.0	7.5	3.1	3	.
23	35.5	7.5	3.1	3	.
23	47.0	7.5	3.1	3	.
23	59.5	7.5	3.1	3	.
23	70.5	0.0	3.1	3	26.6
23	71.5	7.5	3.1	3	.
23	84.0	7.5	3.1	3	.
23	95.8	7.5	3.1	3	.
23	107.5	7.5	3.1	3	.
23	120.0	7.5	3.1	3	.
23	132.5	7.5	3.1	3	.
23	140.0	0.0	3.1	3	27.7
24	0.	63.0	3.2	2	.
24	0.7	63.0	3.2	2	.
24	2.0	0.0	3.2	2	37.3
24	6.5	32.0	3.2	2	.
24	16.0	10.0	3.2	2	.
24	28.0	10.0	3.2	2	.
24	40.0	10.0	3.2	2	.
24	52.7	10.0	3.2	2	.
24	64.0	10.0	3.2	2	.
24	76.0	10.0	3.2	2	.
24	79.0	0.0	3.2	2	41.7
24	88.0	10.0	3.2	2	.
24	100.0	10.0	3.2	2	.
24	112.0	10.0	3.2	2	.
24	124.0	10.0	3.2	2	.
24	136.0	10.0	3.2	2	.
24	147.5	10.0	3.2	2	.
24	176.0	0.0	3.2	2	38.1
25	0.	15.0	0.7	1	.
25	2.0	0.0	0.7	1	13.7
25	12.0	1.9	0.7	1	.
25	18.5	7.5	0.7	1	.
25	21.0	0.0	0.7	1	21.8

25	23.7	1.5	0.7	1	.
25	35.8	1.5	0.7	1	.
25	48.3	1.5	0.7	1	.
25	60.5	1.5	0.7	1	.
25	61.5	0.0	0.7	1	16.7
25	70.7	5.0	0.7	1	.
25	72.0	2.0	0.7	1	.
25	84.0	2.0	0.7	1	.
25	90.5	0.0	0.7	1	29.8
25	95.8	2.0	0.7	1	.
25	108.0	2.0	0.7	1	.
25	120.0	2.0	0.7	1	.
25	121.5	0.0	0.7	1	38.0
25	132.0	2.0	0.7	1	.
25	138.0	0.0	0.7	1	31.3
26	0.	70.0	3.5	9	.
26	11.5	9.0	3.5	9	.
26	23.5	9.0	3.5	9	.
26	35.5	9.0	3.5	9	.
26	37.5	0.0	3.5	9	28.6
26	47.5	9.0	3.5	9	.
26	59.5	9.0	3.5	9	.
26	71.5	9.0	3.5	9	.
26	83.5	9.0	3.5	9	.
26	95.5	9.0	3.5	9	.
26	107.5	9.0	3.5	9	.
26	110.5	0.0	3.5	9	34.9
27	0.	35.0	1.9	5	.
27	1.7	0.0	1.9	5	26.4
27	12.4	5.0	1.9	5	.
27	23.7	5.0	1.9	5	.
27	35.2	5.0	1.9	5	.
27	48.0	5.0	1.9	5	.
27	59.7	5.0	1.9	5	.
27	71.7	5.0	1.9	5	.
27	83.2	0.0	1.9	5	33.3
28	0.	60.0	3.2	9	.
28	2.0	0.0	3.2	9	16.9
29	0.	20.0	1.0	7	.
29	12.0	2.5	1.0	7	.
29	23.5	2.5	1.0	7	.
29	36.5	2.5	1.0	7	.
29	47.5	0.0	1.0	7	22.9
30	0.	18.0	1.8	8	.
30	2.2	18.0	1.8	8	.
30	6.3	0.0	1.8	8	17.9
30	15.3	3.5	1.8	8	.
30	26.3	3.5	1.8	8	.
30	38.8	3.5	1.8	8	.
30	50.8	3.5	1.8	8	.
30	62.8	3.5	1.8	8	.
30	75.3	3.5	1.8	8	.
30	87.3	3.5	1.8	8	.
30	98.8	3.5	1.8	8	.
30	110.8	3.5	1.8	8	.
30	123.3	3.5	1.8	8	.
30	134.8	3.5	1.8	8	.
30	226.3	0.0	1.8	8	16.5
31	0.	30.0	1.4	8	.
31	1.0	0.0	1.4	8	25.3
32	0.	70.0	3.6	9	.
32	6.5	0.0	3.6	9	12.7
32	12.0	7.5	3.6	9	.
32	21.6	35.0	3.6	9	.
32	24.0	0.0	3.6	9	22.1
32	24.3	7.5	3.6	9	.
32	35.6	7.5	3.6	9	.
32	48.0	7.5	3.6	9	.

32	61.0	7.5	3.6	9	.
32	72.0	7.5	3.6	9	.
32	83.5	0.0	3.6	9	21.2
33	0.	17.0	1.7	8	.
33	4.0	17.0	1.7	8	.
33	5.5	0.0	1.7	8	21.2
33	16.0	4.3	1.7	8	.
33	28.0	4.3	1.7	8	.
33	40.3	4.3	1.7	8	.
33	52.0	4.3	1.7	8	.
33	65.0	0.0	1.7	8	27.4
34	0.	34.0	1.7	4	.
34	1.8	0.0	1.7	4	22.1
34	11.8	4.3	1.7	4	.
34	23.8	4.3	1.7	4	.
34	47.8	4.3	1.7	4	.
34	59.8	4.0	1.7	4	.
34	71.8	4.0	1.7	4	.
34	83.8	4.0	1.7	4	.
34	86.8	0.0	1.7	4	28.7
35	0.	25.0	2.5	5	.
35	3.5	25.0	2.5	5	.
35	15.0	6.0	2.5	5	.
35	19.0	0.0	2.5	5	25.2
35	27.0	6.0	2.5	5	.
35	39.0	6.0	2.5	5	.
35	51.0	6.0	2.5	5	.
35	63.0	6.0	2.5	5	.
35	75.0	6.0	2.5	5	.
35	87.0	6.0	2.5	5	.
35	99.0	0.0	2.5	5	38.0
36	0.	30.0	1.5	5	.
36	2.0	0.0	1.5	5	23.2
36	12.0	4.0	1.5	5	.
36	23.5	4.0	1.5	5	.
36	36.0	4.0	1.5	5	.
36	48.0	4.0	1.5	5	.
36	60.0	4.0	1.5	5	.
36	72.0	4.0	1.5	5	.
36	85.0	4.0	1.5	5	.
36	96.0	4.0	1.5	5	.
36	108.0	4.0	1.5	5	.
36	120.0	4.0	1.5	5	.
36	132.0	4.0	1.5	5	.
36	134.0	0.0	1.5	5	28.9
36	304.0	0.0	1.5	5	12.7
37	0.	24.0	1.2	9	.
37	2.3	0.0	1.2	9	19.5
37	11.8	3.0	1.2	9	.
37	24.3	3.0	1.2	9	.
37	36.3	3.0	1.2	9	.
37	48.3	3.0	1.2	9	.
37	60.3	3.0	1.2	9	.
37	72.8	3.0	1.2	9	.
37	84.3	3.0	1.2	9	.
37	96.3	3.0	1.2	9	.
37	108.3	3.0	1.2	9	.
37	119.8	3.0	1.2	9	.
37	132.3	3.0	1.2	9	.
37	144.3	3.0	1.2	9	.
37	156.3	3.0	1.2	9	.
37	159.8	0.0	1.2	9	33.4
38	0.	26.0	1.3	8	.
38	1.8	0.0	1.3	8	17.9
38	11.6	3.0	1.3	8	.
38	23.3	3.0	1.3	8	.
38	35.3	3.0	1.3	8	.
38	47.3	3.0	1.3	8	.

38	59.3	3.0	1.3	8	.
38	71.3	3.0	1.3	8	.
38	83.3	3.0	1.3	8	.
38	95.3	3.0	1.3	8	.
38	107.3	3.0	1.3	8	.
38	118.8	0.0	1.3	8	21.6
38	119.3	3.0	1.3	8	.
38	131.3	3.0	1.3	8	.
38	143.3	3.0	1.3	8	.
38	155.3	3.0	1.3	8	.
38	167.3	3.0	1.3	8	.
38	183.3	0.0	1.3	8	30.5
38	310.3	0.0	1.3	8	13.0
39	0.	56.0	1.9	10	.
39	1.4	0.0	1.9	10	30.0
39	12.7	5.0	1.9	10	.
39	24.4	5.0	1.9	10	.
39	36.4	5.0	1.9	10	.
39	48.4	5.0	1.9	10	.
39	60.4	5.0	1.9	10	.
39	72.3	5.0	1.9	10	.
39	84.8	5.0	1.9	10	.
39	96.4	5.0	1.9	10	.
39	108.4	5.0	1.9	10	.
39	110.4	0.0	1.9	10	37.7
39	120.4	5.0	1.9	10	.
39	132.4	5.0	1.9	10	.
39	260.4	0.0	1.9	10	18.4
40	0.	19.0	1.1	3	.
40	1.0	0.0	1.1	3	13.7
40	2.0	3.0	1.1	3	.
40	3.8	12.0	1.1	3	.
40	4.0	0.0	1.1	3	25.0
41	0.	34.0	1.7	7	.
41	2.0	0.0	1.7	7	18.6
41	7.3	4.0	1.7	7	.
41	12.0	4.0	1.7	7	.
41	24.8	4.0	1.7	7	.
41	33.9	4.0	1.7	7	.
41	36.0	0.0	1.7	7	21.0
41	48.3	4.0	1.7	7	.
41	58.7	4.0	1.7	7	.
41	59.0	0.0	1.7	7	26.4
42	0.	28.0	2.8	9	.
42	12.0	28.0	2.8	9	.
42	14.0	0.0	2.8	9	13.3
42	23.7	7.0	2.8	9	.
42	36.2	7.0	2.8	9	.
42	47.8	7.0	2.8	9	.
42	60.0	7.0	2.8	9	.
42	72.0	7.0	2.8	9	.
42	84.0	7.0	2.8	9	.
42	95.5	0.0	2.8	9	13.9
43	0.	18.0	0.9	1	.
43	2.0	0.0	0.9	1	22.3
44	0.	14.0	1.4	7	.
44	5.0	14.0	1.4	7	.
44	11.0	0.0	1.4	7	17.8
44	17.0	3.5	1.4	7	.
44	29.0	3.5	1.4	7	.
44	41.0	3.5	1.4	7	.
44	54.5	3.5	1.4	7	.
44	65.0	3.5	1.4	7	.
44	77.5	3.5	1.4	7	.
44	89.0	3.5	1.4	7	.
44	101.0	3.5	1.4	7	.
44	113.0	3.5	1.4	7	.
44	125.0	0.0	1.4	7	27.6

44	125.5	3.5	1.4	7	.
44	292.0	0.0	1.4	7	13.5
45	0.	16.0	0.8	2	.
45	4.5	0.0	0.8	2	16.6
45	12.5	2.0	0.8	2	.
45	24.5	2.0	0.8	2	.
45	36.5	2.0	0.8	2	.
45	48.3	0.0	0.8	2	20.2
45	48.5	2.0	0.8	2	.
45	60.5	2.0	0.8	2	.
45	72.5	2.0	0.8	2	.
45	84.5	2.0	0.8	2	.
45	96.5	2.0	0.8	2	.
45	106.5	0.0	0.8	2	24.5
46	0.	11.0	1.1	8	.
46	0.5	11.0	1.1	8	.
46	2.0	0.0	1.1	8	20.1
47	0.	40.0	2.6	9	.
47	9.3	6.7	2.6	9	.
47	19.3	6.7	2.6	9	.
47	33.3	6.7	2.6	9	.
47	36.3	6.7	2.6	9	.
47	38.3	0.0	2.6	9	25.1
48	0.	14.0	0.7	8	.
48	2.8	0.0	0.7	8	12.9
48	11.3	1.7	0.7	8	.
48	23.3	1.7	0.7	8	.
48	28.8	10.0	0.7	8	.
48	35.3	1.7	0.7	8	.
48	47.5	1.7	0.7	8	.
48	59.3	1.7	0.7	8	.
48	65.8	0.0	0.7	8	41.1
48	71.8	1.7	0.7	8	.
48	84.8	0.0	0.7	8	40.3
48	112.3	0.0	0.7	8	36.8
48	137.9	0.0	0.7	8	35.8
49	0.	26.0	1.3	8	.
49	2.0	0.0	1.3	8	18.8
49	12.0	4.0	1.3	8	.
49	24.0	4.0	1.3	8	.
49	36.0	4.0	1.3	8	.
49	48.0	4.0	1.3	8	.
49	60.5	4.0	1.3	8	.
49	72.0	4.0	1.3	8	.
49	74.0	0.0	1.3	8	25.1
49	84.0	4.0	1.3	8	.
49	96.0	4.0	1.3	8	.
49	108.5	4.0	1.3	8	.
49	120.0	4.0	1.3	8	.
49	132.0	4.0	1.3	8	.
49	144.0	4.0	1.3	8	.
49	150.0	0.0	1.3	8	37.2
50	0.	20.0	1.1	6	.
50	3.0	0.0	1.1	6	22.2
50	12.5	2.5	1.1	6	.
50	24.5	2.5	1.1	6	.
50	36.5	2.5	1.1	6	.
50	48.0	2.5	1.1	6	.
50	60.5	2.5	1.1	6	.
50	72.5	2.5	1.1	6	.
50	81.0	0.0	1.1	6	30.5
50	84.5	2.5	1.1	6	.
50	88.0	30.0	1.1	6	.
50	89.0	0.0	1.1	6	67.9
50	96.5	2.5	1.1	6	.
50	108.5	2.5	1.1	6	.
50	120.5	3.5	1.1	6	.
50	132.5	3.5	1.1	6	.

50	144.5	3.5	1.1	6	.
50	157.0	3.5	1.1	6	.
50	162.0	0.0	1.1	6	58.7
51	0.	18.0	0.9	9	.
51	3.0	0.0	0.9	9	12.7
51	11.5	2.5	0.9	9	.
51	12.5	9.0	0.9	9	.
51	24.5	2.5	0.9	9	.
51	36.5	2.5	0.9	9	.
51	49.0	2.5	0.9	9	.
51	60.0	0.0	0.9	9	31.3
51	60.5	2.5	0.9	9	.
51	72.5	2.5	0.9	9	.
51	84.5	2.5	0.9	9	.
51	96.5	2.5	0.9	9	.
51	108.5	2.5	0.9	9	.
51	120.5	2.5	0.9	9	.
51	132.0	0.0	0.9	9	31.1
52	0.	9.5	0.9	7	.
52	2.0	0.0	0.9	7	14.3
52	4.0	9.5	0.9	7	.
52	12.5	9.0	0.9	7	.
52	35.5	2.5	0.9	7	.
52	37.5	2.5	0.9	7	.
52	59.5	2.5	0.9	7	.
52	71.5	2.5	0.9	7	.
52	83.0	0.0	0.9	7	38.1
52	83.5	2.5	0.9	7	.
52	95.5	2.5	0.9	7	.
52	107.5	2.5	0.9	7	.
52	119.5	2.5	0.9	7	.
52	131.5	2.5	0.9	7	.
52	143.5	2.5	0.9	7	.
52	155.0	0.0	0.9	7	31.2
53	0.	17.0	1.7	8	.
53	4.0	17.0	1.7	8	.
53	6.0	0.0	1.7	8	19.1
53	23.8	4.0	1.7	8	.
53	27.0	7.5	1.7	8	.
53	28.0	4.0	1.7	8	.
53	39.5	4.0	1.7	8	.
53	47.0	0.0	1.7	8	33.3
54	0.	18.0	1.8	8	.
54	3.7	18.0	1.8	8	.
54	9.7	0.0	1.8	8	25.5
54	15.7	4.4	1.8	8	.
54	27.7	4.4	1.8	8	.
54	29.7	0.0	1.8	8	29.4
54	39.7	4.4	1.8	8	.
54	51.7	4.4	1.8	8	.
54	63.2	0.0	1.8	8	29.5
54	63.7	4.4	1.8	8	.
54	75.7	4.4	1.8	8	.
54	87.7	4.4	1.8	8	.
54	99.7	4.4	1.8	8	.
54	111.3	0.0	1.8	8	37.9
55	0.	25.0	1.1	4	.
55	12.0	3.0	1.1	4	.
55	24.0	3.0	1.1	4	.
55	36.0	3.0	1.1	4	.
55	48.0	3.0	1.1	4	.
55	60.0	3.0	1.1	4	.
55	72.0	3.0	1.1	4	.
55	74.0	0.0	1.1	4	20.8
56	0.	12.0	0.6	4	.
56	12.7	1.5	0.6	4	.
56	20.0	0.0	0.6	4	18.8
57	0.	20.0	2.1	6	.

```
57      0.5     20.0    2.1     6       .
57      1.7      0.0    2.1     6      20.2
57     12.2      5.0    2.1     6       .
57     24.7      5.0    2.1     6       .
57     37.2      5.0    2.1     6       .
57     47.8      5.0    2.1     6       .
57     60.2      5.0    2.1     6       .
57     72.2      6.0    2.1     6       .
57     84.2      6.0    2.1     6       .
57     96.2      6.0    2.1     6       .
57    109.0      0.0    2.1     6      27.8
58      0.      14.0    1.4     8       .
58      0.5     14.0    1.4     8       .
58      8.5      0.0    1.4     8      22.4
58     12.0      3.5    1.4     8       .
58     24.3      3.5    1.4     8       .
58     35.8      3.5    1.4     8       .
58     47.5      0.0    1.4     8      27.9
58     48.0      3.5    1.4     8       .
58     59.5      3.5    1.4     8       .
58     72.0      3.5    1.4     8       .
58     84.0      3.5    1.4     8       .
58     96.3      3.5    1.4     8       .
58    107.0      3.5    1.4     8       .
58    120.3      3.5    1.4     8       .
58    131.8      0.0    1.4     8      31.0
59      0.      22.8    1.1     6       .
59      1.8      0.0    1.1     6      22.6
59     12.5      3.0    1.1     6       .
59     24.3      3.0    1.1     6       .
59     36.3      3.0    1.1     6       .
59     48.8      3.0    1.1     6       .
59     60.3      3.0    1.1     6       .
59     72.3      3.0    1.1     6       .
59     73.8      0.0    1.1     6      34.3
59     84.3      3.0    1.1     6       .
59     96.0      3.0    1.1     6       .
59    108.3      3.0    1.1     6       .
59    120.5      3.0    1.1     6       .
59    132.3      3.0    1.1     6       .
59    144.8      3.0    1.1     6       .
59    146.8      0.0    1.1     6      40.2
;
```

From Grasela, T.H., Jr. and Donn, S.M. (1985), Neonatal population pharmokinetics for phenobarbitol derived from routine clinical data, *Dev. Pharma. Ther.*, **8**, 374-383. Copyright © 1985. Reproduced with permission.

Index

Call your local SAS® office to order these other books and tapes available through the Books by Users℠ program: